McGILL-QUEEN'S NATIVE AND NORTHERN SERIES
Bruce G. Trigger, Editor

1 *When the Whalers Were Up North*
Inuit Memories from the Eastern Arctic
Dorothy Harley Eber

2 *The Challenge of Arctic Shipping*
Science, Environmental Assessment, and Human Values
Edited by David L. VanderZwaag and Cynthia Lamson

3 *Lost Harvests*
Prairie Indian Reserve Farmers and Government Policy
Sarah Carter

4 *Native Liberty, Crown Sovereignty*
The Existing Aboriginal Right of Self-Government in Canada
Bruce Clark

5 *Unravelling the Franklin Mystery*
Inuit Testimony
David C. Woodman

6 *Otter Skins, Boston Ships, and China Goods*
The Maritime Fur Trade of the Northwest Coast, 1785–1841
James R. Gibson

7 *From Wooden Ploughs to Welfare*
The Story of the Western Reserves
Helen Buckley

8 *In Business for Ourselves*
Northern Entrepreneurs
Wanda A. Wuttunee

9 *For an Amerindian Autohistory*
An Essay on the Foundations of a Social Ethic
Georges E. Sioui

10 *Strangers Among Us*
David Woodman

11 *When the North Was Red*
Aboriginal Education in Soviet Siberia
Dennis A. Bartels and Alice L. Bartels

12 *From Talking Chiefs to a Native Corporate Elite*
The Birth of Class and Nationalism among Canadian Inuit
Marybelle Mitchell

13 *Cold Comfort*
My Love Affair with the Arctic
Graham W. Rowley

14 *The True Spirit and Original Intent of Treaty 7*
Treaty 7 Elders and Tribal Council with Walter Hildebrandt, Dorothy First Rider, and Sarah Carter

15 *This Distant and Unsurveyed Country*
A Woman's Winter at Baffin Island, 1857–1858
W. Gillies Ross

16 *Images of Justice*
Dorothy Harley Eber

17 *Capturing Women*
The Manipulation of Cultural Imagery in Canada's Prairie West
Sarah A. Carter

18 *Social and Environmental Impacts of the James Bay Hydroelectric Project*
Edited by James F. Hornig

19 *Saqiyuq*
Stories from the Lives of Three Inuit Women
Nancy Wachowich in collaboration with Apphia Agalakti Awa, Rhoda Kaukjak Katsak, and Sandra Pikujak Katsak

20 *Justice in Paradise*
Bruce Clark

21 *Aboriginal Rights and Self-Government*
The Canadian and Mexican Experience in North American Perspective
Edited by Curtis Cook and Juan D. Lindau

22 *Harvest of Souls*
The Jesuit Missions and Colonialism in North America, 1632–1650
Carole Blackburn

23 *Bounty and Benevolence*
A History of Saskatchewan Treaties
Arthur J. Ray, Jim Miller, and Frank Tough

24 *The People of Denendeh*
Ethnohistory of the Indians of Canada's Northwest Territories
June Helm

25 *The* Marshall *Decision and Native Rights*
Ken Coates

26 *The Flying Tiger*
Women Shamans and Storytellers of the Amur
Kira Van Deusen

27 *Alone in Silence*
European Women in the Canadian North before 1940
Barbara E. Kelcey

28 *The Arctic Voyages of Martin Frobisher*
An Elizabethan Adventure
Robert McGhee

29 *Northern Experience and the Myths of Canadian Culture*
Renée Hulan

30 *The White Man's Gonna Getcha*
The Colonial Challenge to the Crees in Quebec
Toby Morantz

31 *The Heavens Are Changing*
Nineteenth-Century Protestant Missions and Tsimshian Christianity
Susan Neylan

32 *Arctic Migrants/Arctic Villagers*
The Transformation of Inuit Settlement in the Central Arctic
David Damas

33 *Arctic Justice*
On Trial for Murder – Pond Inlet, 1923
Shelagh D. Grant

34 *Eighteenth-Century Naturalists of Hudson Bay*
Stuart Houston, Tim Ball, and Mary Houston

35 *The American Empire and the Fourth World*
Anthony J. Hall

36 *Uqalurait*
An Oral History of Nunavut
Compiled and edited by John Bennett and Susan Rowley

37 *Living Rhythms.*
Lessons in Aboriginal Economic Resilience and Vision
Wanda Wuttunee

38 *The Making of an Explorer*
George Hubert Wilkins and the Canadian Arctic Expedition, 1913–1916
Stuart E. Jenness

39 *Chee Chee*
A Study of Aboriginal Suicide
Alvin Evans

40 *Strange Things Done*
Murder in Yukon History
Ken S. Coates and William R. Morrison

41 *Healing through Art*
Ritualized Space and Cree Identity
Nadia Ferrara

42 *Coming Home to the Village*
Aboriginalizing Education
Peter Cole

43 *Something New in the Air*
The Story of First Peoples Television Broadcasting in Canada
Lorna Roth

44 *Listening to Old Woman Speak*
Natives and Alternatives in Canadian Literature
Laura Smyth Groening

45 *Robert and Frances Flaherty*
A Documentary Life, 1883–1922
Robert J. Christopher

ROBERT AND FRANCES FLAHERTY

A DOCUMENTARY LIFE, 1883–1922

ROBERT J. CHRISTOPHER

McGILL-QUEEN'S UNIVERSITY PRESS Montreal & Kingston • London • Ithaca

ISBN 0-7735-2876-8

Legal deposit fourth quarter 2005
Bibliothèque nationale du Québec

Printed in Canada on acid-free paper that is 100% ancient forest free (100% post consumer recycled), processed chlorine free

This book has been published with the help of a grant from the International Council for Canadian Studies through its Publishing Fund.

McGill-Queen's University Press acknowledges the support of the Canada Council for the Arts for our publishing program. We also acknowledge the financial support of the Government of Canada through the Book Publishing Industry Development Program (BPIDP) for our publishing activities.

Library and Archives Canada Cataloguing in Publication

Christopher, Robert J., 1937–
Robert and Frances Flaherty : a documentary life, 1883–1922 /
Robert J. Christopher.

(McGill-Queen's native and northern series; 45)
Includes diaries of Robert and Frances Flaherty.
Includes bibliographical references and index.
ISBN 0-7735-2876-8

1. Flaherty, Robert J., 1884–1951. 2. Motion picture producers and directors – United States – Biography. 3. Flaherty, Robert J., 1884–1951 – Diaries. 4. Flaherty, Frances Hubbard – Diaries. 5. Motion picture producers and directors – United States – Diaries. I. Flaherty, Robert J., 1884–1951. II. Flaherty, Frances Hubbard III. Title. IV. Series.

PN1998.3.F59C47 2005 792.4302'3'092 C2005-901943-3

This book was designed and typeset by studio oneonone in Sabon 10.8/13

In Memoriam

Konstantin Kristoforidhi, 1827–1895
poet, linguist, patriot

Contents

Illustrations and Maps xi

Introduction xiii

Acknowledgments xix

1 The Boy from Iron Mountain 3
"The Islands That Were Not There," 1884–1904

2 The Violin, Camera, and Canoe 23
Diary of Exploration of Lake Nipigon Region, Northern Ontario, 7 September – 5 October 1906

3 From Bryn Mawr to Lake Nipigon 40
Diary of the First Mackenzie Expedition, 5 August 1910 – 14 March 1911

4 Through Canada's Northland 64
Diary of the Second Mackenzie Expedition, 6 June 1911 – 8 August 1912

5 Fellow of the Royal Geographical Society 126
Diary of the Third Mackenzie Expedition, 15 June 1913 – 3 October 1914

6 Frances and the Book of the Heart 201
Diary of Frances Hubbard Flaherty, 17 December 1914 – 22 February 1916

7 Flaherty Island 282
Diary of the Fourth Mackenzie Expedition, 11 August 1915 – 21 September 1916

8 Nanook of the Barren Lands 319
The Port Harrison Diary, August 1920 – August 1921

9 Epilogue 379

Notes 389
Bibliography 439
Index 449

Illustrations and Maps

ILLUSTRATIONS

Robert Flaherty with his father and friends | 9
Susan Flaherty, Robert's mother | 10
Margaret Thurston and Frances Flaherty | 44
Robert Flaherty in British Columbia | 46
Frances Hubbard and Robert Flaherty, 1908 | 47
Frances Hubbard on horseback | 48
Robert Flaherty with violin | 49
Sir William Mackenzie, Flaherty's sponsor | 52
William ("Husky Bill") Fleming | 54
Harold and Mary Udgaarden | 59
Nero Fleming and wife | 61
The Nastapoka Falls | 67
Sledge dog | 68
Hudson's Bay Company post, Moose Factory | 68
The *Sorine* unloading at Charlton Island | 69
Wreckage of *Sorine* | 69

Men icing sledge runners | 70
Omarolluk | 71
Nero Fleming in the mission schoolroom | 72
Robert Flaherty with four Cree children | 74
Robert Flaherty in full native dress | 75
Robert Flaherty in kayak | 76
Robert Flaherty at campsite | 77
Wetalltok's map | 79
Fort Chimo | 105
William ("Salty Bill") Robertson | 137
Noogooshoweektok | 152
Allego | 164
Kanajuq | 169
Sam Sainsbury, who assisted in the filming | 189
Tookcarak Island | 196
Francis D. Wilson of the Hudson's Bay Company | 198
John Hayward, noted as a skilled interpreter | 199
Lewis G. Maver, the HBC trader at Great Whale River | 200
A group of Baffin Islanders | 205
Stewart Gushue and Eugene LaDuke | 206
Drawing by Wetalltok | 292
Wreckage of the *Laddie* | 295
Sam Sainsbury, Omarolluk, William Robertson, and Robert Flaherty | 310
The Hubbard and Flaherty clan | 321
Robert Flaherty and Inuit child | 345
Nanook, Nyla, and Bob Stewart | 369
Robert Flaherty | 370
Alice Nevalinga, who was cast as Nyla | 374
Alice Nevalinga | 375
Allakariallak, who played the role of Nanook | 377

MAPS

Northern Ontario and the southern Hudson Bay region, where Flaherty conducted the first two Mackenzie expeditions, 1910–12 | xxii
The Hudson Bay and Baffin Island area, site of Flaherty's third and fourth expeditions, 1913–16 | xxiii
Hudson Strait and Labrador coast, the route of Flaherty's outbound voyage on the third expedition, 1913–14 | xxiv

Introduction

Every work has an origin, some genesis in an epiphany of sight, sound, or moment. This work traces its moment of origin to a winter morning when a New York City public school outing brought us to the American Museum of Natural History. There are memories of strong scents: my wet woolen jacket, my friend Manfred's salami sandwich. The elephants and dinosaurs were engaging, but the film we saw was riveting, its impression permanent, like an invisible scar. *Nanook of the North* stirred fear and delight, family tenderness, and arctic ferocity. The film wandered through my imagination ever after, and an affirmation of its extraordinary nature occurred in 1989 when it was elected, on the first ballot of the National Film Preservation Board, to the National Film Registry, joining *Citizen Kane* and *On the Waterfront* as films whose merit warranted their preservation by the Library of Congress. This durability of the public's esteem for *Nanook* is reflected in the likelihood that somewhere on this globe, as these words are read, it is being screened in some library, museum, or school, or by some cinema society.

I thus began to ask myself how this incandescent film arose. Since it must have been the capstone of a remarkable process, my interest in its origins became more inclusive and historical. Obviously, the film had had a maker or makers and had emerged from a particular social and cinematic culture, so it was in these questions about *Nanook*'s origins that this book had its inception. The first sources I checked were the early biographies of Robert Joseph Flaherty (1884–1951) and Frances Hubbard Flaherty (1883–1972), specifically the accounts of their lives up to the release of *Nanook* in 1922. With their marriage in 1914, they formed a remarkable and often turbulent artistic partnership. The cultures out of which they arose seemed incompatible in class and education but not in sensibility and artistic imperative. The worlds of geology, geography, and exploration – the roots of both their families – provided a common ground, and they brought into the twentieth century a passion to make cinematic art independent of the studio lot and the conventional Anglo-European location.

This book also makes companions out of two disparate worlds: the Far North and the early cinema. The former was in a state of transformation and steep decline from its indigenous ways, while the latter was in an awkward but nascent ascendancy. *Nanook* comes out of the world of Canada's Eastern Arctic, where by the turn of the century, Inuit and First Nations people were firmly the dependents of the missionary and fur trader cultures that had arrived in force with the decline of the whaling industry after the 1870s. Its isolated trading posts, dominated economically by the Hudson's Bay Company, with some competition from the Revillon Frères' trading company, were accessible only by infrequent boat or rigorous sledge journeys. The posts' managerial officers were of British ancestry, with the Scotsman more often than not providing the European presence. Without the many aboriginal "servants," as the local employees were known, the posts could not have been sustainable. It was in this tight world of northern Ontario and the Eastern Arctic that Flaherty spent nearly half of his career and where *Nanook* became the culmination of his self-directed apprenticeship as a photographer and filmmaker.

Wishing to make films, Robert and Frances had to fathom the bewildering nature of this nascent feature film industry. A year or so before D.W. Griffith's *Birth of a Nation* (1915), Flaherty had included a Bell & Howell motion-picture camera in his kit when conducting an iron ore prospecting expedition on behalf of the Canadian railroad magnate, Sir

William Mackenzie. A flurry of film companies were formed after the dissolution of the syndicated Motion Picture Patents Company by federal antitrust court rulings in 1915, and the footage that Flaherty brought back in 1916 from two of his expeditions was the proverbial orphan in a storm. The pressures of the film industry's search for an identity were imposed on the Flahertys as they too struggled to shape their cinematic expression and execution.

This emphasis on the Flahertys' careers before the release of *Nanook* is an inversion of previous biographical approaches. Customarily, the Flaherty biography regards *Nanook* as the fountainhead of his cinematic career, and the preceding years are treated in quick impressionistic comments about his backwoods upbringing and his first career as an iron ore prospector. This is because the archival research about the first half of Flaherty's life has never been done in detail, and no biographer has followed the advice that Frances herself gave to a prospective publisher of a Flaherty biography in 1957. It would be misleading, she said, to write a Flaherty biography solely from the documentary point of view: "Any definitive biography would have to begin extensively with Bob's experience in the North, his explorations before he made films at all."[1]

The present work seeks not only to rectify the typical approach to the Flaherty biography but also to address the forty-year hiatus in biographical studies of Robert and Frances – a surprising gap, given the continuing stature of Flaherty as a visual artist. The signal exception was the 1979–80 Vancouver Art Gallery exhibition and catalog, *Robert Flaherty Photographer/Filmmaker: The Inuit, 1910–1922*, edited by Jo-Anne Danker. Apart from this, anyone who wished to read the Flaherty story had to rely on several early works by individuals who had been his contemporaries. Richard Griffith of the Museum of Modern Art, a close associate of Flaherty in his last years, conferred with him on a biography that was published posthumously in 1953 as *The World of Robert Flaherty*. Paul Rotha and Basil Wright, both of whom had worked with Flaherty in the 1930s during his association with John Grierson's efforts to build the British documentary school, completed the research and writing for a biography in 1959. But Frances disliked the work and withdrew her support, and the manuscript languished until Rotha agreed to have the research made available to Arthur Calder-Marshall, who published *The Innocent Eye* in 1963. Rotha's original manuscript was later edited by Jay Ruby and published as *Robert J. Flaherty: A Biography* (1983).

Since the early 1960s, then, apart from the Vancouver work, no substantive, scholarly effort has been made to reassess the interpretation of any stage of the Flahertys' biography.

Another biographical concern that previous approaches either minimized or ignored is the scope and depth of the influence that Frances Flaherty had on her husband's early career as a photographer, writer, and filmmaker. In their dealings with the public and with professional associates, the patrician Frances was invariably eclipsed by her Viking spouse. In devoting her considerable talents as writer and photographer to the greater public glory of her more acclaimed partner, she joins those twentieth-century women whose own accomplishments are subordinated to those of their husbands. This total devotion to Robert's success is evident in the diary that Frances kept after their marriage. In the emphasis this study gives to the writings of both Frances and Robert during this early stage of their career together, and the recognition of the powerful literary imperatives that Frances brought as Robert's editor and co-writer, it is hoped that the depth of her engagement in fashioning the Flaherty saga will become evident in ways hitherto overlooked. This work suggests that just as Frances had argued that a biography could not be definitive unless it examined Flaherty's pre-*Nanook* years, a definitive biography about Flaherty must also examine Robert and Frances as partners in life and art.

The structure of this book follows an approach that Flaherty himself favored; it reflects the one on which he collaborated with his first biographer, Richard Griffith. In that work, the narrative included brief excerpts from diaries or narratives written by either Robert or Frances about their film work, or by close film associates such as Pat Mullen during the making of *Man of Aran*. Although Griffith's text gave no citations for the passages (thereby turning the excerpts into historical driftwood), the intention of his approach was to have the Flahertys' story told as much as possible in their own words. The present work gives the autobiographical method even greater prominence by making the core texts the diaries that Robert and Frances wrote during the period 1906–21. The majority are those Flaherty kept during his expeditionary work, but there is a significant diary kept by Frances during the first two years of their marriage, 1914–16. Although other biographers have used snatches of these narratives to illustrate their texts, this is the first to use them extensively, and it is the first to transcribe the remarkable diary that Flaherty kept during the year he filmed *Nanook*.

Each of the diary entries is linked by a narrative that seeks to provide a more detailed biographical context for the autobiographical passages. Throughout the text the reader is provided with enabling critical notes to clarify references in the text to persons, places, and events. Particular effort is made in these notes to give identity and character to the many Native people and ordinary white folk upon whose services and loyalty Flaherty relied and without which he would not have been able to accomplish all he did.

A Note on the Text

In editing the material, the goal was to provide the reader with a text unobscured by a blizzard of editorial notations. Readers are apprised of whether a diary exists only in Flaherty's own hand, in his own hand with a typescript, or in typescript only. The typescripts were prepared by typists that Frances retained, so they are replete with typos and errors by persons unfamiliar with Flaherty's handwriting (which was notoriously crabbed) or his vocabulary. These have been silently corrected wherever possible, including the spelling of some place names.

Flaherty's (or the typist's!) spelling of Native names is especially challenging, since the usages were idiosyncratic or crudely phonetic. No effort has been made to revise them to contemporary spellings in Inuktitut, nor has the term Eskimo been banished. Within the context of Flaherty's world, "Eskimo" was a legitimate term of reference, and he often used it to denote both singular and plural. The word itself was not prejudicial, though the consciousness of its user may have been.

Where there are disputed renderings of the same passage, the original handwritten diary, if available, prevails. Flaherty used a host of abbreviations, no doubt a consequence of keeping a diary in sometimes subzero conditions. Such scribal habits as "arr" for arrived, "pn" for point, and "X" for base camp have quietly been regularized.

Acknowledgments

Given the far-flung character of the Flahertys' enterprise, the search for resources on their life and career relied upon the cooperation and generosity of many individuals and institutions. With apologies in advance for any unintended omissions, I wish to acknowledge the following for their assistance.

The two major U.S. archival centers for the study of the Flahertys are the Rare Book and Manuscript Library of Butler Library at Columbia University, and the Robert and Frances Flaherty Study Center in the School of Theology at Claremont University. The director of the Claremont Center, Professor Jack Coogan, provided inestimable assistance at all stages of this project. I wish to thank the Flaherty Center and Claremont University for permission to reproduce the photographs and written material used in this book. I also wish to thank Sally Berger of the International Film Seminars for permission to copy Butler Library's Flaherty material. The staff at Butler Library, particularly Bernard Crystal and its director, Dr Jean Ashton, aided me in more ways than can be noted. Study at these archives led to trails that brought me to other resources in North America and Europe. Included among these are Library and Archives Canada in Ottawa and the British Library in London, where James Egles and Annie Gilbert lent me considerable aid in negotiating the Canadian Copyright Collection. Cheryl Siegel of the Vancouver Art Gallery, Tory Tronrud of the Thunder Bay Historical Museum Society, Donny White of the Medicine Hat Museum, Anne Morton and Debra Moore of the Hudson's Bay Company Archives in Winnipeg, Michel Chevalier of Revillon of Paris, Leo Dolenski of the Bryn Mawr College Alumnae Archives, Trevor White of the BBC Written Archives in Reading, Cathy Anderson of the Harry Ransom Humanities Research Center at the University of Texas in Austin, Paula Lucas of the Royal Geographical Society, and Charles Silver of the Museum of Modern Art are all individuals who have provided invaluable guidance and support on behalf of their institutions. For his skilled assistance in the preparation of the maps, I would like to thank Chris Johnson.

Other scholars who have contributed to our collective understanding of Flaherty and northern studies deserve mention for their role as mentors. To one, whom I regard as the Dean of Flaherty Studies, Edmund ("Ted") Carpenter, I owe more thanks for his encouragement than can be counted. Jay Ruby of Temple University in Philadelphia, Jonathan King and Henrietta Lidchi of the Museum of Mankind in London, England, and Dorothy Harley Eber of Montreal are all individuals whose scholarship on northern studies has provided me with signatures of excellence. Two of my students, Marlene Clark and Elizabeth Cusack, were important early supporters and aided me in transcribing the texts of the Flahertys' diaries.

It was my distinctive good fortune to receive important guidance from immediate and extended members of the Flaherty family. Their recollections and photographs greatly aided me in understanding the early years of both the Flaherty and Hubbard families. Therefore, I wish to thank Mrs Vernon Barber of Mohawk, Wisconsin, Mrs Lee Erhartic of West Chelmsford, Massachusetts, and Mrs Frances G. Hoffman of Bradenton, Florida. To the first- and second-born daughters of Robert and Frances Flaherty, Barbara Flaherty van Ingen of Brattleboro, Vermont, and the late Frances Flaherty Rohr of Putney, Vermont, I owe special thanks for their willingness to share their family history. Frances Rohr in particular was an early and enthusiastic supporter of this project, and for that generosity she will always be honored in my memory.

For research funding, I wish to thank my home institution, Ramapo College of New Jersey, for its willingness to support interdisciplinary research through the Faculty Research Fund augmented by support from the Ramapo College Foundation. My Ramapo colleagues have aided me by their example and commitment to interdisciplinary research, but I wish to make a special acknowledgment of my colleague Carol Duncan. A grant from the National Endowment for the Humanities allowed me, at an early stage of this project, to benefit from a summer seminar on "Primitivism" with the late Stanley Diamond at the New School University.

To my wife Dr Frima Christopher and our children Nina and Noam I owe the special thanks given only to partners in life, love, and work. Their loyalty and forbearance have helped to smooth the rough patches that accompany any extended project. We cemented our bond with this project when a Government of Canada grant permitted us to spend an extended summer at the West Baffin Eskimo Art Cooperative in the area of Amadjuak, where Flaherty conducted his first filmmaking in 1913–14. There we lived the spirit of Flaherty and came to know the people and landscape he so vividly captured for us.

ROBERT J. CHRISTOPHER
New York City

Northern Ontario and the southern Hudson Bay region, where Flaherty conducted the first two Mackenzie expeditions, 1910–12

The Hudson Bay and Baffin Island area, site of Flaherty's third and fourth expeditions, 1913–16

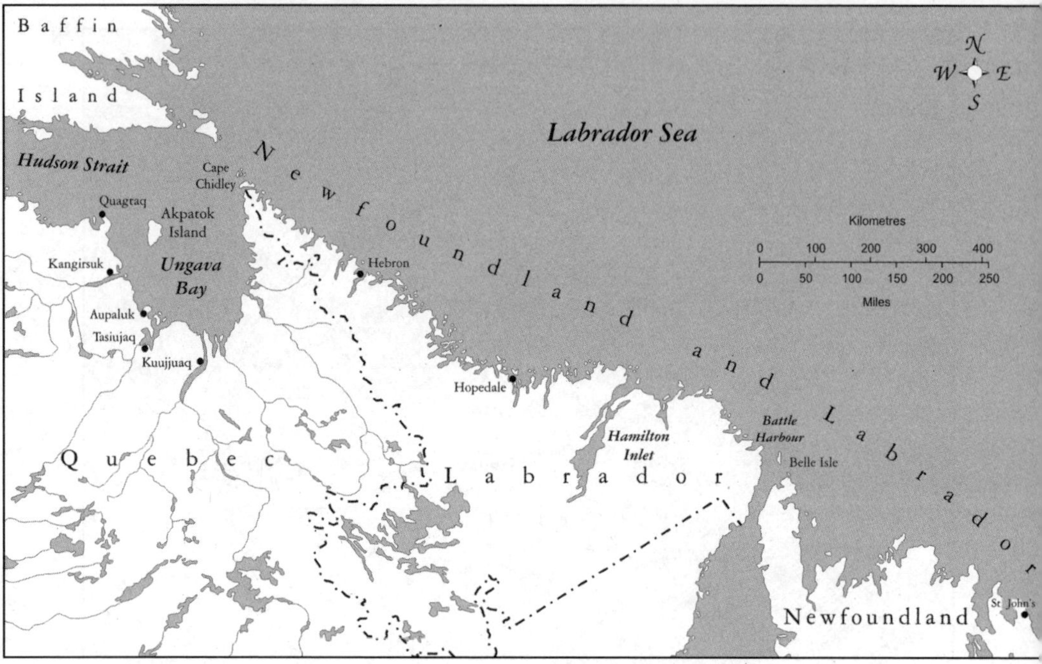

Hudson Strait and Labrador coast, the route of Flaherty's outbound voyage on the third expedition, 1913–14

ROBERT AND FRANCES FLAHERTY

1 The Boy from Iron Mountain

Robert Flaherty is best known as the maker of *Nanook of the North*, a film now regarded as seminal in American cinema history. Its release in 1922 made "Nanook" a novel international word upon which the makers of ice cream, refrigeration, and fur products pounced. It also made Flaherty the latest cinema celebrity, though he realized little financially from the film; but he did gain a contract from the Hollywood impresario Joseph Lasky to replicate the success of *Nanook*, this time in the south seas. Thus began the public cinema reputation, at the age of thirty-eight, of a man who over the next thirty years made only a handful of films yet set the standards of independent filmmakers for generations. This story of the post-*Nanook* filmmaker, whose defiant imagination and singular vision made him an American film icon, is now canonical – so much so that his life before 1922 is almost invisible.

Apart from the first chapters of an unfinished autobiographical narrative, "The Islands That Were Not There," Flaherty's earliest boyhood years were not often the topic of his prodigious tale-telling capacities or published writings. An early Flaherty biographer, Arthur Calder-Marshall, speculated on the meaning of this scarcity and observed, "It would be interesting if we had details of his early life. That we haven't indicates that in his early years, he had a sense of security. The incidents of happy childhood are as hidden as the bricks in the foundation of a good building."[1]

It was in fact a childhood not of singular happiness but one of cycles of security and dislocation, of migrations and resettlements, movements that in large part were the consequence of the erratic economic conditions that prevailed in the last two decades of nineteenth-century North America. By the early 1880s, the Flahertys were in northern Michigan, the state in which Flaherty's father, Robert Henry (1856–1923), was born. His paternal ancestry was that of Irish Protestants, who in the famine of the 1840s had originally migrated to Canada East (Quebec). His mother, Susan Klöckner (1858–1924), of German Catholic origin, traced her ancestors to Koblenz. It was in Iron Mountain, Michigan, on 16 February 1884, that Robert Joseph was born. A first-born daughter died in infancy and Robert, now the eldest, would experience the death of two brothers, one from diphtheria, the other from tonsillectomy complications. A sister, Frances, and two brothers, David and Arthur, reached adulthood. How Flaherty senior acquired his considerable skills as a prospector, surveyor, and mining engineer is not clear, but it is certain that he was the central influential figure in shaping the values, education, and first vocation of his eldest son. The first sentence of Robert's "Islands" autobiography declares with rocklike certitude, "My father was a mining man." In Flaherty's early years, the father's vocation was the son's constant amidst his family's nomadic resettlements.

It is worth tracing Flaherty senior's mining career from the Iron Mountain period onwards, because we can note the milestones of Robert's upbringing and the cultivation of both his explorer and his artistic inclination. As Flaherty observed in his "Islands" narrative, by the late 1890s "a financial panic had swept through the country," and the mine that his father managed, as well as many others, closed. Flaherty's terror at the miners' rage is vividly recalled in his remembrance of their dismantling that symbol of company authority, his father's office shed. Before 1896, Flaherty senior's name is associated with the Hamilton and Ludington mines located along the Menominee Iron Range. In January 1892 these mines were crippled by flooding, and "the work of getting the water out was done under the direction of Superintendent Robert Flaherty."[2] The panic that followed the closing of these and other mines led Flaherty senior in 1896 to relocate to the more promising goldfields in the far southwest corner of northwestern Ontario, the area of Rainy Lake and Lake of the Woods.

Particulars about Flaherty senior's employment over the next decade can be gleaned from the annual reports of inspectors of the Ontario Bureau of Mines, a provincial agency seeking in the late 1890s to regulate claims, safety, and productivity in the wildcat goldfields of northwestern Ontario. Into the midst of this boom, Robert H. Flaherty arrived in early 1896; the inspector's report for that year recorded him as being superintendent of the Foley mine in the Rainy Lake area. The report gave Flaherty high marks for his accident-free management of the two shafts, the Bonanza and the Lucky Joe, and their twenty or so miners whom he supervised.[3] It was into this frontier and volatile world of gold claims and counterclaims that the young Flaherty was brought at the age of twelve in early 1896. This world's landscape is depicted in an inspector's photographs showing the Foley mine as little more than a cluster of crude log structures, muddy pathways, and equipment-strewn suburbs.[4]

By July 1897 Flaherty senior had left the Foley works. The inspector's report for that year listed him as manager of the Yum-Yum gold mine, a new claim, also in the Rainy Lake area.[5] As Flaherty reported in his "Islands" narrative, the Rainy Lake mines were played out, and his "father and many others were ruined in the end." In late 1897 his father left the Rainy Lake claims, relocating farther west in the Lake of the Woods area, where he was again associated with a new claim, that of the Burley Gold Mining Compnay. The Burley site was unusual in that it was situated at the bottom of a lake bed. The company's claim was challenged in court by the holder of the adjacent claim, but it was vindicated, and Flaherty's father was made superintendent of the mine. The inspector's report for 1899 tells us that the superintendent's house and storehouse were nearby, on the *Chien d'Or*.[6] It was to this "Isle of the Golden Dog," as Flaherty narrates in "Islands," that the entire Flaherty family relocated in 1898.

A photograph of the Burley mine reveals how complex the engineering features of this site were.[7] Standing mid-lake, the structure has the look of a North Sea oil rig, rising as it does on a platform of logs with an upper palisade of machine sheds, amidst which stands the central shaft and down through which Superintendent Flaherty had to drill into the lake bed. The drilling proved to be disappointing, and with the nimbleness of the rock-skipping stream crosser, Flaherty left the Burley works in April 1899. These apparent setbacks do not appear to have disabled Flaherty's reputation. In fact the reverse was true, for in July 1899 he was made superintendent of the premier gold mine in the Lake of the Woods area, the Golden Star mine. But although it had a history of greatness, the Star was in eclipse. Its original owners had plundered it without reinvesting the profits in repairs and equipment, and although the inspector's report credited Flaherty with making improvements in safety and productivity, there were difficulties in reversing the decline of the mine, among which, Flaherty noted in a January 1900 letter to the inspector, "I am handicapped for want of skilled miners."[7]

The year 1900 proved to be a transitional one for the Flahertys. In the opinion of the outgoing inspector, James A. Bow, it was a negative-cycle year for the goldfields of northwestern Ontario. More claims, he reported, were being abandoned than being registered, and venture capital was increasingly difficult to raise. Investors were more knowledgeable about the hazards of mining and more savvy about assaying the profitability of a potential claim. Also, the turn of the century was a period of drought, so the lower water tables restricted both transport and power. Bow also reported more serious troubles at the Golden Star in the form of flooding, an increasing accident rate (including one fatality), and the absence of a competent blacksmith to repair and sharpen tools and drills.[9]

Meanwhile, there were larger forces at work that led to yet another relocation for the Flahertys. The age of gold was devolving into the age of iron, and the great capitalist troika of coal, iron, and railroads offered vaster profits than the mostly chimerical search for gold. In pursuit of this new cycle of opportunity, the Flahertys moved to Port Arthur (renamed Thunder Bay in 1970), Ontario, a Lake Superior port that was fast becoming an important transportation point and a gateway to northern Ontario and its unexplored mineral resources. These resources, as Flaherty noted in "Islands," were regarded by many as the northern extension of the rich Minnesota iron ore fields. In the next decade, it was this search for the northern finger of the Minnesota lode that brought the younger Flaherty to the waters of Hudson Bay, for the experience that Flaherty senior had acquired as a mine manager and engineer had made him ready to ride this wave of opportunity. Thus, in 1901, Robert and Susan Flaherty left their American roots behind and made Ontario and Port Arthur their home for the remainder of their years. The following year, the younger Flaherty left his boyhood behind. He entered an apprenticeship, under his father's guidance, as surveyor and geological prospector – a training that eventually equipped him for his future vocation as a northern explorer.

The inspectors' reports during the next decade show that there were many opportunities for an apprentice such as young Flaherty to learn and test out new skills, for they indicate that Flaherty senior prospered, gaining a reputation as a highly regarded iron ore and mineral prospector to whom professional geologists turned repeatedly for advice, maps, and surveys. Taking advantage of a provincial scheme to promote mineral prospecting through cost sharing, Flaherty senior leased a government diamond-drilling rig and drilled many exploratory boreholes in the Lake Nipigon and Loon Lake areas.[10] The reports frequently referred to the "Flaherty Syndicate," suggesting that Flaherty was now less a company employee than an independent contractor working on behalf of but not specifically for any particular entity. The assignments mentioned in the reports included surveying and staking claims for the Lake Superior Power Company and the planned Grand Trunk Pacific Railway. During the 1906–7 season, a report noted that Flaherty was conducting exploratory drill operations for the United States Steel Corporation in the Red Paint River area.[11]

It would also appear that Flaherty senior had a growing circle of employees, including his son. Captain H.E. Knobel (whom Flaherty junior recalled in his "Islands" narrative as an early mentor) was associated with the Flaherty syndicate as early as 1901. The inspector's report for that year observed:

> Mr. H.E. Knobel, superintendent of the explorations for R.H. Flaherty, with headquarters at Atikokan, has completed a road from this station north to Steep Rock Lake, about six miles distant ... to transport the drill machinery to the northern locations and intends to put in another diamond drill in addition to that belonging to the Government now in his employ, as well as two stand-pipe drills to explore the underlying rocks of the clay lands.[12]

To sustain new opportunities, Flaherty not only needed skilled crews but he also had to solve transportation challenges. That he was an inventive and determined problem solver is evidenced in the admiration an inspector had for his ability to move drilling rigs around, as he did when he moved his operations from the Lake Nipigon to the Red Paint area: "The complete drilling outfit was transported up the Red Paint and down the Johnson Creek a distance of about 55 miles by the use of canoes and backstraps, a feat which is probably unique in the history of mining in Ontario, if not in that of Canada."[13] As well as solving his own transportation needs, Flaherty became skilled at serving the needs of the booming traffic on Lake Nipigon. A report notes that in the winter of 1906 two small steamers were built to service this traffic – one for the trading company Revillon Frères, to supply the Nipigon post it had established to rival the Hudson's Bay Company's presence; the other for Robert H. Flaherty.[14]

The younger Flaherty therefore reached adulthood on a crest of progress and prosperity that gave the first decade of the new century an expansive mood. This was also the period that saw the Flaherty family graduate from a seminomadic life of impromptu housing and muddy mining camps to the middle-class solidity of Port Arthur. It was a world in which ambition could have its rewards and in which striving was a creed; and it was a time, under the protecting shadow of his father, that served as Flaherty's initiation into independence and into his vocation as prospector and explorer.

The Islands That Were Not There[15] 1884–1904

My father was a mining man. His profession took him to many parts of North America – always to some new frontier, some new country, as he used to say. At the time of the beginning of this story he was in charge of an iron mine on a recently discovered iron range in Northern Michigan. I was very young at the time, and we lived, to be precise, at a point where a water-power plant was being installed for the mine. The power that was being harnessed was called Quinnessec Falls; it was a sheer break in the winding, foam-flecked river called Menominee, which not only turned wheels for mines and was a grand stream for driving logs, but served also as a boundary between the state in which we lived and the more sedate Wisconsin to the south.

It was in the first half of the 'eighties when all this happened, but I can hear even now the thunder of the broken Menominee. It throbbed far into the forests, which crowded mysteriously deep and dark to the river's shore line and made picture-books in the water … Through the window we used to look at it together, my mother and I, as it danced in the spray. But the place where our log cabin stood was not far from where the river began to gather speed for its plunge; and, romantic though it all was, my mother was glad to leave, she said. For I was always getting into mischief, and that brink was altogether too close for a boy of three years to be playing around the river.

"If it hadn't been for your father, you would have gone over that fall one day," she said. "You don't remember it, of course; but when I looked out and saw you riding on that log – and shouting that it was

Robert Flaherty (upper right) and father (kneeling) with friends, in northern Ontario, 1900–3
(courtesy of the Thunder Bay Historical Museum, 972.255.17E)

a canoe, you young scamp! – I called your father not a second too soon. I've never had a moment's peace after that."

A convulsion came to this little mining town a few years later. A financial panic had swept through the country. All the iron mines closed down. Month after month passed, and not a wheel turned. In the course of time the poor miners became desperate. Relief stores were opened; every now and then I would meet one of my playmates, half-bent as he

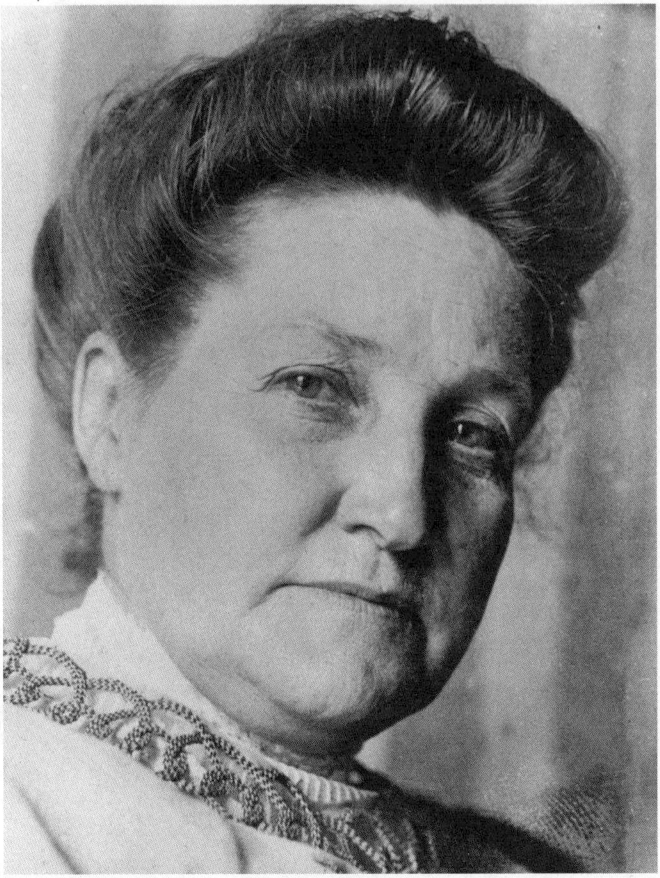

Flaherty's mother, Susan. Flaherty affixed this photograph to the inside cover of the diary book he kept for the 1911–12 expedition (courtesy of the Rare Books and Manuscript Library, Butler Library, Columbia University [Butler]/photo Robert Flaherty [RF])

hauled along on a sled a sack of flour which he had got at one of the relief stores for his family.

My father had to leave us in the desperate town and go to another mining field. One morning, just as I was getting ready to go to school, I heard my mother scream. She was looking out of one of the windows. I ran up to her and looked out. In the background loomed the idle mine – the towering shaft-houses with huge wheels on their head-frames, and on one side the enormous black stack of the mine's power-house. In the foreground stood a little building, now deserted, which was my father's office; and around it the ground was black with people. They were doing something to the office.

Suddenly I heard the splintering of timber; and then the ground immediately in front of the office began to fall back. I realized then what they had done: they had torn off the great steps which extended the whole length of the office front. Others of the mob were hurling stones through the windows. I knew that if my father had been there they wouldn't have dared, for his face when he was angry was like the sky at night with lightning in it – no, he would only have had to come out on those steps, that was all. But the procession began to march towards the house in which we lived. I shrank with fear; but beyond shaking their fists in our direction, they did no further damage as they marched on. There were boys in the procession, as well as men, and not a few desperate women.

It seemed an eternity before my father came home again, but at last he did. How thrilled I was when he said that we were all going to a new world, to a fabulous gold-field that had just been discovered in Canada!

"Are there Indians?" I asked him.

"Yes, there are Indians."

"And birch-bark canoes?"

"Yes, birch-bark canoes."

There were still a few Indians living beyond our own town, but they were pretty much civilized. They wore no feathers, no moccasins, and not one of them had a birch-bark canoe.

My father had brought back with him exciting pieces of gold ore with shining yellow nuggets in them as big as peas. His friends would come to the house and talk with him half through the night about the new land that had been discovered in Canada with real Indians in it and no end of gold. The country was too wild and primitive to take the family there yet, my father said. They'd have to wait a little while.

"How about me?" I asked, "I was twelve years old yesterday, wasn't I?"

Everyone laughed then. But two weeks later when my father left, though my mother was in tears, I went with him …

From the north shore of Lake Superior my father and I journeyed west by rail. To my staring eyes the country grew wilder with every mile. At every point where the train stopped there were Indians. What was more, they wore beaded moccasins, and their hair was long – and at one place I saw one of their birch-bark canoes!

At last after a long night's journey, we reached the first town we had seen since leaving Lake Superior. As the huge, lumbering train slowed down and came to a stop, the little station alongside of it was packed with men that were different from any other men I had ever seen. They wore rough costumes, and knee-length hob-nailed boots. They were prospectors, my father said. I was quick to notice that there were Indians amongst them too. The town was the center of a new gold-field, and its name was Rat Portage. It was a haphazard collection of shacks and houses, its population numbering several thousand souls. The place seethed with excitement, for news had just come into the town of a gold strike, and the news, as news always does in a new gold camp, had spread like wildfire.

The little frame hotel where my father and I stayed was so crowded with prospectors and mining men that guests were sleeping in the halls, and even on the floor of the dining-room.

I have never forgotten the man who owned that hotel. To this day I think he was one of the finest-looking men I have ever seen. His face was swarthy, his eyes piercing like an eagle's, his hair and moustache dark iron-grey. He stood straight as a tree and towered over everyone. Even before I knew who he was, I couldn't keep my eyes off him; there was something so arresting in the way he walked and held himself in that wild and woolly throng. I remember overhearing one prospector say to another as the tall man passed by:

"No man in these parts gets fresh with *him* – not with Jake Godard!"

Jake Godard! Could it be possible? Everyone in those days knew who Jake Godard was – the champion oarsman of the world. Before my father and I left, he actually took me into his office to show me some of the cups he had won in his rowing races in many parts of the world. One trophy he won in the mouth of the Mississippi, I remember; and another in Australia.

The new camp to which my father was taking me was far beyond Rat Portage; we would have to go across the Lake of the Woods and on up the Rainy River, two hundred and fifty miles away.

The river boat on which we embarked was the old paddle-steamer *Monarch*. The gold prospectors, the traders and the trappers and the Indians, that boarded her, made her more overcrowded than even Jake Godard's hotel. The traders and the trappers interested me most. They might have stepped out of the very books by Parkman and Ballantyne that I had pored over ever since I had learned to read.[16] There was one huge, ruddy-faced Scotsman who was the factor of one of the country's

Hudson's Bay Company posts. We became friends, and he told me many tales of his life in the wilds. He hadn't seen "the old country" – as he called his native Scotland – since he was a boy. For thirty-five years, he told me, he had been a trader at God-knows-how-many different posts in the North. One of his posts had been way up on the northern Pacific coast; another, three thousand miles across the continent in northern Labrador.

There were two days of journey from the Lake of the Woods up the Rainy River before we at last reached the new gold country and the mine in which my father's fortunes lay. The mine was on the shore of a four-mile-long lake; Shoal Lake it was named, because only in its center was there enough water to allow the river boats to steam through. The mine had only a year before been hacked out of the spruce forests which hemmed it in on either side; it was still filled with scars of stumps and fallen logs. About a half-mile in from the lake stood the first shaft – a giant frame of timber – and beside it a huge pile of white quartz and green rock. The white quartz was gold ore. Beyond this first shaft-house, half a mile farther on, stood the second shaft – a deeper one, with a still larger pile of white quartz and green rock beside it.

The mine's power plant was at the first shaft. In it was an air compressor which furnished air to the pneumatic drills deep down in the mine. Its slow, measured exhaust re-echoed through the forests night and day. I have never forgotten that sound. No matter how far I wandered away from the stump-scarred mine clearing, I could always hear that slow throb. A long wooden trestle led from both shaft-houses down by a slope to the shore of the lake, where, for months past, a huge stamp-mill was being built. When this stamp-mill was ready for it, the gold ore would be shipped to the mill by cars along this trestle railway. The stamp-mill was the first to be built at any of the mines in the country. It was known as the "Twenty-Stamp Mill."[17] Each stamp had a huge steel rod, heavily weighted, which, through a curious technical device, moved up and down, and with pile-driver force crushed the gold ore, which became a fine sand and was carried off by water over a wide plate charged with quicksilver. Whatever metallic contents were in the sand were caught by this quicksilver. There were other weird mechanical devices, such as vanners – huge tables of rubber; or rather, endless rubber belts which slowly travel lengthwise, but being jigged sideways at the same time. These vanners caught whatever metallic contents escaped the quicksilver plates. I shall never forget the result of its first run of ore from the mine. When I saw it in the Assay Office, whither I had followed the mine assayer and my father, it looked like a huge cheese, bigger around than my arms could span. It was yellow like cheese, too, and full of sponge-like holes. Indeed, I believe that the eyes of any mouse would have lighted at the sight of it. The assayer carried the big sponge of gold to the center of the floor and laid it down reverently on a big sheet of iron. Then, taking up a mallet and a cold-chisel, he began to cut into it. Wherever the chisel cut, the sponge no longer looked the dull yellow of cheese, but shining, gleaming gold. As the assayer kept on chiseling, in order to break up the mass into small pieces to be put into retorts and melted into bricks, pieces of the yellow stuff as big as birds' eggs would fly out into the various corners of the room. After them I'd scamper like a dog after a ball. I just couldn't understand my father refusing to let me keep any of them.

"Not one piece?" I begged. "One little piece?" I was holding in my hand a lump as big as a hen's egg.

"You go over to Goldbug Jimmy's mine," my father teased. "He'll give you some."

There was great excitement in the camp after that first run. Everyone said that in a few years the mine would be turning out tons of gold. But it never did. My father and many others were ruined in the end. One by one, all the mines in the country closed down, and finally my father departed for the Lake of the Woods to begin all over again.

My mother and my younger brothers and sister came up from Michigan then. We all lived together on a little spruce-tipped island that was just one of thousands in the wonderful Lake of the Woods. It was called the Isle of the Golden Dog. The mine was on another island about a mile away. In another direction, not more than two miles away, stood a scattering of birch-bark tepees, with always columns of blue smoke rising from where the tepee poles met and crossed at their tops. On the white beach before the tepees lay the inhabitants' birch-bark canoes. These inhabitants, of course, were Indians. They used to paddle over often to visit our island and trade with us whatever they might have – big birch-bark baskets heaped with blueberries in the early summer, and with raspberries later on; and often some pairs of beaded moccasins, or beaded belts. In winter they would snow-shoe across on the ice, with strings of rabbits or of partridge on their backs. None of them ever seemed to smile very much. Their furtive faces were depressing. Their terrible poverty was only too evident in the hopeless-looking rags of white men's clothes which they wore. They were indeed a far cry from the Noble Red Man I had conjured in my mind.

"It is too awful what the white man has done for them," my mother used to say. More than once I noticed tears in her eyes. Some of the Indians had hacking coughs which frightened her. They always wanted to come into our kitchen and just sit silently on the floor, and while they were wreathed in the smoke of their long wooden-stemmed stone pipes, they would stare at the cook bustling at the stove. It made my mother uneasy to have them there, they coughed so much. Finally my father had a little hut built for them near the kitchen, where they could congregate for their smoke and biscuit and mug of tea. Many times I tried to make friends with them, but they were always too shy. It was all very sad. My younger brothers and I used to feel very lonely at times on that little island. I had conjured up such visions of hunting with the Indians, of going out in their birch-bark canoes, and I even had the hope that one night I might sleep with them in one of their wonderful birch-bark tepees before the leaping flames of the tepee's fire, and listen to their hunting tales and their stories of the Great Manitou, or Spirit. But the nearest I ever came to realizing any of the romance of their lives was lying in my bed and listening to the throb, throb of their tomtoms floating through the still air. Those dances of theirs were night-long. When I awoke in the morning, the throb, throb still kept on. I used to wonder what the meaning of it all was, that endless slow, fateful dance of theirs all through the night. It would depress me profoundly, and I would think of my mother and the tears in her eyes.

One day the chief of the reservation came over, an old man with a tired face. He said he wanted to see my father. My father was busy, someone told him – would anyone else do?

"No," he answered, "not anyone but him."

At last the old man was shown into my father's office.

"My son – the best hunter of all my people – is sick," he said. "It is here" – and he pounded on his chest. "You white men, you make many miracles – the great iron horse, the swift canoes with smoke pouring out of them, many things – you must make just one more miracle: make well my son."

He would not accept my father's remonstrances that he was not a doctor. Even if there were a doctor anywhere near, my father told him, there was little chance that he could do good, either – for it is very bad when one has a sickness in one's chest. But the old man persisted. Just to please him, my father got into the old man's canoe and went with him to the reservation. ("You stay where you are," he said, when I tried to get into the canoe with him.)

The old chief's expression when he brought my father back haunts me still. He said only one word – "Maguetch" – when my father got out of the canoe. "His son was dead, poor devil," I overheard my father tell my mother.

I saw the old chief but seldom after that. When I did, he never came inside, but while the others did what trading they had to do, he would sit alone on the ground in front of the house, smoking and staring into space – wondering, I often thought, why we white people could do so many miracles, yet could not cure his son.

As time went on, the shaft my father had sunk hundreds of feet into the ground showed poorer instead of richer results. I couldn't help noticing my father's increasing concern. It had been that way, too, at the other mine on Shoal Lake – brilliant showings of gold on the surface, and then as the shafts went deeper, a gradual decline. Was it to happen again at this new mine? I wondered. It did.

We left the Isle of the Golden Dog. Years afterwards I heard that the head-frame of the shaft was still standing, its timbers bleached white like bones by the years.

An entirely new field now opened for my father. It was a far cry from gold. One of the steel corporations of the United States wanted to carry on, between the great plains of the West and the unexplored interior of Quebec in the East, an exploration for iron ore. It was foolish to think that the fabulous iron deposits of Northern Minnesota stopped at a boundary; there must be rich deposits in Canada as well, everyone said. This exploration would take many years, for the country, more than a thousand miles across and hundreds of miles deep from the frontier of Canadian civilization in the south to unknown regions in the north, was at that time virtually unknown. The exploration would have to be made by many expeditions. It was decided that the headquarters for this exploration would be on Lake Superior, at the then quiet little town of Port Arthur. It was to become our beloved home town, in which some member of my family has lived ever since, and where my father and my mother both ended their years ...[18]

One of the centers of the exploration was Lake Nipigon, a hundred miles long, and fifty miles north of the central part of the north shore of Lake Superior. It must be one of the most beautiful lakes in the world, its waters near shore as green as green, and the bluest of blue beyond. There were lovely spruce- and birch-clad islands, and great traverses, with the land looming faintly on their rims; and other traverses with no land visible at all.

The maps of the country around Lake Nipigon were vague. Each of my father's explorers had to make his own map of the country he traversed. I cut my teeth on this exploration with a mining engineer who had come to the country from the fabulous Rand gold-fields of South Africa, which still produce almost half of the gold in the world. He was one of the mining engineers who had become involved in the famous Jameson raid and been captured by the Boers, barely escaping with his life. His name was Captain Knobel.[19] I was seventeen years old then. One day I was seated with Captain Knobel at the camp mess at the mouth of the Sturgeon River, which was then the center for the explorations of the Lake Nipigon country. He was to leave the next day in a big birch-bark canoe with one Billy Shaw, who was one of the best canoemen in the country, and an Englishman named Kyle, who, as he himself put it, had "fooled around a good bit with gold" in the Lake of the Woods country. All morning I had been watching them getting their outfit ready for the expedition – weighing out sugar, beans, flour, bacon, dried fruit and tea; deciding what blankets to take, and how many cartridges; and getting their big birch-bark canoe pitched so that she would be seaworthy in the morning. As we dined, Captain Knobel talked of the trip; they were going right up, he said, to the last trickle of the Sturgeon River, across the Divide and along into the waters flowing north.

"It's no man's country," Billy Shaw said. He didn't think that even an Indian had been through it for many years. Captain Knobel said they would not be returning by the Sturgeon; but after they'd found a chain of lakes along the Divide which they had heard about, they would swing over to a lake called Long Lake, and after they had traversed it they would strike south until they reached the railway on the north shore of Lake Superior. This was going to be something like an exploration, I thought.

"You wouldn't take me, I suppose?" I ventured timidly.

Captain Knobel looked hard at me for a moment, and then in his cryptic way said:

"Well, why not?"

"You mean it?" I asked, holding my breath.

"Yes."

In my excitement I spilled the big mug of coffee I was holding in my hand, all over the rough board table. With a bound I left to get my things ready then and there – blankets, shoe-packs, an extra flannel shirt, thick socks, a needle and a bit of thread, soap and towels, and so on – the usual outfit of the country.

The next morning before the sun cleared the trees, and while the mists were still curling up from the black, foam-flecked surface of the Sturgeon, the canoe was launched and loaded, and we were off …

For a few miles the river's flow was quiet; but even in this easy water the clumsy birch-bark paddled more like a tub than a canoe. It was big and cumbersome, and "not a hell of a straight keel, either," as Billy Shaw said from his place as steersman in the stern.

We paddled on. The river's meandering curves began to straighten out; the flow got swift. We had to hug the shore-line, crooked though it was. At last we came into a mile-long straight reach, the distant head of which looked like a high bank of snow. A cat's-paw wind began to ruffle the black polish of the stretch that intervened; and then came the roar of the river's first white water, which meant our first portage.

We found the portage much overgrown. It was just a short jump, however. In an hour we had packed the outfit and canoe across and launched into the swifter stream.

Within a few miles the river was broken by more white water – in some places but short tumbles, and in others wild rapids a mile or more long. One portage ran up hill and down dale for nearly two miles. To pack the canoe and outfit over it took most of the hot, still, fly-ridden day. The mosquitoes were out in millions. Each of our packs weighed upwards of two hundred pounds, carried in the usual way by shoulder-straps and a tump-line, which is a broader strap, the strain of which is taken on the forehead. There was one hill on that portage which I could only climb slowly, foot by foot, by grasping branches that overhung the trail, and with these branches in either hand pulling myself up. There is no harder job in all the world than portaging. A two-mile long portage means, with two trips across it, six miles of walking – four of them the hardest kind of strain. Carrying a two-hundred-pound load one cannot go more than a quarter of a mile without a halt; and if the portage is rough, with many falls and rises, and with fallen trees lying across the trail, the stages are shorter still.

We had one portage over four miles long. "Waterloo," Billy Shaw called it. "Yes, sir – Waterloo." It took us a day and a half to cross it. "A tough nut to crack, all right," said Billy, panting and wet with sweat as he dropped his huge pack to the ground and joined us who lay on the ground, fly-bitten and played out.

Our Waterloo was really the last of the Sturgeon River, up which we had been fighting for nearly two weeks; for now the river had dwarfed to nothing more than a meandering little creek connecting a chain of shallow little lakes. The lakes began to dwarf, in depth as well as in size. The last one had only a few inches of water over its bottom of soupy, stinking ooze. Though we paddled hard, we could barely move the canoe across it.

From this lake we portaged through muskeg so soft that we had to lay spruce poles end to end to walk on; otherwise we should have sunk waist-deep in the muskeg. When we had crossed the muskeg we came to another little lake, and we knew then where we were; for ahead there was a little opening in the lake's grass-grown shore – a creek, which was the lake's discharge. The creek was flowing north – we had crossed the Height of Land separating the waters flowing southward into Lake Superior from those flowing north to the great inland sea of Canada, Hudson Bay.

From that moment, the flow of the little creek, each little tree, and the very ground I walked on, became strange and new. Everything ahead was indeed new land, spreading on, God knows how many miles, into the mystery of the North.

In quick succession one little lake followed another in this strange, solemn new country. The little northward-flowing stream which connected the lakes grew stronger with every mile. Suddenly Billy Shaw, who was the leader of our single file, threw his pack from his shoulders, and pointing, said: "Look!"

Ahead through a break in the trees lay a big lake.

"That must be it, sir!" said Billy Shaw, turning to Captain Knobel.

Captain Knobel pulled out of his pocket an old torn and tattered map. On it I read the legend: "Little Long Lake." If the scale of the map was right, Little Long Lake was twenty-five miles long. After the shallow little lakes, the sponges of muskegs, and the endless portages, how we looked forward to getting on a long, unbroken stretch of water! And what might it not hold for us in the way of exploration and adventure!

We launched the canoe. It was a beautiful day, with just enough wind to keep down the flies ... During the course of the next three days, we found outcrops of ore extending inland from the lake's shore in several places – one of the best of all on the very island where we had camped that night. We located altogether five paralleling lodes by the spinning little compass, and staked over five thousand acres of iron ore-bearing land!

Within a week we pushed on, for our food was getting very low, and more than a hundred and fifty miles of unknown country still lay ahead of us. Our first objective was the head of Long Lake, where there was a

Hudson's Bay Company's post. Here we hoped to replenish our diminishing food supply.

Instead of the two days we thought it would take us, it was a week before we came at last in sight of the post, with its group of red-roofed buildings and a great flag-mast standing before them.

"Now," said Billy Shaw and Kyle together, "for one great big fire and grub enough to cook on it!"

What kind of stock of grub had they at the post? we wondered. Our mouths began to water.

As we drew near the post, servants came out of their cabins to watch our approach, as well as some Indians from the doors of their tepees, which were pitched on the ground near by. An army of dogs gathered on the shore and began their long, mournful wolf-howl. We landed and walked up towards the waiting, curious crowd on the bank, keeping our eyes open for the factor of the post, whoever he might be. But no such person showed himself. We walked to the factor's house. Captain Knobel knocked at the door. There was no answer. He tried the door; it was locked. The wondering Indians and post servants followed us at a distance; but none of them said a word.

"I'll bet they don't see a strange white man here, unless he's a trader, once in twenty years," said Billy Shaw. "From the way they're staring at us, we might have come down from the moon."

We walked over to the trade store. There was no need to try this door – for a big old-fashioned padlock stared us in the face.

"Well, well!" said Captain Knobel.

"Hell's fire!" said Billy Shaw.

But now one of the group came forward and addressed us in halting English.

"The boss is away," he said.

"Far away?" Captain Knobel asked.

"Yes – down on Lake Superior."

"Is he coming back soon?"

"Maybe next moon," our informant answered. That was a blow.

"Well," Captain Knobel persisted, "can anyone sell us food?"

No – no one could sell food. The big boss had the keys, our informant explained. And even if he had the keys himself, he would not dare to sell us food with the big boss away.

"Well," said Captain Knobel, shrugging his shoulders, "we'd better save our breath and make camp, and then see what can be done."

So we pitched our tent and built a big fire before it, and Kyle and Billy Shaw started in with the little food we had left to cook. The man who had spoken to us came over.

"Why do you stay here?" he asked. "If you like, you can stay in the big boss's house."

It didn't take us long to make up our minds. We followed him over to the house, and he unlocked the door and led us into a big deal-paneled room. A few old prints and some antiquated fire-arms hung on the walls. There were shelves with a few books on them. All of these things were commonplace enough; but in one corner we were amazed to see a piano.

"Yes, sir," our informant said. "Years ago the boss got it for his daughter."

Now if any post in the Lake Superior country was hard to get to, it was this same Long Lake post. The route to it was up one of the swiftest rivers in the North – the Big Pic, a back-breaker if there ever was one.

"He got the piano up here by canoe?" we asked.

"Yes, by canoe."

"God!" exclaimed Billy Shaw. "How long did it take?"

"Six weeks, I think it was – maybe more. You see, it's a swift river we had to buck, and besides there were some long portages. One of them was like going up the side of a mountain. It took many of us to pack it on those portages – yes, many men."

"Was the big boss's daughter pleased with it when she got it?" Billy Shaw asked.

"Well, not at first – no, not at first. She said it made such funny noises!"

We struck south for Lake Superior the next morning. In two days we saw the end of sixty-mile Long Lake; then we picked up a little stream running into it, that was so shallow there were more gravel-bars and sand-banks in it than water.

After four days with our old birch-bark, holed like a basket by the gravel-bars, at last we saw something high up and far ahead. It looked at first like a spider's web.

"God save us!" cried Billy Shaw. "We're there!"

We were. After a few more digs with our paddles, we were under it – the cobweb being a bridge of the Canadian Pacific Railway, which skirts the north shore of Lake Superior.

Everyone looked pretty hard at us when we boarded the train, for the rags we stood in were as full of holes as the old birch-bark we had left, belly-up, on the bank of the river.

In the course of the next few years I made many such explorations through wide-spread parts of that huge hinter-land of Lake Superior – always new country, new lakes, new rivers; and always the quest for iron ore. But the country that had the most lure for me was the region north, over the Height of Land, where the rivers run down to Hudson Bay – the fabulous land where Indians were still Indians, and where the fur trade went on as it had done for two hundred and fifty years, with some semblance still of its old glory.

2 The Violin, Camera, and Canoe

Since Flaherty's main intention in "Islands" was to emphasize his rediscovery of the Belcher Islands, he omitted many other particulars of his education and upbringing. Before February 1896, when Flaherty at the age of twelve accompanied his father north to Ontario, he had attended local schools in Iron Mountain, Michigan, but his primary education included an avidity for reading, particularly the frontier writers Francis Parkman, James Fenimore Cooper, and Robert Ballantyne. Flaherty recounted few details about his early schooling; but in preparation for an extended three-part *New Yorker* profile, Robert Louis Taylor interviewed him at length, and in the first part of the series, "Education for Wanderlust," he offers the following description of the Iron Mountain period of Flaherty's education:

Robert was put in school by his father and three or four athletic assistants when he was six, and attended off and on for several years. It was an uncommonly rough period for the Iron Mountain scholastic system. The fact is that the Board of Education on three or four occasions indicated publicly that it had bitten off more than it could chew. The boy learned with ease, far outstripping his tractable colleagues, but he refused to observe the rules. His visits to the classroom were spasmodic. When the humor was upon him, he would turn up every day for a week or so, but he was likely to lounge in around eleven o'clock, smoking a cigar.[1]

Both Flaherty's brother David and his biographer Paul Rotha thought that Taylor had stretched the facts. Rotha commented: "Although Taylor's 'Profile' of Flaherty is both amusing and readable, it is not to be taken too seriously. It is fanciful and, in places, inaccurate."[2] Rotha acknowledged that Flaherty was party to the profile and did not later object to the image of himself as a cigar-smoking Huck Finn.

Given Flaherty's history of trying to survive as a filmmaker outside the industry's mainstream, the suggestion that "he refused to observe the rules" would have had a rebellious appeal to him. It did invite, however, the more attenuated perception that Flaherty, hostile to scholastic learning, was the neo-primitive, the anti-intellectual, impatient with theory. Given Flaherty's eventual association with the faraway and exotic, this inaccurate image of him as the unschooled "natural" clung to him.

Antidotes to this primitivistic profile of Flaherty come to us from his sister, Frances Flaherty Ruttan, who recalled incidents from the Iron Mountain period that are probably closer to the truth about his mischievous precocity. Recalling him as "a very lively boy," Frances declared: "He was always experimenting with something and more or less a nonconformist. He wanted to do exactly what he wanted to do. But always trying to invent something ... I know he used to take his mother's jam jars and things and take them out to the garage or back building we had. It was in Iron Mountain, Michigan. I don't know what he was trying to prove with them but he broke a great many by putting strings around them and burning them or something, I don't know. I don't know what he meant, but he always had some vision of something in his mind."[3]

The parents, among others, nevertheless saw promise in the boy and took special steps to cultivate his talents by hiring private tutors. One area where the younger Flaherty's precocity manifested itself was through music, so his parents took special care for this son who, his sister recalls, was "terrifically fond of music." She explained: "Even as a boy, when he was *very* young. How they knew that he had this terrific instinct and feeling for music ... My father could play the violin a little bit he struck a very high note, speaking of Bob would just go into a pet.

So they had a very good teacher for him, a very good German teacher when he was very young and he used to say: 'Mrs. Flaherty, if you could only make that boy settle down and concentrate, he'll make a great name for himself in music.'"

Tutelage and apprenticeship, not formal schooling, were to be Flaherty's mode of learning. This will to achieve was manifested not only in his lifelong love of music and the violin, but also through an equally important instrument, the stills camera. That cameras circulated among the Flaherty family is attested to by his sister, and since the father owned one she surmises that he gave the son his first. The wide availability of snapshot cameras by the 1890s had come about largely through the marketing genius of George Eastman, whose Kodak motto, "You press the button and we do the rest," democratized the taking of photographs. Frances recalls that her brother "loved pictures and he always carried a camera with him as he was growing up; as a young man he always carried a camera, took pictures everywhere." Although a Kodak probably did circulate among the Flahertys, Frances recalled that her brother still favored the older style plate camera with tripod: "He was always interested in very good old pictures, you know, famous artists and all that and he had his room that he had just filled with 'em but he began to carry a camera with him all the time. I don't know just why. He took pictures of everybody, his friends, he'd take them downtown to the ice cream parlor, anywhere. It was a big camera, on a tripod which was awkward to carry in those days. He never was without a camera. As he grew up he got to be 17, 18, 19 years old."

Thus, we would do best to associate Flaherty's primary education with the violin, the camera, and the canoe. They are the rightful tokens of his vocational and artistic imperatives, and they, not school degrees, served him as his primary credentials. In tandem with the apprenticeship under his father as prospector, they formed the three-legged stool of his education.

Just before the Flaherty family relocated to Port Arthur, the parents sent Robert, in 1899, to the prestigious Upper Canada College in Toronto as a boarder – yet another sign of their continuing high ambitions for their first-born. In a BBC memorial program, "Portrait of Robert Flaherty," broadcast on 2 September 1952, Sir Edward Peacock offered the following reminiscences which, though slippery on dates, provide first-hand comment on Flaherty as a pre-university student:

About 1897, when I was Master of Upper Canada College, Toronto, there came to us from the wilderness of western Ontario a tousled-headed boy who had little idea of the ways of civilization. The knife, for instance, usually did the full work of knife and fork at the table, and very expert he was with it. In spite of this, he was so natural and obviously nice, that the boys of the school accepted him at once, instead of making him a butt. This was a severe test, and a small triumph for him. He was strong, healthy, self-reliant, and it was very soon apparent that he was a natural character. But his heart was in the wilds and in a very few years he deliberately took up work that carried him back to the wilderness.[4]

Here is a description of this same period in Flaherty's education as provided in Taylor's *New Yorker* profile:

This was a prep school of considerable swank, run along the lines of Harrow; the boys wore linen caps and Eton collars, and behaved beautifully. They were the sons of Canadian and other British colonial aristocrats. During the Civil War many Southern families had sent their boys there. The elder Flaherty and his wife, in arriving at their decision to enroll Robert, figured that the school would have a refining influence. "After the woods, he'll take to it like a duck to water," his father wrote her. His prediction proved far too optimistic; he should have sensed the truth from the spirit around camp. When the news leaked out that the boy was going, the odds, as posted in most saloons, fluctuated between eight to one to ten to one that the stretch would be wound up within six months, counting travel time. The week he left, the majority of the gamblers hiked the price to twenty to one, with no takers, even among the Indians. Young Flaherty descended on Upper Canada College in much the manner of a cowboy coming into town after a six-week roundup. He preferred Toronto to the campus, he discarded the linen cap for a coonskin job he had removed from the head of a dead prospector, and he smoked like a stove. The authorities tried a number of remedies, including the lifting of his privilege of having a fortnightly spread in the dorm, but nothing worked. Nevertheless, he beat the odds, lasting a little more than a year.

Reminiscing about this period of Robert's life, his sister observed that Upper Canada College finally found young Flaherty too much of a "dissenting element" and asked him to leave, a decision that left his parents "terribly disappointed, terribly hurt." One incident she remembers that capped his penchant for the zany dealt with the demolition of the "water jugs": "In those days they had water basins in the rooms to wash with and he got them to set them all up and he got them to roll bowling balls down and knock them over and break them. I think that was perhaps the climax of Bob's education at Upper Canada."

At the turn of the century, the Flahertys made one more effort to supplement his apprenticeship through higher education. Frances recalls that her brother was "a natural as a geologist. Just as much as my father was." Since he thrived in the outdoor world of geological fieldwork and displayed an aptitude for the science of the work, his parents enrolled him in the rigorous geology program at the Michigan College of Mines in Houghton. The "Register of Students" lists him in attendance for 1902–3 but not thereafter. Flaherty himself made few public references to this final fling with higher education, and in 1903 he was still living in Houghton doing odd jobs. Given his talent to learn without being scholastic, Flaherty no doubt grew as a geologist. Sometime during 1903 he returned to Port Arthur to work for his father, and it was during the next few years – under the tutelage of his father, Knobel, and others – that he equipped himself to be the independent field worker he became by 1905.

For the period 1903–5 there is little documentation on his activities, though he was most likely in the employ of his father. The presence in the Butler Library papers of several diaries Flaherty kept of fieldwork conducted in 1906 allows us to trace his activities with more assurance. The first of the diaries covers the period 6 April to 2 July 1906 and includes mineralogical notes and a mapping survey of the Lake Squirrel region. That he was in the full-time employ of his father is affirmed by a notation on the opening page: "Received instructions from Dad," and a later entry ("camping with my father") also affirms that father and son were surveying together. There is also an entry, on the front inside cover, of Flaherty in a moment of literary flourish: "Take care not to mix up the loose sheets – by order of Sir Walter Shakespeare."[5]

Another diary, which exists in two versions, is of greater interest, since one of them speaks of his relationship with Frances Hubbard, the woman he later married. These diaries cover the period 1 September to 7 October 1906. One version of this diary gives us Flaherty in his work-a-day world, a world of practicalities, of unreliable workers and guides, of portaging and establishing caches. By contrast, the diary written for Frances is a world of lyrical expression, of charged recollections of arousal and longing for union, and such insider memories as "Skookum" being both a pet name for a canoe and a lake name, and the fact that Frances had given him a watch.

Although the portrayal of Flaherty proposed by Taylor is evocative of him as the wild man, the figure in the 1906 diary is a young man of resourcefulness and stamina, a practiced woodsman with a yearning for the transcendent.

Diary of Exploration of Lake Nipigon Region, Northern Ontario 7 September – 5 October 1906

Friday, 7 September 1906[6] Left Jackfish at 9:00 a.m. Had fisherman take us to the foot of the bay. Hired an Indian to help us pack our outfit to Owl Creek. Dinsmore very sick[7] – he played out at McCraig's camp 7 miles from Jackfish – forced to camp there at 2:00 p.m. for the night.

Saturday, 8 September, Trout Lake The night is perfect. We are camped on a long narrow lake girded with magnificent hills. Rough and rugged they are and very high, so high that their reflections almost meet near the center of the lake. The scene looked wonderful at sunset. The foliage of the birches and poplars already turned yellow russet or orange, contrasting perfectly and blending with the dark, velvety green of the firs and pines firs – and then think of the sunset to go with and over it all. We had a hard day of it – Dinsmore is very weak – from Owl Creek to our camp tonight consists chiefly of long narrow shallow rapids – we had to wade and track "Skookum" after us. Dinsmore nearly played out on the way. We were two wet, tired and hungry men tonight when we struck camp. We are sleeping in the open – I think of the night we had in the sand at Obakamiga – this day has been just as hot as some we had together – do you remember them? It is getting too dark to write – good night.[8]

Sunday, 9 September We have put in the hardest day of the summer – Dinsmore had a hard time of it. The heat was terrific and on the portages with our canoe and packs we were almost "in." To illustrate how tired I am, I could not eat any supper! That's a record for me – isn't it? Just think how tired I am – as tired as you were one night at the mouth of the Kimbell River. Do you remember? You helped me carry the canoe that day. We are camped in a log camp at the foot of Long Lake tonight. My man is at the moment baking bannock and I am writing this by candle light. I am too tired to write anymore but not too tired to think of you – what a dream our summer has become – I ask myself – is it possible – is it true that we have been together, seen each other and talked over our plans. It all seems wonderfully mythical because our relations turned out so different than those I was so sure of and craved for – I can't help feeling blue – I must see you this winter.

Monday, 10 September We managed, though it took a lot of yawning and scratching and rolling over, to arise from our floor bed at 7:15 (by your watch). At 8:30 we were in "Skookum" with a fair wind bowling us up the lake. By dinner time the wind increased so that we were forced to put in on shore – so here we are stretched out on our blankets on a sand point, the wind blowing briskly over us (over the lake also). We shall stay here till sundown and then paddle all night. Long Lake is about 55 miles long and averages probably 2 miles in width ... The posts of the Hudson's Bay Company and French Company are on opposite shores at the north end of the lake.[9]

Tuesday, 11 September I must tell you of our paddle last night – We started about 6:00. The lake was like a long mirror stretching away to the north to as far as one could see till it seemed to blend in with a bank of clouds that hung low on the horizon. The shoreline of high rolling hills glowing like a dark, soft, green velvet with the descending sun and seemed double with its reflection in the water – the sunset was over everything. Paddling along on a night such as this is a treat I wish you could share with me sometime.

After the sunset died away and stars began to show themselves, a line of thunder clouds loomed up to the west. The loons began their cry and then I knew our night's work would soon be canceled. Lightning flashed wickedly lighting up the dark, indistinct stretch ahead, showing us islands and bald faces of the cliffs vividly contrasted against the immense mass of black sky. An intense calm and quiet settled over everything – we did not speak – it was one of those times when one cannot speak, it seems. The chunk, chunk of our paddles and the cries of the loons soon reminded us of our position – and with the first loud growl of thunder we turned for the shore.

The night became dark as pitch and we had a great time coasting along the shore looking for a favorable landing, a growling, rumbling storm threatening to break every minute. We would light matches and hold them high above our heads – stare into a blur of foliage and if there seemed to be an opening anywhere we would land and stumble into the woods (my man swearing beautifully every time he stumbled or sprawled among the boulders or underbrush). We were a half hour looking for a place. We finally managed to procure a candle which lay in the *bottom* of one of our packs. We pitched our tent about 200 feet in the woods from shore and tracked our outfit to it. I had a thin pair of moccasins on which came in contact with everything sharp and hard and it was even worse with Dinsmore. After an infinite amount of fussing, tugging and puffing we settled in our blankets and tried to sleep. The night of course was a perfect one – not a drop of rain nor a breadth of wind – but we were fast asleep and unconscious of it all.

Later. The day is dark and somber (so am I). We have been wind bound 3 hours – have had a disagreeable wind to buck all day – towards night it became calm. A magnificent sunset made up for the dreary day – the night was glorious – northern lights, imagine it. At 10:00 p.m. we arrived at the post – we coasted along expecting to see it hours before we did and when we rounded the little point and the quaint whitewashed houses loomed up with their windows alight I can tell you we were glad. The dogs started their chorus which stirred the factor and he came to the landing to meet us. We were ushered into his house and shook hands with everyone. The factor gave us lunch to which I had no strong objections and after finishing everything in sight I produced the long expected bottle and gave them some magazines.

Friday, 14 September A fine clear morning – paddled over to French Company's post for the factor – he is taking a cache keeper to Kawakashgamiga Lake and wants to follow us as he does not know the north. Ten miles down the Kenogami River we met a party of Indians going to the post for their winter outfit – we stopped them and asked for fish – but they had none – they asked us for tea which we gave – after staring and laughing at us among themselves at the white man – to them he is a source of never-ending amusement – he is to them as a circus clown is to a small Tommy. If they happen to run across a white man's fire place or camp ground they laugh and will say see where the foolish white man had a meal or camped.

Fall is setting in the nights are cold – you should be here now and you would know what a snapping roaring camp fire is like.

Saturday, 15 September The legend of Devil Fish Lake. A long time ago a party of hunters were camped on an island in Devil Fish Lake. At dusk they hauled out their fish spears and tackle, lighted decoy fires on the shore and started fishing – they had wonderful luck and the fish they caught were monsters – it astonished them. Never before had they seen or heard of anything like it. When their fishing was finished they all danced and feasted except one young girl. She told them that their wonderful luck was too unnatural – that surely the devil put poison into the fish with which to kill the Indians – and she then jumped into a canoe and alone made her way to the mainland. In the morning those who had partaken of the feast were dead.

Sunday, 16 September Overslept. Up at 7:00 a.m. On entering Head Lake the sky cleared. Head Lake is the only good looking lake we saw since leaving Long Lake – and it seemed like a good omen to see the blue in through the flying clouds – to see cloud shadows crossing the lake and patches of foliage resplendent where the sun struck them on the shore beyond. The patches of orange, yellow and russet – the trees nearly doubled with the gales – the lakes are waves of green and white – and the flying, scurrying clouds – imagine it! There are the winds that come to take the leaves away and the winds that come in spring to take the ice away – that is the Indians' theory.

How we bounded over the lake – a gale sweeping us before it (and "Skookum" didn't buck over). I had a fine bit of rapid running through a half-mile rapid going out of Head Lake. The factor and I took his large canoe over then while the men portaged the outfit. Instead of running them quickly we had to stand up in the canoe and with an oar apiece let it slide gradually down – there being too many rocks for quick running – what finer sport would you desire – we shall do it together some day – won't we?

We arrived at the cache at 2:30 – I met Bill and Lewis, two of my father's men there. Bill gave us splendid information on a part of the area I am going in. It has set my blood agoing and I am anxious to get there. I am sure of winning, of being with you this winter. I am most blue today. A glorious sunset and a clear night.

Monday, 17 September A fine sunrise – away at 7:30. Dinsmore takes stern from now on – studying map upon leaving the lake – ran all the rapids with a loaded canoe today. Had dinner of fresh trout, bannock and berries – "fit for a king." Arrived at Johnson River, a feeder of this one, at 5:00. Camped. Others happened along – camped with us and had supper with me. We are only 15 miles from the Star Company's claims. Fine clear, cold night tonight – had a "pipe" with Acres[10] and then turned in after washing my face in the river.

Tuesday, 18 September A magnificent day. The river is the fastest canoe stream I've ever seen – only for once yesterday in a distance of twenty-five miles. Imagine the blaze of color with leaves lining the river and their reflection in the water – with a blue, clear sky overhead. We had a chattering King Fisher following us a long way this a.m. – but the novelty wore off, I suppose, and he left us along with the river. We ran some cracking good rapids – all with a loaded canoe. Our camp is at the foot of a waterfall. Dinsmore has just landed 5 mackerel and I had a trout almost landed a while ago but he was indelicate enough to break my line and run away with my only fly. This roaring fall is driving me to sleep. Good night.

Wednesday, 19 September   Another perfect day – fish for breakfast. The river gets wider and deeper and swifter as we descend – we ran 6 rapids this morning with our loaded canoe – arrived at Lost Indian Lake at 10:30. That lake is a large one – almost 12 miles long. I have been watching a molten sunset tonight through the door of my tent.

Thursday, 20 September   Fine, clear warm day. Shall wait here for Acres and Indians who are on their way to Ombabika River. I want to get an Indian sketch of the route which he has and go out home that way.

I saw an interesting grave near our tent. It is almost six months old – body lies in box on top of ground – surrounded by a fence – pole near on which is hung the deceased lady's wardrobe of about three pieces – dry fire wood and cup are placed near it.

In the afternoon I sighted 3 canoes crossing down the lake – they proved to be Indians on their way to winter hunting grounds – they were all filled with one family, the buck and his 3 wives who were about 20, 35 and 50 years old. In one canoe I noticed 2 of the children naked – the others were only a little better off – except the buck of course who wore a frock coat and semi-knee trousers, furry moccasins and neckerchief red and white-man's hat!

Acres happened along at 6:00 and camped with us. Had a "farewell to the white man" chat with him over a good old camp-fire. We watched a gorgeous sunset. Why do I see them all when you are not here?

I have indications of carrying out my way. I would like to write of our work (by the word work I mean (to me) everything) but I cannot – how shall we plan this winter – tell you of our woods – the outfit I've designed – my work now that is going to win me everything – I cannot write here of the great things between you and I. But all my thoughts and energies shall be mastered for the final work that shall make our wishes possible. Good night.

Friday, 21 September Acres left this morning – a gray, cold dreary day. We left at seven for the north. We are truly away from white men now, 6 days' journey from Lake Nipigon on the north. The river is a beauty – we had some great rapids to run and in the last we nearly swamped – running this part of it while going like the wind we struck – the canoe was loaded – it swung to one side – broadside to the rapids – freed itself from the rock only to strike a larger one. I jumped and by good luck grabbed the rope and held on for dear life. The canoe meanwhile swung my stern first down the rapid. Dinsmore could not jump and luckily for both he and "Skookum" I managed to take it to shallow water.

I tell you I was glad when it swung ashore. The formation is a monster – I found indications today by which I can almost swear that the range is to the north, I am sure of it.

We are camped near an Indian family tonight. We had fish from them for supper. Three squaws and two boys invited themselves to dine with us. They crouched around us *while* we were eating. They seemed starving, uttering not a word with that blank expression so much part of the Indians – when we finished I let them "go to" – and they went – they gorged.

The lake we are on now is another large one, an extension of the river. My mapping is going to be terribly interesting. A river called the Little Current River flowing into the Albany 200 miles west of the James Bay has been mapped for 180 miles by the Geological Survey – beyond that nothing is known of it – not even the Indians travel it. The river I am now mapping is some other than the Little Current. I shall in going north for the north boundary of the formation get far enough to prove that the Kawakashgamiga is in reality the Little Current.

The Kawakashgamiga as far as this point, I estimate to be 85 miles long! Won't it be fine to be able to join the two rivers in my mapping. Just think – it will mean altogether a river 300 miles or more in length. How I wish you were here – don't know how wonderful this work is and how exciting – at any time liable to find the range.

How we shall talk of our woods this winter.

It is getting very cold – good night. Dinsmore is getting nervous about the freeze up. I hope he will stick.

Saturday, 22 September Awakened partly by the sounds of chattering squaws, howling children and growling "huskies," and partly by my "cold feet." The day is bleak and overcast. I hired Indians to help paddle me around the lake while I did the mapping. I consider my notes thus far have been worth the trip and what lies to the north! The lake is a beauty – studded with rocky islands – the shores high and rolling – the water clear and calm. The formation as far as I've seen today is even more than I dreamed of. I found soft hematite float which proves beyond all possibility of doubt in this formation. I now consider my theory a fact and proven. The Indian bucks arrived home today from Long Lake Post with their winter's outfit – by the way they are the same we met on the Kenogami. Our supplies are very low – we were given short weight in flour by the wily Hudson's Bay. Fortunately I managed to purchase 20 lbs. from the returned Indians for the sum of two dollars. In inquiring about quarries from the Indians tonight and offering $50.00 upon being shown a good area, one of the Indians offered to show me some – we start out in the a.m. It lies northeast of the lake. I hope to have news for you when I next write this diary.

It is cold and dreary without but I am thinking of you intensely.

That means waiting till the ice is solid and hauling our canoe over it or from around the shores. The day after tomorrow I will try to get two of the Indians and a large birch canoe and a week of provisions and strike north as fast as possible – map the junction of the two rivers – and find the north boundary of the formation. We are short of grub and time – but a week's work may turn up a lot.

Think of it – this trip already successful. Good night.

Later. Two bucks came over as I was making tea – they always come at grub time – we all had tea together. You should see their costume – they wear a long outfit of white blanket material trimmed in red and with a hood attached. It resembles a frock coat. Where it narrows in the back at the waist are two flowers – made of the red trimmings. I "swapped" with one of them tonight who had an outfit on.

As we all crouched around the fire the younger of the bucks pulled out a mouth-organ. How good it sounded. The wind is blowing a gale. I hope we have a fine day tomorrow.

Sunday, 23 September A month ago today you left the north country. Think of it!

Indian flunked this a.m. – said the pervabic was only float. However I am not disappointed. We broke camp this a.m. and moved north. I shall not go any further north on Little Current River as it flows east and crosses the formation and the Laurentian rocks.

I shall work back and take cross-cuts so we can cover the formation and I stand a chance of getting the ore body by doing so – I shall also map and choose as extensive a collection of the float ore as possible to take home. I am trying to get the direction of the glacial movement as closely as possible – I am beginning to believe it is more north and south than east and west. If so it may alter things – in my favor perhaps.

What I've seen in the last few days really deserves close investigation and which I shall do – will have to leave in seven days' time – it is cold. My hands are numb writing this – not much heat in a candle. The Kawakashgamiga is in reality the Little Current beyond a doubt. I wish I had the time to map it to its mouth. The river is over 300 miles long.

There is great difference in climate between this country and along Lake Superior – colder – like November in white man's country.

Monday, 24 September Just to say good morning – girl. About to load "Skookum" to start north. I am thinking to finish and dig for home and farther. I am feeling sure of my work and still have better prospects ahead. I hope this week turns up something for you and I. Cold morning. You would be hugging our fire if you were here. I had *dreams* last night!

Tuesday, 25 September Blue sky this a.m. but still windy. Nightmare last night – walked over Dinsmore – getting warmer and it doesn't make it less lonesome – it is lovely, lovely country.

Started out but had to put back to shore – gale winds and heavy sea. Rain all afternoon – supper in tent. Nothing to do but pace the tent and sleep. Water everywhere – in the blankets, in the grub, in the tent and in the lake!

Wednesday, 26 September Gale staying right with us. Asleep at 2:00 a.m. Dinsmore says I kick in my sleep – it's a story – is there anything more crazy and lonely than lying in tent two days at a time with nothing to read or do – just listen to the monotony of the breakers on the beach, the gusts of wind, the rustle of leaves and the patter of rain on the tent? I think it will be fairer tomorrow.

Saturday, 29 September Cold and gale wind. Made fire and had breakfast – first ice forming – 1½ miles long and 1 foot deep. Camped at far end at 10:00 a.m. Wind-bound for the rest of the day. Imagine how I am thinking of you, girl, these cold, lonely days. I shall see you soon. Most anxious I am for your letters and those photos! Do you remember the ones I took of you?

7:15, Campfire. Can't you feel the heat, hear the cracking sparks, feel the smoke blowing in your eyes. I am writing this by fire light. We have our blanket all spread out before it – we sit looking into it – dreaming and wondering if the wind will ever go away – hazarding guesses on how long we may be in crossing Lake Nipigon.

The night is clear and cold. It may be a fine day tomorrow.

If I could only speak to you now. Good night.

Sunday, 30 September Broke camp at 7:00 – cold and clear. Crossed Devil's Lake in good time. In the creeks ice has already formed – 2 or 3 nights will freeze them solid. We must get a "move on" – this is one of the few routes that freezes in places before the 20th of October. In the rivers and deep lakes, of course, they remain open till at least the 20th – but ice in just a few small lakes and creeks is enough to stop traveling in canoes on along north ... Wind-bound from 12 till 4 o'clock. Dinsmore made a lucky find – a magazine "torn and tattered" but readable which Acres had probably thrown away. Camped at far end of the lake, 7 miles from formation.

Monday, 1 October Awoke expecting rain – some fell (sometimes sunny). A typical full morning – calm and cloudy and intensely still – the sun trying hard to cheer things up. How melancholy the dying foliage, the silence, the stillness made me feel – but with that how magnificent it is. Even the rushes, the reeds and the lily pads have changed their color. This summer has gone – our summer, never to return.

Only the startled ducks feeding in amongst the wild rice break the stillness – the weird loneliness of the day as we suddenly loom in sight around an island or point. Then a roar of wings and a hundred and more ducks will rise – we watch them as they make their circle, finishing it by flying over our heads, curious, I suppose, to find out who it was who spoiled their feeding. I never saw such a duck country. Wild rice abounds along the Ombabika River – it is not found everywhere through the country – and for that reason we usually see larger numbers amongst the rice where it grows at this time of year. Wild rice is a very good treat – it is like barley. Clouds of small birds feed at these patches too – sometimes they are so many as to force the ducks and the geese to move to a fresh patch as they consume more than their share. This is truly an Indian's country.

Camped at Crow Lake. Ombabika River at least for today was without frost. Two men and 6 or 7 squaws – bought a fish from them – and you know I am sure I saw the old squaw you photographed at Wabimash – do you remember?

Tuesday, 2 October Another cloudy morning, cold, cold heavy rain started when we were at dinner and we hunted up a camping ground. It is lonely and dreary – gives me such severe "blues."

Met a fur brigade going inland for the winter. They were Nipigon House Indians. Stopped them and inquired about the Steamer *Ombabika*. They said it would arrive in Ombabika Bay Friday – that means we will catch it at the French Company's post and ride to Virgin Falls. I can tell you the news cheered us up a bit.

It is late. I sit by the fire, or rather lie before it, trying to catch light with which to write to you. I dream of you and me sometime together before a fire – the same as it is tonight. The ghostly trunks of the trees and bushes forming a circle around us and the night beyond – over everything – you and I writing in music a story of our days traveling in the woods or of a lesson we had learned – perhaps reading of your work, or talk or plan of a *million* things (it seems to me now). Then think of our maps, of our work and that mysterious circle of our music.

But what a lot there is to do as it is – how much I have "staked out" and with the vein still to be found.

The fire is a bed of glowing coals like the trees, resplendent while going away.

Good night.

I have been reading "Robin Goodfellow" and his friends by Kipling in the "torn and tattered" magazine – have you read any of these stories?

Wednesday, 3 October We paddled and paddled and portaged (and paddled some more) – we worried and estimated, looked at my watch and looked at the map a 1000 times – how one longs toward the end of a river mouth – how anxious one gets in the last few miles – Old Christopher himself was never so anxious as we were for the sight of "Young Superior" and the cache at the mouth of the river.

At 4 o'clock through a long straight avenue of river we saw the far-off green and blue – the high hills and islands a little nearer and the cache loomed in sight – the keepers shouted and so did we. I finally broke the silence and in an everyday, ordinary tone told them that I thought it was not a bad day.

They invited us to supper – gravy and potatoes, "jungle" corned beef, bread (real bread) and tea. Did I eat?

Thursday, 4 October   Ice clear again but a gale of wind – will try to cross to the post 12 miles up the bay tonight. *Ombabika* leaves there in the a.m. At 8 o'clock started for the gap, or rather a narrow mouth of Ombabika Bay through which the steamer has to pass ultimately, to catch her there – far too heavy a sea to get to the point. The gap is 6 miles from the river.

It was pitch dark when we left the river and a sea again starting to make things "warm" for "Skookum." We sailed out of the river into the lake (the only lake) and glanced back upon a scene I shall never forget. Our fire lighting up the tall growth of trees – the little cache – its one window alight – the dark mysterious stretch of river and such a musical chorus of howling huskies that gave me a weird lonely feeling. We could see only the high rounded nose of the point standing out against the gray blank sky and which gave us our direction – all else seemed black – unreal. The wind, tired of blowing a gale from the east, shifted westward and gave us a "terrifying" sea. It gave me (in its force) a dunking every three seconds or so and I was wet too and cold. We dug in, fearful lest we should be forced to put back to the river and therefore miss our boat. The night was cloudy and squalls of rain made it impenetrable at times – we were anxious but of course didn't say a word to each other – at night everything – the waves, the wind and distances seem magnified. As I looked into the water it seemed as if I were high and far above it – it was distorted like something unreal far below and away.

We paddled (and busily paddled some more) without any stop till we were well within the lee of the bluff – we could tell when we reached it by the sound of the wind and foliage. We coasted along in the shadow of the cliffs till the gap was in sight and beyond it the far expanse of water to the north. The real trouble is in crossing the gap to scrub island which is in its center ½ mile from the either shore. We made it ("like a dancer") as Dinsmore said.

I purchased two ducks during the day from an Indian for a piece of bacon and 50 cents. We gathered a bit of dry wood and made a crackling fire, got 'em defeathered and threw in our ducks with just enough feathers remaining on them to keep them from burning. This was at midnight. How we circled around that fire peering on that pair and wondering if they would ever be cooked – about two o'clock we hauled them out, flopped in our blankets and had a feast – ah me, I can't say any more.

Friday, 5 October   Such a wreckage of feathers, bones and bannock strewn around. We arose feeling "funny." I had a "feathery" taste in my mouth. Dinsmore asked if I cared for any breakfast. I said: "pass the pain killer please."

It was cold and cranky morning – both of us a little like it. The boat happened along at 10:30. We were soon aboard snuggled in our blankets in the hold trying to sleep. We called at Wabimash and as I looked around some I felt lonely – do you remember our swim there? It seemed years ago. Swimming today!

Laid up at Nipigon House for the night. Blues with a vengeance.

On Train. Arrived at Virgin Falls at 12:30 – saw pervabic and got our knife a trifle soiled and dull but that does not matter. I started down river at 1:00 p.m. and didn't we fly. Am at Nipigon 9:00 p.m. You should see the lake and river now – all the colors imaginable in the foliage – not a tarnish to mar things – it all seemed so deserted – I feel lonely. Everything we did together along the river and lake wildly came to me again as I passed along the places and camp grounds.

We crossed Alexander Point just at dark – it was glorious going downstream and how dark it was. We would once in awhile bump shore when we were sure we were in the center of the river.

Mr. Kirby hasn't received the baskets or moccasins yet – I gave him "old Harry" for it though – promised to look into the matter again. However, I purchased that pair for you at Nipigon House – hope they will fit. I tried them on and they were a little large!

I am "worked up" – what a feast of letters I will have tonight and those photos!

I am anxious to see the "kids." Have them get up a pajama tossing match for my special benefit!

Met Alex the Picturesque on the river on his way to Virgin Falls.

Summary Located north boundary – have settled the float question. Joined the Kawakashgamiga River to the Little Current – mapped an unknown route across country to the head waters of the Ombabika River and mapped the Ombabika as well as country further east. Have definite maps and information of the Huronian formation and the area surrounding it in the east, north and west, the whole being south of the continental divide. Just in to see how the pictures are coming out. They are alright. I will send you a set tomorrow.

Please excuse the grubbiness in this edition. It is hard to keep one's writing clean in the woods.

3 From Bryn Mawr to Lake Nipigon

The preceding diary as intimate narrative documents the relationship that Flaherty and Frances Hubbard began in 1903, pursued intermittently throughout the decade, and affirmed through their marriage in 1914. It was a lifelong partnership, for after 1914 Frances was a continual influencing presence in the Flaherty enterprise. The origin of his association with the Hubbard family deserves note, as do the early years of Frances Johnson Hubbard. Her fierce advocacy of Robert Flaherty and her own contribution to refining and promoting his work as photographer, filmmaker, and writer did much to shape the character of his artistic career.

The second daughter of Lucius Lee Hubbard (1849–1933) and Frances Lambard Hubbard (1852–1927), she was raised in a household of comparative privilege and affluence. She had two sisters, Charlotte, the eldest, and Julia. Her mother, with ancestors of wealth from among the Irish whalers of Belfast, was raised by a grandfather, Allen Lambard (her mother having died in childbirth), who made a fortune as a sawmill and wholesale hardware proprietor during the California gold rush.

A vivid source of details on the upbringing and education of Lucius L. Hubbard is that provided by his youngest daughter, Julia Hubbard Adams, in her "Memories of a Copper County Childhood":

My father was born in Cincinnati in 1849, and was graduated from Exter Academy, Harvard [Phi Beta Kapa, 1872], and the Boston Law School. Finding the practice of law uncongenial he turned a hobby into a profession by taking his Master's Degree [and PHD, 1886] in mineralogy and geology. Having a wife and two children by this time, economy made it necessary to go to Germany to take his degree at the University of Bonn.

Dad was a collector at heart. His first real love was books. (His collection of first editions of *Robinson Crusoe* and *Gulliver's Travels* were given to the University of Michigan at his death.) His mineral collection was left to Michigan Tech [Michigan College of Mines]. He collected stamps and coins and even the envelopes he received for their possible postal cancellation value. Mother said that in Germany he would come home happily bearing beautiful Sèvres soup plates when, too often, the money for soup to put in them was lacking. But we were all eventually the fortunate owners of a few priceless things that represented this passion for collecting. He was a Regent of the University of Michigan for twenty two years, and died in his eighties still absorbed in projects of one sort or another and active to the very end.

In reviewing my father's life I like to remember the following event. During his college years and well in the married ones Dad had camped every summer in the Moosehead Lake region of Maine. He knew the area so well that he had made a map of it, a map that is still being used.[1]

In 1891 Hubbard was appointed state geologist of Michigan and was associated with the Michigan College of Mines, serving as a trustee of the college from 1904 onwards. Mrs Hubbard passed the winters in Cambridge, Massachusetts, to be near her daughters and their education, spending the summers in Houghton, the site of the college. Resigning the post of state geologist in 1899, Hubbard (paralleling the career path of Flaherty's father) took up duties as mine manager and engineer for the Copper Range Mining Company, moving to Painesdale, ten miles from Houghton.

Into this household of erudition, gentility, and privilege was born Frances Johnson Hubbard. The 1916 alumnae register of Bryn Mawr College provides the following particulars:

Mrs. Robert Joseph Flaherty. Residence: 36 Roxborough Drive, Toronto,

Canada. Born December 5, 1883, in Bonn, Germany, the daughter of Lucius and Frances Lambard Hubbard. She is a member of the Episcopal church. Prepared by Miss Ingol's School, Cambridge, Mass., and by Miss Florence Baldwin's School, Bryn Mawr, Pa. A.B. 1905, group, History, and Economics, and Politics. Special student, New England Conservatory of Music, Boston, Mass., 1905–1906; student of music, New York and Paris, 1908–1913. In February, 1911, she cruised to the West Indies and the northern part of South America.

On November 12, 1914, in New York City, she was married to Robert Joseph Flaherty, of Port Arthur, Canada, an explorer.

The paths of Robert and Frances crossed sometime in 1903 when Frances had concluded her second year at Bryn Mawr, and during or just after the seven months of Flaherty's participation in the mineralogy program at the Michigan College of Mines.

According to the journalist Robert Taylor, this was just another flamboyant phase of Flaherty's benighted academic career: "The trouble was somewhat the same as at Upper Canada College; he had found the place confining and, among other things, had taken to sleeping in the woods. Also, in classes he drifted into nostalgic reveries, answering questions, if at all, in Chippewa. Upon his expulsion, he received a letter from his father wishing him the best of luck in whatever he elected to do, on his own hook, in the future."[2]

A letter that Frances wrote to her friend Margaret Thurston on 22 December 1903 indicates that Frances and Robert were already acquainted and that he was employed at a lumber camp near Painesdale.[3] They had arranged to go ice skating together. In addition, there are letters from Frances to her mother, undated but also written on Bryn Mawr College stationery, which refer to correspondence between Frances and "Rob." As if in his defense, Frances comments that "his life really seems to be getting more balanced and regulated" and that given all of his survey work he has no time to practice the violin. She closes one letter by saying, "He's a dear boy, *isn't* he, Ma?"[4]

Despite the view among Flaherty's biographers that Flaherty met Frances in Houghton, in fact they met in Painesdale when Flaherty was in the employ of Lucius Hubbard. In the memoir of her childhood, Julia Hubbard Adams recalled:

> Before I leave Painesdale I want to tell how Robert Flaherty came into our lives. Dad came home from the office one day saying that he had just hired a young man by the name of Flaherty to do odd jobs around the mine principally the

care of the street lights on the expanding mine locations. Young Flaherty said that his father had staked him to an education at the Mining School explaining carefully that he considered it his last parental responsibility in connection with his son. If he couldn't stay in college he was on his own. As it turned out when he presented himself to the Painesdale mine for a job he had just discovered what "being on his own" meant. He owned only the clothes he wore and the violin which he carried carefully under one arm. They put a cot up for him on the third floor of the new office building and hung curtains around it. Here he sat long hours playing to himself until he discovered the one local saloon and then he played for the miners assembled there on Saturday evenings while they passed the hat for him.

Dad thought my sister Frances and Bob would have their music in common. And so it proved. And this is where the romance got its start. But it saw a good many years of rough going before it finally led to their marriage. Bob didn't like my little friends because they threw snow balls at him and yelled, "Hit him again, he's Irish!" He blamed me for it for some reason! Anyway, Dad heard him swearing at me one day and shortly after that Bob left Painesdale and it was a number of years before any of us knew where he had gone or what he was doing. Either by accident or by design – I never knew which – my sister Charlotte and her husband and some friends asked Frances to go on a camping trip to Canada with them, and who should be one of the guides but Robert Flaherty![5]

There is an evident connection between this meeting (most likely engineered by Charlotte) and Flaherty's recollection of Frances being his companion on a journey, to which he referred in his diary of September–October 1906. In a letter of 29 August 1906 to Margaret Thurston, Frances alluded to "others" indolent enough to be paddled about by guides in Peterboroughs [large wooden canoes] and to Charlotte's playful and clearly first-hand view of Robert as the "spitfire."

The passionate yearning for union that pervades Flaherty's 1906 diary was not to be satisfied. Given Flaherty's dismissal from Hubbard's employment, what chance of union could there be? – especially in view of the force of Edwardian proprieties, ready to challenge the union of a just-graduated woman of twenty-three and a lumberjack-handyman, with or without violin, of no means and few expectations.

This proved to be a shock point in Frances's life, so much so that by the summer and fall of 1907 she was a resident of a sanatorium in Dansville, New York, where she wrote to Margaret Thurston: "This is strictly between thee and me; nothing is likely 'to come out' for some years and marriage is still a long way off in the dim and unknown region of the

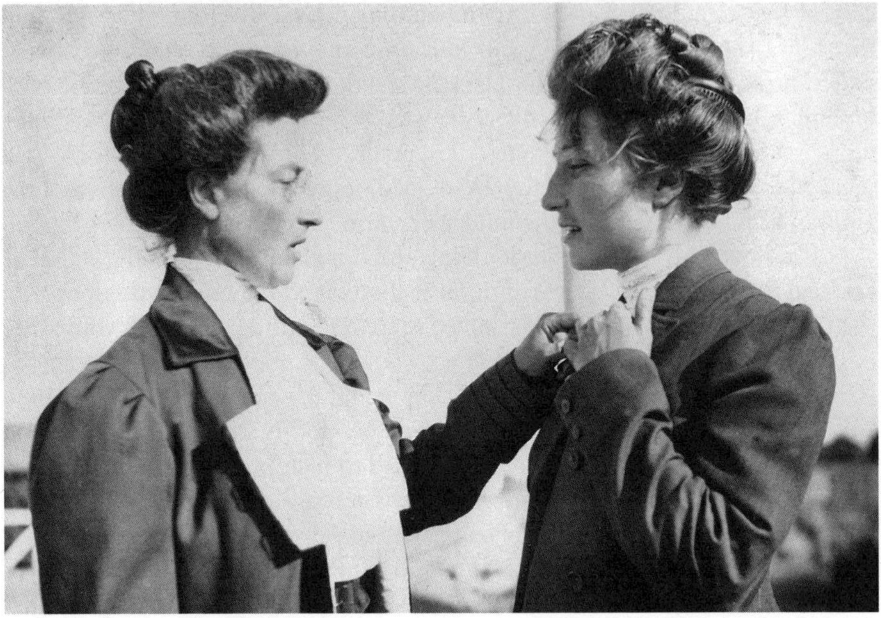

Margaret Thurston (left) and Frances Flaherty, James Bay 1915
(courtesy of the Flaherty Film Study Center at Claremont University [Claremont] and Library and Archives Canada [LAC], PA147414/photo RF)

future. I am content to have it so."[6] Among the Hubbard Family Papers there is an envelope from a Dr Charles Stockton, on which Frances has jotted, "A letter to my sister Charlotte from Dr Stockton, the physician who saved me from invalidism following a 'nervous breakdown' after college." On the back of another envelope, this one a 1906 letter to Frances from Stockton, she noted, in 1966, "If I wanted to meet anyone in heaven it would be Dr Stockton."[7]

If Frances took flight through nervous illness, Flaherty took flight physically by going in late 1906 to British Columbia. Of his stay there, Paul Rotha reported the following anecdotes, based on letters he received in 1958 from H.T. Curtis:

H.T. Curtis, a retired mining engineer, remembered meeting Flaherty fortuitously about November 1906 at the Balmoral Hotel, Victoria. Curtis, who was assistant to the resident engineer of the Canadian Pacific Railway (Island Division), found the young man "a most likeable soul, kind-hearted, generous, but improvident." He appeared to receive an allowance from his mother, but although he paid the hotel bills, he spent the remainder on books, fancy ties, socks, and the like. He and Curtis went on canoeing trips, in which Bob was expert and altogether in his element, though he showed no enthusiasm for fishing.

Curtis introduced him to various people in Victoria, among them a well-known architect, Sam MacClure, whose wife was musical. Flaherty often brought his famous violin to the MacClure house, where he met Mr Russell, the conductor of the local Musical Society. This acquaintanceship resulted in Flaherty and Curtis sharing a house with Russell and his brother. "We more or less mucked together," says Curtis, "and Bob filled the role of house boy."

On Christmas Day 1906, Bob and Curtis went canoeing toward the Indian settlement on the other side of Victoria Inlet. Flaherty was captivated by the Indians' music and songs.

Curtis adds, "He talked at one time of going to Alaska when the spring set in, but to do what I don't remember. He never needed to have any special aim as to occupation or employment. In fact, work in my idea and experience was right out of his ken. However, I learned in later years of his success as a film-maker, etc. I left British Columbia in Easter 1907 to follow my profession and had the occasional breezy note from Bob but finally lost contact."[8]

At the opening of chapter 4 of "Islands," Flaherty tells us that he spent three years in British Columbia before returning to the Lake Superior region. In the Flaherty papers in Butler Library there is a report Flaherty wrote for a J. Herrick McGregor, on whose behalf he did marble and iron ore surveying work along the Tahsis River on the west coast of Vancouver Island. Leaving Victoria on 1 April 1908 and returning on 15 May, he did not offer encouraging findings to his employer:

> Any discovery one might make above the head of the first canyon would be situated in a very disadvantageous position, as the topography of the country being such that an outlet by road or tramway to salt water would entail the ascent and descent from the nose of a foot hill that descends to the canyon, which would prove a very costly operation as conditions in mining on the West Coast now obtain. Unless a very exceptional area in copper, iron or gold were found tangent or near the east fork of the Tahsis River, operation there would be a useless affair.[9]

In addition to the formal report, there exists a fragment of a diary that Flaherty kept as a means of sharing with Frances an extended narrative of his impressions about the culture and history of Vancouver Island. He told her:

Robert Flaherty, in British Columbia 1906–8

(Claremont, LAC, PA147352)

Nootka was a Spanish trading post and garrison in the days when the seaboard of the Pacific states was a mystery, when all the seaboard between Panama and Sitka was a series of far-off unknown regions.

The keel of the first ship to be built on the north Pacific was laid at Nootka. The massacre of the "Good Ship Boston" occurred in that Friendly Cove! It is all steeped in history – a romance – and so little known. Today it is a mere shadow of the wonder days, a village of degenerate Indians, a lone white trader and a priest who fights a hopeless cause. If you wander about the village you may find pieces of the old Spanish tile of the forts, a few chiseled pot holes in the masses of granite that were used in the old days for water. And near the Chief's house a few traces of bones dug out of the ground some years ago when the Indians were excavating for a cellar. That is all that marks remains of Nootka – the first port in all the north Pacific.

The history of it all is a long story – you shall hear and to the better advantage when you come. I must not tell you all the story of Nootka, but when you are come and gone and that experience is all folded away in memory, you will know the fascination of its history through all your life, enhanced for the reason that it was so little known – almost belonging to you.[10]

The tenor of this diary and Frances's letters to her friend Margaret

Frances Hubbard and Robert Flaherty, Vancouver, 1908
(Claremont, LAC, PA170913)

Thurston make clear that Robert and Frances were not to be diverted in sustaining their relationship. Frances visited him in British Columbia during the summer of 1908. Writing on 8 April to Thurston from Buffalo, where her sister Charlotte resided and where Frances was under the care of Dr Stockton, she confided:

You know, I should just like to try to fool myself into thinking I was going to see you before I go West. It's the real, truly Westest West I am talking about now

Frances Hubbard on horseback, Vancouver, 1908
(Claremont, LAC, PA147512/photo RF)

– the Pacific Coast, British Columbia, the Rockies, the Yellowstone. Such are the landmarks of a two month trip I am planning to take in July and August … I am wild. Oh, I can't tell you about these past three months here in Buffalo. In part they have been so ghastly – but now I am really getting WELL – better every day, and I am beginning to live again. Lots of the good has come through medical gymnastics and Mrs Manken who has been giving them to me is to be my traveling companion next summer. So you see it is a trip "for my health."[11]

The impression the trip made on Frances and its aftermath are recalled by Margaret Thurston in her own autobiography, written in the mid-1970s. Frances, she tells us, did go to Vancouver Island with her companion-therapist Manken: "I can still remember Frances's happy expression as she described the pristine beauty of Vancouver Island: the clear tumbling streams and marble pools, fringed with maiden hair fern, the birds and the flowers. All this was a joyful experience but Bob had not grown up. Frances told me he had been childishly jealous of her companion, the doctor. His letters had been deceptive. Frances broke her engagement and returned to the East."[12]

Robert Flaherty with violin, a photograph Frances declared to be among her very favorites of "Rob." Vancouver, 1908 (Claremont, LAC, PA114960/ Frances Hubbard)

Over the next few years, Frances traveled to New York and Paris to continue her conservatory training in music and piano, and in 1911 she visited the West Indies and South America. During the same few years, Robert returned to Port Arthur and then moved to Toronto, where in 1910 his father joined the firm of William Mackenzie and Donald Mann as director of their mining department.[13] Through his father, Flaherty was retained by Mackenzie and Mann to conduct the first of four iron ore surveying expeditions to Hudson Bay and Baffin Island in the Eastern Arctic. With a small outfit, one assistant, and a cash reserve of $450, Flaherty struck out by canoe from Ontario to begin a series of expeditions that would preoccupy his energy and talents for the next six years and serve as milestones in his evolution from prospector-explorer to photographer-filmmaker.

Diary of the First Mackenzie Expedition 5 August 1910 – 14 March 1911

Friday, 5 August 1910[14] Engaged with William Mackenzie to examine the iron ores of the Nastapoka Islands.

Saturday, 6 August I went to Ottawa with a letter to A.P. Low.[15] I found Low out of town. However I obtained the data required satisfactorily. After return to Toronto from Ottawa, delayed there for about two weeks.

Sunday, 21 August Finally left for Cobalt and completed arrangements for trip.

Saturday, 27 August Engaged Alec Crundell for the trip.

Monday, 29 August Left Cobalt for Cochrane.

[Tuesday], 30 August Left Cochrane for Ground Hog. Left Ground Hog at noon with George Friday as passenger to Grand Rapids and also in company with McNab brothers, and May.

Friday, 2 September Arrived at Grand Rapids at noon. Cached canoe at south end Long Portage and came down in canoe cached at other end.

[Saturday], 3 September Portaged over Grand Rapids and started with Indian family for Moose. Made map of balance of Mattagami River and Moose to mouth of Abitibi. Arrived at mouth Mattagami River at two o'clock.

Sunday, 4 September Arrived at French Co. post at six o'clock.[16] Camped. Next a.m. continued to Moose Factory, three miles away.

[Wednesday], 7 September Stayed at the Factory outfitting, etc. Took and developed very good photos of the place and people. Were treated very kindly and assisted in every way. Left by sail boat for Charlton Island with strong fair wind and four man crew. Arrived at six o'clock in evening. Crundell sick. A record trip. Met Mr McNab, the manager and staff, also Mr Gillies of Albany. Advised to wait here until Griffith of Fort George comes from Rupert House, where he went to be married.[17] Advice re trip, from all concerned, seems to be against our going at this time of year. Saw my first "Huskie" at Charlton. Interesting.[18]

Wednesday, 14 September Griffith and bride arrived from Rupert House. Have secured two Huskies for trip and now waiting for schooner *Pride* from Fort George. Huskies went back on their "contract" and must now wait and get dog team from Fort George.

Tuesday, 20 September *Inenew* with Mr and Mrs Crundell, Mr McNab, Mrs Turner and passengers left for Moose six o'clock.[19] Partner and self with the Griffiths alone now. Unusually bad, windy and stormy weather, ever since our arrival here.

Wednesday, 21 September *Sorine* sighted, distress signals.

Thursday, 22 September *Sorine* came in post with Miller,[20] going to be abandoned sprung a leak. *Pride* of Fort George arrived.

Saturday, 24 September Turner arrived from Moose. Amazement at *Sorine*'s return. Waiting for wind for *Pride*.

[Sunday], 25 September Awakened at 5:30. "Fair wind." McNab volcanic, lice in his bed from me, astounded – very small – parted minus formalities. Fine day and splendid run. Mrs Griffith and Crundell sick. Camped at sunset at Long Point, great dinner.

[Monday], 26 September Up at sunrise, clear day. Handed ½ lb. of flour to Indian family. Took picture, Mrs Gillies. Fair wind. Indian made us present, ducks, trout and white fish. Camped at Grey Goose Island at four o'clock. Mrs Griffith sore throat. New wrinkle in goose hunting. Indian givers. Small progress today. Light wind. Indians came down from Fort George, called at dark for visit and tobacco. Showed them our outfit, we are wonder workers no doubt!!! Much interested, gave them bread and syrup.

Tuesday, 27 September Splendid day, north wind. All Indians hunting geese. Took three pictures. Indians came along at dark with five geese.

Sir William Mackenzie, Flaherty's sponsor and, according to Frances, his nemesis. Toronto 1914 (LAC, C23691)

Wednesday, 28 September Up early, light west wind, beating our way north to post. Slow work. Camped at Grey Goose. Mrs Griffith still ill. Cold wind and weather.

Saturday, 1 October Warmer, fine day, little wind, headache. Sunday dinner!! Goose and dried beef. Southeast wind tonight. No goose hunting today. Expect Fort George tomorrow.

Sunday, 2 October Up early, cold, fine wind, bowling along. Reached mouth Big River at 11:30. Tide and wind against going up river to post. Gale blowing, rain, stayed in forecastle till 7:30 at night, then managed to beat to post.[21] Will remain at post till freeze up. Living at Aldridges, Crundell at Griffiths.

Monday, 12 December Preparing for trip. Am going to "Gulf" alone. Crundell will take January packet for "Moose" and await me there. Go to Cape Jones with "fur" team and thence to "Great Whale" with "Huskie Bill." Fall has been unusually fine and freeze up normal. Expect to arrive again in Fort George 20th of Jan., at latest. "Drifter" delayed our start.

Friday, 16 December Started at nine o'clock. Outfit complete. Nine dog team. Alec and Teddy (drivers).[22] North wind, cloudy day, "rime" very bad. Lunch at 11 o'clock, currant biscuits and tea. Covey of ptarmigan watched us eating. Arrived at "Cook's" camp at Brandy River about 2:30. Camped. News of silver fox to northward for Hudson's Bay Company. Johnny Inlet arrived at five o'clock. Good weather, good outfit. Report of starving "Huskies" on the Cape, and impassable deep snow on the headlands and points. Richard and Johnny traveling with us with six dog team. Great outfit in beans and bacon, few canned luxuries and presents for natives (knives, tobacco, mouth organs, needle cases, matches, etc.). Earth-shoeing and icing is a novelty. Salt water rime the bane of travelers. Country or coast line, same as to southward of Fort George. Good tent or "marquee." Snow during night.

Saturday, 17 December Awake at 5 o'clock. Intermittent "snacking" till day break. Present of tobacco to "Cook" and sons. A splendid dog of Cook's died most unexpectedly during night. Most trying traveling during journey today. Deep snow and rime. Dogs played out at noon. Stayed in tepee with Indian friends for the night. Present of "sweets" for the "ladies" and children. Clouded windy day and snow.

Sunday, 18 December Away at daybreak. Better traveling, wonderful sunrise. Snack with Indian friends at 11 o'clock. Left again at noon amid racy sendoff from the "ladies" who chased after our sledge only to fall short and fling themselves prostrate into the deep snow. While crossing a headland struck a boulder and ground away a good part of our earthen sledge shoeing – thereafter travel harder. Fair wind, have left the salt water. On Cape Jones Peninsula now. Camp with Indian friends, who helped put up my marquee, fetch wood and water, etc. Windy clouded night fairly cold. Men all in tepee. Abandoned my beans, gave them to Indian friends of last evening, too bitter.

Monday, 19 December Wind and cold, snow very deep and drifting, very cold. Arrived at Matowkum's camp at noon. Camp is a log hut on Bishop Roggan River, a river of some size. Very crowded indoors. Wind too heavy now and will stay here all night. Very kindly people, two of them afflicted with an incurable cancerous disease. One a man and other boy of fourteen or thereabouts. Poor old man's wife cried when I examined him. "Benjamin" gave a sermon to us (about twenty) at night in "Cree." Very picturesque and original. Will always remember it and

William ("Husky Bill") Fleming, who with his brother Nero provided Flaherty with inestimable assistance. Great Whale River 1901–4

(courtesy of the A.A. Chesterfield Collection, E2-3, Queen's University Archives/photo A.A. Chesterfield) in the part where he went wrong on the hymn, singing the first half of the song and form and leaving out the completing form throughout the hymn. (Like sea-sawing all in one side.) Wind increased. Sleeping in "Matowkum's" bunk.

Tuesday, 20 December   Awake early, cold night, gales of wind. Going around by coast line as lake route is too deep in snow. Gale of wind and very cold, though clearing. "Matowkum" and son started out with us but broke their earth shoeing a few miles out and had to go back. "Benjamin" accompanying us as far as his brother's at the "Cape." Traveling vastly improved. Barrenness of the country is felt now, in miles of country devoid of all vegetation. Had noon "snack" at Indian camp, took picture there of Indian boy, and dog pictures later. Afternoon beautifully clear and cold. Learned of "Husky Bill" going south to Fort George, disappointing. Arrived at Huskies ("Showuk") about 3:30, which is end of trip with the half breeds, thence farther with "Huskies." After long "palaver," "Shank" and "Teddy" took self and outfit over to "Tucktoo's" camp about four miles away. Arrived at dark, about 6:30 o'clock, "Teddy" as interpreter arranged details of balance of trip as far as Whale River. Will use flour as dog food, as seal meat is unobtainable. Teddy and Shank left after snack for Shank's camp. Slept with Huskies in their camp. Much impressed with "Huskie."

Wednesday, 21 December   In camp all day waiting for start. Leave in morning early. Have Husky women making biscuits for me. Good weather till night fall. A blowing gale set in about midnight, the fore part of my tent gave away and I was forced to spend balance of night under half the canvas while the fore part and part of outfit drifted in snow. Bitterly cold. Huskie came over in morning, fixed up tent and stove again. Gave him breakfast.

[Thursday], 22 December   Shank came finally though I did not expect him in such weather. After handshake all around with the social dames of the camp, we started with a fresh ten dog team, my first Eskimo sledging over hill and lake country which hardly held a tree, we made our way. We are indeed getting out of the tree limit and into the barren area. We reached the coast at noon and traveled on the ice along the tide mark. About 1:30, we hailed an encampment of Huskies in two tents. Lunched with them. Gave them some small presents which made them effusive. Lunch in good order and (odor!), then away till about four miles on we broke our earthen shoeing. Forced to camp (about three o'clock) and men went after moss for "patching." Windy but not cold (south). We are into Hudson Bay now and the character of country is changed to high rugged and barren hills and rocky country. It is more interesting than to southward. I am glad to be rid of that monotonous country. Huskie just making the patch shoeing as I write. He mixed moss and flour and water into a dough, to be put in the broken gap and allowed to freeze. In a.m. it will be planed down and iced with warm water as is usual in icing the earthen shoeing. A wonderful and ingenious affair. The "Huskie" is all that an Indian isn't, and then some. They have the ingenuity of the Jap, the strength that is par with any man's, are fearless, open and frank and (important!), grateful for kindness shown (not so the Indian) damn him! This trip is accumulating interest in every mile. A south gale of wind as I write, shaking the tent like a wobbly jelly, and the stove (the heart of it all) crackling, the sparks from it chasing madly as they shine in streaks and flashes through the bellying canvas. Camp at White Bear Hill.

Friday, 23 December Awake early. Wind veered to north, snow. Awake at daybreak. Heavy traveling along sea ice, drifts of snow and jagged ice fields that appear as masses of frozen waves from 3′ to 6′ high. Snowing steadily and heavy wind. Made "Sapper" and "Huskie Bill's" camp at noon at little Cape Jones, into the finest Huskie outfit I've seen. Out of grub and naturally glad to see us. Gave them presents and small amount of grub. One fine type of woman amongst them, really fine looking. An Indian – Huskie diet of six months may alter viewpoints of beauty in natives' favor. "Sapper" a fine type, like him. About five or six miles on from our lunch place, and while trying to navigate some frozen seaway, an earthen shoeing broke again. We had to make shore and into a patch of stunted trees for camp about three o'clock. Vexations, damn! My two Huskies are splendid and work like "nailers" always in good humor. A virtue of Indian and Huskie, a white man could copy. Fine camp. Made stewed peaches and gave my "Huskies" a fill of them. "Na-kung-mek" and smiles. Showed the men a safety razor and demonstrated it. Much surprise and curiosity. Won't see Whale River Post till Xmas night (if then).

Saturday, 24 December Northwest wind and fairly cold. Our camp at Little Cape Jones, on the open coast line of Hudson Bay. Very difficult traveling. Ice fields impassable and forced to keep along tide mark.

Between bare rock cliffs, boulders and sea ice and salt rime, we found things interesting. It is wonderful how my men navigated the sledge through seemingly impassable places. I narrowly escaped breaking my leg and falling into a crevasse which was innocently coated at surface with a crust of snow and ice. Our sledge is average size of about 14′ long, is carrying about five hundred pounds. How my men ever brought it through the ice field and rock shore line and handled our ten dogs, is a marvel, and so apparently impossible. Our travel average about a mile per hour this afternoon. We are camped in a grove of stunted trees near Bear Islands and about fifteen miles from Great Whale River. Passed the famous Sucker Creek, where Leith tried to ford. Cleared this afternoon, a brilliant and original sunset, color everywhere. The great saw-toothed ice field offshore was a splendid sight, with here and there pillars of ice resplendent in the glare of sun and color and looking like gothic spires in the distance. The black bare rock of shore line and receding hills was contrast to the illuminated ice and snow. Gave my men a big feed tonight of my rations, syrup and raspberry jam. Clear night, Xmas eve, thinking!

Sunday, 25 December   Off at daybreak, clear and cold and off shore breeze. A glorious sunrise. Expect to make Whale River today. More ice work, very difficult travel. Thankful my legs are not broken. We reached a Huskie encampment at noon and "snacked" with them. Gave them presents, pipes, matches, tobacco, fancy soap, and biscuits to youngsters. Away in short order and into the ice work again. Again I marveled on how we ever get through. Along a tide mark of jagged ice with lanes of open water off shore, over black bare rocks that threatened every minute to demolish our sledge. Our earthen shoeing was half off early in the game and part of the sledge was down to the ivory shoeing underneath, which the rocks quickly ruined. There is no control of the dogs in the work and they strain for speed continually. It is up and down, racing pell mell ahead, crashing into cakes of ice and ever on one runner, then a drop, sheer away from rock to ice. I scramble after blindly and catch the sledge on an even sheet, try to recover a breath for the next "chop" and through it all these "Huskies" steer on either side in straining, tugging, heart-breaking work, both hurdle and run, freeing entangled lines that run out to the fan of yelping dogs and admonishing and coaxing the "leader" the while. A little after four, darkness came, the wind increased and Whale River seemed never near. My men could not tell me where we were, by sign or otherwise, and when night descended I made motions for camp but they would not hear of it. It became bitterly cold. We rounded headland of point, straining for a sign of light along the black shore line ahead. We came upon drifted black ice of the river's mouth, which our dogs took at a gallop, only to plunge into the wind-packed drifts of snow which we would barely strain them through at speed, over another glare sheet with the same result tiresomely recurring. Of a sudden our ten dogs are howling madly with energy redoubled, the lights of Great Whale Post glow out to the night, with a cheer indescribable. We arrive, a fire, pints of tea, warmth and rest. The population (in toto) encircles me, Huskie and Indian.[23]

Monday, 26 December Whale River Post. Making arrangements for trip northward. Nero will go with me. Greatly interested in the "Post" and people – "Harold" the clerk is a character, married to a Huskie (sister of Nero's).[24] Have picked up some splendid curios. Developed pictures. Heard story about the finding of Leith's bag, containing over a hundred dollars in bills, which the Huskies and Harold thought were no good after being wet. Accordingly threw them away!![25]

Wednesday, 28 December Stayed at Great Whale River two days. Left for northward with Nero and six dog team. Expect to pick up another Huskie and two more dogs tomorrow and seal meat for dog food. From Whale River north the country is high, barren almost and impressive, a relief to the dreary flat of James Bay area. Camped near Paint Island, about twenty miles from Post. Splendid day. Killed ptarmigan with a splendid shot.

Thursday, 29 December The trip today was good, made about twenty five miles. The towering masses of sheer cliff on the seaward side of the sound in which we are traveling are magnificent. About noon met a Huskie and son going south with kayak on their sleigh. Gave them something to eat and bought a dog for ten Beaver.[26] Made an encampment of Huskies just over the neck of land at the end of sound. Arrived about seven o'clock, dark, tired and hungry. Calm all today, but heavy wind tonight. Nero held service. Gave Huskies I am staying with presents, purchased another dog, and secured another Huskie for trip.

Friday, 30 December Away at 8:30. Wonderfully rugged high and barren coast line. Towering cliffs a thousand feet high and farther inland hills of three thousand feet. This morning Nero found a fresh seal hole.

Harold and Mary Udgaarden,
Great Whale River
(LAC, PA136292/photo Olaus J. Murie)

Waited for seal to come up which he did – fired and missed an easy shot. We tried out gun, I won in the shooting contest and chaffed Nero about it. Saw a red fox on ice but could not get near him. Calm day, though foggy from open water not far to seaward. Camped near Little Whale River. Windy tonight. Barrenness increases. Bad traveling, broken ice field.

Saturday, 31 December Started late this a.m. Nero is slow in breaking camp. Clear, cold and drifting wind from southward. In my deer skin coat and Huskie boots I nearly froze. About five miles from camp came to a Huskie family. Decided to fix sled and cook up biscuits and beans, therefore camped. Calm at evening and cold. Gave youngsters sweets for "value received," sewing and water.

Sunday, 1 January 1911 When I woke up an "easter" with snow was blowing. Nero did not want to break camp. At noon it cleared, nearly calm and brilliant sun and clear sky. After lunch started. Made another encampment of Huskie and family and camped. Camp is off Belanger Island. Had men cut tent poles for balance of trip north for well out of the timber. Scenery today was splendid. The coast becomes higher and masses of wind swept rocks rise in cliffs to over two thousand feet high on the sky line inland. They looked wonderfully fine in the brilliant sun, their satin snow patches and red-black masses of rock. Gave the Huskies presents and left order for some Eskimo snow goggles and a doll of seal skin. Nero held a service in the Huskies' tent tonight. Clear night. The boys saw a silver fox while we were travelling.

Monday, 2 January Calm and clear, finest day of trip so far. Passed Richmond Gulf entrance, or rather Hazard Gulf, safely over new ice. Nero on foot ahead testing with a seal spear. The beauty of the coast line is still more bold, rugged and high as we go north. Richmond Gulf entrance marks the last of the trees and henceforth we use drift wood for fire. Made our course along the lee shore of the Islands. Expected to come upon an igloo encampment about noon somewhere on Inlet Island. When we arrived at island saw two Huskies at gap of open water hunting seals. Had our lunch near by and invited them to it. They are original Huskies with no sign of white man's cloth in their costume. During lunch we spied an Arctic fox making a meal off a seal which the Huskies had killed but couldn't get, so the hunter and I went out and practiced on it with the rifle I got at Fort George. Nero came along and finding the ice field moving down from north, it very soon had the lane of water and thin weak ice nearly closed, so after a few trials he speared it and we dragged it to the field ice we were on. That Huskie hunter was pleased. I bought the seal for dog food. We made for mainland and camped. Gave a banquet to my men – beans and bacon, condensed soup, jam and tea!! Northern lights. Took photo of the Huskies.

Tuesday, 3 January After a mile of our travel this a.m. came on an igloo encampment. Took photos and visited the four igloos and distributed sweets and tobacco. The men all off seal hunting. Had tea in one of the camps. Most interesting camp. Wish I had a hundred films. Made south end of Gillies Island and camped. Drift wood fire and snow floor. No let up to the cold.

Nero Fleming and wife, Great Whale River, 1910–11. He was one of the Inuit who were associated with Flaherty. (courtesy of the British Library [BL], Canadian Copyright Collection [CCC], 23989.46/photo RF)

Wednesday, 4 January   Away at sunrise. South wind, fairly cold. Met inland Huskie family coming down to the post from the north. Took pictures and gave them tobacco, sweets, tea and sugar. Arrived at north end Gillies Island at 1:30. Camped. Away to northward some fifteen miles we could see the spray of Nastapoka Falls towering on the horizon. Good camp, warmer. Examine Taylor Island tomorrow.

Thursday, 5 January   Took Nero and went over east side Taylor Island. Warm and snow too much for pictures. Will examine southeast end of Taylor and northeast end of Gillies Island tomorrow. Then south to Clarke Island. Took a few samples (subject to sorting). Stormy tonight.

Friday, 6 January Examined southeast end of Taylor Island this a.m. Took average sample near summit, near southeast point and photos of jasper. Fine day though colder and west wind. In p.m. went along northeast shore of Gillies Island and took photos of jasper and of Taylor Island. Saw a red fox. Fine night. Shaved!

Saturday, 7 January Gale of east wind, cold drifting. Delayed as I want to photo the jasperlite cliffs. Cleared tonight.

Sunday, 8 January Left this a.m. about 9:30 for Husky encampment, near Salmon Fishing Cove. Have finished my examinations. Clear cold day. Arrived at encampment about 6 o'clock. Staying in igloo for the night. Surrounded by curious Huskies, large and small. "Nero" held service tonight. Cold, clear, windy night. Took samples on Gillies Island today and on Clarke. Photos of jasperlite on Gillies Island.[27]

Monday, 9 January Great sleep, igloo warm and not too smellie. Photographed this a.m. Started about 10:30. Very cold, wind west and drifting. Made our old camp ground of New Year's night. Decided not to go into Richmond Gulf, "Hitting it up" for Whale River Post. Dangerous crossing at Gulf Hazard.

[*Between 10 January and 4 February, Flaherty has only abbreviated notations of his rapid trip south from the Nastapoka Islands to the James Bay area.*]

Sunday, 5 February Sunday. Cold day, wind, snow getting deeper and slower traveling. Arrived at East Main about three o'clock p.m. Mr Jobson the factor, a fine old man. The Bonards of Revillon Frères are a boon and treated me royally.[28] Waiting till Saturday for McNab – monotonous time of it. Cannot wait longer.

Sunday, 12 February Left for Charlton Island today, cold and deep snow. Arrived at Revillon Frères depot at the Struttons at dusk.[29] Stayed with caretaker, enjoyed a few glasses of claret and made ourselves at home generally. Clear cold night.

Monday, 13 February Left for Charlton about 9:15 taking caretaker and wife as passengers. A few miles out we struck exceedingly rough ice and deep snow. Our travel was slow and very hard. We arrived at

Charlton at dusk. Learned that McNab had passed us today, they going to Struttons and we to Charlton, very disappointed. Visited ship after tea and had a great "soirée." Shank bucking on going to Moose but is taking me to Rupert House instead.

Tuesday, 14 February Resting, leave Tuesday for Rupert House. Glorious weather.

Wednesday, 15 February Away with twelve dogs. Splendid day. Arrive at post at eight o'clock at night. Waiting till next Monday before I can get a team for Moose. Rupert House quite the finest post I've seen. Most important on James Bay.[30]

Monday, 20 February Left at seven for Moose. Cold, "rimy" day. Met Revillon Frères inspector and three white men on their way to Rupert House at lunch time.[31] Had afternoon "snack" at Indian tepee. Camped halfway over Cabbage Willows.

Tuesday, 21 February Away at 6:30. Forced to camp at noon near East Point. Heavy weather and dangerous to cross Hannah Bay. Snowing.

Wednesday, 22 February One of the heaviest drifters of the year. In camp all day.

Thursday, 23 February Away at 5:20 a.m. Squally day. Alternate snow and sun. Arrived at Moose about seven o'clock at night. Great time.

Wednesday, 1 March Left for Cochrane.

Saturday, 4 March Clear cold day. MacAlpine caught us as we were just camped about 3:30 p.m.[32] My feet nearly done on the snowshoe work.

Sunday, 5 March Cold clear day. Started en masse at a strong pace. Played out completely at noon. MacAlpine's party gone on. We camped. Caught returning supply team and obtained three of their dogs. Lucky!

Tuesday, 14 March Arrived at Cochrane.

4 Through Canada's Northland

Upon his return to Toronto in March 1911, Flaherty lost no time in submitting his final report to Mackenzie, completing it on 3 April.[1] In the seven months he had devoted to this expedition – the shortest he would do for Mackenzie – he had proved that his practiced woodsman's skills could also function in a subarctic environment. Although he had used a sledge and dogs in northern Ontario, the icescape of the Hudson Bay terrain could impose formidable physical hardships, and in his report to Mackenzie he gave these harsh conditions as the reason for his decision to send Crundell back to Moose: "Bad ice conditions along the northern route made me decide to take the trip alone, in order to save weight on the sledge and facilitate traveling." Conditions apart, a more compelling reason was the opportunity that this first expedition gave Flaherty to make imaginary travel real, to fulfill an ambition of "getting north" and, as a white man, to do it by keeping pace with the rigors of dogsled travel, first with Indian and then with Inuit guides. In Flaherty's wish to realize this vision, the sodden Crundell was nuisance baggage.

When passing beyond the treeline into the Barren Lands, Flaherty had entered a culture that he had only imagined. Thus, recalling the more denigrated condition of the Indians of his boyhood, it was inevitable that he would compare them with these "Huskies," who "much impressed" him. The latter were more primitive, more vigorous in their sense of duty, more grateful to the white man for his material resources and the opportunities to obtain them through service. Even thirty or so years after the fact, Flaherty's residual memory, even of the dogs, reflected his cross-cultural unease when he recalled in the "Islands" narratives, "Here and there dogs lay sprawled on the grass – not slinking Indian curs, but splendid, thick-coated huskies brought down from the barren lands of the Eskimos far in the North."[2]

A long and at times murderous history of Indian-Inuit encounters tended to sharpen the cultural fault line. The worst of the hostilities had subsided by the 1850s, when the increased presence of missionaries, traders, police, and – to even out the odds – a more equitable circulation of firearms had muted the more dangerous aspects of the hostility. But in this hierarchy of Indian-Inuit worth, the Indians, as the far more defeated people, ranked lower, as they did in Flaherty's social imagination. In this, he was of his culture; but as an artist, he was outside its faults. In Flaherty's visual imagination, Indian and Inuit alike were figures of dignity, and though they show the mark of different cultural influences, the eye of Flaherty's stills camera was democratic, free of prejudicial judgments. To see this, we need to shift our gaze from the narrative to the photographs he took during the first expedition, which in the spring of 1911 he assembled into an album of 102 photographs, entitled, "Through Canada's Northland."[3]

The title and content of the album suggest that Flaherty saw himself as working in the recognized genre of expeditionary photography – field photography, as had been practiced by Albert P. Low, Robert Bell, and a host of others ever since the stills camera became a standard item in expeditionary kits. In addition to its scientific purpose, expedition photography found itself catering to the vast appetite the public had during the nineteenth and twentieth centuries for images of the faraway and exotic. But the traditional imperatives that drove this genre emphasized the scientific, the ethnographic, and the scenic. As Flaherty noted in his diary, he photographed the geology of the Nastapoka Islands and the grandeur of its mighty falls, so the imperatives of the scientific and the picturesque do make their presence felt in the album.

Since the album commemorates a journey through a distant world, modes of transportation over land, water, and ice are represented, with clusters of images of canoes, schooners, kayaks, sledges, and dogs, the last being so ever-present that one out of every six photographs includes a dog. There is also the suggestion of a larger, more global journey with ambitious commercial imperatives. Flaherty's photographs make the Euro-Canadian presence evident by portraying commercial settlements whose transportation networks reach out to Montreal, Paris, and London. We are thus invited to view the sturdy Hudson's Bay Company buildings at Moose Factory, beside which stand two ceremonial cannons, relics of the earlier struggle between the English and French for control of Hudson Bay. These commercial centers serviced ships such as the *Sorine*, seen moored at Charlton Island to unload annual cargo for the network of trading posts and, in turn, to take aboard the principal harvest of the Arctic, the furs. One photograph portrays two traders discerningly examining a fox pelt (they themselves dressed in tastefully tailored furs).

While the commercial presence in the album is strong, even stronger is the impact of these forces on the northern people in all their variety. Flaherty depicts a culture of polarities, part indigenous, part western, its hybrid identity often denoted by clothing and objects of utility: an elderly Cree hunter smokes a European pipe; a Cree woman, Madonnalike, is wrapped in a trade-cloth shawl; a family group is seen in a crazy quilt of fashions, styles, and garments; and the bipolarity of all these identities is further signified by the pervasive evidence of interracial unions.

Part of Flaherty's fascination with the Inuit was his view that the distance between them and these cultural forces was greater than that permitted to Indians. But the Inuit were not immune, so the disparity of images that Flaherty constructed of them was even greater than the more mixed, blended, and westernized identity of the Indian. We thus have striking contrasts of image, which take the form of strong, full-faced photographs of individuals, such as Omarolluk of the Belcher Islands, whose penetrating gaze stares out at us from a frame of textured and angular skins; or the photograph of Nero Fleming and his wife, whose awkwardness before the camera is offset by a gaze that is direct and assured – standing with solidity in clothing free of western tokens. But Nero is a man who signifies two worlds, one traditional and one emergent. In the photograph of him standing, Bible in hand, in the Anglican mission church at Great Whale River, Flaherty clearly acknowledged the presence of the educational and religious forces at work. The church itself stands as the institution prepared to lead the Inuit out of their old

Nastapoka Falls, Nastapoka River, 1910–11
(BL, CCC, 23989/25/photo RF)

ways, and the world map and Anglican creed on the wall behind the altar signify that through the Word and through knowledge of God the larger universe will prevail.

The album includes a series of photographs of Flaherty himself and thus we can witness his efforts not only to document his journey but to affirm his affiliation with a world that hitherto he had only imagined. To do this, he had to invert the cultural process, showing himself, as a white man, becoming the insider in a world whose indigenous culture was dissolving. We thus have a photograph – taken on Charlton Island by someone to whom he had surrendered his camera – of Flaherty hunched behind a group of standing Cree children. His hovering figure suggests paternal protection, an alliance he later featured in a lifetime of films featuring the young guided by wise adults. Another photograph shows Flaherty manfully piloting a kayak, the only incongruity being his wide-brimmed hat, the same he wore in the Charlton photograph. The third and last self-portrait in the album is of Flaherty in full native dress, standing heroically amidst the barren landscape, assured of his place there.

Sledge dog, whose peaked ears and erect tail signal that he is ready to race, 1910–11
(BL, CCC, 23989.37/photo RF)

Hudson's Bay Company Post at Moose Factory, 1910, the administrative center for the Eastern Arctic. Its cannons celebrated the victory over the French for control of the region.
(BL, CCC, 23989.30/photo RF)

Above: The *Sorine* unloading cargo at Charlton Island, 1910–11
(BL, CCC, 23989.6/photo RF)

Left: Wreckage of the *Sorine* – scuttled, it was suspected, for its insurance. Charlton Island, 1910–11
(courtesy of the Hudson's Bay Company Archives [HBCA], 1988.51.467/photo Hugh Conn)

Men icing sledge runners, a necessary preparation for traveling on dry snow, 1910–11
(BL, CCC, 23989.28)

In the history of Flaherty as a visual artist, the 1911 album ranks as an important milestone. Given the great difficulty in placing and dating photographs taken in these early years, the album provides us with an anthology of Flaherty's photographic styles, a baseline that is invaluable in evaluating the other photographs of the North that Flaherty took through to 1921. Although he never found a publisher for the album, he did receive some public recognition, most notably in Augustus Bridle's article, "Fur Folk of Labrador," which was illustrated with thirteen Flaherty photographs and was published in the large-circulation weekly, the *Canadian Courier*.[4] Bridle observed that the featured photographs were but a sample of "an astonishing collection of northland pictures." Other particulars in the article suggest that Bridle had seen not only the album but other photographs Flaherty had taken, as well as the diary itself. The Bridle article was the first significant public debut of Flaherty as explorer-photographer. Although its publication did not bring Flaherty

Omarolluk, another significant contributor to Flaherty's expeditionary work.
Great Whale River, 1910–11 (Claremont, LAC, PA500137/photo RF)

Nero Fleming, Bible in hand, in the mission schoolroom-church at Great Whale River, 1910–11
(BL, CCC, 23989-97/photo RF)

the wider audience he wished for, it is clear that he viewed it as an artistic first harvest. That the album fell out of sight for seventy years is a token of how Flaherty's early work as photographer has been eclipsed by the more pervasive publicity photographs of *Nanook*.

Flaherty's success in obtaining a second round of support from William Mackenzie – not an easy man from whom to gain a deal – can be teased from the way in which Flaherty evaluated the outcome of the first expedition and the need for a second. In reporting on the core goal of the expedition – whether the iron ore deposits on the Nastapoka Islands were commercially viable – Flaherty was cagey. Of all the islands in the Nastapoka chain, he observed, only Taylor and Gillies contained "the ore bearing series of economic interest." Besides, following Low's earlier survey work of these two islands, other development syndicates had already staked out mineral rights claims, claims which Flaherty suggested were chimerical, since "no ores are developed in individual areas to a sufficient size to be properly called ores." Flaherty was shrewd enough to know that in Mackenzie's world nothing came of nothing, so it would be best to suggest something beyond the Nastapokas, something contiguous from a mineralogical perspective, and, best of all, unexplored:

> I secured information and data from the Eskimo along the coast concerning the chain of Islands which parallel the coastal chain some sixty miles off shore. This Island system is much larger than the coastal chain, and probably has a length of some 400 miles paralleling the coast for that distance. They are unknown and no record at any of the Posts along the coast show that they were at any time visited or examined by white men. Probably the parallel chain of Islands are formed of the same rock system that occurs on the Nastapokas. I understand from the Eskimo information that I have received that these Islands have the same physical character. The Island chain is probably the western edge of the fold of these islands which at this eastern edge forms the Nastapoka Islands. I believe that an exploration with a proper equipment along the Nastapokas and then through the Island chain would be advisable. The Nastapoka ores are certainly inducing enough in both size and extent to warrant an extended exploration through that country.[5]

The "Eskimo information" he alludes to here (about which the 1910–11 diary is silent) was expanded in later publications and narratives, appearing as a full-blown event associated with Wetalltok, an Inuk from Charlton Island, whom Flaherty met in the fall of 1910, according to the "Islands" narrative:

Robert Flaherty with four Cree children on Charlton Island, 1910–11
(Thunder Bay Historical Museum, 972.255.175PP)

Robert Flaherty in full native dress, dramatically scanning the landscape, 1910–11
(BL, CCC, 23989.48)

Robert Flaherty demonstrating his kayaking prowess, 1910–11
(BL, CCC, 23989.33)

One morning, for want of something better to do, I walked over with Johnny Miller to look in on Wetalltok, the Eskimo. His hut was more of a den than anything else – ceiling, walls and floor cluttered with harpoons, spears, nets, dog-harnesses, seal-skins, seal-skin boots and kooletah, and the Lord knows what else. As soon as I had sat down on the box which Wetalltok's wife bashfully placed before me, Wetalltok started talking to Johnny Miller in Eskimo. His wife, with her back turned to us, went on sewing the seams of the seal-skin boot she was making. From odd, dim corners of the hut her children peered at me furtively out of their little slant eyes. A nest of new-born puppies near the stove yelped now and then. Wetalltok kept on talking with Johnny, until at last, turning to me, Johnny said: "Wetalltok is full of stories of the North, sir. He has just been telling me what a long time it is since he was there."

"What part of the North does he come from, Johnny?" I asked, hoping it might be somewhere around the region for which I was bound. "Is this country of his anywhere near the Great Whale coast?"

"No," Johnny answered. "He says his country is far out from the coast – on islands out at sea."

"Where are they?" I asked, pulling out my map and spreading it before Wetalltok.

Robert Flaherty at campsite
(courtesy of the Mashantucket Pequot Museum and Research Center, Archives and Special Collections, MSS 43)

For a long time Wetalltok studied the map – at a loss, I thought, to understand. Finally he pointed to a group of little islands in dotted outline – the dots showing, of course, that they were unexplored – marked on the map as the 'Belcher Islands.'

"Wetalltok says his land is here, sir," said Johnny, "where these islands are; but the way the white man draws them is crazy. It's a big land that's there, Wetalltok says."

Wetalltok pulled out an old sea chest. He opened the lid, and after rummaging through odds and ends of tools, some old carvings in ivory, harness toggles, harpoon-heads, and so on, he finally took out a tattered and yellowed piece of paper. I asked him to let me look at it. It was an old missionary picture of the Good Samaritan.

"No, it's *this* side he wants you to look at," said Johnny, turning it over. A map had been drawn on its blank side in pencil. "It's Wetalltok's map."

It was well done. The land was leaded in with pencil; the sea was simply the blank paper.

"He says this is what his island really looks like," said Johnny.

"Is there any scale to it?" I asked.

"I think the only way we can get a scale to it," said Johnny, "is to ask

Wetalltok the travel time from one point to another. That's the only way I know of getting a scale from a native map." When Johnny asked Wetalltok how long it would take to travel from the southern extreme of the land mass he had drawn to the northern end, Wetalltok said: "If I go fast by kayak, two days."

"Two days!" I exclaimed.

"Yes," said Johnny.

"Would Moose be close to here," Johnny asked Wetalltok, "or far?"

"Close," Wetalltok replied.

"Good Lord!" I said. "If that's true, this land of his must be upwards of a hundred miles long!"

But of course I knew that what Wetalltok said was preposterous. It was impossible that there could be a group of islands upwards of a hundred miles long outlying the east coast of Hudson Bay, and not known to the white man. I thought of the once-a-year ships which had been sailing into the Bay for more than two hundred years. Certainly many a time they must have passed not far from this group of islands. I looked again at my own map, at the place where Wetalltok claimed there was land. My map showed soundings! Johnny told Wetalltok it was impossible that this land could be so big; but Wetalltok, laughing a little, said "Yes, it was possible. The white man doesn't know everything," he added, with a grin.

Before I left, I asked Wetalltok if he would lend me his map so that I could make a tracing of it.

"Here, take it," he said. "I have others."

I put Wetalltok's map among my notes, and for the time being forgot the matter, for that same day the boat from Fort George came in.[6]

Flaherty claimed that this chance meeting with Wetalltok provided a critical clue about the existence of the Belcher Islands, which the Admiralty charts did not even acknowledge. In "Islands," Flaherty presented himself as being initially incredulous that an Eskimo map could trump the charts. But this encounter, as well as information he received in 1910–11 from other informants, confirmed his belief that the islands did exist, and the promise of their rediscovery was the lure he used in his attempt to persuade Mackenzie to sponsor a second expedition.

Flaherty succeeded in persuading Mackenzie that the Belchers held the promise of an important mineralogical find, thereby hitching his ambitions to his sponsor's wish to make Hudson Bay a new-age investment zone that would enable Mackenzie to become, as Flaherty put it, the

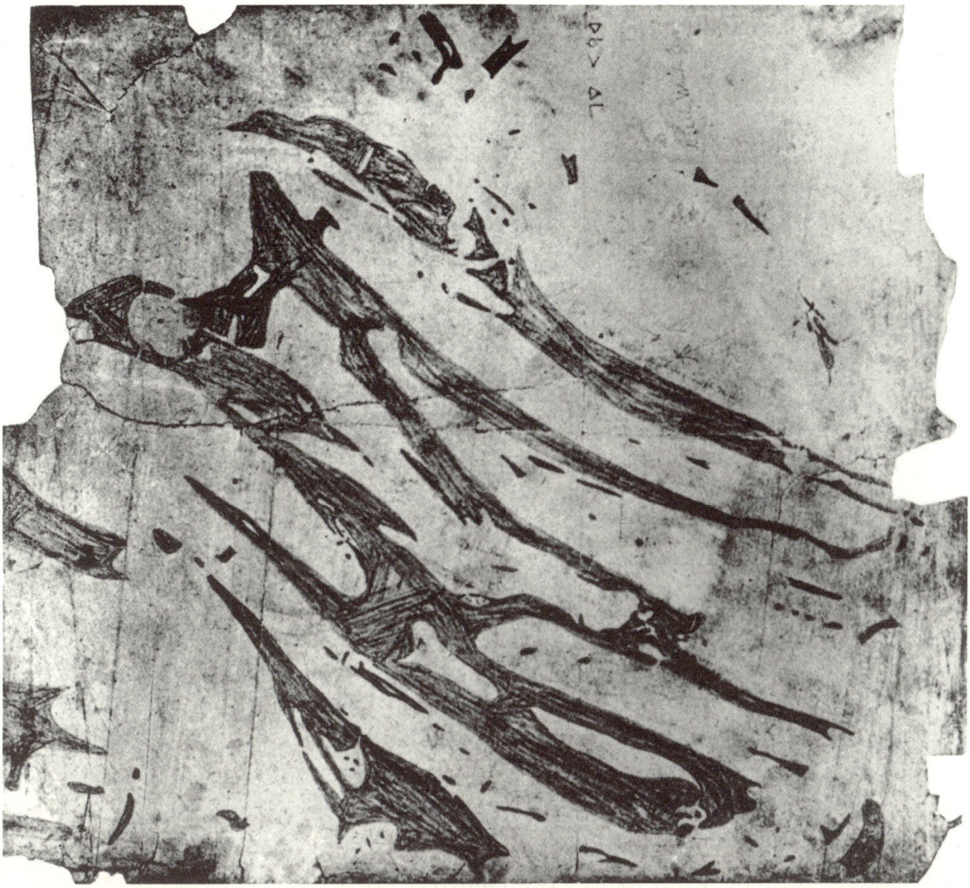

Wetalltok's map of the Belcher Islands, a document which, Flaherty claimed, motivated him to rediscover the Belchers. Later expeditionary work led Flaherty to affirm the accuracy of the map. (Claremont, LAC, PA114361)

"Cecil Rhodes of Canada." Although Flaherty made no mention of photographs in his formal report, they were part of his planning for the second expedition, in that Mackenzie's support included five hundred dollars' worth of camera and photographic equipment. Mackenzie's proposal stated that the majority of the exploration was to be done by motorized launch, rather than dogsled. In order to purchase and outfit such a boat, Flaherty set out for Moose Factory in June 1911.

Diary of the Second Mackenzie Expedition 6 June 1911 – 8 August 1912

Tuesday, 6 June 1911[7] Left the Grand Trunk crossing of the Missinaibi Railroad this a.m. at 11 o'clock, with E.E. LaDuke as assistant, R. Crowell as engineer on our engine plant, and four Temagami Indians as guides: "Joe Friday, Tommy Potts," and two names unknown as yet.[8] We are well loaded and better in that regard than we anticipated. We have two twenty foot Peterboroughs and a seventeen foot "Chestnut." The engine plant is ideal for canoe transport. Our gramophone is a boon. The river is swift, not as wide as the Mattagami. Its banks show the usual forest growth. The day was fine, fair wind. Toward evening flies were very bad. Came over two short portages; camped within sound of last one. Evening cloudy. Poker.

Wednesday, 7 June Clear warm day. Flies not so bad today. Many rapids, but not heavy ones; ran many. Camped for the night on portage next to Conjurer's House portage; played our gramophone and then poker. River getting larger, and in burned country.

Thursday, 8 June Many flies, partly clouded. Made three portages today and have the last and long one tomorrow. Took photos of Conjurer's House rapid.[9] River banks becoming high, showing approach to the Devonian coastal plain. Camp at top end of Long Portage. Caught brook trout. Rain shower during night. Many flies.

Friday, 9 June The long portage is good, and all our outfit was over by five o'clock. Camped at foot of portage. Many flies, showery weather. Fished at foot of portage in evening.

Wednesday, 14 June Away at 5:45, clear, cold north wind. After a hard time, against head tide and wind, we pulled into Moose at 6:30. Apathetic welcome as usual.

Thursday, 15 June Installed in the old mission hospital. Very comfortable. Have started on boat.

Tuesday, 18 July The *Nastapoka* was completed and ready for sea.[10]

Wednesday, 19 July We left Moose for the Ungava coast with an Indian crew of two men, E.E. LaDuke and self. Morning nearly calm and balance of day a light head (north) wind. We had to coast along the Hannah Bay shore. We anchored in the mouth of an unnamed river, about 14 miles northeast of Hannah Bay River, at seven thirty o'clock. Engine working well. The day's run gives us a better idea of what the boat will do. Water and oil supply is found to be ample. Fuel tank is too small.

Thursday, 20 July Overslept. Fine clear day, light variable winds in the morning, east and northeast in the afternoon, freshening at 2:30. In full sail from 2:30 with engine running. About six miles off the southeast shore of Charlton, the engine broke down, and had to finish balance of trip to the depot by sail. [William] Miller and a Huskie hailed us in a canoe and came in with us; arrived at depot at 7:45. Miller gave me the news of Olive Walton's death. Evening heavy and wind from eastward freshening.

Friday, 21 July Awake early, worked on engine and tanks. LaDuke put engine in shape again, and we showed our speed to the interested islanders. Later in the evening we gave a gramophone concert, and had a deck full of listeners, Indian and Eskimo.

Sunday, 23 July Clouded day, fog banks in distance, wind north by northwest. After bedtime, voices from ashore warned us that we were adrift. A scurry into a few clothes and we then hoisted sail and we worked her back to her anchorage. Tried to start this p.m. but engine plant out of order. Was righted too late to start out. We took Mr. and Mrs. Miller out for a run instead, with Huskie Tommy in the engine room, steeped in wonder and amazement at the engine's performance. About dusk the *Inenew* was sighted, arrived about dark. We went on board, to bed at 11:00.

Tuesday, 25 July A gale of wind and heavy sea. *Inenew* laying too. Wind shifting in afternoon westward. Rain. Developed pictures in evening.

Wednesday, 26 July Bright and clear and quarter wind, west, northwest. Away at ten minutes to six. Arrived at the Strutton (Revillon's) depot at nine o'clock. Only stayed ten minutes, then away. Made a low lying island, northeast of Strutton Islands 6 miles and anchored. Heavy weather again, and rain squalls. Anchored all night. Dangerous place.

Friday, 28 July Awake at 4:30, took on water, hard time getting out of anchorage. Went aground, took off ballast, and made deep water at high tide. Anchored until 1 p.m. Wind slackened, under sail and steam. Camp at Grey Goose Islands. Party of Indians encamped, windbound, came on board. Played gramophone, gave bread, tobacco and sugar. Gave us smoked fish.

Saturday, 29 July Away at seven with all the Indians on board. Ten women and children of assorted sizes in cabin. Heavy weather and rain. Arrived at Fort George about 3 p.m. under sail and steam. A crowd lined the banks to see us land. Stayed at Fort George getting outfit and plant in shape.

Sunday, 6 August Set sail about 6:45. Breeze freshening, fog coming up at noon. Passing Cape Jones. Arrived at Dog Island. Long Island Sound at one o'clock. Met the Whale River boats on their way to Charlton, Harold, Nero and half a dozen Huskies. Invited Harold and Nero to a snack on board. Nero and Shawuk took our boat twenty miles farther on to Shawuk's camp. Obtained Shawuk and partner for trip to Bill's encampment.

Monday, 7 August Fine day. Under sail until 9:00, then steam. Arrived at Bill's woman camp at two o'clock. Bill at Sucker Creek. After various signals in sign language we went on, and arrived at Bill's fishing camp about seven o'clock. Bill cannot take trip on account of his son who is dying of consumption. Giving us his son and man of his camp. Feasted, cigar'd and wined Bill, and gave candy all around. Wonderful sunset and warm. The day is as tropical a summer day as one could wish for, even in Lower Canada. Bill gave us some fresh trout and white fish. Arrived off the south point of Whale River mouth, and had to beat into a northwest wind, on account of our oil giving out in the fuel tank. Shawuk at helm could not handle boat, and we were into the coast, reef infested, and breaking over with a sea that mysteriously came out of the north. We dropped anchor less than one hundred yards from shore and put our faith and all into it till steam was up again. Darkness came on, the sea increased, our boat pitched head on, and almost under, the engine was started and raced wildly with the wheel merely churning foam, as the stern rose with the sea. We crept ever so slowly out from shore, raised sail, and beat into the wind paralleling the coast line, which seemed a huge thundering shadow to windward. We were into shore, till out of the darkness the surf showed itself, we anchored and trusted to it until morning. We spent from sunset till midnight weaving along less than two miles of coast. At daylight we beat out, but the men could not handle the boat. We ran before the wind a short distance, and into a horseshoe cove and anchored. Sent the crew of scarecrows ashore for water for the engine – get under steam and with a dead sea to run into, made Great Whale River post.

Wednesday, 9 August The post is the most picturesque on the Bay, and unutterably lonely. The great high rolling country is almost barren. The buildings of the post look down on the river from high sand banks, which became higher in the distance, and accent the curve of the river shoreline. Great lonely granite hills rise inland to the horizon. The wind plays about the buildings of the post in sand storms which in summer cooperate with the flies, and both sting unmercifully. We are windbound until Monday. North winds and very cold. In the meantime put on a larger propeller and successfully tried it out.

Sunday, 13 August Our crew (Bill's Infantry) gave us cheering word Saturday that they must go back. Two girls from Bill's camp came into Whale River, Saturday for them, having walked some fifty miles along a rugged coast and into the post. Bill left for Fort George; his harem became uneasy (lack of food probably), hence the girls' jaunt to Whale River. Glad they had to leave, were useless, but dared not fire them as I may need Bill next winter. Secured a new crew, good men, Mulucktoo (Capt.), Nucktie's son, and Awayak.[11] Left Whale River at one o'clock. Camped at Paint Island (Log: 17 knots).

Tuesday, 15 August A clear morning, a Breeze northeast. Men on board at 5:30. Away at seven o'clock. Manitounuk Sound would harbor the vessels of the world. It is thirty odd miles long, and some three miles wide on average. The great high granite range of the mainland descends gradually to the water's edge, the slopes here and there marked in green of little clumps of stunted spruce, oasis upon a rugged waste of rock, sheer cliffs of white, and red and black of their strata unfold their profiles to us on our journey northward. They stretch away into a haze of distance like sentinels of this silent unknown coast. Their contours, the great long folds of the strata and capped with jet black columnar sills of diabase, were an interesting study. We got through the last boat opening when we were forced to stop on account of the engine. Anchored all afternoon. At evening ran into harbor close by. Developed films.

Wednesday, 16 August Away at seven, glorious day, warm and summery as in Lower Canada. The wild, rugged and semi-barren coast line, with its long terraced slope, green-gray in a dazzling sun, and over it all, great cloud shadows ever changing and to the horizon of the island slopes are unforgettable. Then the long line of reef sparkling white that bounded it all, it kept me on deck. Two Huskies put out to us in kayaks when opposite the north end of Manitounuk. Gave them tobacco, matches and took photos. Arrived at Little Whale River at five o'clock. An encampment of Huskies; five kayaks put out to see us; gave them tobacco. Little Whale Post is very picturesque, barren and lonely.[12] Many flies. Wind bound two days. In interval Gene repaired engine and adjusted it. Obtained some splendid pictures of Little Whale River.

Saturday, 19 August Left for the [Richmond] Gulf. The Gulf is really a tidal lake, separated from the sea by a gorge averaging not more than 500′ in width, and about two miles long. Sheer cliffs on either side rise to more than five hundred feet. The rise and fall of the tide (6′) makes this passage at certain times most dangerous. Indeed we had to wait for our chance of getting through over night and until nine the next morning. The Gulf is thirty miles long, sixteen miles wide, and seems countersunk into a great basin, the edges of which rise some few thousand feet in one place, and to great high hills generally. The country is semi-barren, merely patches of stunted spruce, along the tawny slopes of the hills, and at the foot of the long lakes, slopes of high sheer cliffs. On our first day on the Gulf we ran east through the river north to Ungava Bay, a beam wind bowled us along and part of the time uncomfortably tossed in a choppy sea. Our canoe dipped under and we had hard work saving it. A lovely waterfall 315 feet high pouring out of the gorge of the high rock, and cliffs showed us the eastern coastline of the Gulf. We could see the white spray of the fall miles away, asparkle in the western sun. We anchored for the night at the river's mouth, and the white bottom of shells and sand showing itself through emerald green water.

Sunday, 20 August Splendid day, light westerly winds. Away about nine o'clock, through the islands and horizons of great hills of cliffs of the shoreline. Camped and anchored just inside the Gulf's mouth. Awayak tried to show us a lead deposit. We walked over tiresomely soft moss, and scrambled over cliffs of rock only to find he had lost the location.

Monday, 21 August Splendid day, light variable west wind. Met the kayaks of the Little Whale River as we passed down the Gulf entrance. We called at Salmon Fisher Cove for water – three kayaks came out to meet us – gave them tobacco, matches and took photos. Our run in the afternoon was splendid, a calm sea. We anchored at second harbor on Gillies Island. At dusk an east wind sprang up and a choppy sea came in on us. Glass low, storm tomorrow.

Tuesday, 22 August Storm arrived, tempestuous seas, our anchor could not hold her and we gradually drifted into shore, the boat striking occasionally between high seas. We managed to beach the boat, stern on, on a steep inclined bottom. We hung that way all night with seas breaking over her bows. I stayed on the boat, the crew on shore. Gene watched her through the night. Bitterly cold, everything wet. Unloaded most of our grub and instruments.

Wednesday, 23 August In morning the wind shifted to westward putting us in shelter. At high tide, at seven p.m. we got her off and into deep water. Cook very sick, he and Awayak stole a lot of dried apricots, probably ate too many. We have had a close call; will be more particular of our harbors hereafter.

Thursday, 24 August Splendid day, steamed up along Gillies and Taylor Islands, went ashore at Taylor and took photos. Arrived at the Nastapoka River about 4:30. An encampment of Eskimos on the south shore. All the hunters are away inland. Glass going down again, more bad weather, light south wind. After anchoring we went up to the falls, just around the curve of the river. As I rounded this curve the great towering mass of white water, swirling towers of spray, and a deafening roar just ahead struck me with amazement. Surely one of the most lovely waterfalls I have ever seen. The river compressed into an inconceivable narrow granite canyon, plunges over a sheer precipice one hundred feet high, then surging through a canyon still lower and narrower and with great express speed shoots out into the broad river's mouth in circles of foam and current and eddy. Afterwards paid the encampment a visit with candy and tobacco as presents. There were none but women and children, but they were unafraid. Scrambled candy and threw tobacco on the granite ledge. They were in great excitement, and their "ah's" resounded.

Friday, 25 August Rain and an east-southeast wind, no day for pictures. Went inland along the river a way. The country of granite hills, and rolling sand plains, and terraces with patches of Arctic vegetation, moss and berries and flowers look picturesque and desolate, indescribably lonely. The Eskimo hunters come home this afternoon. They came on board, four of them, gave them food and tobacco and photographed them.

Saturday, 26 August Photographed the falls, and measured them by aneroid, 138′ fall sheer. Went over to encampment in afternoon, photographed.

Monday, 28 August Better weather. Took pictures in morning, and in the afternoon started. Skirted the Nastapoka Islands, and anchored at Anderson [Island].

Thursday, 31 August John and I went over ridge on north side of river to the mountains up at bend, took photos. At crest of mountain found remains of an old flag pole, rotted to the ground, must be fifty years old; barometer showed mountain to be 800′ high. Developed pictures in the evening.

Monday, 4 September Went along north ridge with John for photographs. Picked raspberries and wild currants. In the afternoon at 3:45 we started for Manitounuk Sound. Arrived at Bottom of Bay Cove at seven o'clock, twenty-one miles in three hours. Rain tonight, almost calm. Poker.

Tuesday, 5 September Cannot get out of harbor. In afternoon much colder, and the hills are white with snow. At dusk a tempestuous gale set in, very cold full moon, and partly clear with scudding clouds. Took photos and developed. Poker.

Tuesday, 12 September Men awakened us at six o'clock. West-north-west wind. Under sail and steam. Cold and partly clear. Bar. low. Made Whale River at eleven o'clock in the morning. Very heavy seas and squalls. When entering river mouth, heavy seas swept two of our tanks away. West wind. Cold.

Wednesday, 13 September Waiting for the schooner from Charlton; staying with factor.[13]

Saturday, 16 September Southeast wind. Nero, Harold and Omarolluk arrived from Charlton Island in their boats.

Monday, 25 September Omarolluk's and Nero's boats left for Richmond Gulf Bay. Interesting departure. Both boats crammed with men, women, children and dogs, and camp impedimenta. Catamarans of kayaks towing astern. The noises of wailing dogs and children and excited parents colored the scene and not forgettable in a hurry. The affectionate leave taking amongst the natives struck me very much, and there were many over-kissed babies. These dangerous over-crowded boats are off to their winter ground, happy with their outfits, unmindful of the winter before them, and what it may mean. Their foresight is "Unto the day." Nero has promised to engineer my trip to the Belchers next February.

Sunday, 1 October Left Great Whale River for Fort George with LaDuke and man. Ran into Black Whale Harbour under sail. Wind bound two days, then made Otaska Harbour and camped. Made Sucker Creek two days later, late at night in cold east rain. Had some trouble finding Sapper's camp; fired off gun which he answered. Wind bound two days. Arrived at Bill's camp at noon, and left there at two o'clock, with Bill and son and Tucktoo, for Huskie camp at Cape Jones. Arrived there about midnight. Next morning, Bill and outfit left us to walk back to their camp. We proceeded with two Huskies to Seal

River; arrived at dusk in splendid fair wind. Great contrast to see Indians again. Great time of it, many presents. Parted next day with three Indians for Fort George. Arrived two days later, 13 October, after exciting sail.

Friday, 20 October[14] Left for trip up the Big River, with Walton and David and son. Ascended about fifty miles, magnificent stream and splendid trip. Wintering in half breed cabin.

Wednesday, 3 January 1912 LaDuke left for Cochrane on very cold day, -25° with high wind.

Saturday, 10 February Supplies arrive from Moose Factory.

Thursday, 15 February Mavor left for Great Whale River.

Monday, 19 February Departed for Great Whale River with two teams and four men as drivers, "Long Sam" and Tucktoo and two Indians of Snowboy's Paint Hill Camp.[15] Clear fine day, slight head wind, travel medium. Camped in Jimmy Salt's tent for the night.[16] New moon. News of three Eskimo dying of starvation, north of Great Whale River. In this tent I note the following: a six year old bastard boy crippled with a deformed spine, two bastard children, a motherless infant of about four months, being reared on a scanty supply of frozen condensed milk, and flour soup with lard and sugar admixed. A young girl of some seven years, a helpless idiot; total number of occupants approx. seventeen. Four stoves respectively, diameter of tepee twenty-five feet.

Tuesday, 20 February Squalling babies and red hot stoves prevented sleep until after midnight. Roasted by night, frozen by day. Awakened by Long Sam saying a storm was on, head wind for the dogs, etc. Waited until 7:30, and with moderating weather started. Tucktoo with cramps: gave him beef tea at "snacking" time which cured him. Drifty day, what Long Sam calls a "North cracker," but not very cold. While Sam was taking out the tangles of the "Peetow" and his dogs showed signs of restlessness, he turned to me, "My goodness Sir, these mixed teams Sir, they has no manners whatever Sir. I don't like to make a brag of myself Sir, but I'm not the one to care about driving them Sir." "Oh they are all right Sam. Say, what weather tomorrow?" "Well Sir, I don't like to be too knowing Sir, but maybe it will be fine, if we don't have a head wind, Sir." We arrived at the mouth of Bishop Roggan River about 2:30 and Sam wanted to put up, rather than try for Seal River, some fifteen miles further on. Disappointing head wind, and weakly agreed. Ran into an Indian encampment of three families and three widows. Comfortable and way ahead of pitching camp. A hunter came in at dark, with a red fox, which is promptly skinned, and part of it forms a snack for the people at supper tonight. After supper shaved, with a safety razor, to the amusement of the people. Afterwards washed hands and face which was promptly imitated by the people. It matters not whether a family bowl of crockery, its regular occupation being sugar, is the utensil used, or again, a lone towel makes the rounds of the encircled people, but sufficient to show the "Ouchinaw" a rather aristocratic accomplishment, a hallmark of native gentility. But Ouchinaws are few. They are delightfully unconventional, the tooth brush, the high water mark of native gentility, isn't nearly as exclusive an affair as it is with us. After an interminable series of prayers, sermons, and a slow syrupy hymn, enhanced artistically by our dog drivers's well used voices, we all turned in, in comfort be it said, with no squally babes to bother our snoring chorus.

Wednesday, 21 February Awake at 5:30. Tried to force a mucky plum pudding that was presented before leaving Fort George, and copious draughts of tea, into my inner storage. Away at daybreak with the usual throng following to the edge of the wood to see us go. Stopped to snack near the Seal River Indians' tent. Long Sam went into their encampment while we ate. Brought back 40 partridge for dog food and presents of salmon for me, for which presents the men wanted sugar. Encamped in grove of stunted trees on north side Cape Jones. Beautiful night, cold and calm.

Thursday, 22 February A north cracker on. Started at 7:30. Were a mournful looking outfit bending into the white swirl of snow as we forged ahead. The drift was so thick that it was difficult to keep the leading team in sight, though they never were more than a hundred feet ahead. Tucktoo was our hope, how he guided in that drifter is a mystery. He hit the trail (under drift) into Bill's camp from the coast, to a dot. Though we were traveling along off the coastline, we were never in sight of it. The two Indians are sure having an experience, never in the Eskimo area before. How meek and humble they look tonight in the Huskie encampment, with their detested foes of not many generations back. I think today's work gave them a vast respect for Huskie dog driving, and Tucktoo is to them now, no doubt, a marvel. Long Sam dropped back to my sledge to inquire in his over solicitous way, if I could stand it. All of which meant in fact his anxiety for our course, and also wanted me to suggest camp. When we arrived at the Eskimo encampment and were thawed to a talkative mood by draughts of tea, he was a changed man. His courage rose in a ratio to the security of his surroundings. "Well Sam, bad storm, you fellows did well." "Oh nothing Sir, I don't like to make a brag of myself Sir, but I didn't find it bad Sir, not what I might call bad Sir." Big encampment. Six families, noted two beautiful girls. Visitors coming in to see me (for sweets). Alone in tent. Men sleeping with Huskies. A devil of a storm raging.

Friday, 23 February Storm still on. Here for the day. Visited the various tents. Opened the gramophone and played to an enthusiastic audience. Nothing else but interminable snacking and tea drinking the live long day. Tea drinking in the country is an industry. Bill's mind is made up to go with me, as far as Lake Minto, on my overland trip to Fort Chimo. Clear tonight and blowing moderately. Learn one of the Indians' "froze up some" yesterday.

Saturday, 24 February Awakened at 5:30. Off at seven with a large and picturesque assortment to see us off. Splendid "going." Arrived at "Nucktie's" at 4:00. Played checkers with Nucktie.[17] Fine lot of people.

Sunday, 25 February Away at seven. Arrived at Great Whale River at 10 o'clock. Mighty glad to see it all again.

Monday, 26 February Had some fun with a mad dog. Johnnie left for Fort George today.

Tuesday, 27 February Long Sam and outfit left for Fort George. Starving Indians came into post for relief – provisioned them. One of my men, Omarolluk, has been ill. Waiting for ice fields to close again – were broken by a north cracker some ten days ago. An unusual occurrence at this time of year.

[Saturday], 2 March Huskie came in from the north with news that the fields did not drift, though badly broken. Expect to get away Tuesday.

Tuesday, 5 March Thick weather and men won't attempt to cross today.

Wednesday, 6 March Still thick, snowing with northwest wind. Outfit as follows: Flour, beans, bacon, pork, dried fruit, desiccated potatoes, tea, sugar for three men for five weeks. Presents of tobacco, matches, mouth organs, knives, needles, fish-hooks, and candy to Eskimo. Two Cameras, 5 × 4 Eastman plate, and 4 × 5 Graflex with 200 exposures. Two compasses, aneroid, thermometer, sextant, cross section books, 100′ steel tape, two dozen sample bags. Deerskin clothing, coat and pants, "hairy leg" moccasins, dogskin "overshoes," 12 × 11 tent, stove, oil stove and oil as fuel.[18]

Thursday, 7 March Harold came in this evening with the joyful news that the returning team from Little Whale River say the ice fields are really broken. Some Eskimos north of the Sound saw two dogs in harness on ice floe. Were starving. It all means my trip is impossible. The "Islanders" may starve as no relief can be sent until July by open water. Keenly disappointed after eight months of effort in trying to get out there. Fortunate I was delayed at Fort George by the Moose packet, or would never have returned. Have decided on going through to Fort Chimo, via Lake Minto by dog team, and leave on Monday, 11th.[19]

Omarolluk and Wetunik and twelve dogs, good ones. A supporting team of ten dogs with Nero and partner go into Lake Minto with us.[20] Well outfitted and the best of men. Expect to return by canoe to Great Whale River and go to those damned islands with the relief boat next summer, which will go out to relieve the unfortunate Huskies.

Later. Two Huskies from the islands came in on Saturday after a dangerous trip. They run a good chance of going adrift on their return if a land wind springs up. They report the ice fields badly broken. Gave all the people a feast on Friday night. Much fun, gramophone, Huskie and white man games. Scrambles for sweets and tobacco.

Monday, 11 March The people in toto assembled to see us go and to ride a quarter of mile or so to the edge of the plain. Well-loaded sleighs. Encamped early near Paint Islands. One of my team shows signs of the madness. The dog sickness is the one great danger. We depend greatly upon meeting with the barren ground caribou inland, and indeed is a great inducement for the men to go on this trip.

Tuesday, 12 March Glorious spring day. Went asleep too early and consequently awakened too late. Breakfast is a bore, no appetite and have to cram my food. Met "Red Man" and partner off Big Rock with a light sledge and two dog team. Were dressed as all the Islanders are in feather coats made of eider duck skins. On their way to Great Whale River. About 11 o'clock met a lone Eskimo traveler on his way to Great Whale River. Adjourned to shore for the noon snack and invited him to it. Very "rimy" this a.m. with southerly wind. Prevented me taking some of the picturesque cliffs of Manitounuk Sound. Took two dog pictures and one of Nero wielding a frying pan. Encamped at Second River. A group of Eskimo children, boys and girls, came over as we were making camp. Photo'd them. Their igloos a short distance away. A picturesque bunch – gave them chocolate and they scoured the rocks for brush for the tent. To our great relief the sick dog is well again. Splendid traveling and dogs working well. I gave Wetunik a watch yesterday and he is immensely proud of it, looks at it every half hour or so though he can't tell time. Many visitors, gave them snack. Nero very fond of army rations which he calls sweet meat. All the coast we journey by brings back hunting scenes to Nero, he tells me as we pass: Here one time deer kill 'em four and so on. Coast getting very barren now with stunted trees that hardly afford firewood.

Wednesday, 13 March Nero holding service, his tent crammed with Eskimo, one I noticed kneeling outside with his head in the tent door. A late start. Away at 8:30. Into rough ice. About ten o'clock we came across a group of seal hunters. Photo'd them. Nero broke his sled in the rough ice. We had to turn in at Jim Crow's encampment and secure another sledge.[21]

Pitched camp at noon as the new sledge we have secured has to be relashed. Gun shooting in afternoon and showed them my auto revolver. Astonished. Photo'd snarling dogs and shoreline. Wetunik in great dismay. He came to me with his watch and pointed out with a long face, a tiny fracture of the watch crystal, done with traveling through the rough ice today. Reassured him and he is happy once more. Purchased another dog for twenty beavers from "Jim Crow." Nero is holding service as I write in one of the camps. The people of all five tents are there, imagine it; the strains of "Pull for the Shore Sailor" came to me between squalls of a drifter, and snarls of the dogs tethered close to my tent, and if they are not friends very soon! This is the last Eskimo encampment we shall see until we are over into the Ungava

Bay country – glad of it in a way, will travel faster now. The coast is gradually becoming barren though, higher and more picturesque. The coastline ahead, shaded far away to masses of steel blue and white, and great masses of pressure ice scintillating in the sun, reared up in acute contrast to the long slopes of the shoreline. I noted some wonderful varieties of agate in the dark green trap along the shoreline near here. The trap was water worn to a slippery smoothness and some of the agate masses had a partial polish. Another photo of a boy at 5:30. Groups clustered about me as I hung the thermometer on the ridge pole of the tent tonight. Of course I had to explain it all to Nero in our amusing "Pidgin English" fashion. He in turn explained to his friends. But Omarolluk couldn't understand him very well, couldn't see that if that slender thread of mercury went down, all water would freeze, etc. He thought that the cold made water freeze, not my thermometer.

Thursday, 14 March Nero had service this a.m. It seems impossible to make an early start. A virtue of the Indian. Huskies are heavy sleepers. Nero when at his winter hunting grounds rarely wakes till nine or ten a.m., though he hunts later than the others by far. Away at 8:30, after saying goodbye to the last people we shall see until we are over into Ungava Bay ... A hard day's work today through dangerous ice fields off Gulf Hazard. We made a circuitous crossing of the Gulf currents by going about nine miles off shore and traveled through pressure ice and ridges that delayed us a great deal. We encountered many delays while Nero went ahead with a seal spear to test the rime ice and find passage for us through the ridges. The drift was blinding at times. More than thankful we have crossed the Gulf current without breaking through. The men worked hard. Had an extra meal tonight. Encamped on sea side of Anderson Island. Snow floor and driftwood tent poles of fantastic design. North of trees now and will have to travel on sea side of islands in order to obtain driftwood for fuel. Dogs in bad temper after a hard time in the ice. Fighting murderously the whole day. In passing Flint Island, noted a rocky mound and went to it with Nero. Made by Eskimo "very near thousand year" according to Nero, as he said he could remember it when a small boy! Clear and cold.

Friday, 15 March Clear overhead. Very cold. Strong wind all night. Away at eight o'clock. About ten o'clock, Omarolluk spied an encampment of Huskies to seaward of us. We went there. Much surprised to see strange Eskimo, for as it turned out later they are traveling south to

Great Whale River from Hope's Welcome where they have abandoned their hunting ground. Five families, four igloos. Nero secured a new sledge from them in lieu of "Jim Crow's" which is too short for his load. Gave them tea, flour and tobacco, and they are very happy. They say there are more families traveling south but further out to sea, hunting seals enroute. Took several photos. Recognized a family amongst them which I saw at Salmon Fisher Cove last winter. Broke away about seven o'clock a.m. Dogs fed at 7:30 amid devilish fighting, on every side of my tent it seems. When one is tired after a long day's work and just dropping off to sleep, the quiet of everything is shattered by a pair of dogs, within say two feet of where you lie, fighting and snarling as only they can. Perhaps the canvas sinks suddenly where you lie, it's nothing, merely the dogs arrived at the rolling stage of a fight. One doesn't care about going out, or you'll spend a shaking interval, getting warm again. The moon not only affects tides, but also our dogs it seems, and their worshiping is a tidal wave. One gets to know each of the team's voices, from base to tenor. But after all, were there no dogs, half of the color of the north is gone. How Wetunik gloats over that watch. He carries it swathed in a yard of cotton print, and watches the hands and compares with Omarolluk to be sure they both are equal. There will be trouble in Wetunik's face, the day both watches do not tally. The jealousy of Eskimo is subject for a volume.

Saturday, 16 March   Very fine and clear. As we skirted along the Nastapoka Islands, we came across many deserted igloos. There was quite a village of them at one place. They looked indeed deserted villages as Goldsmith never imagined. Took many photos, igloos and dogs and jaspilite cliffs of the islands. Very fine traveling underfoot, after the two days of drift. Learned something about whales, cod and ore body from Nero. Omarolluk says the Belchers have the same type of rock groups (i.e. jaspilite of Gillies Island). The Nastapokas are a cod fishing ground of the Eskimo, who fish for them from kayaks. Omarolluk says the whale country is the Ottawa Island group (has hunted there). The mainland looked desolately picturesque. The great glaciated granite hills of fantastic outline and swathed in steel-blue haze that comes with spring sun. (Wearing goggles now.) Not a tree in sight and driftwood is hard to find. I learn today from Nero that there must be a hundred Huskies migrating to Great Whale River. The number of igloos we saw today shows it. Encamped on the shore ice of one of the Nastapoka Islands, opposite the Nastapoka Falls. They showed up brilliantly this evening across the four or five miles of Sound, and the spray seemed like the smoke of a forest fire on the side of the huge sloping mainland. Last winter we saw the spray of the falls more than thirty miles away. Big supper tonight. Cooked dried apricots for all hands.

Sunday, 17 March Just enough driftwood to carry us through breakfast. Nero holding service as I write. How my men can sleep with one 3½ point blanket is beyond me. But I understand that in the old regime while traveling they had no blankets at all, but snuggled up to the barricade fire, which they kept going all night. Indians same. Nero expects to be ordained next summer when the Bishop arrives and great things will happen (in the native's eyes). Left Hudson Bay at White Whale Point about 1:30 and commenced on journey across Ungava. Had dinner near the crest of the coast range and in view of the Bay, which spread out below us in a splendid panorama. Our route to Lake Minto lies through a chain of lakes, sunken into the pockets of the scarred desolate granite hills. Some of the lakes we passed through today appear like the canyons of a large river, the bare and almost sheer granite rising to five hundred feet. As we speed down the pass to a new sheet of ice, its snow surface all drifted into hard packed hummocks that catch the shadows of the western sun, it seems not a stone's throw to its far end. We were however a half hour traveling across one of them, a surprising deception to me. Not a tree to be seen. A more barren country is not possible.[22] Nothing but intensely glaciated granite hills snow patched to a great contrast and everywhere that lodgement is possible, glacial boulders, great and small, which gives chaos to the depressing desolation. We camped late as we could not find trailing fir for creepers for firewood. When at last we came to some on the slope of a high hill, it took the men more than an hour digging up enough out of the snow for our fire tonight. The trunk of these trees is not more than 2½″ through, gnarled and full of sap, and cutting them is a tedious piece of work. As we go further inland, we shall come upon stunted trees such as we found south of Richmond Gulf. Fed the dogs on seal blubber tonight. The dogs were tired and ravenous. Having no convenient way of tying them for the night, they were free. The scene just before feeding time was unforgettable. Omarolluk had to stand guard with his 20′ whip while Wetunik cut up the blubber. The dogs acted for all the world like wolves, crawling up to the meal on their bellies from every direction. They braved the whip in more than one instance and a cut from it is certainly a painful affair. Omarolluk constantly cut them with terrible blows. Those dogs were certainly in a murderous temper. They are quick as lightning in snatching, a wolf's trait, to the ground. Their fierceness and desperate temper as the odor of the seal blubber came to the crouching circle of them, is beyond the telling. What would happen to us without them.[23]

Monday, 18 March Our Waldorf fare of army rations, jam and canned steak will soon be exhausted, then beans forever. Omarolluk cut his hand at breakfast, but fixed it up with a poultice of butter and tobacco. He tries so hard to do as the "angarooka" (master) would do. Nero told me of the salmon north of Portland Promontory while riding on his sledge yesterday. How the Eskimo live on them all winter, spear them through the ice, in far greater numbers than when the Hudson's Bay Company fished for them in Richmond Gulf and Salmon Fisher Cove. He said the great place for them was in Mosquito Bay. I believe there are possibilities in that regard. Nero spoke of the flies inland, that in many instances kill the deer. He has seen them inches deep on the deer, the deer's face being raw and the eyes swollen by their work. In July this happens when there are hot days and calm. The deer's coat is at that time at its thinnest. He has seen them after being killed and says they are bloodless through the flies' work. The Eskimo, it may be noted, keep their dogs in their tent at this time – imagine the smell. Along the crests of the ridges he said the flies would look like fog. 6 p.m. Ther., 20-; Bar.; 29.18. We traveled through a perfect maze of canyon lakes today. They nestle in the sockets of the coast range of granite hills everywhere. Never have I seen a more likely country to get lost in, nor a more desolate one. The men on three occasions were confused, notwithstanding that they have traveled to Lake Minto before. The short portages between lakes seem like miniature mountain passes. The ascent and descent often very steep. At one point this a.m. we reached the summit of one and started descending, but barely managed to stop short of a 75′ precipice. With our 900 and 600 lb. sledges and teams that continually strain for speed, it was no small matter to stop in time. We also shortly discovered that while we were looking over for a new course, we were standing on the snow overhanging, which projects from the cliff edge about 25′. There are many snow formations like that in the rugged area here and south along the Richmond Gulf country. The snow is everywhere wind driven and packed to a picturesque extent, such as is not possible southward. This overhanging of which I speak resembles the eave of a house on a huge scale. Many a hunter has lost his life through unconsciously walking to their edge, then suddenly breaking them. Two men of Little Whale River post plunged hundreds of feet to their deaths, while traveling to the post in a drifter, in the manner I speak of.

[Tuesday], 19 March One of the coldest days we have had so far. The ther. at lunch registered 12-°, with heavy head wind. I realize now that there must be a vast difference between the climate of Hudson Bay and this Ungava interior. On traveling inland to Lake Minto the coastal height of land is very narrow, approx. 35 miles, where we crossed it. The rise therefore is rapid. We felt a vast difference in the cold of the coast and the height of land, and there seems no difference in the incessant winds that sweep Hudson Bay and make the low temperature so difficult to us there ... This entire area is barren of soil, silt and trees. The snow of the shadow sides of the lakes and slopes and cliffs of the hills never disappears ... The country looked desolate and dreary with clouded day, the outlines of the low sweeping hills and jagged edges of the cliffs, blurred by the drift of the wind. We saw two partridges, one of which Nero shot. It was given to "Beauty" tonight for supper. Would an Indian give his dog a lone partridge? Big supper tonight of canned beef and evaporated potatoes amalgamated into "hash."

Wednesday, 20 March Seven a.m. Near our camp I noted the very old poles of an Indian tepee, which surprised me greatly as I thought we were north of the Indian country. It seems, however, that some Indians trading into Great Whale River post came north this far with the deer herds, many years ago. A few Eskimo families hunt here and trade into Fort Chimo and Great Whale River.

Felt the cold very much today ... The tree limit must be but a short distance to northward. Nero shot partridges as we camped, gave them to dogs. Nero cached 50 lbs. of flour at lunch time for his return journey to Great Whale River. Big supper tonight and long talk afterwards, covering the route, etc.

Thursday, 21 March Omarolluk gave further information concerning sperm whales last night. He said there were many whales there in open water, that they were black, had divided spray, white about their mouth and very large. These are the Ottawa Island group of which he speaks and other unknown islands west of Hope's Welcome. At one time the

Eskimo there managed to kill one and the bones of it are there still. A large whale was seen in Manitounuk Sound about five years ago, though unknown to the Hudson's Bay Company men. Was seen by Huskie Bill at the "boat's opening." These islands are also a great country for walrus and polar bear. This is Nero's last day with us traveling. He turns back tomorrow for Great Whale River. We estimate having traveled about 30 to 35 miles so far ... Camp will remain here for tomorrow. Dogs will have a rest which they need as they are very thin. Hope we get to the deer herds soon so as to get dog food. Will then be able to travel faster. Wetunik says we are more than halfway across the lake now. Very fine day, brilliant sun which hurts my eyes very much though I wore goggles part of the time. Aurora and sun dogs during the day.

Friday, 22 March Sun and snow reflection almost blinding. All but Nero off to north and south of lakes after deer. Nero baking bannock and fishing through ice. Hunters returned at sunset, and Wetunik saw fresh signs of about 80 deer. We push on tomorrow for east end of the lake, there men will hunt for a day. Nero returns to Great Whale River tomorrow. Nero drew map of lake for me in evening and we had a conference together afterwards in Nero's tent covering route, deer herds, etc. Dog food is our greatest worry but the men are sure of getting deer within a week's time.

Saturday, 23 March Said goodbye to Nero and partner at eight o'clock, then started on our way to Fort Chimo. I felt lonesome at seeing him go. No one to speak to now. My men cannot understand a word of English and I have a vocabulary of about twenty-five Eskimo words.[24] Nero will arrive at Great Whale River in about seven days' time. He is one of the most remarkable men I've seen. Clever, a Jap's keenness for novelty and information, the greatest Eskimo hunter of his people, a dare devil on ice or in kayak, and the model generally of all his tribe, always smiling, and alert, likes to be on journeys with white men, admires them but with all intensely. Nero is simply an illustration of the development the Eskimo are capable of. I parted with him this a.m. with regret indeed.

Wetunik confused again and later completely lost. We have traveled some 40 miles today and are now camped within two miles of last night's encampment ...

Sunday, 24 March   Head wind made a disagreeable day of it. About one o'clock Wetunik became confused again and the men climbed one of the high granite hills for a sight. Omarolluk returned alone and we went on further northeastward. Began to feel that it would be yesterday all over again but at three o'clock ran into Nawri's abandoned igloo and we felt good all over. Straightaway camped. Wetunik returned from his scouting among the hills a little later. The lake is a monster and will prove to be the largest in Labrador, not excepting Lake Mistassini, I think. A storm about to arrive.

Tuesday, 26 March   Passed another abandoned igloo of Nawri's this a.m. Arrived at the end of the lake at ten o'clock. The discharge is a small open rapid. Omarolluk tried for fish but caught none. We traveled on a mile further, then camped as the drift is blinding and wind very strong. Trees are increasing in size and number and camp in quite a grove. The country appears more low and even now. I estimate the lake as being the longest in Labrador, having a length of more than a hundred and fifteen to twenty miles.

Wednesday, 27 March   Very cold day with a typical March wind and blinding drift. Became snowblind partly and eye is very sore indeed this evening. About 2 p.m. came across deer tracks on river ice. Omarolluk went after them and Wetunik and I went on with the team. Camped at three o'clock and no more than had it up when Omarolluk came with the news of two deer killed. He was as happy as a child over it as he has never even seen deer before, being an islander of Hope's Welcome. It means a great deal to us and nothing could have been more opportune. We all shook hands in high glee over it. The men returned at eight o'clock with the deer, cut and quartered, having given the dogs a feast when cutting them.

Thursday, 28 March   Laid up with snow blindness and a painful affair it is. The men are off after the deer with dogs and sledge. It seems Omarolluk wounded one besides the ones he got. It being a very stormy day, the deer will not travel but keep in the valleys. Omarolluk killed his deer yesterday with 30.30 shells in a .303 gun. He gave me to understand the bullets were very loose ... The men at supper tonight tried to tell me in signs and our limited vocabulary that the dog I purchased from Jim Crow died today, but I thought they said that they were going back to Great Whale River. For a moment was alarmed and angry but I caught their meaning in time – much laughter.

Friday, 29 March Traveled eleven miles for the day, and all of us done up. Wetunik with snow blindness, Omarolluk with a lame knee and I with cramps and headache after snow blindness of other day. Have never seen such a continuously long rapid and of such size (apparently) for its length. No doubt we are on one of the great rivers of Ungava. River is very picturesque. Trees increasing rapidly, noted one spruce 6″ through its butt. Wetunik making me a pair of Huskie goggles. Cached 80 lbs. of dog food at noon. Sledge is very heavy.

Tuesday, 2 April A late start, nine a.m. Wetunik in bad way through snow blindness, cannot open his eyes and racked with headache ... The men were in high glee over being through and they explained to me that the big water (Ungava Bay) could not be far away. Have just put poor Wetunik in his blankets, a very sick Huskie. Trouble at noon today. The men, as I discovered, have been keeping their sealskin boots in the cooked bean bag! The day is the warmest we have had, but with a thick drifting southerly wind. The icing on our runners wore off quickly and part of our earthen shoeing is gone. Noted Omarolluk's method of baking bannock this evening, thus – two handfuls of baking powder to about four pounds of flour, and we live!

Wednesday, 3 April Clear day with light south wind. Started early 7 o'clock. Ruined our earth shoeing and had to run on the runners today. Tonight the men have made new earth shoeing. The beauty of the river is beyond description. The wonderful high hills stream down to the river for all the world like a fiord. This p.m. we thought we were arrived at the mouth but it proved a long river traverse (about eight miles) stretching away to a faint horizon ahead with the great canyon-like hills making a frame for it ... A glorious day and our first day of spring really. At feeding time one of the dogs mistook Wetunik's hand for deer meat and consequently made a considerable mess of it. It's one damn thing after another with Wetunik. He is quit of his snow blindness. Omarolluk's knee is giving him trouble.

Thursday, 4 April Clear overhead. Men finished off the earthen shoeing and departed at nine a.m. A fine day with warm south wind and slight drift. Noted some more splendid examples of marine terraces today, about 250′ high. Last evening at camp noted a Canada Jay (Whisky Jack), first bird other than ptarmigan seen on the trip on a small poplar bush. Travel very tedious and slow owing partly to the spring day, which makes both men and dogs very sluggish. We are all on edge now expecting and wondering when we shall come to the sea.

Saturday, 6 April One of the most trying days we have had. We camped on the sea ice last evening and broke camp this a.m. at eight o'clock. Very soon were into impassable and treacherous ice, where at times we had to literally chop our way. Heart breaking work. Left the team and climbed the hill side of mainland and saw our course was helpless. Open water in the distance and detached floes packing toward us. There we were like a fly in glue. Retraced our steps and arrived at last night's camp at one o'clock. We made for shore and with infinite and trying labor arrived at three o'clock (a half mile). Men and dogs done up. Pitched camp on mainland and tomorrow will attempt to travel overland and come out on southerly side of the bay, and clear of the rough ice fields. Work tried our temper but all right now. Camp located ¾ of a mile from last night's camp. Omarolluk baking bannock and singing fragments of Eskimo songs and every little while humming the tune of "Waltz me around again, Willie" which he has heard on some phonograph at Fort George or Great Whale River. Great to see him imitating a seal today to decoy the dogs while we were trying to get over hummocks and crevices. Our very limited conversation bear altogether on Fort Chimo and our arrival.

Sunday, 7 April Snow during night. Stuck here for the day, a miserable camp with everything wet. Men off in the hills looking for a course for our travel tomorrow. Slight snow blindness again. Men returned at noon saying they have found a course over the hills to the Bay, but cannot tell whether the ice in the bay on the far side is rough or not. Wetunik went off again this p.m. to see the ice fields from the top of the range. Returned at 5:30 saying ice was all broken. Expect we shall have a hell of a time tomorrow. Omarolluk and I poring over maps this p.m. The most miserable of all days, everything melting.

Monday, 8 April Gloomy and overcast. Started on our cross country travel to avoid the rough ice fields at 9 a.m. About 100 ptarmigan assembled on a distant knoll to see us go. Very hard and long climb to an altitude of about 600′ accomplished by noon in 100′ jabs, with the usual Huskie dog conversation at each one. In the true barrens now and away from trees. The country traveled today has an exceedingly desolate appearance. One long climb was compensated by a galloping coast down the long slopes of this side of the range. Encamped on the main coast of Ungava Bay with another broken ice field staring us in the face. Fort Chimo seems farther away every day. Noted the long looked for Cambrian series and crossed some of them this p.m. Noted float off the distant Cambrian hills which showed you the large pieces of good looking hematite. Hope and expect to find this the most interesting iron country of the north. The range is certainly well located to shipment and avoids 1000 miles of doubtful ice navigation, as is the case with the Hudson Bay area. Surprised to find this ore series on tide water and of course much pleased. This is the area to explore. Low's map of the Cambrian ore series most misleading. Cannot stay to explore now, but will return after reoutfitting at Fort Chimo.

Tuesday, 9 April Snow during night. Upon looking around this a.m. were pleased to find the ice fields are not broken far from shore so that after we are through the fringe along shore will have fine traveling.

Later. Wetunik confused and does not know the route from here to Fort Chimo. He is certainly a useless guide, and "attullie" had been his cry ever since we left Nero. It seems from what I can gather from the men that the sea coast is impossible to travel by sledge and that Ungava Bay proper is open water. As Fort Chimo is more than 75 miles away in a straight line it is most important that we find the trail. It is made difficult owing to the heavy snow fall of the last few warm days (6 inches). The maps are misleading *extremely*. Traveled inland no more than a mile when in a clump of stunted trees found fresh Eskimo cutting. Camped, then looked around for tracks underneath the new snow. Found many Eskimo tracks but none of a sledge and as yet cannot tell if these cuttings, etc. indicate a sledge or not, which is an important thing to know. Two signs indicate the Eskimo have camped here about seven or eight days ago. While pitching camp thought I saw smoke in distance which put everyone in excitement. Looked through the glass but could discern nothing. Wetunik went off to a distant mountain with glass to scout, but returned with no information. Our grub looking ill. Wetunik is pin head, I'm thinking. He has hunted this country and should know about it. But Omarolluk makes up for him, full of resource and brain, a good "Huskie." Storm brewing. The Cambrian series here are on a vast scale and will have a job of it later when I return to explore. The iron bearing series are no doubt well represented ...

At breakfast Wetunik happened to peer out of the flap and who should be coming but two Eskimo women floundering along in a halting fashion and not knowing whether to advance or not. We called out "Chimo" with vigor and they came up and into our tent. After all we are encamped not a mile from an encampment of four or five families. We gave them something to eat and then came on with outfit to their encampment. We are certainly relieved of some worry and feel good all over. Now at dinner in a small hut of one of the families, which is 10 × 12′ and crowded with visitors of the other tents to peek at the "angarooka." Will camp here as the deep soft new snow and warm weather is impossible for us to travel in. All the men are away hunting deer which we learn are in great numbers and may not be back for some days. The first humans we've seen since leaving Hudson Bay.

Thursday, 11 April After a short debate in signs, etc. we started on our way to Fort Chimo. I was in favor of starting, notwithstanding the almost impassably deep snow, as the fearful alternative of living another day in that filthy hut was too much. Last night the visitors numbered more than twenty (hut 10 × 12′). One of the inmates, a man of about 25 years, is dying of consumption and showed symptoms similar to those seen with the Hudson Bay Eskimo, i.e. blind and partially deaf, body becoming benumbed as the disease gains headway. These Ungava Bay Eskimo have not as yet created a very favorable impression, are certainly more unclean, but too early to judge conditions.[25] Our travel very hard, the snow soft and at this time about 1½′ deep, i.e. above the winter snow level. We barely strained through it at times ... Tealess supper, not enough wood. Overcast and gloomy.

Sunday, 14 April Travel fast and the excitement of nearing Fort Chimo a stimulus, to even the dogs I believe. We plied Charlie with anxious questioning all through the day trying to fix our location and nearness to the post. At 3:30 or thereabouts we came to the crest of the river valley of the Koksoak and commenced our long descent over beach country toward the river. About 4:30 we suddenly stood out on the last of the terraces. Fort Chimo, the great broad river and a valley stretching to a blue haze of the dazzling sun, lay before us. The white buildings of the post from our vantage look like a strange far-off village.[26]

The descending sun shot into the innumerable windows bolts of light and cast the surging figures of Eskimo, men and women, now aware of the arrival of a strange party, into vivid profile. The day and hour were made for our entry there, and the color of sunset of the sky caught by the snow plains and broken ice of the river, affected us strongly. The white mass of days and days travel was over.

Tuesday, 23 April Expedition to Hope's Advance, Leaf Lakes and Ungava Bay coast. Left Fort Chimo at 9:30 with an eleven dog team outfit for two weeks travel. Mr. Parker, Hudson's Bay Company's clerk, and Dave Edmonds, Hudson's Bay servant, and self comprise personnel.[27] Very beautiful spring day, clear, calm and warm. Camped at 8:30. Splendid outfit of grub and equipment. Traveled about eighteen miles.

Wednesday, 24 April Beautiful clear day with light westerly wind. Traveling very slow. Dogs in a spring fever. Camped early to await the Huskies who leave Fort Chimo today for Leaf Lakes.

Thursday, 25 April In camp all day waiting for the Eskimos who left Fort Chimo later than we did. Want them to take some of our heavy load and guide us over the barrens which commence a few miles from here. They came along at 3:30 and encamped a little further on.

Monday, 29 April Tent nearly burned at breakfast. Had Eskimo woman over to repair it, and then made us bannocks. Borrowed Shenowgook's gramophone which brought on a fit of homesickness. A northern Huskie prepared to visit our tent, but refused him admittance which put him in sulks, which he wore off in circling walks about our tent. Is a filthy specimen, and named him "Grease Spot." Have arranged for a four day journey north of this camp and taking another team with wood, etc.

Saturday, 4 May Am at Fort Chimo.

Wednesday, 19 June Expedition to Great Whale River via Payne Lake. Outfit of 4 Eskimos, 25′ canoe and grub for two months. Flour, beans, pork, smoked deer meat and dried fruit. Canoe adaptable for coast work, 16″ draft on 4500 lb. load. Nuckyuillik, captain; Nechyveluak, Nungunguck, Partridge's son, Anghick. The *Walrus*, a 30′ schooner,

Fort Chimo, Flaherty's destination on his west to east transverse of the Ungava Peninsula (Claremont, LAC, PA115067/photo Olaus J. Murie)

with Eskimo crew and wives, and two kayaks taking us north to Payne River. Under Palliack as Captain.

Left Fort Chimo at 3 p.m. on the ebb tide.[28] The population in toto lined the banks to see us go. They were a motley throng of Nascopies, Crees and Eskimos. Flags of Revillon, Hudson's Bay and the Mission aflying: the port seemed en fete. Reached Partridge's sealing camp, north of the river mouth, some fifteen miles, about six o'clock.[29] Anchored for the night. Made a quick run with east wind and splendid current. Enormous tides produce a racing current in the Koksoak and along the coast. Slept in Partridge's tent or rather tried to. Partridge and wife join us on the morrow. We are a happy family of four women and four babies and eight men all told; not to omit about two dozen Eskimo puppies in the hold. The *Walrus* takes us to Payne River, then to send them way back to Fort Chimo.

Thursday, 20 June Arose at four o'clock and away at six o'clock, after saying good-bye to the encampment and to Parker. A fair catspaw wind and ebb tide, but only made some ten or fifteen miles. Light rain about four o'clock, then cleared ... We are only a few miles south of the Leaf Lake entrance. As our craft drifted lazily along the men made hunting excursions in their kayaks and the big canoe. Killed five fish, ducks, and got pails full of gull and duck eggs, which they boiled and ate on board ...

Friday, 21 June Started about eleven o'clock. Wind soon died down, and balance of day and evening was flat calm. The two boats drifted along, with fitful rowing at times by the women. The men in their kayaks scooted along the mirror of water, and in amongst the ice floes after seal and ducks. The deck was in "négligé," babies, dogs, ducks and dishes, and women in tousled hair, gossiping over their sewing, cooking and fowl cleaning. The men had a great seal hunt which took an hour or so of chasing and maneuvering for the spear throwing at a large seal. They would follow up much the same as in coon hunting. When the seal rose to the surface they kept up a great noise, which in the distance seemed like a ball game at home. This row kept the seal in curiosity so that the speedy kayaker got his chance for a throw. However, there were many dives and following throws before Annotook hit his mark, "Ahonna." We all straightaway proceeded to an ice cake, where the seal was carved. The dogs formed the outer circle of interested spectators. Every part of the seal was used for dogs and men, and Partridge as chief, offered me the liver and a bit of seal pup that had been killed earlier in the day. I accepted diplomatically and told my tummie not to butt in. They jarred the blood, stretched out the skin to dry, and made fires on the ice cake and boiled some of the meat. We have anchored, eleven p.m., to a floe for the night, or rather the twilight. Everyone sleeping on board. Should not like to think what would happen if a gale came on.

Sunday, 23 June Rain squalls, cold. Our harbor is badly choked with ice. At high tide the men tried to shove the outer cakes out into the currents and make a clearing: not successful. Partridge and I went for a walk in p.m. He showed me the ruins of an old Eskimo village of stone igloos. They were about twenty in number, evidently of great age. We noted an Eskimo skull nearby. He showed me some old stone fox traps built on the dead fall system. We burrowed around for arrow heads, but found no good ones. We gazed with his telescope at the ice fields a long time. He did not say anything encouraging about them. They worry me not a little. Partridge is a splendid old fellow, and most solicitous about my comfort. He is one of the real types of his people. A bleak desolate night, very cold.

Tuesday, 25 June Wind northeast, and strong with rain squalls most of day. Ice closing all along coast and packing in from seaward. If there was ice in Hell it would be here too. Am resigned to indefinite waiting.

It is vital to our trip overland to get a clear passage soon – we may be short on our food supply through it, among other things. Nothing to do but sleep, then read, then visit the people in the tents which isn't charming, as I can't speak to them nor they to me. As leaven to this damnable monotony is my reading. Two books of Mark Twain, one of Balzac and two contemporary novels of Churchill and John Fox, Jr. and three old Scribner's magazines.[30] They are nearly done. Note: Duty-bound to read. Opportunity, etc. Have struck up companionship with Palliack's three year old son. As he isn't arrived at the fluent stage of his own language yet, we hit it off very well. Showed him my safety razor and after seeing me shave intimated that he wanted one, which I carried out amid great laughter from the circle of onlookers. His mother showed signs of anxiousness during the operation. He knows all about my biscuits, syrup and canned fruit. Took him into cabin and gave him a half can of raspberries and biscuit, which put him way off his seal meat diet. Half suspected his mother thought I tried to poison him. Haply he came round again in short time, and greeted me with his quaint "O Kshurie" when I came up to the tent this morning. The men and women played at skipping the rope this p.m. Two women operated a ten foot seal line, the men jumping. The rope is turned very rapidly, the men skip one foot at a time and alternate from one foot to other according as they get tired. The longest skipper wins amid hearty laughter and applause. Beached the boat at five o'clock, as the ice is closing into it ... I note many peculiar stone monuments four and five feet high on these islands, of Eskimo origin. Possibly many are modern. Similar affairs in Hudson Bay on Great Whale River coast. A blizzard now and very cold. One needs winter outfit the year through. Good old Partridge noted me shiver while writing this, and straightaway fetched me one of his "Koolituck's" (moleskin capote) all washed and clean and let me understand it was a present. These people are considerate of my comfort. How such kindness is valued up here away from everything, can be imagined. Several seal alarms during day, but none killed. To hear the excited Huskies gesticulating and scurrying to and fro for their guns, the good wife not the least active, with youngsters bobbing in the hood like a tourist on a camel – the rapid launch and the scooting of those shark-nosed kayaks to the rings of water of the seal's last dive – spear poised and ready – is not easily forgotten.

Wednesday, 26 June Wind abated to moderate northwest. Ice everywhere and no land in sight. Rain and snow squalls during day. Have been carrying on some experimental cooking to pass away the time. Inflicted the results on some of the men. They are good subjects. At high tide the ice closed in on the boat while the men were hurrying to take her cargo and ballast out of the hold. The boat was broken amidships, but not so badly as we thought at first. Will be able to fix her up again in some two days' time. It looks as if we might be here for weeks now. Ice looks hopeless. Noticed that Partridge gave me the only capote he had other than his deer fur one, and going around with that on, which isn't very comfortable at this time of year. Men killed another large seal today. At present men and women out on rocks cutting them up, and packing and preparing the skins. Had a shooting match this evening. Great fun. Finally brought out my automatic pistol. Palliack hit the bull's eye two out of three times, and was the only one who did so. Remarkable as his first experience with revolver. Is a fine all round shot.

Saturday, 29 June Heavy squalls of north-northeast wind all night. Started about seven a.m. An Eskimo of the encampment we spied last night visited us just as we were boarding boat – gave him matches and tobacco and flour. Crimped along at a good rate with double reefed sail. Exceedingly cold. Anchored off the Eskimo encampment for few moments, and were given three or four sealskins, dressed. Our women to make boots of them for our overland trip. Eskimos living in skin tent ... A hungry crowd after our disagreeable journey. Noted a very fine stone monument near our camp, and remains of Eskimo camps, stone fox traps and seal caches. Men went over the rise and report ice close inshore. This wind and ebb tides should put it seawards by a.m. No driftwood. The women scoured the plain for fire moss with which we cooked our supper. While the women were putting the finishing touches to supper, we had putting the shot and throwing at targets. The Eskimos are expert at throwing stones at targets, etc. They practice it by the hour.

Sunday, 30 June Wind bound. Nuckey and Palliack went north along the coast and report bad inshore ice, and also suggested that we go ahead balance of journey to Payne Bay with canoe, if wind is not favorable in a.m. Some of the people washed themselves, it being Sunday ... Palliack played his hornless and battered gramophone out on the rocks this evening. The women played ball, and general revel all around, followed by their service in one of the tents. Palliack's son comes into my tent on visits now, gravely and laboriously takes off his kooletah, calls for a piece of paper and pencil and draws pictures and the like. The pet of the camp.

Tuesday, 2 July This a.m. we went off in canoe from the boat to a small island alive with eider ducks and their nests of eggs. The men killed many which fell into the tide race and carried away. Carried off some of the hundreds of eggs and eiderdown that lines the nests. While we anchored this p.m. on account of heavy tide, a similar affair occurred, so that now the canoe is loaded with eider ducks. The scenery along the bay this evening is very fine, more than welcome after the low monotonous coast. We are merely drifting in with the tide, the mirror of water half covered with the pan ice from sea and occasionally huge blocks 20 to 40 feet high. The descending sun enhanced the beauty of it all with warm yellow and long slanting reflections and shadows. Anchored at eleven pm. The people sleeping on the rocks ashore.

Wednesday, 3 July A beautiful day, and to us the first warm one. The men and I climbed a high bluff to see how the ice looked ahead. The upper reach of the bay is choked from shore to shore. Men saw three deer about 1½ miles away on the south shore ... At noon sighted them to northeast about a mile away. Palliack, Nawri, Long Hair and Partridge worked into them, the remainder spreading out south of valley, in case they took the alarm. Not long before the shooting commenced – they literally poured lead into them with their repeating rifles. Two cows and a bull. Noted that their winter coat was still on and horns in velvet. Palliack easily plucked the winter coat off and obtained a splendid summer deerskin. It wasn't long till they had them cut up and packed in their own skins, strips of the hide being cut with which to tie the whole and pack them. Nuckey was busy breaking open the leg joints and knuckles and eating the marrow with gusto (so he appeared). Returned about three o'clock to find our harbor a raging river of rapids in islands of boulders. The women were scattered about the granite ledge in various degrees of dress amid a rubble of dishes and things. Sundry articles of their personal adornment were plastered to boulders drying. We are a happy family, surely! The sun is hot, the rocks enhance it and we are bathing in it, awaiting in lazy apathy the flood tide. Ambrose killed two ptarmigans with stones. At five o'clock a few of us went fishing at the rapids, but caught nor saw nothing.

Upon returning had a shooting match for plugs of black tobacco, with Ambrose, Palliack and Partridge. Lost twenty plugs which covered the prize list. Palliack's gramophone on the rocks playing to an interested audience. The affair is as ancient and out of date as a street car horse, but withal (under the circumstances) more than tolerable. Though they don't understand the dialogue records, seem fond of them extremely. The first flies today in considerable numbers, but not biting. Noted that we saw none till we came up with the deer. Numerous preparations made this p.m. for the trip overland. Canoe touched up, etc. Boots and duffles made and washing of clothes by the women. Numerous rock throwing contests with matches as prizes at sunset. Calm evening, the roar of two or three waterfalls on the north side of bay are distinctly audible. The sunset a disc of red blazed a trail across the bay, colored the ice pans and has ended a paradoxical day of ice and cold breeze from the sea, a hot sun and heat waves on the upland and rocks, so that on the lee side of the winds we broiled, on the hills we shivered.

Thursday, 4 July Last evening was expecting to start when the tide came in, consequently was furious when they lay down on the rocks to sleep. Discovered today how badly in error I was, for the distance to the mouth of Payne River is three or four times what I had reckoned. We started with the flood tide, but had a wind head on. At noon decided to go the balance of journey by canoe. Went ashore, sorted and culled our outfit, wrote letters to Fort Chimo and departed about 3:30 with tide and wind against us. I felt sorry to see my good friends sail away. The *Walrus* and her mass of women, babies and squealing puppies is surely a memory. Anghick, Partridge's son, is the youngster of the outfit. To see his kind old mother packing his duffle – with bits of advice here and there – his father looking on silently, though reinforcing his mother's words, was for all the world the same as we have it. His young wife of about seventeen and son went aboard with the first canoe, so that she didn't figure in the final farewells; I guess she felt it though. I shall never get over finding out the goodness of these people. Gave "Jimmie" handkerchief. Nawri is the silent steady chap with the strength of a bull, Ambrose, the comedian, though all this subtle brilliant work is in understandable Eskimo. Nuckey is bow and captain – the early riser and soothsayer, Heaven knows we need an early rise – heretofore is in many ways our prima donna ... Had supper on the boulders at the first tidal rapid about seven o'clock. At the head of this rapid, stopped at an island over which swarms of duck and gulls were flying. We found countless eggs and eider down, and men killed three ducks with their Savage rifles. Nawri and I found an Eskimo grave on the top of island with some of the old trappings still there. A kettle lamp, remains of a bow and arrows and two long topek [tent] poles which we took off for fuel. I peered into the grave in a sort of box of boulders on the granite ledge, but there was nothing there.[31] Nawri explained by pantomime that foxes had eaten the body. Later, a short distance away found some of the bones. At 10:30 camped, or rather effected a landing, under the nose of the frowning shore line, and spread our blankets on some cushions of moss over the rocks. Finished an ancient Scribner's and turned in. Evidence of plentiful fish is shown by increased numbers of duck and gulls. Many seal seen also. So far no flies, therefore our travel surely ideal.

Sunday, 7 July Overslept and consequently late start. I wonder when the birds sleep, there is even but little twilight. I heard them at two o'clock this a.m. Men had service after breakfast, evidently Omarolluk's warning about the end of the world is having its effect.[32] Very hot sun and light easterly wind. Short portage at noon; had dinner there. Noted large bumble bees and "bull dogs." Recent Eskimo footprints in moss. Passed an apparently recent stone grave ... About 4:30 on rounding a sweeping curve of the river Nawri spied three Eskimo topeks ahead. As we neared them, saw a kayak pull out from some shore ice toward us. As we drew near a tiny island, he landed on the other side of it, crawled to the crest and peered at us. He finally stood up and called out "Chimo" which we answered. He was all amazement which we could note from his slightly trembling voice. And no wonder – a twenty-five foot Peterborough sail up and five paddles in this country, where no white has ever travelled. We scared him all right. He paddled alongside in his short little craft and became quite chatty. As we neared shore he called to his women jokingly about the "Adellite" (Indian) coming. I rather imagine he really thought it was a war canoe of Indians at first, and how even to this peaceful day they dread the Indians. They were an embarrassed crowd of women and children, huddled together in front of one of the topeks as we came up to shake hands. Went into one of the tents to greet an old woman and saw a caricature that made me cold with horror – withdrew rapidly and ungracefully, stumbling over a tame sea gull enroute. Ugh! Note there are two men, about five children and four women. Salmon trout are spread out drying and nets set in the river. They are living on deer and fish in plenty. Three dogs running about in sniffing inquiry of our arrival. Surprised they don't eat all the fish that lay out to dry, I suppose they are allowed to help themselves. This is the first time I've known a Huskie dog to "have enough." Noted two ivory shod sledges, and Nuckey says they have traveled to this country overland from the south in winter, also the head man's name is "Gwack" of Great Whale River, many miles to southward. Pitched camp near them and gave them tea, sugar, tobacco and pipe. Little girl came over with a salmon trout. Nuckey is holding a service in their tent – strains of their singing come to me as I write. Would rather it went somewhere else. Getting a map from Gwack of territory to south. Top of Gwack's head is bald! first instance.

Monday, 8 July   Warm sun. Trout breakfast and part of the encampment forming the outer circle of our repast. Gave them scraps, some needles, thread and hooks and tea. Learn that they are going to Ungava Bay to seal hunt. Gwack could not make map, much confused. Gave us a large white fish, two salmon trout and one lake trout. The river teems with fish. At noon came to the forks of the river, and now learn from my men that the best route lies along the north fork, thence over the divide to the head waters of the Povungnituk River. They know part of route, no doubt they expect to meet with inland Eskimo later on, then balance of journey will be all right. At the forks there is a large Eskimo monument on the crest of a knob of granite ... This is sure a naked country, nude and barren. Not even soil other than the superficial sands and gravel about the river way ... When we reached the head of the long rapid, I saw along the plain of the high bank the queerest array of what we thought were innumerable Eskimo monuments. They were deer decoys, so Nawri said, made by the Eskimo. On boulders men placed in upright position slabs of granite, so that from a distance the boulder looked not unlike the deer body, the slab forming the head. The boulders were in natural position of course, averaging about four or five feet through, and both stones were gray – the color of the deer in winter coat. The array of them spread over three or four acres of ground, and spread apart so as to be at a distance very distinct; really looked not unlike a band of deer grazing on the plain.[33] Nuckey rigged up a line and hook, inflated a trout bladder, attached it as a float about four feet from hook, cast it all out from shore, fastened the line to a boulder. This is a resource, there are no poles here. The crew were a dripping, melting bunch today.

Thursday, 11 July West wind, clouded, threatening. Another shivery breakfast. Nuckey had a lovely little trout fried for me, which represented his catch with night lines. Have been through another series of rapids, have tracked and portaged all day with seven miles to our credit. While lining over a rapid cellar, the canoe swamped and was very nearly lost. The men are learning, but are prone to take too many chances. The river has a most erratic course, bending to every point of the compass. The country is changing rapidly in appearance, lower with sweeping uplands and valleys. Supper at 7:30, then camp beside a wild booming rapid. Just after the snack, Nawri and Ambrose went off to the hills to try for a sight of the route ahead. In forty-five minutes they came back in great excitement, calling over to me, "Tooktoo!" I told them "Tooktoo Kokpunga." Shouldered their guns and away again. Poor Jimmie wanted to go too, his gun was shouldered, and on his way when Nuckey called him back to help make camp. He came reluctantly, smiling sheepishly. Later Nuckey came to my tent announcing the welcome killing of a deer. Outlook is changed now. Men expect to meet with more deer later on. Saw many decoys today. Some we saw just along the profile of a long curving hill. The effect was odd. Perhaps the deer are decoyed through curiosity to see at close range the caricatures of themselves. Deeply worn deer trails along the river banks. So far no flies. Expect them with the break of the cold weather. Nuckey baking his bannocks. Jimmie fishing along the rapid. Very cold west wind.

Friday, 12 July Forgot to say the day was ushered in with a deer meat breakfast, cooked in Nuckey's only and original way. At noon Nuckey succeeded in raising a fish. Jimmie next tried, caught two whoppers about ten pounds! We thought at his first catch he intended pulling in the head only, he hauled so rapidly. He was excited and beaming with the glow of a sunrise. Lost no opportunity for chaffing Nuckey of Jimmie's immensely superior powers as a Nimrod, etc., the whole carried on in pantomime of course ... Camp on second expansion at 4:45 on account of strong head wind. Canoe shows many bruises after her week of tracking. Paint is nearly scraped off the bottom, and is waterlogging rapidly. Nuckey says moss and willows are used in winter as well as summer for fuel. It means a trip by sledge could be taken across this area without difficulty ... Thirty-five miles plus in four days. Not quite nine miles per day! I hope the worst of our rapid work is over.

Sunday, 14 July Flies. A morning's travel through mirror lakes all silvery with clouds of a showery sky. The moss and shrubs scented from the rain. Idle ducks and gulls, with no wind for their sails. Nuckey spied some "keeyook" ashore, went after it, found it was an old sledge runner. Started dinner at twelve o'clock, but not ready till after one o'clock, notwithstanding the aid of our valuable find. We have three fires in use for our cooking. A tiny furnace is made of three slabs of angular granite blocks (millions everywhere). The penance is constantly feeding the spasmodic flames with moss and willows, green and dry. It represents calm indeed to coax our large teakettle to boiling point. At noon the flies were very thick ... We are putting the canoe in fearful shape with the tracking and lining up rapids. No one seems to know where they will end, or how far we are from the upper waters of the Povungnituk River. Nuckey says, "Eeteeveerunte Thiahke owerik-tock mana," "the Fort Chimo Sea (Ungava Bay) is far away now." In other words, he thinks we are half way across the peninsula. Noticed millions of flies on the calm surface of lakes this a.m. Camp at foot of portage, where I saw ruins of a very old stone igloo. Nuckey caught one pike during supper. Men cooking bannocks. Ambrose with his usual grace of movement broke one of the spoon oars during the excitement of lining canoe into rapid. He apologized in pantomime. Had to forgive him; it was so funny. Would let him break another one provided he asked another apology so funnily. The men imagine these spoon oars are valuable.

Thursday, 18 July Heavy gales of northwest wind with rain squalls. Coldest day so far. Men had baking fest. Ambrose washed some of my clothes. Went over grub which didn't please me much. Flour nearly half gone. Had a long conference about route. Find we are but a short distance south of Hudson Straits. Nawri says will reach head waters of Povungnituk River in three days with good wind. Will be on short rations if weather doesn't turn soon.

Friday, 19 July Snowfall today was completely unlooked for. No such occurrence this time of year on the Straits, Hudson Bay or Ungava Bay, I think, due to our altitude. Are not far from the divide. Wandered over the boulder plains during twilight, taking advantage of the first good weather after the extensive staying in tent. Condemned to a sleepless night. This is the fourth day we've lost – a serious matter. Nuckey went after deer, saw none. Balance cooped in tent. The differences between Eskimo travel and white man's are many – mostly in favor of the native. The one great quality they possess, never do they fume, swear and worry about those things that occur during travel: cold, flies, storms and the like. How much better they are for it. Therein lies the advantage of a single man traveling with them. Having no one with whom he can share his grievances he gradually adopts their mode of looking at things, i.e. a joke for every mishap.

Saturday, 20 July Frost, ground covered. Not far from start came upon a long portage, three-fourths of a mile, which carries us over a local divide. Could see the creek running in opposite direction from the hills. Completed the portage about ten o'clock and had dinner, as we breakfasted about 5:30. Spent a sleepless night and felt the effects today. Have found that the men have loaded the bannocks with baking powder – has raised the very deuce with me. As fizzy as a soda fountain ... Millions of flies on the lake surface trying to rally against the cold, so far so good, but by Jove when they do start we will long for the freezing days again. Decoys have ceased to be a novelty or even a scenic effect. We came across a winter camp of Gwack's today. Found his tent poles, a bag of fox traps, etc. We enjoyed a comfortable, quick service lunch through our wood find.

Sunday, 21 July A head wind all day. Did not get away until 10:30. Very cold. Passed the divide at noon much to our satisfaction. It is a very short portage, upon which there are many signs of Eskimo camps. The lakes today are very shallow and contain numerous boulder islets and reefs. The deer decoys are so numerous that one is struck by the innumerable generations of Eskimo hunters required apparently to make so many. The lake we are now encamped upon marks the end of Nuckey's and Nawri's travels here in former years. From now on it is an unknown affair. Overhauled the grub again tonight. Surprised at the limited amount. We will surely run short. That voyage on the *Walrus* to Payne Bay settled it, I am afraid. They probably treated the others with stuff, etc. unknown to me, though their proverbial improvidence may be the larger factor. A calm evening, cold. Cooking beans and bannock. Nuckey went off with telescope to look for deer. I realize the value of a telescope to the Eskimo; they doubtless locate many a deer with them which otherwise would be unseen. Told Nuckey that first man to kill a deer would get a present. Nuckey just pulled in a whacking big fish on his night line. Last of the syrup this a.m. Beans and flour enough for two weeks. A small fragment of ham left, but ample tea, sugar, tobacco, matches and hunting and fishing gear, and some patent beef extract, soup, etc. But three hundred and fifty or four hundred miles yet to finish.

Monday, 22 July Came to final traverse of lake shortly and climbed a low hill for a sight of outlet. Noted ice-fields all about the lake. Nuckey told me that deer pass here in their migrations. Eskimo spear them while swimming across the narrow gap. Later on saw a loon put out from shore to an islet – went there and found her nest with two eggs in it. Ambrose dipped them in the water and seeing that they didn't float, replaced them in nest ...

Tuesday, 23 July Few drops of rain in early a.m. Some very large fish caught last night, six or more. One is more than a meal for five of us. Has been a day of portages ... Flies had an innings today and this evening. Has been warm and semi-sun. When at foot of portage, suddenly saw canoe with men shoot out from shore to apparently the crest of a very heavy chute, was horrified of course, but the canoe crossed the crest to the other shore. The illusion was complete. I could not see from my vantage that a large area of easy water lay above the chute. Camped at six on a portage. The men done up with the hard work. One fish tonight. Baking bannock.

Wednesday, 24 July Clear day with southeasterly breeze, light and warm. Flies had a feast today. This a.m.'s work was principally portages. This p.m. were much pleased to launch out on two very large lakes, separated one from the other by a beautiful fall. We are encamped on second one ...

Thursday, 25 July Morning principally portages. At noon after running a short rapid in light canoe with Nawri, came out upon a long lake. This p.m. at three o'clock had traversed it, and came out on a big body of water, like Fort Chimo sea, said the men ... A most gratifying p.m.'s travel. A delightful breeze. No flies. No paddling. Every one but steersman cuddled up in bottom of canoe, droning and humming in monotone. Sailed on till 6:30, then camped not far from lake's outlet. Greatly puzzled about lake. In keen curiosity to know if it is the large one as indicated on the Eskimo sketch. Prepared a bang up meal of emergency rations, potatoes and carrots which put a smile on the men all right. Service as I write. Still filing on the same hymn in long-drawn "sand in the break" melody. Men set net.

Friday, 26 July One fish in net. Men went off for sight of route. Returned in hour saying a large river way ahead with a small lake expansion. Later Jimmie and Nuckey went off to where river discharges from this lake for fish. But a scanty supply for breakfast! Nuckey and Jimmie returned at noon with six fish, one a monster weighing about fifteen pounds. After an early lunch we packed up and were off as weather seemed all right again. The river at discharge was a surprise, a mighty size, so that we are no longer in doubt as to our position now. It discharges in magnificent wide island rapids ... Evidently the lake discharge is a great fishing ground for the Hudson Bay natives. The river, after rapids, flows with a strong current among islands of a small lake expansion. We camped again at discharge of expansion (more island rapids). At three o'clock a rain came down heavily. Rain most of day and fog. Nuckey caught two small trout at foot of rapid here. Men and I have been practically living on fish these last ten days; easing up on our limited supply of flour.

Saturday, 27 July Rain and heavy east wind during night, and rain till 10:00 this a.m. Breakfast at ten o'clock and as fuel is so sodden with water that a fire from it means a long, tedious and blowing operation. Have been running rapid after rapid. All of them splendid curving sweeps of deep water, as green as an emerald, so that underfoot we see the boulder masses flash up through it, for we have been traveling at times so that the wind cut our faces. Our big ungainly canoe walloped the cellars and rapid tails that seemed to toy with her, but with deep water what did we care? We were sliding down to Hudson Bay, our portages and lining and wading were a mere memory ... While we landed above a draw this a.m. in order to spy out some doubtful looking water, Nawri went off to a hill with telescope and returned, saying, we were near the "Big Water" ... Have been through another series up to seven o'clock tonight, and now encamped at a waterfall, a very fine one and with a most surprising volume of water. Immediately canoe was unloaded tonight, men ran off to a near-by cliff with telescopes. With their glasses rested on a boulder in front, and lying prone on the cliff edge, the whole hooded row of them are a picturesque sight. It is not so much a sight of the Big Water they are after as it is to see any Eskimo encampment ahead. The days are getting shorter most rapidly. Three weeks ago there was hardly any darkness, in fact only twilight, but now at nine-fifteen must light a candle. The country traveled is a low rolling plain area, much finer than the rugged, desolate boulder-strewn interior.

[Monday], 29 July The loveliest day of the trip. A southeast wind made the lake all blue and white and mottled the surface with the squalls that swept them. After our gorge portage this a.m. came out upon a large lake, and following the south shore or rather fighting our way through seas and wind, we are at the southerly end, only to find there instead of a discharging river, two rivers, one of considerable size flowing into it. We have the consolation of now, however, sailing with the wind we fought all a.m. to the westerly shore, where no doubt the river lies. Lunch before start. As we near sea coast the country improves in appearance. There is no longer the chaotic boulder country, but splendid velvety plains and valleys and down-sloped hills ... Became cold toward evening. Are in luxuriant willow growths now which form delightful green patches along the banks and slopes of the tawn and russet slopes. Our fuel supply is much improved. At six o'clock came to a gorge, high banked and exceedingly narrow – in places less than 40′ wide. The volume of water and the speed of it most impressive. Camped at head. Men portaged canoe over after supper. About three-fourths to one mile portage over high granite ledges. Men went off to a vantage point for a sight of Big Water, but nil.

Tuesday, 30 July After lunch started, a gale of wind with us and bowling us down a large lake expansion. Running a rapid series; at the discharge came out on big water with a far off horizon of blue hills. The men were sure we had come to the sea. Sailing along some four or five miles, the outlook wasn't improved ... Climbed another hill, men preceding, and from the crest, called to me, "Tiahoke tavary" (the sea over there). Sure enough, there it lay, far off to the southwest. The river in the middle distance curving towards it. Camped at seven o'clock. Very much pleased. Cooked a bang up supper, a wonderful soup and a fragment of plum pudding powder that made Jimmie smile all over.

Thursday, 1 August Strong easterly wind. Rain squalls set in at noon, still unabated. This a.m.'s travel was through a bewildering series of island rapids very long and very swift. At the head of one flushed two young geese which put us in great excitement. So much so that we nearly went down a rapid broadside on. Nawri went ashore and balance went down rapid after geese. Closed in on them, but the rapid cellar shook the canoe too much for an accurate shooting. After a final sharply curved rapid of size and speed that made our running it exciting, we shot out upon the long road of Povungnituk Bay – the sea in the distance. Sailing before a gale of wind (have never had so many fair winds before) we shortly came in sight of two large Eskimo topeks which sure keyed up the men. Sailing into the shore Ambrose called to them, "Ho! Ho! Ho!" They began presently to come out and down to the shore, a motley array of men, women, children and dogs. Camped here as wind is too strong. This p.m. a kayak went over the Bay to tell a large encampment there of our arrival. Later seven or eight kayaks came to see us. During supper a porpoise appeared near shore. The men went along shore, and Jimmie managed to hit it, but it sank before it could be reached with kayak. This evening had a long conference in large tent with maps laid out on a deerskin; have decided upon going to Cape Wolstenholme and to catch the ship there, that being the safest course to take.[34] From information I could gather, there are sea run trout without limit all along our course. Only deer in winter, and but few then, mostly north near Kovik. Eskimo say Povungnituk is the largest river. Many porpoise along coast and seal of course. Appears principal food is fish and duck during summer. Many presents of fish given us; we gave them tobacco and sugar. Were exceedingly pleased to obtain salt and about seven pounds of flour for tobacco and sugar. It seems we passed but short distance south of a high range of hills or mountains while descending the Povungnituk River (Inquire). Eskimos say there are no large lakes inland and northward. Service as I write – the usual hymn singing of four voices is tonight reinforced to band size.

Friday, 2 August Bade the encampment good-bye at nine a.m. They were a grotesque array outlined along the crest of the low point, with the gray sky behind throwing their waving arms and lolling figures in comical relief. Have had a beam and quarter wind all day, which has given us a glowing impression of the coast travel to come. Lunch on Cape Anderson. Reached Magnet Point for the night (thirty odd miles travel). Have taken two Eskimo along for the first day's travel; they return on foot tomorrow. While the old tub waddled along with a light breeze this p.m. amused ourselves shooting at sea pigeons which would hover above us no more than forty feet upward. Saw several seal, but couldn't get near them. The old Eskimo with us today gave me some information concerning mica inland from Kovik, also *supposed* silver inland from Cape Smith. Camped at 7:30 with a surplus of driftwood close by, a luxury indeed! A flock of ptarmigan on the rocks which the men tried to kill with stones. Any amount of ducks and pigeons today. Flies worse than ever before. Ducked into my tent in short order. We were practically free of flies on all our trip to this point, and I had imagined all sorts of things about them. Failed to connect with our salt and flour this morning. Will get to the bottom of it when I see an interpreter at Cape Wolstenholme. Flour will soon be gone.

Saturday, 3 August A splendid clear day with light easterly winds until one o'clock; then in afternoon gradually veered to north. Many flies. Nuckey outdid himself this a.m. by having breakfast ready at five o'clock. Took our two kindly Eskimos on to a further point. They started on their tramp back about eight a.m. with a letter to clerk of Great Whale River. Eskimo intends going there with dogs in winter. Coastline traveled this a.m. very low and monotonous. Eternal granite. Men caught two cod last night which pleased me immensely. They are the true deep sea cod without doubt. Eskimo catch many and very large ones. Say there are many off shore and in deep water. Had Nuckey skin one which I will take to Toronto. An important find. The coast and rivers from Cape Dufferin northward to approximately Cape Wolstenholme contains immense numbers of sea run trout or salmon trout. They with the sea fish (cod, etc.) form the chief source of food supply to natives. This p.m. had to row with light head quarter wind against us. Saw several seal and countless water fowl. At noon Nuckey caught a sea pigeon and obtained two eggs from nest. While idling time away about five o'clock by shooting long range at a seal, our north wind suddenly stiffened, were about three miles off Cape Smith and had a time of it getting into shore. Had we been out but little farther, would have been swept out to sea … Landed on a trap island close in shore, and while looking for drift wood, Nuckey spied two white whales traveling close in shore. He wounded one of them. The blood and oil of it showed vividly at surface, and gradually made a long, calm track to seaward. All was excitement now. We jumped in canoe and after it. Nawri rigging up an improvised landing harpoon out of a tent pole and large cod hook. Was soon up to him and alongside. Jimmie held his gun ready in case whale started bucking very much and shot to kill as Nuckey threw harpoon, and harpoon failed and all thought he was lost now. But Ambrose took harpoon and caught him as he was sinking in about fifty-six feet from surface. He soon slipped a sea line noose around tail and towed him ashore, not before Nawri put another bullet into him just at top of head. Men told me exultingly what splendid meat they would have to eat. They straightaway cut him up and squatted down about the carcass and guzzled some part of it raw, with a kettle full of another part cooking on every fire. Have never seen them so happy or greasy.

[Sunday], 4 August Clear and warm. Many flies. Very warm at noon. Started at eight o'clock amid swarms of devilish flies, with a calm sea all of a.m. We felt the warm day. It melted my buttery men to inaction. We managed to amble along with our "billiard table" between seals and there were many. Every one within any sort of shooting distance came in for attention, though nary a one was hit. I was an apathetic onlooker, though contributed to the sport by scratching and rapping along the gunnel of canoe while the battery waited in half pointed position for seals to rise, in curiosity, of course, of my subtle decoying. They didn't rise! We saw a very large harp seal near a small ice floe. Ambrose climbed on to it and started decoying by raking the ice with a paddle. I being next to steersman had to hold to a crevice of the floe with my hand acting as an anchor while the sportsmen waited, and they waited until I started explaining in heated English that holding ice cakes was no hell ...

Monday, 5 August Rain showers in early a.m. ... Walked along shore with sample bag for some distance, crossing the formation. Noted no important variations to part previously seen. The flowers along shore are most surprising in color, in number and in variety. Walked the banks of them, yellow, purple and white. In the distance the brilliant colors melted into masses of vivid lines and contrasts. About eleven o'clock Nawri spied (Nawri always does the spying) three topeks (tents) on a long low-lying point some distance ahead. As the detail of this scene gradually came into view, could see the scurrying figures going from tent to tent, and peering from nests of boulders at our approach. Coming up within hailing distance not a native could be seen. Innumerable dogs lay scattered about asleep or too warm to rise at our arrival. All was quiet and undisturbed apparently as the mirror sea. Not until we landed did a tousled head emerge from the cavernous depths of the hood – waiting for the stranger's handshake. I imagine this is some of their past training, have been struck by it everywhere. A babe not a year old poking out its fist for a handshake. My men stood there dignified and reserved, gazing at the horizon, apparently hardly venturing a word. The men of encampment opened a disjointed conversation. After a proper interval during which my men and the people melted into a more cordial assembly, I threw out the magic word to

Nuckey – tobacco – instructing him to give them some, with sugar and matches. Nuckey keenly alive to his role, gravely opened grub bags and from the canoe distributed the presents. Nuckey capped it all by dramatically holding forth the white whale tail to them, and they were pleased in something of the way children are when the door is finally opened to the lighted tree and presents. All was good fellowship now.

Bade the encampment good-bye at noon; two of the men coming with us to a long point to show us where to find drift wood. Gave them more raw whale meat and tea for their lunch. These summer days are not traveling days. Again there were many seal, waterfowl and schools of salmon trout. The sea was burnished steel and silver, which caught the heavy cloud shadows and mirrored the glinting green and white ice floes. We couldn't paddle continuously – the warm sun and languid air, with innumerable seals large and small popping their heads up at close range kept us from it. After several volleys of spattered lead at several seal, as a joke I asked Jimmie if he was really, "Kokpunganetsuk" (hungry for the seal), answering with that smile of his, I said, "Very well your master will kill one for you. Now you see that small one over there – call him!" Borrowed Ambrose's cheap little "trade 22" – which we've all (but Ambrose) taken turns at ridiculing, waited expecting to miss so badly that the absurdity of it would convulse them. The seal came up at seventy-five yards. I fired. After an exclamation of the crew had exploded, realized I was sublimely wonderful (to the men). Not only did I hit that seal, but kill him instantly. The only spirited paddling of the day occurred just then to reach him before he sank. Whether they were more pleased at the feast to come or amazed at the freak affair would be hard to say. Took full advantage of this chance to tease them unmercifully. We landed on a large floe later on for water, and took pot shots at several seal (nary a pot). Camped at seven o'clock at a point midway between Pecten Harbour and Kettlestone Bay.

Tuesday, 6 August The a.m. was warm and very fine, but by three p.m. the cold wind was icy. Reached an Eskimo encampment on north side of Kovik Bay at 4:00, the most primitive of all so far seen. They numbered about twenty-seven, and lived in one large sealskin topek. Kept well to windward of it. There was very little constraint about the meeting with them as was the case of yesterday. Two kayaks put out to meet us. The spokesman wasn't long in getting the appeal for tobacco. Gave them tea, saccharine and matches also, which pleased them mightily. Disappointed in not being able to obtain deer meat from them. None about. Living on fish and occasional seal. Departed shortly and sailed on to north end of large islands (nameless). Camped at 8:00.

Wednesday, 7 August Breakfast at six. Fog clear at seven-thirty. Have had the best sailing wind of the trip, but very cold and uncomfortable. About eleven a.m. while sailing along the lee side of a large floe, Nawri suddenly shouted, "Nanook! Nanook!" Just some polar bear a hundred yards ahead. I saw him swimming for the floe; he landed in short order, galloped across it and took to the water again, we sailing for him with a beam wind and large sea running. Overhauled him shortly and he headed for shore. Crew now took in the sail, and we followed the more slowly swimming fellow with paddles keeping a respectful fifty feet or so behind him. I got out both cameras and went up near the bow. Asked the men to close in a little more which they reluctantly did, until our quarry came around with a snort, whereupon we fell back to the old margin. Much surprised he did not swim faster, didn't seem to have nearly the speed a moose has. Men waited with rifles ready, and as he landed took my pictures as they fired. Ambrose firing first with his "22" in order to bay him on the rocks, but Nawri and Nuckey followed too quickly and spoiled my chance for a most interesting picture.[35] They at once started in skinning and cutting up the carcass, Nuckey and I getting dinner ready. He is a fair size and in good condition. Taking pelt and skull and part of meat. Ice is packing in shore rapidly. Saw many seal and one white whale, which went by us at about forty feet, which made the men regret that their guns were not in readiness, but for my part glad as we are surfeited with seal, whale and bear meat and salmon trout. Have made a splendid run. Am at Nuvuk Bay at seven o'clock. All through the balance of our day's travel every peculiarly shaped outline on the ice floes was a bear.

Thursday, 8 August Ice floes. Light clouds. Cleared at seven o'clock, but wind is very strong ... At noon while rounding a high island point, came in sight of an Eskimo encampment but a short distance ahead. Put in to them, Ambrose calling "Inuit! Inuit!" Presently three men and their families appeared. Surprised to find them the finest lot so far met with. Two of the men in fact were very Canadian, one part Negro I suspect, the other part Scandinavian, of gray saucer eyes and light hair. Stopped for lunch and to get data on route. Owing to scanty supply of driftwood and damp moss, lunch was not ready till two o'clock. The people were very hospitable and kind – a fine looking lot. Stayed in one of their tents for lunch, the wind outside being very strong and cold. They proudly showed me their two slips of paper certifying to their baptism last fall by a traveling missionary on the Hudson's Bay ship at Cape Wolstenholme. Persuaded the head man to travel with us as guide to Cape Wolstenholme. Departed at three o'clock with a still heavier wind. The old billiard table has shown a cardinal quality to us now and we sure needed it. The sweep oar rigged as rudder couldn't hold her and I went close astern to Ambrose, who was steering and helped him with the "augunk" (paddle). We rapidly came into a bigger coastline of high sheer cliffs and granite gneiss domes, mightily picturesque. Soon Digges Islands, some seven miles northward, came into a near range. Then the cliffs and headlands of Cape Wolstenholme of a thousand feet sheer – their crests overhanging and bowing to sea level – the shoreline an apparently hopeless mass of sheer walls without even a footing or talus slope landing hove in sight. Stratas of water fowls and gulls contrasted these profound and splendid heights. The rusted immense gneisses rocks of them fall in sheets of browns and greens and yellows, cross sectioned and streaked with dykes innumerable, gave them the appearance of an Italian vari-colored veined marble. Snow patches in steep valley seams and furrows, bathed in a haze heavy and ever changing as the scudding clouds raced between them and the western sun, created a fusion of color. All of our journey in one held no scenes like this one gave us, by the way of a few moments so critical. The wind now swept down off the cliffs and tore the water into sheets of flying foam and curled and eddied so that we at one time lost control and shipped water with a seaway, owing to the undertow and heavy currents. It seemed as dangerous to attempt lowering the sail as to continue as we were, but suddenly we scudded into a flat calm lee of the nearby sheer walls, lowered sails and paddled in along the base of the shoreline some distance, where in around a sharp nose a tiny cove opened to us. Upon landing Nuckey held council with our guide which ended in deciding to abandon the canoe and outfit, climb the range and walk overland to Cape Wolstenholme Post, a distance as we then thought of some six miles. Note waterfalls. Arranged the cache of outfit and canoe to be called for later, if possible. We commenced the walk at 5:30. The first part of journey followed the deep, canyon-like valley of boulders, talus and sand with a rapidly descending brook, formed of the snow fields of the range. In an ascent of a mile or thereabouts, we climbed 1500 feet, then continued over a cobbled, rolling, pond dotted area toward the port. The snow fields have covered more than half the ground surface and are the source of innumerable torrents that tumble in narrow deep valleys to the sea. The men started off at a stiff pace, Nuckey and I bringing up an ever lengthening rear. The cobbled and bouldery country devoid of even moss for the most part, gradually made the walking most trying. I regretted starting away with only one pair of duffles and Husky boots. As we kept on the pain increased, so that when stepping on the more angular stones I was almost doubled with pain. Twilight had turned to night and still no sign of the port or bay. Our guide gave but little satisfaction when questioned; merely laughed or smiled accommodatingly. It was over hill and valley, around tiny lakes still half covered with winter ice, over deep long snow fields that never disappear. The footing underneath was no longer firm. I stumbled over the never-to-be-forgotten pavements, at times coming up with a maddening bruise. Deep valleys and sunken lakes appeared in the gloom of a clouded night while a high cold wind from the south gave a sense of desolation not experienced on the travel over the divide of the interior. It was about eleven-thirty when a sharp descent was commenced down a steep snow banked valley which farther downward had melted into a tumbling torrent. Unexpectedly we stood out on a valley height of Erik Cove, the post a half-mile distant. Now learned that a small river lay between it and us. The men signaled by firing their guns, which after an interminable time was answered by a hail of an Eskimo and his wife on the other side of the river. The pastor and his servants were roused and came to us with a boat, and the men were shortly installed on either side the servants' mess table with piles of sea biscuit and pots of tea that spelt a long looked for luxury.[36]

5 Fellow of the Royal Geographical Society

Nearly two months passed between Flaherty's last entry of 8 August 1912 and his arrival at Moose Factory. In his final report to Mackenzie he observed that the original plan had been to meet the HBC supply ship *Nascopie* at Cape Wolstenholme on its outbound passage and thus reach the south via Labrador and Newfoundland. But the *Nascopie* was delayed and arrived at Cape Wolstenholme on 20 August, a month behind schedule. Flaherty boarded her nevertheless, and steamed west across the Bay, an area he had never observed, to the posts at Fort Churchill and Chesterfield Inlet, then south to York Factory and down into James Bay to the terminus at Charlton Island, where the *Nascopie* began its outbound passage. Flaherty reached Moose Factory on 2 October 1912. He reported to Mackenzie that overall "this expedition was an invaluable one. I had now become acquainted with every post on the coastline of the Ungava and James Bay with the exception of Fort Albany."[1]

Flaherty's claim to an expanding understanding of the Hudson Bay region is affirmed in the many ways we can observe his growing skill as an interpreter of his own work and the culture within which it was occurring. The diary that Flaherty kept for the second expedition reveals him as more relaxed and reflective as a writer, and his entries go far beyond the workaday matters that prevailed in the first expedition. There is evidence of Flaherty's increased efforts to obtain more facility in the Inuktitut language. Although he never attained any significant fluency as a speaker of Inuktitut, he did work to build a core vocabulary of words and phrases, such as those in the lists he included as subset entries in his 1911–12 diary and the presence among his papers of sixteen pages of English-Eskimo words and phrases, which are typed and dated 2 September 1911. As he spent more time with companions who were not bilingual, his use of gestures and his grasp of the context of their words no doubt made him a more understanding listener. There are some semicomic moments in this process, as in Flaherty's entry for 28 March, when in the calm after the panic he recalled: "The men after supper tonight tried to tell me in signs and our limited vocabulary that the dog I purchased from Jim Crow died today, but I thought they said they were going back to Great Whale River. For a moment was alarmed and angry but I caught their meaning in time, much laughter."

Just as Flaherty made efforts to gather and grasp language, there is also evidence of his efforts to collect the intellectual and material culture of Native peoples. Although he never thought of himself as a professional ethnographer, he had the instincts of one. There are repeated entries of obtaining by barter or gift items such as tools, clothing, and carvings, which he gathered, on behalf of Mackenzie, for a "curio" collection. The first distribution of these items occurred in August 1913 when, following the second expedition, Mackenzie donated what Flaherty had collected to the institution that eventually became the Royal Ontario Museum of Archaeology. Flaherty also made an effort to collect and transcribe examples of cultural narratives, such the Cree legend of "The Man in the Moon," "The Ungava Legend of the Flood," and "Beliefs of Arctic Eskimos."[2]

This imperative to be observant and informed about the world he was exploring is most powerfully manifested in the identity of Flaherty as scientist. The diary of the second expedition provides us with an image of Flaherty as the observant and concrete analyst of geological terrain. For him, the landscape becomes animated by the nature of its rock formations, the layers of its strata and folds, the scoring and scars of geological time, and the promise, overall, of its extractive worth. These are the clues not only of a process of seeking mineral wealth but of the great skills that Flaherty demonstrated throughout his career to view reality as dynamic space, full of motion and vector, charged by its shapes, contours, and contrasts.

In the unexpected division of his second expedition into two parts, chance had given Flaherty the premier experience in his career as a geographer-scientist. The first and shorter half of the second expedition was a reprise of the first in that he re-examined the Nastapoka Islands, this time by boat, and returned to spend the winter of 1911–12 in the Fort George area. Then, not being able to make the ice crossing to the Belcher Islands in the early spring of 1912, he set out to traverse, west to east, the upper Labrador peninsula across the Ungava to Fort Chimo and then returned, east to west to Hudson Bay, all in one season. In recognition of this second part of the expedition, he was elected a fellow of the Royal Geographical Society.

His nomination, as was the custom, was entered by two fellows of the society, the two being Harold A.C. Machin (1875–1931) and Arthur Albert Knight. Flaherty's election occurred on 5 May 1913. Machin, the primary nominator and in whose hand the application was completed, gave as warrant for the nomination that Flaherty "made two journeys into Ungava for Sir William Mackenzie and penetrated the Barren Lands of Canada."[3] Flaherty's crossing of the Ungava Peninsula, touted as the "first" for a white man, was really a semi-first. Two HBC explorers, James Clouston and William Hendry, had independently traversed the Ungava in the 1820s at a comparable or lower latitude; and in 1884, with the help of four Cree guides, the Reverend Edmund James Peck had crossed by canoe from Great Whale River to Fort Chimo in twenty-five days. The uniqueness of Flaherty's journey was that his west to east crossing was at the highest northern latitude and that he apparently was the first white man to cross the Ungava by canoe along the Payne and Povungnituk rivers.[4]

To his generation, this feat gave Flaherty significant status as an explorer, the recognition of which he was enormously proud, adding the letters FRGS to his name in most of his publications and publicity profiles well into the 1920s. In 1940, an especially difficult year for Flaherty economically, his name was dropped from the Society's rolls for non-payment of dues.

In trying to affirm the significance of what he had accomplished on the second expedition, the report Flaherty submitted was the most comprehensive he ever provided to Mackenzie. Another motive for its comprehensiveness was no doubt his sponsor's wish to obtain detailed information on a host of potential economic resources in the Hudson Bay region. In addition to its primary objective of attempting "an exploration of a series of unknown islands which parallel the Nastapoka group," the purpose had also been to investigate "the fisheries of James and Hudson Bay, particularly the whaling, of which superficial information had been obtained on the previous expedition. The physical characteristics of the country and meteorological records bearing particularly on the ice movements, the differences in season of the coastline and the usual barometer, thermometer and wind observations were to be obtained and information generally as to the territory explored."[5]

Given the extreme ambitiousness of the objectives Flaherty took on to satisfy Mackenzie's craving for hard economic results, his findings, unsurprisingly, fell far short of expectation. The timber, fishery, and mineral resources of the James Bay area were, in Flaherty's view, negligible. There was noteworthy potential for fishery harvesting in the Hudson Bay region, but not a match to those of the Labrador banks. Walrus and white whale abounded along the Ungava coast, but by 1912 the market for tusks and whale byproducts bordered on the moribund. There remained mineralogical possibilities, but only along the coast and outlying islands that formed the southern extension of the Nastapokas.

Eager to prime the pump of success, Flaherty offered Mackenzie the following as evidence of the value of the second expedition: "This expedition has resulted primarily in determining the location of those areas likely to be of economic interest and with exploratory possibilities, or in other words, of narrowing an area of vast extent to definite and defined territory where an exploration can be undertaken with a minimum of time and with effect."[6] He was, of course, arguing for a reprise of the failed primary objective of the second expedition – finding and assessing the presence of iron ore on the Belcher Islands:

> The experience acquired by the two expeditions undertaken to Hudson Bay on your behalf [he told Mackenzie] has placed the writer in a position to continue the exploration with results that should finally be of economic value. With the proper outfit this work can be made to at least pay for itself by the furs, ivory, and data accumulated during the expedition, with a possibility of making a surplus that would materially help out the expense of the exploratory work already incurred. As a further exploration would concern original or unknown ground, the natural data alone should be of great interest and value.[7]

Although this report was undated, we can assume that it was in Mackenzie's hands no later than November 1912. Unlike the time between the first two expeditions – a matter of months – Flaherty received no immediate reply regarding future expeditionary prospects. By December he was in Toronto living in the Queen's Hotel, and it was only on 26 May 1913, when Flaherty forwarded to Mackenzie a memorandum of proposal, that the matter of a possible third expedition was again broached.

In the memorandum Flaherty retraced the points made in his final report. He was, he said, in seasoned readiness for the next venture in that the past expeditions had provided "comprehensive experience into the ways and means of travel, the general knowledge of the physical characteristics of the seaboard of Hudson Bay."[8] Again he proposed that the Belchers and their discovery offered the most promising opportunity to find viable ore resources akin to those of northern Michigan and Minnesota, and like those found earlier, though not at commercial grade, on the Nastapoka group to the north:

> This island range is a series of island groups outlying and paralleling the Ungava Coast of Hudson Bay. They have a length of more than 350 miles and are completely unknown and unexplored. Large land masses occur there which sustain an Eskimo population peculiar to these islands and of whom little is known. The greatest inducement to an exploration of the Eastern or Ungava coast of Hudson Bay occurs here. These islands are formed of the identical rock series which form the iron ore and silver lead bearing series of the Nastapokas, of which they are a seaward extension.[9]

With two expeditions behind him, Flaherty could be forceful regarding his experience and his confidence that the Belchers did exist and were mineralogically promising.

But his experience had been gained at a cost – a real investment cost to Mackenzie and Mann – and the issue of money therefore began to shoulder its way into this process of persuasion. To gauge the economic costs of Flaherty's explorations, we find help in two memoranda that were written after the third expedition (of 1913–14) but before the fourth (of 1915–16).[10] In the first of these memoranda, dated 16 November 1914, Flaherty advised Mackenzie that the total cost of the three expeditions to date had been $75,000, a figure that he revised upward to $100,000 in his memorandum of 24 February 1915. In both estimates Flaherty reported that the second expedition had cost $30,000 (at best, a low-end calculation).

Thus, at the time that Flaherty was attempting to persuade Mackenzie to sponsor a third expedition, some $40,000 to $50,000 had already been invested in the first two ventures, no mean sum by 1913 standards. Flaherty's efforts to anticipate this rising red ink was evident in the mention above of "furs, ivory and data" as a source of "surplus" for costs already incurred. In the proposal for a third expedition outlined in his memorandum of 26 May 1913, the matter of recapturing investment was given foreground attention: "The complete cost of the expedition will be defrayed by the furs, ivory, whalebone and motion pictures obtained on the cruise ... Moving picture outfit can be obtained by a purchase or a royalty agreement with the Edison Company of New York City. A general trading outfit of walrus guns, small arms and ammunition will be included with a list of the provisions for the cruise. The geological survey of Ottawa will purchase any nautical or natural data resultant of the expedition."[11]

From the perspective of cinema history, the flashbulb in the dark is, of course, the mention of motion pictures. Sometime between November 1912 and May 1913, the notion of the economic promise of filming the Inuit intruded itself into Flaherty's public thinking. In later years (for instance, in the "Islands" narrative), he ascribed to Mackenzie the suggestion that he include a motion-picture camera in his outfit: "When I was outfitting the [third] expedition, Sir William had suggested that I get 'one of those affairs,' as he called it, which made motion pictures. 'You will be seeing new country,' he said, 'strange people, wonderful wildlife, and all that.' I needed no urging, for already I had become deeply interested in photography, particularly as it related to the Eskimos; and a motion picture camera became part of my equipment."[12]

On a number of levels, the ascription of this idea to Mackenzie makes no sense. There is nothing in Mackenzie's profile to suggest any prescience about the future of cinema or an awareness of its technical particulars ("get one of those affairs"!). There is also documentation showing that it was Flaherty who actually proposed motion pictures as a source of income – a move very much in character for Flaherty the poker player, who in this game of betting and bluffing wanted to strengthen his hand in his negotiations to get supporting capital. There is more than enough suggestion that the source of cameras had been investigated by Flaherty, and though he eventually turned to Bell & Howell for a camera, rather than to Edison, he had investigated obtaining equipment and licenses. Finally, there is the strong linkage to photography which, as is evident from the journals of Flaherty's previous expeditions, "deeply interested" him.

Although we may never be able to unravel this question of who actually fathered the idea of taking a motion-picture camera along, the nexus here of exploration, economics, and filmmaking was a paradigmatic moment in Flaherty's career. After 1922, when he ceased to be an explorer in actuality and became an explorer of cinematic metaphors, he struggled for a solution to the same paradigm he faced here: how to persuade sponsors that this "Belchers on my Mind," this mirage seeking actualization through exploration, could pass the test of skeptics and bookkeepers. The Flaherty legend chimes on the triumphs of such films as *Moana* (1926), *Man of Aran* (1934), and *Louisiana Story* (1948), but these successes of persuasion overshadow the many deadends, dropped projects, and the litter of polite refusal letters that he received during his career. Although in this game of bet and bluff Flaherty lost more often than he won – to the diminution, some would say, of North American cinema – he was a persistent, inventive, and bold player, and he won the game in his proposal for a third expedition.

Not only did Mackenzie agree to it, but he sponsored the most ambitious expedition Flaherty would ever conduct. The *Nastapoka*, the 36 ft "jigger rigged boat" that Flaherty had commissioned at Moose Factory for the second expedition, had proved unfit to explore the unchartered Belcher Islands, so it was to be replaced by the deep-water schooner *Laddie*, a 75 ft ship with an adequate 75 hp engine. It was to have a crew of ten, including a professional skipper. The expedition had a dateline of nineteen months, an ambitious exploratory program, and a cargo list that detailed the scope and depth of its resources:

> The cargo consisted of provisions, clothing, lumber, coal, etc. for 11 men and 19 months, with Eskimo trade outfit and exploration outfit including dynamite and drill steel, salmon and cod nets, jiggers, etc. to be used in connection with the fishing investigations; a comprehensive motion picture and camera outfit including 1,000 lbs. chemicals, 25,000 ft. film and 2,000 dry plates; hunting outfit, including one whale gun and equipment; four #303 British Winchester Rifles, one Mauser, one Manlicher, four shot guns, 2 Colt Pistols, and 600 traps; also a mineral testing outfit and a comprehensive range of reference and general literature.[13]

Flaherty had made the passage from canoeman with companion to expedition commander. In the process, the photographer was to evolve into the filmmaker, and the rooting of the Flaherty legend of cinematographer as explorer was to have its first planting.

Diary of the Third Mackenzie Expedition 15 June 1913 – 3 October 1914

The actual outfitting of this expedition commenced at St. John's, Newfoundland on the 15th June 1913 and was completed on the 12th day of August 1913 at St. John's.[14]

Thursday, 14 August 1913 Departure was delayed by heavy weather until August 14th. The cruise finally had its beginning at 10 a.m. with fine weather and light southerly winds favoring us. All hands were more than glad to be under sail after nearly two months of outfitting and delay at St John's and at Toronto.[15]

The crew had shanties for every job from the hoisting of the anchors to the coiling of ropes and stowage of deck gear, and we all felt mighty glad to be out of the tangle of accounts, settlements, checking of cargo, and the tiresome worry of making final purchases.

The tiny imp of a tug that towed us from our berth to mid-stream waved us a farewell as she cast off the tow line, and the clumsy old *Laddie* heeled to a light draft, the auxiliary engine started up a clatter that gave new life to the ship and to us, and at last, though it seemed too good to be true, we were under way, free of the greatest hardship of any cruise, that is, the outfitting, the vexatious delays, worry and a thousand and one things.

Friday, 15 August Another splendid day with light southerly winds. Two large icebergs were sighted at 4 a.m. Developed departure photographs during day.

How good it is to be away from smelly old St. John's and its grimy waterfront, but above all to be free of that damnable outfitting.

LaDuke and I are strangers to deep water cruising, which will make the ship cruise part of this affair the wonderful part of it all. Some large bergs sighted during the day along the horizon to eastward.

Saturday, 16 August Last evening's breeze stiffened to a gale during the night from SE. Galley was flooded from the seas off her bows which almost dove under oftentimes. Had to turn out at 11 p.m. in order to secure innumerable sundries that had broken adrift in the cabin. Sky cleared at 9 p.m. with brilliant moon.

Sunday, 17 August A splendid day – The ship wallowed along through the heavy glassy swells of yesterday's breezes. Belle Isle was sighted all through the morning far off to westward. Many icebergs, some of them quite near, and huge affairs they were. LaDuke tried out one of his new rifles this a.m. – plugging away at a school of porpoise and later used his "toy" 44 gauge shot gun on a sea pigeon saucily perched on the main mast head. His gun would not reach it, much to the amusement of the watch and, I believe, the bird! Played gramophone on deck and lolled about enjoying the glorious a.m. Southerly breeze started at noon and gradually freshened during balance of day, so that by dark we bowled along at 8 knots through a wonderful moonlit night.

Sighted Battle Harbour coast of Southern Labrador. Printed photos – gramophoned and played "Mousie" with LaDuke.

Monday, 18 August A dull grey a.m. – wind southerly and moderate. At 10 a.m. rain set in, and wind slackened considerably. Towards nightfall ran in amongst a nest of bergs and detached floes which gave the skipper an anxious night of it, with all this fog and rain. Land was reported several times before dark but always found it to be bergs looming gray along the mist of the horizon. Rain and fog.

Tuesday, 19 August Heavy fog in early a.m. Sighted land about 7 a.m. off the northwest entrance of Hamilton Inlet. Made for an anchorage owing to threatening weather and numerous bergs and floes to seaward. Arrived at Indian Harbour, of Hamilton Inlet, at 11 a.m. to find it crowded with Newfoundland fishing schooners all weather bound. We ran in amongst them, rather recklessly I thought, and anchored. Our flags were flying and many of the skipper's old fishing friends answered and others along shore fired volleys from their rifles. Went ashore during the day and visited Dr. Grenfell's Mission Hospital.[16] French, one of our seamen, was sent ashore to the physicians in charge of this hospital with a badly poisoned finger. The doctor pronounced it a dangerous affair, were it left much longer without medical treatment. Had a most enjoyable visit to the mission hospital and met the officials in attendance, Dr. Paddon, Misses Hillcrest & Smith – and two Harvard medicos, volunteers during the present summer season. I invited the two latter aboard for dinner with champagne and gramophone – later a chafing dish supper. The Champagne was a brilliant idea – they stayed with us all night, sleeping on the cabin floor – for our bunks are only three, and they would not hear of an offer of them. All breakfasted together on bacon and eggs of which they had not tasted since leaving civilization.

Wednesday, 20 August Fishing friends of the skipper's were entertained during day which was principally a drink. Dined at the mission during evening. After dinner, which by the way was a pleasing contrast to our Newfoundland cookery aboard the schooner, we all trooped aboard the *Laddie*. Gramophoned them with Grand Opera and the like, showed off our cabin outfit and finally all hands fell to on a Welsh Rarebit operation, conducted for my future benefit in part. An enjoyable evening – gave them a roast of beef, oranges, bon-bons, and nuts at parting – for their "civilized food stuffs" are hard to obtain in these parts. Perhaps the last bit of civilization until return.

Friday, 22 August Departed under sail and engine at 8 a.m. Fine and clear. Put in for Turnavik at 2:30 p.m. Anchored in harbor just in time for a wicked "nor'easter" swept down upon us, with great force so that close-hauled and with engine we barely made the harbor – a snug little horse shoe cove. Anchored at 4 p.m. At 8 p.m. a heavy gale with sleet and rain and a thundering of breakers on the reefs outside.

Weather bound at Turnavik until Wednesday August 27th. Five days of most valuable time, as we may have more than 1200 miles to travel. We are woefully late and the accomplishment of reaching Repulse Bay seems doubtful.

Wednesday, 27 August Tuesday dawned fine and clear which put us in good humor and more hopeful once more. At 8 a.m. another delay caused a deal of vexation. The ship swung far out on her chains and grounded on an unusually low tide. Cleared the harbor on a rising tide at noon. Turnavik proved a most trying delay. A desolate barren island with a few ramshackle unpainted houses of the fishing station there, a rickety old wharf and tumble-down fish sheds. There were about a dozen fishermen and two Newfoundland servant girls, who came aboard one day and visited us. They marveled at the cabin, which I've found all along the coast is considered a most splendid affair by the fishermen and "livyeres" who all know the old "tub" of former days. No doubt they think we are made of gold for did not we have oranges – a mahogany gramophone, modern rifles – a green velvet table cover and a cabin done up in white enamel!

I must repeat how gladly we took our leave of Turnavik and its desolate mass of rocks – its hopeless poverty stricken air. All of it is a relic, however, of days gone by when it was one of the great fishing stations of the Labrador, its tiny harbor crowded with fishing schooners and innumerable fishermen who didn't always "fish" at Turnavik.

Thursday, 28 August William Robertson, cook, laid up with a bad cold.[17] Sainsbury taking his place as cook.

Saturday, 30 August Engine again stopped for repairs. The high bold coast looms up to westward, its boldness increasing to northward. Day's travel spoiled by that damned engine or rather engineer – still out of commission.

Cook very ill – lumbago – is the skipper's hazard of his case.

Sunday, 31 August It seems we have over run our course and instead of making the Button Islands off Cape Chidley, the SE entrance to Hudson Strait, we made the southern coast of Resolution Island, which marks the NE entrance to Hudson Strait. A mighty tide with rips and overfalls and churned to a nasty cross sea by an east wind – sucked us into Hudson Strait, literally speaking, for it was not good navigation that did it.

We sailed along off this high bold coast of Resolution Island with good speed – but so strong was the tide which swirled in circles and eddies at times that the ship would momentarily lose steerage way so that we made a corkscrew course of it most of the a.m. and the ship pitched in all manner of ways in the choppy seaway. The error in our course (more than 30 miles) was due to a fouled log which I found was trailing kelp on its spoon.

Note: Refer to Sir John Franklin's *Journey to the Polar Sea* (1819) for an account of shipwreck on Resolution Island, etc.[18]

Newfoundland sailing methods have given me no glowing impression of what we might be up against on the crossing of Northern Hudson Bay later on. I have an idea that courage and hardiness minus brains is a crime.[19]

Monday, 1 September At 5 a.m. off the Saddle Back Islands. Cook improved. A few icebergs seen which are carried into Strait along north coast by tides from Davis Strait. A large one overturned not far from ship later in day. Afforded a most impressive sight. Its overturning

William ("Salty Bill") Robertson, 1913–14, who served as cook-seaman on two of Flaherty's expeditions (Claremont, LAC, PA500687/photo RF)

spread out radiating circles of swells for more than a mile and the thunder of it gave us a respect and awe of icebergs and of their mighty size and displacement. I believe that berg turned out of vanity for with its turning it presented a new face to the world – of wonderful greens and blues like a mass of emerald and sapphire combined in one. Its seams and edges glistened brilliantly white in the sunshine which was rather a contrast to its old weather worn face from which the greens and blues had long melted away to a monotonous mass of gray and white. Steamed on through the night close in shore at an attempt to reach an anchorage off the entrance to Lake Harbour. Sainsbury having spent the previous winter at Lake Harbour acted as pilot. The night was pitchy blackness – the sky heavy and overcast – the sea calm and motionless. The skipper and watch had an anxious time of it, but at midnight the ship crept into a temporary island harbor in which after too little precaution in sounding the anchors were slipped.

While preparing to turn in after a "mug up" of cocoa the keel at the stern almost imperceptibly grounded. We rushed out on deck but the darkness was impenetrable.

We could hear, however, the rapidly receding tide swirling along the ship's sides. In an incredibly short time the ship was grounded from stem to stern and heeled rapidly outward away from shore. The deck load of coal oil and gasoline in nested casks – 3,000′ lumber, the launch and canoe and sacked coal gave us much concern, and it seemed a question of when it would break adrift with the rapidly heeling ship. We gingerly picked and climbed our way over the deck load which seemed like climbing a steep embankment to the inshore bulwark and there clung on to the ladderways, etc., helpless in the dark night and wondering what the deuce was going to happen. After a long time it seemed then a streak of dawn appeared in the east and in the gray light of a dismal chill morning we made out an absurd situation for we were a funny looking row of shivery blackbirds clinging to the bulwark and ladders. There lay the old "tub" careened on her starboard side at an angle of at least 40 degrees and high and dry and with only her stern post in a stranded pool of water. We slipped over the side with ropes and walked about the hull. She nestled into a mud and sand flat which was barely large enough to hold her while some 20 ft. farther out where she stranded there would have turned her completely, and right alongside she barely missed a reef, which would have surely broken her back. As it was she was unbent and there was nothing for it but to await the return tide. One could not imagine a more narrow escape. I estimated this fall of tide at 45′ though I understood later that at Lake Harbour the maximum is over 50′. This is one of the greatest tides known in the world which is common with the enormous tides of Ungava Bay, which lies across the Strait to northward, where it attains a maximum of 60 ft. And we had anchored at half tide in 5 fathoms of water!! Robertson on duty again.

Tuesday, 2 September Clear at 9:30 a.m. and underway for Lake Harbour. Engine disabled – under sail. Anchored at Lake Harbour in 30 fathoms at 11:30 a.m., eight miles distant of last night's anchorage. Lake Harbour is a two year old trading post of the Hudson's Bay Company, which in common with Cape Wolstenholme and Chesterfield Inlet represents the "Company's" new venture into exclusively Eskimo territory. Since the time of their charter in 1670 their operations have been confined practically to Indian territory, or rather within the north limit of trees.

This new venture is interesting as the idea has always prevailed that trade intercourse with Eskimo for furs were not in the main profitable – and also from the fact that the fur varieties and values are far less in Eskimo territory. How hopelessly desolate the two or three small buildings which constitute the post looked, squatted in the valley of a colorless wilderness of barren rocks, and at such a place the factor and his young Scotch clerk of from 15–20 years of age will live in complete isolation except at "ship time" once a year for from 3 to 5 years! It seems to me that hardships (so-called) of explorations are as nothing to that. We were visited yesterday shortly after anchoring by Messrs. Fleming and Bilby of the Mission, and they stayed with us to dinner. Later on Parsons Jr. and his clerk, Mr. Cantley also visited the ship. I learned of them of the *Pelican*'s arrival only a week before.[20] This is the Hudson's Bay Co. ship on her annual voyage from England to Hudson Bay. Water was taken aboard during the afternoon which by this time was little enough, and that being bad owing to defective casks taken aboard at St. John's.

Wednesday, 3 September Clear day with northerly winds. LaDuke and I went ashore during afternoon, and traveled inland a mile or so on a tour of Capt. Murray's mica workings, being guided to those various places by an old Eskimo who had been in former seasons one of the native workers there. He was kindly loaned to us for the purpose by Messrs. Bilby and Fleming of the Mission.

Lake Harbour has for more than twenty years been a rendezvous of the whaling ship *Active* of Dundee, Capt. John Murray, and at this port usually secured her complement of Eskimo crew preliminary to her advance to the whaling grounds through Hudson Strait into northern Hudson Bay.[21]

During the last seven years he has equipped the Eskimo not undertaking his whaling cruise with a few crude tools (for digging, cutting, etc.) and an outfit of rations – sea biscuit and tea with which they were ordered during the open season to collect mica which they have run across at different times during hunting trips and had reported to Capt. Murray. This work was carried out under the direction of Scotch miners – from 2 to 7 men in different years.

Seven men at one time directed the work and wintered at Lake Harbour, erecting a small portable house for the purpose with a tool shed – portable forge for sharpening drills and mica cutter, etc.

The output that year was "13 tons of excellent mica." All the mica collected was transported in baskets and bags by the Eskimo 1–2 miles to Lake Harbour. This mica mining was carried on behalf of Kinness of Dundee, Scotland.

The extreme shortness of the open season, July 15th – Oct 15th, and the absence of anything like a mining plant were sufficient to preclude of anything like a large tonnage being mined.

The advent of the Hudson's Bay Company to Lake Harbour and gradual decline of the whaling industry accounts for the termination of this mica operation some two years ago ... Purchased a few provisions and sundries, etc. and mailed letters to return by the Hudson's Bay Company ship *Pelican*. We departed from Lake Harbour at 3 p.m. under sail and with engine. Took an Eskimo pilot with us as far as the mouth of the harbor, distant 12 miles.[22] Dropped the pilot and his friends at nightfall.

Thursday, 4 September A heavy gale of north wind sprang up shortly after nightfall. Were soon into heavy seaway through which the old wagon waddled with little concern. Later on during the night the deck load gave us some anxiety.

Friday, 5 September Still a gale with snow squalls. Ship working well, deck load giving her a port list notwithstanding. At noon sighted the coast of Ungava – of sheer bold cliffs of granite – snowcapped and barren. Sighted Wales Island at 2 p.m. With engine and sail wore up to it, finally locating the entrance to Wakeham Bay at 7 p.m. Entered at a 9 knot clip with a wind astern – (all sail and engine) at nightfall.

Anchored off the fur post of Revillon Frères – seven miles in from the entrance of a wonderfully fine harbor – snug and comfortable with high rounded granite hills and velvet moss grown valleys surrounding it. We soon discerned the yellow lights of the post windows, a half mile away, which brightened up everyone. The skipper, LaDuke and I made short work of dinner then went ashore to the post where we were hospitably received by Monsieur Devine, the factor, and I met an old friend of Fort Chimo – Sam Ford – acting here as interpreter. I invited them aboard – wined and gramophoned them.[23]

Saturday, 6 September Clear, fine a.m. Wakeham Bay is a splendid harbor, having a complete length of about 14 miles. High granite-gneiss hills surround. The hills and valleys are velveted with fawn and russet moss, contrasting to the streaks of jet of the cliff faces and snow capping of the dome-shaped hills.

Devine and Ford came aboard with us at noon to dinner. We purchased some specially made ice chisels and walrus harpoons and a few sundries when ashore in the morning. We cleared Wakeham Bay at 4 p.m. but were barely past the entrance when we again encountered thick weather.

Sunday, 7 September The wind increased over night with flurries of snow during whole of the following day. I had of late been feeling doubtful as to whether we could make Repulse Bay without very considerable risks, which would from now on increase as the season advanced for we were now more than a month late on the Hudson Strait passage. A westward passage at this time has seldom been attempted by a sailing craft and the stout old *Laddie* is in poor condition with her doubtful deck load to withstand much rough handling on the crossing of Foxe Channel – northern Hudson Bay and up the Sir Thomas Rowe's Welcome to Repulse Bay still distant about 800 miles. A deck load of petroleum, gasoline carbide, sacked coal, lumber, 27′ launch, canoes, three dories, and miscellaneous gear occupies every inch of deck room save at the bows and astern at the wheel.

After a conference with the skipper and LaDuke we decided not to attempt the journey westward, afraid of heavy weather and probable loss of the deck load and also of new ice in Sir Thomas Rowe's Welcome.[24]

I decided to winter on this Baffinland coast and attempt to carry on an exploration of the mica bearing gneisses that had impressed me so favorably at Lake Harbour and have that work in a more or less defined state by the time the ice had cleared the following July of 1914.

I planned to cruise westward off the Baffinland Coast and in amongst the innumerable islands that fringe it, in which connection the launch would be used as pilot in advance of the ship. The ship would continue westward in this manner until we fell in with natives, to obtain from them an idea of their numbers, locations of their winter encampments, of the game resources, general information of the country, etc.

It was my object to erect our winter base in good hunting country and where we could have intercourse with them throughout the winter for trading, hunting, sledging and motion picture purposes. Sainsbury had spent the previous winter at the newly established Hudson's Bay Post, Lake Harbour, and would probably know some of the natives, which we expected to fall in with, a great advantage to us in our preliminary arrangements with them. We made the high bold snow covered coast off Fair Ness at 4 p.m. We were feeling our way slowly through fog and rain, when suddenly a high rugged coast line stood before us. The launch was slung over and LaDuke, the mate, and Sainsbury went ahead in her through the outlying channels in search of an anchorage which was found at dusk. The coast here about is bold, rugged and boulder strewn – of such folded and banded gneiss which characterize practically all of the Hudson Strait seaboard of Baffinland. We scanned the coast enroute to the anchorage for a sign of Eskimo encampments but without success.

Monday, 8 September At daylight LaDuke, Sainsbury, the Mate and Engineer went off to westward with the launch on a cruise for possible Eskimo encampments. The day was cold with an east wind and heavy sea and snow squalls which gave the launch party a cold wet time of it. They appeared long after dark, a dripping shivery outfit. They sighted no sign of Eskimo.

Tuesday, 9 September Hoisted anchors and sailed westward, the launch in advance. Lolled about deck during the summery day – took pot shots at seals and water fowl with the "Manlikler" – brought out the gramophone and played hornpipe for the crew. Skipper in "Crow's Nest" during day scanning coastline and islands for Eskimo. The coastline of today's cruise is a most dangerous cruising ground …

This enormous rise and fall is a trap to mariners. Even Eskimo are of little use as pilots here and the one way of navigating is with a launch or a ship's boat with a sounding complement and signals working in advance of the ship. With this advantage, the advance should be made, in narrow passages, only on a rising tide, so that the margin of rise in case of grounding would be large enough to clear away with. We slowly cruised westward some 30 or 40 miles to a group of small islands inshore from Macdonald Island.

At 4 p.m. the launch was sent on into them to sound for an anchorage which after many trials and just at a time when the skipper expected to have to put out to sea and "hove to" for the night, a harbor was found and the launch signaled us to advance. This was at dusk and a difficult affair it was, crimping into a keen north, or offshore wind under engine and sail to a canal-like passage separating two small islands. This passage afforded us a secure berth for the night though its entrance was not a 100′ in width and almost proved too narrow for the old tub as she was heeled to a stiff beam wind on the turning under topsails, foresail and jib. The berth was mighty narrow so that she was moored to either shore by bow and stern hawsers.

Wednesday, 10 September The following day the launch proceeded westward on a further cruise for Eskimo, the ship remaining at anchor. This cruise was rendered more difficult and rather confusing by an intricate island studded coast line, in which there were innumerable blind channels and passages, the navigability in some instances completely depending on the tides. The cruising party returned shortly after nightfall unsuccessful but brought back a most acceptable half dozen or so of ducks and an Arctic hare.

Thursday, 11 September The following day at dawn LaDuke, Sainsbury, the mate and I started out with the launch. We ran into innumerable groups of water fowl (gulls, eider, black ducks, loons, and Arctic terns). Took pot shots at them occasionally with our 303 British Winchester Carbines with which I made the two "freakiest" shots imaginable. Seals came in for "target practice" as well, though we bagged none.

By noon we had traveled some 20 miles and just about to ascend an inlet which had suddenly opened up before us, as the launch rounded the nose of an island, when Sam spied masses of white along the shore line, which looked like the usual blocks of tide stranded ice. We were sure of it, but he persisted in his belief they were topeks of the Eskimo. Wearily directed the launch's course towards them expecting the usual disappointment. But he was right after all, and we were soon able to make out figures scurrying about amongst them. With a will we made for them, cheered beyond measure with our fortunate discovery. Even an Eskimo fireless topek or his igloo of snow and ice holds the same cheer that the lonely traveler experiences the world over, though here perhaps that feeling is still stronger or more acute for it is given by a violent contrast to natural conditions, the desolation of which is unequaled in more habitable latitudes. As we neared them and the details of the scene came into view the scurrying from one tent to another ceased, all was quiet, the natives were within their topeks – even the dogs were apparently undisturbed by our visit. Not until Sam called out "Chimo!" did they slowly emerge from their tents and haltingly came forward as we were effecting a landing to shake hands with them.[25]

There were five tents, or topeks, some of them seal and walrus skins sewn together with sinew and other of cotton duck, torn and bespattered with seal and walrus oil about their doorways. They were patched and sewn in innumerable places. No doubt, they had traded for these cotton tents with some Dundee and New Bedford whaler at one time or other.

To my disappointment the present occupants comprised only the women and children of the encampment and the men were inland hunting deer, having but left this morning, so they said, but added that they would probably return at dusk. We decided to await their arrival. After the preliminaries of greeting were over they gradually thawed a little from their embarrassment and showed by innumerable signs their deep curiosity and amazement, but were withal glad to see us which part was not a little influenced by presents to them of tea, biscuit and tobacco. They were indeed elated when later on Sam told them that we would winter amongst them, that we had great quantities of food, beads, "sweeties," guns, knives and the like. We lolled about the rocks the whole afternoon – scrambled chocolate with the youngsters (most of them looked like shaggy young bears in their deer fur clothing) and watched the women scattered about on the rocks busily sewing or chewing sealskins. They were a dowdy lot and very very unclean, or rather seemed so to our civilized eyes! This feeling of repugnance is merely a novelty however, which a little residence amongst them wears to nothing – at which time your own state of civilization had been adjusted to a standard in harmony with the north and its people.

At length one of the younger wives proudly displayed an old accordion, another donned a pathetic bit of old red calico, which she draped about her over her deer fur trousers, skirt fashion, and at intervals afterwards would insist upon using the hem of it as a handkerchief. The accordion lady finally started a diffident operation on the leaky old instrument, just a hint to us of rollicking sailor hornpipes and the like. We demanded music to which native fashion she acceded with the inevitable preliminary fumbling and embarrassment. Was soon launched into the thing, with downcast eyes and looking tremendously serious. The rest of the women and children quickly circled around her. The mate in top sea boots, sou'easter, and jersey jumped into the circle and stepped the "Sailor's Hornpipe" to the infinite delight of the women, and added embarrassment of the musician.

We waited until 6 o'clock but no hunters appeared at the crest of the cliffs which back the tiny bit of low-lying shore and upon which the encampment is situated. We had just waved farewell and the launch was under way, when a figure was seen descending the hills. It was one of the returning hunters – a young fellow and husband of the musician.

We gained much information from him of the country, its game, resources, of his people and most important our present location, which proved to be Amadjuak Inlet of the Admiralty Chart.

With darkness coming on Sam's party was cut short and we were forced to hasten, for 20 miles lay between us and the ship, which might be impossible to accomplish. Sam told him finally to have his people ready for the coming of the ship on the morrow and to line us to anchorage just off the encampment with their kayaks.

Darkness came before the ship was reached, but with only one miss LaDuke hit the narrow entrance to the ship's anchorage where lay the good old *Laddie* with signal lights on her ladderways.

Friday, 12 September The following day at daybreak we weighed anchor, bade farewell to the secure little anchorage. The launch advanced as pilot. We reached the encampment shortly before noon. A half dozen kayaks skimmed out toward the ship. The ship crawled slowly up to an anchorage already sounded by the launch. The kayaks were spied by one of the crew in the Crow's Nest coming down toward the ship from the head of Amadjuak Inlet to northward. This was indeed good fortune for it meant that other encampments were near at hand. The natives lost no time in boarding – men, women, children and dogs, who could not be trusted ashore at the unguarded tents.

The dowdy women of yesterday's meeting were spruced up a bit – their hair braided, and bits of finery about them, copper pennies, pewter spoons an their kooletah tails and the like.

Of course they were hungry – (when isn't an Eskimo hungry?) and lost little time in making it known. Gallons of tea and tubs of sea biscuit were placed on deck, around which they circled, in an orderly way more or less, but crammed themselves of rubbery sea biscuit with such industry that they could only squeak to each other from their overburdened mouths, which indeed seemed like overloaded jaw-crushers, and how they managed to drink the quarts of tea the while is another story, for much of it was wasted and trickled down from their mouths in rebellious streams.

LaDuke turned the gramophone on them from the cabin deck starting with Caruso of whose work I believe they thought merely an exhibition of the rude vocal strength of the Kabloona. To their eternal credit be it said they object to music at meals, though the concert shaded down to Lauder minstrels and reels to which they tried hard to listen but their former distraction overruled.[26]

Everything is via the stomach with an Eskimo and therein he shows a characteristic that makes him the primitive of all the savages in the world. After much handshaking a few of the head hunters were called by Sam and questioned about the country, people, game resources, etc. I find that the head of Amadjuak Inlet offers an advantageous site for the winter base. It is a rendezvous of the Eskimo along this seaboard – a good game and fur country, according to the Eskimo. The one point about it which has most influence in our deciding to winter there is from the fact that fresh water is obtainable throughout the year from a small river, the discharge of several interior lakes. It enters the tidewater in a series of rapids, and at these rapids water is obtainable the entire winter.

Great quantities of fresh water will be necessary during the winter for the development of the motion-picture films of which it is anticipated some 15000 feet will be exposed. LaDuke and Sainsbury went in the launch up to the head of the Inlet during the afternoon and located a site for the winter base.

The natives of the encampment opposite the anchorage were ordered to have their gear, etc. aboard by daylight. After a supper to them on deck, they were sent ashore for the night, much pleased with their eventful day, and of the prospects of having a post in their country the ensuing winter.

The day was silvery gray and very calm. At night it cleared with a gorgeous sunset that splashed reds and purples over tiny islands far to seaward and over the near high snow capped hills and blazed an undulating trail over ice-pans and water right up to the anchorage. The wolf howls of the dogs ashore all through the night sounded like the old days in Hudson Bay and we were glad of it – the old longing realized at last!

Saturday, 13 September There was a noisesome bustle at daybreak.

The Eskimo were hurried to the ship – breathless, confused and half-awake, with squalling babes and bad tempered dogs. Their kayaks, a half dozen, were lashed in a catamaran and towed astern, while their gear and camp impedimenta was piled in confusion on deck. Anchor was weighed and the *Laddie*, under steam, and with flags aflying slowly stemmed the tide toward Amadjuak Inlet. The gramophone again did the honors from the cabin deck, much to the delight of our passengers. It seemed not a little like one of those crowded, unhappy affairs – which Sunday schools call excursions. Anchor was dropped in 15 fathoms close in shore and just off to eastward a short distance of the mouth of the river, near to which the post sight has been determined.

This was the last anchorage of the cruise, a relief in a way but withal some attachment had warmed us toward the old tub, the month's experience had been interesting indeed! But now nearly a year of wintering would pass before the ice would give her passage way again. Amadjuak Bay is a secure land-locked harbor, about 4 miles in length and 1–2 miles in width. Rugged barren hills of gneiss 100′–500′ in altitude surround it. The shore line is generally abrupt and boulder strewn, with here and there tongues of jagged rocks reaching out beyond its general margin.

The post site is located on band rock, though indeed it was difficult to find an area of 40 ft. sq. sufficiently level for the post site, while the shoreline in front of the post is so boulder strewn that the landing of cargo will be worked only with the tides.

The tidal rise and fall is approximately 30 ft. On its ebb it exposes great areas of chaotic looking shore line.

With Sam as interpreter many interesting statements were made by the Eskimo about the game, resources, etc. of the surrounding country.[27] The river near which the post is situated teems with Arctic salmon during the spring and summer and in spring time are particularly numerous as they ascend the river from salt water to spawn along the sand and gravel beds.

Deer are plentiful throughout most of the winter but particularly so in summer as they graze along the head lands and hills of the seacoast in order to escape as much as possible from the flies.

Walrus are obtainable from the late fall throughout the winter off shore from the outer islands of the coast. Their presence is not always certain, however, as it is dependent on ice conditions off shore – that is to seaward of the outer islands.

Seals – square flipper – harp, harbor, jar are numerous (harp excepted) and generally obtainable throughout the year. Few, if any ptarmigan winter here and bear are not numerous. Hare are plentiful as are white foxes with blue foxes in lesser variety. According to friends, the game outlook is surely inducing.

Soon after dropping anchor and while preparing the running gear, etc. preliminary to discharging cargo, the balance of the Eskimo from the head of the inlet in two omiaks [umiaks], filling to overflowing with men, women, children, dogs and camp gear joined the ship. In little time a tiny village of Eskimo topeks sprang about the post site – all was bustle and activity and a curious confusion of Eskimo and whites on this desert rock of an hour ago. The Eskimo omiaks and our own craft as well were lashed in catamarans – and platforms of the post lumber laid over them – the work of discharging cargo had commenced.

The women, even mothers with their babies bobbing in the hoods of their kooletahs as they worked, labored with the men.

Rations were doled out to them of sea biscuit, tea, sugar, and tobacco. They formed picturesque circles scattered about on the rocks at meal times with half-starved dogs prowling about the outskirts of them. Two very old women ("too old to work") act as planners to the community. Sam is their "angarooka" to whom they must look for food (the all-important affair). This gives him prestige over heaven itself.

Sunday, 14 September I decided this morning after a conference with LaDuke and the skipper to return the *Laddie* to St. John's, retaining all of the outfit and cargo other than a necessary outfit of grub, etc. for the return cruise. This course would effect a slight saving in salaries to crew during the winter – would enhance the value of our exploring and trading outfit which would be augmented by the crew's provisions, etc., saved by their return to Newfoundland. The prospect of a considerable fur trade with the Eskimos during the coming winter influenced me in that respect considerably – as the trade outfit in itself is not a large one, provided this winter proves a good fur year.

Another serous factor was in wintering a crew of 10 men – most of whom would be unemployed during the winter season, or rather till May at the earliest, and all the attendant dangers of sickness and dissension which would at least be reduced in percentage of chance were we to winter alone, and the ship returned. I decided to retain the 1st Mate – Stewart Gushue along with Sainsbury as assistants to Mr. LaDuke and self.

The crew were rather mutinous when their Captain gave them such unexpected orders to return with the ship to Newfoundland. Only after much wrangling and dissatisfaction amongst them were they induced to an agreement to return and at that only after they were promised a bonus for doing so, the amount of which was more than unreasonable. As I had no legal right to retain the Mate of the ship here, according to the Board of Trade Regulations, they had a legal right to refuse to sail – a point they were not long in discovering and of making the most of, though it was purely a lever in the bonus affair. As the ship can reach us on or about the 1st of August at the latest (possibly the 20th July, 1914) that date would be no more than ten days later, at most than the ship's departure were she wintered here.[28]

Upon return of the ship the westward cruise of the Ungava Coast of Hudson Bay and the northwest coast of Hudson Bay would be again undertaken. In the meantime the mica exploration and a general one of the coastline and certain portions of the interior would be carried out. It is to be hoped indeed that sufficient mica will be opened up in that interior to form a cargo of several tons for shipment when the *Laddie* returns.

Nearly all the motion picture and photographs will also be completed during that interval as well – the fur returns also.

The work of discharging cargo was rushed with all speed and the erection of the post was carried on apace by Mr. LaDuke and the Mate with an array of Eskimo men and women as helpers.

The Post is 30′ × 15′ in size, one story of dressed matched lumber with tar paper (roof and walls). It is divided into a large living room-kitchen, a large studio tent and two of 10′ × 12′ to shelter the general outfit.

In the course of construction the wits were nearly scared out of the natives working by a sudden collapse of the walls. As they were working on the roof at the time – their precipitate plunge to earth amidst a tangle of lumber and rafters dumbfounded them. They talked of it all through the winter – to every stranger of their kind that they met with.

20 – 25 September[29] The post was completed on the 5th day and cargo discharged a day later. Ballast was taken aboard (40 tons), and the ship made ready to sail.

After a delay of several days due to foul weather – heavy winds with snow squalls – the *Laddie* finally cleared the harbor at 10 a.m. September 27th, which was a rather lonely affair alright, for she will be nearly a year away. However, so much remained to be done about the Post to get everything in shape that it seemed to offset any depression about the *Laddie*'s departure. Sam and the Mate with launch piloted her out to sea – distant nearly 20 miles – and returned the following day. Many of our Eskimo friends had departed ere this for their winter hunting grounds, not a few of whom were outfitted with rifles and traps etc. from the trade outfit. A staff of Eskimo as servants were retained by Sam for the post during residence here.

The post was gradually whipped into shape through Mr. LaDuke so that by October 1st we were at last settled with a tangle of outfit, more or less classified and much to our relief. Nothing could exceed the pleasure we all took in the building and furnishing of our post. It is mighty comfortable and altogether a delight after the cramped and stuffy cabin of the ship.

The living room is about 17′ × 15′, in the centre of which is a billiard table which when not in use serves as a reading desk and table generally. The table has a dimension of 8′ × 3½′ – all through the long winter afforded the chief source of amusement both to players and our native spectators. Its only rival was the gramophone for which we had a library of over 400 records, numerous enough to cover the complete scale of musical taste which indeed ran to extremes in Amadjuak.

The library was the usual affair for this sort of work: text books, geographical references, etc., natural history, botany, a fairly comprehensive list of works on northern exploration, on photography, etc., fiction well chosen and not too great in quantity. The house was divided into two rooms, a small kitchen and a large living room; Sainsbury and Gushue bunked one above the other in the kitchen, LaDuke and I in the far corners of the living room.

Within a week of the *Laddie*'s departure the ground was permanently covered with snow.

LaDuke and I remained about the post most of the fall getting the outfit in order for winter and carried on a few excursions inland of the shore line, on Eskimo mica reports. A few trials were made of the motion picture outfit as well.

I had my little studio tent erected near to the house and plunged into the portraiture of some of the Eskimo who were retained here for that purpose.

Stewart and Sam made launch excursions to the seaward islands. When at one island they made a promising fox discovery. It seems that some Eskimo had killed a white whale round about there – cached a part of its carcass on the island. The resultant stench of its summering attracted a colony of foxes – Stewart and Sam caught fourteen all told – most of which were brought into the post alive.

An attempt was made to pen them and try our hand at fox breeding, but through carelessness and bad trap wounds they all eventually died off. It was also hoped that some motion pictures of them might be obtained.

Friday, 26 September Trading tents erected. Sam tossed candy amongst natives after work. The natives were so excited the men bolted and bumped the women right and left stretching them out at full length on the ground. A dog got into trading tent and ate a whole ham, from the effects of which it died next day, causing great excitement amongst the natives.

Saturday, 27 September Fine day, *Laddie* weighed anchor for Newfoundland at 10 a.m. At noon wind started – followed by blinding squalls of snow. *Laddie* departed under steam and canvas at 10:15 a.m.

Sunday, 28 September *Laddie* put out to sea in early a.m. Fine day – evening calm and cloudless.

Tuesday, 30 September LaDuke, Stewart and I with Noahasweetow and his two "kid brothers" went to look over a mica discovery of Eskimo situated some 2 miles inland of head of Amadjuak Bay.[30] Too much snow overground to enable me to form much of an idea of it. Deferred till spring. We left the boys in charge of launch whilst away – returned to find it stranded high and dry and they off bird hunting. Walked home – Sainsbury went after it at high tide.

Wednesday, 1 October Sam, whilst hunting, came across 7 Eskimo, brought them into post. Some of our Eskimo visitors departed in their omiaks [umiaks] today for winter quarters. Turned motion pictures on their departure.[31]

Thursday, 2 October One of the servants brought in live fox, which he had caught in trap, leg slightly bruised. Sam fixed it up. In evening held a drawing room to our friends – great time – billiards, gramophone and games.

Friday, 3 October Sam and Stewart with 4 Eskimo and launch went

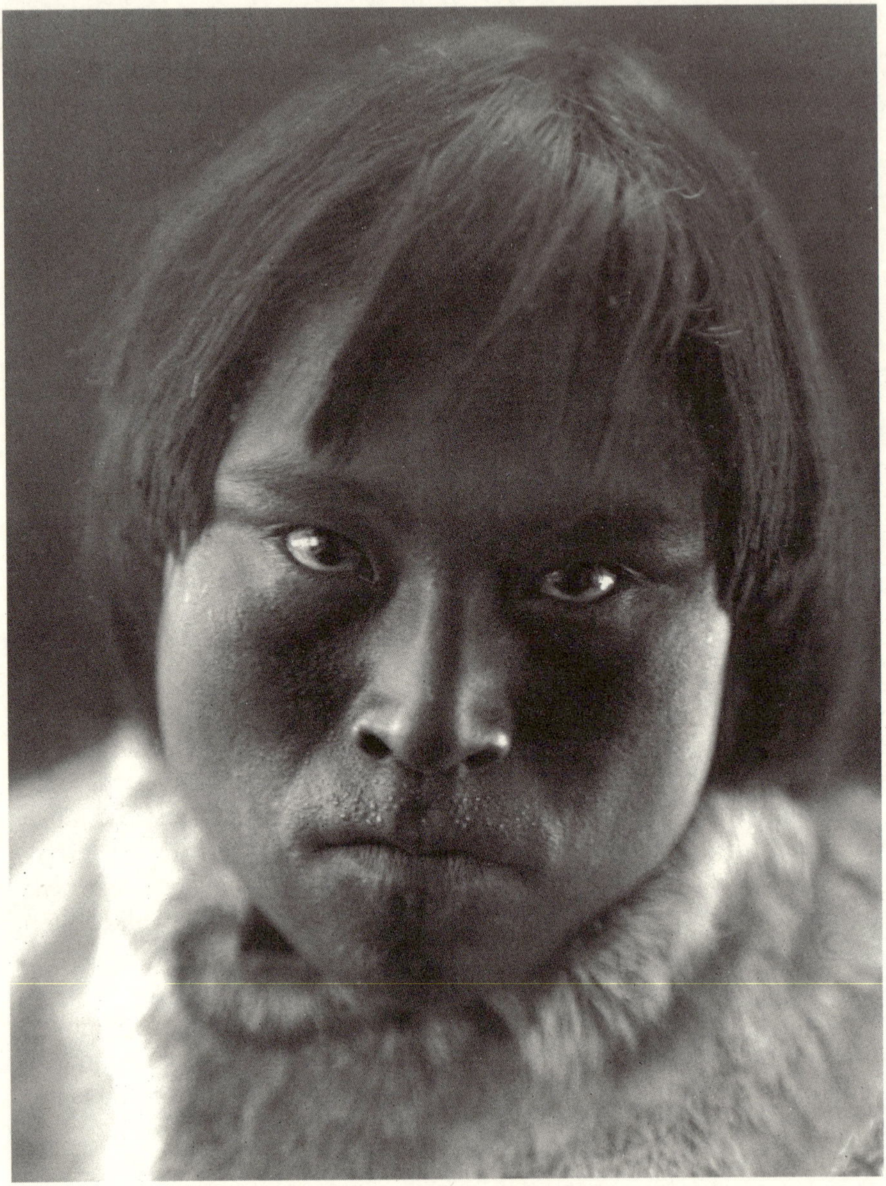

Noogooshoweektok, Baffin Island, 1913–14. Flaherty refers to him as Noahasweetow in his diary. The drawings which Flaherty published privately in Toronto in 1915 were by him. His son Anunglung played a feature role in the Baffin film, a counterpart, as it were, to Nanook.

(Claremont, LAC, PA500678/photo RF)

out to Islands and setting fox traps on some of them, just now seal and walrus are scarce – not enough to bait fox traps.

Sunday, 7 December[32] On Friday last I made a sledge trip to the walrus grounds situated some fifteen miles southwest of this post, where Sam and Stewart are walrus hunting with the Eskimo. As Sam had taken all the decent sledge dogs, I had to be content with a make shift team of young dogs and pups. Took Yew's son, Jack Johnson, with me as driver.

The day was clear and warm, which with some light undrifted snow just lately fallen, made our travel rather hard. We started at dark, four o'clock, just as two sledges of the returning walrus hunters had reached camp. Sam was much surprised to see me. Cordially greeted by the hunters and their families, some fifteen people all told. I put up with Sam and Stewart in Anunglung's igloo; this is where my men have been living during the walrus hunt.[33] Charlie and his wife and child, Anunglung's wife and two children, and together with we three men completed the list of occupants. I was most agreeably surprised to find it most cleanly and neat.

As this was my first travel of the year, my condition wasn't up to much. All my clothing was wet with perspiration, so that in a little time after arrival became chilled through, and straightway had to get into a deerskin sleeping bag. Gave the people presents of tobacco and candy and to the men pipes. Sam reports poor success.

Sam had a narrow escape from being caught on a drifting floe, but was warned of the danger just as the sheet parted.

During the evening I decided to arrange for a sledge trip eastward to Lake Harbour, ordered Sam to arrange with the Eskimo. Stewart and I with Jack Johnson's team departed for [base camp] post the following a.m. after a hearty send off by the people of the encampment. Sam sledged out to Simonie's igloo with Poodlak, as he intends arranging with Simonie for the trip. He returns to the post on Monday.

Stewart and I arrived at the post at 3:30. Had a most glorious day for the journey. Shortly after arrival LaDuke called me aside and told of "Joseph," one of the post servants, and of a row that occurred during my absence. It seems that Joe has been nursing a series of imaginary grievances, against me for the last week or more, all of which were capped when I used his sledge for the journey to the walrus grounds. I had not known that he objected to my using it. As to his other grievances I had no knowledge of them. He is probably consumptive and of little use as either a hunter or servant and has even shirked chores about the post. We have tolerated him and kept him and his family in food solely on account of his supposed illness.

After my departure LaDuke noticed that he sulked and angrily mentioned something about my taking his komatik [sledge], all of which LaDuke could not understand. He and his wife hung about the house most of the day. Joseph finally demanded that he give him a pail of molasses, in payment I suppose for the use of his komatik. LaDuke very rightly refused him.

Sometime later LaDuke reading on his bunk suddenly looked up to see Joe making for him from the kitchen doorway with a 303 British Winchester rifle. Yew's wife, who was in the kitchen at the time, was clinging to his coat tails trying to dissuade him from shooting. This fact combined with LaDuke's quickness in covering some fifteen feet that lay between them, saved his life. He wrested the gun from him, but most wisely offered him no violence. He hid the gun, then loaded his own gun and kept his "weather eye" open for future disturbances. Joe again attempted to steal a shotgun that hung up in the kitchen but LaDuke prevented him. His wife during this disturbance attempted to steal a carving knife that lay on the kitchen table, but was prevented by Yew's wife. Yew's wife finally quieted her, as she later explained to us, by beating her on the chest.

We were not expected back until Monday, so it was rather fortunate that we turned up on the following day. He had a rather nervous sleep of it that night. It seems that Joe went completely out of his head, which is typical of Eskimos when they start gunning. His wife, we believe, influenced him in making his attempt on LaDuke. I remember now that during the last week or so that he has acted strangely. On two different nights he stood out from his igloo, blazed away cartridges at nothing apparently, and to no purpose.

We have suspended judgement, and rather restless until Sam's arrival Monday, as he understands Eskimo, and will probably unearth much interesting data connected with the affair.

Preparing to depart for Lake Harbour on Wednesday. Have decided to hold our Xmas dinner tomorrow night upon Sam's arrival, as we will not arrive back here again until sometime in January. We couldn't help opening the Xmas box tonight, and looking over the list of eatables. Part of them we made into a midnight supper which was most thoroughly enjoyed.

Monday, 8 December Cooked up beans and biscuit for the trip to Lake Harbour; also got together the greater part of the required provisions. Much to my surprise Sam and Jack Johnson did not turn up today. Joe is sulking again, neither he nor his wife has put in an appearance today, which is rather a nervous affair for us. Yew and his wife and son have been hugging the post pretty well all day. Last night he and wife stayed till very late. I think they are frightened alright.

Tuesday, 9 December Sam arrived today from the walrus grounds with Jack Johnson. Cunayow's father followed with his own team and Ayowningnung of Simonie's encampment came in with me also. Sam reports traveling improved but still hard. The coldest day of the year, -40°, but clear and fairly calm. Sam has completed arrangements for our trip to Lake Harbour with Simonie. Will have a fifteen dog team, all in good condition. Has also obtained Simonie's whalebone sledge. We commence the journey on Thursday.

Sam was dumbfounded when he learned about Joe and the gun racket. We tried to get at the affair through Sam as interpreter, but it ended with everything hopelessly confused, through many contradictory statements. Incidentally I have learned something of "Huskie lying" and deceit. I decided to send Joe and his outfit away and make him understand that no further relations would be opened with him at anytime.

I decided to hold our Xmas dinner tonight as we would not return from Lake Harbour before the 7th January. It was a sumptuous affair, LaDuke did himself proud in the Xmas box purchase. It contained everything it seemed: Jellied Chicken, Jellied Pigeon, Ox Tongues, Oxford Brains, Boston Brown Bread, H & P Cherry Cake, Plum Puddings, Heinze Cream & Tomato Soup, Huyler's Candy, Dates, Figs, Preserved Candied Fruits, Ginger, Raisins & Nuts, Olives, Prize Packages, Champagne, Port, Brandy, Scotch, Sarony's Cigarettes, Cigars, Dutch Cheeses – Roquefort, Biscuits and decorations, which were mostly recruited from the trade outfit, beads, etc.

The dinner was laid on the billiard table, and it was large enough to crowd it. During the dinner Yew's wife gramophoned us. The champagne made a hit with Stewart. It was a glorious night – even the handful of Eskimo who happened to be around the post at the time stayed feasting in the kitchen on the aftermath until the small hours of the morning. The feast was followed by poker, at which poor Stewart and I were gloriously walloped. The aroma of Turkish cigarettes and champagne.[34]

Thursday, 11 December Left this day 10 a.m. A few miles out Sam found a hare in one of his traps. Charlie came along with his wife on way to the post to trade. Had a ten dog team. Sam turned back with them. I went on to the first walrus camp, Sam following later and at night. Stayed the night in Billy's igloo. Cold and clear. During the evening "Auntie," Bill's mother, pulled out an old seal skin pouch which contained one of the old time fire making outfits of large pieces of pyrite, and the white dry down of the willow as tinder. She showed us the way of making fire, which consisted of striking together the pieces of pyrite, which after a bit produced sparks – they collected of course on the outspread willow down. After a lot of striking the down finally caught, burning as cloth will. It was then vigorously blown upon and gradually spread until flames burst forth. The process completed took about ten minutes. Sam received the fire pouch for me as a curio.

Our demonstrator, by the way, is a character. As old as the hills and older, almost blind, as all Eskimo become through exposure and snow blindness. Cataracts invariably appear during middle life. She is still vigorous, most of which during our stay in her son's igloo was expended in begging tobacco, matches, sweeties, biscuits and tea. Even after I had presented her with a few nuts (relics of our Xmas feast) she insisted upon her inability to eat nuts without sweeties. Noted a peculiar Eskimo custom: Old Auntie sleeps with her little grandchild, a boy of about six or seven years; as he is her favorite of one of her daughter's families (Poodlak's wife), she exercises this old Eskimo custom.

Sam says that at Lake Harbour two winters ago, Mrs. Ford, an expert Eskimo linguist, and native of Labrador, found out some surprising details from a very old Eskimo woman of cannibal feasts of the Eskimo. These she declared occurred as recently as fifty years ago. Through old Auntie, Sam tried for information along similar lines. She said that these feasts occurred, one of their number being sacrificed, but was always prompted by impending starvation. It seems to me that the Eskimo character is near enough to the animals or animal nature to make an exhaustive investigation along these lines most interesting. How very near they are to that nature can hardly be realized.

Friday, 12 December Breakfast at six, away at daylight, nine o'clock. Two walrus hunting sledges. Poodlak and father preceded us for a part of the journey, then branched off for the open water to seaward. Forgot a dunnage bag but was hailed in time. Two of our dogs missing, expect to find them at Simonie's tonight. The day proved cold and trying, with a stiff east wind, which drifted the snow, soft and lately fallen, into clouds that were almost blinding at times.

We made Eliza's igloo at noon and lunched there. The encampment consists of three igloos – some of the people I have not seen before. Eliza's igloo is most cleanly, the interior is all lined with canvas, which prevents drops of melting ice in warm weather from falling. The men were all out walrus hunting. They have seal and walrus in plenty which is to them everything. I noted a most interesting walrus-skin bucket in the stranger's igloo, which was secured as a curio. Noah's little son Jacob hung around me during lunch. (Thermos tea and chocolate.) Taught him the art of winking to the immense amusement of the assembled people. Eliza and I are great pals. She is wife of the chief, one of the heads of the Eskimo, along the coast and is moreover famous for her pretty daughters. She calls me her "pickaninny" and pretended to cry when we said good bye. She and her husband are making curios for me during the winter.

Made Simonie's encampment of three igloos at dark, but while going through the rough ice along shore, the master line broke as the sledge collided with a set ice block. The dogs nosing the encampment, made for it, most of them becoming hopelessly entangled with their harnesses and dragging traces enroute. It was an hour's cold and fumbling work, returning them and untangling their traces. We made the encampment finally at dark.

All the men were away walrus hunting when we arrived, but the large female population assembled about the sledge whilst unloading. There were many familiar faces, and cordial greetings. We ensconced ourselves in Simonie's young wife's igloo (he has his wives, in separate igloos of course) though they were away hunting walrus at the time. The igloo is small, but proved a blessing, for but a few of the curious and hungry are able to congregate therein at one time, so we are comparatively free of over crowding with all its attendant evils, particularly smell.

Whilst in the midst of dinner Simonie and his wife returned from his walrus hunt and exerted themselves to show us their hospitality and welcome. Simonie is one of the finest type of Baffin Eskimo, a mighty hunter, which here means affluence and plenty. The criterion to his prowess is reached perhaps when one considers that he heads two domestic establishments, in which he alternates his residence, day by day. He it is who has been secured for our important sledge trips later on this winter. Sam satisfied that he will prove the right man for it. He is young and exceedingly active, a handsome type, very popular with his people.

He shows singular enterprise, perhaps audacity, in taking his nineteen year old wife with him walrus hunting, which of all things is a mighty cold and dangerous job. They hover about the edge of the set ice fields nine miles or so distant from land, awaiting an opportunity to creep up in close quarters with a two ton walrus asleep along the edge of the ice fields. The greater danger is of course from the ice fields becoming broken into sheets, and moving out with the enormous tides so particular to this coastline, which with its strong, steady Arctic currents that sweep through Hudson Strait would carry them oceanward in short time indeed.

Nuckey, Sandy and Sharkey called after grub, and smoked a pipe with us. Micky harpooned a walrus today as it lay sleeping along the ice edge with only its head above water, secured to the ice by his gleaming tusk. In some instances one can approach without the least fear of his awakening. The great idea in walrus hunting is to harpoon him before shooting, as otherwise in most cases he sinks before a line and float can be attached. Nuckey was successful in securing, but found it impossible to haul him up onto the ice, though there were other hunters with him. He severed his head and had to be content with that as the result of his hard day's work.

While they were at this hunting we were sledging through the storm of drifting snow. It was such a day as few white men would care to undertake a hunting excursion. Sam says that Poodlak killed a walrus outright with only his lance, a week or so ago. I find that the Mauser Pistol will penetrate a walrus skull at close range, which is certainly surprising. Sharkey had an experience with a bear a few days ago and right in at his igloo, the bear attempting to break through but was finally driven off by the dogs. It might have proved embarrassing to Sharkey seeing that his gun and harpoon were outside on the roof of the igloo. This is always the case – were they brought inside they would rime upon coming in contact with the warm air.

Sam slept in Simonie's elder wife's igloo, and that is too small to accommodate all four.

Saturday, 13 December   Repairing sledge and harness. The women all busy sewing and mending garments, etc., though not too busy to hover about in long continued spells for sweets and tobacco. Simonie made a dog whip during the evening, large enough to handle our fifteen dogs. We have an unusually fine team. These providential winds have made this snow-covered ice sheet hard packed so that our traveling will be much improved. Simonie is not taking his younger wife with him after all, as her winter deerskin clothing is still uncompleted. She is much disappointed, so are we, as a woman in the igloo is much to be desired in patching and mending and drying our clothing and softening frozen sealskin boots on a cold a.m.

Sunday, 14 December Breakfast at six o'clock. Just as we were making ready to depart, two strange Eskimo came in with a ten dog team from eastward. We adjourned to Simonie's elder wife's igloo to learn the news from the strange arrivals.

The younger was Pitseolak's son from Fair Ness, out on a wife hunt. I suspect he is after my very pretty photo model, who is the only young marriageable prospect in the Amadjuak country. The elder of the two proved to be a new arrival on the Strait's coast, having emigrated with two omiaks of Eskimo from Frobisher Bay last summer. We learned from him of the Whaler *Active*'s arrival at Lake Harbour last fall, landing there thirty Eskimo hunters and wives before proceeding to Dundee after a year and a half cruise in Hudson Bay. Captain Murray died on its cruise, the most successful he has had in twenty years in Hudson Bay, killing six right whales on the Ottawa Island group, which ground he ventured in and tried out for the first time.[35]

We also learned that Shepherd and Willie Ford of Cape Wolstenholme were swept out into Hudson Strait last summer and lost. Shepherd's wife died the preceding winter of consumption.[36] Sharkey told us that about the time the *Laddie* cleared the islands for the Strait homeward bound last fall, that she was in a very heavy storm. The two strangers are going into the post. Gave them an order for food. They stated also that Parsons was successful last fall in establishing Dorset Post.[37]

Finally departed at 10:30. The population turned out en masse to see us go. Simonie's younger wife who seems madly in love with him followed the sledge to the shore ice, very loath indeed to see him go. As we drove away she sat down in the snow and sobbed heartbrokenly, Simonie calling for her to never mind. The while, Simonie must be some diplomat with these two wives of his, as both are devilishly jealous of each other.

We were no sooner into a gait before realizing the vast improvement to our travel underfoot since the big winds of the last few days. The dogs maintained a smart pace which elated Sam and myself. The day was glorious, calm and clear, thermometer about -30°, but the Eskimo saying that it is never cold until the wind blows is true. We traveled in and out of islands the whole day, with a splendid smooth ice sheet underfoot ... Our igloo was built too small and proved very uncomfortable. Sam spent a sleepless night of it. Imagine it very cold but thank God I stopped carrying thermometers, which are altogether too stimulating to one's imagination.

Monday, 15 December Shortly after the start, a ten dog team and single driver came towards us, streaking over the crest of a hill ahead and toward us at a gallop. It proved to be a Lake Harbour Eskimo with the Lake Harbour mail, enroute to Cape Dorset. We struck the sea ice again at two o'clock, continued after a new icing of the sledge runners toward the big Eskimo encampment. We arrived at dark, about 3:30. This is indeed the largest encampment so far seen, of more than nine igloos. The population formed an interested crowd around our sledge and welcomed us warmly.

I repaired to old Mary's igloo, a kindly old soul, whom I had met at Lake Harbour enroute there. The igloo was large and comfortable, with three occupants besides old Mary and the husband. Mary's son is an invalid, suffering a paralytic stroke, which had permanently blinded one of his eyes. I gave his wife, a good looking girl, with a half breed child with large wondering eyes and curly hair, an antiseptic outfit for washing her husband's eyes, and explained its use to her. She has been Captain Murray's concubine on the last two whaling cruises of the Whaler *Active*. Much impressed with the encampment and their welcome to us. Simonie's sister here is not seriously ill as he imagined, influenza.

Tuesday, 16 December Away at daylight, a northerly wind, cold. The encampment as usual assembled to shake hands. Two of the girls and a young boy piled on the sledge and rode on the sea ice with us half a mile or so. We have the great advantage today of traveling with a returning Lake Harbour team, twelve dogs and his Eskimo. Hit off at a smart pace, only to be plugged at times during the day by vast fields of salt rime, over which the sledges crawled at a walking gait. The coastline here abouts is higher, bold and rugged and very picturesque. Towards nightfall it became very cold – even the Eskimo complained ...

We decided to keep on until the next Eskimo encampment was reached, though the Eskimo said we could not make it until late at night. We kept on a cold shivering outfit in the brilliant moonlight. After an interminable time, the cutting cold of which will not be easily forgotten, the warm yellow light of little rectangles of ice windows of Eskimo igloos showed up to us a short distance ahead – the dogs at the same time nosed the encampment and galloped towards it howling the while. Once there on the shore ice they piled into a tangled fighting mass, for their hard day put them into a murderous temper, and the keen cold made them ravenous. The encampment of some eight or nine igloos were all retired nor did they hear us till I crawled into one to announce to the sleepy occupants our arrival.

Thursday, 18 December   Hit up and maintained a smart pace in the hope of reaching Lake Harbour tonight. While running rough tidal ice my Mauser got lost. Will send first Eskimo back for it. Lunched at noon at Eskimo igloo, fifteen miles from Lake Harbour. Arrived at Lake Harbour at six o'clock after a rather cold time of it.

Sunday, 28 December   Day's travel is devilishly slow, deep snow and overfed dogs who had diarrhea from last night's guzzling of seal meat ... At dark, about 2:30, we sighted two teams ahead. It was Cantley and two servants and an independent team enroute to Lake Harbour, Timeloo by name. We all decided to put ashore and camp, but had a most difficult time climbing up over the tidal ice (75′) to land. The dogs were almost played and in a fighting temper ... Have arranged with Timeloo to put back with us and take portion of our load to first Eskimo camp. All hands encamped at 5:30, in four igloos.

Monday, 29 December   Timeloo has gone back on us this a.m., will spare us two dogs instead. Tried to force him but couldn't work it. Regretfully said goodbye to Cantley and struck off westward, he to eastward, at nine o'clock a.m. The dogs scented deer off to nor'ward at noon. Made west end of Long Port at dark and camped. Simonie built us a sumptuous igloo, large and comfortable, but by a.m. had proved a mighty cold one. Cold and clear and calm.

Tuesday, 30 December   Off at daybreak, one of Timeloo's dogs broke away and galloped off to eastward on the scent of his old trail. The day, though cold, is very calm and beautiful. Two portages, the last one very steep on its approaches, have given us a hard day of it. Arrived at Euytoo's encampment at dark. Well received, igloo all tidied for our arrival, the house wife's hair as well. Sam has secured another team to help us on to Ekecktillik, [Fair Ness] tomorrow.

Wednesday, 31 December The last day of the old year. Sam secured dog food alright, and a small amount of deer meat. He secured Anunglung as one of our dog drivers for the sledge journeys this winter. He comes with us as far as Ekecktillik now with an extra ten dog team. Later he will move with his family to the post. Is a likely looking chap. As I write Simonie shows an original method of cleaning his teeth by picking out a long hair from his abundant crop and saws it between the crevices of his teeth ...

Travel underfoot much improved, the additional team is a big help. I hear that a bitch of Ishanalook's team the other day gave birth to a pup while running, which was promptly eaten by the following dogs in harness ... Met Pitseolak and boy enroute to Lake Harbour this afternoon. Sent letters by him to Parsons, etc.

Thursday, 1 January 1914 Camped in a comfortable igloo last night. As we are only a half day's journey from Ekecktillik, the dogs were left in harness all night, but found that many of them had partly chewed or eaten their harness. We had no dog food for them, but expect to secure some at Ekecktillik. Simonie and one new man travel without sleeping bags, simply lie down to sleep on a winter deer-skin robe, though I fancy their night rests are broken with innumerable short naps.

Simonie awakened Sam at four a.m., saying that the early a.m. frost would cover the salt rime to some extent, which of course would make the sledge travel easier, and also that Pitseolak of yesterday's meeting said that the rime ice near Ekecktillik was breaking. Of course these were excuses as Simonie and one new man weren't altogether comfortable, minus sleeping bags and felt the cold night. We were off at dawn. The day cleared beautifully with the same brighter sun of yesterday unobscured by the usual towering spirals of fog from the open water to seaward. I know of nothing so desolate or forbidding as the dark cloudy fog swept horizon that lies to seaward, and seaward means a line 150 miles longer, outlying from the Baffinland Coast, which we have continuously paralleled on the sledging to Lake Harbour.

Arrived at Ekecktillik at noon, the inhabitants swarming about the three sledges as we drew up at old Mary's igloo. Overhauled some of our outfit, and immensely relieved to find nothing broken. Sam secured two new men and eight dog team to relay us on to the post. The other man returns tomorrow. Sam has also succeeded in purchasing four new dogs and secured a servant of the post.

Friday, 2 January Off to a good start at dawn. I shall never forget the scene. A swarm of Eskimo waving goodbye, the galloping of the four teams across the tiny pond, then plunged down the steep embankment to the rough tidal ice. Simonie's brother and wife and boy are coming with us as far as Simonie's camp. He will winter there to supply Simonie's wives with seal oil, while he makes the sledging trips with us ... Have been out of sorts due to constipation all day, and traveled minus breakfast, which make the cold cut some. A most glorious day, calm, very clear, with the ice-fields and far off shore line a fantasy of most delicate coloring, wonderful snow white grays and light blues, and the rugged bald Fair Ness headland, swathed in purple. Camped at dark in an island gutway, the party divided in two igloos.

Saturday, 3 January Away shortly after daybreak, a mighty cold gray dawn, clouded with a drifting north wind. Intensely cold in igloo last evening, which completely spoiled our sleep. Allego stayed on my sledge and kept me warm, or tried to rather.[38] Fastened a dog tail muffler about my throat, which proved a splendid idea. The wind died as the sun rose. Kept up a smart clip all day and arrived at Simonie's encampment at dark, amidst much rejoicing and excitement from the Huskies, whom we looked on as *our* people more or less.

Stayed in Simonie's elder wife's igloo for the night. His other and newer one opens off from it. His two wife idea is certainly an outrage. His elder wife became furious during the evening, indeed one cannot blame her. Her youngest boy looks seriously ill, inflammation of the lungs, so are taking them into camp for treatment, such as it is. Stayed up till midnight. Nyla played the accordion, whilst Sam played off a few steps on the ice floor of the big igloo.

Sunday, 4 January Away at daybreak, very cold with keen off shore wind. Enroute to post. Simonie and his new wife must needs stop at Eliza's igloo, his mother in law, whilst we waited in the biting cold and re-iced the sledge runners. Impatient with the delay, I climbed the shore ice and crawled into their igloo, where Simonie and his wife were calmly guzzling raw walrus meat. His elder wife, whom we all like, stayed in the sledge and the little invalid son who is traveling into the post for treatment. Never was a day's sledging so long, and was I ever so impatient to see the good old camp again.

At last, and just at dusk, the blood red sky to westward, the new

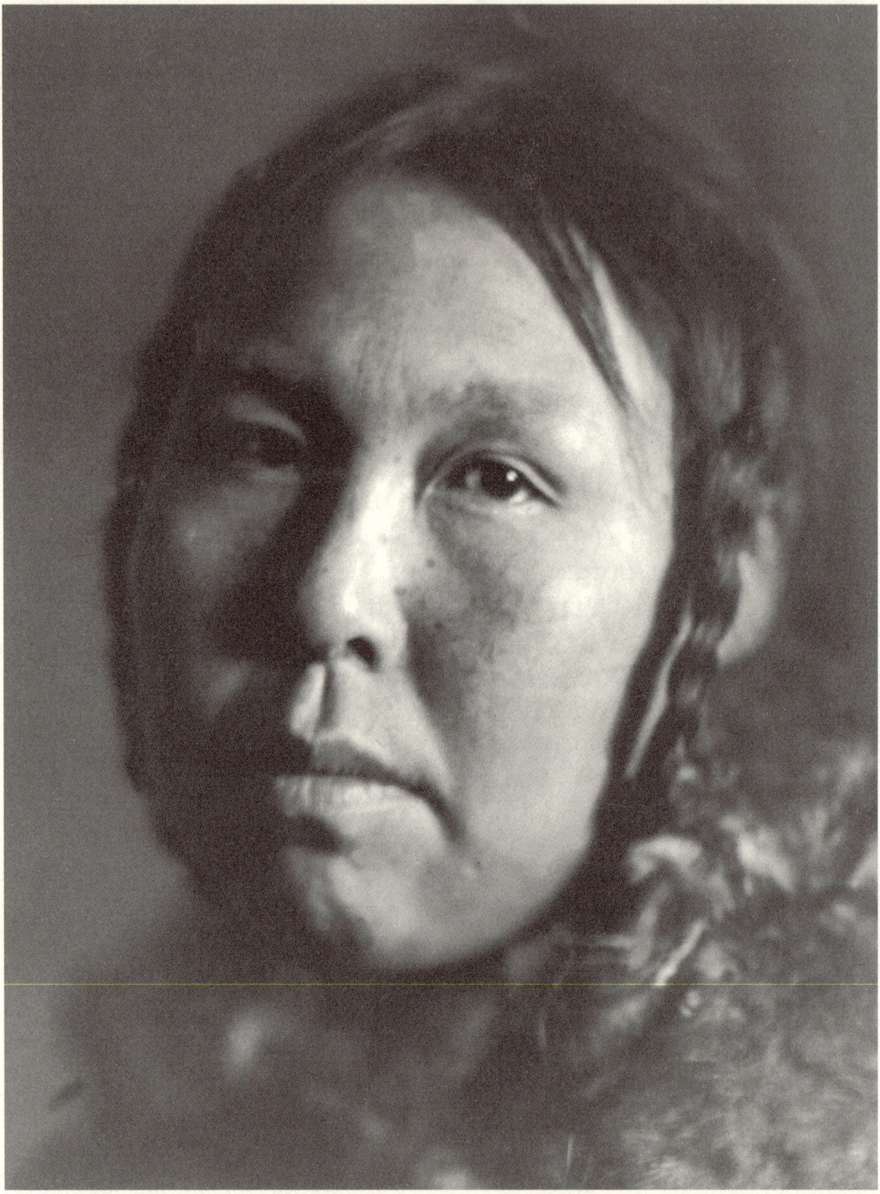

Allego, 1913–14. She assisted Flaherty in his laboratory work and, according to her descendants, was smitten with Flaherty's gramophone.

(Claremont, LAC, PA500739/photo RF)

moon creeping up over the horizon of scored snow swept hills, the camp was sighted. The light of its windows shone out almost brilliantly. The dogs caught the scent, and we galloped over the remaining distance, and scrambled over the rough shore-ice hewing madly the while. The men were about as glad to see us as we were. They must have been bargaining hard for our homecoming, for they were four days out in the month's reckoning!! We had another Xmas feast at midnight, which it is hoped will be final.

Tuesday, 6 January LaDuke and Stewart off at sunrise, the Ekecktillik men followed shortly. A typical January thaw. The house leaking most damnably. LaDuke and Stewart returned from Fair Ness on 12th, bringing a packet and a few articles sent up by Parsons at Lake, via Eskimo. They also picked up Anunglung, our new dog driver at Fair Ness enroute to this place. We decided to have the much talked of Eskimo feast on the 13th, the day after LaDuke's arrival. This had been promised them last fall, and up to this time they have been looking forward to it, always reminding us whenever we meet with any of them. During the interval that LaDuke and Stewart were away at Lake Harbour, Sam was up to his neck cooking currant biscuits (bushels).

Preceding the great event, sledges of Eskimo came into the post from the hunting grounds on the islands to seaward (15–20 miles). Jack Johnson, the servant, stuck a tent pole into the snow and flew two of the *Laddie*'s ensigns from it. Some sixty persons gathered here, which with their dogs and ours, over-ran the place.

The feast lasted two days, one continual cramming of biscuit, tea and rice, and meat (deer and seal). And there were scrambles for buckets full of sweets and tobacco and matches out in the snow with the pack of them (60 remember), piling over one another in confusion. Then there were races, men's, women's and children, out on the sea-ice. At the post we gramophoned them to their hearts' content, with minstrels, the "Preacher and the Bear" and the like, reels, jigs and Lauder, and they were fascinated with the billiard games. On the eve of departure, we had dances, men and women singly, for which prizes were given. Then followed one of their native competitions: guzzling, of which more will be said later at length.

That final evening was indeed a success. We bade them goodbye the next morning. Glad they came, for it cut into the dragging time. Anunglung departed for Ekecktillik (Fair Ness) before starting with me to Polar Star Bay (Cape Dorset). Sam made two trips to the Eskimo camps for dog food, and secured about six hundred pounds of walrus meat. Have decided to start for Polar Star Bay (Cape Dorset) with two teams, with Simonie and Anunglung as drivers.

Wednesday, 28 January Sainsbury and I with Anunglung and Simonie as drivers with two eleven-dog teams, started this morning for Cape Dorset and Foxe Channel. This is an exploration, one of a series which will be from now on undertaken until open water, next June or July. The first inducement of this affair is to try and secure a certain Eskimo, now at Cape Dorset, who has knowledge of large mica outcrops, in our own Amadjuak country, then an investigation of what is believed to be a Huronian rock area, near to Cape Dorset, though the information is from Eskimo wholly and of course very speculative. Then an exploration of the Foxe Channel Coast of Baffinland which even from Cape Dorset to Penguin Point, was only superficially coasted by Luke Foxe in 1631, which country he named Foxe Land ...[39]

It is even expected that we may run into Eskimo, wholly isolated from intercourse with whalers and Hudson Bay natives. Expect the expedition to last approximately six weeks. Cape Dorset now contains a Hudson's Bay Company post, an extension from Lake Harbour. It was established last September 1913. Two white men in charge. At that post I expect to reoutfit for the trip northward along the Foxe Channel Coast. A fine day, clear, 25 degrees, with light wind. Travel very heavy, encamped some eighteen miles from post, in two igloos as there are two wives in the party. New moon, cold night and clear.

Thursday, 29 January Little sleep last night. Breakfast at six o'clock, away at dawn, exceedingly heavy travel, deep snow which makes for frozen feet, both dogs and men. Some of the dogs were shod today, on that account. During travel today Simonie and Anunglung, with the wives and my assistance had to perform a surgical operation on one of the dogs, whose feet had been badly frozen ...

Arrived at Mucktoo's encampment of four igloos at 3:30. We had expected to make it in one day, but this heavy travel has delayed us to that extent. Got up spanking fine supper of beans and bacon, and stewed apricots, biscuit and tea. Note one of igloos here which is most surprisingly warm, positively comfortable, due to a construction of walrus and seal skins sewn topek fashion and lining inside of igloo, so that the sea oil lamp can run full blast, no dripping from overhead, due to seal walrus skin lining. Have gained most interesting information here from

Pudlat and Simonie. They have seen large icebergs in Amadjuak Lake in summer while deer hunting, as large, they say, as the icebergs of salt water. This must mean that glaciers discharge into lake, and lake must be of great depth. Hope to investigate on return from Foxe Channel. "Old Auntie" the prize grafter is pestering me as I write. How these people eat, like feeding a rat hole, their stomach is surely more than the ruling passion. They really live to eat.

Friday, 30 January Very cold, with high west wind and blinding drift. Travel underfoot frightfully hard, moved at a snail's pace. Mostly everyone frost bitten today. Dogs were done up at 2:30. Built two igloos which was a more comfortable operation for builders than we who had to stick it out in the bitter wind and swirling snow, and no shelter … Igloos most comfortable.

Saturday, 31 January Tomorrow we essay the crossing of Chorkbak Inlet, of which we have been hearing fearful tales of swirling tides and treacherous ice from the Eskimo. The prominent hardship of this travel is the tedious and chilly waiting while our Eskimo are building the igloos. They take the better part of an hour while we have nothing to do but stamp cold feet and rub noses and look on. Eskimo women, contrary to a former idea of mine concerning their efficiency as part of a travel outfit, are a bother, which even their sewing and lamp handling cannot offset. Travel approx. fifteen miles, mighty slow. Expect good traveling underfoot to westward of Chorkbak Inlet.

Sunday, 1 February A sparkling calm day, a blood red sunrise and sun dogs to either side of sun (equidistant) all morning … Anunglung pointed out a series of islands that follow one another to seaward in a particularly straight line, and at an almost regular distance apart from where we viewed them, and told of a shipwreck there many years ago. That was, he added further, the first time the Eskimo of this coast were enabled to procure sledges of wood, which formerly were made of whalebone, ivory and driftwood, and even some of them wholly of ice. Later in day, he told of the trail of two strange sledges, which were sighted by Eskimo hunters along this coast long ago. The Eskimo far and near along the coast discussed amongst themselves this strange occurrence. He said they could not account for their disappearance, only knowing that they came from westward along the coastline. Probably a shipwrecked crew, and died whilst sledging in looking for Eskimo.[40]

A bitch of our team gave birth to a pup last night and one at noon today, the latter being promptly torn to pieces and eaten by the dogs. These premature births are caused by intense cold, say the Eskimo. Think that hard work on a sledge has something to do with it. Comfortable igloo tonight and encamped in good time. Clear, calm and cold. It seems now that our five day reckoning of sledging to Polar Star Bay and Cape Dorset will stretch out to ten. This is the fifth day. Anunglung says that in the old days before firearms came, that Eskimo killed too few deer for clothing, having only bows and arrows to kill them with. They made kooletahs of Arctic fox skins, pussy seal (fetus), trousers of dog skins, seal, and bear, and seal skin kamiks (boots) with bear skin tops. Will attempt to have these things made on return as curios. Next month there will be many seal, says Anunglung (they pup in March).

Anunglung and Cunayow sleep in their traveling clothes and without cover, but drawing their hands well up into the sleeves of their kooletahs, they manage to spasmodically sleep away the night.[41] It is not comfortable, however, even to them. I had occasion today to severely "jack-up" one of the men who had been an uncomfortable sulk. I did so by declaring that he would receive no food until all was well again. Sam acquainted Simonie with this proposition first. He seemed almost horrified and quick as a flash wanted to know if the "Kabloona's" God could countenance such a thing. To deny a man food, from an Eskimo point of view, is apparently atrocious. Though Simonie, his wife and Annyow, knew him to be in the wrong, they unhesitatingly stood up for him under such conditions. This partly goes to show to what an extent the stomach rules these people – they live to eat, for it is their life and more, an intoxication. For instance it is hard to comprehend their thirsting and craving for their various foods, seal, bear, deer, hare, white whale and fox, whale, narwhal, etc., etc., the amounts they guzzle when a killing is made.

On the former expedition I managed to secure Omarolluk, an Ottawa Islander, for the sledge journey across North Ungava, which would mean to him separation for five months from his family, a mighty hardship to an Eskimo. He came not because he was to receive a (to him) princely wage, have his family rationed at Hudson's Bay Post, Great Whale River, during his absence, eat the Kabloona's food enroute, but simply to eat deer (tooktoo) knowing that near to our destination, Fort Chino, we would be in time for the southward immigration of the barren ground caribou. They speak of suddenly being possessed of a craving for a certain meat and it may be merely a hare, a fox, a crow or a deer, but that craving will oftentimes send them to great extremes in order to satisfy it.

Kanajuq, Baffin Island, 1913–14. Her photograph first appeared in a Toronto newspaper article in 1915 and was circulated widely thereafter, making her an Inuit poster girl.
(Claremont, LAC, PA121988/photo RF)

The more I see of these people, the more I realize that their friendship varies as the amount of food they receive at your hands, that their whole estimation of you will hang on that as a base. In at least several instances good feeding has been their ruination, for while in the first stage of our acquaintance, they were all that could be desired, full feeding soon made them indifferent and arrogant. But after all they are children, mentally in particular and should always be treated as such, for like children are their petty faults and jealousies, demanding much patience and consideration from their Kabloona.

Monday, 2 February Away at sunrise. A calm clear day overhead, but many fog banks to westward, which in the afternoon became general, so that we could see no more than a half mile or so ... We hope for and expect good going from now on to Cape Dorset, which distance should be completed in three more days. The Esquimaux we met with today returned to their encampment tonight at dark to find us comfortably ensconced therein. They were successful in killing a large seal, which they and my men have been guzzling for an hour or more this evening.

Tuesday, 3 February Simonie sulked this a.m. and refused breakfast, but seeing us in negotiation with one of the Eskimo of this encampment, he came around in short order. He delayed our start by more than an hour. Departed at 8:30. Fine day and nearly calm. Secured eleven fox skins from one of the Eskimo of this encampment who traded with us in the fall ...

Travel underfoot much improved. About 2:30 sighted three deer on the sea ice, about a mile ahead. Anunglung and Sam went ahead with their rifles and managed to stalk one who let them approach to within 300′. They fired at least fifteen shots at their large target, but only hit twice, wounded him slightly. The deer acted like a fool, seemed hypnotized, for at each shot he merely danced in a circle and then presented a broad side, stock still target. Buck fever and intense cold accounted for their poor shooting. Even when we came up with the frantic teams of dogs he seemed transfixed with curiosity. Sam and Anunglung saw that he was fatally wounded however, and Anunglung cut the traces of the master dog of my team, but the deer showed his heels to him, and we are minus deer and dog. We iglooed to a short distance away, in hopes of our dog returning overnight. Clear cold night with the old cutting wind that usually comes up at sunset.

Wednesday, 4 February A premature breakfast owing to Anunglung's inability to sleep on account of the cold. Away at 8:30. Another calm clear day, spoiled by the fog bands to seaward, which would occasionally sweep in and blanket the landscape. Slow progress and overfed dogs and deep snow. At lunch the deer dog returned much to our satisfaction for he was badly needed today. He killed his deer alright for he was strewn with hair about the muzzle. At 2:30 we reached the Eskimo encampment of Annyow's aunt, the men being all away hunting. This point marks the end of Simonie's wife and Annyow's journey. Simonie has erected a permanent igloo for them this afternoon. Sam and Anunglung left shortly after arrival for another Eskimo encampment, which is a short distance to seaward on a small island in order to interview Evaloo, the man who has the knowledge of the Amadjuak mica. Getting mighty short of fuel and grub, thanks to our female friends. These women eat more than the men, one good reason why they should never be taken traveling. Are a nuisance generally. Sam and Anunglung returned at 9:30 p.m., having lost their way on return in a heavy fog. Saw Evaloo whose mica information looks good indeed. He may return with us later on. All the people here have suffered serious losses of dogs, most of whom died through exposure, i.e. frozen feet.

Thursday, 5 February A "shukalee nami" start with Simonie sulking. Refuses to go westward of Cape Dorset on the Foxe Channel trip. Is wife ridden with those two "mule" females of his, but they are all mules, these women. Their votes in the affairs of men in Eskimo "noona" (land) is a mighty power. So soon as the traveler comes to realize this, he is acquiring real experience. At three o'clock sighted the wreck of the Whaler *Polar Star*. Judging from her position and locality of wreck, it looks as if she were wrecked for the insurance. The Whaler *Active* was here at the time, rescued the crew and took out her engines. They were here killing walrus, there being a wonderful ground for them. Since the wreck, which happened several years ago, this bay has been known to the Eskimo as Polar Star Bay (Gordon Bay). The wreck has afforded the finest of teak, pine and oak to the Eskimo for sledge runners, spear and harpoon handles, kayak and omiak frames, and the like. A veritable treasure indeed for it attracted the Eskimo of three hundred miles from the country around.

Near the wreck stands the largest Eskimo encampment encountered since leaving Amadjuak Bay. Some half dozen igloos, and fine and large and comfortable they are. What a comfort it is to strike one for the night's rest, rather than shiver in the cold while a traveling one is being built, while the warmth of an old one which gradually turns into an ice shell inside, through the constant use of the lamps, is much greater than a new one which is always a shivery affair at best. The Eskimo burns his seal oil lamps constantly day and night, so that they are always lighted. As far as uncleanliness is concerned, I fail to see it. Certainly if we lived under their unavoidable conditions, we should be no cleaner. I rather suspect that the native has quite as marked an opinion regarding our cleanliness, at least during winter traveling, as we generally have of theirs. The women regard one who is unshaven with no small amount of repulsion. Natives are practically beardless.

How soon they tire of the Kabloona's food or his presents generally (hunting gear excepted!). Their great food is seal, to the exclusion absolutely of the white man's "nucky." They are wonderfully self contained, particularly so when one considers their country, its dearth of metals, wood, vegetable growth (willows and mosses excepted), its merciless climate when all the energy and nervous force is used to fight the constant cold ... During evening in the igloo showed natives specimens of galena, hematite, magnetite and native copper.

Two of the women recognized the native copper and state that it occurs in this neighborhood and on the north end of Nottingham Island. They state that it occurs in small nuggets, splattered throughout the rock faces. Have arranged that one of them secure us some samples and forward some to Cape Dorset, our headquarters, at once. Some of the natives claim that iron ore, red in color and very heavy, occurs near here. The pyrite deposits occur near here also, as well as to westward of Cape Dorset. They have been for centuries the source of supply of fire stones for the Eskimo. The chart of this coast is quite useless and is impossible to locate ourselves by it. The only location I can give these rocks at present is among the islands near the mouth of Gordon Bay (Polar Star) and a day's journey by sledge east to Cape Dorset.

The country today is markedly lower, no doubt peculiar to this rock system. Is a wonderful game country, enormous herds of walrus in summer and plenty in winter with innumerable barren ground caribou. Salmon also obtainable winter and summer. The Eskimo are in plenty. Must depart for Cape Dorset tomorrow as we are now out of fuel and grub. Expect to return in a few days to make investigations of the natives' mineral reports, though no serious work can be done till April, May, June.

Friday, 6 February Went off into Johanessie's, our host, while the team were being harnessed, to look at some rock exposures where my Eskimo friends say there may be an iron deposit ... Promised the copper lady a sewing machine, if her find is good and to Johanessie a rifle.

Struck a final Eskimo encampment enroute to Cape Dorset of about six igloos where we had lunch. Finally arrived at Cape Dorset Post (at 4:30 p.m.) at dark. An old woman of Johanessie's encampment told same a piteous story of her only son Shee, who was lost on field ice last October or November during a walrus hunt. The ice field upon which he was hunting being suddenly detached from the fixed ice of the coastline, by an off shore wind, and swept out into Hudson Strait. He probably died of exposure and starvation.

A few days before Xmas, a walrus hunting party, Luketak, Senejot and wife, and Luketak's son were swept out into Hudson Strait in the same way, but after a frightening experience of hardship and exposure and starvation, their ice field again closed into the main fixed field, upon which they landed and returned to their people who had given them up for lost. They were prisoners on this ice field driven haphazardly to and fro, according to the winds and tides, for two weeks. During this time they subsisted chiefly on seaweed (kelp), which is an article of Eskimo diet being valued and eaten occasionally to effect their almost continuous fresh meat diet. The salt which it contains is another attraction. Still another instance can be given of a walrus hunting party being caught on drifting ice this winter – during the time they were adrift (about two weeks) they prevented starvation by eating seal skin harpoon lines.[42]

Saturday, 7 February Resting today and having our clothes overhauled, etc. This post was established last September by the Hudson's Bay Company ship *Pelican*. Consists of two flat roofed buildings, and the factor's dwelling and store. Mr. Parsons, Ralph Parsons' brother, in charge with a young Scotch clerk as his assistant; interpreter, John Edmonds, a Labrador "livyere" of Davis Inlet. The post seems to have possibilities, for to my mind it is situated in the finest game area of the Hudson Strait coast of Baffinland. Probably no post of the Hudson's Bay Company in Canada has the walrus resources which are to be found tributary to this place. This post's location here is a distinct help to me in the exploration of this seaboard, particularly to west and north westward.[43]

Monday, 9 February Enjoying the luxury of Turkish cigarettes (Sarony's), Bass's Ale, and Hudson Bay Port. Very lazy and comfortable.

Stewart, the clerk and interpreter, went off to westward some twenty miles with sledge to fetch Mukpollo, who has some knowledge of the coast line to north westward of this point, which may help me in estimating for the sledge journey to Foxe Channel.[44] The weather at this post this winter has been quite as remarkable as that which was obtained at Lake Harbour and Amadjuak Inlet, i.e. a succession of calm days, or nearly so, with clear skies overhead and a complete absence of heavy winds, or an amount of winds which obtain in Hudson Bay. On this account I believe the winter climate of this coast to be much more endurable than that of Hudson Bay, particularly the Ungava coast line, where it is hardly ever calm or nearly so. The Eskimo of this coast, who in former years have wintered in Hudson Bay at various points while cruising with Scotch and American whalers, complain of the cold there, and invariably state that this is much the warmer country. Winds determine the cold and the amount of exposure a man can resist, and not the degree mathematically by temperature ...

Mukpollo came in from his encampment last night bringing us discouraging news that his encampment are almost starving, so that my expected source of dog food supply (walrus meat) has failed. He states they have killed neither seal nor walrus lately, and are out of seal oil, so that they have no fuel for their lamps, their igloos being in darkness. The dog food as usual, will be the one factor that will determine the amount of travel to westward. If meat supply fails will attempt to cook up corn meal and grease at this post, freeze it in sacks and use that for dog food during the trip.

Saturday, 14 February Preparations practically completed for the trip to Foxe Channel. Have engaged Elie, a Dorset Eskimo, for the trip, as partner to Anunglung. Simonie is being returned to Amadjuak. Will travel with two teams in charge of Anunglung and Elie respectively. Outfit of bacon and beans, dried fruit, tea and sugar, three Primus Stoves, fifteen gallons fuel, one Eskimo stone lamp, 700 lbs. dog food, walrus and deer meat, with an emergency supply of 50 lbs. cornmeal. Estimate supplies enough for six weeks for four men and dogs. One 303 Winchester, one Mauser pistol, seal, harpoons, etc., ice chisel etc., extra nails, screws for sledges in case of breakdown, with a piece of runner wood for splicing, etc. Two thermos bottles (qts.), tobacco, needles, beads, saccharin, B&W, medical kit (small pocket), Chloradyne and Friar's Balsam. Fish-hooks and line, three compasses, stationery, sextant, thermometer, aneroid, magnifying glass, sample bags, range finder, telescope, waterproof match safes. One Graflex camera, 4 × 5, six dozen plates, one film camera, 3¼ × 4¼, twenty five films, one tripod. All dog food chopped up and put in bags. Bacon sliced and in bags. Beans cooked and frozen in bags. All canned goods in bags minus cans. Emergency supply of rice, flour and saccharin and etc., etc. Have arranged that a relay team will leave here two weeks after our departure, travel six days west, then cache an outfit of dog food and grub, marking it with a cairn and flag.

Later. Have decided to abandon the relay team idea, as we expect to return to Amadjuak via Nettilling and Amadjuak Lakes. Have tried two loads on the sledges today and weighed them, checked over outfit finally before start tomorrow a.m. Short on alcohol for lamps, using spirits of peppermint and some Florida Water instead which is, of course, sold here to Eskimo, being a highly desirable luxury to them in the bead, mirror, and mouth organ sense of the word. The women of the post have been working overtime on boots, sleeping bags, socks, etc., bustling activity in this sleepy country.

Monday, 16 February A glorious calm day, the sun so bright as to make us realize that soon we will have to wear snow goggles. Had a great old shooting match during the afternoon. My birthday. All in readiness for departure tomorrow, a.m. Passed a jolly evening with a cheap fiddle and autoharp accompaniment.

Tuesday, 17 February A fine clear day, -20° in a.m. and zero at noon. Finally cleared the post at twelve o'clock, after a final, more elaborate than usual dinner. Parsons flew the Hudson's Bay ensign for us with rifle salute and rang the dinner bell. Simonie departed for Amadjuak at same time.

Our dogs are picked teams and have already shone up well this p.m. The sledges, 14′ and 12′ in length, whale-bone shod with icing. The 14′ sledge is handling a load of 900 to 1000 lbs., the smaller approx. 800 lbs. Our food supply should last with full rations at least six weeks or two months, so that with good travel underfoot we should cover 1000 miles within that period. The outfit is practically self contained even supposing that no game is at any time secured.

Anunglung's widowed sister accompanied us today. She has been employed this last week at the post making boots, mitts and fur clothing for my men and self. Ensconced in her igloo for the night. Arrived here at 6 p.m. This encampment is the last human habitation to westward.

We may see no Eskimo until return to Amadjuak. The encampment consists of some seven or eight igloos, some of them containing three chambers or rather separate igloos, nestled together with a common entrance. The hunters of the encampment returned shortly after our arrival, were successful in killing some seals today. Sometimes they feed their dogs in the igloos, usually when it is too dark to feed them fairly out of doors. It occurred in this igloo tonight with a devil of a row, snarling half famished wolves they were. Cape Dorset is noteworthy as marking the highest point of seacoast between here and Fair Ness. Max. Altitude – 1,000′ ... Cape Dorset, Gordon Bay and the coastline between this point and Cape Dorset, is perhaps one of the greatest walrus grounds of the north. Has been much hunted by Dundee whalers for walrus, though their numbers have in no way diminished. Just at present while there are great numbers off the set ice fields, the ice itself is very dangerous, so that the natives here have had a stiff time of it trying to keep from starvation. Have until very lately been without fuel for their lamps, with their igloos in darkness.

At just about sleep time last night, the population must visit me (of course sheer curiosity), an old accordion was dragged out and the belles of the encampment took turns with it, playing old sailors' jigs and reels, which they have picked up from the whalers probably. No matter what they play a droning bass is carried with the air, just a tinge of their ever primitive and savage color. There was much dancing by the younger folks, like so many shaggy bears in a rough and tumble shuffle.

Wednesday, 18 February   Breakfast at 7 a.m. Find that we broke a part of whalebone shoeing yesterday on big sledge and some of lashing parted. Being repaired now. Anunglung is icing the whalebone shoeing, of both sledges as I write. Preparatory to the actual icing he squirts seal's blood on the shoeing, for as it freezes to the shoeing it forms a pasty coating of red and to which the icing will adhere much better than if it were put on alone. He takes huge mouthfuls of seal's blood from a walrus skin bucket, and squirts it in streams on the shoeing ... Splendid coastline and sharply sloping inland to maximum height of 600′. It seems strange indeed that we are the travelers of the coast charted by Luke Foxe in 1631, the first to use this chart. Anunglung pointed out an island (Mill Island, I think), some fifteen miles to seaward, said that in open water there are great numbers of narwhal there, which the Eskimo have hunted from kayaks with harpoons. Took several photos this a.m. before departure. Encampment assembled en masse to say "too hewtill." The last humans, for some time. Exchanged sledges, a large one for our small one, with Mukpollo.

Thursday, 19 February Three dogs chewed themselves out of their harnesses during night and made merry with the walrus meat dog food. The men had to dress, cut open the door of snow and catch the dogs whom they relashed, also bound their muzzles with sealskin thong. While preparing for start, Anunglung saw a bear walking along the field ice towards open water one half mile distant. Sam, Anunglung and self, went after him leaving Elie to watch dogs.

We jogged over from ice field to two reefs that lay between him and the open water, and waited in ambush for his coming. Peering over a final ridge of the island we saw him, an enormous fellow, slouching lazily along, but Anunglung thought that he would detour away from our place of ambush to an island nearer open water, so we abandoned our position and made for the other island. We arrived there breathless and white with frosted perspiration, only to find that he had gone along the original way after all. We found out afterwards that as soon as he came across our trail he ran to open water in short order and plunged into it. Anunglung was in time to see him swimming in the distance away from land. We returned to the igloo almost played out with the stiff chase over crusted and deep snow drifts, over rough ice and rocks – one knows at such a time the handicap of fur clothing. Anunglung states that a bear is more sensitive to smell than a deer. We had no difficulty in picking out the bear from his background of snow, there was no sun at the time. He was a distinct yellow, against the contrast of pure white snow.

We had a light lunch before starting, as it was nearly noon when we returned (from the hunt). The morning's hunt proved disastrous to Anunglung, who lost his dollar watch during the chase, and also shortly after the bear hunt and while watching him swim away, he killed a huge square flipper seal; he lost that as well having no harpoon to land him with. Continued journey during afternoon, but some four miles westward came to impassable field ice …

From my native informant Mukpollo, we understood the coastline to be low and quite navigable by sledge wherever the rough ice extended to actual shoreline, but such is not the case. Mukpollo is a liar, and we have journeyed 350 miles for nothing. There is nothing for it but to return and attempt via an overland route to reach the northwest coast of Foxe Channel, for I feel confident that the Foxe Channel coast from

Cape Dorset to Penguin Point is impassable by sledge. A bold abrupt coastline. Almost continuous open water to seaward and rough inshore ice. The fact that the native has never traveled it and is unknown to him guarantees this statement for he is always a traveler and in touch with his own people over vast distances. So we returned to last night's igloo, sick with disappointment, stayed there for the night. Pored over a chart with the men and discussed a plan of attempting an overland crossing via Chorkbak Inlet (some 100 miles to eastward) thence north-westward over the interior, coming out on Foxe Channel north of Penguin Point (Foxe is farthest north). Will sleep on it, is Anunglung's advice. Clear calm night, dogs all tethered by burying their coiled trace into the snow, a secure anchor, hope for an undisturbed sleep.

Friday, 20 February Clear, slight west wind -20°. Constant boom and crack of grinding ice during night. Away at eight o'clock with a stiff portage to start with. Delayed the usual preliminary of icing runners till after crossing portage, on account of rock ground. A light, drifting northwest wind during day, cold. Enroute to Mukpollo's encampment, our first sleep from Dorset westward. Sam had some trouble with Elie, which finally meant that he would not go without his wife and child to keep him warm, his clothes dried and mended, which is the Eskimo way of refusing. He has a nasty looking sore breaking out on his chin, which may be his real reason, for the real reason to anything an Eskimo never gives. Both men I believe are afraid of the Chorkbak trip, for Chorkbak has a nasty reputation, treacherous and dangerous ice. It extends some two to three days sledging into the interior, is uncharted and unknown. The country inland of its head is low and level and should be a feasible route for sledges to Foxe Channel. My own time is becoming dangerously limited for I must return to Amadjuak by, at least, the 15th April ...

Arrived at Mukpollo's at 4 p.m. Anunglung's sister, who gave us such glowing information of copper and of mica, which her children used to build toy igloos with, now laughingly tells us that it was all a lie. She no doubt expected a present for her invention at the time. The people having a nightcap and raw seal, as I turn in for sleep. Purchased two deer from Senejot, who with three others killed a dozen today. Secured a whalebone dish as curio.

Saturday, 21 February Away at 8 a.m. for Dorset post. Mukpollo is coming with us with a thirteen dog team and one of his wives. Is helping us with our load. Arrived at post at noon with tail between our legs and had the pleasure of listening to the "I told you so's" of the post. Received lately some Bass's Ale and Sarony's cigarettes. Elie has bucked in earnest and will give up Chorkbak Inlet scheme of going overland. Will return to Amadjuak, as soon as possible. Send LaDuke overland to Foxe Channel via Amadjuak and Nettilling Lakes. Will devote my time to motion pictures and to exploration of east coast of Amadjuak, later its mountains and glaciers.

Note on climate of Hudson Strait: I can only account for the comparatively mild climate in winter along this coast (from Foxe Channel to Lake Harbour, possibly to Resolution Island), comparatively mild according to Hudson's Bay and Rowe's Welcome standards, by the fact that all along this seaboard, some 450 miles open water exists in all cases to within an average of eight miles to seaward of the average coastline. This open water renders the winter temperatures very even, constant and equable.

Monday, 23 February Departed from snug little Cape Dorset post rather reluctantly and not before Parsons and I had a final shooting match with Manchester rifle, which he used very easily. As soon as we cleared the sheltered harbor, ran into a stiff drifting west wind. Stayed at Elie's camp for the night and collected further interesting information concerning the rocks of this locality etc. Sam went off in late p.m. to look at an island of so-called "white rock" (marble). Returned at dark without reaching it.

Tuesday, 24 February Away at eight o'clock with the two sledge loads on the sleigh. Broke a five gallon oil cask whilst trying to navigate the overburdened affair, through rough ice. A seventeen dog team, culled from thirty or more. Reached Johanessie's camp at 4 p.m. ... Stayed in Johanessie's camp for the night. Our copper friends have failed to come up to the mark. Their desire to please Kabloona overcomes their sense of honesty. Had occasion to call down "Johnnie" who has now arrived at the well fed stage and consequently inclined to be fresh at times. He sulked over it, refused to come further, offered to return his treasured 303 British Winchester and said he would live here in the future and would not bother with his wife and two children, who are at the post under rations. There is the real Eskimo to a dot. He came around however, the rifle loss being too much to him. Old Elie is another wily affair.

Wednesday, 25 February Met Parsons at noon enroute to Dorset post.

Took Saila and team to help us today as far as Evaloo's igloo – enroute he told Sam that from head of Chorkbak Inlet a crossing overland could be made to Foxe Channel in two days, fast traveling. Reached Evaloo's at sundown, engaged him to come with us to post with his team, also show us his mica discovery. He killed fifteen deer yesterday, his party killed twenty altogether. Finest day of winter.

Thursday, 26 February Arrived at Chorkbak Inlet at 3 p.m. Camped with Tuckpannie for the night.

Friday, 27 February Tuckpannie coming with us to post, taking part of load (Note: Tuckpannie-Parsons affair).[45] A remarkable sunrise, clear and brilliant sun. Travel underfoot very heavy, big team in poor condition, nearly played out on today's journey and could not keep up to other teams, deer meat and underfeeding the cause. Leader played out and had to be carried on sledge. One of the dogs died earlier in the day. At feeding time tonight were ravenous. Built igloo on sea ice at dark.

Saturday, 28 February Anunglung says that igloos made of this salt snow off sea ice are warmer than one of land snow, which forms into ice more quickly. Our dogs cannot keep up on frozen deer meat, two or three days more of this would kill them all. Deer meat frozen is of no use without seal and walrus meat. Even when thawed it requires more in bulk, by far, than either seal or walrus meat. However, crossed the rough ice and not without great danger of getting hurt, and once across soon found Mulucktoo's encampment. Had nineteen dogs on Evaloo's sledge, which we took into camp with our sleeping bags and grub. They were frantic and unfortunately broke Evaloo's sledge while crossing tidal ice on approach to camp. Found Fleming there and the usual Eskimo groups (all hungry).

Sunday, 1 March Turned in at 1 a.m. Breakfast at five a.m. but our sleepy Eskimo made another "shukalee nami" start of it, which was at nine o'clock a.m. Cold day, foggy with southerly winds. The usual throng assembled to see us go and some of the women riding on the sledge to the tidal ice. Hard day's travel and very slow on account of deep snow, which almost played out Evaloo's team of dogs. Struck Foxe Island at sundown, which was a beauty, orange red with the ice field leading to it charged with blue gray shadows in its fissures and scarred surfaces. Clear night, unusually brilliant stars, moon of new quarter.

It was night when we hit the mouth of Amadjuak Bay. The aurora was playing off toward the east southeast coast horizon, but as night deepened it seemed to marshal the few bands of white and cream colored ribbons into a northeast and west formation, then one after another in several rows, like regiments they started northward. They narrowed with astonishing rapidity and even dissolved into huge flickering masses, then reformed and took up the march again. Soon they were overhead and like successive curtains, the bottoms of which sharply spired fingers, undulated in glorious sweeping curves, the undulations often culminating in a maelstrom of swirling light, not light but wonderful apple greens, lavender, old rose and cream, and through it all the stars shone. It wasn't a riot of color of indefinite movement, but color and movement of perfect harmony. So low did the fingers hang to our moving sledge that they seemed almost in reaching distance. We had been sledging six weeks, anxious to make Amadjuak once more, cold and tired out with our long hard day, but it was all forgotten now. We had seen an aurora of such rare beauty that the Eskimo (Evaloo and Anunglung) "kapayed" in sheer astonishment.[46]

In the midst of it all the sledge stopped, the dogs were baying frantically, and along a point of the shoreline two tiny squares of yellow light marked the post, for we had reached the rough tidal ice leading to its shore entrance. We had forgotten our journey. Out of doors we reluctantly left the aurora and its festival, marking the moon and stars, the light of which paled before it, lending to the rugged hill horizon to eastward a pale, uncanny green light. It was good to see the post once more, the affairs of which had been undisturbed during our absence. LaDuke and Stewart had painted the interior during the interval and otherwise effected improvements that to our igloo eyes, seemed mighty fine.

The following day Evaloo and Noahasweetow, with LaDuke and Sam went over to Evaloo's mica discovery, which I am glad to learn is only three miles from post, and inland of the neighborhood we prospected superficially last fall. Evaloo's description of the outcrop is confirmed, but the deposits can only be definitely estimated on disappearance of snow next June. Samples returned here from the surface areas are up to 8″ × 8″ in size. Paid Evaloo for his information, traded with Tuckpannie for a part of his dead whale at Chorkbak, sending Yew and Noahasweetow back for a sledge load with our returned team.

Anunglung arrived at post with Tuckpannie and a bunch of badly used up dogs, on day following our arrival. The dogs played out just a few miles from post which forced them to igloo it. So much for frozen deer meat as dog food! Simonie has been again raising trouble by leaving without my permission for a sledging trip to Poodlak's "noona" with his younger wife. His excuse was that he went after his deposed wife whom he abandoned at that point enroute to Amadjuak from Polar Star Bay, in order to transfer her to the outer island encampment where his young son is ill with consumption. He returned after three days' absence, bringing in his brother, both wives and the invalid, asking us to look after the elder wife and son whilst he and the younger wife went on another trip seal hunting. I fired him and his entire outfit, after taking away the 30-30 Savage rifle and shells which I had given him in fall – the latter action was some punishment.

His sick son's case is pitiable, but were he to live here we could extend him no aid that would be as beneficial as his living where he is, in an igloo. The day after their departure, the astonishing news leaked out that his brother sleeping in Noahasweetow's igloo with young Anunglung and Noahasweetow's wife, Luliakame, raped her during the night, bruising her severely, scared young Anunglung not venturing to interfere. Noahasweetow, and Yew his father, arrived a day later at midnight. Without sleeping he reharnessed the team and with his wife stole out of camp (quite unknown to us). At breakfast when we had learned that he had gone it looked to me like a gunning affair. We anxiously awaited his return to camp, which occurred at night. We missed our guess and learnt of another item of the Eskimo character, and of the hot headed and jealous Noahasweetow. He accused his man in his own igloo in the presence of his wife. He made no answer, but turned to him and proposed that they exchange wives, at which Luliakame raised some row, though the other wife seemed willing enough. Noahasweetow finally accepted, but just as he was departing, his anger apparently quite dissipated by the arrangement, he refused her, and departed with Luliakame. He finally revenged himself enroute to the post by beating Luliakame.

Noahasweetow's and Yew's trip after the whale meat dog food was a failure – they brought only two hundred pounds on the sledge and were forced to abandon a like quantity some distance west of here, owing to deep snow and over-worked condition of dogs. This means that the projected expedition across Amadjuak and Nettilling Lakes to Foxe Channel is also a failure, for the time being at least. The Eskimo state that along in March there will be many deer in Amadjuak, which is now our only hope.

Parsons arrived here with two sledges on March 9th, enroute to Lake

Harbour post from Cape Dorset. It was of course an interesting day, seeing we have so few visitors. He settled the crooked Tuckpannie by breaking up both of his rifles with an ax, to which Tuckpannie (noted as a hard nut) made no interference. Parsons departed on 10th. Took motion picture of his teams going through the rough tidal ice. Arranged with Parsons to purchase a cook stove at Dorset post, ours being done up. Sent Sam to Cape Dorset for it this a.m. with a fourteen dog team and Anunglung. Noahasweetow and Yew finished off the studio igloo today.

Splendid clear calm weather since 1st of March, mercury averaging zero, a surprising winter. Innumerable Arctic trout have been seen in the lake through the water holes. LaDuke and the women have been angling for them this last week, though LaDuke only has been successful, catching a few fine meals of them. They refuse bait, spoons or fly, but are at this time very sluggish so that LaDuke gets them by jigging them up with hooks, a cold job. Anunglung and Jack Johnson managed to saw a trench in the ice. It has not proved successful, only catching one six inch trout so far.

[Saturday, 14 March] Sent Noahasweetow out to Ishawongatock's camp this a.m. in order to secure his aid for the moving pictures. He returned at night with Joe and his dogs. Ishawongatock will follow tomorrow. Joe is nearly gone with consumption. Tried out the new studio igloo on 13th with motion, unlimited patience picture machine. Staged an interior igloo scene with Yew's wife and child and Annyow. Tried again in p.m. but light failed us. Ishawongatock arrived with wife and children in afternoon, brought me a present of deer meat. Sending Joe back tomorrow as it is impossible to feed so many starving dogs of his.[47]

Friday, 20 March Sam arrived from Dorset fetching the much desired cooking stove, etc.[48] Reports good traveling; made this post in four days' time. Since Sam's departure have taken quite a series of motion pictures, about 4,000′ in all. Successful in having a very large igloo constructed which measures 15′ in diameter and 12′ high, a record for size. It only stood a week however. Secured some fine pictures of Ishawongatock's wife and child. Shortly after Sam's arrival a row occurred with Noahasweetow and wife. Tried to get poor Noahasweetow to shake his crooked wife who was responsible for his failure. He broke down and cried, saying he would kill himself if she went away. We were melted and relented toward expelling him, but later next day he decided to go away (due to her influence with him). Gave over all his things including his beloved harp and gun. Leaves tomorrow and Ekecktillik Eskimo came in today. Will probably leave with him tomorrow. March has been wonderfully mild, a succession of dull, warm, melting days – the entire month to this date averages no less than +10°. Waiting for picture weather.

Thursday, 26 March Got a splendid day and secured 800′ interior igloo, subject of Allego fire making. Whilst in the midst of operation loud thunder and a perfectly clear sky. Ther. about +32°. Thunder, said the Eskimo, was loath to go. Charlie and his wife left with Jack Johnson and one of our sledges and dogs. Following day Yew arrived with a load of dog food from Poodlak's noona. Are killing walrus there now and occasionally bear. Billy and Katarina narrowly escaped drowning other day while walrus hunting. Day following Yew's arrival, Sam went out to Kingwackshaw's camp to fetch in the old ivory carver and wife. They will arrive on Monday. Waiting for more picture weather. The spring weather is too heavy. Have spring fever and bad cold.

Sunday, 12 April Have been taking motion pictures up to this date, total exposure to date about 15,000′. Wonderful weather since 1st of March. Have almost completed motion pictures.[49]

Yew and Anunglung were sent deer hunting a week ago, secured eight deer near post. Yew returned snow blind, and fear one eye is permanently blind. Yew's wife suffering much from rheumatism. Kingwackshaw and Noahasweetow happened into post about time of Yew's and Johnnie's return. Went after more deer and secured nineteen.

Wolves very troublesome, a pack of ten were prowling about the igloo the other night. Made a pitfall but was unsuccessful. Seem to be badly starved. Sent Sam and Jack Johnson off to Amadjuak Lake to get information, preliminary to trip later on.[50] Sending Anunglung eastward a hundred miles for his kayak and tent, as per promise to him. Sam and Jack Johnson arrived home unexpectedly today from the Lake Amadjuak trip. He was successful in reaching the lake. Enroute he was attacked by the wolves which left this bone of contention to follow. He killed one and wounded another. They were desperately hungry and approached to a short distance of sledge before being shot at. The sledge journey from this point to Amadjuak Lake can be made in two days' time. The country surrounding is very low and flat. To northward nothing can be seen but a blue horizon. Anunglung left on Monday, April 13th, for his kayak and tent. Still storming as yesterday with drifting snow. March weather in April.

Sunday, 31 May[51] Departed at midnight with three teams of 9, 9 and 11 dogs with LaDuke, Stewart, Anunglung, Annyow, Mary, Allego, Noahasweetow and wife for Ekecktillik, or Fair Ness. Samples of graphite had been sent in to me from Eskimo of an encampment there that looked promising and induced me to take the trip. Traveling by night we were enabled to take advantage of the frozen snow crust and made great speed thereby, arriving Ekecktillik the following day at five p.m. Distance fifty miles. Warmly greeted by the encampment, who turned out en masse as our three sledges galloped pell mell into the encampment ... Have worked up the Eskimo to exploring the country around when snow is gone. It is possible some discoveries may be there made. Returned, starting Tuesday 3rd June, at midnight. Arrived following day at noon. Secured valuable curios from people. A most enjoyable excursion, with delightful weather, and fast travel. Secured fine photos of iceberg, etc. Enroute home came upon two komatiks ambling aimlessly along, the occupants of which were sound asleep, man and wife on one and (Elie's son) and Mulucktoo's son on other. They awoke with a start to find our dogs and theirs at war. All hands breakfasted together, they felt so jolly over it that on departure gave us the old Inuit farewell.

Saturday, 6 June As the snow is still too deep for explorations, advantage is being taken of the interval to attempt to explore and map Amadjuak Lake, make soundings of its west and east coasts and determine if Eskimo reports of glaciers exist along east coast are true. They report seeing icebergs in lake. Explorations divided into two parties, Anunglung and I taking east coast, LaDuke, Stewart and an Eskimo taking west coast. I started at 9:30 p.m. June 6th. LaDuke delayed with neuralgia. At about midnight came across deer. Shot three. One killed from sledge, dogs and deer on a gallop. Traveled until noon following day. As I made camp Anunglung went after deer few hundred feet ahead, killed two. Cold weather and head winds with snowfall making travel bad underfoot. Weather extremely variable.

Wednesday, 10 June Cleared, but very gray heavy looking day. Enroute up the lake a small group of deer came across our trail diagonally and completely unaware of our approach, till within no more than 150′ of them. I then learned the pleasant news that our cartridges are reduced to one for Anunglung's 303 British, and only one for my Mauser. As we must kill deer for dog food, it will mean a return unless we can intercept

LaDuke's party. Made for a prominent island short distance to northward. Pitched camp in commanding position while Anunglung erected a double stone windbreak on an elevation near tent. He lies there wrapped in deerskins, and through the day on the lookout with telescope for LaDuke's crossing of Mingo Lake. An amazingly long winter, there is more snow now than at any time of winter, chill and bleak wind …

The deer are indeed plentiful, we saw them on every side. They are easily hunted, which is mainly owing to their unquenchable curiosity. Even after alarmed they usually retreat by a short distance and fitfully trot in circles about the object of their curiosity. The mothers are heavy with young at this time. To the Esquimaux they are the prize, for the fetus deer's coat goes to form the finest of their clothing. Anunglung says that before guns came to them, they hunted them with dogs, dogs run them down in deep snow. The old driftwood bows were of most limited range indeed. I suppose none were so primitive. Saw many deer decoys along lake shore similar to those I've seen in North Ungava.

Thursday, 11 June Very bad headache last night took six tablets of calomel and four of quinine. Cured! Snow blind in one eye. This a.m. very fine and warm. Went up to head of lake for deer that we cached in snow. Secured two, two were eaten by fox. Sent Anunglung off on a cross section of lake for signs of LaDuke's trail. No luck. Must return to camp tonight, secure cartridges and oil. Oil can burst yesterday, which under some circumstances would be a serious affair. A hundred miles of travel for nothing. Damn it! …

Noted LaDuke's trail, missed him after all. He probably got out of course to Mingo Lake for Anunglung swears he could find no trail. Anunglung came across a doe and fawn which must be newly born indeed. He could not capture it, the mother defended it so ably. He called out to me to unleash the dogs but I was at full length on the sledge fast asleep.

Friday, 12 June Warmest day. Snow [melt] has started in earnest, with a sun so hot it burned my face intensely and blinded my eyes partly, in spite of glasses. We noticed no great softening of trail until we struck the third and last lake. It was here announced rather vividly by a sudden plunge of the dog team through the ice. Barely stopped the over running sledge in time.[52] Anunglung became panicky. Pulled them out all right and went on our course. Succeeded in crossing the lake, but very hard travel, deep snow and water through which the dogs had to waddle belly deep at times. Decided to wait on portage for the night's frost. Boiled the kettle and stretched out on deerskins for a two hours' nap. Started again with snow slightly crusted with frost. Forced to travel shoreline of two last lakes into camp. Arrived at two a.m., very tired and wet after a continuous travel of thirty hours.

A hell of a spring. More than a month late. The snow is not half gone. LaDuke states that he saw a robin at Amadjuak Lake. Geese are seen every day, starving, the Eskimo say, through lack of open water. Departed with Stewart and Simonie, two dog teams, moving picture and camera outfit for the icebergs off from Kingwackshaw's encampment. Heavy travel through slush ice and water 4″ deep on Amadjuak Bay. Camped first night at Anunglung's camp. Following day proceeded to Kingwackshaw's encampment. Arrived too late to obtain berg pictures on that day. Noted many stone graves and monuments at Kingwackshaw's of slab gneiss and mica schist. As we arrived the hunters of the camp came in with three sledges of walrus meat – they had just killed a large one a mile away in open water.

Open water extends all along the north side of straits probably. Had some trouble crossing a tidal crack, between two small islands near to destination. Following day succeeded in securing moving pictures of dogs and iceberg, also camera studies. Splendid day. At midnight departed from Kingwackshaw's, after scrambling some excess grub and cartridges amongst them. Arrived at mouth of Amadjuak Bay to find it flooded with water, forced to travel tide mark. Arrived at igloo at 6 p.m.

Friday, 3 July Avalishia came in with a monster square flipper seal for which we have waited so long. Gave him a rifle (.44) for it.

Saturday, 4 July Though foggy went out with two teams, Ishawongatock, wife and child, Cunayow, "Jack Johnson," Anunglung and Sam, secured moving pictures of Eskimo fording stream, etc., enroute to mica. Most interesting pictures I think.[53]

Sunday, 5 July As luck would have it this day turned out a beauty. At once started preparations for the moving picture of the big seal hunt. Took two sledges, about twenty-two dogs and a half dozen Eskimo. Secured what I think will prove a fine picture. In the midst of it, a runaway team of dogs came galloping along with part of a sledge. It proved to be LaDuke's outfit coming from the mica. LaDuke has not been successful in finding any large mica, though snow interfered with that possibility to a large extent. It seems that exploring conditions will be good about the time our ship comes.

Tuesday, 7 July Sent LaDuke with Ishawongatock and Quewencktow and wives to Anunglung's island to do some surface trenching on garnet and beryl outcrops, etc. Noahasweetow hurt by sledge in rough ice. Joseph failing every day. Sainsbury giving him hypodermics occasionally. Secured a second picture of fording stream, which should prove highly successful. Young Amelia, twelve years old, killed a deer the other day while out salmon hunting with some of the women. Presented them with a .44 rifle.

Saturday, 11 July Fairly good weather last few days and have developed some 1,000 odd feet of films. River a roaring torrent now and sounds very distinct at camp. Expect to depart for Metuck noona tomorrow with three sledges, five Eskimo, Sam and I. Hope to get pictures of Eskimo duck and egg hunting. The *Laddie*'s arrival is discussed ever hour of the day. The time drags like the devil, which isn't altogether conducive to good temper.

Sunday, 12 July Left at noon with Anunglung, Noahasweetow, Annyow, Luliakame, Amelia, Nyla and Sam, three sledges and twenty-five dogs, for the eider duck breeding grounds, for motion pictures … The Inuit were excited as at our approach to the island countless ducks flew up from their nests, or scurried over the rocks. After pitching camp, advanced with population in toto to motion picture machine but found that the duck are much too scary for pictures. The Eskimo like hounds in a leash, were given the freedom of their island. They scattered in groups for their egg gathering whilst Sam and the men went gunning. A rare day's sport indeed. Departed following day for Amadjuak not a day too soon for it turned out later the ice field broke the next day. Found Stewart at camp upon return. LaDuke came in four days later with his outfit. Sam outfitted and repaired dory for island beacon expedition and departed on the 19th with Queweneccktow and wife. He will camp on Duck Island and erect beacon there. Will remain till *Laddie*'s arrival.

Saturday, 25 July We found five feet of ice in harbor. Our Eskimo friends now predict the opening of navigation on or about 20th of August, which puts us in some temper. Sent out Allego, Annyow and Anunglung to Duck Islands to gather eggs with dogs and sledge. They

Sam Sainsbury, an unacknowledged contributor to Flaherty's Baffin Island filming. Flaherty included this photograph in a Bell & Howell camera testimonial with the caption "At the ford, Kokjuak River, Baffin Island, March 1914."
(Claremont, LAC, PA114947/photo RF)

returned on 31st with Queweneccktow, who brought me a note from Sainsbury saying that Hudson's Bay Company launch *Darrell* passed bound to Dorset on 30th. They told him the Whaler *Active* passed in first week of July bound for Ottawa Islands. The egg hunters brought back a most acceptable large number of eggs. They report the ice in shaky condition which about ends dog sledging.

Wednesday, 5 August   Secured motion picture of omiak.

Friday, 7 August   A heavy gale southeast, with rain, has at last started the eternal ice – there are open spaces of water here and there. Its final disappearance is not far off. Developed omiak pictures, 7th and 8th The ice finally broke on the 11th August, so that a ship could enter the harbor on the 12th Ice all disappeared on 15th. Joseph died of consumption on 12th August at night. Was buried at daybreak on the rocks to eastward of his topek. Two births occurred on the 16th.

Tuesday, 11 August Ishawongatock says that he sighted beacon signal, signifying ship's arrival from his lookout on the mountain, but it proved a false alarm.

Wednesday, 12 August Ford of Wolstenholme came down coast in sail boat enroute to Lake Harbour. Sam departed for islands on following day. Waiting for ship is very hard, being long overdue. We are running up to limit of our food supply. Will have to strike east for Lake Harbour by 1st September, and abandon our outfit. Auction Bridge is the one antidote to our tedious waiting.

Wednesday, 19 August A warm summery morning. Awakened by the excited announcement of the ship's arrival. Noahasweetow went over to lookout mountain at daybreak and reported her from there by firing off a dozen or more rifle shots. We soon returned to post carrying back a lot of the deer hunters, who also saw her. Our spirits fell to zero, however, when Noahasweetow arrived for he said she left a long cloud of smoke behind her. Could only see her spars over the outlying Islands. *Laddie* is an oil engine auxiliary. At once dispatched him with Atcheak for another lookout on mountain with orders to fly a flag if it proved to be the *Laddie*. After a heartbreaking wait, and when I had given the affair up for a steamer bound into Hudson Bay, the flag was furled and Noahasweetow and Atcheak fired their guns, every shot exultingly and music indeed!

This was at ten a.m. How we put in the balance of the day waiting her arrival into Amadjuak Bay can hardly be described, but principally spent in fitful hands at bridge. Just before dark she rounded the point. We all went slightly off at that time, such a night it was. The Eskimo seem more exultant than us. Stewart ranged our Eskimo stalwarts in line, and gave a rifle salute. The *Laddie* sent us blasts of her fog horn and ran up her ensign. The day closed in rain and fog with northwest wind, strong at times. The *Laddie*'s anchor was hardly slipped before all hands were on board. I was indeed glad to see them all again for she carries substantively the same crew as last year. She left St. John's on 15th July, had a hard passage with much ice. In Gray Strait off Cape Chidley she was ruffed in ice and narrowly escaped. The ice rafted to either side of her as high as her yards. False beams were installed in her this spring and which alone saved her.[54]

Three busy days were spent in loading vessel, preparatory to departure after ship was beached, her bottom inspected and spare propeller installed in lieu of one badly bent by ice. Her bows were badly cut by ice, also several places along her bottom. Greenheart sheathing saved her much damage. Magazines, papers, our much-longed-for mail, oranges, cigars, cigarettes, and wine were some novelty. With more reluctance than I can describe we bade farewell to the Eskimo, for whom we really learned to care. They were sorry too, always asking anxiously were we coming back again. Owing to a shortage on board ship and at camp, we are forced to steam to Cape Dorset in an attempt to buy flour of the Hudson's Bay Company there.

Sunday, 23 August We departed from Amadjuak at noon with a northeast wind and clear sparkling weather. One year of waiting ended. We arrived at Cape Dorset at noon following day after a splendid run, with little ice, all in loose pans. Several walrus were sighted enroute. Dorset post thought that we were the *Pelican*, much disappointed, as she is long overdue. Eskimo population of the country round are encamped at the post awaiting ship's arrival. Secured flour fortunately and departed for Wolstenholme at seven p.m.[55]

Tuesday, 25 August Splendid clear day, high west wind. *Laddie* hardly holding her own against it and Ungava coast sighted at dawn.

Wednesday, 26 August Awakened by skipper saying steamer was in sight coming eastward. We hailed her and she held up while skipper and I clambered aboard. Proved to be *Belle*, a venture bound to Sydney. Capt. Randell regretted that he could not take my motion picture film negatives, developed samples, etc., in charge of LaDuke to Sydney. Were much disappointed. She is in government service bound for Nelson River. Arrived at Cape Wolstenholme at noon. Chalmers in charge whom I met two years ago aboard S.S. *Nascopie*.[56] Usual thing of Eskimo awaiting ship's arrival. Ice cleared from Erik Cove latter part July. At Dorset conditions much worse. Not navigable for ship until 5th August. *Nascopie* arrived at Erik Cove 15th August, eleven days enroute from Cartwright.

Thursday, 27 August Gale southwest wind, rain and fog. Nervous about harbor which is open to northerly winds.[57] Captain had anchor watch all day and night. Arranged to send Sainsbury out to St. John's with results of expedition.[58] People here suspect Eskimo of murdering Grant and crew.[59]

Friday, 28 August Departed at six a.m. Light head winds, moderating during day. Later cleared. Took panorama of Wolstenholme cliffs and tidal race. Took panorama of Wolstenholme post. *Laddie* doing surprisingly well. Exhausts cleared out yesterday which accounts for it. Boys played football ashore yesterday. We were entertained at post. Wonderful numbers of birds about Cape Wolstenholme coast, large rookeries said to exist near Cape. Sighted Eskimo near Nuvuk country at 4 p.m.

Sunday, 30 August Gray, hazy and partly foggy. Light fair wind. Cleared of fog at two p.m. Sighted Cape Smith thirty miles to southeast. At eight p.m. estimated our latitude at or near north extreme Ottawa. Hove to. Fog at times. Offered a .44 Winchester to any of the crew who caught a cod. Men jigged for hour or more, no luck. Sea Pigeon sighted at nightfall. Expect near islands. Hove to at 8:30.[60]

Monday, 31 August Engine started at daybreak. No islands sighted. Course was accordingly east-southeast, no chance that ship was too far to westward. This was at seven o'clock. Fog at daybreak. At eleven a.m. low lying mainland with outlying islands and reefs sighted ... Laid course to westward for Ottawa [Islands] ... Engine stopped at eight p.m. Hove to, till daylight. Islands show up to westward, clear cut blocks of blue and grays. Smoke sighted on or near one of northerly islands. Believe it is Whaler *Active* of Dundee. Jimmie and French jigged, say water is too deep hereabouts. Finest sight of all the summer. Note great difference in temperature here and in Hudson Straits.

Tuesday, 1 September At daylight found ship about five miles to westward of northerly range of Ottawa ... [*Flaherty then took to the launch to scout the islands.*] Coasting southward along east coast of islands some six miles suddenly came on a group of men outlined along crest of island hill. At once knew they were crew of Whaler *Active*. Soon came upon *Laddie* and *Active* anchored side by side in a secure harbor. The harbor is the *Active*'s whaling station on the Ottawa Islands. They have a house erected ashore, with beacons, etc. Captain Murray stated that no whales had been seen. Attempted to reach islands on 1st August, but failed on account of ice, finally reached them on 17th August, with Fullerton natives aboard. Secured some motion pictures of them. Claims there are many whales here, but seen in spring, up to July, in late fall and winter, off edge of ice fields. Whale foods are plentiful. Economic whaling is impossible, owing to impossibility of getting natives to winter, as islands are particularly barren, though many seals in winter. Mate of *Active* claims to have seen large and interesting deposits of asbestos on small island some two miles southwest of Murray Harbour. Ballast taken aboard on second day. Gale northeast wind sprang up continuing until 11 a.m.

Saturday, 5 September Cleared Murray Harbour finally at 11 a.m. Stewart noted further occurrences of asbestos while on line bear hunting one day. Sent LaDuke, of small extent, interesting samples. Cruised southward along east coast Ottawas.[61] More islands than there are on chart. Good speed with brisk northeast breeze. Islands sighted continually to southward, unusually low lying barren and up to 3–4 miles in diameter.

Monday, 7 September Lighter northeast wind, gray day. Low lying islands sighted continuously to eastward-westward on our southerly course today. None very large, max. about 3–4 miles. Shoal ground and reefs skirt them as shown by breakers. Few sea pigeons, only life seen. At night fog came on with rising glass. Men jigged for cod over ship's side. This was also carried on at Ottawas. Rock cods are plentiful there, but no deep sea fish have been found, never tried for according to Captain Murray.

Tuesday, 8 September Engine started at daybreak. Foggy, light air from northwest. Passed Bakers Dozen at 6 p.m. on port and starboard bows. At eleven a.m. sighted a low lying island to southward. Hove to and landed in launch. Examined rock series, massive trap, fine grained with gashes and stringers of calcite, is a phase of the Manitounuk Series, the usual Manitounuk float occurs, including jaspers, clouts, etc. Noted signs of very old Eskimo camp grounds and a human thigh bone. Driftwood in quantity, vegetation more luxuriant than at Ottawa. Heavy banks of fog at intervals all day with light northwest wind. Believe ice is not far to seaward.

After clearing island, decided to lay course for Great Whale River in order to obtain pilot, as these low lying islands look like dangerously shoal ground. Made 7 knots balance of day, with engine and sails wing and wing. At eight p.m. LaDuke, Stewart and I were at bridge when the ship struck, head on. A heavy night, but noted land short distance ahead. Sounded ground around ship, find we've run on a bar at approx. high tide. As ship was not making water, Captain decided to hold over discharging ballast till daybreak. All hands asleep at one a.m., a surprised and crestfallen outfit.

Wednesday, 9 September Awakened at daybreak by Captain and mate saying the ship was a wreck. However, crew were put to work discharging ballast and oil, was finally lightened by some 30 tons, including 30 tons oil. Launch, dory and canoe were put in commission, taking food and clothing, etc., ashore. Day finally cleared of fog at six a.m. with sun. Saw land on every side but northwest. All of it low lying reef a mile to seaward with one exception to northward, where high islands occur, ten of them and look for all the world like the high islands of Manitounuk Sound ...

One of crew cheered us up considerably by saying he saw Eskimo ashore, but later found it false alarm. At nine a.m. tide reached flood, and higher than we had hoped for. We set topsails and foresail. After a hard session discharged more ballast and breaking in additional water and oil casks. Finally after several short jumps, a foot at a time, the good ship cleared. We soon slipped anchor and swung in deep water once more. We were more than anxious to see what water she would make, for she was earlier in a.m. reported broken along her starbilge. There sure was ground for it for she strained horribly, her bottom heaved upwards to such an extent that it seemed impossible not to break. There was no water in well. Like to sun breaking into our fogged and gray morning, came a smile to our much worried skipper. A drink smile the crew called it and such it was.

We find we are temporarily safe, but reefs on every hand. The launch was sent out to sound for a channel. They returned with a minimum of 11′ at half tide on the bar we struck. We must cross it to get to sea. Fog came in thick at three p.m. which put a stop to any attempt to get to sea today. A heavy northwest wind will fix us good the next time in this anchorage. All hands tired and asleep at seven p.m. except a watch of course. Barometer high, light north wind.

Thursday, 10 September Heavy fog, light southerly wind. Succeeded in crossing with two feet to spare and dropped anchor half a mile farther out to sea. In afternoon went ashore in launch, noted copper pyrite, etc., and have secured sample. Many new varieties of plants. Saw innumerable remains of stone igloos, wind break cairns, etc., some very old. These islands are wonderful breeding grounds for geese. Men saw some today while ashore for water. Fog all day, very heavy, so that we could not venture inland on island. At eight p.m. a clear moonlight night and brilliant aurora.

Friday, 11 September Sent launch away at daybreak to sound for harbor, which was reported by watering crew yesterday. Returned at ten a.m. saying harbor is impossible. They traveled over to high island, climbed it and away to northwest lay a large high island, distant about thirty miles. Its extremes took in nine points of compass. Their point of observation was about 400′ high. This is surely the large island of the Eskimo. Weighed anchor at eleven a.m. and proceeded north-northwest. Will endeavor to cruise along off shore of big island. Southerly wind, clear sparkling day. At twelve miles on course veered to west and ran in for the large island which was seen by men this a.m. Arrived at an open anchorage in six fathoms about half a mile off shore at six p.m.

LaDuke, Stewart, French and self put off in launch for shore. We ascended over barren trap rocks to the crest of shore slope, scared up an Arctic hare enroute who gave "Rusty" some chase. Finally gaining the crest, which proved surprisingly far and high (some 500′), an amazing panorama spread out before us. Long sloped hills, barren with some moss grown valleys amongst them, soft green and russet, streaking the orderly ranges of gray and black rocks. As far as the eye could see to westward, range succeeded range, ending in a gray blue line. And over it a sunset, its colors like the foreground. Blood red, orange and yellow and over all three Mare's tails of a windy sky.

As we stood there the wind swept strangely across the foreground, warm and summery, unusual in this country. Southwest and north ended in blurred blue haze. Innumerable small points of silver showed graphically their relative levels amongst the pockets of the hills while deeper than all to eastward lay the sea, veiled almost in blues and silver grays. Through the center of the panorama lay a large waterway running north and south to both extremes of the land mass, though its width is not greater than four miles. Surely this is the great lake of the Eskimo, who told me of their two days' journey by sledge, traveling its length. Never have I been so impressed, that indescribable panorama! Returned at night. Wind increasing, southerly. In for a strong blow (a la every September).

Saturday, 12 September Splendid day, clear, southerly wind. At daylight went off to southward along coast with Stewart, Bill and Dick, some seven miles, where we discovered a splendid harbor. Sounded it and its entrance. Returned to ship at 9:15 a.m. Breakfasted, then went ashore with moving picture machine and made panorama of country seen last night. In meantime ship proceeded to southward to harbor and steamed very slowly against stiff head wind. Arrived at four p.m. enroute to anchorage with launch engine broken down.

LaDuke went ashore and started breaking rocks – ground looks like red shales I had noted in a.m. on west side of harbor. Finally went ashore myself. He showed me hematite, amazingly good, red and blue, far finer than any of Nastapoka series. Went over to ship for dinner at 4:30. After it, sent Stewart and part of crew with launch farther off to southward to explore coast. LaDuke and I went above the south side of inlet. Discovered another series, separate and some half mile from shore. Many geese enroute, and LaDuke shot at black fox enroute. Shot duck enroute, back to ship. Tea at seven p.m. Went alone again after it, but too dark to see much. Stewart returned at 8:30. Cruised seven miles to southward, bold coast farther to southward outlying islands with "streaks of red." Clear night. Aurora.

Sunday, 13 September   Succeeded in getting crew to work today, they started at six a.m. Ballasting ship and watering her. LaDuke and I went

Tookcarak Island, Belcher Islands, 1914 (Claremont, LAC, PA114274)

ashore to southward over iron formation, took panoramas of country formation, etc., with moving picture machine. Sampled ore body and erected monument. In afternoon went northward along harbor shore, then across to number one, and sampled and photo'd it. Noted Eskimo stone marks. Men had half holiday. Scared up white fox. Traveled to hill on eastern skyline, vast area and very high to westward they report. Returned to ship at 5:30 p.m. Bridge at night. LaDuke scared up two acceptable bottles yesterday. Three or four whales were noted from launch, bowhead, according to Stewart. Very heavy wind, then blew scattered. Very near launch. Clear night aurora, windy.

Monday, 14 September   Away at seven a.m. Hazy a.m. Clear and warm, light south westerly wind. Course east-northeast. Sighted mainland at twelve noon. Noted islands on south with dip to westward (not certain). This may mean completion of fold to eastward. At 7:30 forced to hove to, as darkness came on, seemed to be some 12–13 miles off mainland of Richmond Gulf. Southeast wind with little rain at night. Stewart and party in launch yesterday, traveled south along island coast, some eight miles. He noted ore, etc., on beach of landing. Could see southward to blue horizon.

Tuesday, 15 September   During night found that ship was again in sight of Wreck Island, course laid too far to westward. Balance of day spent in getting into mainland islands, with southeast wind on our quarter. At 4:30 p.m. while cruising off shore of islands, a heavy squall carried away two jibs tearing them in tatters, and halyards of mainsail parted. Things looked interesting for a while. Finally ran with wind northward and successfully navigated a gap between two islands. Anchored in lee of one. Heavy weather.

Wednesday, 16 September   Whilst boating down Nastapoka Sound this a.m. spied an Eskimo camp on mainland. Put ashore with launch. Found two men with a lot of women and children etc., in a semi-starving state. Inquired for Nero and Omarolluk. Anchored off mainland till three p.m. Engine cleaned. At dark anchored but a few miles further on. Terrific gales of wind, thunder and lightning. Very close and sultry.

Thursday, 17 September   While off the entrance of Richmond Gulf this a.m. spied a small boat rushing for us. It proved to be Renouf, clerk of Great Whale River, with Nero and bunch of Huskies, wind bound and

Francis D. Wilson was serving in 1915 as the HBC inspector for the Hudson Bay region. Robert and Frances both met him on several occasions.
(HBCA, 1987.14.19, N14625)

waiting for favorable wind for making Great Whale River post. Took them aboard, i.e. Nero and Renouf as passengers to Great Whale River, the sailboat to follow later. Noted Omarolluk and Wetunik, my Fort Chimo traveling friends of former expedition. Forced to anchor in lee of Belanger Island for night.

Friday, 18 September Departed for Great Whale River at three a.m. Calm clear. Nero as pilot. Beautiful run, light southerly wind. Arrived at "Ship's Cove" at dark. LaDuke, Stewart and I and Renouf immediately

John Hayward, an Anglo-Inuk reputed for his skills as an interpreter. Lake Harbour, 1918–19 (HBCA, 1987.257, N98, N8120/photo James Cantley)

left in launch for Great Whale River. Became badly mixed up with sandbars at mouth of river. Fired guns and waved lanterns, but no response from lights ashore. Finally rounded a troublesome bar and made for westward light. It proved to be an Indian encampment, the chief of the occupants came forward as we landed, acted like a crazy man. He piloted us over to post and we could see figures outlined against windows as we approached, but all deserted when we landed. They were badly frightened, taking us for a German landing party.

We later heard the astonishing news of war, dated to 12th August. Found Tees, Aman and party of post enroute to Moose Factory. Discharged all instruments etc., at Great Whale River took on necessary provisions, and on a.m. of 22nd, departed for Moose Factory. North-

Lewis G. Maver served as HBC trader at Great Whale River during the period of Flaherty's expeditions along the eastern coast of Hudson Bay and therefore would have had frequent association with him. (HBCA, 1987.14.38, N14626)

east gale and glass upside down. Arrived at Charlton Island two days later to find the *Nascopie* still there, etc. Departed on Sept. 20th at six p.m. with Messrs. Mackenzie and Wilson aboard and a fifty ton cargo for Moose Factory.[62] Arrived off Moose River Oct. 2nd. Cleared bar with 10′ water and slight bump enroute. Two glorious days, warm south winds into the most summery weather since leaving St. John's more than a year ago.

Thursday, 8 October   Departed from Moose Factory at 8 p.m. with small launch towing us to first rapid. Leaving LaDuke, Bill and Mike to winter at Moose.

6 Frances and the Book of the Heart

Upon his return to Toronto in late October 1914 after completing the third expedition, Flaherty provided Mackenzie with a short summary of his accomplishments. But between the time of his return and the submission of that summary on 16 November, he and Frances Johnson Hubbard had been married. The wedding took place on 12 November 1914 in a civil ceremony at the New York City residence of her cousin, Dr Royal Whitman. According to the biographers Paul Rotha and Arthur Calder-Marshall, the proverbially broke Robert could not fund the customary marriage tokens of ring and license, and they were paid for by Frances. He was thirty, she a few weeks shy of thirty-one. How their extended relationship suddenly arrived at marriage vows is a matter of speculation. Legend has it that she sent him a congratulatory telegram on hearing reports of his return with the rediscovery of the Belcher Islands confirmed; and he shot back a reply that included a proposal of marriage. If we accept an anecdote told by Ernestine Evans years later, the reaction of his potential in-laws was cautious, as it had been ever since the Painesdale days. The Hubbard family, solicitous of their daughter's interests and uneasy with Flaherty's vagrant vocation, were prepared to secure him a Ford motor-car sales agency.[1]

In the end, Flaherty neither sold Fords nor remained the itinerant prospector. Instead, he made films, and in the design of his subsequent career as writer and filmmaker, Frances was a significant architect. The diary entries that follow demonstrate all too clearly Frances's determined aspiration to partner, protect, and promote her husband's career, whether as diarist, writer, photographer, or filmmaker. He was the genius, she his helpmate. By choosing this role, Frances subordinated her own notable talents to advance her husband's career. In this regard, she joined the ranks of other twentieth-century women whose more acclaimed spouses overshadowed their own contributive and creative roles in the work of their husbands. The diaries kept for the first two or so years of her marriage document the depth and intensity of her wish to become her husband's collaborator and, initially, to assist as his publicist, editor, and business manager.

At first glance, the marriage of Robert and Frances might appear to be an improbable match. Superficially, Frances could be perceived as a Miss Baldwin's School bluestocking, the daughter of an erudite collector who regularly sent her books, such as *Lamb's Tales from Shakespeare* and *The Arabian Nights*, as Lucius Hubbard did at Christmas in 1893. In letters to her mother from Bryn Mawr, Frances wrote about her recently purchased horse, Rex, of attending a poetry reading by W.B. Yeats, and of hearing a lecture by Henry James. Later, after her graduation, she wrote of her role as secretary to the Houghton Suffragette Society, hosting and introducing the English suffragette leader, Mrs Emmeline Pankhurst.[2]

But Frances herself regarded her marriage to Robert not as an act in conflict with her culture but as one that fulfilled her desire to put her previously near-useless education in the service of his "natural," non-institutionalized genius. In a self-profile prepared for the tenth reunion of the Bryn Mawr class of 1905, Frances wrote of the six years after graduation as a time when "we really must do something." She explained: "So our large vial of well-meaning missionary zeal pours out upon the defenseless heads of our long-suffering family, friends and fellow citizens and everybody's business is turned inside out in the energetic quest for our rightful own." Feeling that her own "philanthropic-social-service-career" had left her "a rampant alien in a righteous community," Frances departed in 1912 to study in Paris, and in so doing, as she said, "gave myself up to music and in that blessed single-mindedness gathered all my forces together again and bound them up neatly in several philosophical essays on education."

In closing this reflection on upbringing, education, and vocation, Frances declared that she had found the resolution to her longing for purpose in her marriage to Robert Flaherty: "Coming back for a visit to my own country last July, I found myself caught by the war, and doubly caught in the toils of an old romance. I married my husband for several very plain and simple reasons: 1. Because an innate sense for the preservation of his own genius has saved him from all educational institutions or instruction of any kind. 2. Because that genius is for (a) exploration, (Profession: Exploration and Mining), and (b) music and the arts, (Avocations: playing the violin and portrait photography)."[3]

Frances's marriage to Robert Flaherty was the perfect duet of pianist and violinist. Patrician classicism was wedded with natural genius, and art and social purpose found their creative resolution. But the marriage gave Frances even deeper fulfillment – the realization of a fairy story:

> In all things of a lesson nature, I was conscientious to a painful degree, was possessed of an abnormal passion for perfection, and a reputation for being the best scholar, to preserve which, I wore my spirit to the bone, hiding my secret conviction of the sand upon which it was founded. I liked writing fairy stories – but the great, the truly thrilling joy in life was to get away, far away with the sun's sweep where hill beckoned to hill, and the horizon stretched endlessly – to unknown lands of delight, through dark woods of mystery and teeming silences. Of known paths I would have none, beyond the known my feet got wings – I would explore, and by myself alone![4]

Marriage to Robert Flaherty was the public fulfillment of a "secret conviction" – that "thrilling joy" of finding her fellow explorer. Whatever the complex of motives that shaped this relationship, when Frances Hubbard slipped her bluestocking feet into Robert Flaherty's seven-league boots, it became a partnership for life.

Upon his return from the third expedition in 1914, Flaherty received little public recognition for his geographical work, even less for his work as diarist and photographer, and of course none at all for his filmmaking activities. Although his election to the Royal Geographical Society had given him some stature among the professional explorer community, his public identity was minimal. Flaherty's entry into the celebrity circle began in 1915 for two reasons. First, his rediscovery of the Belcher Islands gave him a celebrity in the form of a byline that was most attractive to the press. Second, both he and Frances devoted themselves to learning the art of public relations, working together as a team when that was possible and with Frances continuing as his public relations agent when he was in the field.

Flaherty's increased visibility is demonstrated by the difference in the attention he received from the press in 1913 and in 1915. In the summer of 1913, when he was about to depart on the third expedition, he received minimal press notice. What coverage there was in local Newfoundland newspapers – or in more influential Toronto papers such as the *Star* – made Mackenzie, not Flaherty, the person of the moment, with such headlines as "Mackenzie Finances Expedition to Arctic" or "Sir William Is Seeking New Fields to Conquer." Worse yet, a Newfoundland paper found ships more newsworthy than people when it headlined an article "Schooner *Laddie* for Far North."[5]

By the time of his departure on the fourth expedition in the summer of 1915, there had been a dramatic increase in the incidence of Flaherty-centered newspaper publicity. Major Toronto and New York newspapers, as well as those elsewhere, made Flaherty's exploits the lead story, featuring him as explorer and rediscoverer of the Belcher Islands. During March 1915 the Toronto papers – which, incidentally, adopted Flaherty as a Canadian – set the tone of enthusiasm through such headlines as "Lost Land Found in Hudson Bay" which the *New York Times* trumpeted in a major Sunday magazine section. This theme of rediscovery was also taken up by Toronto's *Globe* when it featured Flaherty's accomplishments under "'Lost Islands' Found Off Shore of Ungava." The *Evening Chronicle* of Port Arthor, not to be outdone by the big city press, applauded Flaherty as the local boy made good: "Port Arthur Boy's Great Achievement: Found the Lost Islands in Hudson Bay."[6]

As Frances's diary entries for March 1915 indicate, they struck pay dirt when they persuaded the *New York Times* to feature Flaherty, as it did in its Sunday Magazine section of 14 March, under the familiar lead, "Lost Land Found in Hudson Bay." What one realizes when surveying these clippings is that there were designing hands behind this process of self-promotion. Although no press kit survives among the Flaherty papers, in the Butler Library, the Flahertys must have prepared one or more press kits, since across the span of the clippings there are so many similarities in narrative details, anecdotes, maps, and photographs. These articles, then, did not only spotlight Flaherty's work as an explorer and geographer, but for the first time they gave his photographs wide public exposure.[7]

Published in the *Courier*, 27 March 1915, this 1913–14 group photograph of Baffin Island Inuit with two of Flaherty's crew – Stewart Gushue above and possibly Sam Sainsbury below – is here reproduced for the first time.
(courtesy of the General Research Division, New York Public Library, Astor, Lenox, and Tilden Foundations/photo RF)

Faced with the large and growing body of Flaherty's photographic work and his diaries, Frances eagerly took on the combined duties of archivist, secretary, copy editor, publishing agent, and literary provocateur. Flaherty's photographic plates and negatives, for example, were in disarray, susceptible to damage and loss, so Frances devised a system to clean, identify, and store them.[8] They deserved such care not only for their aesthetic value but also because they were fungible. Given her growing realization that marriage to Flaherty was likely to be a cash-poor enterprise, she exhorted him, "And remember those negatives are all the working capital we have. Many of them should increase in value with time."[9]

As noted earlier, in order to prepare the diaries for circulation, Frances arranged to have them transcribed, and she devoted herself to their editing, in the process learning to use a typewriter. "I am getting fairly expert with this machine," she commented on 7 January 1915, "and shall probably prefer to use it exclusively in time – it saves lots of hand cramp." But

Stewart Gushue and Eugene LaDuke positioning Bell & Howell camera, 1914. Flaherty included this photograph in a 1915 testimonial for the Bell camera with the caption "Setting up in field ice of God's Mercy Hudson St. April 1914."
(Claremont, LAC, PA500181/photo RF)

the machine's power was not simply that of utility; it empowered Frances to be the processor of Robert's literary potential. Continuing in the same entry, she observed: "Robert's chief aversion to literary effort is the actual writing, he talks better, remarkably well, in fact, so I am preparing to be his literary secretary, to take his dictation and then type it. We have outlined two 'efforts,' one for the lecture to accompany the moving picture, the other for the Royal Geographical Society."

Between the time of their marriage and their departure on the fourth expedition in the summer of 1915, Frances helped put in motion the first wave of their shared ambition to find publication outlets for Robert's exploratory experiences. To nurture his status as a fellow of the Royal Geographical Society, they prepared two short informational notices for the "Monthly Report" section of the *Geographical Journal* (May and September 1915), both of which emphasized Flaherty's Belcher Islands work in Hudson Bay. Frances was also developing outlines for articles that would not be actively worked on until the fall of 1916, after the end of the fourth expedition. But the literary vision was already being cultivated. On 30 December 1914 she wrote in her diary: "I have been working out suggestions for a paper for Robert to write for the *Journal*; my heart is set on it. Subject: Discovery of an unknown land area in Hudson's [sic] Bay."

In the meantime, it was Robert's diaries that Frances regarded as the literary jewel, the work from which she hoped they would fashion what she called in her diary a "Book of the Heart."[10] The phrase was used in connection with her efforts to obtain the support of Irving Putnam, father of her Bryn Mawr classmate, Avis Putnam, and president of the Putnam publishing house. Although Frances reported Putnam's receptivity to the diaries and the photographs, no firm proposal materialized. The Flahertys had a similar disappointment when they visited the literary staff of Scribner's, a meeting that included the presence of a recent newcomer to Scribner's, Maxwell Perkins.[11]

Frances not only helped Robert take the offensive in creating recognition for his work, but she also defended him from those who sought to benefit from his accomplishments. Her scorn was withering for Captain Harold Bartlett's efforts to present himself, in a New York City lecture, as the leader of the third expedition.[12] When the Canadian writer Alan Sullivan offered to "edit" Robert's diaries and photographs, Frances was as wary as a snake: Who was this intruder? What were his motives? Did he plan raids on the Flaherty capital? Flaherty's insouciance about such matters caused her to burst out: "The whole affair has been miserably mismanaged, and only confirmed me in a resolution I had taken since coming to Buffalo of talking a more active part in Robert's affairs. There was Alan Sullivan stealing our ammunition, and I had begged Robert not to send him the portraits. I would market Robert's material myself, everything – I was as capable as the next person."[13] The crudity of the Bartletts and Sullivans was not to be allowed to interfere with the purity of the Flahertys' creation, one that was to be carried out in an imagined pastoral setting: "We are quite capable of editing the diaries ourselves, and I am already picturing in my mind's eye, a little log cabin in the heart of the woods where we shall work the matter out to our own pleasure and profit."[14]

While Frances was bringing her substantial literary editing skills to advancing the publication potential of Flaherty's work, his attention was almost exclusively devoted to editing the film footage he had shot during his third expedition in the Amadjuak Bay area of Baffin Island and his brief exploration of the Belcher Islands. Flaherty offered a brief comment (dated 24 March 1915) about his initial experience with filming, which appeared in the promotional pamphlet "As to the Best Means of Taking Motion Pictures," prepared by the Bell & Howell Company, the manufacturer of the camera that Flaherty had taken with him:

> I have been fully satisfied with it and believe that for our particular work in Baffin's land, where the wooden box cameras warp very quickly, due to intense cold and dry air, your camera is quite the instrument to use. We left here with very little knowledge of motion picture work and had to thresh a good deal of the subject out when we erected our Wintering station in the North, but we have been quite successful and have secured some very interesting film – 14,000 feet. It is hoped that this film may go well toward defraying the expenses of the expedition.[15]

Writing to her sister Charlotte on 13 December 1914, Frances commented on the status of the film and her new husband's preoccupation with it: "Later we took a couple of reels of the moving pictures to project them in a little theater to see if the printing was satisfactory. The printing was not satisfactory. But from the point of view of interest and photography they were certainly unique. It will take from four to five months to get them ready for market. He is wrapped up in them day and night, dreams of nothing else, oblivious of everything, too absorbed to take any notice even of brand new bride, hearth and home!"[16] At the beginning of the New Year, while Robert was giving his attention to the printing and editing of the film, Frances was devoting her skills to constructing a lecture narrative to parallel the showing of the film: "A most interesting morning. Planning the story of the moving pictures for titles and lecture material. Printing expected to begin this Tuesday, " she wrote on 3 January 1915.

By the beginning of February, the printing phase was all but done and the editing was about to begin. Standing as we are at the headwaters of Flaherty's film career as we read the entires in Frances's diary, her assessment of the footage in its still unedited form is noteworthy. She and Robert disagreed over whether the screening of the Baffin Island film should be accompanied by a lecture. This was more than a disagreement over whether a still untitled silent film should have verbal accompaniment. The footage, at this moment, was in search of an audience and if, as Flaherty wished, it was to capture a "general public" audience, then somehow it had to be given "thrill" and "spectacle." Frances argued that the footage itself did not create that engagement; it required the narrative intensity of a human presenter to animate the "existence of the slow-moving Eskimo." Although the film's values were sufficient to meet "scientific, ethnological and geographical" ends, it lacked human drama.[17]

Flaherty's initial rejection of the lecture solution arose partly from his habitual unease with public presentation, a view affirmed by his sister.[18] His hesitancy also arose in large part from the absence of a cinematic solution to the problem he was facing: how "to make the actors in the drama human." That, according to Frances, was "the idea Robert has been working out in his mind."[19] Thus, Flaherty was only partially in search of an audience; he was primarily in search of a story, one that could be used to animate a heightened level of human interest in his footage.

That there was a conflict of definition between the Baffin footage as an ethnographic scientific product and as a dramatic photoplay venture is manifested in a variety of ways. To get others to support their efforts to market the Baffin film, the Flahertys enlisted the aid of, among others, a Mr Kimball, a Buffalo friend, who on 6 March 1915 wrote a letter to Mr Grosvenor of New York City: "This will introduce Mr. R.J. Flaherty of Toronto who has a most interesting series of ethnographic moving pictures of Eskimo life which show the primitive existence of a people in the way they lived before being brought into contact with explorers."[20] Although this is a comment by a second party, it does suggest the ways in which Robert or Frances were trying to interpret the Baffin film to prospective advocates.

The two different visions of the film are even more pronounced in two different drafts which the Flahertys wrote,[21] not as explanatory accompaniments to a screening of the Baffin film but as summary narratives of what they thought it was trying to accomplish. Both drafts have been entitled (by David Flaherty) "Early Account of the Film," and both show Frances's editing hand. One begins: "The keenness of which the people themselves took in the filming work had much to do with the successful results." It then proceeds to describe the escapades, successes, and mishaps that Flaherty experienced while working with the actors as collaborators. It seeks to describe the process as a human interaction.

The other begins: "An interesting part of this experience grew out of the filming work. I had planned to depict an ethnological film of their Eskimo life covering various phases of their native hunting, traveling, domestic life and religion in as much of a narrative form as was possible." The remainder of the narrative uses the cycles of the four seasons to describe just those "phases" in an educational manner, without the intrusion of human characters.

In this bipolar vision of the film and its intents, it is striking how even at this early stage in Flaherty's career, the primary terms of critical discussion about his work overall have been anticipated. Should our primary appreciation of the film be as ethnography? If it is a documentary, what does it "document?" Does the power of the film reside in the force of its human fable, with the ensuing suggestion that Flaherty is less the documentarian than the fabulist, a "poet of the cinema" as his brother David called him? Flaherty scholarship is still tangled in these issues. But here, in 1915, all that Frances could do was draw upon the strength of her sensibilities and urge her husband to seek a literary solution to the dilemma. If the film lacked drama, they should write an accompanying literary narrative to give its actions and characters focal strength.[22]

In the end, Robert and Frances crafted just such a presentation outline, and he accompanied both of the Toronto screenings with a lantern slide lecture. The screenings proved to be a major debut for the Flahertys. An important Toronto mentor appeared in Charles T. Currelly, director of the Royal Ontario Museum of Archaeology, who was responsive to the ethnological value of Flaherty's film – and keen, no doubt, to continue to have the museum be the recipient of the many artifacts which Flaherty, on behalf of Mackenzie, gathered on all of his expeditions. Currelly arranged for the first public screening of the Baffin Island film, which was held at Convocation Hall on the campus of the University of Toronto on Tuesday, 30 March 1915. It was followed by a second screening later that week at the Toronto Arts and Letters Club on Saturday, 3 April. Flaherty's performance as lecturer went badly at Convocation Hall but was much better at the Arts and Letters Club.[23]

These Toronto screenings are important not only for the way they helped Flaherty build a reputation among the elite of Toronto but also because, given the press coverage, we can roughly reconstruct the content of the Baffin film as it was finally edited. The notice in the *Toronto World* informs us:

> The motion pictures series started with the picture of the family rising in the morning in their snow huts. It went on to show them eating their breakfast of raw meat. Following this came the pictures showing the Eskimo building the hut, including the cutting of the snow blocks and the putting of them together. It also showed the oil lamps, the only source of heat and light the Eskimo knows.
>
> Other intensely interesting pictures showed the hunting of seals, the Eskimo finding the seal breathing place in the ice and waiting until the animal appeared and then the actual harpooning. It also showed the pulling out of the large animal and then the cutting up process and the feast that followed the success.
>
> Another interesting feature was the motion pictures of the dances and festive occasions of the Eskimo. The dances, if such they may be called, were not unlike the sun and other dances of the North American Indian.
>
> A decidedly human touch and one that the audience appreciated was the Eskimo flirtation, which was a decidedly rough affair, winding up with the lady in the case wielding a stick rather handily.[24]

Additional details can be gathered from other press notices: the installing of an ice window during the igloo-building sequence, sledging scenes over rough terrain with dogs straining in their traces, the launching of an umiak (flat-bottomed open boat), the spotlight on the "toddler," and general scenes of family life. It is difficult to piece together a narrative from these descriptions, apart from the statement in one notice that "the spectator follows the simple and sometimes adventurous life of Anunglung, his wives and his dogs with ceaseless attention." There is a suggestion that Anunglung and his entourage are the focal characters. We can also catch glimpses of Flaherty's sense of playfulness and his great capacity to get people to unfold before the camera: "The picture of the men, women and children shown were exceptionally strong types, not the low beetling brow or sulky faces one associates with the Eskimo. Happy, sturdy children were pictured with all the curiosity in the world in their eyes as they faced the camera."[25]

What we cannot obtain from these press notices is the actual context from which the film arose, and in this regard the third expedition diaries kept by both Flaherty and Sam Sainsbury are invaluable. In the face of Flaherty's frequent vagueness about the particulars of a shooting on any given day, Sainsbury's entries were at times surprisingly sharp and specific, a fact that reflects the zeal with which he participated in the filming. It is doubtful that Flaherty brought to the Baffin winter camp a plan of what he wished to photograph; therefore the diaries invite us to experience the often impromptu approaches that Flaherty and Sainsbury brought to their camera work. For example, the surprise arrival and departure of Parsons, the HBC man from Cape Dorset, stimulated Flaherty to take a "motion picture of his team going through the rough tidal ice" (1 March 1914).

It is Sainsbury, in fact, who tells us that Flaherty's debut as a motion-picture cameraman in the field occurred in the impromptu circumstances of being present as a group of Eskimo, about to depart for their winter camp, launched umiaks. "At this opportune moment," wrote Sainsbury on 1 October 1913, "the motion picture camera was raised for the first time and several hundred feet of film was taken of the Esquimaux and the way they travel with their families at this particular time."[26] The success of a chance shooting did not prevent Flaherty from following up on a later occasion when there was an opportunity to shoot retakes of the same event, as he did on 5 August 1914: "Secured motion picture of omiak [sic]."

On those occasions when Flaherty attempted a preconceived shooting, a host of contingencies often marred its execution. In a burst of exasperation, Sainsbury complained, "The Governor and myself began to take pictures but before we could get the Esquimaux ready the sun closed in again, and remained unseen for the rest of the day. This is the seventh attempt to take this picture but it had to be canceled every time owing to the dullness of the weather" (18 June 1914). If the vagaries of light plagued them in June when the Arctic daylight period is extended, the short winter light with its intense temperatures caused other reversals of intention, as Sainsbury reported on 21 November 1913:

> On the morning of the 21st started taking moving pictures. When everything was ready, camera was set up at a given distance from the subjects that were to be taken. In order to get a good igloo view with the Esquimaux performing in the background, the camera had to be set up in another place in order to get this picture. While operating the camera some little thing went wrong with the film that could not be fixed in the intense frost but had to be taken into the house, which hindered us from doing any work during the forenoon.

On another occasion Sainsbury simply reported: "Trying to take moving pictures of the Esquimaux but the static spark was too great and the camera had to be put aside until warmer weather."[27]

If the weather did not prove to be compliant, neither did the human actors. Sainsbury alludes to the ill-temper and mutiny of the actors (17 November 1913) and of performers who, despite the most elaborate preparations and "rehearsing" (23 June 1914), could not grasp the basics of theatrical timing: "On the morning of the 25th a series of pictures were taken of the Esquimaux making a fire with pyrites and willowdown, which was specially prepared for the purpose. This picture took quite a lot of film owing to the slowness of the woman operating the [oil] lamp – one needs much patience in taking pictures of the Esquimaux, who are the slowest people under the sun" (25 May 1914). Flaherty's skill at using the right balance of cajolery and incentive ususally succeeded in obtaining cooperation from his actors, as he was able to do for the stream-fording episode of 4 July 1914.

If people, on occasion, prove to be slow or resistant, the animals moved like furtive lightning. All of Flaherty's designs to get footage of the Eskimo hunting eider duck were futile, as he noted on 12 July: "Found that the duck are much too scary for pictures." On another occasion, Sainsbury described preparing for a dog-feeding scene. They built a snow platform upon which to mount the camera so that they could shoot, in raised safety, the frantic scene of snapping dogs. But as they were doing so, other dogs plundered the provisions tent (24 May 1914).

While the diaries reveal many of the exigencies that Flaherty encountered in attempting to film both impromptu and preplanned scenes, these journals also persuade us that it is the igloo – its construction and the social life that occurs within it – that is the centerpiece of Flaherty's Baffin Island film. The igloo, and the ritual of its construction, is emblematic of Eskimo culture itself. It is more than shelter. For Flaherty, it signified that element of human culture that defines a group's attachment to craftsmanship – a measure of culture that was to prevail throughout his career as a filmmaker. He celebrated this ethos of masterful skills cinematically in many forms: in the shaping of clay in *The Pottery Maker*; the making of tatoos on the human body in *Moana*; the blowing of glass in *Industrial Britain*; the building of an earth garden in *Man of Aran*; the plowing of fields in *The Land*; and the sinking of oil pipes in *Louisiana Story*. But it was the experience of the North that shaped the Flaherty ethos of the snow house as the archetype of human craftsmanship.

Thus, we find many entries by both Flaherty and Sainsbury that describe their efforts to build and utilize the snow house as a film setting. During the months of October and November, Sainsbury mentioned repeated efforts to build an igloo sufficient in size, 22 ft in diameter, to serve as a performance stage for "the natives who were acting on the raised floor of the igloo, in the first interior scene" (31 October 1913). The igloo settings became even more elaborate as efforts were made to build adjoining domes so that the camera could be provided with an adequate shooting field: "On the morning of the 15th we started again to build a large igloo for moving pictures. The igloo took quite a long time to build owing to the softness of the snow. After that one was finished another one was started. The second being attached to the large one enabled the Governor, who was operating the camera, to get sufficient space from the background to the outer dome" (15 November 1913). To improve the lighting, ice windows were installed in the shooting studio.

When the severity of winter weather subsided in early spring, Flaherty returned to the igloo setting, as he reported in March: "Tried out the new studio igloo on 13th with motion, unlimited patience picture machine. Staged an interior igloo scene with Yew's wife and child and Annyow." A week later, on 20 March, he noted: "Successful in having a very large igloo constructed which measures 15′ in diameter and 12′ high, a record for size. It stood only a week however." Before the spring weather became "too heavy," he "secured 800′ interior igloo, subject of Allego fire making" (26 March 1914). By the end of the month, the igloo had dissolved and outdoor shooting predominated. By 28 May, Sainsbury was reporting that nearly eleven families were in camp "for moving picture purposes," and Flaherty was soon giving attention to such scenes as seal hunting and stream fording.

In this remarkable burst of filmmaking we should not loose sight of the equal zeal with which Flaherty pursued his photographic endeavors. He continued as in the past to make the stills camera a tool of his scientific and geological interests. We can also observe that many of the subjects and activities that had received Flaherty's still photography attention in the first two expeditions had now migrated to the domain of motion-picture subjects. This shift is evident in the way that while the movie camera studied action, the still camera studied character. The third expedition diary reveals Flaherty's intense interest in portrait photography of the kind he had experimented with in the 1911 album. Later, when he and Frances had the opportunity in New York to compare his Eskimo photographs with those of Native Americans by Edward Curtis, Frances observed that, by comparison, Robert's revealed "interest centering in personality independent of race, costume or detail of any kind."[28]

Because of the semi-permanent structures Flaherty had built at Amadjuak and because of the duration of his stay on Baffin Island, he had been able to create a working studio environment for taking portrait photographs. Access to such studio-like conditions had led Flaherty to recruit, wholesale, sitters for his portrait work: "I had my little studio tent erected near to the house and plunged into the portraits of some of the Eskimo who were retained for that purpose" (20 September 1913).

Dorothy Harley Eber's interviews with Baffin Island residents led to this striking piece of eyewitness recollection by Simonie:

> They had to take them inside, in Flaherty's house. I don't recall them having flashes with the camera. They used kerosine lanterns, and I remember three lanterns being placed in special places on the wall. I remember a camera with a cloth that had to go over the head. Maybe that was because they had to prevent any light coming to the photographer's vision. It took a long time before the photographer could actually take a picture. They couldn't take a picture of a person as soon as he sat down. They had to relax him first. The man sitting on the chair had to be very relaxed ... If he was liable to move at all they couldn't take his picture. That's what I remember.[29]

These studio-type photographs reveal Flaherty reaching for a more pictorial style, a style that uses side lighting and softer focus to portray a more evocative personality in his sitters. In his entry of 12 June 1914, Flaherty even used the term "camera studies" to describe his photographic activities. (My use of the plural here is simply incidental, since we begin to observe that Flaherty is photographing his subjects in multiple exposures, sometimes taking as many as five different renderings of the same sitter.) While the third expedition brought Flaherty to the threshold of his career as a filmmaker, as a portrait photographer he was at the apex of his powers – as is evident from the predominant presence of his Baffin Island portraits in the 1979–80 Vancouver exhibition. In 1915, the year in which Flaherty's filmwork received its first showing, his photographs also received their first public exhibition; they were shown at the Toronto Arts and Letters Club in January.[30]

When Flaherty brought the Baffin film to its first public audience at Convocation Hall in Toronto, he would have been be possessed by both fears and expectations, aware that more than two years of frustrating, risky experimentation was now going to be scrutinized by an audience largely unaware of the difficult context in which the film had been made. Although there is a tendency – even in Flaherty himself – to romance the North, the technical challenges of shooting and developing nitrate film in 1915 in the hairy, freezing universe of the Arctic were enormous. In the two Toronto screenings there were some who were bored, some riveted, but the person whose opinion Flaherty knew would be crucial to the prospects of a fourth expedition – and his future as an explorer and film-maker – was William Mackenzie. The presence of journalists at both screenings benefits us in providing the following vignette by Augustus Bridle of the *Canadian Courier*:

> On a winter evening in 1915 Sir William Mackenzie went to an art club in Toronto to behold a set of moving pictures. It was the first film drama he had ever seen. The human figures on the screen enacted the struggle for existence in the most primitive form remaining on the continent of North America. They drove frantic dogs drawing walrus-laden sleds; sat by the hour over lone holes in the ice waiting for seals; rolled themselves to sleep in deerskins bags, and when they got up gnawed raw meat and went on long journeys. All these things the head of the greatest railway-building organization in the world watched with uncommon sympathetic interest and an occasional enormous yawn.[31]

We can forgive Sir William the yawn as the fatigue of a harried man who, in the year he yawned, opened the Canadian Northern Railway from Quebec City to Vancouver. As a major CNR shareholder, he and the railroad were both on the threshold of insolvency, a fiscal crisis that was eventually averted by 1917 legislation that nationalized the CNR. An arbitration hearing determined that the value of Mackenzie's CNR shares fell short of outstanding notes to the Canadian Bank of Commerce. Mackenzie was broke.

Although by 1915 Mackenzie was shrewd enough to realize that his dream of a transportation empire was unraveling, some "uncommon sympathetic interest" in Flaherty endured, and despite Frances's frequent impatience with Mackenzie's hard-bargaining style and her devoted wish to be "free of Sir Bill" and "this slavery to salary," she had to report on 21 July, "Sir William gave Robert $1,000 out of his own pocket for his photographic outfit. He seems keen about the moving pictures on Robert's account."

Mackenzie's decision to refinance Flaherty gave him a reprieve at a time when the war was beginning to drain the resources, both fiscal and emotional, of Canadians. The United States was not yet "over there," and it was to the movie industry centered in New York that Frances and Robert turned their energies in the spring of 1915. As she so energetically depicts in her diaries, they made many efforts, shuttling between Toronto, Buffalo, and New York, to gain public recognition for the Baffin Island film and to find a distributor. Frances reports of screenings arranged on several occasions in New York (13 April 1915, 17 and 18 January 1916) and in New Haven (30 January 1916), but it was certainly the screening in New York on 13 April 1915 that proved to be the high point of the Flahertys' efforts to validate the worth of the Baffin film. The screening, "before an audience of experts," had been arranged by Edward Curtis, the photographer whose portraits of North American Indians the Flahertys had seen and compared with Robert's Eskimo portraits the week before the screening. Curtis, too, had recently completed a film, *In the Land of the War Canoes*, which he had made in the Pacific Northwest, and like Flaherty he was seeking wider distribution. It is hard not to imagine that Curtis saw the screening as a comparative performance, his film matched against Flaherty's, with the expectation that the striking ceremonies of the Kwakiutl would eclipse the "slow moving" Eskimo. As Frances reported,

> Mr. Curtis showed his own film first, all taken in and about our old hunting ground, that wonderful west coast of Vancouver island, vivid scenes that were like flashes of memory; and our old friends, Sutor's kinsmen, the Salish Indians, were the actors. It was a story of the customs and ceremonies of the old head-hunting days a generation past, with a thread of romance running through it ... By the time our pictures were called Robert and I were prepared to see them fall perfectly flat on tired eyes and brains. They didn't; everybody asked questions galore; and though as Robert said, it was an acid test for them, putting them with all their crudities in juxtaposition with an elaborately toned and perfected film such as Curtis's, it was a curiously happy one, in all their crudity they stood out human, real, convincing and big in contrast to the spectacular artificiality of Curtis's, wonderful as they were as a mere spectacle. As Mr. Curtis said of our pictures, there was an "intimacy" about them; but he also criticized them as "monotonous."[32]

Frances's response to Curtis's reaction is ambivalent. She was prepared to defend Flaherty's film on the strength of its "human appeal," an appeal which she believed would capture the attention of the general audience. But Curtis was a gentleman, not just a rival: "He has been lunching with me here at the hotel, been talking to us like a father, with such infinite tact, too, giving us all the benefit of his experience in the moving picture world;

we swept it all, sweeping away lots of illusions in doing so, and finally getting down to what it would be best to do with our film."[33]

The Flahertys eventually followed the advice of Curtis and others who suggested that Flaherty obtain more footage on his next expedition – the kind "with the real human punch in it" – and that the new footage and the Baffin film evolve into a more sharply realized product. The realization of film as commodity was an additional piece of the Flahertys' education. So was the information they also received from Curtis and others: "The market at present is chaos, demoralized by over speculation and the war; the whole business is a new headlong phenomenal thing, which nobody really knows anything about."[34]

It took Frances about ten months to process her insights into the feasibility of marketing the Baffin film. On 22 February 1916, when Flaherty was in the Belcher Islands, she told him (in the last of the diary entries in this chapter): "I have decided beyond doubt now in my own mind that it would hurt your next film to have this one put out now. I regret nothing of the experience either in its main or its side issues, because in the main I have acquired a few useful ideas and a certain philosophical point of view that may apply to the situation in the fall when you come down."

Among its many points of light, Frances's diary is a portrait of persistence – hers as well as her husband's. As a couple, the patrician Frances and the viking Robert formed an impressive duo as they attempted to power their way into the offices, studios, galleries, and meeting halls of such luminaries as Franz Boas, Alfred Stieglitz, Edward Curtis, Felix Adler, and others who in their fashion were shaping modernity in such fields as education, photography, anthropology, finance, and movie making. The Flahertys were a force not easily diverted, and although they fell short of their goal of distributing their film, they themselves are a portrait of a family determinedly in search of an artistic destiny – but one that would have to wait another cycle.

As it happened, the persistence did weaken, though not in the artistic domain. Although, in view of Flaherty's absence, Frances accepted the postponement of their efforts, she was quite prepared to regroup her energies on his return and renew the quest for literary, photographic, and cinematic accomplishment, even by going with him to the Arctic. But during the spring of 1915, when the likelihood of there being a fourth expedition seemed more certain, she began to have second thoughts about accompanying Flaherty to the Belcher Islands as she had originally intended. In a letter of 20 June 1915 to her Bryn Mawr friend, Margaret Thurston, she wrote: "We are not at all sure if it will be wise for me to winter with him or even to go on the ship from Moose [to Charlton Island]. I haven't given up the idea entirely by any means and at the last minute I may decide to go with him."[35] She then told her friend of a "compromise" plan: Frances would accompany Flaherty by canoe from Cochrane to Moose Factory, where she would remain until he departed for the Belchers on the *Laddie*. But a month later, on 18 July, she wrote in her diary about preparations "with a view to the possibility of my wintering with him in the islands, and talking about it." In this same entry she announced that she was in the first term of her pregnancy: "If I can't winter with him, it would be the one ample compensation."

The final compromise involved Frances traveling by ship from Moose Factory to Charlton Island, accompanied by Margaret Thurston as well as Flaherty's brother David and his father. After Flaherty's departure for the Belchers, they were to await the arrival of the HBC supply ship and take it outbound through the Hudson Strait to Newfoundland. We can only speculate whether Frances would have persisted – or her husband relented – in her wish to accompany Flaherty if she had not become pregnant. Flaherty's resistance to her participation was grounded in reasons that included but went beyond those of her pregnancy. On her outbound journey Frances reflected on what his motivations might have been: "I have felt enough of the country to know both its fascination and its fear. Neither are describable or explicable. One must come and see for oneself, in the face and fashion of the people, the inexorable toll that the country, the cold, the desolation, solitude and isolation, exacts of those who brace and stay them. It was fear of this influence that made Bob refuse so long to listen to any proposal of my going with him – he was afraid for me."[36]

A month after returning from the Arctic, Frances underwent surgery on her hand. Brooding, as a pianist, on a potential disability to her finger, dosed with codeine, fearful of losing her child, and profoundly lonely for her absent husband, she was still capable, in the fashion of a life review, of reflecting on the outcome of the plans she had crystallized a year ago as she walked, after music practice, along Riverside Drive in New York City. Writing in her diary on 26 October 1915, she noted that her plans, which "have come true," had been to marry, "with Bob as the instrument of my desires, such a nice healthy, interesting, convenient 'tool'":

And so we lived together – and something happened, and swallowed up all that pretty little scheme of mine – new desires, new creeds – I would have no life but his, risk everything, endure everything, give everything for the sake of that perfect sharing of life in all things great and small. We were so passionate toward each other, and with all the superficial differences between us in breeding, education, disposition and temperament, fundamentally we believed and loved and desired life of the same things. Between us were the makings of a rare relationship, a wonderful passionate partnership. I would throw myself and all I possessed, my mental equipment and my heart's enthusiasm, into his work and its fulfillment; his the conception, mine the detail; his the sowing, mine the garnering; surely as my nature and gifts were complementary to his, I could be a real and valuable partner. All my heart was in this new ideal; the winter at the Belchers would be the first step, the definite beginning.

Then fate stepped in; and even before we started out on the great adventure, I knew that I must at the threshold turn back. Shall you ever forget that night, my Dear, on the deck of the *Laddie*, with the sky above and the water beneath like the hollow of a great star-studded bowl about us, how I yearned clinging to you and the adventure, how helpless and afraid I was and incoherent against fate, because I saw as you couldn't, how it was a crisis in the direction of our lives and the quality of our relation – that it was too truly a parting of the ways. I know how I, coming back, would inevitably drift back into the channel of my old individual life. For you, living alone again crudely and carelessly would only deepen those differences between us, differences that with a passionate consecration to one and the same life and work could count for so little, but that on the lesser more conventional plane of a less absorbing bond would count for only too much.

The passage has the force of an imploded ideal in which the loss of not accompanying Flaherty to the Belchers challenged her vision of a partnership. In less than a year of marriage, Frances had exerted great surges of will to overcome these "superficial differences" – but they proved to be neither superficial nor easily dissolved through a passionate commitment to a partner's creative life. The result was the realization that, as an explorer, Flaherty had another life, one Frances had not included in her equation as she took her afternoon walk along Riverside Drive. It was a life that could be "crude," she realized, one that would include relations with Eskimo women. This proved to be the case, since during Flaherty's stay on the Belchers he fathered a son with an Inuit woman. This relationship is affirmed by contemporary Inuit in the French Canadian film *Nanook Revisited* (1998). As the outsider to this other life, and as a secret sharer about this unspoken Inuit family, Frances could feel herself trapped within this all too inclusive devotion to an ideal that contained less substance than can be constructed in an afternoon's reverie.

In a lifetime of trying to sustain this partnership, Frances was to demonstrate great power to rebound, to re-engage. Thus, as her diaries moved ahead into 1916, she quickly reasserted the partner role that she had perhaps inconclusively defined for herself in her marriage to the charming but now absent Robert Flaherty.

Diary of Frances Hubbard Flaherty 17 December 1914 – 22 February 1916

Thursday, 17 December 1914[37] It is an anxious time. Today may decide many things. Sir William returns from Ottawa and Robert will know whether or not he intends "to come there"![38]

We were talking this morning about the land discovery, its importance to Mackenzie, Mann & Co., to other interests and to the country in general. Its importance from the geological point of view lies in the fact that the formation is the extension of the iron-ore bearing rock of Minnesota and Michigan. It is, moreover, the only man-sized iron ore proposition so far discovered in Canada.

Besides the Canadian National Railroad with its terminal at York Factory on Hudson's Bay, a Sea Company proposes to run a line from Cochrane to a terminal on James Bay. Robert has a letter to the Premier of Ontario in the interest of this Company. The question is whether Sir William will, or has been able to put through a deal at Ottawa excluding other interests from the territory in question. It was Robert's opinion this morning that the Government could grant him rights over only so much of the land as had actually been seen, i.e., seven miles of seaboard, the merest fraction of the whole. If this is so, and Sir William does not come through, Robert can take his information to the other interests and still hope to continue his exploration of the islands.

The whole crux of the matter of sticking by Sir William lies with the moving pictures. What they have meant in work can only be realized by reading in Robert's diary the story of his winter at Amadjuak Bay where they were taken. They are unique in subject and in treatment, and from the point of view of photography, I judge their excellence by the opinion of those in the business and by the few feet I myself have seen. We hope that they will attract a great deal of attention, be widely shown, and gain recognition for Robert as an explorer, as an artist and interpreter of the Eskimo people, and consequently bring him greater opportunity.

So the matter stands; and meantime, our exchequer is down to a few dollars!! The time is critical indeed.

Friday, 18 December Last night Robert brought out the last consignment of prints of his Eskimo portraits. Two of them at least and perhaps three will be included in the final collection of the ten or twelve best. We have been talking about what would be best to do with them. Wouldn't the National Geographic Magazine take them together with other pictures of Arctic scenery, Enooesweetok's drawings and the ivory carvings, and feature them in a number devoted to the Eskimo? I hope Robert will open up a correspondence with them immediately. It would help advertise the moving pictures.

The proof sheets of the drawings look very promising. I should have preferred to have the legend at the bottom of each page written in by hand rather than printed, but it is too late now. Now, I want Robert to write a preface to go with them; they need to be interpreted in detail, and the nicest form of interpretation it seems to me, would be a little account by Robert of his personal relations with the artist, his experiences with the people, incidents, etc., explanatory of their life and customs.[39]

Monday, 21 December Mr Alan Sullivan and the book.[40] Robert has come home much "enthused" Saturday afternoon announcing that Alan Sullivan had spoken to him at lunch that noon at the Arts and Letters Club about working up his diaries and pictures and all the geographical and geological data of his arctic expeditions into a book, a book on the order of the old books of travel, such as Sir John Franklin's Voyages, etc.[41] Mr Sullivan was prepared to devote all his time to it for a year to come. Robert was impatient when I did not immediately fall in with his enthusiasm; but I thought perhaps, I smelled a rat. I am jealous of those diaries. Robert would be just as careless and prodigal about throwing away or giving away his work and all the credit for it, as he is about everything else. I seemed to see Mr Alan Sullivan walking off with all Robert's wealth of material, putting upon it the stamp of his own literary style, floating it on his own literary reputation and getting all the credit and applause. I had read some of his short stories and poems and found them undeniably clever and well written. Eskimo, Indian trapping and trading stories with just the sort of local color that Robert's diaries are full of, with the same feeling for elemental natural things. Later, when we discussed the matter with Olive and Louise, I think they were inclined to agree with me until Robert explained that the diaries were to be used simply as a reference and one source of material together with many other reference books on the subjects that the book was to cover, and that the book would be written entirely by Mr Sullivan, probably in collaboration with others who would be authorities on these special subjects.

Very well then, that didn't interfere with my plan for the diaries. For I intend that they shall be printed exactly as they are, even if only for private circulation. I was most curious to meet Mr Sullivan. We were invited to tea there yesterday afternoon. We found Wychwood Park at dusk, quite the most attractive wooded Park in Toronto I have yet seen. We were hesitating, wondering which house to try, when a head poked out of a window above us spoke, "How do you do, Mr Flaherty. Wait, I'll come down." It was Mr Currelly, Curator of the Museum.[42] He had us come in through a dark passage into a most interesting high studded room, all wood paneled, with a great open fire. After introducing his wife, he immediately launched on the subject of the moving pictures, and his plan to show them at Convocation Hall under the auspices of the University and the Archeological Institute of America, with a wide circulation of invitations and advertising, something that would give them a good "send off." Mr Currelly, by the way, is a dear. He directed us "over land and sea" (just next door) to the Sullivans' house, a large square grey stone affair that might pass for a latter-day French Chateau. We were going up the steps when a voice called behind us "Bonjour, Bonjour." After tea, Mr Sullivan took Robert to his study, while Mrs Sullivan entertained me until supper time. I had come with the express intention of finding out Mr Sullivan's real idea about the book, but the opportunity did not come until after supper, when he afforded it himself by asking me my opinion. I asked a leading question, and sure enough, it transpired even as I had thought. The book is to come out in diary form, Robert's own diary, culled, cut and amplified, and illustrated with his photographs. Mr Sullivan thought it would make a volume of about 120,000 words, or twice the size of an ordinary novel. Said Mr Sullivan, "I shall simply be taking your husband's material and editing it." The time of bringing it out was then discussed; whether to wait a year from this next Spring in order to include the further material that Robert's next expedition to the Belcher Islands will undoubtedly bring forth. How interesting to wind the book up with an additional chapter on a hitherto unknown tribe of Esquimaux, now visited for the first time, a tribe all dressed in feathers.

Well, the whole scheme seemed to me quite ideal, and I began to look upon Mr Sullivan as an instrument sent by Providence to do this work, so perfectly qualified is he in every way to carry it through; for not only has he the dramatic sense and imagination and background of north-country story and history that he has absorbed for his own writings, but, being by profession a mining man, he can as well appreciate the purely scientific value of the material. Besides, his standing with Harper's, who have been taking his work regularly, will be a help when it comes to finding a publisher. So we left the house mutually enthusiastic, and walked home through the night much pleased with ourselves, and the universe in general.

I now know, with the exception of "Stewart Gushue," all the Amadjuak Bay family. Mr LaDuke, "Gene" of the diaries, just arrived from "Moose," where he was left in charge of putting the *Laddie* into winter quarters, and Robert brought him up to dinner. His man, with a twelve-dog team, is waiting at Cochrane to take him back to "Moose" as soon as the plans and outfit for next Summer's trip to the Belchers shall be completed. He is a dusky, crude, shy, inexpressive individual, Robert's antithesis in every particular. Robert asked me afterwards what I thought of him. Said I, "Mr LaDuke has a head on his shoulders" but did not add that I now understood several things that had been puzzling me!

Tuesday, 22 December More serious discussion over the financial situation, and more light on Sir William as a general crook and side stepper, the kind that invites a credulous creditor to dinner, and sails for Europe before tea. So are the mighty fallen, and Robert's hero, "the Cecil Rhodes of Canada," found stuffed with saw-dust. It seems that even the "milk-fed, home grown protege" of the Company can't collect his dues and predicts the downfall of the Company within six months. But it is doubtful if the government could afford to let the Canadian Northern Railroad fail; the Bank of Commerce, the fourth largest banking concern in the world would tumble with it. So strongly is Sir William entrenched. I have no idea whatever that Robert will get his salary, not having a scrap of paper to prove anything, nothing but promises. His debts already amount to approximately $4000. Pockets turned inside out to find even $75 to pay on a note for $240 due today.

"Little Paul Hahn" came to dinner last night. Little Paul Hahn has already paid me two morning calls, in regard to my piano, and taking it from me in part exchange for the beautiful little Mason and Hamlin we are renting from him. The first time he came he told me his life history. I hadn't asked him to take off his coat, expecting the conventional brief business call. The second time I began with the familiarity of the coat, and we spent the morning mending and talking music. So he came to dinner and brought his cello. After dinner, we turned out all the lights, and by the light of the fire, Paul played to us. It was not the pure delight that it sounds ideally; as Robert says, Paul is "gusty," and again, gusty. The interesting part of the evening came later when we began with some simple trios and trio arrangements, and worked up to the, to OUR Beethoven B flat. It was a joy to have Paul struggle with Robert over the time, and make him stick to it, repeating the same passage again and again. It did my heart good. Paul left at 10:30, and we played and talked until after one.

Wednesday, 23 December Cleaning day for the sitting room yesterday. I escaped early in the afternoon, and at 4:30 met Robert at the office. We went first to see about frames for the ice and snow pictures, to try to decide on a standard frame for all of them. It is a much more particular business than might seem, as we have learned from having already made several mistakes.

Then came my long promised visit to the Arts and Letters Club. Half a dozen members were gathered before the broad open fireplace. We looked at the exhibition of pictures on either side of the entrance-wall, landscape sketches by Beatty, typical Canadian scenery, very well done. I wanted one badly, to own it. Other Art members of the Club were represented on the walls. I took the occasion to become acquainted with Messrs. Jackson and MacDonald who were hung in the little room where we had tea.[43] Robert brought in Mr. Bridle, and we talked and listened to someone playing the piano in the big room. The club is a lunching and lounging place for its members who are exclusively the votaries of the arts, letters and science. I heard the fire-side group talking about Nietzsche and German Militarism as I passed. The fireplace is the magnetic center of the room, a high old room that used to be the Court of Assizes, a dusty gray, hung with large paintings; plain black oak tables and chairs occupy the floor space, at the other end is a raised stage. I was an intruder in the club, and quite irregular, being a mere woman. This is my first coming up against the Englishman's attitude toward his mother and wife and sister. It makes my blood boil.

On the whole, I was very favorably impressed with the general atmosphere of the club (it reminded me more than anything, of some of the old Halls at Oxford) and its artistic standards. Yet Robert says he never feels quite at home there, seems to detect a trace of artificiality and pose. I can understand it perhaps from the taint of the modern

French influence I found in Jackson's canvas. Mr Beatty, on the other hand, has kept all the freshness of his point of view. He used to be on the Toronto Fire Force, Robert tells me, self educated with some European study.

Had dinner at the "Queens" with Mr Wiley. Mr Wiley is the man who told Mr Currelly, who told me, who, etc., etc., to the end of the fateful story.

Finished off the evening with a good show.

Friday, Christmas morning A glorious morning, clear, cold, sparkling, below zero. I pulled the sitting room curtains, and the morning star shown in out of a sea of purple above the bare trees and the blue-greens and green-yellows of the dawn behind them. Ran up again to call Robert. The furnace man came creaking in rubbing his ears as we watched at the window.

What do you suppose Robert brought home to me last night? My picture, Mr Beatty's picture, the one I wanted, and have been wanting more ever since. And now that it is here, I love it more, the more I look at it; the snow slope in purple shadow, the sunlight that grows more intense, and the four patches of the sky that grow deeper the further away you look at it. To my mind it is a little gem. You see in the morning, we had decided to make picture buying a part of our program, just the things we like regardless of the artist's name, school or reputation, trusting for guidance entirely to our own taste. Robert's particular ambition, of course, is a collection of good photos. He could hardly wait to show me some portraits of Coburn's at Tyrell's. We bought five of them, Masefield, Shaw, Rodin, Bennett and Chesterton, respectively in order of excellence.[44] The Masefield is in a class by itself, with Whistler's portrait of his mother. They were delivered late last night. We had gone to bed overcome with sleep very early, but through our dreams ran the undercurrent of a continuous procession of delivery wagons outside. Suddenly, Robert shot out of bed to the window and downstairs, and returned bearing the prized package of photos. We arranged them on the bureau where we could view them from the bed together with three of our own "masterpieces," and studied and ruminated, and were well pleased. By that time, the first hour of Christmas day, we were so wide awake that we slipped on some clothes, and came down to try over a Bach and Schumann trio that Paul had left with us in the afternoon, together with a beautiful blue moth from his collection.

Monday, 28 December "The Remarkable History of the Hudson's Bay Company" is circling through my head to the tune of a Beethoven Sonata. I'm thinking of the trouble Groseilliers and Radisson had to find any one to finance their expedition to Hudson's Bay in the year 1664; I'm thinking that in this year of our Lord, 1915, it may be much the same story with one R.J.F.[45]. Robert saw Mr. E of the "other interests" yesterday. Mr. E could not give definite promise of sending Robert out this year until he had consulted his colleagues. Agreed that Robert should see Premier Hearst today.[46]

Everybody broke. Mr LaDuke housed all Christmas day for lack of funds, and Robert had to borrow five dollars from his father to feed him today, the Company, meanwhile, owing him $2,500. Of the salary Robert received before Xmas, he distributed half of it among the office force out of Xmas charity. Whatever money Robert may ever have will be everybody's money. He just naturally feels that way about it, more simply than a child, more rightly than the philosopher-economist of a hundred years; for if all the world felt as he does, there would be nor poverty nor war nor lawyers; we would live like the Esquimaux with whom all the glory is to the successful hunter, and all the spoils to all the people even to the least. Yet half the world and more, steeped in its petty morality, would point its finger at Robert and call him an improvident fool.

This is my idea of the war: it is the natural, inevitable result of the mad desire of all the nations, the desire for material wealth. We are destroying ourselves through this false ideal. Tolstoy felt it coming; he was like a St. John crying in the wilderness: "Divest yourselves, give up your wealth or it will destroy you. Can't you see where the world is going, the brink toward which you are rushing?" Did he not prophecy the war, and also that a man should come "out of the north" to save? It is a world crisis, a moral and ethical crisis, greater than we can realize. The world is mind-sick from thinking false and evil thoughts. A great healer must come, a savior, a master-mind. Thank heaven that my own mind was not so far gone but that it is already a little clearer and lighter through contact with Robert's and my one idea for my children from my first knowledge of their coming will be to make them men and women of the New World, the New Morality.

Wednesday, 30 December Very restless this morning. Looked over some thirteen volumes of the *Geographical Journal* (Royal Geographical

Society), picking out the articles on arctic and antarctic exploration: full accounts of the Scott Expedition; Dr Mawson's report of his work; notices of the Stefansson Expedition as they came out to the final rescue of the survivors of the ill-fated *Karluk*; and the plans for the Shackleton Trans-Antarctic Expedition which left this fall.[47] All with a view, of course, to getting a perspective on Robert's work, its relative importance, and its original and unique features. By the time I had gotten through half the volumes, the whole story of Arctic and Antarctic exploration seemed to be one continuous din of hardship, starvation, freezing, death. It got on my nerves. "ALL BUNK" Robert calls it, having no patience whatever with "heroics." Says that such hardship is entirely unnecessary, due only to ignorance, and should be considered a disgrace to the commander of the expedition. Certainly in comparison to the tales of these others, Robert's is a smiling, happy tale of comfort and snug quarters, of delight in the beauty of the country, and of kindly sympathetic association with a kindly primitive people; and yet with no lack of exploits that are noteworthy in themselves, as, for instance, the sledging trip across Ungava – 35 days alone with two Eskimo without any intermediate base of supplies, and the summer trip back again by canoe, when often all their hope of subsistence depended on the rope that held the canoe tracking through rapids of rivers never traveled before. Once, waiting for the Eskimos with the canoe he thought to see them carried over a fall, leaving him alone in a thousand miles of barren wilderness. As for the land discovery, that certainly is as romantic, if not more so, as one more remote, from a geological point of view no less interesting, and economically far more important.

I have been working out suggestions for a paper for Robert to write for the *Journal*; my heart is set on it.

Subject: Discovery of an unknown land area in Hudson's Bay.

A. The Idea.

Traditions and reports of the Belcher Islands that made Robert think there was something there to be discovered. Maturing of the plan to explore them.

B. The Attempt.

Second expedition: sledging and canoe trips across northern Ungava, alone with two Eskimos. Hazards of the trip.

Third expedition: Wintering in Baffin Land. Attempted exploration of the unknown coast of Foxe Land. Mica, graphite, and dichorite.

C. Success.

The stranding of the *Laddie*. Exploration of the coast. Old Eskimo map and official map compared. Sir George Simpson's Diary.

D. Results.
   Geological; ore-tests.
   Economic.

The paper all through would be a manifest of Robert's imagination, versatility and daring, and in spirit and point of view would be a welcome contrast to the general run of Arctic literature.

Thursday, 31 December Good Heavens! Listen to this: Mr Annesley, Sir William's secretary, showed Robert a letter today from the Canadian Camp, an explorer's club, enclosing copy of a letter to "Commander" Bartlett of Sir William Mackenzie's Expedition to Hudson's Bay, expressing great interest in the wonderful land discovery about which Captain Bartlett had written them, and asking if it would not be possible for him to prepare a lecture with moving pictures to be given at the meeting of the club to be held at the Hotel Astor on Feb. 23rd, holding out as inducement the opportunity of meeting several hundred of the best known explorers of the world. So Bartlett, skipper of Robert's ship, the *Laddie*, and a poor sort of skipper at that, had not only given out the discovery, breaking faith with Robert, but had given it out under his own name as commander of the expedition! You see, the name carries a certain reputation with it through his cousin "Captain Bob" Bartlett of Peary fame.[48] Bartlett is evidently making capital of the discovery on his own account hoping to get an expedition to the islands next summer. Robert thinks he is probably also negotiating with the government.

Sunday, 3 January 1915 A most interesting morning. Planning the story of the moving pictures for titles and lecture material. Printing expected to begin Tuesday. Robert decided some time ago to take the printing away from the Conness Till Co. and do it himself. Accordingly sent to Chicago for printing outfit, which has been lying at the customs ever since for lack of funds to clear it. Sir Donald [Mann] has finally come to the rescue. A young Dutchman, ex-employee of the Conness Till Co., has offered to do all the printing in return for the use of the plant for some work he is doing on his own account. Ridpath of Potters is providing the studio conveniently near the office. Robert's portraits to be hung at the Arts and Letters Club this week. Telegram from Bartlett this morning, replying to protest from Robert, to the effect, "Where do I come in? and what about my little bill?"

Thursday, 7 January Tottie dear, I wish you were here with me now. The wind is blowing outside a terrific gale, it is dull and wet and chilly. The house is cheerless, sitting room all torn up waiting for the chimney sweep, and I skeptical as to his coming after all. I am whiling away the morning in the dining room, busy correcting the typed copy of Robert's last diary which came in yesterday, and planning my own plan about it. From it I turned to Stefansson's book, and came across this passage which you will be interested to hear apropos of the present we sent you yesterday (we've been waiting for the wherewithal to pay for the express!). "This wolf," – speaking of the white wolf he had killed – "was not only fat and excellent eating, but its skin was of great value, either scientifically or commercially; scientifically because the animal is rare, and commercially because a wolf skin of this type can be sold for as much as twelve fox skins, which being translated into dollars at the prices quoted in 1912 would mean from 100 to 120 dollars for each wolf-skin."[49]

Tottie, why don't you come to Buffalo? I could have walked that far! Why didn't I know of this back-ache before. Write me. You know there are some times when there is no one in the world I want but you, and this is one of the times. A big kiss for the Cabot book and the *Atlantic*.[50] Robert devours current literature, mostly between the hours of 11.30 p.m., and 1 a.m., and I really rather prefer the flavor of it second-hand as I get it from him.

This is just a stupid letter, dear, but you don't mind if I just ramble on about anything that comes into my head. I am getting fairly expert with this machine, and shall probably prefer to use it exclusively in time, – it saves lots of hand cramp. Robert's chief aversion to literary effort is the actual writing; he talks better, remarkably well, in fact, so I am preparing to be his literary secretary, to take his dictation and then type it. We have outlined two "efforts," one for the lecture to accompany the moving pictures, the other for an article for the Royal Geographical Society.

Dear, I suppose I do seem terribly egotistically absorbed. I know I have a terrible egotistical streak in me, and it is such a relief to have it have a legitimate outlet about somebody else's personality. I am willing to slave to the bone for it, i.e. for my ambition for him. I think it is not a bad thing that we can't do the thousand and one things we'd be wanting to do if we had money, it helps to concentrate on the really vital things. We are doing with one presentable table cloth, but not counting cost in the printing and framing of the photographs, engraving of Eskimo drawings, typing of diaries, and generally developing and bringing out the results of his work in the best form possible. All this, too, forms a solid anchor for all the adjusting necessary during the first year living together, no matter how congenial two people may be. I sometimes think he is selfish, and he sometimes thinks I am, when we don't agree about this or that detail. Of course most of our differences have to do with finances. Thank heaven that in the large our tastes and ideals and ambitions are so identical that there can be no question of difference, but in the lesser things Robert has never thought of denying himself anything he happened to think of wanting in any quantity it pleased him to want it, without a thought of the cost, either before or after consumption; and his wants are the wants of a physically sensuously luxurious person. With an identical appreciation of real values, still he is a sensualist and I am the ascetic. And sometimes I must admit that when I see perfectly good money going into his overly fat and capacious "tummy" in the form of the most expensive candy and drinkables on the market, I am inclined to be somewhat disgusted. Motor cars and front-row theatre tickets are another bone of contention. As a matter of fact I suppose we are both extremists.

There is the loveliest bowl of flowers on the side-board, snapdragon. I wish I could send them to you just so, they appeal to me indescribably. Good-bye, dear, for I must go and dress to go out. Write very, very soon, to "your own Patsy."

Sunday, 17 January Robert working at the "studio" today; whole office force busy printing. A most fascinating process. The current turned on, the machine begins to click, the reels to unwind, and the miniature pictures flash out click by click as the negative and positive together pass before the little square aperture in front of the lamp. The negative flows down into a bag, while the positive is gathered in long loops, wound on a reel and plunged into the developing tank, washed, fixed, and then wound on a revolving drum to dry.

Monday, 1 February Moving pictures still the under-current of life. Printing almost finished and editing begun. Robert refuses to let me see them projected until the first edition is in shape. A title for them under discussion Sunday evening at the Annesleys. Mr and Mrs Annesley asked us to supper to meet Mr and Mrs Moore especially, I think, to bring Mr. Moore and Robert together on the subject of the pictures. Mr Moore is a Canadian National Railroad man, very clever.[51] His suggestions were good: "The Baffin-landers." Something easy to pass from mouth to mouth: "The curious inhabitants of the second largest island in the world," anything to arouse sufficient interest to get people there. Once there, will the pictures hold them? Robert thinks they can be so amply titled as to be successfully presented without a lecturer. I think not; I think the lecture is going to be the important part of the show, and that on the lecturer will depend the success or failure of the pictures in so far as their appeal to the general public is concerned. The public demands some sort of thrill, either the thrill of sheer beauty, or the thrill of battle. Sir Mawson's pictures of the antarctic had both; his ice pictures were beautiful beyond words, those of the violence of antarctic tempests were spectacular, and the animal pictures were unique in that they were taken in the only spot on the globe where animals have no fear of men.[52] Robert's pictures cannot be compared to them in any sense; there is nothing spectacular about them, the climactic conditions are not seen as a spectacle, they have to be realized by the imagination; there is nothing spectacular about the daily struggle for existence of the slow-moving Eskimo, its appeal is to a broad human sympathy; their general interest is the interest in any curious, unusual, little-known thing. The chief object of the lecture, therefore, is to create the atmosphere of the north country, and to make the actors in the drama human, and that is the idea Robert has been working out in his mind. The real intrinsic value of the pictures is, of course, scientific, ethnological and geographical, and their real place is with schools and universities and scientific societies. I am not at all sure but that they should be exploited from that point of view alone.

Robert is full of the idea of the use of moving pictures in education, in the teaching of geography and history. Someone might well make it a life work. Why not we? At least he has been sketching out in his mind a most alluring project and one for which he is most eminently fitted; it involves the Canadian National Railroad, and much money and every facility of course, and perhaps two or three years' work, but what glorious fun it would be, rolling around in a private car and yet being right out in the woods at the same time. The project is a moving picture story of the development of transportation in Canada, from the time of the early voyageurs to the present. As Robert says, the canoe has been to Canada what the camel is to Egypt; it is passing, in a few years it will have been superseded everywhere by the rail. Even Obakamiga, way up there where we felt so isolated only six years ago, is now sandwiched in between two transcontinental lines. Robert knows the waterways, knows a good rapid when he sees it, is familiar with every detail of that mode of travel, knows the stories of all the early travelers, knows the Hudson's Bay Company country, knows the Indian customs, etc. It would not be hard for him to stage and carry out the purely historical part of the story. The rest of the story would be in pictorial form all that passed through the minds of the promoters of the railroad inducing them to venture their undertaking; they saw the grain fields waving in the West, they saw the grain being transported in slow freighters down the Lakes, they saw in their minds a new route, shorter, by rail and through Hudson's Straits. And then there would be the romance incident to the actual building of the road, etc, etc, etc. I know it is stretched out much farther in Robert's mind than in mine.

On the subject of Sir William, Robert blows hot and cold. I am beginning to balance up and get a pretty fair idea of the whole situation. Robert says truly that there are mighty few men who would have been willing to do as much as Sir William has. The first expedition was fruitless, the second failed of its object. Says Sir William: "All you brought down was a lot of damned curios and we had to give those away!"

(We went to the museum, by the way, to take a look at those damned curios, and had a talk with Mr Currelly, their curator. On his own responsibility Robert gave over the material from the last trip to be added to the collection, which is to be called the Flaherty Collection, and is to include, at Mr Currelly's request, a full set of the Eskimo portraits. D—d proud we'll be of those d—d curios! I was much surprised by the museum, it is worth coming from Europe to see.)[53]

To resume: It naturally took some persuasion on Robert's part to induce Sir William to send him out a third time. Robert's stipulation was that in the event of the success of the expedition he should be given an interest in the results, and have his salary doubled. Fourteen months later he returns flushed with success to find – the war, the syndicate defunct, its members unable to pay up. After all, what would Sir William do? The whole burden fell upon him. There were no funds even to meet the expenses incurred. Undoubtedly it was Sir William personally who had to meet the Cochrane note that Robert almost got arrested about; probably everything that Robert has been getting has been out of Sir William's pocket. He is seeing Robert through, even to his debts such as the Ramsey bill for pictures of the last expedition ... They tell me that Sir William likes Robert, that Robert gets more out of him than most people can, and I believe it.

As for the moving pictures, Sir William has been inclined to class them with damned curios, skeptical of the value Robert puts upon them. To get from him driblet by driblet the money necessary to produce them has been like pulling teeth and has involved all this killing delay. Plainly, absolutely everything depends upon their success. Certainly neither Sir William nor anybody else has at this time money to put into expensive expeditions to explore remote Arctic islands. If, however, it should be demonstrated that such an expedition can be made to pay for itself???? To us, of course, it wouldn't matter whether the pictures were a primary or secondary object.

Mr Sullivan has gone to New York. Once more and more deeply do I distrust Mr Sullivan and his conspicuous interest in R.J.F. He proposed to "help" Robert with the pictures, in just what capacity was rather vague, but Robert seemed to think he would be a valuable associate, and suggested him to Sir Donald [Mann] as a collaborator. Sir Donald, instead, and very wisely, put Mr. Moore and the machinery of his office (Mr. Moore is secretary of the Canadian National Railroad) at Robert's disposal. Mr Sullivan on the eve of his departure for New York himself had an interview with Sir Donald, hoping to be authorized on COMMISSION to negotiate for the sale of the pictures in New York. He appraised the pictures to Sir Donald in most enthusiastic terms, and got for his pains – nothing. Neither did he take Robert's portraits down to show to Harper's, as had been definitely planned. Of this I am distinctly glad; for one thing, the portraits are not yet copyrighted, for another, I do not propose that Alan Sullivan shall make capital out of them by launching them simply to float articles of his own in connection with them. Besides, my opinion of Mr Sullivan's literary ability has suffered two distinct shocks, one being his latest book *Blantyre Allen*, and the other, a dramatic sketch lately given at the Arts and Letters Club, a discourse on love, so trivial, worse than trivial, it made me squirm to listen to it. His offer to edit the moving pictures for Robert and draft the lectures for them showed about as much perception as offering to finish an Artist's picture for him.

So I conclude (1) that Mr Sullivan has no sense, (2) except a mercenary sense, and I am determined first and last that he shall not be afforded the chance of making hash of Robert's good material. We are quite capable of editing the diaries ourselves, and I am already picturing in my mind's eye, a little log cabin in the heart of the woods where we shall work the matter out to our own pleasure and profit.

Tuesday, 2 March, 36 Roxborough Drive Packing for an early start. Left poor Louise to grub for her own breakfast and shut the door on an empty house. Robert much concerned about my health.

Noon, same day, Buffalo Tottie and I, tongues wagging over the lunch trays at 77 Linwood.

Tuesday – Friday Three good tongue wagging days, renewing old friendships and dispelling the phantom of ill-health. Thursday evening took portraits, maps, and moving picture outline to Mankells; much enthusiasm and interest; plans hatched for a dinner Saturday night for Robert and a Mr Brooks to talk moving pictures.

Friday evening. Went down to meet 8.35; no Robert; pretty mad; went to "movie"; Robert turned up at 77 soon after we got back, and we went over to the Lenox. Snowing. Memorable night: report of the Canadian Camp affair. You see, a clipping from the *N.Y. Times*, dated Feb. 19th, announcing Bartlett's proposed lecture on the island discovery in Hudson's Bay, had come to hand on the very day of the lecture.[54] To the letter from the Canadian Camp in which Sir William had referred to Robert, Robert had never paid any attention other than to write to Bartlett reminding him of his promise to secrecy. From Bartlett's reply Robert inferred that the matter of the lecture would be dropped; when clipping announcement came to light Robert's only course was to expose Bartlett by telegraphing the Secretary. Well I remember my feelings that night listening to Robert snoring beside me and thinking of Bartlett holding his audience in New York. Now it seems that the telegram was handed to the secretary just after the lecture and naturally the secretary was wrathy, wrathy at Robert for ignoring his letter, and inclined to take Bartlett's part. The whole affair had been miserably mismanaged, and only confirmed me in a resolution I had taken since coming to Buffalo of taking a more active part in the business end of Robert's affairs. There was Alan Sullivan stealing our ammunition, and I had begged Robert not to send him the portraits. I would market Robert's material myself, everything – I was as capable as the next person.

Saturday, 6 March Breakfast on the top floor, beautiful snow-white scene from the window. Spent an hour or so at the Albright Galleries;

much excited to find a Beatrice How; man new to me, Watson, had an interesting portrait; Hawthorne and Sargent.[55]

Dinner at the Mankells: Mr Brooks a funny little undersized wall-eyed person, unattractive until through his enthusiasm, his genuineness and simplicity shine out: his quick comprehension of and homage to Robert's nature, spoken to me, made him noble in my eyes. The dinner party soon resolved itself into a mutual admiration meeting, the talk centering about Robert's work and how to handle it. Why not go to New York? Mr Brooks had already given me addresses of people in the moving picture business, and would be glad to introduce us to Mr Harrington, sub-editor of the *Herald*.

A restless night for all concerned, Robert in particular. Decision taken Sunday morning, influenced largely by the idea that information had probably already leaked out through Bartlett's lecture. Lukes telephoned; gives sanction to go ahead.[56] The rest of the day spent with the Mankells and Mr Brooks until tea time when we adjourned to the Stocktons and held another meeting over the portraits and moving pictures. Two more letters of introduction, from Dr Stockton to Mr Walter Clark, banker, portrait painter and inhabitant of the Adirondacks, with J.P. Morgan; the other from Mr Kimball to a Dr Grosvenor, chemist, in touch with the moving-picture game.[57] Farewell supper at Statlers on Tottie and we were off on the 10.35.

Monday, 8 March, New York City The Babes in the Woods. Installed ourselves at the "Biltmore." Our room was on the 21st floor overlooking all the city sparkling against a blue sky and morning sun. 10:30, "the time has come the walrus said," and we sallied forth to the *Herald* office clutching our open sesame letter to publicity. Fresh, keen, New York air. Mr Harrington was not in his office, and a telephone call to his house divulged that he was far out of our reach, in Bermuda. Hesitation, should we confide ourselves to the Sunday editor? Decision, we would consult with Mr Clark. Accordingly we dropped down into the subway, emerged on lower Broadway, past Trinity Church just at the hour of the noonday service, slipped inside long enough to sing a hymn, the church was packed, and finally after many inquiries found ourselves in J.P. Morgan and Co.'s new building opposite the Stock Exchange on Broad Street. Mr Clark was engaged for the moment, would we be seated, and for half an hour we sat breathing the same atmosphere with the Financial Great. Bull-necked and pot-bellied they passed in review. Then came Mr Clark, wiry, clean-cut and keen, fit in every fibre of his physique. By that time we were so bottled up with waiting we were almost too full for speech: Mr Clark helped us to be brief, and promised his good offices in our behalf.

So we turned our attention to shirts, hats, ties, and something to eat. More adventure was in store for the afternoon, meeting the Sullivans at tea at Cousin Julie's. I had been at much pains turning over in my mind how I might most politely snatch back from the clutches of Alan Sullivan the diaries and portraits. Should I use diplomacy and kiss his hand for his "kind efforts in our behalf," or come right out and tell him that we had to have the money ourselves? However, tea time brought no Sullivans and passed pleasantly as also did dinner with the family. Arrangements were made for us to see Mr Miller of the *Times*, editor in chief, the following afternoon. That evening we went to see the great film play, *The Birth of a Nation*, three hours of absorbing soul-wracking melodrama.[58]

The steam heat in the hotel made both Robert and myself wretched. Robert tossed on his bed because the people were so busy outside, could hardly enjoy his own accustomed laziness. But what am I to do about his wanting to eat and sleep all the time? Cousin R. examined his feet and said he would probably have no trouble but for his weight, and read us a wholesome lecture on eating as a mere habit and the benefit of never wholly satisfying one's hunger.[59]

Tuesday, 9 March Before breakfast the telephone rang: Mr Crockett of the *Herald*, advised through Mr Clark, would call at 10:30. What about newspaper etiquette and our appointment with Mr Miller? However, Mr Crockett was coming.

10:30, the much anticipated interview at last. Followed tense hour and a half; the story stumbled all over itself in clumsy and over-bulky fashion, and we both heaved a mental sigh half of relief, half of misgiving when finally Mr Crockett departed with reports, maps and a couple of pictures under his arm. A more satisfactory session was held that afternoon at the *Times* office following our call on Mr Miller.[60]

We could now give our whole attention to the moving pictures.

That evening at dinner at Cousin Julie's we met Stephen Galatti, a school friend of Armit's, a dusky, shy, young man, very much Armit's type, with an air of very sufficient money and nothing much in the way of back-bone.[61] He had invested some of his money in a moving picture concern. Robert "got him going."

Wednesday, 10 March A most instructive morning at Scribner's; we passed in review before three departments and talked with Mr Chapin, art editor, who knew Robert through a letter from Mr Heming in Toronto, with Mr—, literary editor, and Mr Perkins of the book department.[62] They were most evidently much interested in all we had to show them; it was too bad the war was taking up all their space; *Harper's* was not running any war stuff, we might try them; and certainly the *National Geographic Magazine* would receive us with open arms; of course eventually we should want to make a book, for the sake of putting ourselves on record and not for the money in it for even with a successful sale with 15% royalty we couldn't expect to make more than $1000 out of it; they would be glad to consider the book when we had it ready but advised giving several years and careful work to it and making it a valuable contribution to the literature of exploration and ethnology.

For the rest of the day Robert and I parted company. I met Isabel, who took me to Dr Adler, who gave me a letter of introduction to Professor Boas of Columbia University, "the foremost ethnologist and authority on the Eskimo in America."[63] Robert knew him immediately by reputation. Later in the afternoon I went to the Natural History Museum whither Molly had paved the way. There I saw Mr Sherwood and Mr Whistler, and the gist of the visit was that they would be glad to see a few reels of the pictures run, that their lecture program for the year was filled, but that Professor Osborn on his return might consider a special lecture.[64]

Meanwhile Robert had been spending the afternoon with Stephen Galatti at the offices of his company. It seems that they usually do business on a 50-50 basis, 50 for you and 50 for them, reckoning 35% as the cost of advertising etc., and 15% net profit for themselves, while you reimburse yourself and realize your profit out of the remaining 50. Robert telephoned Mr. Galatti about some detail and the latter came flying down to the hotel like a jumping Jack on a string: they propose to meet Robert at the train when he returns with the films; so much eagerness is a suspicious thing. Robert left on the 8:20, and I came over here to the Club.

Today I sought out Dr Grosvenor for possible light on the "moving picture game." Finally reached him by telephone: How could we get our film before the market for open competitive bids? Suggested making arrangements with some theater manager to run our film at a certain time and send a circular letter to moving picture companies inviting their inspection. Suggested also writing to Sir Douglas Mawson who was "in touch with the New York market for educational films." Dr Grosvenor had a nice voice and the construction of his sentences was beautifully clear and concise. I should like very much to have seen him. From all accounts of his colleagues he must be quite the busiest and most hard-working man in the city.

Thursday, 11 March, Bryn Mawr Club, New York [to Flaherty] Your telegram came in the nick of time; I was just about to telegraph you. Just the same, I think I will send you a little dissertation in three parts that I wrote last night, because, for the good of the family I think you ought to know.

Let me tell you about yesterday. I went to *Harper's* and received back a package of Eskimo portraits. Mr Wells was very nice indeed, said they were certainly the best of their kind he had ever seen, but that the public was surfeited with Eskimo stuff, and he for his part didn't care how soon the race became extinct.

I was due in Brooklyn for lunch and having some time to spare, took the train for Flatbush to see Miss Bertsch of the Vitagraph Co., in whose judgement in all matters pertaining to the movies Mr Brooks had expressed so much confidence.[65] Miss Bertsch was not there, but my errand reached the ear of a Mr Williams of another department, and I was advised that they would be glad to run our film on trial any day after eleven o'clock.

Later: Ever since your letter came, about an hour ago, I have been debating in my mind whether, since you are uncertain about when you will be down, I had better come home tomorrow night? I have about done all I had planned to here. Of course if you are sure about being here this week, I should stay without question. And if I came home I probably couldn't come down with you later on account of the expense. Of one thing I am sure – that there is no hurry about articles for the magazines: there will be a much better market for non-war stuff next fall. Still, it is never too soon to begin, and I have already made arrangements to have the rest of the diaries typed. You see how I am wobbling.

The best news in your letter was Englehardt's promise; but, is it for this year or next? Let me go on with my yesterday's adventures. Late in the afternoon I reached Columbia for an appointment with Professor Boas. I'd have given anything if you had been there in my stead, he would so gladly have talked with you, had read the article in the *Times* – "very interesting" – and the portraits were "beautiful," just where did you winter and how far had you penetrated? Amadjuak Lake, yes, it was he who had discovered it thirty years ago – and what could he do for us? I mentioned how anxious you were to go back to the islands; yes, it had taken 20 years to get that same call out of his own blood, and how desirous it seemed to bring your work to the attention of interested people. Had I seen the Museum people? Yes, and I told him the result, and did I know of Capt. Cromer and his work on Southampton Island? His own greatest interest lay in the region north of Southampton Island on the mainland. He thought it would be most advisable to get in touch with Capt. Cromer and his financial backer, Mr Ellsworth.[66] Thought that in conjunction with them and the Museum, the chances for arranging an expedition for next year were excellent, as next year the Museum would be "very rich." He gave me Capt. Cromer's address.

I wish you were going to be here tonight. I am dining with the Mankells to meet Mr and Mrs Lund and another man, the director of the galleries where Mr Lund's exhibition is to be held.[67] Nothing is much fun without you anyway, I have discovered that much. Never mind Alan Sullivan, we'll write a better one.[68] Much love from your dutiful wife.

Friday, 9 April, The Stratford House, New York City Here we are again. I have quite a different feeling about this visit. When I got home, and from the safe, assured ground of vegetable-paring and dish-washing, took stock of our last. I confess it looked to me like much mis-spent energy; my idea had been to push Robert's work, – better perhaps just to have let it carry us along by its own sheer weight; an ounce of influence is worth pounds of energy. Better first to have worked up a solid bridge of influence by strong letters of introduction from prominent local people and press notices upon which to make our entree into New York.

Mr Currelly certainly did well for us at Convocation Hall; the pictures could not have been brought out under better auspices, the University of Toronto, the Archaeological Institute of America, and the Royal Ontario Museum of Archeology; the tickets were printed in the form of an invitation with R.J. FLAHERTY, F.R.G.S. in large type, another one of Mr Currelly's nice ideas.[69] Then the introduction by the Lieutenant Governor Hendrie, even though nobody could hear a word of it, was of course entirely appropriate. The really vital moment of the evening came when after the pictures had run their course (a most feeble and disappointing course; the lantern was all to pieces and so was poor

Robert), Sir Edmund Walker, Toronto's foremost banker and art collector, addressed the audience with a note of thanks that embraced every phase of Robert's work, the size of it and the quality of it, in a fine and just and most sincere appreciation, the kind that makes one feel humble. President Faulkner of the University standing out from the front row seconded the vote in more or less set form.

Were the pictures a success? During one of the extra long lapses of the lantern, under cover of the dark, numbers from the audience had been slipping out. Had the pictures failed to hold the audience? I myself was sick with disappointment, and chiefly resentful that there had been no rehearsal for either lantern or lecture. Robert's remarks were few and forced, none of his usual engaging spontaneity, no hint of interest in his subject to carry his audience along with it, it dragged along, stilted and stale. What would the papers say? and the people? Mr. Currelly had placed "ears" all through the house to listen for comments; their reports were unanimously favorable. The next day Robert telephoned up that the office force and friends were congratulatory and the press notices good, also that the Arts and Letters Club wanted him to show the pictures there on Saturday. "Never again," Robert had said in the cab after Convocation Hall! But I already foresaw a triumph for the next time. About six o'clock Saturday night Robert telephoned that as Sir William was bringing his family I could come too. Walking toward the Club we caught up with [Flaherty's] Father R. and Mr. Annesley, and I waited outside with them while Robert went in. Sir William and family arrived in their car, and I was duly presented, at last! Upstairs in the hall I found refuge between Mr and Mrs Ely, and the meeting opened with a few remarks from Alan Sullivan, prompted by Robert and tactfully directed at Sir William, hoping he would not fail to continue to promote a work of such importance to the whole country. Then came the first slide and so on with a fine brilliance and a fine flourish, not a hitch, not a lax moment, and a lecture that even I couldn't have improved upon!! The Mackenzies with Mrs Sullivan flocked around to congratulate me while Robert was mobbed by the members. Two especially nice tributes I remember, one from Mr Defries who called the pictures "a great human document," the other from a chorus, voiced by Alan Sullivan when he said that he hadn't heard a single first person pronoun throughout the whole lecture; "Don't spoil him," they said shaking their fingers at his worldly-wise wife. Sir William shook hands, again with silent scrutiny; Lady Mackenzie had invited us for tea the following afternoon.

The following afternoon came, we managed to survive the tea-test.

The daughters and their husbands were there and a few guests; of these the first are very pleasant, the second perfectly impossible, and of the third I can only remember a dear sweet Mrs Smith, and Mme Rochereau, wife of the French Consul, who talked about the Secours Nationale. It was suggested putting the pictures on for a benefit.

Wednesday morning we arrived in New York. At the station Robert and I parted company, and I did not see him again until about four o'clock he appeared, Mr Galatti with him, hot, tired and dusty and worn out with the adventurous business of getting the films through the customs; together in company with a faithful taxi-driver they had lunched from a soup-kitchen counter! But there it was, our "little box of tricks." I am beginning to have a most personal and affectionate feeling for Anunglung and Allego and Kellepellie and all the family, our children. The next morning they started out to work for us. Robert had come back about 2:00 and we went across to the Astor for lunch. The Picture Playhouse people had estimated the film to be worth about $50,000. This was far under Robert's own calculations and much figuring did we do. (It is a circus to see Robert figure; when he wants to divide 2400 by 10 he does it all out by long division!) We decided to walk up the avenue and call upon Lee Keedick, Mawson's agent; we were kept waiting in the outer office for some time, and when finally Robert sent in his name and errand we were informed that Mr Keedick was not interested.[70] (It was undoubtedly our own fault, we should have written, enclosing press notices; this we subsequently did.)

Much crest-fallen, to console ourselves, we stopped in at Curtis's studio on the same floor. We were shown the portfolio of photogravures for the 10th volume of Mr Curtis's colossal work on the North American Indian.[71] Five hundred sets at $4200 and $3500 per set, his life work and one to stir the imagination. The same thought crossed our minds at once: why not the same for the Eskimo? We learned that Mr Curtis too had ventured into moving pictures and just put out an elaborate Indian Drama film: the World Film Company, 50-50 royalty basis, 20 copies routed.

From that moment Curtis became *the man to be seen.* Would he be interested in us? Robert was sure of it. We made comparison between his portraits and Robert's:

INDIAN PORTRAITS: flat, toneless quality of drawing, interest decorative, and dependent upon picturesque costumes and other details.
ESKIMO PORTRAITS: depth and tone quality of painting, interest centering in personality independent of race, costume or detail of any kind.

On the whole the Eskimo portraits were "bigger"; the question in my mind was whether Curtis was a big enough man to interest himself in Robert's work.

Tuesday, 13 April Surely our "stop in" at Mr Curtis's studio was a lucky chance. Yesterday Mr Curtis saw Robert by appointment, and arranged to have the pictures shown this morning before an audience of experts, including besides the unapproachable Mr Keedick, a Mr Whitney, a broker for the European market, a Mr Collier of the board of censors, and several others.[72] Cousin Julie and Molly came bringing Mrs Damroschi; I rather took satisfaction when they came in, turning a retaliatory back on Mr Keedick.

Mr Curtis showed his own film first, all taken in and about our old hunting ground, that wonderful west coast of Vancouver Island, vivid scenes that were like flashes of memory; and our old friends, Sutor's kinsmen, the Salish Indians, were the actors. It was a story of the customs and ceremonies of the old head-hunting days a generation past, with a thread of romance running through it.

It ran through 600 feet: by the time our pictures were called Robert and I were prepared to see them fall perfectly flat on tired eyes and brains. They didn't; everybody asked questions galore; and though as Robert said, it was an acid test for them, putting them with all their crudities in juxtaposition with an elaborately toned and perfected film such as Curtis's, it was a curiously happy one; in all their crudity they stood out human, real, convincing and big in contrast to the spectacular artificiality of Curtis's, wonderful as they were as a mere spectacle. As Mr Curtis himself said of our pictures, there was an "intimacy" about them; but he also criticized them as "monotonous." Blood and thunder and the "punch" again; but it is my belief that the punch that the "yap" audience demands is not necessarily the blood and thunder for itself but the human appeal it has in it. And that is just where I think Robert's film would "get across" where Curtis's wouldn't. Mr Curtis told us how a little upstate New York town, a Texas town, and Rochester, N.Y. itself had turned his film down as high-brow stuff. He has just been lunching with me here at the hotel, been talking to us like a father, with such infinite tact, too, giving us all the benefit of his own experience in the moving picture world; we swept it all, sweeping away lots of illusions in doing so, and finally really getting down to what it would be best to do with our film. I am inclined to think he is right, absolutely, to hold them over until we can reinforce them with more and better material from the next expedition, the material with the real human punch in it. Sir William would do it undoubtedly, has already himself suggested holding them over for a better market. The market at present is chaos, demoralized by over-speculation and the war; the whole business is a new, headlong, phenomenal thing, which nobody really knows anything about.

Friday, 16 April Robert is as good as a whole show. Our entire stock of cash at this moment consists of one dollar bill, one nickel and 29 pennies. Robert telegraphed last week to have his April salary advanced and sent, received word that it had been requisitioned, but has since received neither money nor any answer to two urgent telegrams. We've had a beautiful time on what's gone, no stint on taxis or theatre, to say nothing of after-theatre-suppers and every indulgence under the sun. Robert has taken the most whole-hearted delight in donning full dress every evening. Our theater tickets are all ordered through the hotel from Tyson's, nothing less than orchestra seats on the aisle, and likely as not with Robert's fooling up to the last minute we have to go in a taxi. We are out for a regular back-from-the-Klondike-spree, you see!

Our first three theater parties were really worth while: Arnold Daly in *You Never Can Tell*, Granville Barker's *Androcles and the Lion*, with a curtain raiser by Anatole France, *The Man Who Married a Dumb Wife*. Robert nudged me to notice the novel and striking stage effects, grouping of figures and colors, etc., the unforgettable blue of Androcles's robe. As we drove back that night we remarked how fortunate it was that our taste in pleasure-taking was so perfectly one. Our third was *A Pair of Silk Stockings* at the Little Theater, clever beyond words and cast to perfection.[73] To take Robert to the Little Theater was like tasting the fruit of youthful dreams, dreams dreamt in Painesdale days when my picture of Heaven was two front seats in the highest and humblest balcony of Boston Symphony Orchestra Hall and Robert and myself holding hands: I lived again the enjoyment of my first impression of the Little Theater, the soft lights gently lowered, the musical curtain signal, all the intimacy and "atmosphere" of the place. Down in the coffee room during the entre-acts we came upon a still more substantial reminder of the past, a Mr— of Victoria, B.C., and the Tahsis marble quarry; he wants Robert to see someone here about it this week!

From the Little Theater we drifted into Castles in the Air; Ralph had already given us a taste of the dance delirium at Maurice's. Robert has a little Broadway high-life curiosity still unsatisfied; last night after dinner at Cousin Julie's, what should we do? I suggested, considering our slender purse and the beauty of the spring night, a truly romantic walk across Brooklyn Bridge. No response. A little later he announced he was going over to the Waldorf to see Hiam. Would I be lonely? *Would* I be lonely? Would I surely not be lonely? I don't know what time he came back, but half waked out of my slumber I gleaned through a million prodigal embraces that he had got as far as Broadway and indulged in a plate of bacon and eggs!!! Shades of Romance!

Thursday, 22 April Robert has gone to the New York Athletic Club to see the Barnes South Africa pictures. Mr. Barnes is lecturing with them. Robert lunched with him today at Delmonico's, at Wyllys Terry's invitation.[74] We dined with Marie and Wyllys last Monday. That dinner and the opera Saturday afternoon in Katie's box marked the high watermark of Robert's career to date! Our grandchildren shall hear of it, of an Arctic evening.

We had our walk across the Brooklyn Bridge the other evening. Alas! the incessant ear-racking rumble of the trolley spoiled all the romance of the place and the hour, the moon and the sky-line. So we philosophized: what would an Eskimo think of all such sights and sounds? He would die of trying to think at all – something like Robert's own state of mind on previous visits. This one has been so nearly normal, we congratulate ourselves. No wonder instinct compels me to go north and savor myself all these priceless months of labour in husband-making. Without me it would be all lost; he would run all wild again, all to be done over again. Only I wouldn't! At the first bruit of his coming I would run in a corner and hide, and not love or money could prevail to drag me forth to the fray!

According to Mr. Barnes we have nothing to expect from anyone in the moving picture game but lying and cheating and stealing and every sort of crooked dealing. We know nothing of Hendricks or his company.

For several days last week the pictures lay idle. Robert was busy making appointments with Mr. Mein and others connected with the Nickel Trust hoping to interest them in the ore samples from the islands. They were interested, but not to the point of doing anything about it. Then came this Hendricks affair and we thought we had surely fallen in with our luck, except that it sounded almost too good to be true. This Mr Hendricks, it seemed, was a prominent lawyer about town, who, for the sake of doing good to his fellow men, had formed a company for the sole purpose of promoting the educational moving picture film. His contract terms were most fair and full of promise. It was a big idea; it made the other companies and their offers look small and paltry. Robert's information came through a Mr McCord. Mr McCord was representing a film taken in South America. I made the little man's acquaintance in a cab going out to the Museum; little slack moustache, cane, Australian accent and no manners. Surely nothing would come out of such an ill-shaped head. And when he began to talk about "our company" I began to have my suspicions.[75]

Wednesday, 28 April, Stratford House Looking back on it, I think that one of the strangest dinner parties that ever happened, took place in our rooms last night: McCord and Hendricks, the one an Australian adventurer, the other little runt of a man, of unhealthy pallor, unkempt hair, ill fitting clothes and generally ungroomed appearance, supposedly a prominent lawyer, a trifle eccentric if you like, member of a prominent club, writer of books, and signer of government treaties and conventions. Robert planned dinner in the room the better to talk business. We began with opera and the drama, from the Greeks to Ibsen; Mr Hendricks seemed well-versed, had written drama himself, cited part of it to illustrate some ethical point. How was it that his plot sounded so strangely familiar? I could almost see the cover of *Lippincott's Magazine*! Mr McCord appeared to rather better advantage this time, telling something of his roving life and literary career. I tried hard to make him out the real "litterateur" as he talked. Both departed in due time. Robert and I just looked at each other and laughed. What were they? We gave it up.

The next day I saw Mr McCord's Amazon film. Robert had reported it as quite equal in interest to Barnes'. My rose-colored glasses were not on: I saw that the photography was abominable, the subject matter entirely superficial, the whole film merely so much newspaper copy. It and the shape of Mr McCord's head measured up perfectly. Robert meanwhile had been sifting down Hendricks. So that deal has fizzled out, even as I had anticipated; but Robert was quite shaken and down-hearted.

But today we are up again. We have at last succeeded in reaching the Paramount people, recommended by Curtis and others. Mrs. Johnson, reviewer for the company, seems to have a great deal of sense, proposed using the story of the expedition to advertise the pictures through the medium of *National Geographic Magazine*. That surely is the way it should be done. But time presses. Mr Lukes visited New York on Sunday. Robert spent the morning with him. I came home from church to find him in a dream. Paced the floor and sat in turn in every chair all afternoon. Much talk of the expedition this summer; a new company to finance it, a three years' base on the islands! Wily Lukes! He was very kindly about the film, too kindly altogether, about not worrying about it any more, holding it over for a better market, etc. Just the little game I thought they would be playing, sending Robert off north again WITHOUT his money, knowing full well he'd be only too glad to get back there at any cost and then handling the films at their own convenience and in their own interest. They have been very loathe to send Robert any expense funds for this sojourn in New York. Lukes consistently ignored Robert's repeated messages requesting an advance of his April salary. Since the first week we have lived, one week on my allowance drafted from Boston, this last week merely by courtesy of the hotel management! The check from Toronto finally came today.

Friday, 30 April, New York City   Red Letter Day! Visit to "291." While I slept yesterday afternoon, Robert went to Brentano's and came back with an armful of photography periodicals, filling our room with treasure. Of the lot the pearl of great price, reverently displayed with all the pride of new discovery, was *Camera Work*, edited by Alfred Stieglitz.[76] We forthwith resolved to see Mr. Stieglitz, hence our pilgrimage to "291," a little old building on Fifth Avenue, the ground floor of which was given to the sights and smells of a Third Avenue back alley, bearing out Robert's impression that "they were a bohemian lot, anarchists and all that, ultra-modern."

The visit turned out to be a peak experience for me. I look back on it now with worship in my heart. Bare walls and scant furnishing, a few pictures, a few prints, but the place is hallowed, for there is Reality and Truth and Soul, Love and the Labour of Love, and the deep spirit of Rest. And the spirit of the place is the Man: I saw him in a golden aura. It was all so simple; we began immediately talking about *Camera Work*; he beckoned, leading us on into his mind, to see the priceless labor and love he has put into it. It is the record of the birth and development of photography as an art, as a medium for expressing the soul in things, in the work of the great photographers from the time of D.O. Hill. Our eyes were shining with the recollection of his enthusiasm, and I was bursting with impatience to go get our portraits and bring them into the magic of this hour; I was sure of their welcome. Robert went; I stayed. We talked of this and that; it was not so much the subject, it was the sympathy. We talked of the City, of our dissipated energies. He too is an apostle of concentration, it is the motive of his life and work, his message and his mission. How well I understood the way he spoke of his student years in Germany and the utter misery of the first years of struggle here, against ill-health, with his work, the intense, body-shattering excitement of it; and then, little by little, the gathering of the thirsty about him, himself the spring in that oasis of the great American desert of mediocrity and commercialism. Our conversation became almost as one thought, we took the words from each other's mouth.

Robert came back. Mr. Stieglitz looked over the drawings and the portraits with interest and appreciation and words of kindly encouragement.

Two little shining souls (at least mine was) went back to the city streets, with two large autograph copies of *Camera Work* tucked under their arms. And what he had said to Robert's expostulation at the gift, but: "You don't know what YOU have done for ME this morning" (!), and wrote: "To Mr and Mrs R.J. Flaherty, as a souvenir of a very Real and Live Hour at 291."

Sunday, 16 May, 36 Roxborough Drive, Toronto Such a funny time; I was left in bond, so to speak, in New York, trunks held at the hotel, etc., while Robert hurried back to Toronto with a contract offer from the Paramount Company. Expected to be sent right down again to close the deal. I knew he wouldn't; however I finally agreed to try his way. Cousin Julie harbored me. A delightful peaceful week with Armit, taking good care of my finger. Of course at the end of a week, no husband. So, leaving half my clothes behind at dressmakers and laundries and my shopping all at loose ends, I paid the hotel bill, and after a hectic day gathering together into some travelling capacity all Robert's slides, pictures, albums, and ore samples, I got off, with great difficulty making an early train in order to arrive at 8.40 in the morning in time for breakfast. Funny, it overcame me as I sat in the train passing the outskirts of Toronto, that Robert would oversleep. I hardly even looked for him on the platform, and went right up to the hotel, slides under one arm, ore samples under the other, just as MAD! Breakfast, where he joined me, was not a hearty meal (on *my* side) and somewhat strained on both. However the drive up in an open motor through the new glistening green and the sweet air and getting home to a lawn all yellow-starred with dandelions, seemed to help matters. Or perhaps it was the sight of the soldiers swamped all minor emotions. The news of the Canadian casualties was still fresh, and poignant at sight of the men of the next contingent training for their turn. There was a note of fate in the sound of their marching, a note of mourning in the music and the drums, against the buoyant beauty of the May morning something heavy and full of doom.

No, I don't believe I blame Robert for being willing to go at any sacrifice, only to GO. The ranks of the bread-line are growing day by day. I notice changes, men every day at the shelter begging for work or food. The lighting up of the furnace man's face when I told him he could go ahead with the job of fixing up the yard. The old char woman with her 8 grand children and the tears in her eyes. Mrs Wilcox herself, there was something almost pathetic in Mr Wilcox's thank you reply to my check for the rent. It was my last cent. I have $10.12 in my purse, all we have to live on until Robert gets some more money. And money at the office is harder and harder to get. All the promise of the next expedition, like most of Robert's dreams, has fizzled out to a bare skeleton. Robert having reduced his estimate of cost to a minimum, cutting out salaries, relinquishing past claims and with them all hope of paying his debts, is now turning every stone to get enough cash to get the expedition going. Wired to New York offering the pictures for cash: $5000 was the most the Paramount Co. would even consider paying outright. From $100,000 (dreams of an earlier day) to $5000! My trouble is that I haven't yet got used to this eternal discounting, to covering the liabilities of the discount, paying the mortgage on Robert's dreams.

Sunday, 23 May, 36 Roxborough Drive Mother Darling, I am exploding with things to tell, not the things particularly, but the telling. My "dour" old Scotch woman left the house Friday night with her week's wages (in her stocking, I've no doubt) and has been seen no more. I like these spells of doing my own work. Each spell finds us both handier. Robert got so enthusiastic this morning over washing up last night's dinner dishes that nothing could stop him, not even the sizzle of hot breakfast in my frying pan. The critical moment of the whole day is when we taste the coffee. This morning it was pronounced "man's coffee" (woman having made it!), and conduced to an extra session over the cups, when we discuss men and nations in general and our own affairs in particular.

The Company wants a favorable report on Robert's discovery from Mr Flaherty Sr. before putting up the money for Robert to winter on the islands. It seems perfectly reasonable. But Robert, realizing that his own salvation depends upon the winter and the moving pictures, is bound to get the money and make final arrangements *now* for at least a year to come. I left him in a most unhappy frame of mind, torn between exasperation with the Company and loyalty to Sir William and the possibility of making a deal with another company. He had even gone so far as to promise himself conditionally to the other company, and send in his resignation to Sir William. The immediate result of resignation was that two checks were hurried through on Lukes' personal account to cover LaDuke's expense account and a letter of credit on Revillon Frères for $2000. The feeling at the office was that Robert's resignation was an act of ingratitude: "Think what Sir William has done for you," etc. As Robert himself says, he will be branded forever if he goes back on Sir William now. Finally Sir William could protect himself by getting an injunction restraining Robert from going out. So there you are. The great and only injustice Robert has suffered through Sir William this winter is Sir William's repudiation of his promise to double Robert's salary and give him an interest in the expedition. His salary on the old basis, $250 a month, has been paid regularly. The real rub has been on being on a salary basis at all! For exploration work, of course, for a man without capital, there is no other way, because there is no immediate return to live on. The whole idea of the islands was original with Robert, but it took $85,000 of Sir William's money to carry it out, i.e., Sir William bought Robert's life and brains at $3000 per annum. By virtue of the wage system, therefore, that organization of industry that makes some of us masters and the rest of us slaves, all the return of Robert's life and brains belongs to Sir William. It is the same with the pictures: Sir William's money again and Robert's brains and personality. But here is a difference, there IS more immediate return on the pictures, and the capital required is not so great. This sort of work need not of necessity, therefore, come under the wage system. There are two alternatives: to obtain a loan to do the work himself, or to go into partnership with somebody on a percentage basis: the difficulty with the first being the matter of the security required. Robert's propensity for getting away with money, his own and everybody else's, certainly is phenomenal. If he had saved one quarter of the money he has wasted in the last four years, he would have enough on hand now to finance himself twice over as far as the pictures are concerned. It makes me angry to think of it. His wastefulness, carelessness, extravagance, and irresponsibility about money matters, taken together, is one great flaw in his character that threatens to defeat all his life and work.

Written on the train: Tottie dear, reunion was *great*! I wouldn't have missed it for the world. The only fly in the ointment was not having

Jaynesie there. Between 40 and 50 of us there were, however, and never before in the history of the class, I am sure, were so many of us so generally gregarious. The first meeting, perhaps, was something of a shock; they all seemed so frightfully thin and pale and wornish. Gertie got quite depressed, wished they'd all go home! But we got used to that and a few blooming members arrived later to take off the curse. The days were beautiful, a feast of sunshine and green. We spent all Tuesday morning, Margaret and I, in the grass under the trees, she to prepare for her role of toast-mistress for the class supper, I to prepare my toast – but we didn't, we just talked – and when supper time came it was all the better, I hooked her into her dress at the eleventh hour, and we made our entree before the company all ready seated, late. Noways could there have been a nicer supper. We all felt it to the cockles of our hearts; it was mellow, as we were, and surprising things happened, so many of the shy, uncouth members of the class had come into their own, and stood up and made themselves felt, I, perhaps, as much as any, so they were pleased to say when I had finished telling them the story of the islands and what we were going to do. I know, from the way they listened and looked and spoke afterwards, that I had made them feel something of the romance and the bigness of it. And when time came for me to go next morning, they all assembled in the hall and gave two cheers, one for Hubbard and one for Flaherty; half a dozen piled into the station wagon with me, Bess saw me into Philadelphia; Margaret, bless her heart, couldn't bring herself to be parting and stayed behind the station door. How I was in love with the world![77]

And here I am at Hamilton, almost back to Toronto. The whole trip cost me less than $50.00. It was worth while, wasn't it? Bless you for your little note, Sister Mine.

I didn't tell you about my traveling companion down to New York, Mr. [Frank D.] Wilson, Hudson's Bay factor at Moose, he whose invitation Robert had at the time of our wedding to bring me to Moose this summer, a pleasant florid-faced gentleman, clothed in the fashion of the prosperous farmer of some years ago. It was his first trip to New York, some special call to meet his superiors to discuss the condition of the fur trade produced by the war. There practically is no market, the furs are rotting, and 3000 souls, Indians and Eskimo, hunters and trappers for the company, are facing a winter without provision. The same with some six or seven hundred dependent upon Revillon Frères. It will be a winter without precedent in that region.

Another scrap of news. Every report of a north-bound ship fills

Robert with dark forbidding. We recently read one of the *Neptune*, an old ice-breaker, chartered by some American Moving Picture Company for a trip around the world, "leaving six men in Baffin Land for ethnological record of Eskimo," Captain Bob Bartlett in command. They may be making straight for the islands and the ore, for all we can tell. To have them duplicating our film is bad enough. (And the war we have always with us!)

Tuesday, 15 June 7:30, on the porch. Such a glorious morning! The birds heralded it with an ecstasy of song. I lay in bed concocting the most agreeable things to do. Yesterday was dull and devoted to clothes, sorting and mending and packing away. Today I would call up Miss Weil, would ask her if she liked paddling and suggest a real adventure, up the Humber.[78] We motored there last Sunday afternoon, our first, one, and only motor spree, and my own idea. It was hot, the first heat of summer, a day made for the occasion. It was also my first sight-seeing expedition beyond the city limits. I had not guessed the beauty of the country. We picked butter-cups and stopped at a little tea-house on an old mill sight for tea. It was a beautiful day to remember. I went on with my musings: Mrs. Tapper would roast the chicken, cold chicken, toast and bacon sandwiches, lettuce ditto, cucumbers and eggs, tea, mmmmmmmmm! If Miss Weil were not in there was still an alternative, the hydroaeroplane; last year passengers were taken up for 50 cents. Robert and I watched it once from a bridge near the harbor, mount, wheel, drop and alight like a gull on the water, and then turn plowing to its shed like a great sea-beetle. My watch had stopped. I went down in my wrapper to consult the kitchen time-piece: 6:20. I opened all the shutters and doors, breakfast on the porch! After my nice bath and cold douche I set the table there. The sun gave me a warm salute as I pulled down the porch screen, promise of singing locusts and shimmering air. I lit the gas burner, and somehow it smelled like camping!

And here I sit, the breakfast dishes before me in the dappled sunlight, and here I come to the real matter of my story. The other morning I had a most mysterious visitor, heralded by a prolonged ringing of the bell. I went downstairs; through the door the man looked like a mendicant. I opened it, he seemed to know our name, but without stating his errand requested to speak with me INSIDE. Once inside, he began fumbling in his pockets, he had "had great difficulty in finding the house." Probably he had some paper stating his case for charity. He laid it on the table saying, "I have a judgement against your husband for such and such a sum." "Hunter vs. Flaherty," I read. The only Hunter I knew anything about was an old friend in Port Arthur. It must be a mistake, the wrong Flaherty! "No, oh no." He could not enlighten me on the case, probably I could find out by telephoning Mr Flaherty, and probably Mr Flaherty would want to speak to him, and he followed me upstairs. Robert was not in the office, I left a message and then turned to my visitor. He seemed much embarrassed, rocked back and forth on the arm of the Morris chair, his hands about his knee. His embarrassment increased as I proceeded to question him; he put out a deprecating hand as if to shield himself, and only after my assurance that I "wouldn't take it personally," did he come out with the fact that he was the bailiff. That somehow seemed to open a flood-gate, and he talked steadily of his experiences and misadventures in the pursuit of his office. I think it was one of the most vivid half hours I ever spent. I had read of bailiffs in books, here was a real live one, and I was talking to him, or he to me, telling me all the intimate, the shabby, the tragic little stories of real life to which his calling gives him the key. I think he will be telling someone of his visit with me as not one of the least surprising of his receptions in strange houses. Finally he took a book and I went back to my typewriter. Mr. Flaherty meanwhile was on Bob's trail. The second scene, after I had made out my check on the State Street Trust Company and it came to listing our belongings as under seizure until the check should be honored, was no less amusing than the first. I indicated our few possessions; "Poor pickings for a bailiff," said I, and he ended by putting down a few hypothetical tables!

Monday night we started the evening with an argument, on the question of stimulants, alcoholic liquors. I couldn't see why Robert got so heated about it, as in the end we seemed to be of the same opinion, that drinking does so much more harm than good, we should all vote for prohibition, could it be made effective. The butter-cups had all straightened up on their stems and made a glory of yellow and meadow sweetness in the house. I had thought all day of taking them up to Mrs Murray, sick and suffering and probably dying, but had put it off until evening thinking we could go together; they were Bob's friends from Port Arthur, but the suggestion made no appeal to him except as something to spoil his evening. And then I lit into him. He keeps talking about the war, the horror and the suffering, and our lack of imagination and cold-blooded attitude toward it. Here was a woman, a woman he knew, suffering agony equal to any soldier's, fighting her last fight, and he wouldn't even bestir himself to show her the slightest attention. He would "order flowers sent to her." That made me angrier still, his way of always "having things done," as though the money value were the only thing that counted. I used to resent it when, the first month or so here, huge boxes came to the house, expensive flowers, some office boy's choice, often as not half-faded. And yet he rails at money, and the evil of money, the great god that rules civilization and our lives and breeds wars; and I told him it was exactly the soul-less attitude that was in him that bred war. For the rest of the evening he sulked, and an evil temper lurked ready to spring out at everything I did or said. It was so unlike him; I had thought I was the only one afflicted with just that kind of devil, and I remembered his patience with me under similar circumstances. Perhaps it would be good for him to go down to the club; he thought of it too, but didn't go.

Yesterday, as I say, I spent the day with my clothes. Half past five o'clock came, and I left my mending to get supper, white fish, beans (Robert is particularly fond of beans) and a delicious snow pudding. By 6:30 everything was cooked to a turn and ready. Mr. Flaherty had telephoned to locate Robert; he had $50 for him for his expenses to Montreal. He was evidently leaving by the night train I was surprised to hear, as Robert had not given me any notice of such an intention. About 6:45 he telephoned that he'd be starting up at once, going to get our Pullman accommodations. We both had passes (my first present from the Canadian National Railroad). A little after 7:30 the telephone rang again; he would stay down town for dinner. I was angry with disappointment, but told myself he probably had some good reason. So I grabbed a hasty bite, and began to make my preparations for going. I had trimmed myself a hat, out of all the odds and ends I had been overhauling. Not a bit bad either, in fact I was rather puffed up about it; I would show it off when he came. Last time the passes had come too late for me to go with him; better so, we would enjoy it all the more this time. We were to buy all the stuff for the expedition. He came about nine, found me upstairs by my desk. He was very affectionate, "had to eat my dinner all alone, etc." His voice was strange, his endearments overdone; I looked at his face and saw that his eyes were queer and his skin blotched, and, yes, he speech was decidedly thick. To make sure I smelled his breath, it was reeking of whiskey, "a Scotch and soda at the club." I got up, remembering that I had left the dinner dishes on the table. He followed me downstairs helping me clear the table, and then went up to lie down, "awful headache." I kept on with my sewing in the billiard room, hearing his heavy breathing. He lay like a log on the bed. I was determined he should keep his engagement to go to Montreal. At ten o'clock I went in to rouse him. Shaking would not do, and I brought in a wet cloth, which he seemed to resent; he was all right, he wasn't going to Montreal, and I saw that ugly petulant curve and protrusion of the lower lip. I had done all I could. Finally about 10:30 the telephone rang, a man wished to speak to him. Again I tried to rouse him, then went back to ask if I could take a message. "No, No," the tone at the other end was impatient and not polite. I sat for half a minute. If Robert came to the telephone he would betray his condition, and what other excuse could I give. In desperation I went back, and lashed Robert to his senses. It was Mr Campbell at the other end, he knew the whole situation (the irony of my panic!). A little later a cab drew up, sent by Mr Campbell I supposed. Robert left.

That was last night.

Sunday, 18 July Mother Darling. Three letters I've started to you. Our state of mind is hardly transcribable, and life is too d— full for adequate expression.

The trunk arrived yesterday afternoon, such treasure as you never imagined it to contain! We are taking it all up to the Eskimos, all that truck, to trade for priceless fur. Robert waxed fairly profane at the sight of it. We packed a trunk full of it, and Robert is taking it up to Montreal tonight to ship with the rest of his stuff in the morning.

We are arranging our packing all with a view to the possibility of my wintering with him in the islands, and talking about it. The little house, the little oil-stove for me to cook on, the piano – yes, actually; all our music is packed and gone. Won't it be fun concocting dishes out of powdered eggs and powdered milk and preserved butter and what not. We tucked in a kitchen diary, and the record we propose to keep in it ought to be unique in the annals of culinary art. Did I tell you what a cracking good cook I've proved myself to be? Ask the old man, if anything can beat my pie and cake and salad and little home dinners. I'm getting fat on them myself, so fat everybody is remarking on my blooming appearance. I feel too fit altogether, suspiciously so. In fact, Mother dear, what do you suppose has broken in upon all this packing and planning? – a strong suspicion, amounting almost to conviction, that there is going to be another one of us! Now isn't that almost too much, truly. What's the use anyway. I always said that would be my luck. Of course we, Robert especially, are consumed with curiosity to know what our prospects may be in that respect, and the certainty would be a tremendous relief to our minds. Robert has been adorably ridiculous about it all day, already sees himself miraculously transformed into the most responsible and provident of beings (parents?)! There is no doubt about his enthusiasm, and for me, if I can't winter with him, it would be the one ample compensation.

My diary has been sadly neglected. I am going to begin again today. A week from tomorrow we shall probably be leaving for Cochrane. I promise to keep you posted.

Squeeze Tottie for me till she begs off, bless her. And Julia too, whether she will or no! What news? Your own, Patsy.

Wednesday, 21 July, 36 Roxborough Drive Tottie Darling. What am I thinking and doing? Thinking – what and how; doing – now and next. The whence and whither flew out the window when Bob came in at the door. Perhaps they're just sitting on a bough, two large owls, or a raven and an owl, winking and croaking till the day of the broom is past and they come into possession again.

Today? – the squirrels are turning somersaults and the very stones bid fair to blossom. We had our breakfast betimes. It is the most self-satisfied meal of the day for Robert because he gets it and consequently is full of the philosophy of life, coffee, and smoke. We are the diplomats, the generals of war and finance, the prophets and seers and what not, of the breakfast table behind the porch screen! He gets very much excited and pleased, then I wash the dishes and boil the rags, and scrub the sink, and sweep the floor. No dinner to get today; we are having it at the studio with the girls. Frances Loring I met at the Arts and Letters Club last winter. We exchanged calls and courtesies, and I saw little more of her or her companion, Florence Weil, until that memorable time recorded in my diary (which I think I will send you, because it all isn't anything now, and I've a notion it is rather well written?). They live in the upstairs of a little old house downtown: beams, rafters, and sky-light, and the floor littered with casts and models and swathed clay figures; a bedroom partitioned off, and a diminutive alcove kitchen that welcomes and provides for any number of guests at all hours of the day. For a dinner table, if you please, they roll a barrel out into the middle of the floor and nail a big square board on top of it. Since the picnic up the Humber, for I carried out to the letter all my elaborate scheming, we have been back and forth in the free-est and friendliest fashion. It was their picture I sent you; Florence Weil (in the kimono) is going down the river with us.

Now I must go back to my broom, Tottie dear, and get the guest room ready for Margaret [Thurston] coming tomorrow. Isn't it too good to be true? Bob will be lying down on his chores now, I plainly see. He is a joy to me. Such habits of neatness and care and attentiveness as he has developed are the pride of my heart. No more clothes to pick up or papers or matches; he helps make the bed and sort the clothes and I like to wait dinner and get it after he comes for the fun of bossing him around in the kitchen. And he is just as proud of himself, too, – fairly *likes* to have neighbors see him take in the clothes, and laughed at his foretime idea of a proper wife and how she should "crawl" to her lord and master. Extravagance is still a problem, not a worry, though heaven knows why I *don't* worry. We have spent $3000 of mine, including gifts (your blessed check, dear, just covered the rent arrears with a little welcome cash to spare), my savings (on carfare!) for the last ten years, and $400 worth of piano, and NOTHING to show for it. But I've a clever little scheme for NEXT time. No bills and no worry for Wifie; the bank account is going to be in Hubbie's name, and Hubbie is going to get a monthly allowance from Wifie and not another red cent, and PAY ALL THE BILLS! And strong-minded Wifie is not going to stir a finger to save the ship even if she sees it going straight to smash!

We need $3000 before we can leave Toronto: debts. That's the rub just now. Robert has been trying every way to arrange a loan on his contract with Sir William (pending) and insurance policies, but nobody'll take it, banks or insurance companies either, simply because it's Mackenzie and Mann and their security is no good. Everything else is well settled and away, as fine and complete an outfit as Robert could imagine, and that's going some, gone on Revillon Frères' steamer which sailed yesterday from Montreal for the Bay. Sir William gave Robert $1000 out of his own pocket for his photographic outfit. He seems keen about the moving pictures on Robert's account; I was for basing his whole future on them, wrenching them free of Sir Bill somehow, and developing them by and for ourselves, gradually weaning ourselves away from this slavery to salary, Mackenzie and Mann, or anybody else; make the pictures pay for future expeditions of our own. But Sir William won't give them up and he won't do anything with them, just sits on them as though they were a mineral claim, while the reels reel on! Judge of his appreciation of Robert's work when he didn't even know it was Robert himself who took the pictures, had no idea where the Belchers were or anything about them.

Well, dear, here I have been writing far into my busy morning.

A thunder storm has rumbled up and passed on. I wish you were here – to rub noses. Big hug, Patsy.

Friday, 23 July Margaret's initiation. Bob still trying to get his salary contract with Sir William – $6000. $3000 in advance to pay his debts.

Monday, 26 July A.m., while dressing, I to Bob: "Feel it in my bones you are going to get 'fixed up' somehow or other today." P.m., while dressing to go out to dinner, Bob to me, read copies of two following telegrams:

Toronto, 26 July

R.H. Flaherty
93 North Algoma Street
Port Arthur, Ontario

So that you may carry out understanding of leaving here tonight, we are mailing you today care Revillon Frères, Cochrane, cheque to pay Indians at Cochrane and for Gushue's salary. Your report will be upon ore-lands, and LaDuke has knowledge of their location. We also have enclosed order on LaDuke for use of letter of credit and to accept our instructions – also copies of invoices covering supplies shipped by the *Bonaventure* to Strutton Island, and order on that post to use any of these supplies if you arrive there before Mr. R.J. Flaherty. Also a copy of the location of the ore-deposit as filed with the government. Signed, Lewis Lukes

Toronto, 27 July 1915

R.H. Flaherty
93 North Algoma Street
Port Arthur, Ontario

Documents mentioned in my telegram yesterday have gone off to Cochrane. Would it not therefore be better for you to get to Cochrane unless you are obliged to come to Toronto on other business. Signed, Lewis Lukes

Which being interpreted, meant either that they were intending to "shake" Bob, or were putting up a bluff to scare him out of the fight for his salary, etc. Monstrous, laughable.

Wednesday, 28 July Two more days "up in the air."

Dinner time. Standing over something steaming on the stove, spoon in hand. Bob bursts in, bills bulging from every pocket – $1500. Had seen Sir William; Sir William had given him this amount and made him sign a statement acknowledging it as a satisfaction in full for all past claims. Not a scrap in writing from them to him as to salary, interest in the picture or anything else. And Bob, his face wreathed in smiles to think what an astute piece of business he had put through, told me how he had signed the paper and been thoroughly delighted with himself!!!! Sold out! the picture we had lived for and lavished for and worried over all winter, all the assurances of the promised $3000 we had alternately hoped for and despaired of with heart-burning and stormy rending of the domestic heaven(?) – all reduced to a smile and sold out for $1500. Joke! (And wait until you hear how that $1500 went!)

Thursday, 29 July Fever of packing, hoping to get away as fast as possible before any more untoward event could possibly happen. Departure set for Saturday night, 9 p.m.

Saturday, 31 July Late afternoon. House clear and swept clean, Trunks all packed. Bob at telephone trying to get a dray. Going to the Queens for dinner. Said Bob, the fatal words fell on my ears like doom, I knew they were coming, I knew it, I wanted to dodge. "We may be held up again, a constable at the train." And then came out the tale of the Ramsey Bill.

Bill contracted after the second expedition – settling time put off as usual until point of departure – settlement as usual subject to mortgage on the future in the form of a note on Bank of Ottawa, accepted by them on signed statement from Lewis Lukes that salary of $250 would be paid to the bank monthly. Bank lent Bob $1,100 on same guarantee. Bob left and trouble began. The bank got back its $1,100 by fighting for it, but not another cent to satisfy Ramsey.

So this trip Ramsey got a judgement against Bob. Bob was for giving them another of those convenient notes, and they were threatening to detain him until a sufficient and satisfactory guarantee should be attached thereto. The threat had been served that afternoon, and our train time noted. But, as it happened, we never got to the train, not a berth to be had, and the Queens harbored us for the night.

Monday, 2 August The fever of delay under the shadow of the law! Bob's pockets empty again, $50 of the $1500 left. NO, he had not paid his debts, not at all – only a few sundry insignificant few by cash, the rest were to be settled by that famous note system, including the balance of some $800 or so on the violin (and wait till you hear what happened to that violin!). All that $1500 had gone toward various salary and outfit items incident to our departure – all Mackenzie and Mann accounts of course.

Scene: room in hotel. Bob sprawled out disconsolately on chair. How much had I left from the account I had garnished for household bills? I reluctantly pulled forth a hoarded $200. Energy and enthusiasm return to Bob, out of the chair and out of the door at a bound.

Scene 2, later in the afternoon: return of Bob and Margaret from a motor drive seeing Toronto. A certain belligerent I-don't-care-if-you-don't swagger about Bob. Explanations finally forthcoming. He had bought, against all my dissuasions – a nasty little brute of a monkey – $30 worth of ugliness and bad temper, led, misled, by visions of a motion picture coup.[79]

Monday, 2 August   On the Grand Trunk Pullman. David joins our party.[80]

Tuesday, 3 August, King George Hotel, Cochrane   Bob buying river outfit, paid for by his father, Bob being once more out of pocket. Margaret and I seeing the town – one main street and several side issues. Supper time enlivened by another disclosure: all our goods, shipped from Toronto by express, under seizure to Cowan of the Hudson's Bay Company, held on account of $400 contracted by LaDuke on his way down the river in May. You see, I'll have to explain here that if I haven't before, that the Hudson's Bay Company had refused to give Mackenzie and Mann further credit until an outstanding bill of some $4000 should be paid (contracted by Bob on former trips). Mackenzie and Mann, loath to losses up, in spite of the fact that Sir Bill is a director of the Company, done the Indian trick of going over to the other company, Revillon Frères, gaining credit from them. Cash payment is therefore to be required in all Hudson's Bay Company transactions – awkward business in a region where the Hudson's Bay Company reigns in monopoly supreme.[81]

9 a.m. Mixed local on the Grand Trunk pulls out westward bound. Bob waving to us from station platform, left behind as hostage for the $400, and to keep the wires hot to Toronto.

Evening, in camp on the banks of the Ground Hog, waiting for Bob.

Would he come tonight or would it be tomorrow, or not until next week! Nothing to do but meet all the trains.

Wednesday, 4 August Supper time in camp. Sounds of the motor canoe returning from the line. All hands to the bank. Only two men in the canoe – another disappointment. And then Bob bounced up from under a blanket amidships arms waving. All clear, at last, relief unutterable. What ho, now and henceforth, for light hearts and romance unalloyed!

Our trip divides itself into four well-defined chapters, beginning, chapter 1, "The River Trip," 185 miles downstream from Ground Hog to Moose Factory, then – but you shall hear in detail.

From river to river we came wending down, by the little shore-shadowed Ground Hog, the wider flowing Mattagami with its high granite banks and boulder-strewn stream, foam and rapid and fall, and then the Moose, wide, shallow rapids and rapids, silvery and shoal, of grey shores of limestone and fossil, being the ancient bed of the Bay. Tide water and current meet far upstream, threading a maze of waterways. Here one glorious morning, Saturday, August the fourteenth, we came singing along between the wooded islands, rounded a point of land, and there were people, squaws on the bank, a curious crowd, haystacks, and cows, and a church, and then a row of white houses, Moose Factory, the Hudson's Bay Company Post. And chugging toward us came a launch, bearing welcome – Sam's beaming smile, even LaDuke's sombre countenance twitched at the corners, and Bill, the Captain, was frankly grinning from ear to ear.[82] Alongside and over and we went chugging merrily on, past the Post, ringing twelve o'clock from the carpenter shop belfry, three miles further where the fringe of an out-lying island the topmast of the good old *Laddie* pointed against the sky.

The *Laddie*! and our clambering on her solid black hull and over the rail! and how we sat all that afternoon dangling our legs over the edge of the afterdeck, chin in hand gazing, speechlessly gazing, up at the queer old-time square rigging, down at the cluttered deck where our pack sacks and dunnage lay jumbled up with water and beer and oil kegs, loose lumber and a various assortment of baskets and pans and pails collected about the little 2 by 4 galley, from the open door of which Sarah, the squaw, our Indian guides and swarthy fire-rangers, with a motley collection of Indians and half-breeds from the Post were lounged about the deck in various attitudes of pipe smoking. A canoe came alongside, another dusky face appeared over the rail, and Bob with much ceremony brought up and presented to us Tookalook, an

Eskimo. We found nothing the least incongruous about this formal hand-shaking: we took to Tookalook at once, short and bow-legged and shuffling as he was, there was something about him of self-possession and dignity; Tookalook was a gentleman.

And so passed ten sunny days and mirrored sunsets, lying at anchor, the *Laddie* marking time to the ebb and flow of the tide, Bob buying out the store. Margaret and I busy in the berry patch, while the real business of the trip went on below the decks where all day and overtime besides, Walter and Stewart struggled manfully with the *Laddie*'s outworn engine. Not a ship's length from our berth could we stir without it; a narrow channel, two bars and clearing them save at the moment of high tide. We put our house in order; Sarah, the divine Sarah, as M. the gallant chevalier of the French Company called her, bowing low, while Sarah snickered behind her hand, was dispatched. We entertained and were entertained by the pale post superintendent and his half-breed wife and their two little Indian faced children. We danced with Bull, our comely faced guide, in a room reeking Indian to the fiddle and the drum squatted cross-legged against the wall. Finally came the day and the pilot, the engine gasped and chocked and blew clouds of villainous smoke through all the afterhold, chasing us from our cabins like bees smoked out of a hive, and with a creaking of the anchor chain we were, as last, off and away.

Now Sam and Bill and Stewart are three as sturdy, handy, willing lads as ever sailed out of St. John's; but Bill had shipped as a cook, and Stewart was never an engineer and all that any and all of them together knew about navigation had been learned within sight of land. So it was with the Labrador fishermen – sail with a fair wind and the harbor at night. So we anchored that first night, and Jocko, the monkey was all the anchor watch we kept. Dawn was gray when I awoke to the bumping of the keel beneath my bunk. Wind and weather were blowing and beating outside. I heard the engine, and slept on again in security. False security, for morning found us hard and fast aground, a mile to leeward of the channel beacons, with a half a gale blowing, and a ring of boiling surf all about us, and the engine room flooding fast! That was a day – pumping by shifts, hoisting the mainsail to steady her, and still as the tide went out and the storm continued, little by little she keeled, settling in the mud, and more and more desperate seemed our plight. We cabin passengers were ordered ashore. That night, the retreat to the Post will ever remain lurid in my mind – the cold, the storm, clouds and crimson rifts, the turbid tumbled water, and suddenly, glowing in the sky, embracing the poor old *Laddie* all forlorn and aslant, a great, glorious rainbow arc. Was it a beautiful requiem, or was it really an omen of good hope?

The next days for us were blind days, interned in comfort and security in the old Company house at the Post, guests of Mrs. Wilson, our wonderfully kind hostess. But our hearts were with the *Laddie*, lightening and patching and getting her afloat. Came a fearful storm one afternoon, tearing roofs and trees, churning the bays, and when it cleared, there, upright in the offing stood the masts of the *Laddie*!

Our final crossing of the bar was the actual realization of my pet recurrent nightmare, wherein I am in a water craft perilously navigating dry land. Once again we barely missed disaster, the engine balked at the bar like a balky horse at a fence and we had to turn narrowly grazing a shoal and try again. And then how for hours we bumped, bumped, bumped, tethering on the waves, creeping over the ground, shaking and shivering, lagging far behind the fast out-flowing tide, while Sam in a fateful, sing-song called out the falling fathoms!

But oh, sailing in the *Laddie* before a gentle wind and a gentle sea had a salt and savor about it that can never be again when the good old sailing ships and the seas they sailed have passed into tradition. How we loved to waken in the morning to the chanties of the men as they hoisted anchor and sail, and how we loved to sit on the aftercabin deck at night with Sam at the wheel and listen to the tales of the Labrador. It was all too short. A week and a day and we had to say good-bye to the *Laddie* and watch her sail away with a last ahoy at the ropes and a last chug of the engine, and fading row of faces at the rail-bound for the Belchers – without us. Never shall I forget that last evening, sitting on shore, the *Laddie* dimly outlined in the channel before us, the quiet of the evening broken by the gentle grating of a boat on the beach; we looked down on a procession of figures bearing burdens; they filled the canoe and pushed off, a row of silhouetted heads above the gunwale, and glided out into the deepening twilight toward the schooner. "There," said Bob, "goes an epic." It was Tookalook and Wetalltok and "Tommy," their wives, children, dogs and household goods, and they were going back to the land of their fathers, the Belchers – Bob was taking them.[83]

So ended the second chapter of our adventures. So we were left cast up on an island while Bob and the *Laddie* and the main current of adventure sailed on! But little time had we for repining; we had to hustle to keep ourselves in food, firewood, and make provisions against wind and weather and threatened cold. Never before have I been left so entirely dependent for subsistence on my own efforts and faculties. Mr. Flaherty is an old hand in the woods, and fashioned all sorts of convenient and indispensable articles out of old boxes and bow-wire, gallon cans and scraps of iron. My province was the cooking, my larder a high platform or cache made necessary to keep our staff of life, consisting of a variety of cans, from the ravenous, marauding, four-footed visitors – nothing more alarming than the thievish pack of dogs that prowled about the Hudson's Bay station a mile down the shore, but quite as dangerous to our well-being as the wildest beast. Day and night we had to be more watchful than they. There were fish in the streams and birds along the shore. Mr Flaherty got the fish and David the birds and great was the rejoicing and feasting on fried trout and "bully for all" after a day's fortunate catch or hunt. And then the berries, Margaret's and my quarry – more berries you never saw, the ground, the bushes, the trees were covered with them – currants red and black, gooseberries, blueberries, and a dozen more varieties unfamiliar to us, among them a little red berry growing in the moss that made a more delicious cranberry sauce than was ever tasted further south. Our limpid, cold-as-ice water supply flowed past the camp just two steps down a mossy bank. There we squatted, Indian-fashion, and scoured our pots and pans with moss and sand. But oh, the sparkle of the mornings, the cold and the dew and the freshness; and the wind on the beach, and the buoyant, spongy caribou moss inland. Sometimes we tramped all day, and every day was a new glory of color – fall, with its Midas touch over the tinkling aspen, with a delicate palette over the gray moss, tinting it pale lavender and sage green, painting every little leaf and the low-lying bushes until they glowed like rubies aslant the sun. And the vivid northern sky by day and the eerie northern lights by night. Two weeks of perfect weather and then came a lowering sky, a rapidly falling barometer, a new feeling in the air that made us want to fly to cover with the birds and puff our feathers for downy comfort, and the equinox burst upon us. Our poor tent! We called it Lydia Languis, for, for all we could do, it would flop and sag in the most disconsolate fashion, and now the wind shook it and beat its flapping sides together, and the rain wept through it, and it was a sorry enough cover, forsooth! And the wind lashed our fire, and flame and smoke and ash darted and whirled out and blinded and singed us as, in gleaming raincoats and with all our eaves dripping, we bent over our supper pans. Those were the days! The ship was due, overdue; our neighbors down the shore, a government party of surveyors, were folding their tents for departure south; conjectures were rife as to possible mishaps of the ship, and we began to feel something of the grip, the inexorableness of the country. We pictured ourselves and the island wrapped in winter snows, a few fateful flurries had already drifted over us. Our neighbors took their chance with the first fair wind; we saluted them bravely as they passed us by, watched them come to anchor off the point held back by the heavy sea, and, still watching, saw their flag travel up the mast and down and up again and remain floating from the masthead. Fearfully expectant we waited and watched, until, sure enough, above the horizon appeared two masts and a funnel in between, and we knew that anxious waiting was over.

Sunday, 3 October, Aboard the *Nascopie* She's a comfortable craft, and it's a friendly company, passengers and crew, all of the country and the Company, most of them known to Bob and familiar to me in his diaries. We passed the Belchers some several hundred miles to eastward, night before last. Yesterday we sighted land again, the sheer, snow-capped cliffs of Cape Wolstenholme. Utter barrenness and desolation, snow-drift in the air – our first typically Arctic scenery under a typically Arctic sky. The Post, of three houses, one of the most remote in all the Bay, and according to report the worst conditioned, lies in the hollows of a gloomy fiord on an ancient glacier-bed. Here it was that Bob came out to "Civilization" from his second expedition through the interior. Today we are due in Lake Harbour, Baffinland, and perhaps to see some of Bob's friends of last year, the Baffinland Eskimos. Then on to Chimo, another one of his milestones. Altogether, by the time we are at St. Johns, I shall have much of the story of his last four years at first hand in terms of people and places. In this respect the trip through the Straits has been most fortunate, and taken altogether the experience has been of vast value toward understanding. I have felt enough of the country to know both its fascination and its fear. Neither are describable or explicable. One must come and see for oneself, in the face and fashion of the people, the inexorable toll that the country, the cold, the desolation, solitude and isolation, exacts of those who brace and stay them. It was fear of this influence that made Bob refuse so long to listen to any proposal of my going with him – he was afraid for me. And it is for that now that I want to pull him out or stay with him to fight it off, because now I can read the signs and I am afraid for him – afraid that this winter lost means never-to-be-regained advantage given to this intangible, insidious foe. It is the final, the most sinister phase of the country, its death grip.

The salvaging of the *Fort Churchill*. Most unexpected news at Moose, for us to speculate upon and while away the time; Mr. Wilson was away in the *Inenew*, gone to the Belchers! Disquieting thought, especially taken in conjunction with his winter trip to New York, quite unprecedented. Something important afoot without a doubt. Two tourists accompanied him, from New York, more disquieting thought. The aim of the trip was apparently perfectly straightforward, being the salvaging of the *Fort Churchill* stranded on the islands, so reported by Island Eskimos to Great Whale River and located by Renouf of that post with sledge and dog-team during the winter season past. A two years' wanderer in the Bay, the *Fort Churchill* had slipped from her berth at York and, like a wraith in all her winter shroud, been swept away with the ice to be seen no more. A maiden voyage this of hers, having been but just come from her launching in England.[84] From her salvaging expedition the *Inenew* was already overdue home again. We looked for her with every horizon unrolling northward, but passed Charlton and on to Strutton without sight or sign of her; and then she passed us on to Moose with her quarry in tow, and we knew nothing of it until we were back in Charlton channel. But then the whole tale was told, told by Renouf himself, hero of the winter expedition and party to this most successful second. We baited him in the cabin with oranges and claret and marveled inwardly at his immaculate white sweater and sundry other niceties of costume. Absorption held us, the afternoon passed and the evening – the scene shifting to the deck, main boom and a coil of rope – and still the subject grew and the chase waxed ever more keen, over land and sea, sailing and tramping, fixing land and water marks – such tokens as the barren land afforded – marking off the days by weathers and tides, piecing out all the puzzling scraps of circumstances and evidence, until there mapped itself out some sort of picture of harbor, ship, and ore location. And the finished picture was to a mile or so a perfect replica of all Bob's representations. It was acknowledged to be the truth; doubting Thomases could talk no more; crew and company alike had increased in wonder and amazement as, day and night and still by day again, they sailed this undreamed length of land. Jobin, scoffer in chief, must needs now with Captain Redfern's data to help, make calculations and charts to take back to his department, that same Hydrographic Survey of Canada at Ottawa that had so laughed Bob to scorn so short a time since. How were our enemies refuted and brought to naught.[85] Bob glowed inwardly with the fullness of his satisfaction, and Mr Flaherty was a changed and sanguine man, an ear-witness if not an eye-witness to the prospects of the land. That last morning on the beach they sat and talked, father and son, as bound together at last, in the common undertaking of their lives and its near goal. And I, sitting by, listened, all thought of the near and year – endless parting swallowed up in these men's affairs, and knowing myself and my feelings as but a small and inconsiderable matter tossed on this advance wave of the slow, age-long, world-engulfing tide of Humanity and Civilization rolling up over the North Country. Of what moment might not Rob's work be, should high expectations be fulfilled!

Open the Bay, which o'er the Northland broods,
Dumb, yet in labor with a mighty fate.
Open the Bay! Humanity intrudes,
And gropes, prophetic, round its solitudes,
In eager thought, and will no longer wait.
(From "Open the Bay" by Charles Mair)[86]

On board the *Nascopie*. Dear old Boy. I'm blue. I want you, oh I want you; and I don't know whether to shake off my mind and laugh and go out and play cards, or stay and talk to you and wipe my eyes. I want to put my head in the hollow of your shoulder and my arm across your chest and have you kiss my hair. Will you, when you come back? I wish I could go to sleep until that time and dream, as I have dreamed these nights, that we were in each other's arms again, the warm comfort of it. Do you ever want to be separated again? Is it worth it? If I had only dared to dare. Perhaps it will be different for me when I begin to feel the quickening of that other life; I hug myself even now sometimes and feel full and serene and satisfied; and I picture all that's going to happen at home, and when you come back – my room with the big four-poster and a crib beside it, and the little room which will be yours and the bathroom in between, and the fun we'll have in the morning with a jolly wide-awake crawling over us and sliding down your knees.

Keep us in your dreams too dear, and in your arms, all the nights. Your wife.

On the Intercontinental to Montreal. Dear Boy. I am dazed; so was Margaret. I can understand how you must feel – only 1000 times more – when you come down; I don't seem to feel any excitement, incapable of it. And something has happened to the whole trip, it has faded away like nothing. I shan't be able to talk about it even.

We left Margaret at Halifax yesterday afternoon. Had a day and a half at St. John's and loved it! Sail into St. John's harbor at eight o'clock some misty October morning and you will never forget it either. The harbor was full of shipping, fish, salt, and seal. We went to see Bill's wife, and a happy thought it was. The poor woman was all in a muddle, expecting Bill back and getting only a note, and thinking from the newspaper report that you were back and he left behind. She felt much better after seeing us. And I sent the kiddies some fruit.

We took the *Florizel* to Halifax – heaven, after the unspeakable filth of the *Nascopie*; and here we are, what's left of the party, including Mr Fleming and your friend Mr Mackenzie.[87] Your father and the latter seem to have struck up a great friendship, wining and dining together as thick as thieves. For my part, the man effects me like some leprous beast. Mr Fleming I love, and love to be with. He has been a great companion all through the trip, and perhaps I shall go down to Port Hope as his and Mrs Fleming's guest before I leave Toronto. Telegraphed the family from St. John's – mother in Boston, Dad on his way to Ann Arbor, and Charlotte and the children, bless them, "waiting for me at the old stand." But I am not at all sure that I shall stay with them after Christmas. I have vowed a vow, in sweat and anguish, last night; my finger is troubling me, pains way up my arm; I asked a doctor on the train – bone involved, finger probably have to come off. I thought I wanted to die, nothing seemed to count, you or your child or anything. I was ready to give them all up only to have my finger and the keys under my hand; and I vowed to God in prayer that if my finger were spared, I'd devote myself to my music first. And I know I shall.

Sunday, 24 October, Wellesley Hospital   Waiting to have X-ray taken of my finger before I go to bed. Operation in the morning, good thing to have it over with. Dr. Caven has been a trump to put the whole thing through in such short order for me. I called him the first thing when I got in this morning, and here I am. Spent the day at Queens sorting baggage. Whole staff much interested in our arrival and the fate of the monkey.

Had a talk with Louise. Poor child, as she looks better herself, but hasn't had any picnic at the office. Your father wired her for money ($250) from St. John's; she was refused it on the grounds that salary being charged up to the account of the Northlands Exploration Co., Mackenzie and Mann had nothing to do with it. She stuck it out, managed to extract $100 which put your father under the I should think galling obligation of borrowing from me for himself and David. As for your affairs, it is just as I anticipated; not a red cent has been paid in to your account on the ground that the $1500 paid to you before you left was advance salary and that they were under no obligation to pay any more anyway. Your creditors are howling around their ears threatening suit, Paul Hahn the loudest among them! They go to Mr Lukes and are referred to Mackenzie and Mann who know nothing about the matter and refer them back to Lukes – the same old game. I guess they are trying to shake you, Bob, as too expensive a proposition (and I must confess I have a sneaking sympathy with them!). Only I advise you this time to do the shaking first and let them fight for their goods.

Now for bed and slumber. The nurse has just brought me a nice brimming glass of orangeade – don't you wish you were in a hospital!

Monday, 25 October Afternoon. All over – none the worse. "Going under" (the Anesthetic) is the weirdest of all un-real sensations. One thought I clung to, as a drowning man to a straw, repeating to myself, "God" and "I love my husband," "God" and "I love my husband," a woman's two anchors, I guess, to carry her through any storm and stress. And of course the first thing I thought of when I "came out" was to wiggle my finger to see if it was all there. It was!

Tuesday, 26 October, Wellesley Hospital Another agony, another cup of fear to drink – the fear of losing the babe. They've given me a codeine to avert the threatened disaster – my head is thick with it. This cup perhaps was not quite so full of anguish as the other – the finger would have been so irrevocable, this perhaps not, though at my age? (Poor little Julia; but she is still so young) I've smiled so often and with such complacency to think how all my plans – the plans I planned last autumn as I walked between practice hours along Riverside Drive! – have come true. I would marry Bob, said I to myself, and that was long before he'd remembered me – and we would live together, and by the time it came for him to go away I should have my wish. And I should have my music too; and then, while Bob was away year and again, we, my wish and I, left behind, would have such a wonderful time, growing up and being educated, with our music and languages and traveling abroad.

And so we were married. I could hardly wait to begin my plan, my beautiful new scheme of life, with Bob as the instrument of my desires, such a nice healthy, interesting, convenient "tool."

And so we lived together – and something happened, and swallowed up all that pretty little scheme of mine – new desires, new creeds – I would have no life but his, risk everything, endure everything, give everything for the sake of that perfect sharing of life in all things great and small. We were so passionate toward each other, and with all the superficial differences between us in breeding, education, disposition and temperament, fundamentally we believed and loved and desired of life the same things. Between us were the makings of a rare relationship, a wonderful passionate partnership. I would throw myself and all I possessed, my mental equipment and my heart's enthusiasm, into his work and its fulfillment; his the conception, mine the detail; his the sowing, mine the garnering; surely as my nature and gifts were complementary to his, I could be a real and valuable partner. All my heart was in this new ideal; the winter at the Belchers would be the first step, the definite beginning.

Then fate stepped in; and even before we started out on the great adventure, I knew that I must at the threshold turn back. Shall you ever forget that night, my Dear, on the deck of the *Laddie*, with the sky above and the water beneath like the hollow of a great star-studded bowl about us, how I yearned clinging to you and the adventure, how helpless and afraid I was and incoherent against fate, because I saw as you couldn't, how it was a crisis in the direction of our lives and the quality of our relation – that it was too truly a parting of the ways. I know how I, coming back, would inevitably drift back into the channel of my old individual life. For you, living alone again crudely and carelessly would only deepen those differences between us, differences that with a passionate consecration to one and the same life and work could count for so little, but that on the lesser more conventional plane of a less absorbing bond would count for only too much.

Thursday, 4 November Dearest, I thought I wasn't going to think about you very much, with the result that I think about nothing else all the time. I thought I wasn't going to care about writing to you, with the result that I seem possessed to share with you every insignificant detail of the passing of every day. Your misfortune, not my fault.

Today I am on the Canadian National Railroad, the "rocky road" to Port Arthur, with a car load of other husbandless women (men at the front), each one with a handful of young children, poor souls, all eating and yelling in chorus – bedlam. Your father got me the pass, and saw me off at the station last night with a delicious basket of fruit. David went off Monday night on the first through train.

Yesterday I spent in Port Hope with Mr and Mrs Fleming. Took a drive about the country. No thank you, no living in or about Toronto for me, if choice be mine. The country is deadly uninteresting to me. Better by far a shack in such woods as we are passing through now; it's more like home. I should be happier roughing it anywhere out here, than hanging onto the skirts of civilization in a dead-level town like Toronto. The only thing that made Toronto bearable to come back to was the old Queens [Hotel]. It seemed as nearly like home as any habitation there could be. I went to the studio for tea; Miss Young was there of course; no, nice as they were, the air, the talk, everything about it bored me to tears. Dear Mrs Caven and good Aunt Emily – I did enjoy their call. And what do you suppose they brought me – a wooly, white, hood affair about as big as a minute. I hardly know which way to look at it, it made me feel so queer.

But most of the time I spent in the office looking over your negatives, etc. The negative of the one I consider your best portrait, far and away above the others, is missing. Small wonder when such wonderful care is taken of them. Your friend, Mr Booth, and I had a conversation on the same subject, both foaming at the mouth, with the result that I am having some boxes made such as he has for his plates, and have plans for a cataloging system to keep track of them.

I called up Mr Currelly to ask him about treating a feather dickey I got at Chimo to preserve it properly, and received from him with a package of arsenical soap a very nice note all about my "wonderful husband"! People are still talking about the moving pictures from Baffinland, Mr. Fleming tells me. Percy A. McCord sends you a letter under heading of his new company asking about the films; hardly to be regretted that of course no notice was taken of it.

Wednesday, 10 November On the Canadian National Railroad, going back to Toronto. Just a line before I go to bed. Have been pegging away at my diary all day and am almost pegged out as to brains. It has been a wonderful day – Thunder Bay and Nipigon. Was there ever a more wonderful country. I have the same thrill as always, coming home to Lake Superior; it isn't Houghton or any other place – just the Lake; Port Arthur is as much home as Houghton. Can't we have Sam Mark's bungalow and live in it summer and winter, and sail and paddle, and camp about with our packs and babies on our backs. I'm dying to. I saw Long Lake; I remember your diary and the threatened storm and the loon!

I am going back to Toronto to try for the marketing of your film.

Wish me luck! I'm so glad I had my visit with your Mother. Arthur is having a hard time not wanting to go to school – got suspended for copying (!), and so is trying a job at the railroad yards.[88] I guess he is better off so. David lost all his good camp appetite. Both those boys ought to be out chopping wood, and no more hanging around idle indoors.

Next Morning. I've had such a nice encounter with such a nice fresh-faced lad; the porter was our go-between and "Hudson Bay" the open sesame to conversation. He is, or was, one of the Mounted Police stationed at Fort Churchill, wanted to go to the war, started off on a supposed bear-hunt, left his boat and Eskimos at Cape Churchill and walked alone, along shore, all the way to Port Nelson, carrying only bear meat for grub and no gun – 19 days. Tells how he met a bear, a nice fat young white one, which fortunately took to the water instead of to him; his knees wouldn't hold him for the rest of the day! And now he is bound for New York, across the border, before they pinch him and lock him up in the Police "pen" for a year. He's a great lad, N.C. Orden.

Monday, 22 November, The Selby, Toronto Well, Old Man, I'm full of schemes. I've been talking to Sam Marks. That Nipigon idea appeals to me more and more. Sam says he has a 26 foot launch that'll go anywhere on Lake Superior in any weather, makes 12–13 knots an hour. Where better could we live and establish our family homestead? In reaching distance of both Houghton and Port Arthur, in one of the most beautiful nature spots in all the world (of that I am sure), an ideal place to bring up children (and, between you and me, I think there are going to be lots of them – boys!). We could live there simply and economically and as we liked, and come to the city for things of the city whenever and for as long as we liked. I am going to talk to your father about it next.

I am going to hear Paderewski (!) tonight, and I'm going home tomorrow to be with the family on Thanksgiving Day.[89] My cataloging stint is done. Mother and I did much of it together – numbering the negatives and the "bags," as Mr Booth calls the envelopes. I have followed his suggestions right through, and half a dozen boxes made, handy for carrying, and discarded all those miserable tin-fastener envelopes that have been scratching your plates and buckling your films by the score. What a pity that all the negatives shouldn't be clean and without flaw, when it is such a joy to have them so, and only takes a little more care. What you must do first thing with the negatives you bring down next time is to have them all re-washed and well washed and then put right from the racks into envelope, number both negative and "bag" and keep them so. I have also had cards printed, like this, to be in the place of any negative that is taken out for any reason at all. That should keep track of them. And remember those negatives are all the working capital we have. Many of them should increase in value with time.

I wonder if Sir William may yet have read my letter. Your father took it up to the office this morning and Mr Annesley promised to push it through. It was about the Moving Pictures, of course.

Oh yes, and I have a new acquisition that I love, a picture of David that David himself cut out of an old album for me. It is like a D.O. Hill, do you remember it? The little boy in the big leather arm chair with the buttons on his coat and the book in his lap and the hobnails in his shoe. It is a little gem – I love it! Mr Raw framed it well.

You should feel Robert Allen kick, and you should see the socks I'm knitting for his knickers. Love from your Old Woman.

Sunday, 28 November, HOME I've had such a good time today. Up in the third story this morning where there is no steam bath and one can think without suffocating. I've decided that most of our ills, particularly nervous affections, come from overheated houses; takes all the freshness out of one's skin, for one thing, makes it dry and wrinkled and old – like a nervous person's. Conversely look at the English skin and the temperature of their houses. How much better it would be if we were to keep the indoor temperature as even as possible with the outdoor, and regulated our clothing instead. We wouldn't suffer half as much from stuffed noses then or a thousand other troubles. I nosed about the bookshelves putting mental labels on various volumes to be included in Dad's present to us when we do get a home – the stocking of our library shelves from his own. You would probably have pounced on some of Pa's pet Americana and Indian portraits, but my covetousness was eclectic, omnivorous. The old *Robinson Crusoe* I read as a child, bird books and flower books and fairy tales, mythologies; I wished I could find some of the old German fairy-tale books my old nurse used to read to me, and the "Max and Moritz" pictures! I started to read Dad's *Woods and Lakes of Maine*. I wanted to see what he had made of his record of camping experience. He published the book at his own expense and lost money on it, but has made a matter of $100 a year on his map. If we only could have been here at home together for a little while last year, you could picture it now and share, even by letter, a little of the stimulus of it. I came early Thursday morning; the house was so spacious and spotless, the floors so polished, everything so shining and orderly and complete – all the tempting new books keeping up with the latest discriminating thought. At Charlotte's I wandered about for an hour from room to room, upstairs and downstairs and in my lady's chamber, with new eyes taking note of the daintiness of the ruffled counterpane on Bobbie's bed, the perfect taste framing of all the pictures, the kind of "de luxe" perfection bought "at the right place" with all the assurance of a full purse. A new Edison diamond disc machine in the sitting room, and upstairs a new black seal suit-case marvelously fitted out with every conceivable *article de toilette* in ivory, each one marked with a blue monogram – the enviable joint achievement of imagination and means. At dinner the children sat at a little side table and ate each course as we did with all the proper formality of china and glass and shining silver, individual jelly moulds and nut baskets, and a stately Italian silver salt-cellar.

Such a romping and a roughhousing as there was afterward though! They are a noisy, all-over the place crew. I brought them little dolly Thanksgiving hampers from Chicago, and they loved them just as much as if they had eaten their dinner with a wooden spoon. Charlotte went to Chicago that afternoon. In the evening Dad and I talked Robinson Crusoe, his latest enthusiasm; has a collection of over 250 volumes and an especially engraved book plate for them. Then we drifted on to your work, lots of keen and interested questions and several details I was rather put to it to answer definitely. If you had only been there to seize the mood in its freshness and fullness, you and he would have talked all night.

"Al" came to see me. You certainly made a hit with Al. She asked a millon questions and wanted to see your picture – how you looked now. I am always glad of an excuse that I haven't any, for of course by the time you come down again you will have regained all your youthful fairness and frugality of face and figure, and won't be such a shock to their sensibilities. I am feeding my fancy day and night on a picture of you I had at college – Mother put it on my bureau. If you don't appear before me in its exact image, I shall die of heart failure on the station platform.

Thursday, 2 December In bed on the Pullman between Chicago and Toronto. Oh how much rather I'd be with you tonight. I'm tired to the point of tragedy. There's only one place I could forget about it – a pleasant valley somewhere about east and a little south of your chin! I suppose you have drifted contentedly back into the old bunk-it-alone ways; but I haven't, I don't like this alone business. I didn't like leaving home yesterday. Charlotte had just come back from Chicago, and it was like pulling teeth to leave them all again. I was full of misgivings besides. I had misgivings when I left Toronto, all that night on the train, whether I was doing right in keeping my promise to Mother to be home for Thanksgiving, whether I ought not rather to wait in Toronto for the next move in the Moving Picture business. You see, I wrote Sir William, and called on Mr Lukes, and they seem to have found my arguments convincing, for when I went in to see Sir William that night (I saw him at 5:30 and my train left at 6:30!), he acquainted me with Mr Lukes' intention of taking up the matter in New York and suggested my leaving a note for Mr. Lukes with Mr Annesley. There was time only to leave a verbal message with Mr. Annesley, then I sent the note later from home. Day before yesterday I received a letter from Mr Lukes asking me to make it convenient to come to Toronto for an interview. So here I am. The fact that they are taking the matter up with so much alacrity makes me almost suspicious of my own idea. Was it such a good one after all, and will it work out as I reckoned for our advantage? Would it have been better to wait until you came down next year? Will marketing this film help or harm the next one? The reasoning that inspired my letter to Sir William was this: from the way things are going, the fact that your salary is not being paid, that even your father's salary is being held up, that Sir William and Lady Mackenzie are being sued for petty tradesman's bills in the Division court, etc., etc. I saw that when you came down next year things were going to be even worse than they were last year, and that your only recourse would be to hold up everything until your salary, your expense account, and every item for which you could be held responsible, either sentimentality or actually, is paid up in full and in cold cash. Under those circumstances, any value that could be attached to your new film through the production of the old would be worth fighting for; and any bit of reputation you could gain thereby, too, would be an asset for the future when we are done with Mackenzie and Mann and want to go on with pictures.

Now suppose all my reckoning should be wrong after all, and that the production of this film instead of creating a further demand should satiate what demand there is and so kill your next film! Or suppose I should bungle my part and the pictures be badly put on and you get no reputation at all! Nothing to do but to go ahead. Thank goodness you are not one to cry if I do make a mess of it. We won't care about anything. So put out the light and good-night.

P.S., in the dark: Isn't it funny – how we used to talk about "our work" and here we are about it, and we don't know it yet!

Friday, 3 December Darling, I adore you. It's all right, everything is all right. I talked with Mr Lukes this afternoon for two solid hours. He was his very most agreeable self. We went over the whole file of correspondence re the picture; I have it now in my possession to take down to New York with me for reference, and with it carte blanche to go ahead and do what I can. Whether or not it is going to be advisable to produce this film now, in advance of the one you will bring down next year, is to be left entirely to my judgement, Mr Lukes' idea coinciding exactly with mine, that this film should be used only as it may serve to promote the next! He really seems both keenly interested and wholly reasonable, brought up the matter of my expenses himself and gave me a check for $100 on the spot. You should have seen your father when I told him that. He gave me a nice big squeeze around the waist when I came in (I've kissed him twice!), and then we went out to tea, and I ate all his toast; and then I ran for a car, and I think he was almost alarmed – but Robert 3rd. is a duck, lots of company and not the least trouble in the world. Your father has about made up his mind to leave Mackenzie and Mann the first of the year, says he has several other prospects and several commissions that he could put through if he were free. I shall be glad if he does. Harry has joined the 94th battalion and will soon be off for the front.[90] I can hardly bear to think of Frances' feelings just now. Arthur has a job in the shipyards making ammunition. And that's all the news for today – except that I saw Mr Annesley for a minute and had a nice chat with him.

Saturday, 11 December, The Bryn Mawr Club, New York An interesting evening yesterday; stayed at home for dinner and who should come in to share my tete-a-tete table with me but Mary L. Jobe, she whose account of the climbing of an unexplored peak in the Canadian Rockies last summer I read in the *Bryn Mawr Quarterly*.[91] She showed me her pictures of the trip (3A Kodak), the mountain pictures taken in series to form panoramas, the others all splendidly thought out and taken to tell a consecutive story. I admired her skill in getting such a clear and comprehensive illustrative series. But then, she has been at it, in that country, working along those lines for eight years; she has "had experience." She had an article in *Harper's* last May, consequently she knew exactly how to go about it to get the maximum of "copy" out of her trip. And then a trip like that, straight to a goal and back again all in a summer's vacation, is of itself such an easy thing to handle. I thought of all our mountain-mass of undigested material and envied her compact little portfolio. Ours has just got to grow into shape, slowly and naturally, without forcing. That is the way I intend to try to handle this affair of the pictures. I wrote to the Paramount Co. that I was here ready to take up negotiations where we left off last spring. That was Wednesday a.m., no reply yet. I learn from one of the girls in the house – secretary to the President of the New Netherlands Bank, a girl of awfully good family connections in Boston, who has built up for herself business connections here – that back of Paramount Co. is the Guaranty Trust Co.; she can give me a letter of introduction to one of their staff. Also, she knows well Mr. Grosvenor, brother of the Grosvenor of the *National Geographical Magazine*, a New York lawyer who has been handling cases against the "Movie Trust;" she will put me in touch with him.[92] It all means, simply, camping on the ground, meeting as many interesting people as possible, and seizing every opportunity that comes along.

I seized what I thought was an opportunity in Houghton – read in a booklet sent out by the *National Geographical Magazine* mention of their interest in a biological survey of Hudson's Bay, so wrote, asking for information, explaining the grounds of my interest and referring to the account of your work that is in the September number of the *Royal Geographical Journal*.[93] I send you a copy of that account, suggesting that they will probably be glad to receive your story *direct* of the exploration of the islands and that any material you can bring down in the shape for publication will be much to the good. Miss Jobe gave me a letter to the American Geographical Society, which published the official account of her ascent with maps, etc. Paid her $30 for it. *Harper's* is paying her $150.

Going to New Haven today for over Sunday with "Jaynesie." Her husband is Leonard Tyler, descendant of Audubon. Jaynesie saw the picture catalog and Eskimo drawings and almost had a fit over them – it was a gold mine, she declared, and when I bewailed how you smashed and wasted and threw away your gold mines, she lit into me for a poor sort of wife! Alan Sullivan's article with your pictures came out in the September *Century*, by the way. I glanced over it but not to read it. I send that too. Cousin Julie was so disgusted that you should have let him have them. Jaynsie knows the Putnam family, publishers, very well, and I am looking forward to an interesting talk with Mr Putnam sometime. See how much there is in the New York air!

Wednesday, 29 December, Bryn Mawr Club, New York Just been reading the prospectus of the "Scenograph Feature Film Co." Percy A.

McCord, Secretary and Treasurer, Robert W. Priest, Esq., Vice President and General Manager. Our old acquaintance, Mr Hendricks has nothing to do with it; he "fell down," as Mr McCord expressed it. I had a talk with him yesterday morning in Boston at his office – a neat and unpretentious affair, the office – and in spite of myself I was rather taken with the little man this time. His talk was straight forward and straight out, and I couldn't help admiring the stick-to-it-tiveness that after four months fooling around the picture corporations, and four more months wasted over Hendricks, kept him at it until he had formed a company of his own to handle his film and others like it on lines entirely outside the main "movie" system.

With the Movies all drama this year, harder than ever, with one exception, the Paramount Co., and you see by the enclosed clipping what they are doing. Was much interested in that notice for the reason that Mr. Louis Francis Brown is the man I saw at the American Play Co. where I was recommended to go by Miss Anne Morgan through Molly. I found Mr Brown on that occasion in the act of getting on his overcoat to catch a train to Philadelphia and our whole interview took place in the elevator on the way down from the tenth story; but from it I gleaned the fact of his connection with Burton Holmes and on the strength of it went home and wrote him a letter, giving all the explorational circumstances of the film.[94] Then Mr Brown went and got sick like everybody else in this miserable pest-ridden city, and I have not seen or heard from him since. It is no use bothering him again until the film comes anyway. Spent this afternoon at the customs, and delivery is promised for the first of the week. Then it's got to be cleaned up somehow before I show it.

I think the Paramount and the Scenograph Feature Film Co. are our only hope. Mr McCord had the assurance to the Mackenzie Expeditionary Film in his Company's prospectus, so of course they are keen to get it. They would route it as a separate theatrical venture, like Mawson, Scott, Rainey, etc., putting out ten copies, each with a lecturer.[95] I shall hear more about it when I see Mr Priest, their theatrical manager. The plan is ideal; its working depends on the truth of that little statement on page four of the prospectus to the effect that a growing and eager public is waiting for just this sort of educational film food. No figures are given as to the "fortunes" so far made out of expeditionary films; we could name several that failed to make a red cent. They were attended in any case by a spasmodic public attracted through special advertising means. The success of the Scenograph venture depends upon making of that spasmodic public a better class of "better movie" patrons. I certainly do wish them well – I certainly do believe in the idea and its eventual success, but that this particular company is destined to be the one to lead the way to that happy consummation I have every doubt, for the reason that I think neither its personnel, judging from my measure of Mr McCord, nor its wares, judging from my view of the South American film, nor its backing, judging from the "names of the interested Boston people" Mr McCord gave me, are strong enough.

Mr McCord is, distinctly, uneducated, illiterate; the South American film has no artistic or literary merit above the merest newspaper "copy"; the names given me are chief stock-holders and directors in the Scenograph Co, are not names known to "anybody who knows" in Boston. I'd rather those with known reputation and weight in educational matters were chiefly concerned in the affair, together with somebody else with the same sort of standing financially, and then a good business manager – such as Mr Priest *may* be.

The Paramount Co., then. They have signified their desire to see the film again. I'd give a good deal to know what arrangements Burton Holmes has made with them. I'd like to meet him personally. They would probably cut the film up, probably not run it all until they had your next to work in with it.

From my Line-a-Day Diary, 12 January – 20 February 1916:

12 January Films received from Express Co. after much fuss and fuming.
13 January Gave film to Joseph Fitterman to clean.
17 January Burton Holmes Lecture – ran reel number 1 for him to see – very enthusiastic. This happened at the Candler Theater as a result of dear Dr Coggeshall's interest and effort in securing me an introduction to Mr Holmes through his patient, Mr Kramer, Mr Holmes's understudy. Showing the film was Mr Brown's happy suggestion. Nothing came of it but a few minutes talk with Mr Holmes on the subject of lecture films and lecturers.
18 January Pictures (4 reels) shown to Mr Eaton, in charge of news and travel Department of Paramount Co.
24 January Letter from Mr Eaton. They turned us down, gently, advising us that the film would be just as valuable, "if not more so," six months or a year hence. The facts of the case are that they have under contract with Burton Holmes all the travel material they can use for more than a year to come. Mr Holmes is supplying them with 1000 feet per week from his studio in Chicago.
30 January Sunday. 5:30 p.m., picture on at Globe Theater (New Haven), audience of about 30. I was just visiting Jaynesie, the party was here, and just for fun.

20 February Interesting talk with "Brother Phillip" about film. Phillip Salisbury is a wide-awake young business man employed in the advertising department of the Ingersoll Watch Co., in which capacity he has had to do with the Movie Companies, writing scenarios for animated cartoons (Edison Co.) and negotiating for a film of the plant in operation with some other company (at $700 per 1000 feet) for the Mutual Exchange. He thought the Pathe Co., Hearst-Vitagraph and Selig-Tribune the most likely people for us to deal with. But strongly advised against pushing this film now, in the interest of the next.

Tuesday, 22 February 1916, Bryn Mawr Club, New York Here is a pamphlet after our own heart, a dream come true; my brain is all chaos with the bigness of the Idea, and the Spirit of it, and the Working of it. Read it ALL.

I took the film to Pathe Frères yesterday – my last move in the matter because I have decided beyond doubt now in my own mind that it would only hurt your next film to have this one put out now. I regret nothing of the experience either in its main or its side issues, because in the main I have acquired a few useful ideas and a certain philosophical point of view that may apply helpfully to the situation in the fall when you come down.

Today is Washington's Birthday. How is it with you. Sunshine here, with wind and cold and slippery side-walks. I am barred out of the studio for the morning – did I tell you that I found a place just across the way to practice, a Steinway grand in a studio setting and practically unlimited hours; and that I had been having a lesson every week with Mr Swayne. It grows, I can feel it and see it, and it keeps me excited and happy. We read over an old violin and piano sonata last time, by Locatelli, and he heartily acquiesced in my want to study it – you will like it.[96] Are you practicing?

I told the old story of the Guanerius to an absorbed and sympathetic listener the other day – Avis Putnam's husband, Edouard Dethier. I had just heard him and his brother – at the piano – play in concert.[97] Edouard is no genius, his brother is the artist, but they will be interesting people for us to know. Edouard seemed to think he knew of just the person to put the poor old fiddle together again. Avis was a classmate of mine, her father is head of the Putnam Publishing Co., and that brings me to another interesting matter: I took him the Eskimo drawings to ask his opinion of their publication possibilities, and incidentally, too, lugged along some of the portraits. You should have loved to see the expression of his face when I showed him those. Here was the real material for a real book, a book of the heart, a book with a soul! Wasn't he nice? And then he talked to me for an hour and more reviewing the whole subject of Arctic literature, and analysis of failure and success that was most illuminating. The upshot of it all is that he now has the diaries, looking them over. After what he saw in the portraits I was not afraid of unsympathetic criticism; and whatever he says about them should be a valuable guide as to how to go about the text for the "Book of the Heart."

I thought of you last night as we all sat before the fire at 283, reading aloud to us while we worked on Bob's trousseau, Cousin Julie knitting and Molly and I diligently sewing. Cousin Julie has loved managing the whole affair with all her native skill and pride of daintiness. We owe her several debts of gratitude, don't we.

I know I should be keeping you "au courant" with the events and developments of the war – somehow I can't. I delegated the task to Olive, to send you clippings, etc., and hope she has taken it seriously; she seemed pleased with the idea. Myself, I can't fix my mind on the war, and perhaps it is just as well, it is too full of other and happier things.

7 Flaherty Island

The third expedition – from June 1913 to October 1914 – had been the longest, most ambitious, and costliest that Flaherty had conducted for Mackenzie (an estimate of $50,000 would be safe). Yet he had not really carried out the original goals. It will be recalled that the initial plan had been for the *Laddie*, with a crew of five, to leave St John's in early July 1913, then pass through Hudson Strait and into Hudson Bay, where the expedition was to divide into two parties – one with the *Laddie* to survey fishery resources, the other led by Flaherty in a motor launch to explore the Belcher Islands. In late October the parties were to reunite and proceed north to Southampton Island, where they were to establish a winter base. With the arrival of the spring, the copper resources of Chesterfield and Rankin inlets on the western coast of the bay were to be explored, as well as the Southampton area, and the entire party was then to leave on the *Laddie* in October 1914, outward bound before ice blocked Hudson Strait.

As we saw in chapter 5, the delays in commissioning the *Laddie* upset the proposed timetable. Their departure from St John's in mid-August, rather than early July, made passage through the straits impossible, thereby forcing Flaherty to winter on Baffin Island. The return of the *Laddie* late in the summer of 1914 did permit Flaherty (but only by a kind of nautical forced march) to reach the Belchers late in the season, but only to bring the *Laddie* to near wreckage and to conduct the hastiest survey of the islands.

Although this course of events bore little resemblance to the original plan, Flaherty's determination to get to the Belchers, despite Bartlett's and the crew's opposition, had vindicated all. The location, size, and ore potential of the islands exceeded his expectations, and with the passage of time, his elation at having reached the Belchers was magnified, so that he recalled years later in the "Islands" narrative: "I had been in new country before, but this time it was as if I were standing on the threshold of a new world."[1]

Eager to document this new world, one of the first things Flaherty did once the *Laddie* was in secure harbor (on 12 September 1914) was to take the motion-picture camera ashore and shoot panoramas of the island, of which he said, "Never have I been so impressed, that indescribable panorama!" Throughout both the second and third expeditions, visual art in the service of exploration had been a constant. This was because Mackenzie had continued to finance this aspect of the expedition's goals and because Flaherty, in turn, had viewed his visual products – photographs and moving pictures – as potential revenue sources to offset expeditionary costs. This imperative to raise revenue no doubt stood high on the list of incentives that moved the Flahertys so zealously to seek a market for the Baffin Island film.

In Augustus Bridle's feature article on the 1911 album, he had noted that Flaherty was taking with him on the second expedition "five hundred dollars worth of camera and photographic equipment." This consisted of "two cameras, 5 × 4 Eastman plate, and a 4 × 5 Graflex with two hundred exposures."[2] As on the first expedition, the context for picture taking was often opportunistic, with Flaherty seizing occasions as they arose and invariably rewarding his subjects with gifts: "Two Huskies put out to us in kayaks when opposite the north end of Manitounuk. Gave them tobacco, matches and took photos."[3]

There is one opportunistic photo situation in the second expedition that is worth revisiting because it crystallizes the issue of cultural collaboration that arose when Flaherty's goal, taking a photograph, collided with the Inuit's wish to make a kill. On 7 August 1912 he wrote the following description:

About 11:00 a.m. while sailing along the lee side of a large floe, Nawri suddenly shouted, "Nanook!" "Nanook!" Just some polar bear a hundred yards ahead. I saw him swimming for the floe; he landed in short order, galloped across it and took to the water again, we sailing for him with a beam wind and large sea running. Overhauled him shortly and he headed for shore. Crew now took in the sail, and we followed the more slowly swimming fellow with paddles, keeping a respectful fifty feet or so behind him. I got out both cameras and went up near the bow. Asked the men to close in a little more which they reluctantly did, until our quarry came around with a snort, whereupon we fell back to the old margin ... Men waited with rifles ready, and as he landed took my pictures as they fired. Ambrose firing first with his "22" in order to bay him on the rocks, but Nawri and Nuckey followed too quickly and spoiled my chance for a most interesting picture.

This is a benchmark moment in the development of Flaherty's grasp of cultural collaboration. In stalking the bear, he and his companions were working at cross-purposes, each encapsulated by his particular expectations. All saw the occasion as a hunt, but with a goal appropriate to their cultural context: while the Inuit wanted a dead bear, Flaherty wanted a photograph, and their shots deprived him of his.

We can look at a similar occasion nearly ten years later, from an alleged conversation that Flaherty and Nanook had during the fall of 1920 at Port Harrison. In reply to the suggestion that they go on a walrus hunt, Flaherty said:

Suppose we go, do you know that you and your men may have to give up making a kill, if it interferes with my film? Will you remember that it is the picture of you hunting the iviuk [walrus] that I want, and not the meat?

"Yes, yes, the aggie [the film] will come first," earnestly he assured me. "Not a man will stir, not a harpoon will be thrown until you give the sign. It is my word." We shook hands and agreed to start the next day.[4]

In the intervening decade, Flaherty had learned the art of participatory exchange. The cultural agreement was grounded on collaboration in that Nanook's hunter expectations were synchronized with Flaherty's hope to shoot a picture. Through the participatory agreement there was a cultural merger, one that successfully brought meat to the mouth and movies to the eye. In 1912, in that bobbing boat off Cape Wolstenholme, Flaherty had also been shooting pictures – snapping scenes, recording geology, appreciative of the human tableaux – but the cultural collaboration was not yet there. Instead, material incentives, tobacco for photographs, appear to have been Flaherty's usual normative currency of cultural exchange.

For the third expedition Mackenzie had continued his support for Flaherty's visual work. The extent of Flaherty's camera outfit is revealed when, on 14 January 1914, he listed the equipment he had assembled for a journey to Foxe Channel: "One Graflex, 4 × 5, six dozen plates, one film camera, 3¼ × 4¼, twenty five films, one tripod."[5] As we saw in chapter 5, during the third expedition Flaherty had redirected his visual interests to moving pictures and modified the emphasis he gave to still pictures.

Although Flaherty continued to regard photography and filmmaking as potential sources of income, he realized that he had to seize on the geographical and mineralogical potential of the Belcher Islands as the premier outcome of the third expedition. The short memorandum he wrote to Mackenzie on 16 November 1914, soon after his return, emphasized that the discovery of the Belchers was "in every detail ... original with us." Urging Mackenzie to seek Dominion support in Ottawa for permits and mineral rights to the Belchers, Flaherty provided only sketchy details of the expedition itself and instead stressed the cumulative investment of the first three expeditions: "These foregoing and general details of the exploration, that is the great length of time, the expense and general difficulties of our four years' work is mentioned to show we are deserving of government assistance in connection with land grant, etc."[6]

There was a long period of silence before Flaherty submitted his final report to Mackenzie on 2 February 1915. Soon afterwards, on 24 February, the earlier memorandum resurfaced, now stripped of any reference to government assistance but otherwise only moderately altered. In the interim, what may have transpired is suggested by what Flaherty related much later in the "Islands" narrative:

> If Sir William had made the exploration himself, he could hardly have been more excited. No we shouldn't say anything about the ore discovery now; the geographical side of the expedition was one thing; those iron-bearing rocks another. It might be good plan, he suggested, if we went together to Ottawa. The officials there might be persuaded to give us some kind of prior right of exploration.
>
> But as it turned out, no government blessing was forthcoming.

"What," said the official in charge. "You want us to give you a blanket grant of the mineral rights of the islands."

"That's right," we said.

"But look here gentlemen! *There are no such islands*. Here's the chart. You say it's land. Well, look at it – soundings!"

No argument that we could think of was of any avail.

"Sorry," the official said at the end, "but if you won't believe the chart, for your private information I might tell you that I have consulted the Geodetic Survey about it. You know the survey work they have been doing on the Bay? Well, they say the same thing – soundings!"

Fortunately the rebuff made no difference to Sir William.

"Never mind," he said, turning to me with a grim smile. "We'll show 'em!"[7]

Given these setbacks and the reversal of plans experienced on the third expedition, Flaherty was more subdued in his 2 February report. There is a general air of caution about it, as can be seen from the several drafts housed in the Butler Library, which show scattered suggestions for editorial change in Frances's hand.[8]

In the report, Flaherty glided over the delays related to the commissioning of the *Laddie*, and he justified the wintering at Amadjuak Bay by saying, "The good impression I had received of the mica bearing areas at Lake Harbour and the interesting Eskimo tribes of the Coastline from which the chief value of our motion pictures depended, were the important reasons for deciding to winter on the Baffin Island Coast."

On the matter of fishery resources, he noted, "Owing to conditions beyond our control, an investigation along that line was impossible to carry on." He gave an equally dismal forecast about harvesting whales: "Captain Murray says that this water abounds in Whale food, and that no doubt many whales school here at certain times of the year, times that necessitate the wintering of a whaling outfit. Owing to the present low market for whale bone and oil the whaling has been discontinued."

If Flaherty had not landed on the Belchers (regardless of how nearly catastrophic that landing proved to be), the expedition, from a mineralogical view, would have been worthless. But the modesty of the survey work itself formed the ground for future expectations, as Flaherty suggested in the report:

As we have touched nearly seven miles of the Seaboard, which is upward of 100 miles in length in a straight line, and succeeded in discovering an ore in which in all its characteristics is identical with certain ore types of economic importance in Northern Michigan and Northern Minnesota and with their mode of disposition identical, it would seem to be good ground upon which to base future large and comprehensive exploration of that country. Eskimo information leads us to believe that the ore occurs at widespread points. It is probable that large ore bearing areas will be found there, and that the ore discoveries so far made, though in themselves of economic importance, are but a fraction to what future exploration will disclose.

Despite the setback of receiving no assistance from Ottawa, and the very short opportunity that Flaherty had had to explore the Belchers, Mackenzie continued to show confidence and agreed to sponsor a fourth expedition, one with a single dominating purpose: to reach and winter on the Belcher Islands so that a comprehensive survey could be made of its mineral resources. Since the *Laddie* was under repair at Moose Factory, it was already at a propitious point of departure for reaching the Belchers – far better than having to come from Newfoundland. For the sake of economy as well as because of Flaherty's apparent dissatisfaction with Bartlett, there would be no professional skipper. The crew would be a smaller, more seasoned group, with Flaherty being joined again by Eugene LaDuke, Stewart Gushue, William Robinson and Samuel Sainsbury.

Diary of the Fourth Mackenzie Expedition
11 August 1915 – 21 September 1916

Wednesday, 11 August 1915[9] Departed from Toronto for Cochrane and Moose Factory. R.H. Flaherty, David Flaherty, Miss Thurston, Mr & Mrs R.J. Flaherty, Walter MacCangren, Engineer; Stewart Gushue, two Temagami Indians, Fred Potts, Joe and two "Fire Rangers," Charlie Moore and Ernest Prophet. Departed from Ground Hog, crossing at noon on August 6th.[10]

Saturday, 14 August Arrived at Moose Factory at noon. LaDuke in the red launch met us as we came in view of Moose.

Work at once started on the ship's engine. She was not ready for sea, however, before the 26th of August. We departed then for Charlton Island.

Anchoring at the mouth of the Moose river, a southwest wind came up during the night. The anchor dragged and at day light we had the pleasure of seeing the ship drive ashore.

This kept up the whole of the day. Sent off the passengers during a lull in the wind at 5 p.m. to Moose Factory. The hold was making water faster than the pumps could keep it out. At 5 o'clock the tide receded, leaving us stranded well keeled on an apparently endless plain of tidal flats.

We discovered that the anchor had jabbed a hole in the port bow. It was patched with canvas that night. Following day at low tide we managed to patch her securely with planking. Her cargo and ballast were lightened and on the third day, despite the gloomy forecast of our Moose friends, she came off. She limped half keeled over to an anchorage at ship sands in the face of a most ugly looking thunder storm whose look was worse than its bite. But as it was, the first squall caught her hard and she came dangerously near having trouble.

Went up to Moose in launch the same evening where the folks were most comfortably situated at the Wilsons and Snapes.[11]

After further re – outfitting and the departure of the two Indians and Walter, we reembarked aboard the *Laddie* and she cleared for Charlton Island.

We are two days later under sail to find the *Inenew* not returned from the Belchers. Secured remainder of Eskimos there and loaded them and dogs aboard ship and cleared for Strutton Islands, at which point supplies had been discharged by Revillon Frères.

Glorious week of clear, fine weather. In 5 days returned to Charlton where the folks disembarked and camped about a mile down from the post on a most charming ground.

Saturday, 25 September Departed for Great Whale River. Cleared Sevik Sound following day at 5:30. Arrived at Schooner Opening of Manitounuk Sound at 3:00 p.m. after a short sail across – proceeded down Sound to Boat Harbour, which after dark was with some difficulty located.

Snow squalls also during the day.

Following day Bill, Sam, Sevik, and Doc and I tramped into Great Whale River, taking a route which led us on a heartbreaking journey over hill and muskeg.

Saw good old Mavor again. He put us up – a bath included. The men returned. Following day started cutting wood. In a week's time *Laddie* was filled to hatches with a deck load also to her rails. The *Nastapoka* in the meantime was landed at Great Whale River and put in shape for her tow across to the islands. We cleared Boat Harbour and sailed up the Sound, anchoring on island side near Schooner Opening where we were storm bound until the 10th. We cleared at day light with apparently a splendid favoring wind and even weather.

Just clear of Schooner Opening, we spied our lost dory. Dropping anchor, Stewart and Sam put off for it but found it too badly battered for further use. This was the ship's standby – her only life boat.

At 11:00 the wind increased to a gale. We were forced to stow the mainsail as it was too rotten to risk.

We carried as passengers 5 Eskimo men, 4 women, children of unknown number, 8 Eskimo dogs, a deck load and a 36 foot sailing craft in tow. The Huskies lay along side of the after cabin deck clinging to life lines while Bill, Sam and Stewart handled ship and at that Sam, aloft working on the top sail yards, was sick as a dog the while.

The gale steadily increased – we were crossing an unknown water with dangerous reef infested ground on or near a course which we had sighted when landward bound.

At 2 p.m. things looked bad. The Eskimos were helpless with fear. They sang hymns and "kapayed" when the old *Laddie* was walloped broadside on.

The clinometer needle under the binnacle bumped the end of its scale – the main boom went under, and through it all the ship would rise in a dazed sort of way all a tremble. But this wasn't all. At 2:30 we knew we were nearing the island land coast of the Belchers. Whipped along on the gale came a blinding sleet of snow. We had to run on – and take the risk of hitting an island lee or running ashore where some opportunity offered of saving at least a part of our varied and helpless assortment from the surf. We strained our eyes for sign of land through the drift for two hours, expecting it at any time to loom up almost under us.

At 4:30 and just at about the end of daylight a humpbacked mass of island rock loomed up off the weather bow some 200 feet away (we could see no further). A moment longer and a similar one came up on our lee – there was no turning back – on we went with all our eyes glued on the spray driven sheet ahead. With the islands astern, a shore line stood out ahead – a long low line of foam. The rest of it is hard to describe but we made a harbor amongst it all and anchored. Some luck. The men tumbled into the cabin and fell asleep while they sat – wet clothes and all. I say we in this narrative – it was Sam and Bill and Stewart manning a 100 ton ship in Arctic weather and in unknown country. A passenger list of panic stricken Eskimos and wailing dogs. Some job!

Monday, 11 October At dark we anchored once more at camp. LaDuke with his Eskimo helpers had the house practically complete.

Thursday, 14 October I departed with Sevik, Omarolluk and two other Eskimos for a so-called new discovery of "seviks" [iron rocks]. Upon arrival found a new area of ore series but owing to high gales of wind were prevented from carrying on an extensive search.

Returned on the 16th. Saw the large lake while on trip.

Tuesday, 19 October Trouble with LaDuke. Gave him launch to make the trip to Great Whale River, then to Toronto at first opportunity. He departed two days later with two Eskimos.[12]

Busy two weeks putting the place in shape.

Sent Sam on further exploration of ore series of Sevik's discovery and to establish camp at the north extreme of the island. October 28th, returned in three days, reporting a big find.

Sunday, 31 October Left with Sam, Tommy and outboard motor. Discovery certainly a good one. Spent three days making notes and samples of the outcrop.

Thursday, 4 November Returned only to be greeted by the news that one of our Eskimos had drowned while with three others that went over to creek ½ mile from camp for water.

Young Allego, a boy of 15, rescued two of them, swimming ashore with them some 200 feet in the water. Bill and Stewart had an excited mob on their hands.

The unfortunate one was laid out in state in my photo room. Following day his funeral – his coffin a box covered with scotch plaid and a dismal procession up to the rocks on the hill – the outfit followed in the rear by sniffing dogs of the place.

Some more Eskimos have reported ore to southwest some 40 miles away.

Since the 22nd of September not a day of sunshine. Windy eternally – so much so that we are virtually prisoners here these two months gone. The natives say it is most remarkable. How it has played on our nerves is beyond description. Here it is November and the larger fresh water lakes are not even frozen. In all this period of time the thermometer has not gone below zero – average about +30°.

The ruggedest part of British Columbia doesn't come up to Belchers for dearth of sunshine and the wind.

Last week crossed the Sound by canoe to examine another Eskimo discovery of ore. Found it even larger – more accessible and better than anything hither to.

Friday, 12 November Celebrated our wedding anniversary. Sports. Baseball on the snow – football – running races – shooting – and at evening the population in toto assembled in our quarters. We had games, augmented by the pianola and gramophone and, of course, a day long feast which took two native cooks the previous day to prepare.

Wednesday, 1 December Sam left today for last ore discovery. Stewart and I expecting to leave on sledge trip with two teams to north end of island.

Thursday, 2 December Stewart, Omarolluk and I departed today at 1:00 p.m. for north end *Laddie* Island with a spanking 11 dog team. The first sledging of the season for us. Our sledge, which was fitted with an odometer, works splendidly. Camped on north end *Laddie* Island for night. Calm night.

Friday, 3 December Departed at 9 a.m. Splendid day – nearly calm with a blue patched sky (rare in these parts). Traveled to end of Island. Camped 3 miles south of end. High winds sprang up at nightfall. Colder – two days respite at most is all we get from winds.

During evening Omarolluk regaled us with stories of the winter he spent on Seahorse Islands which lie to northward some 50 miles where he said he killed 6 walrus in one day.

Saturday, 4 December Snow squalls again. Making for base – useless to work further in this weather. At 11:00 a.m. cleared gloriously – the first sunshine in two long weary months – some day! The heavy clouds that have enshrouded these islands this long time have been a trial. Up to now the thermometer has never reached lower than 22° of frost, but with clear weather the much longed for ice will come.

Returned at 3:00 to find Sam returned with additional exploring news of importance. He secured two live white foxes for our motion picture.[13]

Wetalltok's drawing of a Christmas celebration, Belcher Islands, 1914
(Claremont, LAC, PA114363)

Monday, 6 December Sam, Stewart and Bill left today with the teams for *Laddie* Harbor. Omarolluk, Wetalltok, Tommy and Tookalook left with canoe on seal hunt to south end. Splendid clear day again.

Boys returned three days later. Also Omarolluk and party who brought in a strange Eskimo – they saw ore which is probably a southward extension of the Mukpollo Sound area – if so that area has a length of over 40 miles. Slab ice at sea appeared on 21st.

Xmas Celebration started Xmas eve. We faked a tree of spruce boughs which had been sent from Great Whale River for spruce beer purposes. Lashed the boughs to a pole – the usual candles lashed on also.

Stewart acted Santa.

We gave them all presents, candy, tobacco, etc., then musical chairs – "London Bridge Is Falling Down." Then square danced – music supplied by pianola. At midnight a feast of split pea soup, sweets, currant buns and tea. Bill and Stewart and I rendered sea shanteys, all about "her faithful sailor boy" – "the briny foam, etc., etc." The feature of it all was this bottle of brandy carefully unused through nearly 4 long months of monotony and brought suddenly to light Xmas eve as a surprise to me. I must say that lone bottle went well. It is such times that that sort of thing is made for.

Wednesday, 29 December At 7:00 p.m. the thermometer went to -2°. Started one of the largest of the pictures. Sam returned on 28th from day's trip to Fair Weather Harbour and reports some ice.

Thursday, 30 December The clearest day of all – during day attempted another igloo picture – dismal failure. Will try again tomorrow. Dogs broke into trade tent last night – dragged out the two caged white foxes and (serious loss) chewed up Sam's fur kooletah. First sledges of the season came in today.

In afternoon played another game of baseball out on the ice near the *Laddie*.[14]

Wetalltok's girl wants 2 shawls and an accordion.

Sunday, 2 January 1916 Started today on journey from the east coast of Mukpollo Sound in two sledges – Omarolluk, Tommy, Stewart and Bill.

In forenoon previous to departing took another picture film of igloo building.

A glorious, clear day with calm wind. Another crowd of Eskimos in today. Sam had trouble with Wetalltok – the Eskimos all seem dissatisfied.

Encamped on portage of Mukpollo Sound 6 miles southwest of camp.

Ice all rime covered and hard traveling. Oil stove a prize indeed – a warm camp. Wonderful warm weather. Thermometer at -2°. Clear and calm. I cannot understand it – and this is the sub-arctic!

Tuesday, 4 January Away at 9:30 – reached Omarolluk's ore discovery [in] an hour. Later found the ore body improved (i.e., jaspers) but not of commercial extract at surface. A sad, dull proposition. Crossed over plain and saw the Mackenzie Sound side.

At open tidal pool Tommy and Omarolluk killed two seals and a duck. Reached Thomas' igloo at 3:30. Thomas away hunting. Returned at night fall. He has found ore at western side of inlet which I will inspect tomorrow.

A gale of wind during night. I thought the tent would surely go.

Wednesday, 5 January A clear a.m. but wind still blowing this a.m. so strongly. Went over with Thomas and Stewart to west coast of Mukpollo Inlet to see Thomas' ore discovery but saw nothing but float. Returned in two hours.

Poor Thomas' family are in a bad way. No cartridges and hardly any food with a tent covering them that has seen 3 years hard service – a freezing affair. Not in all the wide world is there such poverty – poverty so near a real and actual death. And through it all they seem happy – all smiles and good humor. Gave them a few cartridges and one of the *Laddie*'s sails for tent.

Friday, 7 January Wetalltok affair is smoothed over and he is alright again. One of the Island Eskimos went for Sam the other day, finally told him that he wasn't "King" of these islands, etc. Seems they are all thinking along that line.

The people are starving and beg us for food we dare not give out – even our matches will be gone by spring.

Put the whole thing up to Omarolluk. He with our dog sledges and an outfit is going to take the south encampment north to the walrus grounds as they are reported in great numbers – the first time in 3 years. Only a few of all the families on the island have enough dogs for traveling.

Omarolluk once before saved them from starvation through his skill and fearlessness in walrus hunting.

A big, heavy gale all day, -10°. In a.m. provision tent burst with the strain of it.

Saturday, 8 January Omarolluk leaves today. Tommy came to Sam this a.m. asking for some white cotton with which to make a pillow slip for his traveling outfit! A little Eskimo from the west coast of the island wanted a rifle for a sledge dog, saying he was "starving for a gun." As this was too much for a dog by miles, but feeling compassionate for his acute starvation I compromised by offering a very good but second hand .44 Winchester. He refused it and left this a.m. empty handed – probably on the thin edge of starvation, as they all are at present.

Wetalltok greatly injured by being refused the walrus hunt. Afraid of trouble with that outfit. The possibility of being forced to burn the ship looms nearer every day – all the wood was discharged on to the ice today. It can hardly last more than 6 weeks. There will be nothing for it but that this poor old *Laddie*'s carcass burns to keep ourselves from freezing.

It seems like cannibalism – our discussions about how long the spars, the yards, "the cabin of experiences," and all of it. The clumsy, smelly old tub seems half human after all.

The capsized *Laddie*, stripped of its upper works for firewood, Belcher Islands, 1914–15
(Claremont, LAC, PA143612/photo RF)

Winter here at last – the 4th of January recording the first low temperature.

Wednesday, 12 January The time is racing now. Sam went off this a.m. to Fair Weather Harbor with Casey and dogs. Thomas came in at noon having run from his camp 35 miles away and after an hour's stay went home again. Poor devil looks starved alright and has a bullet in his hand where he some time ago shot himself – he suffers much from it today.

Grub looks pretty bad. Stewart and Bill say we may get caught. Only one day so far unfit for outside work.

Thursday, 13 January A blizzard today – very high wind. Minus 22° tonight. Grub tent in bad way – men strengthened it during day – prudently transferred package goods into house.

Doc staying up tonight to stoke stoves. Blizzard abated somewhat at 12:30 a.m. Minus 20°.

Several discussions about our food and fuel. We figured out the running feet of the *Laddie*'s masts, booms, yards and bowsprit. The fuel situation looks grave indeed. Sam came home at dark. His team went through the ice at the narrows – a close call – not much wet however – rubbery ice.

Saturday, 15 January A wonderful day, calm. Minus 10° with those blues and white-grays that come only to the North.

Started some more movies today and built another igloo studio.

Omarolluk and Tommy returned today saying ice fields too broken for walrus hunting now – saw a band of Eskimos who didn't know we were here. Their trip has again extended the boundaries of this island – the farthest point of travel being more than 125 miles away.

Now we are worrying about the fields to mainland – not frozen yet. Will this be another freak year?

Monday, 17 January Minus 12°. Heavy south wind and swirling drifts. Started at 11:30.

Before start an old man came in on foot from south end of Big Lake. He was in starving condition. Almost died on journey which he made in little under 24 hours. Relieved his wants somewhat which pleased him mightily. Omarolluk says that many years as the vast deer herd of these islands were starved by an unusual rain that fell in winter and glazing all the moss in ice to such an extent that they could not eat it.

Ice in lake about 2 feet thick. Omarolluk says winter ice (for fishing) is about 3 feet. Sea ice is more thin – less than 2 feet.

Tried sail on sledge today with good results.

Sunday, 23 January Started at 9:30 in the heaviest blizzard of the year – a heavy southeast wind. Traveled some 7½ miles in the teeth of it on sea ice in the trail of the old man. Omarolluk, who started earlier than we with his wife and child and household effects, is joining Mukpollo's village at south end of Mukpollo Inlet.

We suddenly made out the forms of Omarolluk and wife in the swirl of driving snow building an igloo on a small island. He gave up the journey and so did we, building an igloo beside them. Hellish weather!

Monday, 24 January A gale all night – one of the heaviest of the year. Decided to start – away at 10:00 – a strong drifter from westward. Used a sail on the sledge with very good effect.

Very cold. Made trip worse at one o'clock, thence northerly along the west coast of Mackenzie Sound.

Cooked bacon and beans at Eskimo igloo enroute home. Poor Eskimos on edge of starvation – gave then the balance of the grub.

No seals in sight. Came across some of the hunters on the sea ice marching about with spears after possible seal holes. Poor devils – they're doing this day after day in this frightful weather – a hopeless task.

Arrived home at 5:30 after the fastest journey I've ever made. The sail was a boon – dogs on ground continually. The 8 days of our journey almost a constant gale – thermometer averaging -20° to 25°. House buried in drifting snow – also *Nastapoka*. Two of the trade tents torn to pieces. Wood supply will be ended in two weeks' time.

Thursday, 27 January Two strange Eskimos arrived today from northwestern islands. Also Tookalook's son and father. Wood hunters returned today with load of driftwood. Report only five sledge loads there which wouldn't last a week. Going to make an effort to get wrecked schooner coal on west coast – but some 70 miles away. Starving Eskimos in again today. A blizzard all day. Minus 20°. Some winter!

Friday, 28 January Another stormy day but not so cold. One of the starving Eskimos had a fit in Tookalook's house.

Saturday, 29 January Three teams off today for coal which lies some 70 miles to westward – the last gasp on the fuel question. Took photos. Omarolluk returning from ice scouting trip reports ice is not altogether closed in yet.

Sunday, 30 January Bridge today with dire results to Bill and I. A warm day, +10°, but a storm toward night with wet snow. Our weather eye peeled for another northwest cold "cracker." The eternal war! Discussions about it till 1:00 a.m.

Monday, 31 January A warm, calm day. Too dull for photos. Bridge as usual and eternal (as usual) discussions of the ways and means of life in Toronto. War topics mild – like the day! Snowing again tonight.

Omarolluk off on another scouting trip to the ice field.

Tears in kitchen – jealousy amongst Lucy, Mary and Ananyung. Mary happened to make up and sweep the quarters for me – cause of it all.

All of them like children – and (thank heaven) they are.

Tuesday, 1 February Clear day. Minus 10° with west wind. Omarolluk returned saying ice remains same – seems a bit discouraged about it. Wants to go away – afraid we are running short. Doesn't want to use up our resources, etc., etc.

Wednesday, 2 February High, drifting wind. Minus 20° to 15° all day. Took motion picture panoramas. Wetalltok came back with party. Could not get coal – washed away by heavy sea last fall.

Thursday, 3 February Ice field to Great Whale River looks good according to latest reports. Bath today.[15] Two Eskimos came in tonight from westward. Report Tookalook's camp is starving. No seals anywhere.

Friday, 4 February Awakened at 5:00 a.m. by dogs trying to steal our bacon. Had to get out. Started at 10:30 a.m. for Mukpollo Sound to sample series.

Sunday, 6 February Omarolluk returned – killed twenty seals. Ice alright for Great Whale River. Busy getting ready for crossing. Developed motion pictures.

Monday, 7 February Sam, Stewart and myself with two sledges, Omarolluk and Tommy departed for Great Whale River. We were joined by Nevalinga and partner with another sledge, while we took Attata with us as a passenger.

Sam and Stewart with a self contained outfit, dogs, etc., are to proceed to Moose Factory, thence to Cochrane and Toronto taking my packet (ore samples, plans, data and mail) out to company and to arrange for my father's return here next summer for an inspection of our ore deposits.

We encountered rime ice and rafted fields at the commencement of the crossing which continued almost entire distance to the mainland. We were three days making the journey. Arrived at Great Whale River at 8:00 o'clock at night which much surprised Mavor and Old Harold. Off shore of the mainland we met the heaviest ice of the journey. It was heart-breaking travel for awhile. We noted an outward bound sledge track while in the heavy ice which caused consternation all around. It meant that one of LaDuke's men of last October's journey was enroute to our camp and probably with the mail – the mail we have been worrying and longing for since God knows when.

Upon arrival at the post the supposition proved only too true – our mail was gone – we had passed it enroute to Great Whale River. What a maddening affair. However the mail was not the all important one, for the winter packet had not yet arrived at Great Whale River, but this meant either a tedious wait and which would be dangerous as Sam and Stewart should leave Moose Factory south bound no later than the middle of March.

I decided to go south to Fort George for the packet – a distance of 185 miles – for the packet would surely be there ere our arrival.

Monday, 14 February Omarolluk, Tommy and I with one team and Stewart and Sam with their outfit departed southward bound.

Saturday, 19 February We arrived at Fort George. What a contrast – use of a camp stove and trees with spruce boughs for bedding. The smell of it all seems to change the world. What a contrast to oil lamps – an ice floor partly covered with deer skins and endless wastes of white everywhere with here and there wind barred rocks and scared hills. And later all my old friends – Huskie Bill, Moses, Snow Boy – all of them I saw again. I was a stranger indeed for they had heard of a report of me being murdered – with six of us strewn about the beach of Black Whale Harbour.

The arrival at Fort George was exciting, particularly so for Sam and Stewart – they had never been there before.

More old friends – visits to the Mission and Revillon Frères with grub – real beef and potatoes. Why, Griffiths of the Hudson's Bay Company even had a barrel of Bass's ale. But no packet. That spoiled everything (beef, ale and potatoes). We waited a long week with what speculation of what it might contain – our several personal affairs – the company and the war! Thanks heaven it's over, for never was I so anxious before with the innumerable delays.

Friday, 25 February Said good-bye to Sam and Stewart outbound south on the packet.[16] I intended to start on the return but the heaviest blizzard of the winter set in and raged for three days. It caught Sam and Stewart nicely. In the meantime, Mr. Thevenet, inspector for Revillon Frères, turned up and from him received another letter.[17]

Wednesday, 1 March   Departed from Fort George and arrived at Great Whale River five days later.

Thursday, 9 March   Received mail I had missed enroute to Great Whale River. Two days later departed for camp – arrived on the 10th, just a month since departing, having traveled 570 miles to get my mail with a great loss of a month's splendid exploring weather. Such are the fortunes of an expedition.

Arrived to find Bill with troubles. Poor Jocko the monkey dead – also an Eskimo and no fuel but scraps of half stoked coal which was combed up from the *Laddie*'s hold. Bill's story of his mail and worrying about our whereabouts – the shortage of grub and fuel – a crowd of Huskies always begging him for tea and food – what a mess to come to.

Sunday, 12 March 1916   Dismantled the *Laddie* today – with a motion picture of the affair. The Eskimos in toto assembled to see it – great excitement when the spars and yards crashed to the ice. She looks forlorn looking enough now, but we have enough fuel to last till August.

Sending three families of Charlton Eskimos on to the mainland, for we can't feed them any more – they've been a useless outfit anyway.

Monday, 13 March   Had arranged to go to Great Whale River again today with Levy and Fatty but rather heavy weather – snow and drift.

Tuesday, 14 March   Sending Bill in my stead owing to the necessity of getting picture done before the sun gets too strong.

Bill left at 9:00 a.m. with Levy and Fatty. Minus 15% and drifting. My last mail of winter.

Omarolluk and wife seal hunting. Started painting inside of house and commencing general improvements. Place is frightfully dirty.

Wednesday, 15 March   Tommy and Wetalltok and families left this a.m. for Great Whale River. Moved Tookalook and family aboard the *Laddie*. Using his house for storage. The last of the hang-on Eskimos left today.

Thursday, 16 March   Busy on house improvements – Mukpollo came in – gave him last blanket for a bear skin.

Friday, 17 March   Heavy, typical March drifter. Minus 15°. Still up to neck with "house improvements." Omarolluk came back today – killed several small seals but no square flipper which I require for motion picture.

Discharged the cook who is too fat and well fed for future service. A new cook – Mary – lean but able.

Saturday, 18 March A splendid day – very clear and calm and warm enough to start the rimed windows adripping.

Sunday, 19 March Minus 20° at breakfast time – drifting all day. Further home improvements.

Sugar down to about 20 lbs. and rat holes without number.

Monday, 20 March Omarolluk sulking – along in afternoon he and "Took" came into my quarters. Tookalook as ambassador stated that Omarolluk was most injured over my refusal to allow his women to come into the house (all of it untrue). Cleared the atmosphere by stating so – all well again. Most of these petty affairs originate with the women.

Tuesday, 21 March Glorious day – calm, clear gray-blue and white – the night sky swept with the aurora from rim to rim. Too young ladies and boy visiting today. Pop corn feast at night. Reinstated Lucy as cook much to the delight of every one. Omarolluk off for square flipper seal.

Wednesday, 22 March Another cold, blizzard day. Minus 15° with heavy wind.

Omarolluk returned at nightfall with two Eskimo hunters – they brought in a square flipper seal for motion pictures – but he is disappointingly small.

Thursday, 23 March [sic] Splendid spring day, warm, clear and calm. Put 2 Eskimos to work digging snow and helping transfer stuff from large tent to Tookalook's house which we are now using as workshop and store house, the tent being somewhat scarred after the winter's storms. At 8:00 p.m. weather turned again most abruptly changed – turned and is starting to drift again. Tried carbon printing for the first time today – fascinating work.[18]

Thursday, 23 March Find I've slipped ahead a day on the March calendar. The thickest drifter of the year with gale of wind – but fortunately not very cold. Everyone kept indoors – for the exit to snow tunnel was completely blocked.

At 9:30 a.m. who should burst in upon us but Wetalltok from Great Whale River bringing in local mail from Mavor and Walter. He and Johnnie, his partner, were fed and bed made up for them in the kitchen.

Friday, 24 March Weather cleared – whole camp almost completely buried. Wetalltok left at 3:00 for Great Whale River, taking his son with him. We're practicing carbon printing.

Saturday, 25 March A wonderful discovery. Negatives of 36 Roxboro Drive that I had not dreamed of – rushed a series of prints. What a ray of light![19]

It rained tonight upon all the country around with glazed, shimmering ice, and most effective photographically. The poor old ship is a sight – what a strange feeling about it all.

Sunday, 26 March Omarolluk came back today – reported all the Eskimos but three gone to Great Whale River. Killed 2 seals.

Bill hove in sight at 6:30 p.m.

Great excitement – has successfully arranged everything with Mr. Wilson at Great Whale River post. Finished the last lone bottle so dear to Bill's heart. More conversation than usual all the night.

Thursday, 30 March Another inquiry into the food problem today – the Eskimos have given them everything – all the rations and tobacco which was to last until August. Developed pictures.

Friday, 31 March Preparing for big pictures – iviuk and igloo interior, etc. Improvements in house completed.

Saturday, 1 April Rather a drifting day. Musical chairs and bridge pass the time away.

Monday, 3 April Warm, dull day. Bill started making an engine repair – ship [*Nastapoka*] in the warehouse.

Started thawing out the square flipper for pictures.

Tuesday, 4 April Clear, windy day. Took over 1,000 feet pictures with much loss of patience. Fatty and wife bucked in midst of it all. Told them to return guns and go away. Eskimos here are steeped in quarrels and jealousy

Bridge at night – our life saver. Bill glances at the clock at quitting time and with a sigh – well some more time stowed under.

Wednesday, 5 April Clear, rather cold – drifting wind. Photographed all day. Omarolluk off with Tookalook sealing. Mary very angry when Lucy was allowed to play pianola today – the jealousy of these people!

Friday, 7 April Developed pictures all day. Of all things, Wetalltok burst in upon us just at dark with Nero and Sevik from Great Whale River. We were surprised and pleased – stayed up till dawn just talking – pianola, gramophone and photography.

Stayed five days – the visit a burst of sunshine indeed to us all – Nero did not go to bed until 3 or 4 a.m. Almost like going out to civilization. Departed April 11th after dinner. Omarolluk sealing.

Wednesday, 12 April Finished square flipper and igloo pictures. Departed on 16th for Great Whale River post – arrived two days' time. Very fortunate in securing flour and other necessities, all of which will tide us safely over. Through Walter and Mavor got the Eskimos to take some of the stuff out in their sledges.

Photographed interior of church – also a few panoramas.[20]

Departed in three days' time for camp – arrived on 22nd. Much water on parts of ice and very hard footing for dogs – sharp ice. Expecting early spring. Finished up some pictures and made trip to northwest of *Laddie* Island where I verified Eskimo report of ore body.

Monday, 1 May Some more Eskimos came in today, one of them reports some ore to northward. More news today with Omarolluk. His daughter gave birth to a son this a.m. She is walking about the rocks just now – 2 p.m. Developed motion pictures and photos.

Tuesday, 2 May Cold, raw day. All our visitors left for southwest today – much lending of dogs – bustle generally. Took upwards of 40 portraits.

Geese seen today for the third time. First seen about April 20th. Levy brought one in yesterday – had it for dinner, but impossible – too tough!

Omarolluk and Levy off hunting – also Fatty. Open water in *Laddie* Sound.

Thursday, 4 May Clear day, rather cold. Traveled south along east shore of Tookalook Bay some 25 miles. Omarolluk killed 3 seals en-route. Says it contains seals in great numbers and wonderful quantities of fish – some large as seals. Must be deep sea cod.

Portaged over snow and rock some 1½ miles to an arm of Big Lake. This portage showed qualities of ivory shoeing.

Friday, 5 May Miserable day – feasting on fish. Departed in driving sleet and rain south eastward for Omarolluk's igloo – a half days's journey. Miserably wet and cold. Omarolluk says that past winter was coldest on record – many ducks perished when their open water haunts remained ice bound.

Sea ice broken – gone along south coast of islands. Ice generally breaking extremely early.

Saturday, 6 May A blizzard – tent half filled with drifting snow. All day in sleeping bag – cold – and this snow vapor passes through this tent, it's so old and worn.

Omarolluk has a bad case of dysentery – he is in discomfort. Teased in good natured way Omarolluk about the storm – said every time I came into his land I had bad weather – much amusement.

Told him about the bird that could talk (parrot). Also about the boy that wanted the moon – about Krupp guns and warships, etc.

Storm ended at 8:00 p.m. – thankful as I am out of grub. Thomas is the one who was given a gun last winter when he and his family were starving. He could not use it on account of his shot filled hand (right) and returned it to me. Why not give it to one of his friends?

Sunday, 7 May Clear a.m. but rather drifty, dull day. Arrived at camp at 1:45 p.m. Packet from Toronto brought out by Wetalltok. What luck and news. Changes everything. More to come, expect it tomorrow.

Monday, 8 May Wetalltok departed – took kayak on sledge in case ice breaks. Ice around islands breaking rapidly. Eskimos to southwest of us cannot go north westward to their spring hunting ground – will probably hang around us and try to sponge.

Plans of spring sledge expedition scattered to the winds. On 10th took motion pictures of Omarolluk and seal, etc.

Friday, 12 May Left at seven with Omarolluk, wife and adopted child for company. Bitter west wind. Noted ice fissured enroute to Big Lake River. Will soon be gone. A huge pack of seals were spied by Omarolluk on the ice to seaward – driven by the breaking ice, I suppose. Arrived at Big Lake River at 3 p.m. Walked up to river rapid where Omarolluk did some goose hunting and fishing.

River at rapid discharge about 50 feet wide, with almost 1 foot of water over crest – cannot measure until summer with canoe. Not large enough for power. Can get no farther to westward on account of broken ice.

Omarolluk told me stories of the time he was nearly killed by a bear, of the three different kayaks he has had destroyed by walrus. He told me about the ghost cave near Omarolluk's igloo land – "dojan," he calls them. Noted two very large, interesting fox stone traps which I mistook for igloos.

Departed for camp May 13th.

Cold with drifting snow. Omarolluk killed four seal enroute. Arrived at camp at 6:30.

Casey arrived an hour later. Have made a new ore discovery which undoubtedly proves that the Mukpollo fold underlays the sound and for more than thirty miles north and south. A wonderful field. One of splendid appearance.

Wednesday, 17 May Big quarrel again. All the jealous females sore at our cook – tears and tales galore. What children.

Thursday, 18 May Snow going rapidly – more of it about the house than anywhere in the islands, I think.

Omarolluk and Tookalook returned bringing 2 geese and a mess of splendid trout.

Omarolluk sulking again. Said he would go away. I assented and he crumpled.

Saturday, 20 May Splendid, clear warm day. So warm we can hear the roaring stream a mile around.

Departed with Omarolluk at noon for a final sledge exploration of the Big Lake country, traveling via Mukpollo's Inlet. At departure Tookalook and Fatty with Tookalook's wife and Omarolluk's wife join us with a dog team, wedging in on our trip. Your Eskimo is not made for work in warm weather – what sleepers they are!

Plowed through ice water over our boot tops – miserable traveling.

Encamped for night 15 miles down Mukpollo Inlet. Noted the ore series recurring at this point with deep westward seam of jaspilite.

Monday, 22 May Continued northward along west coast of Big Lake. Omarolluk killed six geese during day. Ice very bad – the dog tracks are blood stained – one of our best dogs has the toe nail of one foot completely off. Encamped 19½ miles north of yesterday's camp.

Omarolluk hunted geese till dark while I cooked another special supper. The extra special was stewed dried peaches which sure put a long smile on Omarolluk's face.

Tuesday, 23 May Heavy, cold wind with heavy fog.

Continued to portage up Mukpollo Inlet, thence home. It took us all day – dangerous ice, almost waist deep in water at times. This is the last sledging alright – we had all we could do to manage today. Found Bill with boat almost painted.

Thomas here from the southward. He came into quarters after tea with the humble request that Bill and I should play him the pianola and the violin, which we did – Sousa marches and all that. He formed all of our almost hysterical audience.

Thursday, 25 May Levy came in from Sentinel Hill yesterday with a bunch of geese which at once put Bill into a hunting fever. So off he went with him this a.m. for a few days hunting.

People much worried over non-appearance of Tookalook's outfit – feared that they have been caught by breaking up of ice.

Clear day but very cold wind. Started a new series of rock pictures today.

Saturday, 27 May The first real day of summer. Bumble bees and a stray house fly or two – warm southerly wind and thick cottony clouds. Bill and party returned at night fall. Only one goose and few eggs. Snow and ice made strides today.

Sunday, 28 May Bill and Doc at *Nastapoka* and launch which are almost ready for sea.

Warm day with showers in afternoon. Fatty returned today.

Wednesday, 31 May A clear, splendid day – summer. Bill all the way out of his skull today – talked about the Indies and Jericho.

Sunday, 4 June Overcast – fairly decent day. At least we got the outboard motors in running order. Bill tried them out in p.m. In evening we all played Duck on the Rock and Bull in the Ring – much merriment.

Tuesday, 6 June Finest day we've had. Eskimos are busy covering kayaks and canoes. Busy with red launch and *Nastapoka*.

Wednesday, 7 June Went down toward narrows in cedar skiff with outboard motor – Levy and Fatty accompanied me. Ran into bunch of geese on the way and found a dozen eggs which were too far advanced for eating. Levy killed two. Left Fatty there to continue hunting. Returned to camp. Fatty walked back at night fall, having killed a single goose. Came into the house with it and presented it to me. His outfit are on short rations at best.

Friday, 9 June Nellie, Omarolluk's daughter, gave birth to a child this a.m.

Saturday, 10 June Another day of summer. Mosquitoes made their debut but not of consequence so far. Transferred red launch engine to the junk pile and installed two outboard motors which should move her along in good style. Preparing for walrus trip to northward. Much excitement among the men. Lucy saw a ghost tonight which had a marked effect on the people. They all say *Laddie* Island is haunted.

Men showed us Eskimo feats of strength tonight – one of them remarkable. Saw that some men can lift four men from a position lying prone on the ground.

Sunday, 11 June Clear, south wind – strong breeze. Tried out *Nastapoka* – a great success. Crossed over to Mukpollo Sound ore deposits and looked over south end. Made cracking good time on return, 33 minutes for 5 miles.

Played ghost at sun down on the river – they swallowed it whole.

Monday, 12 June Clear, sparkling day with wind. Departed on the walrus expedition at noon with motion picture camera and plates and arsenal of guns.

Trouble with cook again – sulking.

Tea completely gone. Last of it given out to the Eskimos today.

Made north outlet of sound and went egg hunting on small island. Gulls' eggs but most of them bad.

Camped on northwest point of sound as field ice is too heavy to northward. Clear, moonlit night.

Tuesday, 13 June Awoke late – turned out of tent by late a.m.

Ice a nasty looking field toward walrus islands, thus attempted to go north westward to Kitieshuk's land but ice began closing in and prevented. Headed toward camp – arrived at 5 o'clock. Heavy east wind enroute, continuing through the night, Clear – moonlight.

Will soon attempt a trip with the *Nastapoka* – outfitting her tomorrow.

Thursday, 15 June Bill putting finishing touches on the *Nastapoka*.

Friday, 16 June People are wailing over fact that tea is all gone – including ours. Omarolluk proposing that three of men kayak in to Great Whale River for further supply and also bring out his boat. Must get at bottom of it tomorrow. They don't seem to exert themselves about the hunting.

Sunday, 18 June *Nastapoka* departed at 20 minutes to one. Took aboard old Attata and kayak. He came into camp yesterday with another chap and reported ore down in Fair Weather Harbour country. Arrived there at 3 p.m. Found the ore discovery merely a part of one I had already gone over.

Wednesday, 21 June Learn from Omarolluk that ice has undoubtedly disappeared for summer. In years of variable winds ice stays around inland all of July so one can imagine how fortunate we are now. Many ducks here abouts. Extremely strong tidal currents about which afford ducks and sea fowl a habitat the year round.

Went ashore after ducks. Have discovered that the 12 gauge paper shells are damp and of course useless. Omarolluk brought in two ducks during afternoon.

Friday, 23 June Light northwest wind – slow progress. At 1:30 ran aground on a gravel shoal – falling tide. Unable to release her until next tide. Went ashore during balance of afternoon – boys goose hunting. Omarolluk secured one. Bill saw nest of young geese – probably 3 days old. Flies fairly active.

Clear evening and gorgeous sunset.

Stayed up for the high tide at 1:30 a.m. but still unable to release her. Have traveled from Fair Weather Harbour to a close lying barrier along coastline with reef infested ground to seaward and reaching out a large distance making it impassable except for small craft. The Fox and Gull Islands wonderful land masses rising high above the surrounding country.

Saturday, 24 June Light variable wind from eastward. Released boat at full tide at noon, but discharged part of ballast. Continued on our course north northwest along coast.

Sunday, 25 June Fog and rain. In afternoon cleared a little. Boys went ashore, succeeded in killing four geese. Omarolluk says geese are shedding their wing feathers now so for next month or so will not be able to fly. Bill went out on a hopeless quest – jigging for cod – but of all things successful brought in only but three small deep sea cod. Have preserved the skin. Water here very deep.

Monday, 26 June Breakfast at 5 a.m. Clear, sparkling a.m. Departed at 6 a.m.

This sound is both largest and deepest of all this island group. A bold shoreline east and west making all of it a splendid water way and harborage for deep sea ships. At 3:30 put into shore of western island and anchored. Bill and I went inland across the island which is more barren than any islands to eastward – a vast mass of ice scarred diabase and dotted with innumerable lakes – one of them at least three miles long. Most impressive example of glacial erosion yet seen – striae north northwest by south southwest.

The island is almost 7 miles wide – fairly flat and desolate in appearance. Noted snow drifts along east coast showing later season to that of eastern islands.

Bill scared up 4 geese yet failed to make a killing.

Good weather in sight at last. These ten days past have been trying. Saw many small trout in lake streams.

Tuesday, 27 June At 2 o'clock saw a kayak in distance – proved to be Tookalook. Took him aboard and proceeded to the encampment situated on north entrance of the big island.

They report seeing no ore – are out of grub, living on fish. Noted some deep sea cod on the decks of their kayaks which we secured. Have salted.

Sam Sainsbury, Omarolluk, William Robertson, and Robert Flaherty manipulating a "spanish winch" to release the *Nastapoka* stranded on a reef ledge
(Claremont, LAC, PA114254)

Wednesday, 28 June Have arranged with Tookalook for the walrus hunt. Omarolluk pointed out small worms that infest stagnant water pools – says that they are fatal if swallowed while drinking. He carries an ivory tube with which he sucks up the water.

It seems that four Eskimos of the encampment left only yesterday with kayaks for the Walrus Islands.

Thursday, 29 June Departed for Tookalook's walrus ground at 8:30 a.m. Arrived at 7:30 at one of probably the "Baker's Dozen" group.

Swarms of sea pigeons flew about us as we anchored. All went ashore hunting ducks and splendid chance for pictures of pigeons – can get right to them with camera. Went aboard at dark with a big bag of ducks.

Wind increased during night. We attempted to beat out but owing to the ground swells were thrown on the rocks where she rapidly punched half-dozen holes into her bottom. We barely had time to save our gear and lost 1,200 feet of motion picture film in the process.

Secured motion pictures of the wreck.

Saturday, 1 July Bill in all kinds of blues. We are some 50–60 miles north of camp on part of the Baker's Dozen group of islands.

Sunday, 2 July Bill rigged up a spanish winch of driftwood and we started with a forlorn hope that she might come out of it – which if so might mean that we could save her. She came after a day's hard pull – succeeded in berthing her on a rock ledge above high tide.[21]

Monday, 3 July Developed some 80 feet of film during day – started our return at 8:30 p.m. Very calm and warm. Arrived at wreck at 10:30 following day – July 5th, bringing Tookalook along as carpenter. Bill had to strip and dive for some of the lost gear.

Friday, 7 July Wind veered over to north – still strong.

Forced to shift camp as big sea flooded it during the time I was in sleeping bag.

Enroute north to this island on July 5th came across carcass of Right Whale on small island. Some of the flesh still remains. Could not find bone.

Sunday, 9 July Wind bound on island to this date – impossible weather. Noted young eider ducks just hatched – a day after hatching were into the water.

Monday, 10 July Departed with Omarolluk and Tookalook in red launch with kayak in tow for the Walrus Island ground to northward. Splendid, clear day with light head (north) wind. Arrived at last – 7 p.m. The western sun was covered while approaching and for a time we all feared that our journey was to be a failure but in drawing closer in surely enough there lay a herd of tawny monsters asleep and taking their ease on its rocks.

We landed well to windward, discharged boat and pitched camp. Then went over to have a glimpse of them – no pictures till tomorrow on account of the light. They lay packed together in a large tawny mass on the smooth, water worn greenstone which rose half wavering from the water. The way they grunted and sighed and slobbered one could not help but see they are working off a gorge of clams and shell fish.

One would turn and scratch with his flippers – it was comical to see. Its ungainly bulk shaky like a jelly. Once in a while one would give another a poke with his tusk and then there would be a row. They are all bulls at this ground and some of them are very large. Omarolluk says that polar bears kill them in the water. It sure speaks well for the bear.

Tuesday, 11 July A splendid, almost calm a.m. About the time we made ready for start of walrus pictures, a slight air from northeast came up which made us very anxious as we were then to windward of the herd.

However it didn't amount to much. We made approach safely. Omarolluk and Tookalook arranged their harpoon line, anchoring it to a huge boulder. We all then started creeping up to the herd – distance 200 feet. Omarolluk led, myself next with camera and then Tookalook. At distance of some 35 feet I stopped. Omarolluk crept on, harpoon in hand, which I filmed. At distance of 6 feet he launched it. The herd, panic stricken, made for the water – presently I heard the square flipper harpoon line snap, our quarry was lost and off into the sea. The herd, their anger aroused, showed their ugly muzzles at the water's edge and even started for the land again, but my own movements with the camera spoiled it. They then went off into deeper water.

Omarolluk and Tookalook called and they came into shore again. We singled out a large one and all fired and in a minute he was dead with half an acre of his blood over the water.

We took pot shots at the herd now at a distance of 1,000 feet distance – at third shot I hit one. They made off then. Omarolluk says they won't come back here.

At 1 o'clock, having flensed the walrus, we started south with about 800 lbs. of meat aboard. Light northeast wind. Arrived at 7:00 p.m. to find the *Nastapoka* in the water once more.

Wednesday, 12 July We departed for camp at 10:45 a.m. Light south wind gradually freshening. Had Tookalook's kayak in tow. At second island south had to put in and land him and tidal sea made it dangerous with kayak. Left him on island with a chunk of walrus meat. He will kayak to camp later. Saw young eider ducks in water. Wind became heavy, shifted to north – big sea augmented by a nasty tide. Made for lee of an island at 5 o'clock and while off the point of it narrowly escaped disaster. The sail jibbed and Omarolluk lost control of it – as it went over to starboard it carried away the frame on keel and at gunwale – the mast fell in water with sail. The motors had been raked with salt water and were useless. Had a time of it getting into lee of the island camp – wind very strong and cold. Omarolluk went off hunting and returned with two geese. Had a cup of chocolate before turning in.

Thursday, 13 July Departed at 6 o'clock. In passing third island from camp – distance some 25 miles – Omarolluk left tiller to me to start pumping out boat – was struggling with outboard at the time – I turned around in time to see us crash into the rocks – a heavy surf – we were soon swamped but managed to save pictures and film gear from the water.

The boat filled – we discharged her with the surf breaking over our hands and shoulders. We got so numb we could hardly move. Later rigged up tackle and hitch anchor – managed to get her on a shelving rock but not before she was stove in in several places.

In afternoon very calm, beautiful day – warm. Omarolluk worked at boat splicing broken planking and caulking while I overhauled engines.

At 7 p.m. we launched her again. Tookalook hove in sight in kayak. Found it impossible to start engines. Worked at them till dark when we abandoned operations and put ashore on a gravel beach, anchoring launch.

A gale of south wind came up early a.m. At noon anchor rope chaffed in two and the launch was wrecked this time in earnest. Saved engines and gear. Miserable day with rain and heavy wind.

Omarolluk saw my grub was getting short so he refused his share, saying he and Tookalook could very well get along with ducks and sea pigeons.

Saturday, 15 July Glorious day. Extremely heavy fog in early a.m.

Omarolluk and Tookalook left at daybreak in single kayak for camp in order to return with large canoe and grub so that I with remaining gear can get to camp.

Sunday, 16 July Southwest wind all day – calm at night – full moon.

Should have been here. Awakened this a.m. July 17th, to find no arrivals. Something wrong somewhere.

Monday, 17 July Steady south wind with driving rain. Grub mighty short – tobacco expires today sometime – would rather the grub went – cold, miserable – incessant surf close at hand. What a summer. Not two days running of travel weather. Eternal wind – these islands are a storm center.

About 4 o'clock I was startled by a hail above the roar and torrent of surf. Jumping out of the tent I saw 4 Eskimos with a big canoe with two kayaks lashed to either side making a catamaran. Some sea and wind for them to be out in. They came of course to relieve me, bringing food and welcome tobacco. The wind abated at dark. Strange news they brought of Sam, Stewart's and LaDuke's arrival.

Started about midnight for home – distance about 35 miles. Much fussing with the outboard motors.

Tuesday, 18 July A wonderful dawn. My anxiety to reach camp and get mail was a strain. Around about 7 a.m. a warm, sunny morning "with gold in its mouth."

Big encampment of Huskies surrounding camp. Mail proved to be a letter from Sam and a few papers and letters for Bill.

But the "family" clears the air – everything.

Bill arrived via narrows at noon. Thought it was Dad at first.

Wednesday, 19 July Developed pictures. Strong, strong wind – gale in fact. Bill's trip from Wreck Island here somewhat strenuous. The boat leaked badly up to the lockers all the way. Men out staking land. Bill and Doc caulked *Nastapoka*. Very warm, close evening – thunder and showers.

Thursday, 20 July Light south wind – warm and close, showers in afternoon. Developed pictures.

Saturday, 22 July Wind abated – west northwest. Bill, Casey and Tookalook leave with *Nastapoka* for Great Whale River today.

Eskimos report having seen smoke of steamer and rockets and fires of distress some 10 days ago. Is it Dad in the *Inenew*? Anxious – all of us.

Omarolluk left for Big Lake geese hunting. Most of visiting Huskies left this a.m. for their summer ground to north westward. Afternoon fine and warm.

Wednesday, 26 July Clear, warm day – westerly wind. Traveled over to Mukpollo Inlet in outboard motor canoe with Eskimo boy. Went over Sainsbury's staking. Put Johnnie and Fatty at work over here erecting monuments.

Thursday, 27 July Went over to Mukpollo Inlet and went into staking in detail with Tookalook and Levy. Returned at dark.

Friday, 28 July Went over probable ore area near camp this fore noon – located 1,500′ claim on outcrop of float and copper.

Motion Picture Subjects
View of driver and sledge
Icing sledge runners
Snarling dog
Opening can of meat
Children with a pup team
The [dog] fight
Shoeing a dog's frozen foot
Harnessing dog
Igloo
Building of igloo
Window reflector and interior view
Interior arrangements – laying bed, etc. Manipulating of lamp, kettle, etc.
Kiddies under cover
Breathing hole

Close up of ice pictures
Frost, salt-rime, effects of
Sketch showing white man travel – frozen beans
Primus lamp, sleeping bag
View of Great Whale River Post
Portrait of Harold [Udgaarden]
Snowed in houses

Wrecked ship [*Laddie*]
Putting bait on spear
Portraits
Omarolluk
Lucy
Mother cild
The flirtation

Square flipper hunt
The hole close up
Approach to hole
Building wind shield
The seal comes – ready
The strike
The fight
The landing
The feast

Kayak building
Close-up
Water tight seams
Ivory tipped paddles
Duck hunting in kayak
Duck spear
Eskimo game of walrus hunt

Salmon fishing, salmon traps

Special
Scene showing Omarolluk/wife and child departing in kayak
Close up of lamp

Portraits
Group showing characteristic Belcherites in duck skins
Panoramas of islands
Nastapoka under sail

Left camp with Levy in outboard motor for the Fair Weather Harbour country at 7 a.m. Light north wind – warm. Arrived about 3 p.m. Very dark night with mist.

Saturday, 29 July Heavy thunder showers through to better part of a.m. Also fog and south wind. Staked three claims in a.m. Left at noon for camp.

Reached camp at 5 o'clock. Heavy fog all the way. Partially cleared at sundown – hazy – almost calm and warm. Found that Omarolluk had returned feeling very embarrassed about sulking fit.

Sunday, 30 July Splendid day – warm almost calm, variable winds. Sent Levy and Fatty off in kayaks to Thomas' land to erect monuments on ore series. Left with Omarolluk and Kitieshuk for Mukpollo Inlet. Staked extension to south. Made panoramas of ore series. Flies especially troublesome. Started for camp at 3:30. Along the shoreline of *Laddie* Island saw a sail boat. It's arrival proved to be Dad and his party.[22]

Friday, 18 August Dad and party departed this afternoon at 4:30 for Great Whale River.

Waited 3 long, weary weeks for Bill's return. Had started preparations to cross to mainland with canoe and two kayaks when Bill hove into sight.

Saturday, 9 September Had to leave the good old Huskies behind. They waved to us till the last gasp.[23]

Sunday, 10 September At anchor 3 days – heavy southwest gale. On 11th clear weather.

Wednesday, 13 September Cold, north wind – overcast. Departed for south in a.m. Somewhat to westward of the Twins following a.m.

Following day made for lee of Discovery Island and anchored 2½ days. Terrific southwest gale while there.

Departed on September 18th – 6 a.m. Heavy squalls with hail. Arrived in harbor at South Twin Island. Went ashore after geese – saw many but not successful.

Wrote story of Omarolluk adrift in calm waters five days in Hudson Bay.[24]

Tuesday, 19 September Arrived at an island of the Solomon Temple group and anchored in lee.

Wednesday, 20 September Southwest wind all day. Hunted ducks –

killed two – or rather one and a diver with rifle from the boat. Bill slightly poisoned – suspect canned apricots.

Thursday, 21 September Fair southeast by south wind. Very heavy with light sea running.

Made Trodely Island – proceeded to anchor there as wind for this part of the course to Charlton is adverse.

8 Nanook of the Barren Lands

Flaherty's return to Toronto in the fall of 1916 closed his career as an iron prospector in the employ of Mackenzie and Mann. The Great War's bottomless appetite for financial resources had consumed any ambitions Mackenzie or others might have had for the economic expansion of Hudson Bay. Although no final report on the fourth expedition is among Flaherty's papers, the geological findings reported in the diary suggest that while the iron ore deposits on the Belcher Islands were interesting, they were no bonanza. The limited commercial value of the Belcher iron deposits would have been confirmed by his father's first-hand inspection. It is noteworthy that for the period of Flaherty senior's stay on the Belchers there are no diary entries, thus no mention of his father's findings.

During his Belchers stay, the first of the three Flaherty daughters was born – Barbara Lee, in March 1916 in New York City – an event Flaherty learned of when he received the mail packet on 7 May 1916. Within a year of his return, the second daughter, Frances Farnham, was born – in September 1917 in Houghton, the Michigan residence of the Hubbard family, where the Flahertys lived and contemplated how they would fashion their lives without Mackenzie's sponsorship. Onerous as this economic relationship had been to Frances, its absence made blunt the truth that Flaherty was an unemployed iron prospector with few immediate opportunities, and was dependent on the generosity of his in-laws.

The year 1917 saw Flaherty shuttling between Houghton and Toronto as he sought to print and edit footage of the Belcher Islands filming and merge it with the Baffin Island footage to produce a new hybrid, the Baffin-Belcher Islands filming. Since this film did not receive the press coverage the first did, we know less about it than we do about its predecessor. Some suggestion of the shots Flaherty may have used to replace or blend with the Baffin film footage appear in the list of "Motion Picture Subjects" that follows his diary entry of 28 July 1916. Although we cannot assume that Flaherty shot all these sequences, there is sufficient corroboration in the diary to suggest that many of them were shot.

We find, therefore, suggestions for retakes of sequences that were in the Baffin Island film, such as igloo building, with the attendant interest in Eskimo domestic life. There is a repeat (again, using a dead seal) of seal hunting through the seals' breathing hole in the ice, with the inevitable tug of war on the harpoon line followed by the communal feast. Flaherty reports that he finished both the igloo and the seal sequences on 12 April 1916. Other episodes reminiscent of the previous film are the driving and icing of the sledge and the dog handling and feeding scenes. The family and kayak departure shots of Omarolluk and his family would, if included, compete with the central role that the Baffin film gives to Anunglung and his family. The most striking potential departure from the Baffin film is the inclusion of the white man, his habitat, diet, and modern field equipment; Harold Udgaarden, the HBC employee at Great Whale River, makes a cameo appearance.

Clearly, it was not Flaherty's intention to do a major remake of the Baffin film but to refine sequences with which he was dissatisfied and to add other brief elements, such as trader episodes, which would give a fresh, distinctive edge to the newly combined Baffin-Belcher film. It was for this film, in whatever final form it took, that the Flahertys again hoped to find a distributor. Working in a Mackenzie and Mann facility in Toronto in the spring of 1918, Flaherty had completed the editing of the approximately 25,000 feet of footage to a 6,000 or so length when, because of a careless cigarette, the small room of nitrate film exploded. A decade later, Flaherty recounted the details to Terry Ramsaye: "There was a burst of flame. Flaherty was thrown across the room, burned deep by the blast, scorched

The family picnic, Houghton, summer of 1917. Back row (left to right): Frances Flaherty, Platt Adams, Robert Flaherty, Charlotte Hubbard Goodell; seated (left to right): Lucius Hubbard, Barbara Flaherty in his lap, Julia Hubbard Adams holding Charlotte Adams, Frances J. Hubbard, Charlotte Goodell, H.S. Goodell; seated on ground (left to right): Ruth Goodell with back to camera, Frances Goodell, and Robert Goodell

(with kind permission of Mrs Lee Erhartic of West Chelmsford, Mass.)

as though he had stepped into the roaring vortex of a giant blow-torch. He struggled out of the room and ran into the street in a frenzy of pain, clothes afire. Weeks later he recovered in a hospital."[1]

The aftermath of the event was described by Flaherty in an earlier interview in the *Baltimore News* of 27 May 1923: "After I came out of the hospital – and I very nearly didn't – there wasn't any negative and the one print we had was too thin for reproduction, but despite this calamity it probably was a good thing because there was little story or continuity to my material." What must have indeed been a moment of calamity for Flaherty and his film ambitions, over time (especially after the success of *Nanook*) mellowed into a fortunate fall, a coincidence that propelled him to leave behind the Baffin-Belcher experience and seek an opportunity to make afresh his vision of the Eskimo. This "bit of fortune," as he characterized the explosion in 1922, became a milestone in his artistic development, as he often acknowledged.[2] In 1950, more than thirty years after the event, he recalled that after the destruction of his footage he still had an edited print of the negative which he had shipped to Harvard for a screening. This Harvard Print, as it came to be known, remained in Flaherty's possession: "I showed it to the American Geographical Society and then realized just how bad it was. It was utterly inept, simply a scene of this and a scene of that, no relation, no thread of a story or continuity whatsoever, and it must have bored the audience to distraction. Certainly it bored me."[3] After Flaherty's death, Frances made this perception of the explosion canonical when she declared in her retrospective, *The Odyssey of a Film-Maker*, that he would have said, "Amateur that I was, I dropped a lighted cigarette on it and it went up in flame. But I wasn't sorry. It was a bad film; it was dull – it was little more than a travelogue. I had learned to explore, I had not learned to reveal."

It was of course easier to dismiss the Baffin-Belcher film in the aftermath of *Nanook*. Between 1918 and 1920, Flaherty had in fact continued to promote his single print, showing it at, among other places, the Explorer's Club in New York. He also showed it to a number of community audiences in and about the Silvermine area of New Canaan and Norwalk, Connecticut, where he and Frances had relocated in the spring of 1918. Apart from infrequent visits to see his family in Port Arthur, the Flahertys never again resided in Canada. Meanwhile, with a family to support and no evidence of a steady income, the Flahertys were in economic straits – so much so that Frances was giving music lessons at three dollars an hour (a tidy wage in 1919).[4]

One of Flaherty's viewers during these two years was Captain Thierry Mallet, an executive of the Revillon Frères Trading Company who supervised the company's northern posts. A seasoned northern hand, Mallet had established many of the Revillon posts, the first at Moose Factory in 1903 and another in 1910 at Port Harrison, where Flaherty later finished *Nanook*. Theirs was truly a kinship of sensibility. Mallet initiated his young friend as a member of the Coffee House Club, where Flaherty established his lifetime cosmopolitan base in New York City (though later he also based it in a suite he kept at the Chelsea Hotel). There is no doubt that it was through Mallet's brokerage that Revillon agreed in 1920 to sponsor Flaherty's proposed northern film.

While Flaherty was seeking supporters for a new film venture by using the Baffin-Belcher film as a sample of what he might do, Frances devoted her energies to being his literary secretary and agent. His experience was the stuff of literary adventure, and the Butler Library papers contain multiple renditions of draft narratives or outlines prepared by her for projects that capitalized on Flaherty's six years of exploration and diary keeping. In letters written to Margaret Thurston throughout 1917, Frances alluded to her work on a "book," though what its focus or content might be was unsaid. There are drafts, edited in Frances's hand – on Groundhog River sequences from the first expeditionary diary, with the working titles "Down River to the Bay" and "River Travel."[5] Frances also prepared an outline as a prompt to Flaherty's memory for a book on his four expeditions, whose title she suggested might be "Six Years of Exploration and Adventure in the Subarctic of Eastern Canada."

Given these efforts to bring literary luster to Robert's working field diaries, the Flahertys began to single out individuals whose characterization were to be given an enhanced fictional identity. This transformation is most evident in the figure of Wetalltok, the longtime Charlton Island resident whom Flaherty met on his first expedition and whose map first prompted him to consider the Belchers as a forgotten island land mass off the eastern coast of Hudson Bay. In the editorial hands of the Flahertys, Wetalltok underwent an apotheosis. There are notes for a "Story of W": "Make W an old man – a patriarch of his people – old, white – pathetically old – his followers and children a new trade generation unused to old Eskimo ways."[6] He is to be given a refurbished history as an eighteen-year fugitive from the Belcher Islands because of a blood feud over a murder he committed. The once great hunter is to become a Hudson's Bay Company servant.

The viewing of Wetalltok's map deserved careful reconstruction, so Frances revisited it: "The map was drawn on the reverse side of an old missionary lithograph and represented Wetalltok's hunting grounds previous to his migration – islands which on the admiralty charts are known as the N. & S. Belchers, shown there in dotted outline, the largest then not more than six miles long. Wetalltok's map on the other hand showed a land mass of surprising extent. He calculated distance from point to point by Wetalltok's reckoning, i.e., travel time for kayak and dog team – it proved that the main islands would probably be 100 miles in length."[11]

The overall portrait of Wetalltok is, of course, only a shadow of the man whom Flaherty ejected from his base camp on the Belchers in 1916 because Wetalltok was unwilling to have himself and his family live in the native style. By fictional reconstruction, Wetalltok becomes a hero. This process of imaginatively transforming the cultural identity of their film subjects and locales became a trademark in the Flahertys' career as fabulists of the exotic.

The most substantial outcome of these efforts to capitalize on Flaherty's experiences occurred with the publication in June and August 1918 of two articles in the prestigious journal of the American Geographical Society, the *Geographical Review*.[8] The June article serves as a summary of all four expeditions. Its dominant theme is the rediscovery of the Belchers, with particular credit being given to Wetalltok, including the map episode that Frances had specifically written to heighten Wetalltok's contribution. In the last sentence of the article there is a flourish of finality: "The Big Islands are ancient history in the bay now, and Wetalltok stands vindicated." Despite this flourish, the tone of the article is scientific and professional, befitting the journal that published it. The August article emphasizes the cross-Labrador exploration of 1911–12 which formed the basis for Flaherty's election to the Royal Geographical Society. That, too, is in the manner of the explorer seeking to credit not his personal exploits but his professional contributions to science.

These two articles constitute the first major publications that recount Flaherty's career between 1910 and 1916, and they thus form a baseline for all the subsequent narratives the Flahertys produced about this phase of his career. Although the articles include a host of photographs, many of which are of maps or are geological in subject, there is no commentary about the picture taking itself. However, in the June article, Flaherty does allude to his filmmaking endeavors: "During the winter we compiled a series of motion pictures showing the primitive life, crafts, and modes of hunting and traveling of the islanders – an improved version of the film we had previously made on the Baffin Island expedition." He also tells us that he showed the Baffin film to his Belcher audience, "purposing in this way to inspire them with that spirit of emulation so necessary to the success of our filming."[9] Drafts of this article show that Flaherty originally wrote "cooperation," which Frances edited to "emulation." The adjustment is interesting in that Frances viewed the Belcher filming process as an attempt to imitate the actions of the Baffin film, whereas Flaherty, as he always did, worked to create participatory contributions to a process. The intention of the filmwork ("we compiled") is securely ethnographic and educational ("showing the primitive life"), and any sense of wonderment about the film is made the experience of the Belcher audience as they marvel at the "strange and wonderful ways of the *kablunak* (white man)."[10]

By early 1920, Flaherty was making progress in persuading Revillon Frères to support his film ambitions. In a letter of 16 February to Mallet he made several proposals for the project while providing as background his earlier exploration and filmwork:

As you know, I have spent six years in geological exploration in northeastern sub-arctic Canada. During that time I did a good deal of photographic work among the Eskimos. Among other things I made some thirty thousand feet of motion picture film, which, just as we were about to place it on the market, was unfortunately lost by fire. Only a partial copy of the film, much worn and flawed remained. This, however, was brought to New York in the hope that it might be duplicated and thereby commercialized. We showed it to the firm of Robertson-Cole who, much interested, forthwith made arrangements whereby they, entering into partnership with us, would duplicate and exploit the film. The deal fell through only when their laboratory expert declared the duplication was not economically feasible. This film Mr Revillon and yourself have seen.[11]

There is a suggestion in the letter that what the Revillon people had seen and what they wanted were not the same. Their interests were apparently in film that would enhance the commercial identity of the fur industry, Revillon's core enterprise. Flaherty, on the other hand, had proposed a film that would "contain no white man or fur trade subject matter" but would "be exclusively the life of the Eskimos as the primitive inhabitants of the land." He added: "The film since it would contain no fur trade propaganda could perfectly well be produced under the name of the firm Revillon Frères, using, for instance, your letter head which in my opinion would lend the film both dignity and prestige."

The dilemma Flaherty found himself facing here was one that would be a familiar nemesis throughout his career: How does one negotiate with a prospective sponsor whose interests are commercial and exploitative when you are striving to make a film whose people and society are historicized to exist in a world predating commercial intrusion? Always the nimble pragmatist, Flaherty resolved the impasse by suggesting, "Apart from this projected [film] of Eskimo life, I enclose herewith a rough draft of a second film, the subject of which is frankly the fur trade, but which also, I believe, would be a feature film quite as big in its way as is the first. In the enclosed draft I believe you will perceive what I am driving at. Please understand, however, that it is only a rough, tentative plan." The outline, which the Flahertys entitled "A Trader's Life among the Eskimo," called for a narrative that began in northern Ontario and took the viewer through the stages by which a trader arrived by ship at the Revillon post at Port Harrison. The scenes were to be variants of what Flaherty had already shot – dog handling, igloo life, beans and bacon – the significant difference being that a white man was the focal character. Given Flaherty's lifelong resistance to being held to a predetermined production script, the trader film outline is unusual. The hedging tone ("rough, tentative") is a sign of his working under compulsion yet leaving himself room to maneuver.[12]

The contract that Flaherty signed with Revillon on 30 March 1920 settled the issue by calling for two films: "The first of said films will picture Eskimo life, featuring exclusively the natural Eskimo way of living in the wilds; while the second of said films will present a picture of fur trading in and about the trading post of the Revillon Frères system at Port Harrison on the East coast of Hudson Bay."[13] Any photographic work associated with the film was to remain the property of Revillon, and once the expenses of making and printing the film had been reimbursed to Revillon, the profits were to be split 51/49 in favor of Revillon. In return, Revillon would provide Flaherty with $10,000 to cover all preparation and equipment costs and $3,000 for the technical expenses of preparing a final print. In addition, it would provide transportation to and from Port Harrison, an advance of $3,000 so that Flaherty could compensate local Native people, and a line of credit at the Revillon post of $3,000 to cover supplies and ammunition at an allowance normally allotted to Revillon agents.

As of 1 April 1920 and through the fall of 1921, Flaherty was to receive a salary of $500 per month, and this salary was to be forwarded to Frances in Norwalk during the time when Flaherty was working in the North. There is a more unusual clause in that it called for Flaherty, at contract, to surrender to Revillon "his damaged film of Eskimo life," which would be returned to him on his departure so that it could "be used by him exclusively in the furthering of the purpose of said exhibition." The agreement apparently protected Revillon from having the "damaged" film becoming a competitor to its own interests, but it also allowed Flaherty to follow his practice of showing the film to his prospective collaborators in the same fashion he had shown the Baffin film to the Belcher Inuit.

With contract in hand, Flaherty had a little over two months to make the many necessary preparations. Although Frances had joined him in working hard for his success, the prospect of his absence for more than a year must have dimmed the brightness. The division of their pathways was made all the more decisive with the birth of a third daughter, Monica Lambard, in early May. Some of Flaherty's movements between his departure for the North and his arrival at Port Harrison can be determined from the diary that Thierry Mallet kept from 13 June to 7 September while on an inspection tour of the Revillon posts on Hudson Bay, a tour that included accompanying Flaherty to the company's post at Port Harrison.

Flaherty had already reached Moose Factory when Mallet arrived on 23 June. While Mallet left to conduct inspections of various posts, Flaherty remained at Moose to finish preparations for his journey to Port Harrison. Among his stops, Mallet visited Fort Albany, where the bulk of Flaherty's outfit (thirty-nine crates) had been sent down the Pagwa River by scow. From there it was to be loaded onto the *Annie Geele* for transport to Harrison. Mallet was worried about the careless management of transporting Flaherty's outfit and was especially alarmed over the absence of two crates, fearful that all or some of Flaherty's 75,000 feet of filmstock might be lost.

Mallet and Flaherty were reunited for their shared journey to Harrison when the *Annie Geele* picked up Mallet at Port Herodier on 6 August. On board, in addition to Flaherty, Mallet found Robert Stewart, the incoming Revillon post manager (who later played the white trader in *Nanook*), Stewart's wife, and a young apprentice clerk from Montreal named Griffith. This party, plus skipper and crew, made for a very crowded ship, and Mallet predicted:

> This is going to be a tough trip, for we are eight in the cabin and there is only room for 4. Flaherty sleeps on the floor in the engine room. [Captain] Nielson on the floor in his cabin beside his bunk occupied by the Stewart couple. Griffith on the floor, under the table, in the main cabin. The schooner is filthy and the cook – Joe Gagnon – does not try to improve matters. The excuse is "too many passengers." That is true. But since the schooner left Moose on her first trip to AY [Fort Albany] this spring, she has not been washed once (outside or inside) when she laid empty in port. Joe Nielson is responsible. He is himself as lazy and dirty as an Indian.[14]

By the time the ship arrived at Harrison on 15 August, the mood aboard was stressed. Mallet, a man not given to gentle opinions, was ready to savage Nielson, and as for Griffith, "He is intensely selfish, lazy and untactful," having annoyed everybody, "especially Flaherty."[15] But Mallet could also say, almost in relief, "I like Stewart. He is as bright as can be, knows his business, and gets along very well with Flaherty (Thank goodness). He has the interest of the post at heart and I am sure we have in him one of the best men who have ever worked for us at Port Harrison. Just now, he is head over heels in love with his [newly married] wife, but he will get over that soon."[16]

The reception at Port Harrison was enthusiastic, and to Mallet's surprise there were more than a hundred Inuit ready to unload the annual supply shipment and Flaherty's outfit. The weather turned foul as Flaherty's goods were being transferred to a barge and there was the danger that the barge, precariously anchored, might capsize. Flaherty, aboard the *Annie*, pleaded with Nielson for help, and the reply he received, according to Mallet, was: "'F— them. They have left my ship. It is none of my business,' and then [he went] on reading." Flaherty did succeed in enlisting the help of two Indian crew members, George Hunter and Joe Trapper, who in rough water managed to launch the lifeboat. "[When] Hunter takes charge," noted Mallet "The Huskies are scared. The jigger is smashed. Hunter repairs it and manages to sail her to the post. Without him, we would probably have lost the barge and a part of Flaherty's outfit, which would have been absolutely impossible to replace here."[17]

Before the *Annie* departed with Mallet and Grasset, the outgoing Revillon post manager, Mallet fussed over ensuring that all of Flaherty's crates had arrived (they had): "Everything OK. Very busy trying out his [projector] motor (for screen) and superintending the four Huskies who are building his dark room and numerous shelves and tables ... I allow him to buy the nine Eskimo dogs belonging to Grasset at $10 a piece (cheap). He must have a team this winter, especially to go to Nastapoka Falls, where we have planned to film a lot of scenes in sight of that enormous waterfall (165 feet high)." His task of being the good comrade and mentor done, Mallet departed, but not before making a forecast more prescient than he realized: "With any sort of luck, I am convinced that Flaherty will give extraordinary good results with his future films."[18]

The Port Harrison Diary[19]
14 August 1920 – August 1921

The up trip over. From the Ontario frontier down the Ground Hog toward Moose and James Bay.[20]

Moose Factory Aboard the Annie northward bound – "The Twins," Fort George and Port Harrison – at last.

Port Harrison A throng of scurrying figures gathering around the factor's house. Slowly, with flags aloft, making anchorage which from the post was not more than a mile away. The flag pole was bare. No sign came from the factor of the post. By the time on deck unlashing boats and launching – Eskimos carried out the flag. To our amazed gaze slowly ascended wrong side and stopped at half mast! Good Lord, was the factor dead was question uppermost in our minds.

Deep in speculation we drew slowly toward the post – watching narrowly the door of the factor's house, hoping against hope for his appearance. Fearful doubt had resolved to conviction when, as keel grounded in the sands, the door popped open and the factor appeared, a huge tripod and camera in hand, the horde of Eskimos behind, and stalked rapidly toward us but without a sign or word of salutation. Stopped off at camera's range, pointed at us his camera lens, face in camera hood, and pretended to photograph!

Embarrassment, no doubt, troubled him – the visitor kind. That comes from living long alone in the north.

Unloading cargo, strewn along wharf – men, women and babes. The *Annie*'s departure. The house and staff. My servants and dogs and boxes and settled for the winter.

The country around Port Harrison, the rivers and heartland unknown. The Eskimos – tribal names and characteristics. Reduced morale due to lack of deer migrations.

Epidemic after ship's departure.[21]

September
The Walrus Hunt
Showing the film[22]
Trading furs
The storms
The igloo camps around
The dogs and their houses
The daily routines – the bell
The evening dog chaos at their feeding
Starvation along the coast
Eskimo trading
Absence of deer skins – after them

Bear tales and hunts
The adversity of Nanook – the bear tales of Nanook Noona
The bear expedition

The long, dreary spring
The migrations
The ice breaks – the long days – sleepless
The flowers – mosquitoes
The elastic ice

Wednesday, 22 September 1920 The narrows – 5 miles northwest Port Harrison. Departed in whale boat with 4 Eskimos this a.m. for Walrus Island – films and exploration. Wind bound at narrows at noon.

Fine clear day – cold northeast wind. Made films of landscape in p.m. and Eskimo dogs and tent life. Sparks from one of my men's pipes burned hole in my focal plane shutter of small Graflex while filming this afternoon. Eskimo in question crestfallen indeed – is a serious loss.

Fine camp – feels fine to get away from the irksome post routine. Among other unexpected goodies, Stewart enclosed a box of bon-bons in my grub outfit.

Eskimo names: Snow Bird, Harry Lauder.

Thursday, 23 September In camp all day – wind head on for course down the Sound.

Changed sail much to crew's delight. The old one being much too large. Would surely have come to grief had we been caught with it in heavy wind. Sent Harry Lauder into post for oil and additional supplies at night fall. Returned in his kayak at 2 a.m.

Friday, 24 September Beautiful a.m. Frost on the ground. Broke camp at 7:30 – light offshore of wind until after lunch. Climbed on surf swept rocks of outside coast. Wind departs at 2 p.m. and have started out for walrus land – the crew loath somewhat to leave the land.

A mere breath of wind all afternoon. The crew had to row part of the time. Finally reached Walrus Island at nightfall. Landed on an extremely rocky surf bound coast. Had to put block and tackle on boat to haul her up beyond the tide.

Reveled in the luxury of a big drift wood fire. We camped on a flat ledge of rock – there being no gravel ground at hand.

All of us elated at good journey.

Saturday, 25 September Sent the men to scout out the walrus ground and found walrus there and went over with outfit of machines.

Saw a whole string of perhaps a hundred walrus skulls or more that some Eskimo of yore had strung in fanciful array along the backbone of the island – also a human skull and on many old trap and stone topek mounds found old bone and ivory relics.

Walrus, a hundred or more, played in the surf but did not land. Filmed them with telephoto lens albeit the weather was dark and drops of rain were falling.

Returned to camp about dark. Above the boom of surf could hear the walrus barking – a sure sign that they had landed. Praying for clear weather on the morrow.

Sunday, 26 September Has been the day of days.

Morning calm, clear and warm. Saw twenty walrus lay sleeping on the rocks. Approached to windward 100 feet and filmed with telephoto lens. Nanook stalking quarry with harpoon – within 20 feet they rose in alarm and tumbled toward the sea. Nanook's harpoon landed but the quarry succeeded in reaching the water. Then commenced the battle royal. Four Eskimos straining for their lives on the harpoon line at water's edge – the quarry like a huge fish floundering and churning the sea. The remainder of the herd hovered around, their "Ook, Ook" resounding. One great bull even came up to the quarry and locked tusks in attempt to rescue. I filmed and filmed and filmed, the men calling me to end the struggle by rifle, so fearful were they of being pulled into sea.

Completed film of men flensing, their gorging.

Tired, returned at dark. The men with their bellies swollen by their gorging after dark. I am certain that each man this day has eaten 30 lbs. of meat.

A tropical thunder storm in night – thunder and lightning would seem strange indeed for this latitude – the island of 100 skulls. This day of days is Sunday which with the thunder growling around them has made them somewhat apprehensive – "the Devil's voice it may be."

Walrus Scenes to Make
Story of journey
The whale boat in sea – kayaks
The skipper
The island – desolation
Old Eskimo camp signs – walrus skulls

Human skull (skull is of Eskimo killed by walrus – harpoon line fouling)
The surf and sea coast – preparations for hunt
Rigging the harpoon line
The harpoon – close up of Nanook belly stalking
Carrying outfit to walrus ground
Camplife

Scenes to Make
Boy eating live sculpins
Children hunting sculpins on beach

Trading as Subject
Detail
Teeth
Chewing skins

One Way of Making the Film
Water carrying
Camping outfit
Eskimo loading camera in cold weather
Filming in drift
Changing films in box in igloo
Transportation by kayak – sledge
The drifted studio
Temperatures
Drying film on rack
Giving sweets for picture

Post Scenes
The *Annie*
Unloading
The post
Winter
"Snowing up"[23]
Trading
The Gramophone
The factor's cook

Post Fashions

Xmas
Trading
The factor's life and field
Sledging
Medicine – castor oil

Monday, 27 September The men gorging while caching in rock mounds what walrus meat we cannot take in whale boat to the post.

Trying to hurry them the while for we must take advantage of the splendid day and wind for our crossing to mainland. The men humming "Pull for the shore, sailor, pull for the shore." We had all the sea we could stand for first half of journey – a big, choppy surf made by northern current and angle of the wind. Though the wind was good we made less than 4 knots an hour – we wallowed so in the seas.

Darkness came when we were less than half way over – the wind dying down – we lay rolling in the swells. By nine o'clock the moon loomed up, then a great bowl of gray cloud and the wind again came along from the southward.

At ten we came into the shadow of the big wall of surf-bound coast and amid the din of booming seas threaded a narrow island channel and like magic swung to anchor in a gleaming, smooth little cove. By moonlight we scoured for drift wood among the tall sea grass, made tea on the crackling fire – a shivering outfit grouped around it. A midnight we established camp, tired and happy. A white ring around the moon is in Eskimo an igloo of the gods.

Tuesday, 28 September We sailed a happy, smiling crowd – a happy, smiling day up the Hopewell Sound – arrived at evening at the thronged beach at camp.

Wednesday, 29 September I was awakened at 7 by excited screams of women out of doors. I thought it was a drowning. Soon I heard the put-put of a motor; it was a landing crew of the Hudson's Bay Company *Nascopie*.[24]

Monday, 4 October *Nascopie* departed at 8 a.m.

Thursday, 7 October In company with the white servants of the Hudson's Bay Company and their motor boat and 8 Huskies departed again for Walrus Island.

A storm caught us at the narrows only 5 miles away. Leaving the Huskies encamped there, the Hudson's Bay Company men and I in launch returned to post following day – to await favorable weather.

Monday, 11 October In launch started out for Walrus Island. Reached it at 6 p.m., the 13th.

Thursday, 14 October Storm bound at Walrus Island.
Implements to Be Made
Bow and arrow for bear hunting
Duck skin towels
Stone pots
Model igloo, komitik, kayak, etc.
Deer bones on top of igloos, etc.

The Walrus Grounds
An island ringed with surf
Landing
The beach in distance – stalking
Fixing harpoon – the kill

Camp Life – Games
Children wrestling
The women playing ball
The boy and his bow and arrow
Catching sculpins (eating them)

Retake
Maggie and Attata – close-up feeding Attata[25]
Spitting on duck skin towel
Boys fighting and tug of war with meat

Films of flora – creeping willows
Maggie pulling off boots with teeth

The wild and rugged coast of Ungava
Seascapes, rock-bound, treeless land
Landscapes

The biggest tree is creeping willow

The only wood is driftwood – only found by the coast – perhaps a cord a hundred miles
There are banks of flowers and moss plains look like cultivated fields

The first sight of Eskimo camp in distance
Scurrying figures as we approach – all is still – indoors?
The old woman and child come forth
The welcome
Port Harrison

Tuesday, 19 October Storm bound 5 days so far. Tremendous surf pounds away within stone's throw of our tent door – its salt spray spume fogging the air.

Storm bound nearly three weeks. Amuse ourselves with "duck on the rock," Eskimo games and desultory reading. Eskimos show notably in their games – in all our games while we often disagree, they never do – their spirit of fairness and sportsmanship is remarkable.

Finally left the Walrus Island after being storm bound three weeks and arrived at camp on last of October. Found the air on shore much more wintry. Permanent snow covers the ground.

Attata has cut his hair.

Stewart's cook burned her face badly with scalding tea. Lay all day in her room without making a sound. Wonderful endurance to pain.

Geographical Article on Ungava
Geographical pictures – indicate limit of trees – its north-south coast
Typically arctic
Interior land, lakes, rivers and Payne. Its rivers: Koktak, Kogaluk and Innuksuak
Geology and topography
Date of establishing Wolstenholme
Date of establishing Port Harrison
Tribal names of Eskimo inhabitants
The island designations which outlie the east coast of Hudson Bay – South Belchers to Mansfield

Film Notes
Eskimo carrying and launching kayak
Fish and bait – close-up
Fish spear showing prongs

Ask Nevalinga how far north trees extend – also location main rocks in interior

Eskimo names and meanings
Portrait split lip
Girls with dolls

Beginning of walrus scenes
Debarkation – approach to quarry

In later writings, Flaherty provided more detail on the exigencies he faced in developing his film on site:

I had no crew for the job; I went up alone with two Akeley cameras, a developing outfit, a miniature electric light plant and a projector. My crew were Eskimos. Nanook himself helped me in the hut which was converted into a laboratory to develop and print the picture. The laboratory outfit was pretty crude: old pin rack developing frames which required 20 minutes to load 200 feet of film. The light of my little electric plant was not steady enough for the printing of the film. To do that I cut a hole in the wall of the hut and let the daylight in through a trap the exact size of the aperture of the printing machine, this machine being an old Williamson printer which was screwed into the wall of the hut and cranked by hand. I used layers of muslin before the printing aperture to regulate as far as I could the strength of the day light.

The little schooner which brought me to my base near Cape Dufferin wasn't big enough to carry all the lumber I needed to build the laboratory, drying room, etc. By the time they were finished I found there was not enough left to complete the all-important drum which I must have to dry the film. The drum was about 8 feet long and some 5 feet in diameter. But Nanook solved the problem. He had to walk a good many miles, but eventually he picked up enough driftwood to complete the job.

I had to have heat in the drying room, of course; but for a stove I had to depend upon one that burned coal, soft coal at that! We lost not a little of our film through soot; more still through stray hairs from Nanook's deerskin coat, which also got mixed up in the washing water which he hauled up from the river from a hole chopped through 6 feet of ice. Whenever the film was drying I had to keep one Eskimo constantly turning the drum by hand. How many times they fell asleep,

I cannot now remember. One time sleep was so deep that the fire went out, leaving a whole drum load of 1200 feet to freeze.

The most serious jam, however, during that never-to-be-forgotten winter, came when I found I was running out of negative. I had taken what I though was ample, 70,000 feet. There was only one thing to do, try the positive film which I used for printing. Only a technician would know the difference. The public never knew, but some of the negative of *Nanook* was made on positive film.

Another difficulty was the cold. The way to know when it was really cold, said Nanook, was to spit. That's what we used to do at starting time of a bitter morning. If when we spit there was a snap, we knew it had frozen before it hit the ground. "Ikee!" said Nanook, which meant, "plenty cold." At such times I couldn't dream of threading the film into the camera; I couldn't even hold a match long enough to light my pipe, my numbed fingers would simply part in spite of myself and the match fall to the ground. Nanook did my pipe lighting and he also threaded the film. There were times however when it was impossible to use the film at all, for the moment I'd begin to crank, it would break up in the camera gate in particles like the shattered crystals of a watch.[26]

Somewhere Enroute by Snow Shoe to Port Harrison   Everything so far seems average. I would not mind being your maid of all work – everything but diapers – for years and years. Yes, I could hang the clothes on the line without turning a hair.

I would like on return to go with you to some old, old farm in Connecticut – deep into some glorious woods – I have no other ambition – not even pictures. Don't tell the Hubbards this!

I think of you most of the time – I have fears and fears sometimes – I am going to help you iron when I am with you again.

Tomorrow's sledge trip will be my first of this winter. My dogs are nearly dead of starvation during early winter and are none too strong now. I have two teams for tomorrow's trip, however.

You and the kids seem a millon years away. We expect a packet by the 1st of April – I can't wait for your letters – to know how all of you are. Don't let the children grow. Are they over running you and who is there to help you? Indeed are you in New Canaan, Florida, North Michigan, with the Gutmans south?[27]

Wednesday, 22 December   The mad man – threatens this camp. Wants cartridges – information. Said the little black balls in his eyes were getting smaller every day. Like a wild animal, running to and fro. People starving, afraid to venture out.

Friday, 7 January 1921 A crowd came and surrounded him. They killed him. Everyone relieved.[28]

The Film
The walrus hunt
The *Nascopie*

Winter
The first sledge of Eskimos

Servant trouble and kinks in native character
Mary's burns
Starvation along the coast – no seals
Billy's tales – starvation tales
"Xmas"
The "maniac"

Cape Smith and the bear

Films
The migration
Omarolluk's belated arrival
The migrant's stories of the hard winter
Starvation – bear experiences

Trade Film
Trading in store
Feasting in store – the lard treat – gallons of tea
The gramophone
Castor oil
Omiak [umiak, flat-bottomed open boat] arrives
Kayaks
Debarkation – skins, skins, skins
Towing the black barge
Ringing the bell
Harry in costume

Attata preparing spear
Show tied wrists
Maggie close-up pulling off boots with teeth
Schooner arrives
The fur press – chewing fox skins

Departure
Icing sledge
Coming out of igloo
Dog fight – away
Cloud views while sledging

The fox hole
The rough ice
Building igloo
The blizzard days
The howling dogs – groups in drift
Nanook in drift – entangled around igloo – off into drift

The ojuk [seal]
Coming into post to trade
Trade scenes

Snow knife
Igloo setting
Stone lamp
Camera tests – try heavier filter

Igloo Interiors
Attata asleep – close-up
Mother and child
Trimming lamp
Putting snow in basket
Fixing ventilator
Putting on boots
Chewing boots
Ice window

Igloo occupants asleep
Awakening – yawning – trimming lamp

Opening ventilator
Dressing
Mother and child – bath – duck skin towels
Child goes out to play
Women go into igloo
Dusting furs – make the beds
Set up their lamp
The men come in – the seal
Dogs in igloo

Trade Film
Castor oil
Maggie as cook in kitchen
The primus stove

Children dancing
Cooties from child's head
Child eating raw seal and suckling breast
Miniature of ice bear
Children hide and seek
Snow-up of factor's house
The trading scenes – furs – barter

Moleskin on screen, brown and black
Catch owl by towing mouse on string along the ground
Nanook and seal meat

The threat of insanity is rather large one

Allie and children playing in igloo
Sliding – komatik and pup
Hide and seek
Suckling breast
Licking snow knife to make it cut
Children dancing

Snow Pictures
Hardness of snow – cuts to an edge
Chink up cracks in igloo
Retake chinking igloo and entrance

Master's departure
Building igloo – he directs
Interior igloo views – master enters
Brushing snow
Supper – primus lamp and beans
Chewing boots – asleep
Dressing boy – the duck skin towel
Ice window out in from inside
Allie and his igloo
Foxes and hole

Build Igloo
Igloo setting
Departure – Attata crawls out
Harnessing long sledge
Lashing sledge
Over bank and away
Chinking igloo
Dogs rush tunnel for seal
Pups in niche in igloo wall
Allie's snow house
His pups and sledge

Trade Film
Building igloo
Master crawls in
Master departing and sledging

The Eskimo have strong teeth
Teeth close-up
Pulling boots off

Bring in square flipper
Look for powder snow

Close-up – Allie and mother awaken
Close-up – spitting on duck skin towel – child's face – duck skin towel

Sledge Construction
Driftwood

Lashing
Ivory shoeing – mud – dug up from bog

Kayak Construction
Frame – sewing seal skins
Ivory tipped paddle

Stone Pot and Lamp Construction
Soapstone – working it with chisels

Shoeing dog's frozen foot
Deer skin shoes for dogs

Master throwing sweets to children

Square Flipper
Approach from sledge
Approach from hole
The hole
Bubbles rising
The strike
The fight
The sledge comes up
Break neck for the seal
Hauling out – the feast
The quarrel between boys over meat – tug of war with meat in their mouths

Shoeing dog's foot
Seal hole with dog – in muzzled snout

Close-up – child and naked arm
Shaking hands
The Eskimo kiss
Pup in igloo
Litter of pups

Portraits
The louse picture
Maggie pulling off boots with teeth

Close-up of cook at stove – dripping nose
Close-up eating seal – cutting off with knife close to mouth
Castor oil
Boys tug of war with seal meat
Close-up – Maggie feeding Attata

Snow Hardness
Snow not soft – stand on it without snow shoes
Cuts to an edge
The knife – from a walrus tusk

Lamp and Stone Pot
Wick – moss – dug up from under snow
Oil – from blubber of seal
Chewing it for oil
Trimming flame
Lamp for drying clothes
Water – giving baby a drink
Dressing and bathing child

Allie and pup – his snow house
Ice window

The Sledge
Driftwood found along the coast
Icing sledge
Getting peat for shoeing
Melting in pot
Putting on runners
Frozen fast
Ivory shoeing – walrus tusks
Fastened with wooden pins

View showing ice window being put in position from inside

Comic Types
Nevalinga's wife
Nanook's wife
The post cook
Gait and posture

List for Bear Expedition to Cape Smith[29]
Beans
Codfish
Sea biscuits
Salt, mustard, pepper
Sugar
Dried fruit
Pork and bacon
Tea, coffee, milk
Candles
Cheese, macaroni-cheese – cooked
Butter, bread, flour, baking powder, egg powder
Tobacco and matches
Deer skin mat
Primus lamp, oil stove
Oil
Tools – flash lamp
Needles, soap, towels
Dishes
Pails, frying pan
Axes, bow and arrow
Film and plates
Filters, changing bag
Books, paper
Hudson Bay chart
Dried vegetables

Clothes to Make
Nucktie's boy
Dan's girl
Billy's wife – pants
Lauder's wife – pants
3 girls
Number of women and Maggie's mother
Maggie
Stone pots and lamps
Attata to see to igloo
John to inquire about clothes

Robert Flaherty and Inuit child, Port Harrison, 1920–21. Flaherty included this photograph in a September 1922 issue of the *World's Work* with the caption "Mr Flaherty and Nanook's youngest son."

(Claremont, LAC PA114945)

Monday, 17 January 1921 Departed for bear hunting expedition to Cape Smith at noon. Drifting head wind, minus 20°. Two teams, very poor ones, and three Eskimos. Enroute over portage to Eskimo igloos overturned large sledge so violently that some of oil, ⅔ of can, was lost. Two of the dogs ran off during the night. Secured two more from Eskimo camp here. A wick of our wonderful stove also lost. Some flour lost by being saturated by oil. Built igloo – comfortable. Cramps in legs, kept me hopping. Am very soft on this first winter trip.

Tuesday, 18 January Met all the northern Eskimos shortly after breaking camp, some ten sledges of them bound for Port Harrison. Secured from them a dog and also got one from encampment where we stayed overnight. Passed the "black barge" and mugged up for trip two hours onward. Camped on Levy Island, or thereabouts, for night. Clear, cold day, south wind and light drift. Could see Walrus and Bear Islands out to sea which are to be a picture possibility for later on.

Wednesday, 19 January Wonderful morning. Light wind, south. One of the finest of these northern winter days. The sky is blue enamel, the wind-ridged snow fields enamel too, and the long slanting shadows of pinnacles and broken ice and flocks of little islands dull gray and blue, some of them almost as blue as the sky. Near snowblind toward evening, snow and light wind.

Thursday, 20 January All day crawling at snail's space, deep, soft snow. The team cannot understand it; they turn around haltingly as we crunch through the deep drift. The drivers must send the whips cracking through the air and, cowered, the dogs strain on, their feet outstretched, bellies near the snow. The admiralty charts of the coast are altogether out, our course zigzags from one deep bay to another. Until Saturday the above traveling continues – "deep snow" – comes constantly from the men.

Saturday, 22 January Has been mildest January I've come across in the North. Today seems like April – still, calm. Sea rime particles, like mica oscillating through the air. The rims of sea and far-off land are softened by the haze. A wonderful sun dog through midday, the most elaborate I've ever seen. Reminded me of one of Nansen's sketches in *Farthest North*.[30] During sundown I stood idly by watching men build igloos, so still was air and warm I could hardly believe we were not in April. The sun sank, splashing the winding track of our sledge trail with copper, as it fell into the black-gray rime of open sea. The night came on serene and still when I crawled into camp. The aurora was playing in the sky.

Sunday, 23 January Calm and still. The great fields of white only relieved by little boulder strewn reefs and little islands. Looked like crumpled satin in the long, weak rays of sun.

Again, a slow, plodding day. Billy lopes ahead – it is the only way to give encouragement to our team who strain, whining the while, through the deep banks of snow. At noon came upon Nanook's old, early winter encampment, a forlorn little village of igloos, their walls dealt gaping holes, drifted high with snow. We determine to camp here until winds shall have hardened the snow, for at our present rate Cape Smith is weeks away. There are foxes here the men will hunt and the dogs will be rested.

As we crawl into camp there are welcome signs – mackerel clouds of wind in the sky. Our igloo tonight is more than ordinary. There are sleeping banks of snow at either side and between us stands our stove. I made beans, codfish and sea biscuit and apples for the crew.

Monday, 24 January Hardly wind enough to move the snow. Sun and very cold. The men sleep under single blanket. The cold had not let them sleep much. They just huddle together shivering while they warmed the tea and silently munched frozen bannock in the middle of night and slept and rose chilled to the marrow at dawn. I wonder for the millionth time how they stand it. Such things are jokes for them. They laid their traps today, the number disappointingly few. I ordered them to bring many when we left the post. Here they have a golden opportunity to make something for themselves (all the foxes they can catch on expedition are their own) and they knew they would have chance to set traps of their choice on one of the best winter fur grounds, but no it seems a few will content them, for their children's minds are on Nanook – bear, bigger game. They need the guidance as do children in exactly the same way. Made a feast tonight of dried vegetables and salt beef.

Wednesday, 26 January When Billy crept out this a.m. he reported a gale brewing, overcast and snow in the air. Nanook, however, said to start. It was warm (by contrast) and the sun barely shone through the haze and snow filled sky. Underfoot was heavy, deep and soft. The dogs, much improved after their rest, strained along at slowest speed. It was sweaty and heavy trudging, the worst kind of day. We camped early, at three, delighted to find we are now off the mouth of the Kogaluk River. Low's map is more in error along this coast than along any other portion of the east coast of the Bay. The land is extremely low lying, boulder strewn everywhere to a more then usual extent for even this country.

Curios
Snow kayak
Willow mats
Wooden trenchers

Sledging on rough ice
Hurdling and crashing sledge
Cooties [lice] – picking of child's head
Bear skin cootie trap

Pictures
Miniatures of icebergs
Igloo building complete – tunnel and vent block

Children huddled up in furs waiting
Steamy ventilator
Making snow bear and ivory for children's (per Nanook enroute to Cape Smith) pictures

Carrying dog on back – to its harness
Wrapping fur spear heads while enroute sledging

Thursday, 27 January A clear, cold day – sun dogs. To our delight are off the Povungnituk River. A slow, toilsome journey, deep, sandy snow. Encamped on a tiny island. It must be heavily grown over with sea grass in summer for they show, silvered by the drift, above the snow. A night of map reading and mending, with ever our talk veering to Nanook and the big Cape to northward. Have taken such heart over the day's progress that we feel sure to reach it in four days.

They made caricatures of how when the bear appears we shall, frightened, run away. And then there were reminiscences, bear tales of other days.

Nanook relates to his fellows – to them the Cape is a strange country

– hunting tales of other days, his seal, and bear and the white whale kills, tales which inevitably end with the details of cutting up and feasting. With smacking lips he tells them how good it all was.

How immaculate is an igloo newly made, all spotless white and clean. It barely lasts an hour: tea leaf stains and crumbs of bread and match ends and dome grayed and smoke begrimed.

Igloos, says Harry Lauder, are always warmer when there is wind. When it is still and cold, as it is now as he tells me this, the cold creeps in from every side, with wind on one side only.

Thermometer, minus 24°, almost calm.

Friday, 28 January So enchanting in the yellow rays of the morning sun seemed the scene of breaking camp, that I called for the motion picture camera. To my dismay so brittle was the film that I could not operate the camera. The stuff broke as if it had been so much thin glass. Abandoned all idea of continuing to Cape Smith until some remedy could be found. So spent the day – successful – by taking the film retorts into igloo and raising temperature. It means that before taking pictures in cold weather that film retorts will have to be warmed to zero or so and left folded within the folds of my eiderdown robe. Men went sealing but returned unsuccessful at dark. "Kapoonganetsuk" (hungry for seal) is the most common exclamation. They cannot stand the gaff of white man's food; they cannot keep warm enough, they say.

Saturday, 29 January Thermometer minus 32°, calm. One of the most brilliantly beautiful days I've ever seen in the North. Mirages wherever lay the mainland (we are out at sea some ten miles) and its outlying islands. The rim of sky silvery, then green-blue, and a blue that I cannot describe. The snow flanks of Cape Smith, sixty miles away, loomed faintly on the horizon. The snow fields, pointed by angular blocks of ice, yellow, green and blue, where the shadow lay of each rift and crevice. Gray walls of rime marked the open sea very far to westward. The air was like wine to dogs and men alike. Though slow journeying to a walk and crawling where the drift banks lay, we made good progress. Still far from land at nightfall, encamped on the ice in igloo of inferior snow. It's cold and drafty indeed, augmented by the cold stillness of the night.

Sunday, 30 January Another windless day, clear and sparkling – sun dogs. All day through fields of rough ice, good progress however.

Encamped on Magnet Point at sundown. The declining sun cast a rose tint over the white and ivory and blue shadows. The night still and clear – aurora. Igloo most comfortable igloo – last night's cold one still in mind. All evening over maps and stories of Nanook's adventures.

Monday, 31 January Coldest wind behind us, thermometer minus 14°. The edges of everything blurred with rime and the drift. Toward mid-afternoon the nose of an island stared out of the blur ahead. We (elated) thought it was Cape Smith. Into a flock of islands toward evening, igloo under the steep brow of one. Angry sky at sundown and wind a little stronger. Brassy winter shows its teeth. Mare's tails and long, twisting folds come up toward us out of the dull yellow sun to westward. Expect a drifter tomorrow. Igloos very cold, fitful sleeping. Just where we are no one knows. Cape Smith may be from one to three days from us still.

Tuesday, 1 February A cold day, a little more wind than unusual. Thermometer minus 26°, 7 a.m. Far off veils and shrouds of drift bank fooled us completely about Cape Smith. One little island we took for its huge outline, only to find it when the clouds swept away to be less than 2 miles off. We came to a big indentation running east at noon. Then our hopes fell for we knew it for Mosquito Bay. The Cape is miles, two days at least, away. Tonight's igloo most comfortable. Only two days' dog food left.

Wednesday, 2 February Thermometer minus 30°. Perfect calm and clear. Mirages all around us. I don't know how many times we thought we saw "Nanook's Noona" (Cape Smith). Another big indentation opened up at noon day which all means that Cape Smith seems to get farther away with every mile. Nanook completely bewildered. Now he is floundering in surmise and predictions.

Blue black walls of cloud lying low to north westward we mistook for the Cape, but the Cape visible sixty miles away some days ago now lies buried in the rime of open sea into which it thrusts its nose for some ten miles out from land.

Billy and Harry Lauder out of patience – showed it unmistakably today. Certainly it is a heart breaking trip. The travel ground as bad as ever and we barely strain through it. Two dogs crippled, their food ends tonight. Discouraged, we igloo'd on a tiny island off the mouth of the new indentation which is, I hoped, Mosquito Bay at last. As the sun declined the rime swept views of everthing became clear and, sure enough, Cape Smith, steel-gray and blue, loomed up to us westwardly. It is still far away, three days or more at our present rate.

Clouds peeled, cleared brilliantly at igloo building time. The usual satiny snow, blue-shadowed. Sun dogs flanked the sun. Encamped on a tiny sea grass island somewhere off the mouth of Mosquito Bay. Suffered very much all day from cold feet. Nanook warms my feet against his belly. Cheeks and nose well bitten. An evening of mending. The men are adept with the needle. Every evening they ply it, keeping their wearing gear in repair.

Harry Lauder told me tonight of he and his mother (he a child then) crossing with a band of Eskimos via the Povungnituk to Ungava Bay. They all starved – two died – he was severely frozen. He says dogs are good eating. Billy told of not having anything but dogs to eat for two months, 30 miles south of Port Harrison, no light for igloos. Harry Lauder would stand strong in a pinch.

Thursday, 3 February   Rough ice to seaward forces us to amend course. The going heart breakingly heavy – damnable toil. Though air is cold as it is, the men came in at night wet with perspiration. The roof of our igloo tonight is festooned with sundry garments drying over our stove. Camped early for we've hit a possible sealing ground. Nanook, the old blunderbuss, slowly built our igloo. It was hours and I nearly froze the while. Billy and Harry Lauder went out for seals. Returned at dark – no luck. Almost out of dog food.

The day, as ever, wonderfully clear, only a drift of air. Mirages and sun dogs. Such weather, such difficult travel, none of us have ever known before.

Friday, 4 February   Igloo all day. The men off sealing. Returned at dusk – no luck. Cape Smith looms up again in the same theatrical way, the same dark curtain slowly creeping northward, the same ever-narrowing margin of yellow sun-lit icefields of sea, until the sun's last glow seems to lodge momentarily on the far rim of sea and sky when out of the welter of the black-gray clouds fragments of blue come out one by one until, as the light dissolves the rime clouds, the background turns the color of an old rose and the Cape looks out through the silence of our darkening world.

Saturday, 5 February   At it again, toil, toil, toil. By three o'clock the dogs are played out and we igloo among the rough, upturned reef ice out at sea. Nanook flounders and flounders in his landmark bearings. He announced in mid-morning that Mosquito Bay still lay to northward. Our jaws fell indeed. He continued, deeply chagrined, with head bowed and steadfastly refused to look again toward the land. Much to our happiness found his prediction wrong. We are certainly within two days of the Cape. The day marvelously still, cold and clear.

The Cape stood out all through the day. I've never seen such still weather in the North before. Igloo comfortable. Down to our last tin of oil. Will surely be short. With the Cape so near we all feel better. Thermometer at 7 p.m., minus 38°, still low for this cold snap. Nanook says very high land exists between Kovik and Sudluk. Maybe land is much higher than geographers have imagined.

Sunday, 6 February At last we feel certain that Cape Smith is near at hand, a day away. Everyone is happy, bear and seals and foxes are the subjects of every conversation.[31] The men seem almost mad for seal meat. Every possible place for breathing holes we scan as we go along and follow a fissure far afield to spend an hour running hard to catch up with the sledge again. A young bear's track today has set the men agog. Wind drifting at dark, and new moon. Going much improved today.

Monday, 7 February Three weeks ago today we left camp. Thermometer minus 3°. High drifting wind, fair. Cape Smith hidden all day in clouds and rime. We looked for it anxiously most of the day. Out of sight of all land. The brown dog again played out so we carried him on the sledge. About mid-afternoon a high, humpbacked land mass loomed up through drift and rime. Nanook knows it well; it is an Eskimo campground in summer. Igloo'd there. Many fox signs all around.

Tuesday, 8 February Day broke, dull, minus 10°, dismal. But a bare sight of Cape Smith, a faint mottled mass of dull blue and white. Dismally we plod along. The poor, starved brown dog, lashed on top of sled, groans and weakly whines at intervals. It surprises the teams. They turn their heads toward in deep surprise and pity it, I almost fancy. All life, everything seems depressing. The vague outline of the ranges become blocked out by banks of rime of gruesome gray. Nothing to watch save the swaying shoulders of the men jogging at the sledge head, and the fan of dogs beyond, their snow swept heads straining low. A wind follows us; it is cold enough; my pipe freezes while alight, and my numbed fingers cannot clear it. Billy fills and lights his – offers it. I take it between my teeth. Our poor dog shows signs of dying. We cast it off. It has run the gauntlet and Billy ends it with harpoon. We halt for a while and debate as to whether to carry the carcass on for dog food, but when Nanook held it up it was a mere skeleton he held; finally we leave it there, a brown patch in the snow.

By noon the leaden pall of clouds began breaking and the rime shrouds around us became golden where the sun shone through. Ahead, out of the welter of gray, loomed patches of shimmering satin which were portions of the gigantic flanks of the Cape. It is near the end of the up end of our long trail. We can easily say the order, but even today we may get seals. We see bear tracks and fox and bear trails as we come into land. We pass slowly on through the gutway which separates Cape and mainland and continue to island in distance off which the water is always open. Here we must igloo until we kill seals. The dogs will soon be starving. Drawing near Nanook gloomily states that all the ice is frozen and sure enough sea ice in pointed spirals and in great crumpled masses to the far horizon. The continuous cold, calm weather has been indeed extraordinary. It means hunting by breathing holes, a week or more, and with luck getting an adequate supply.

Here we are, twenty two days on, at the fag end of everything, and no game in sight. It means something to be "broke" in the North. Discouraged, the men turn to building the igloo. I climb the island's highest vantage. The sun shines gloriously and the deep blue of sky is patched by quick sailing clouds and the great massive flanks of the Cape, blurred by drift, reach straight out until they are lost in the rime at sea.

I turn from the scene with all its color and enchanting light and gaze off over the ice fields of the sea. In amazement I see an open lead and close and near at hand. The island had blanketed it from Nanook's view. Turning, I shout to the men and wave my arms. They drop their knives and come running eagerly. The pleasure in their faces of their sight of open water shows to me the purest emotion on all the trail. Made motion picture tests in wind (thermometer minus 10°) and views of Cape. No more than bedded when gale broke upon us. All through that night the coldest igloo night I've ever had. The roaring gusts of wind came to me through the igloo's almost sound proof walls.

Wednesday, 9 February Clear with north wind and heavy drift. Four bears crossed our little island sometime during a.m. All of us indoors, was too bad to venture out. Sea ice jammed high along the coast.

Thursday, 10 February Cold and clear, light north wind. Myself in igloo all day. Ice bad for sealing, but Harry Lauder secured one. Couldn't wait to flense it in igloo so he and others gorged where it was killed. The dogs huddled in tunnel for shelter fought like demons to get in when Harry Lauder came dragging carcass in. Decided to at last leave for outer Cape and bear ground tomorrow, hoping to kill seals while there.

Friday, 11 February A living gale from southward and extremely cold. Depending now on seal oil lamp for warmth (coal oil nearly gone) but it is giving woefully little heat. All day in my eiderdown; my body has melted molds in my sleeping ground. Nothing to do but huddle from the cold, listen to a bitter wind piping around our snow house, the swish of drifting snow. Shadows stream through the walls when squalls strike it. Nothing left to read, and too damn cold to write.

Saturday, 12 February Sleepless, I listened all through the night for let-up to the wail of wind. Dawn was still, but crawling out of doors found the land, sea and sky blanketed by rime and heavy falling snow. The wind in a moment whipped around to the north and within another hour was blowing another gale. No travel today nor sealing either. Resigned, we return to igloo. The almost week's occupation has begrimed it very much. My snow platform is strewn with tobacco ash, sea biscuit crumbs and match ends on the floor. The seal carcass and heaps of picked bones in the lamp corner is a sight. Harry Lauder has set to work with snow knife scrapping away the dirt. As he brushes it through the door the horde of dogs makes the place one of turmoil and pandemonium with their fighting. They are almost constantly clubbed to prevent them forcing an entrance. Added are the cold billows of steamy air that chill and befog the place. I crawl into sleeping bag and bury head in the folds. Nanook went out at noon for new seal oil lamp wicking. Came back shortly with his tin tobacco box full of hard dung. They all finger it and slip their hands into sugar bag when I call for sugar.

Over two days of south wind which had made the snow as hard as pavement are all for naught. This day's snow is very deep. My birthday is due in 3 or 4 days – just when I don't know. Down again to fag ends of seal. Dogs got at seal lines and bow and arrow case at top of igloo last night.

Sunday, 13 February The weather clear, cold with light drifting west wind. We start along north side of the Cape for bear grounds. One of the traps set a short distance has a fox. Its wild jumping to get free we sight a long distance away. The sight cheered the men. Out of seal (unknown to me), they took only tea for breakfast (Billy sulked). Till noon we continue along the ice foot of the Cape's projecting points when opposite the high, sheer regions of the Cape (2/8 rods of length) we igloo. The fox is no sooner killed and sledge started than Nanook squatted thereon to skin the fox. Numerous rare tidbits of still warm flesh. Blood drops fall over in the trail and on bootlegs are great red splotches.

Igloo is very cold; all night my cold feet prevent sleep.

Monday, 14 February Billy and Harry Lauder go out on ice fields for seal. Nanook goes inland for bear cave. The day clear, cold with west wind. In igloo all day. Our oil, food the cause of some refection. Igloo very cold, nearly zero by thermometer. Can only light stove for shortest intervals. At dark men return, no seals. The ice is very bad and on those west winds half of Hudson Bay is packing in. Harry Lauder and Billy saw tracks of bears going out to sea for seal. Nanook returned late. How we waited to hear above the crunching sounds of his approach some word of bear. It took an hour between gulps of food and sips of tea to get his news. Saw many, many signs of bear but no caves. Says snow is very bad. However, things are hopeful. We shall continue west tomorrow, make another stop and hunt like this one.

Billy tries hard to regain my good will after yesterday's sulk. Cuts my tobacco, overhauls boots and dog-skin mitts, etc.

Harry Lauder and Billy look gloomy. Food we badly need, dogs have been without it for two days. Nanook's cheerfulness, however, never fails. We talk the evening through. Nanook sends us hopeful to sleep.

Tuesday, 15 February The men have just crawled out with the seal skin (the last of the 2 seals in eight days' hunting). The dogs, scenting food, are half crazy – how little they will get!

When I think of it, this cold, the bolts of fog that shoot in this poorly closed door whilst the men are dog feeding, that in this latitude south there is open water and warmth and sun.

A blue, cheerless day – very cold west wind. Meet many bear tracks enroute. A flock of ducks wheel about over the rough ice fields. Elated, think it's open water which means seals, but the men are glum and silent. The ducks starving and nearly frozen. They show it in their feeble flights, are hunting for an open pool. All the ice in Hudson Bay must be packing in. Note that all bear tracks lead out to sea, to an ice edge that must be very distant.

Cape Smith, a chaos of seamed and ribbed lava looks high and close at hand. Every drift seam of its tremendous flank holds the prospect of a bear cave. We scan every profile as well as the spired ice fields for sign of bear. Just before igloo time the dogs sight an unusual dark spot on the snow. It proves to be a duck nearly dead frozen. Encamp near end of Cape Smith. Rough ice fields outlying as far as eyes can see. The duck makes a bully for all tonight plus dried potatoes and pork and Croquettes de Marche. Cold night with little wind.

Coming out of doors
Igloo setting
Kayak on frame
Fox skins – deer horns, etc.

Fox film: eating fox on the sledge
Questions for John

Child asleep in hood
Building igloos
Allie with bow and arrow
Boy building igloo
Close-up of Attata sleeping

Wednesday, 16 February I think this is my birthday. However, a wonderful day, really most remarkable. Still, clear and moderately cold. Have never seen such a day for this time of year in this latitude. The men go off early, Harry Lauder and Billy sealing and Nanook hunting with dog for cave among the ranges. I dare not go away. No matter how securely I block the door the dogs, starving, start digging at snow walls the minute my back is turned.

The men return at dark. No seals but most encouraging for the morrow. Open lanes are appearing on ice again. Wood fire out of doors for cooking tonight. The air so still the smoke curls straight up, as in Indian country. Most unusual indeed. The biggest feast of trip tonight: salt pork, sea biscuit crumbs (the last, alas), codfish Julienne and Croquettes de Marche and dried apples. The sighs and "ahs" resound. What children they are. Igloo roof, which is flat topped, sags. If a dog gets on top he may drop in on us during our slumbering. Igloo most comfortable.

Thursday, 17 February At intervals during the night came the ominous sounds of sagging igloo roof, but, thank God, it held till a.m. when the men got out and put a new roof on. The delay caused was trying, for open, seal hunting lanes show near at hand. They may close at any minute. I took stock of the dogs. They are now badly off, their ribs show. They are cold and restless. The tail of master dog is drooping low. I crawl out in afternoon for sight of fields and men. Not an open lane shows. They've got to get seals.

Day clear again and cold. Perfectly still in a.m. Wonderful weather but igloo is chill indeed. At dark the men returned. How eagerly I listened for word of seals. The dogs made no sound. I resign to the inevitable when two hands open the door, shoving before the carcass of a small seal. Though only one and small, it comes in a trying time. Thank heaven the poor brutes outside, too dull and listless to show signs of interest, will come into their own again. Crawling through tunnel today the dogs who barred my way had to be prodded out. We need eight seals, at least, to see us through. Listless evening, everything read through and through, and ads all memorized. Seal liver for my supper. Clear, cold night.

Friday, 18 February Very cold south wind. Making tea on seal oil lamp. Nearly two hours' operation. Men sulked a bit because I cut off coal oil stove. In sleeping bag all day. Igloo dismally cold. I have figured out grub supply to the ounce. Two square flippers will see us through. Will probably abandon small sledge which is cached 3 days down the trail.

Dark and asleep when men come, but what news, a big square flipper. All kinds of bear signs and trail passing near igloo during night. Eager for open water lanes which are starting on this south wind. Men almost drunk with their feasting. Nanook grunts like a walrus when he feeds.

Saturday, 19 February Never have any of our igloos been so warm. From the hoar-frosted huddled, prostrate forms of the men arise clouds of vapor. It all comes from their ojuk [seal] eating. Not an open lane in sight. Wind from the west, clear cold. Another long, long day in sleeping bag with mittens when I try to read. Worry all day of how my precious time is leaping by whilst we are not even able to hunt for bear caves. The dogs look better, however.

The men returned at nightfall – no luck. I worried over it for the small pile that I thought represented the ojuk I knew was not nearly enough to enable us to continue. On top of it came hints from Nanook to abandon our hunt and start for home, mumbling something about how badly off our dogs are.

What delight was mine when Billy crawled in and I unraveled enough of his speech to find that ojuk lies cached a short distance away on sea ice, so much of it that he fears we will be overburdened.

What gorging the men go through with tonight – intensely animal. They can hardly move heads from side to side.

Sunday, 20 February All day the men have been packing through the inaccessible and rough ice fields [to find] the ojuk seal.

Monday, 21 February Clear with wind and drift, thermometer minus 36°.

We cannot round the Cape on account of heavy, rough ice. We traveled east two miles and strike inland and across. All along the northern flank we are enveloped in drift and whirlpools of snow. The gales are just as much as we can stand. We soon unload sledge and take on a half load, to return for remainder on the morrow. We strain sometimes for only 15 feet at a stretch, two drivers in harness, myself astern and one ahead for decoying.

Nanook says something metal-like is on the Cape in view of rocks white as snow.

Tuesday, 22 February Warm, heavy fall of snow. Men off sealing, Nanook came in early with seal. What a meal the men had. It was a load off my mind to hear shouts, wails and wailing at dog feeding once again.

Sleep comes soon after seal meat feasting. The men are under blankets early. They will sleep warmly now they say with seal meat in their bellies. The sleep I can hardly imagine for those bellies must be strained to a point that is nearly bursting.

High wind again this evening, from the north (first in 3 weeks!).

Tonight's dinner, pork and duck, was my feast portion.

Wednesday, 23 February Men returned after all day cave hunting at dark. No luck. Our trip for nothing – a handful of weather and 4 seals.

Break for the south tomorrow. Men grim and silent, for I can't help looking blue. The strain, worry and surprise, however, are over – it will be a relief to swing out for the homestretch.

Thursday, 24 February A splendid day. Just enough cloud to break the monotony of blue sky. Continued down through old Eskimo Point across the Cape – a deep series of ravines to the sea.

Near sea Nanook and I left sledge to examine what he thought was silver. Nothing but large quartz and calcite veins with some iron pyrite. Poor, stupid old Nanook – feels much chagrined over his repeated failures. Note: told men about cobalt and silver, just by way of conversation what it would mean to one of them if they found some.

The rock examination over, we struck out over the rough ice fields for the south. The Cape, clear cut against the sky all day, became swathed in drift and cloud – only its extremes poking through the blanket as we jogged away. We were in perfect calm.

A reef – rimmed with high rafted ice – was our camp ground. We reached it in evening. The sun, a ball of brass, died to a mere smudge of color on the skyline. All the stars lay mapped out amidst the sky before we igloo'd. The night calm and held a hint of warmer weather, I thought, whilst waiting for the igloo lighted from within – its every block vividly outlined in white and green.

Friday, 25 February Calm – like a spring day – sun bright and snow is starting to kindle. The light draughts of air (north) were cold, but mud on south runner of sledge as we struck east started melting along upper edges.

A devilish bit of rough ground lay between Nanook's igloo – and side-sledge shoeing broke – delayed an hour. We all had to make pools of urine in the snow with which they cemented the broken pieces together again. Reached old igloo island early – camped.

The day is wonderful. The Cape is even playing hide and seek with the clouds and drift. The sky burning with color – the snow is often blue and wisps of rose-red diamonds lay bedded, it seemed, in the depths of blue. Cape Smith is at least 1,800 feet, perhaps 2,000 feet in altitude.

Nanook washed his face tonight – just for me – long since reconciled.

Dogs getting on their feet again – but one of our best probably will be shot – badly chewed up from fighting.

Saturday, 26 February A day of mild winter with touch of spring in the air. Men nor I have ever seen such weather. Haunting clouds, colored delicately like sea shells. Soft blue skies rimed at its rim. The ice fields like sheets of white-blue wrinkled silk. Two sun dogs climbed in the lemon, orange, and rose sky – closely flank the sun, now brighter and warm when we turn toward it.

A long day – tea'd on the ice at noon – broke up boxes for fuel. Encamped at dark not far from Magnet Point – heavy rain and fog until sundown – then partly clearing day like steamer smoke on sky lines. While harnessing this a.m. men shot at fox.

Film Notes
Billy tests ice margin with harpoon – ice breaks
Fussing with snow kayaks
Fur bottomed boots
Making fire on sea ice
Breaking up boxes for wood, etc., etc.
Dogs breaking into igloo at a.m. at moving time
Struggling into clothes

Nanook's laziness reached a climax today. Riding on sledge much too often and not doing his share. Filling his pipe whilst sledge barely strained over heavy drift. Busted him off, scattering his pipe, match safe, tobacco box and him in snow. It woke him up. The balance of the day has worked like a demon. Eskimo in many ways shows surprising lack of initiative and resource. Asking him to dry moss for lamp wicking. Tonight he replied that it was frozen – would mean all night drying if he placed it on drying frame where boots and mitts are kept. Did it occur to him to use frying pan?

Using his seal oil lamps now – my coal oil gives out tomorrow night.

When first going into Eskimo igloos when at post, how noticeable the smell was – now I cannot detect it.

Sunday, 27 February Another blue, clear day. A bit of wind hovering from northeast. Reached komatik igloo and Magnet Point at ten o'clock. Got hold of a fund for wood – an old box of ours and also broke up Nanook's komatik – the mud shoeing also comes in for our big sledge. Tea'd and shaved and continued to last old igloo – the deep igloo which however was buried to top in drift and very cold for first two hours. Buried film to warm it up. Eleven candles and two seal oil lamps doing service tonight.

All of kooletahs and sleeping bags badly frozen. Have line stretched overhead in effort to partly dry them. The heat available for such purpose is feeble indeed.

Ituk, one of the best dogs, badly chewed up and played out, refused service this a.m. Left him but he finally limped after us – is with us now.

Nanook works extremely well now after "jacking up." When I think of how long and effectively he played soldier, I feel like walloping him.

Spending the evening trying to learn how to trim seal oil lamp. Just enough coal oil for a.m.

Cold night and heavy wind. Sea shore close in now but we no longer have use for it.

Monday, 28 February Awakened to find Billy and Harry Lauder wearing clothes – seal oil lamps out and only a few candles sputtering on top of defunct stove. Door badly closed and shafts of cutting cold shooting in. Nanook was outside planing sledge runners. Gave my two aces hell. I believe their gray matter numbs on occasion.

Breakfast of the usual lye tea and two gaseous, musty bannocks. Got away well – clear, cold and slight drift with east wind. The first of all our days when the sledge speed was normal. The dogs were well fed and managed some trotting at a fine clip.

Nanook partially snow-blind – unusually early for that trouble. I am beginning to get it too plus a growl in my broken tooth. But the glory of real sledging – the first in all the days enroute – good ground and dogs made me forget it all. The day too – the wind early died down with blue sky and blue shadowed snow, yellowing with the evening sun. The rime of open sea shined in saw toothed towers and billows of smoke – and hanging low just above them, aflank the sun, "sun dogs," opalescent splashes of red and yellow.

Reached Povungnituk Bay at sundown – a splendid sun. Cooked apples over 24 candles in lard pail in celebration.

Ituk failed to follow this a.m. – probably done for.

Tuesday, 1 March Away early with speed across Povungnituk Bay. Hoping to reach Aggie Island by nightfall where there is a precious cache of oil and flour. We traveled in increasing wind till dark – missed it and camped in darkness with a drifter breaking over us. Headache and tired and disappointed – had visions of pancakes and a warming by our stove. Our flour that is is soaked in coal oil and I cannot eat it.

Nanook after all these many days in sealed housing, spoon licking and the like, tells me he has "sick and hollow here" (consumption).

Our seal oil lamps do hardly heat at all. This new drafty igloo and gale made for a miserable night.

Wednesday, 2 March Gale – igloo half buried. Men had to open new door half way up the dome. No moving today. Port Harrison only 5 days away if the good going holds. My beans and pork are now cooked over seal lamp in defunct lard pail. We have to make the tea in stages – a little water at a time or it won't boil.

This failure of a trip is getting tiresome. Port Harrison is all we can talk about. Sleeping bag an unwieldy frozen thing – the cover is so stiff it might be tin.

I have one redeeming picture in mind – it is a stump of driftwood that lies some two days southward – upended in the snow.

Thursday, 3 March Gale continues. Men went out however and to my surprise located very near at hand the lost (Aggie) Island. Brought in with them our precious cache – some coal oil, a loaf of bannock with currants in it (how I went after those currants), some flour and 3 lb. pail of lard.

The day passes very slowly – this igloo black with smoke is the dirtiest one I've had – the roof drips all day long.

Friday, 4 March No sounds of wind came to us when we awakened. The piping of the gale and swirls of snow had died away. Elated, we made a hurried breakfast and then out of doors but the gale, though abated, was still on the dogs buried in the drifts – igloo nearly covered – and only the black streaks of islands and rocks near at hand showed faintly through the drive of snow. Over land so low I could not tell at times from sea ice and curling wind swept boulders, patches of little islands around ponds and the green of tide flooded gutways, and channels and hummocked ice. Off shore we traveled slowly, our good going shot to hell by drifting snow. Desolate coast and its every inch all alike – not a landmark to fasten on. My piece of driftwood we passed somewhere along the way. The sun a white disk and screened by flying clouds gives us the hope of clear weather by nightfall. It finally sinks, however, into a black, gray bank and we are lost in a new gale of dense, blinding drift. We hit an island by luck and igloo on the spot. Before it is barely up the dogs are buried out of sight.

Saturday, 5 March Better weather and start this a.m. but soon as we were well under way drifted heavily – wet and cold wind.

Fox Island of Nanook's old camp where there was a cache of seal blubber was extremely difficult to find – every mile of land and islands seemed alike. Found it, however, before noon and camped in an old igloo – weather too heavy to continue. Men during day went to the traps set on way up – got 3 foxes only.

Sunday, 6 March   Up early and bustling, hoping to make a record trip so that we might reach camp in 3 days. Our oil, blubber and food nearly exhausted.

But the temperature is even worse today and one of the coldest days we've had. About two hours out we found that our lamp had dropped from sledge – I couldn't contain myself. Nanook blew up, went off into Huskie hysterics brandishing his long snow knife before me like a stage pirate. Billy and Harry retreated from the scene – Harry retreated until he was lost in the drift and Billy back over our trail on hunt of the lamp. Succeeded in questioning Nanook enough so that he went off lurching in his rage and still clutching his knife and muttering. Harry finally appeared from out the driving drift and hesitantly came back. Then came the long, miserable wait unsheltered in the gale until Billy returned – how far he might have to go we did not know.

In about an hour returned, when the cold and waiting had almost passed my limit of endurance. What he carried in his arms was the damned old wooden seal lamp which we easily could have substituted at evening in camp and not my precious container of coal oil as I had imagined. "Much ado about nothing." Continued a half hour and unable to stand it longer igloo'd for the night.

Very cold and no sign of let up to the wind. Nanook and I made up and all spent a happy evening sewing and making wooden goggles. Made up sauce of last dried apples – shared all around – also spread over the last crumbs of our sugar.

It had taken hours in sleeping bag to warm my feet – which are clad in four pairs of duffles. Very cold and I refuse to hang the thermometer.

Monday, 7 March   All through the night the gale stormed and I listened as morning drew on for silence out of doors – but here we are storm bound for the day.

Nanook proved to me this a.m. that why he has been able to do so little has been on account of his lungs. He took the trouble during his coughing spells last night to spit big blood splotches on the igloo walls (near the lamp) so that I could not fail to see them.

Coal oil is low, use it now only at meals. Igloo without it, chill rising affair. Wet fog of our bodies over everything – hard to light matches and my pipe must be puffed like a furnace to keep alight.

Second day of drift and only two days from camp. At 1:30 from our peep hole in igloo's wall found to our delight that storm had considerable abated. Struck out and sure enough by night fall all was clear and wind died to a whisper. Made good progress too. Am now in one of the up trip igloos and a day and one half from camp.

Men's seal meat all gone – oil soaked flour is all they have plus the scraps that I can save. Grub enough, however – dogs in fine shape.

Tuesday, 8 March Up early and out – this a.m. ominous clouds sailed from out of east on light drifting wind which increased as we traveled. By noon the weather was drifting heavily. We reached the Eskimo Whale River at twelve and left the sea – the balance of journey to the west and to camp. Such wonderful pictures of drifting snow – writhing and curling smoke sweeping over the low rounded granite hills.

All afternoon traveled hard – the wind increasing and drift finally blinding. Camped at dark as a blizzard (the worst of the trip) sprang up around us. Scrambled for shelter within igloo walls as it went up around us. Here we are within 5 hours of camp and probably caught for all tomorrow and at the least estimate.

We have so far been out 50 days and only 4 days of them have been normal travel.

Men made mid-day meal of Croquettes de Marche Julienne and seal blubber boiled together. My oil gone. Warmed beans and pork over 3 candles.

Wednesday, 9 March Up at 4 a.m. so as to get our tea water boiled by day light. The wail of wind the worst on trip had ceased but still drifted very heavy. How we watched the barometer and every one taking a turn at tapping the dial in the hope that pointer may jog up the good weather's scale a fraction.

Tea and tin of Harry Lauder's blubber and bannock cooked in lard pail for breakfast.

Nanook's good dog sick – wails all night.

We huddled into our bags – resigned to another day and sleepless night of waiting for this drifter to subside – but at mid-afternoon to our amazement when we peered through the peep-hole the sky is clear and ground is smoking no longer. We decided on the moment to start, though it be mostly travel in the dark; but after an hour on Billy knew the way well. We cached all save what is necessary and starting with a lighter sledge, off go the dogs galloping. Soft blue skies and brilliant stars, wearing rings of white mist, follow a long red twilight. It is calm too. The cold sparkling stars illuminated as the last evening light dies – streams of crimson light out of the north. For a long while, dim and weak, they cast no light – slantingly light the snow very poorly – we stumble sometimes among the high rifts and ridges of our trail until finally the aurora in earnest starts in and we get abundant light from its long streams aswirl – or waving slowly – different banks of their hue through everywhere, making checkers in the sky.

As always when gathering speed and heading into maelstroms and swirls – their color is deeper than rose, apple green. So low came one boiling band that it seemed almost to sweep through us – dogs and men and sledge. The last hour of our journey drew near – the hardest hour of all the trip. The glory of the aurora, the star light and satin slopes of fields and hills – we had hardly eyes for. The high bank which marks the valley of the Inuit camp at last came into view and down over its side pell mell we floundered. The sparks of stove, the winking squares of the post – its lights showed us home again.

Build igloo in drift and showing exit from top of dome
Ungava – coastline views
Ungava – surf views
Burrowing for stunted spruce and driftwood

Implements to Make
Ivory stove and deer bone knives
Walrus skin buckets
Ivory toggles – combs – woman's gear, etc.
Stone harpoon heads
Bow and arrows
Duck spear

Eskimo Seal (Whale) Hunt
Camp scene
Woman spies game
Rushes for hunter
Helps him with his spears
Launches kayak and sends him on his way

Tying up dog's nose to quit it from howling
Woman plucks arrow from bear while son stands off and shoots

Father and Son
Playing with miniature igloo
Komatik, kayak, etc.
Catching fox by the way – owl, etc.

Pictures per John Hayward
Mouth pulling game
Tug of war
Ball games
Cheek hitting game
Knee bending game
Eskimo in trapeze
Face making game

Eskimo Washing
Use eggs, seal fat, urine – duck skins for towels

Bear skin used as louse trap
Eskimo woman suckles pup
Seal skin used as seal imitation in film
Eskimo woman when traveling carries pup in hood
Smoke signals are used to signal hunter's success – meat in camp
Man can run down a fat bear
Bears make their caves in mounds of snow – grottos
Owl can fly with live hare in air
Owl can kill fox when near eggs, etc.
If you kill a bear's young, she is apt to be – John says – "saucy"

Film Points
Glacial striae
High seas
Eskimo women souvenir hunting after Angarooka breaks camp
Tent life with white man
Life aboard the whale boat
Eating various kinds of meat, including sculpins, duck intestines, etc.
The teeth of Eskimo
Chewing gum and candy

Eating mouse
Harpooning white whale
Eskimo playing with Avetuk
Rope skipping
Duck on the rock
Playing ball
Head tug of war
White arctic owl
Kayaker upsetting
Wild fowl and eggs
Moving ice pans
Save walrus skins for walrus skin buckets
Igloo note: rimed face appears at door – view from within and gets bucket of water

Monday, 25 April Thunder and bolts of lightning during heavy fall of snow. 12 feet snow in drifts – average probably 6 feet. Time: 6:30. Temperature: +32°. Barometer: 29.50.

Bear – man's experience

Bear smashed in igloo in dead of night – wife held him at bay by holding a candle in front of his nose while husband got outside for gun – shot him but put out candle in the process. After shot, the bear retreated. Man and wife crouched in broken down igloo till daughter and others found bear dead but a few feet away.

Thunder and lightning in March – last weeks

Friday, 29 April My studio has caved in – a total wreck.

Charla and partner caught on drift nearly two weeks. Rescued on 2nd – all right – by whale boat on Walrus Island.

Wednesday, 4 May The packet came at supper time – a most welcome sight. The slowly swerving chain of dots out on the river – dogs and sledge. The packet all good news.

No seals anywhere, say the packeteers. Have been remarkably scarce this winter. No fur to northward.

Friday, 6 May Partridge migration is on. They alight and perch about our doors – everywhere. Third winter bear story. A bear at Nastapoka River attacked and killed – partly skinned a little Eskimo girl.

Summer Films
Mother washes up child

Eskimo Portraits
Arkpollo with mirror
The white haired man
Attata
Maggie's braiding hair – still pool a mirror
Allie
Minnie
The baby smiling
Showing costumes – the kooletah's tail, etc.

Flowers and Summer Scenes
Child picking flowers and strewn in lap
Eskimo kiss
The kayak construction
Ivory tipped paddle
Paddling
Catamaraned
Puppies

Eskimo chewing fox skin
Bailing fur
The gramophone
The cook
Maggie pulling off boots

Film Portraits
Old man carving and then looking at camera or away admiring work – doll as model?
Maggie braiding hair at pool
Mother with puppies
Allie with bow and arrows
Attata with spear, then next showing his harpoon up at Walrus Island
Annie with child
Snarling dog
Howling puppies

Nanook, Nyla, and Bob Stewart encircling Flaherty's Akeley camera, Port Harrison, 1920–21
(Claremont, LAC, PA114937/photo RF)

Flaherty adjusting his Akeley camera, Port Harrison, 1920–21
(Claremont, LAC, PA114940)

Monday, 11 July With Attata, Nevalinga and Harry Lauder departed in whale boat for the White Whale River. Caught up with Omarolluk and his horde of migrating Eskimos in the Hudson's Bay sail boat and sailed in sight of each other all day. In the evening landed at Harry Lauder's camp which contained some 30 Eskimos.

The women – as per arrangements made at post – had been hunting among the stone ruins of Eskimo camps of former generations and found some most interesting stone curios. Gave tobacco and tea all around and presented Harry Lauder's mother with a tin of cocoa. Sailed again in an hour's time, in the gloom and color of the midnight sky. Rather stiff following breeze as we dodged among ice pans and the narrow shallow inland channels where were ducks and sea pigeons innumerable. We must have appeared like a miniature warship – fire belching out into the dusk from our battery of shotguns as flock upon flock of pigeons and eiders encircled us or flew like arrows close overhead. About an hour beyond midnight pulled up on an island and slept three hours.

A.m., in fog and drizzle, at Nevalinga's encampment – men, women and children, squealing their delight, tumbled over the boulder strewn ground to welcome us. The greetings over, "tobaccomik," as ever, the first word on their lips. Disappointed to learn that this very day Nevalinga, Billy and Omarolluk II left in kayak for post to hurry our arrival. Missed them enroute.

Numberless waterfowl, as usual – what with the keeling boat, heavy wind and quick swerves of course, was kept in terror of my most careful crew's guns. The steersman, gun in one hand, tiller in the other, was suddenly called upon for a heavy swing as a heavy pan shoved close up on the bow. In haste, he shoved the gun out from him for me to hold – triggers cocked and muzzle a foot from my eyes.

The wind swung to the west in early morning – ice pans thickened around us so we made much slower progress; the duck infested islands – with their nests and nests of eggs – were mostly responsible. The evening overcast and gloomy, we pitched tents and had a long, deep sleep.

Third day out – heavy southwest wind and driving rain off and on. Here and there on distant ice pans crouching figures of fishermen, dangling their jigs over pan edges and spear poised ready for strike. Women and children play hide and seek among the boulders, throw at targets and hunt sculpins along the shore line. The dogs, overfed, sleep the day away.

Such is the Eskimo day of plenty – constant laughter and cries of fishermen exulting among the rocks.

Saturday, 16 July A Wonderful day – the Eskimos "are young" in all its glory – cream and yellow fields of ice. The water lanes among them, metal-green and metal-blue. The folds, cream and gray along low shore line, vibrant in the sun.

Made film of salmon spearing among the ice pans, kayaking and the like.

The long, still evening, aglow, ever softening, became ethereal as the sun declined. In the stillness of the night I fall asleep to the faint whispers of the ice as through it the tide floods and flows.

Sunday, 17 July A rare summer's day – calm and still. Blue sky and cotton clouds over land – the pan ice fields wrapped in low banks of fog. The water – mirrors reflecting the green and blue edges of the ice floes. The sky dotted with southward flights of water fowl, from far out come the cries of loons and gulls. Vast bands of pigeons flying low come whirling right amongst us.

Off to the White Whale grounds – salmon fishing.[32]

Locked by the ice – passing time – playing ball – duck on the rock. My daily quota of young visitors.

The salmon fishing
The whale hunt
Omarolluk and Mary – an Eskimo scandal
The return – heavy wind and ice
The baking powder
The night visit to camp of sleeping Eskimo
The post once more

Omiak [umiak]
Launching – away
The steersman
The women rowing, babies rocked to-and-fro.
The kayaks scouting ahead
The head of the rapids
Rapid scenes

The dogs barking

The seal skin tent
Breaking camp
The cobble stove and moss fuel
Launching the Omiak, etc.
Bound down river for the sea – details, etc.
The head of the rapids
Rapid scenes
The walrus land
Reaching the post of the white man
Landing the kayak and its over-load
The trade scenes
Farewell to the post – off for another long year

Autochromes
The omiak
The kayak
Allie
Maggie in costume
Allie with bow and arrow
Pup and sleigh
Mother and child
Topek [tent]
Trade scenes and landscape
Seal oil lamp

Summer Films
Pups – mother guarding pups from ravenous dogs
Dogs fishing along tide mark
Dogs packing overland
Dogs tracking omiak and kayak up river
Dogs – flies
Dogs prowling around tent

The Omiak
Launching
Embarkation – away – rowers and babes in hoods
The steersman – a veteran
The over-loaded kayak
Among the rapids
Tracking upstream

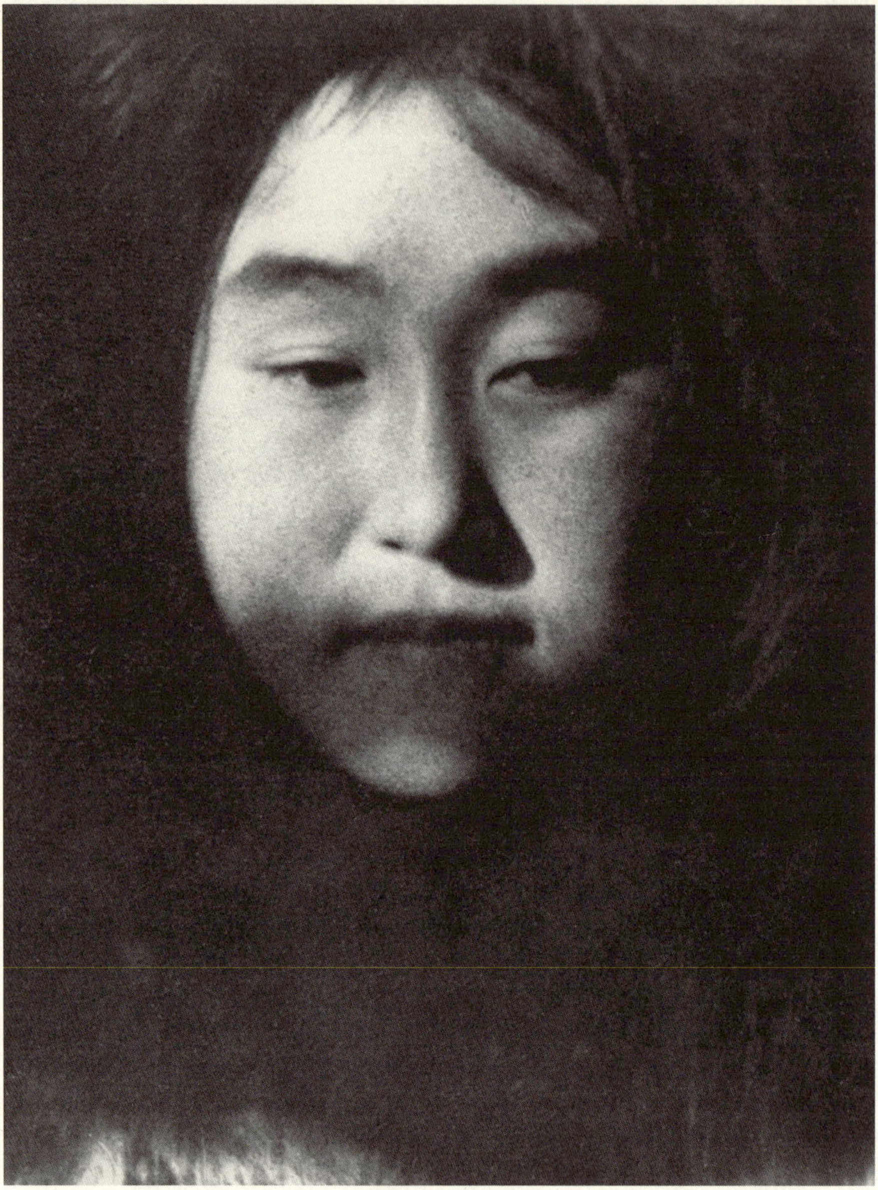

Alice Nevalinga, the woman Flaherty cast as Nyla. Port Harrison, 1920–21
(Claremont, LAC, PA143650/photo RF)

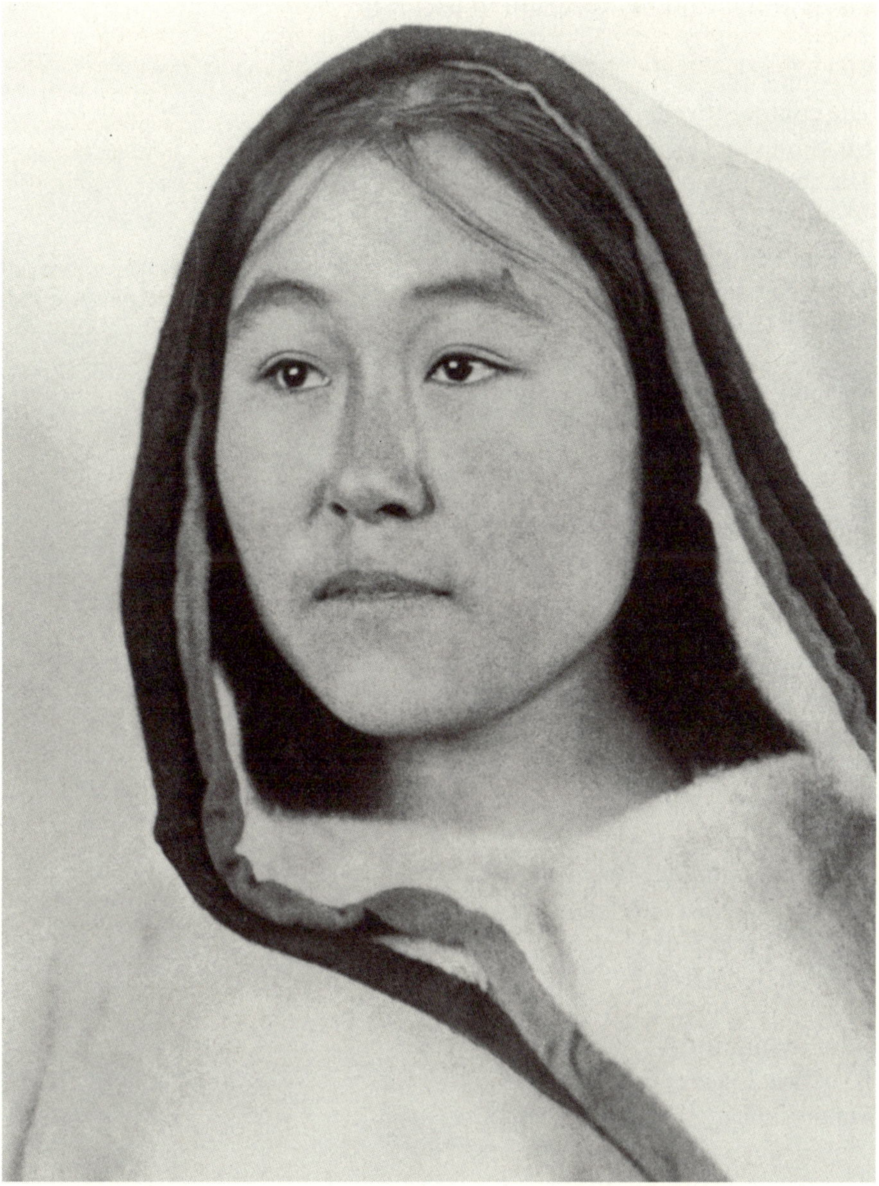

Alice ("Maggie") Nevalinga, Port Harrison, 1926. This photograph first appeared in the September 1938 issue of the *Beaver* with the caption "Maggie of Port Harrison, the Heroine of Robert Flaherty's film *Nanook of the North*."

(HBCA, N14627/photo Bob Stewart)

The portage – Eskimo strength in packing

Making Fire
The cobble stove
Moss fuel
The stone pot and dishes

Flies!, Flies!, Flies!
The sea coast
Seas – kayaks catamaraned

Bird nesting – eider down and eggs – testing them in water
The duck spear – sea pigeons

The White Whale Grounds
Sighting the whale
The scurrying women and children help with kayaks, harpoons and gear
Launched and away
The harpooning
The tug of war
The landing
The feast – the gorging
End of perfect day

Sledging among ice fissures
Crossing swollen streams
Around the rapids
Shoeing dog's feet

John to inquire
Bear skin louse trap
Omarolluk

The Port Harrison diary ends here abruptly, but the Flahertys have provided us with an ending to the story by writing the following in My Eskimo Friends *(1924).*

When August came Stewart, the trader, and I began speculating as to when the once-a-year little schooner, with its precious mail from home

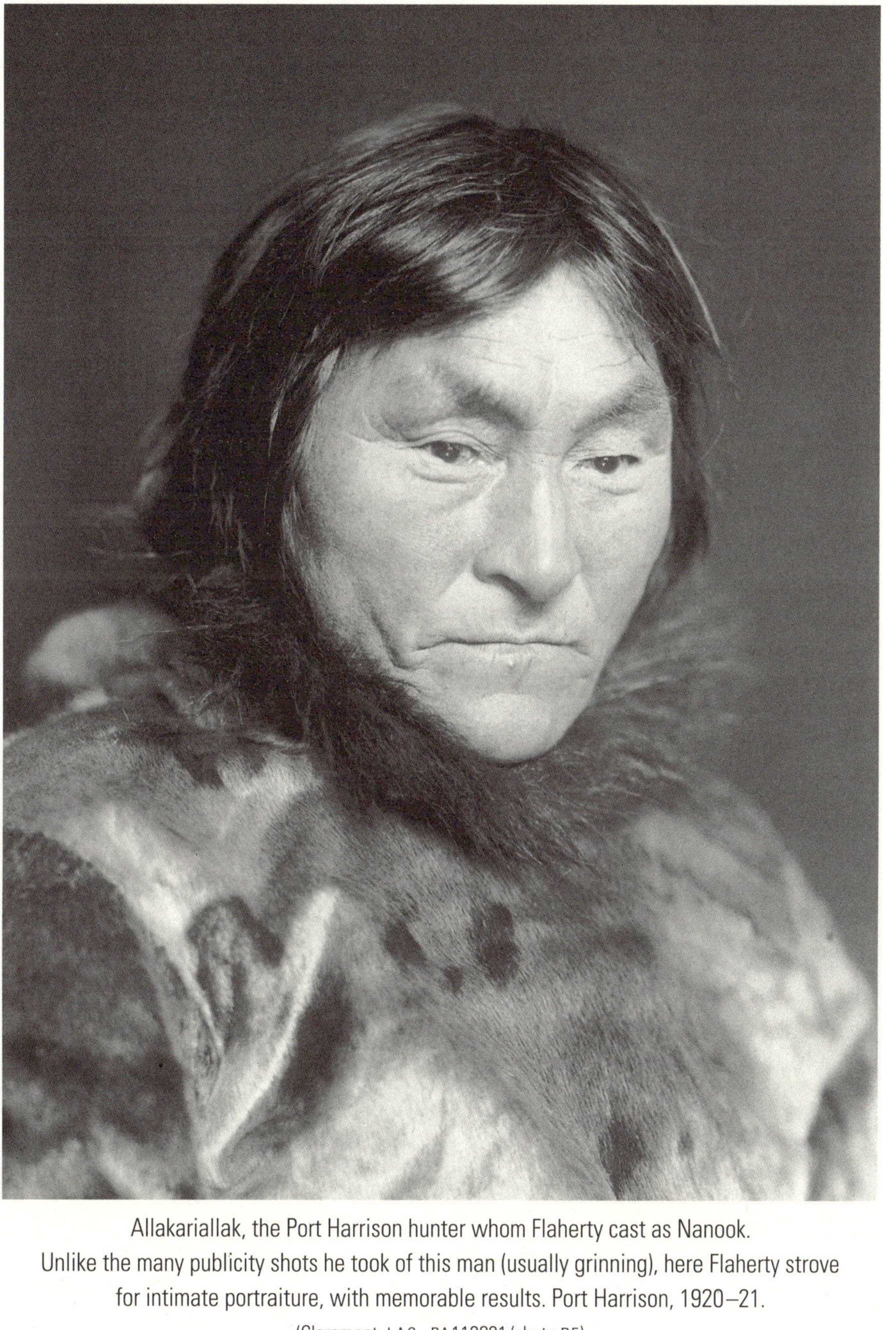

Allakariallak, the Port Harrison hunter whom Flaherty cast as Nanook.
Unlike the many publicity shots he took of this man (usually grinning), here Flaherty strove for intimate portraiture, with memorable results. Port Harrison, 1920–21.
(Claremont, LAC, PA113831/photo RF)

and news from the busy world, would come. We thumbed through the post diaries for dates of past arrivals and, averaging them up, made bets. A lookout was almost constantly on the hills, for a sack of sea biscuit was the prize for him who first should see her sails.

To poor old Nanook the world seemed empty. He hung about my cabin, talking over films we still could make if only I would stay on for another year. He never quite understood why I should have gone to all the fuss and pother of making the "big aggie" of him – the hunting, yes – but surely everyone knew the Eskimo, and could anything possibly be more common than dogs and sledges and snow houses? I tried to give him an idea of the big igloos the kablunak had for showing films. To him, the hundred fifty of his fellow men, as many more at Great Whale, in the distant south, and at far-off Fort Chimo, and at Cape Wolstenholme, were practically the population of the world. The kablunak's movie igloo, into which thousands came, was utterly beyond his comprehension. There were many, I used to say, like the little stones along the shore. "And will all these kablunaks see our 'big aggie'?" he would ask. There was never need to answer, for incredulity was written large upon his face.

At last came the signal from the lookout on the hill. Within two days I was aboard and the *Annie*'s nose was headed south. Nanook followed in his kayak, until the *Annie*, gathering speed, gradually drew away. I saw him turn, still waving, toward his topek, which stood out from the low, melancholy waste of shore – all that he called home!

Less than two years later, I received word by the once-a-year mail that comes out of the north that Nanook was dead. Poor old Nanook! Our "big aggie," become *Nanook of the North*, has gone into most of the odd corners of the world – into the desert of the Sahara, India, Burma, Siam, where audiences must be told that white means snow; and more kablunaks than there are stones around the shore of Nanook's home have looked upon Nanook, the kindly, the brave, the simple Eskimo.[33]

9 Epilogue

The Port Harrison diary displays Flaherty at the height of his descriptive powers as a diarist. Despite its fragmentary structure and the absence of a comforting sequential calendar, for lyric power and acuteness of observation this final northern dairy is Flaherty's apogee. With its mood swings between despondency and intoxication with the very arctic air, the essence of Flaherty's power as a diarist is expressed in the Cape Smith bear hunt sequence of 17 January 1921 to just before the 25 April entry. This expedition just fell short of being a catastrophe, and its rigors pushed men, dogs, and equipment to the limit of endurance. It was during these times of deprivation that the northern landscape took on for Flaherty an extraordinary palette of color and tone, and its shapes became monumental in their presence: "Cape Smith looms up again in the same theatrical way, the same dark curtain slowly creeping slowly northward, the same ever-narrowing margin of yellow sun-lit icefields of sea, until the sun's last glow seems to lodge momentarily on the far rim of the sea and sky when out of the welter of the black-gray clouds fragments of blue come out one by one until, as the light dissolves the rime clouds, the background turns the color of an old rose and the Cape looks out through the silence of our darkening world."[1]

Having discarded the explorer-scientist persona that prevailed in much of the previous narratives, what now comes to the fore is the acuity of a poetic observer. Intent on realizing a visualization of the North, which he believes his experience has granted him, Flaherty strives to observe its landscape with an intensity rarely seen before. But the experience of the diary is fully inclusive, encompassing as well the humanity in the landscape. And so we see a figure at odds with our received vision of the happy and energetic cinema Nanook. We meet instead Allakariallak – the man who played the part – a weary, tubercular figure, nodding at his tasks and embarrassed at his own disorientation about place and direction. The Nanook of the film made this figure of Allakariallak invisible, but he was real nonetheless, and this diary allows us to reflect on what efforts he must have made to realize his vision of himself as the heroic figure whom Flaherty was so desirous of giving to the world.

The Port Harrison diaries also provide us with a remarkable record of notes on filmic process from a filmmaker who never again left such a detailed outline of his visual thinking and planning. Given their largely scattered, unpaginated, and undated presence in the Flaherty papers, these jottings could be viewed as previews of shots or as sequences he was considering, as notes on editing strategies for footage already taken, as "things to do" notes related to accomplished or forthcoming shots, or as reminders to do retakes or to order the making of required implements or clothing.

Given these uncertainties, the safest course is to look at the places where Flaherty did include such notes among the sequential entries. Two such sequences in the diaries are those of 22 September to 19 October 1920 and the Cape Smith bear-hunt sequence noted just above. In the first of these, it is clear that Flaherty was attempting to make two parallel films, since there are repeated entries on trader film notes. How much of these sequences Flaherty actually filmed is not known because the outakes of *Nanook* have not survived. It is easy enough to affirm which of the subjects he noted did get shot and included in the *Nanook* film that was released in 1922 – scenes such as the igloo building and the fox capture. But it is evident that Flaherty made more suggestions to himself than he shot – or than he incorporated into the final film if he did shoot them.

We can observe important practices of selectivity that are evident, for example, in the diary entry of 26 September 1920, where he made a series of notes on "One Way of Making the Film," listing such possible shots as "Eskimo loading camera in cold weather" and "Drying film on rack," both of which would have made the filmmaking itself a subject of the film. Given Flaherty's success at making viewers of *Nanook* feel that it is their eyes, and not the camera's, that are doing the seeing, the intrusion of camera equipment or film processing would have undermined this illusion of the seeing eye. Selectivity also came into play where Flaherty worked with a scene he had already shot – the walrus hunt – and reflected on a series of additional "walrus scenes to make," such as "story of journey" or "camp life," to serve as surrounds to the main hunting scene. In a series of subjects listed under "Post Scenes," there is no surviving evidence that Flaherty included shots of the *Annie* and its unloading or of "the factor's cook," but he did choose to use the "castor oil" suggestion.

Observation and suggestion, not the dominance of planning, are the modes of visual thinking that prevail in these lists. In those following the diary entry of 14 October 1920, for example, the subjects listed appear to have risen from observed daily activities such as game playing or from recalled observations of the *Annie* coming into harbor. But all was not without some calculation, as Flaherty, striving for ethnographic authenticity, noted "implements to be made," such as "duck skin towels" and "stone pots." Flaherty seems to have opened himself to a large repertoire of suggestions as they evolved from settlement and camp activity, and then to have acted on them selectively.

One sequence that Flaherty actually recorded shooting in the diary – the white whale hunting scene (see diary entry of 11 July 1920) – did not appear in the print of *Nanook* that was released and is one of the great puzzles of missing footage. Flaherty elaborated on the excitement of the hunt and its powerful action effect in the article "Life among the Eskimos," which he wrote some four months after the release of *Nanook*. The HBC post manager had even taken a moment to note in his journal, that "Mr Flaherty reports that he was quite successful in getting several close up films of the Eskimo harpooning white whales despite very dirty weather."[2] The absence of this sequence from the film is more extraordinary given the failure of the bear-hunting expedition, which surely had been Flaherty's hope for the consummate action scene. Perhaps it existed in the longer negative film that Pathé eventually contracted from Flaherty, in which case it may have ended up, as much of the raw footage did, on the cutting-room floor. Flaherty's white whale hunt proves as illusive as Melville's, to the greater loss indeed for action cinematography in the first quarter of the twentieth century.

Upon his return in September 1921 Flaherty lost little time in preparing a negative of his footage, since Revillon had promised him only three months of salary. Robert Sherwood, an influential film critic who was among the first to acknowledge the greatness of *Nanook*, interviewed Flaherty in 1922 and reported his early efforts to find a distributor: "He took *Nanook of the North* to five different distributing corporations, all of which turned him down flat. They told him that the public was not interested in Eskimos; the public wants to see people in dress suits. Finally, he effected a deal with Pathé, and *Nanook of the North* was timorously submitted to the exhibitors. Samuel Rothafel of the Capitol Theatre in New York decided to give it a try, although he was frankly dubious about its possibilities as a box-office attraction. The week that *Nanook of the North* played at the Capitol Theatre, it did $43,000 worth of business."[3]

The film was released on 11 June 1922, but the footage that Flaherty brought back from the North underwent a transformation between its first printing and its final editing for release. This early version of a "photoplay" is called "Nanook of the Barren Lands," which was Flaherty's first working title and the one that was cited in the contract he signed with Pathé. Steve Dobi, a film historian who has studied contemporary efforts to restore *Nanook*, suggests that "the picture he first cut was about Nanook the trapper who made his livelihood trapping for Revillon Frères. Nanook's sled was emblazoned with the company's name, and the film itself did indeed attempt to prove the authenticity of the Revillons' claim to that part of the world."[4] The claim that was proving burdensome to Flaherty was the one made in the Revillon contract to produce a trader film. If that was the emphasis of Flaherty's first cut, then it is no surprise that distributors did not wish to advance Revillon's commercial interests by sponsoring the film.

The French connection between Revillon Frères and Pathé Exchange may have helped to cement the distributor's eventual interest in Flaherty's film. However it was made, the linkage was forged when Flaherty, as "producer," signed a contract with Pathé in early 1922. The financial arrangements were industry standard for the time, with Pathé first being reimbursed for the printing, marketing, and distribution of the film, over which it was to retain sole rights for ten years, at which time the rights would revert to Flaherty and Revillon. Once the expenses were paid, Flaherty and Revillon could receive up to $50,000, after which all further proceeds from exhibitors were to be shared 50/50 between Pathé and Flaherty and Revillon. The arrangement also called for Flaherty to deliver to

Pathé "the complete negative of said photoplay," one positive print of the negative, and 250 publicity photographs.[5] Flaherty thereby surrendered control over the final cut of the film, since the contract stipulated that the "Producer authorizes and hereby employs Pathé to cut, assemble and title said negative so as to make therefrom a motion picture of six (6) reels containing approximately nine hundred and fifty (950) linear feet." Pathé assigned to the project the editor of its very successful Pathé News series, Carl Stearns Clancy, and he and Flaherty spent the spring of 1922 editing and titling the film in New York City, leaving in the discard bin not only Flaherty's original title but thousands of feet of takes and retakes, including, it would appear, the white whale hunt.

Upon its release, *Nanook of the North* was quickly featured as the best summertime movie of the year. As the enthusiasm of the reviewers gained momentum, so did the kitsch of the Nanook craze. The ice cream, refrigeration, gramophone, and fur industries pounced on the film's title and its imagery to hawk their wares. The public was invited to consume an Eskimo pie à la mode, to drink a Nanook fizz, to enjoy Igloo ice boxes, to wear Eskimo rubbers, to purchase next season's furs at summer bargain prices, and to be reminded by the Columbia Grafonola Company that "Nanook liked Grafonola so much that he ate the record."[6] Flaherty lent his support to these ventures, going so far as to travel to Milwaukee in 1923 to give a schoolboy a $200 prize for the best essay on the Eskimo. A Fulton Street department store in Brooklyn boasted that its fur display windows contained "relics, sleds, suits as worn by Nanook in the famous photo-play 'Nanook of the North,'" all loaned to it by Robert Flaherty, F.R.G.S. The craze went international with the London opening of *Nanook* in September 1922 amid the following spectacle: "The public, on its way in, passes through a hall whose decorations suggest, with the help of a scene painter, a glacier with stuffed foxes and bears in the foreground."

Amidst all this snow hype, a number of film reviewers sensed that *Nanook* was an important film but one whose identity was so unique that it was difficult to place it within the received film categories. It had the look of a "scenic," that genre of film that took viewers to faraway exotic places, as did Martin Johnson's *Cannibals of the South Seas* (1912) and Paul Rainey's *African Hunt* (1912), both of which Flaherty had seen. These films, however, were episodic treatments without continuity – one person doing this and another that. Such were the characteristics that Flaherty had come to feel beleaguered his Baffin-Belcher film. There were also films of polar snow expeditions, such as Frank Hurley's *In the Grip of the Polar Ice* (1917) and Herbert Ponting's *The Great White Silence* (1911). These, in their way, were films about naval expeditions but without any attention given to people outside the expeditionary team. The travelogues of Burton Holmes and the ultrarealism of George C. Hale's "Tours" come to mind, as they did to John Grierson when he saw the Baffin-Belcher film in the mid-1920s. Pathé itself regarded *Nanook* as a photoplay, but its drama depicted no love clutches and contained no sultry starlets or manly professional actors, only people moving about in the bulky skins of arctic mammals.

Although Edward Curtis had used the term "documentary" to refer to his ethnographic filmwork, the term did not yet circulate as a widely shared categorical term. It began its association with Flaherty's work only when John Grierson used it in a review of *Moana* in 1926 saying, "*Moana* being a visual account of events in the daily life of a Polynesian youth and his family has documentary value."[7] In this use by Grierson, we should remind ourselves that the term had adjectival force. "Documentary" as a noun appeared in the 1930s when Grierson used Flaherty's work to fashion the theory and practice of the British Documentary Movement, a cinema approach that spotlighted the social plight of ordinary people in their homes and workplaces.[8]

The influence of such critics as Robert Sherwood was pervasive enough to raise the bar of Flaherty's immediate reputation, while other reviewers endeavored to critique the elements that made *Nanook* so memorable as a film experience. Francis Taylor Paterson, for example, set high standards for the film, declaring, "Here at last begins our native screen language, as original in concept as the *Cabinet of Dr. Caligari*, yet as natural as that is fantastic."[9] In attempting to realize the essentials of this new hybrid, Paterson anticipated the high points of future Flaherty scholarship by trying to acknowledge the unique vocabulary of Flaherty's visual language, its unity and continuity, its power of composition, and the singularity of his "impressions." By using local players working at their daily activities, Flaherty had revised the dramatic formula for the photoplay, said Paterson, calling the film the "first photoplay of the naturalistic school."

A critique by Bruce Bliven in the *New York Globe* was based on a meeting between Flaherty and Bliven, who had sent Flaherty a draft of his proposed article the previous week. Bliven's main concern in the article was whether the current organization of the movie industry – which placed immense power in the hands of exhibitors – could find ways of admitting for circulation other ground-breaking films. He doubted that the industry would tolerate such independence and such experimentation by risk-taking filmmakers. The industry's tastes were essentially conservative and timid, inclined toward the proven staple rather than to the new hybrid. In attempting to create this hybrid of the naturalistic photoplay, as Paterson called it, Flaherty was aware that he was attempting to join together previously disparate elements. He told Bliven:

> It seems to me that it is possible to record the life of primitive people in such as way as to preserve scientific accuracy and yet make a picture which had vivid dramatic interest for the average man or woman. Plenty of pictures have been made of the life of savages in various parts of the world, especially in the tropics. The difficulty is that such pictures are usually episodic, showing unrelated scenes, with little to hold the wandering attention of one who has not a scientific interest in the lives of primitive people. In "Nanook of the North" by taking a central character and portraying his exciting adventures, and those of his family, in the effort to wrest a livelihood from the frigid Arctic, we secure a dramatic value which is both legitimate and absorbing.[10]

Flaherty was thinking of a marriage of ethnography and drama, with the humanity of a family providing an anchor for the wandering attention of the average viewer. In later years he drew fire on both counts. The drama of the film was challenged for the way in which the Nanook-Nyla family was a staged relationship and, on the accuracy front, for the way he arranged the ethnography of the film to give it an earlier, more primitive presence than was warranted by the gun and ammunition culture that he describes in his diaries. At its time of publication, however, Bliven's article gave Flaherty a platform from which to declare his cinematic goals.

While *Nanook of the North* made "Nanook" an international household name and while it made Flaherty a filmmaker of some reputation, he gained little financial reward from it. Like all such industry agreements between filmmaker and distributor, the latter stood first in line. Flaherty was jolted further down the line by Revillon Frères' decision to hold him to the contracted budget for the film. In his agreement of 7 April 1922 with Revillon, Flaherty acknowledged that he had exceeded costs by $28,000 and that payment would be made from the proceeds of *Nanook*.[11] Another significant bite on whatever payment Flaherty might have received was that sometime between his return from Port Harrison and the release of *Nanook*, he conveyed to Sir William Mackenzie 25 per cent of his original 49 percent agreement with Revillon. No doubt Mackenzie insisted on this as partial recompense for all the outlay he had made to support Flaherty's earlier filmwork.[12] Although the complete financial records for *Nanook* have not survived, given the contracts with Revillon and Pathé, the Revillon overruns, and the Mackenzie cut, it is likely that Flaherty pocketed little income for his work.

Even before *Nanook*'s first screening, Flaherty was planning a sequel, as he confided in an interview with the *Morning Telegraph*: "Mr Flaherty is not through with picture making; in fact, his enthusiasm is gathering momentum every day. He has decided plans for another film of the North, not in Nanook's country, but in the vicinity of Baffin's Bay. This picture will have an original plot and there will be no white man in it."[13] However, the only evidence we have of a sequel is an undated, unfinished filmscript entitled "Iviuk, Son of Nanook." The Iviuk ("Walrus") of the story is a kind of Moses among the bulrushes, except that the baby is found in an abandoned igloo surrounded by his dead family, all of whom have died of starvation. This improbable orphan survivor is happily adopted and grows to young adulthood before the draft of the scrip ends. It includes a white man in the form of a trader, and there are a surprising number of repeat episodes from *Nanook*, including a castor oil scene. After reading the script, one feels glad that the film was not made.

The Flahertys made better use of their new fame by embarking on a cottage industry of publications about Flaherty's crossing of the Ungava Peninsula, his rediscovery of the Belcher Islands, and the making of *Nanook*. They found a very receptive editor in Arthur Page of Doubleday and Page, the publishers of the popular monthly magazine the *World's Work*. In the September and October issues of 1922, two articles appeared recounting Flaherty's year-long experience of making the film at Port Harrison. In the January through March issues of 1923, the Flahertys wrote up two other chapters of the Flaherty saga: the crossing of the Ungava and the exploration of the Belchers. The articles included a rich representation of maps, drawings, photographs from all periods of Flaherty's northern work, and publicity stills from *Nanook*.

The reception of these pieces was so solid that Page urged the Flahertys to compile the articles in a book, which they did, and *My Eskimo Friends* appeared in 1924. In the frontispiece, Flaherty gave Frances formal recognition as his collaborator on the book. This was the only jointly authored book that the Flahertys did, and it represents a distillation of Flaherty's more than ten years' work in the North. The text became the capstone narrative of Flaherty's emergence as a filmmaker and formed the foundation of the saga of Flaherty as cinematic explorer.

The Flahertys' life took a dramatic new direction when they were retained by Jesse Lasky of Paramount Pictures to travel to the South Seas to make another Nanook-like film. The Flahertys left for Samoa with their entire family in April 1923 and returned in 1925 with the footage of *Moana* (1926) in their crates.

With this new world of Hollywood and feature films seizing their attention, the Flahertys closed the door on the northern world that had so dominated their planning and thinking. It was a world to which neither ever returned. Moreover, the North was a world that was rapidly changing as it lost its isolation to the advances of technology. The first recorded landing of a seaplane at Moose Factory occurred in August 1920, carrying as passengers a film crew eager to photograph what to them was the new world of the North. Within the next few years, the isolated posts that Flaherty knew so well were connected by wireless to the larger world, which formerly had made contact only through the annual supply ship and the infrequent mail packet.

There were other legacies, which were known to the Flahertys but were a secret to others. The children fathered by Flaherty during his years of relations with Inuit women were never spoken of publicly, but in the North their identity was absorbed into the embrace of the Eskimo adoptive culture. Much better documented than the son fathered by Flaherty on the Belcher Islands is the son born of Alice, the Nyla of *Nanook*. Rather than allowing their child to be renamed in the process of adoptive integration, Alice stood her ground and insisted that the boy's name be Joseph Flaherty. Joseph in turn fathered a family, and if you travel today to the Arctic settlements of Inukjuak and Grise Fiord, you will meet a large and thriving Flaherty Inuit clan. It is with some irony that the manchild Frances so yearned for in her first pregnancy was born a son of the North.

Throughout his life, Flaherty maintained that within two years after his departure Nanook had died of starvation while on an inland caribou-hunting trip. The story must be apocryphal, since there is no evidence that Allakariallak died in such a way. Bob Stewart kept Flaherty informed about Allakariallak's health, and in a letter of 28 January 1923 he informed him, "Attata is sick just now. In fact he's been in bed all fall and winter. He is just skin and bones and expect him to die any day. I'm surprised he has lived so long."[14] This is a man whose condition would make crossing the room difficult, let alone enduring the rigors of a hunting expedition. Allakariallak died on 26 May 1923, an event recorded in the HBC journal for Port Harrison – an entry itself surprising, since it was not the custom of HBC men to record the births and deaths of Eskimo: "Allakaralook Sr. one of Revillons servants, who has been sick all winter, died yesterday afternoon and was buried shortly afterwards."[15] That an HBC man would note the passing of a Revillon servant is an exemplary final playing of taps for a man who will remain vividly alive for us each time we view *Nanook of the North*.

Notes

INTRODUCTION

1 On 26 January 1957, Frances wrote to Iain Hamilton, editor of Hutchinson & Co., about his interest in publishing a biography by Paul Rotha. Her letter is housed in the Robert Flaherty Papers, in the Rare Book and Manuscript Library of Butler Library, Columbia University, from which this work draws on extensively. References to material from this collection will be cited as Butler, followed by the microfilm call number, which in this instance is MN1937.

CHAPTER ONE

1 Calder-Marshall, *Innocent Eye*, 16
2 Knight, Commissioner of Mineral Statistics for Michigan. *Annual Report for 1892–93*, 67
3 Slaght, *Report of the Ontario Bureau of Mines*, 6:260.
4 Ibid., 6:96–8
5 Bow, "Mines of Northwestern Ontario," *Report*, 7:51
6 Ibid., 9:54
7 Ibid., 9:32
8 Ibid., 9:68

9 Ibid., 10(pt.1):79.
10 The 1907 report documents the first published Flaherty photograph, taken either by father or son, captioned "Flaherty's diamond drill, Height of Land." See Coleman and Moore, "Iron Ranges East of Lake Nipigon, Part II," *Report* 17:171.
11 Hopkins, "The Kowkwash Gold Area," *Report* 25(pt.1):266.
12 Carter, "The Mines of Ontario," *Report* 11:266.
13 Moore, "The Iron Ranges East of Lake Nipigon, Part II," *Report* 17:170.
14 Coleman, "Iron Ranges East of Lake Nipigon," *Report* 16(pt.1):106.
15 The unpublished "Islands" manuscript is housed among the Robert Flaherty Papers in the Butler Library (hereafter Butler), MN1927. It consists of 22 chapters and about 225 typewritten pages and was Flaherty's most ambitious effort to write (in the first three chapters) an autobiographical narrative of his childhood, upbringing, and first career as a mineralogical explorer. Its title reflects Flaherty's view that the major accomplishment of his career as an explorer was the rediscovery and exploration of the Belcher Islands in eastern Hudson Bay. "Islands" was written with a youthful reader in mind in the late 1930s when, given the dismal opportunities for film projects in England, Flaherty seriously considered writing as a career alternative. By the fall of 1939 when he returned to the United States to work on his film *The Land*, he brought the almost completed manuscript of "Islands" with him. But, once in the United States and preoccupied with his new film, he drifted away from this as well as from other pending writing projects.
16 Flaherty is referring to Francis Parkman (1823–93), the historian and traveler who chronicled the exploration of North America in such works as *California and Oregon Trail* (1849). Robert M. Ballantyne (1825–95), a prolific writer of adventure stories for boys, used his six years' experience as a Hudson's Bay Company trader to inform such works as *Ungava* (1858), a favorite of Flaherty's.
17 The mill Flaherty describes is at the Foley Mine, the first mine his father managed after leaving Michigan. The now completed Twenty-Stamp Mill, with railway trestle, is depicted in a photograph found in Slaght's *Report of the Ontario Bureau of Mines*, 6:96.
18 Flaherty's father died on 15 August 1923 and his mother on 29 October 1924, in Port Arthur, Ontario.
19 In the "Notes on Chronology" that David Flaherty prepared in the mid-1950s for the biographer Paul Rotha, David wrote: "Knobel was an English mining engineer who had studied at Heidelberg, an interesting recluse who loved to live alone in the wilds. Wherever he lived in the wilderness he brought his piano with him, and was particularly fond of playing Chopin. Captain Knobel served with distinction in the Canadian forces in the First World War, then returned to his prospecting life in Canada. He died two or three years ago, of pneumonia, I understand, caught on ship on his way to visit his sister in London. He was in his eighties" (Butler, MN1931)

CHAPTER TWO

1 Taylor, "Profile of Robert Flaherty, 32
2 Rotha, *Robert Flaherty*, 9
3 This quotation and the others by Frances Flaherty Rultan are printed with the kind permission of the Vancouver Art Gallery Archives from the audiotape interview with Flaherty Ruttan by Susan Boyd-Bowman for the Vancouver Art Gallery, 23 July 1979.

4 Audiotapes of the BBC broadcast are housed in the Robert and Frances Flaherty Study Center at the School of Theology at Claremont University, California, quoted with the kind permission of the Study Center and Claremont University (hereafter cited as Claremont), audiotapes 94–7.

5 Robert Flaherty Papers in Butler Library (hereafter Butler), MN1911

6 The diary for this expedition was kept in a single leather-bound field book and written in pencil, as were most of Flaherty's diaries. Affixed to selected facing pages are thirty-five photographs of various scenes and panoramas, including an Indian grave (see 20 Sept.) and Dinsmore and Native guides. But there are no photos of Robert or Frances or of the "others" alluded to in Frances's letter of 29 August, quoted in note 8 below. There exists a typescript of the entries up to 14 September 1906.

7 Dinsmore was Flaherty's assistant.

8 This reference and many that follow make it abundantly clear that Frances Hubbard was the intended reader of this diary and that she and her sister Charlotte Goodell had been Flaherty's companions in the month before these September entries. Given the photographs, the overall impression of the diary is that of a presentation album, a format in concert with the tenor of the diary as a private communication to Frances. That she had shared the journey with Flaherty is confirmed in her letter of 29 August 1906 to Margaret Thurston, her Bryn Mawr schoolmate:

> Your letter just came before I started out into the woods, whence I have only just returned, and the interim was not an interim of letter writing. But what an interim!
>
> Would that I had the style of a Parkman, a Stewart Edward White and a Jack London – all in one, and I would tell thee and all the world of that country – its primitive history, its primitive people, its primitive forests and the great elemental force of the wilderness. (For we went where no other white woman had ever been before!) 130 miles by river and lake into the distant, blue mountain country where the only human signs were old Indian traps, and once an Indian grave. And where everywhere were signs of the wilderness – tracks of moose, deer, and bears, mink and otter and wolves. Of the first and last, however, we saw no more than their tracks on the sandy shores of the last great inland lake. Rob was our courier; he being the only one, not excepting our Indians, who had been in the country before.
>
> We had our own little birch bark canoe which we paddled and carried over the portages ourselves. It was good hard work, I can tell you. But it was more like the real thing than reclining as the others did in the big Hudson Bay Peterboroughs and being paddled by guides. We explored out of the way bays and lingered on the cool wood moss when we were tired, and sometimes stopped to pitch our little "cheemaun" [canoe]. I hardly realized what a good time I was having, for it all seemed too good to be true.
>
> Rob is just the same "spitfire" (Charlotte calls him). Just as impetuous, sensitive, quick tempered, as full of moods and inspiration and lovable as ever.
>
> We spent one whole day at his house playing together as of old and now nothing will do but he must come down to Boston this winter if he has to walk. (Claremont; audiotape 231A/side 1)

In the diaries of the mineralogy work that Flaherty did for his father during 1906, there is a gap between 6 August and 6 September 1906, and this would appear to be the period when Flaherty served as one of the guides to the Hubbard-Goodell party. The likelihood that these are the dates is further confirmed by Flaherty's remark on 23 September, "A month ago today you left the north country."

9 These two trading posts, standing opposite each other, reflect the growing competition for control of the northern fur trade between the once monopolistic Hudson's Bay Company and its new challenger, the Revillon Frères Trading Company. Often simply called the French Co., Revillon is also referred to in Hudson's Bay Company (HBC) journals as "the Opposition." For a comprehensive study of Revillon's emergence as an HBC competitor, see Harris, *Revillon Frères Trading Company*.

10 Acres was a native guide.

CHAPTER THREE

1 More details about Hubbard's professional career and writings can be found in a memorial article in *American Mineralogist* 19 (March 1934): 118–21.

2 Taylor, "Profile of Robert Flaherty, *New Yorker*, 11 June 1949, 32

3 Margaret Thurston Holt (1883–1978) was a Bryn Mawr classmate of Frances and a lifelong correspondent. Selections of her correspondence with Frances are on audiotapes at the Robert and Frances Flaherty Study Center at Claremont University (hereafter Claremont). Frances's letter to Thurston cited here is from audiotape 231A/side 1.

4 Frances's letters to her mother are housed at the Butler Library in the Hubbard Family Papers (hereafter HFP), box 1.

5 HFP, Julia Hubbard Adams's "Memories of a Copper County Childhood," 25-page unpublished history of the Hubbard family written in the 1970s by Frances's younger sister

6 Claremont, audiotape 231B/side 1

7 HFP, miscellaneous folder

8 Rotha, *Robert Flaherty*, 11–12

9 Robert Flaherty Papers in Butler Library (hereafter Butler), MN1911

10 Ibid.

11 Claremont, audiotape 231B/side 1

12 From the Hudson Bay chapter of Thurston's autobiography, "People Intoxicate Me," 2–3, quoted with the kind permission of her son, Thurston Holt (private collection)

13 William Mackenzie (1849–1923) and Donald Mann (1853–1934), both knighted in 1911, parleyed a partnership as railway contractors into the construction of the Canadian Northern Railway. Of the many ventures they pursued, one of particular interest to Mackenzie was the vision of a gateway through Hudson Bay by which grain and iron ore would flow to Europe. It was this vision that sponsored Flaherty's four iron ore prospecting and geographical exploration expeditions to the Eastern Arctic. For a view of Mackenzie from a contemporary journalist who profiled him often, see Bridle, "Sir William Mackenzie," and for a recent comprehensive biography, Fleming, *The Railway King*.

14 Flaherty kept this diary in a self-contained leather-bound notebook. There also exists a typescript prepared by Frances. The first pages of the diary contain names of individuals whom Flaherty wished to seek out at various posts, as well as a detailed shopping list of photographic equipment and printing paper. The notes suggest how intent Flaherty was at making photography an essential part of his expeditionary work (Butler, MN1911).

15 Of A.P. Low's work in exploring and mapping the eastern Labrador peninsula and

the Hudson Bay region, Flaherty observed: "For such information as we have of the coast and its interior we are indebted largely to the remarkable explorations of the late [sic] A.P. Low, of the Canadian Geological Survey, whose work covering a period of more than twenty years, has given us the most detailed and reliable maps of the region available. It was Low's detailed reports of the Nastapoka Island discoveries made in 1877 by Dr Bell, also of the Canadian Geological Survey, that formed the basis of the investigations which I had been commissioned to make" ("The Belcher Islands of Hudson Bay," 435). Albert Peter Low (1861–1942) and Robert Bell, MD (1841–1917) were both associated with the Geological Survey of Canada and did influential exploratory work in the Hudson Bay region from the 1870s onward. Both were skilled photographers with whose work Flaherty would have been acquainted, having read their reports. Flaherty most likely had also read Low's *Cruise of the Neptune 1903–4* (1906), in which Low had included over sixty photographs. For a profile of Bell, with a sample of his photographs, see Douglas Leechman, "The Father of Place Names," 24–8.

16 The post at which Flaherty arrived, Moosonee, was established in 1903 by Thierry Mallet, the Revillon executive who was later instrumental in negotiating that firm's sponsorship of Flaherty's filming of *Nanook of the North*. The "factory" in Moose Factory, Flaherty's next stop, needs to be construed in Dr Johnson's definition: "A house or district inhabited by traders in a distant country." The second-oldest Hudson's Bay Company (HBC) post, established in 1673 as Moose Fort, Moose Factory (renamed Moosonee in 1932) served as the administrative center for HBC activities in the Eastern Arctic. It was Flaherty's gateway to Hudson Bay on most of his expeditions. For a detailed description of Moose in 1910, see Anderson, *Fur Trader's Story*, 17–27. For a contrasting view of historical and modern photographs of Moose Factory, see Cotter and Wilson, "Moose Factory: Yesterday and Today," 22–9.

17 His meeting with those waiting at Charlton Island for the annual supply ship, the *Nascopie*, was the first of many encounters that Flaherty would with trading-post employees, upon whom he became reliant for supplies and guidance. These chains of HBC and Revillon posts served as the milestones of Flaherty's expeditions and as points of rest, conversation, resupply, and mail. At the time Flaherty met him, Alexander C. McNab (1859–?) was serving as district manager of the HBC's James Bay posts; Donald Gillies (1859–1935), with the HBC since 1878, was serving as factor at Fort Albany; Neville Owen Griffith (1886–1927), appointed in 1903, was HBC clerk at Fort George and was about to return from Rupert House, where he had married the daughter of the HBC manager at that post, Alan Nicolson (1861–1934).

18 "Huskie" (or "Husky") is a term that was used interchangeably by Flaherty and others to describe both man and dog. In this instance we can presume Flaherty was referring to a person.

19 The typewritten transcription for this entry has many typing errors, which may account for some of the confusion here. Flaherty's hired assistant, the hungover Crundell, is suddenly given a wife. The Mrs Turner mentioned (Mary Louise) was the wife of Robert F. Turner (1886–1916), the son of a Cree mother, Jemima Alisapi, and Robert Turner (1848–1907), himself a forty-year HBC employee.

20 This was William Miller (1868–1928), the caretaker at Charlton Island, who also served as pilot for Charlton harbor docking. Captain Edmund Mack described him as follows: "Miller, the pilot, came out to take us in. This was Miller's field day. He lived on Charlton Island all winter looking after the depot, and had his wife and family with

him. When he came out as pilot for a few hours he was boss. He was a marvel, and could handle a ship well under either steam or square-rigged sail. He read constantly during the winter. There were several men in the James Bay District who could have held their own AB's in the sailing ship days" (Mack, "The Nascopie," 8–9).

21 Fort George (renamed Chisasibi) was established in 1837 and was a main trading post in the Eastmain district. It was also the site of an Anglican mission, and in 1910 the missionary in charge was the Rev. William G. Walton. (1869–1949). There was both an HBC and a Revillon post at Fort George. Aldridge was factor of the Revillon post. Although economic rivals, the managers of the HBC and Revillon posts, along with the local Anglican missionary, banded together to form an Anglo enclave. They are captured in a photograph titled "The Cosiest Interior on Hudson Bay," which shows Walton's cluttered Victorian parlor in which they have gathered for a musicale: Walton with violin, Mrs Walton at piano, Aldridge and Griffith with mandolin. (Leith and Leith, *A Summer and Winter on Hudson Bay*, 46). For a detailed description of the settlement in 1912, including Walton's parlor, see Curran and Calkins, *In Canada's Wonderful Northland*, 115–25.

22 Flaherty's dismissal of the besotted Crundell back to Moose was not only a decision to be self-reliant; he also wanted to rely more on the assistance of local people, as he did here with the seasoned sledge drivers Alec and Teddy – the Louttit brothers of Fort George.

23 Great Whale River (renamed Kuujjuarapik), 180 miles north of Fort George, was established as a whaling station at the mouth of the Great Whale River in 1856. The decline of coastal whaling led to the closing of whaling facilities in 1869, though the HBC continued to maintain a trading post. Great Whale River, as of 1912, is described in Curran and Calkins, *In Canada's Wonderful Northland*, 154–6.

24 "Harold" is Harold Udgaarden (1867–1950), who served for forty-nine years as factor's assistant at Great Whale River. Trilingual in Cree, English, and Inuktitut, he had a legendary reputation as a cultural broker, trapper, and marksman. His wife Mary was sister of the Fleming brothers, Nero and William (the latter being "Huskie Bill," whom Flaherty first mentioned on 12, 20, and 23 December). In the Fleming-Udgaarden family and their extended kin, Flaherty found a profoundly enabling collaborative network of assistance and guidance. As he gained experience in northern travel, he grasped the importance of cultural collaboration, and this served him immeasurably in his photography and filmmaking endeavors. The Leith brothers, who met Udgaarden in 1910, described him in an affectionate profile, "Harold Udgaarden, Philosopher," in their *Summer and Winter on Hudson Bay*, 112–17.

Nero and William Fleming, were already reputed figures. The Leith brothers recalled meeting them in 1910, saying of William, "He was a surprise to us, being neatly dressed, speaking good English and appearing anything but a native Eskimo ... We liked Bill from the start and after the next night, when he took us into Great Whale River [by boat] near midnight in a thick fog, were willing to trust him implicitly" (ibid., 153). Nero had by far the greater influence on Flaherty, who spoke of him here and elsewhere with the highest regard, considering him an example of the most "advanced" Eskimo he had ever met. Nero was also unusual in that he served as the first lay Anglican catechist on the eastern coast of the Hudson Bay. In *Summer and Winter on Hudson Bay*, Charles Leith described a service Nero conducted at the Great Whale River Anglican mission:

Roberts and I attended a service in the chapel conducted by Nero, famous as probably the best Husky guide and hunter on the north coast. We were the only whites in the room. Nero had donned a black cutaway coat but retained his sealskin boots and red handkerchief around his neck. Moreover, his coat collar was turned up. He met us at the door, ushered us to front seats and presented us hymnals (Husky) with the grace of a courtier. The service was earnestly read and responded to. We could not take part, though Nero repeated his hymn announcements in broken English and waited until we had located the place in the Husky hymnal, which of course we could not read. After reading, in Husky, the lesson about Peter denying the Lord, Nero with true courtesy attempted to tell us the story in English. His English, always picturesque, under this unusual excitement and embarrassment, became almost an unintelligible jumble, but he struggled on manfully with perspiration streaming from his face, until he could go on no further, when he stopped with "Me English can no more say him." It was difficult to restrain a smile, but Nero had done his best, and where could one find courtesy of finer quality? (48–9)

During Flaherty's stay in Great Whale, he photographed a seated congregation at the church and also took a picture of Nero alone – Bible in hand and world map and Anglican creed in Inuktitut on the wall behind him – standing in the empty mission room. Charles and Arthur Leith included photographs of both Nero and William in *Summer and Winter on Hudson Bay*, 154.

25 In the entry for 24 December, Flaherty had mentioned "the famous Sucker Creek, where Leith tried to ford." He was alluding to the Leith brothers' near-fatal fording of the creek. They barely reached shore and then with difficulty retreated to Great Whale River, having lost one of their two packs and all their food except for ten pounds of flour and some lard. A son of William Fleming later retrieved the lost pack downriver at Little Cape Jones and passed it on to Flaherty, who found among its contents diaries and geological notes, as well as $300 in bank drafts and $53 in cash. On his return to Toronto in March 1911, Flaherty sent Charles Leith, a professor of geology at the University of Wisconsin, a telegram: "Have sent all of your data, money and drafts to you today. Found at Cape Jones by Bill's son." As if to prove that losing something in the Barren Lands was the surest way to get it back, Leith also tells of caching a crate of tools and supplies when their schooner was wrecked at Little Whale River. In January 1911 he received the crate, item perfect, with a manifest detailing its journey: one hundred miles by sledge from Little Whale River to Great Whale River, then by schooner to Charlton Island, outbound then to London, back from London to the United States, and on to its destination in Madison. The manifest requested payment of $1.20 for freight and handling costs! Leith's narrative of these episodes, together with a copy of Flaherty's telegram and a sample of the newspaper reports that made this event a minor sensation, are in *Summer and Winter on Hudson Bay*, 112–7.

26 Flaherty is probably referring to the brass tokens called "made beavers," which were used as coinage in the fur trade.

27 Flaherty has reached the northern point of his journey. Having accomplished his goal of doing a mineralogical examination of the Nastapoka Islands, he now reverses course and retraces his steps. He had hoped to demonstrate that the finger of the Minnesota iron load did indeed snake northward into Hudson Bay. Only with later expeditions did he come to believe that neither the iron ore grade nor the transportation outlets were commercially viable.

28 Both the HBC and Revillon maintained posts at Eastmain, located at the mouth of the

Eastmain River and due east of Charlton Island. Bonard was the Revillon factor and Christopher J.R. Jobson (1851–1918), in HBC service since 1865, was a man with a long memory about the North. James A. McRae, who met Jobson in 1912 at Eastmain, recalled a number of their conversations in *Call Me Tomorrow*, 151–63. Amidst all this apparent conviviality, it is amusing to observe that the HBC journal entry for 10 February reads: "Mr. Flaherty feeling ready to depart & time too!" (Hudson's Bay Company Archives, B59/a/128).

29 The counterpart of the HBC depot at Charlton Island was the one Revillon established in 1906 on the Strutton Islands, about ten miles due east of Charlton, to receive deep-sea supply ships and to warehouse and distribute goods to Revillon posts in the bay.

30 Situated at the mouth of the Rupert River on the south coast of James Bay, Rupert House was the site of the first Hudson's Bay Company post and was named after the first HBC governor, Prince Rupert, who held the position from 1670 to 1682. Its history is grounded in the seventeenth-century origins of the HBC. Originally named Charles Fort, in honor of King Charles II, it was established in 1668 to command James Bay – which was named by Captain Thomas James (1593?–1635), a Jacobean buccaneer who wintered on Charlton Island during 1631–32. Beyond Rupert House's early strategic importance, in 1912 more bales of fur were shipped out from it than from any other post in the bay. Given its location in the south of the bay, timber and agriculture were also cultivated, and it was famous for the canoes constructed there. For a detailed description of the settlement in 1912, see Anderson, *Fur Trader's Story*, 46–53.

31 The Revillon inspector Flaherty passed was Y. Draulette, a man who had been instrumental in establishing Revillon's presence in the Hudson Bay region. With Louis Romanet he had established in 1903 a Revillon post in the Ungava area at Fort Chimo and had supervised the building of the Strutton depot in 1906. The Draulettes, who worked out of the Revillon post at Moosonee, garnered a reputation for providing a touch of Paris in the North. Of Mrs Draulette, who was noted as a skilled trapper herself, William Tees Curran observed: "There is no woman on the Bay who had entered into the spirit of the northern life with the same degree of interest as Mrs Draulette, which is all the more remarkable when one takes into consideration the fact that she is a lady of education and refinement and came directly from the associations of Parisian society to the Hudson Bay country ... Nothing could be neater than her home, and to be invited to sit at Mrs Draulette's table and partake of the dainties provided by the hostess is not only a treat, but a memorable function for the traveler of that country" (*In Canada's Wonderful Northland*, 296).

32 The MacAlpine whom Flaherty passed was George Emmett (1878–?), an HBC employee since 1896, who in 1910 was serving as a clerk at Moose Factory.

CHAPTER FOUR

1 Robert Flaherty Papers in Butler Library (hereafter Butler), MN1910

2 Robert Flaherty, "The Islands That Were Not There," Butler, MN1927

3 Flaherty's registration for copyright of "Through Canada's Northlands," dated 22 May 1911, appears in the *Canada Gazette*, 27 May 1911, 4010, with the registration number 23989. The copy of the album deposited in Ottawa is now lost, but a second copy was deposited in the British Library, as was then required by British copyright law. This second copy survives (Canadian Copyright Collection, 23989/1–102) in the

form of modern transparencies, the original collection of prints being currently misplaced. For a history and checklist of these copyright deposits, see O'Neill, *Checklist of Canadian Copyright Deposits in the British Museum, 1895–1923*, vol 5. For an anthology of photographs gathered from the entire collection, including fourteen by Flaherty, see Pierce, *Canada: The Missing Years, 1895–1924*. For a detailed analysis of the album and its importance in Flaherty's photographic canon, see Christopher, "Through Canada's Northland: The Arctic Photography of Robert J. Flaherty," 181–9.

4 A well-regarded Toronto journalist and a confidante of William Mackenzie, Augustus Bridle (1869–1952) published his article on Flaherty in the *Courier*, 13 May 1911.

5 Butler, MN1910

6 This passage from "Islands" is a good example of how, after the fact, Flaherty often expanded on an incident, amplifying both its character and its context in order to give it fresh relevance in his narrative. In articles that he and Frances later wrote about this episode, they retold this story twice and published the map. See his "The Belcher Islands of Hudson Bay," 440, and "Wetalltok's Islands, II," 428.

7 For his second expedition, Flaherty kept diaries in four different notebooks. In the fourth, he included about twenty or so pages of Eskimo-English words and phrases (entered when he was at Great Whale River in September 1911). With the exception of the vocabulary lists and a number of "miscellaneous notes" to the expedition, Frances Flaherty arranged for typescripts to be made of all four diaries (Butler, MN1912). On the inside front cover of the first notebook Flaherty, affixed a photograph of his mother Susan.

8 Flaherty was now traveling a familiar route, taking either the Temiskaming and Northern Ontario or Grand Trunk Pacific railway to its northern terminus. From there he went by canoe to Moose Factory along the possible water routes offered by the Missinaibi, Abitibi, Mattagami, Groundhog, and Moose rivers. Compared with the modest outfit of his first expedition, the second was ambitious in its supplies, so much so that Flaherty had to recruit four Ojibwa men from the Lake Temagami region to pilot the three boats he needed to transport his outfit. Crowell's role was to install and service a 25 hp White Steamer automobile engine in the *Nastapoka* – the launch Flaherty was to purchase and outfit at Moose. His other recruit, Eugene E. LaDuke, served as Flaherty's assistant on the subsequent Mackenzie expeditions as well as this one. LaDuke had probably been taken on as a consequence of his having been in the senior Flaherty's employ as a prospector. The relationship was an uneasy one, since LaDuke came to feel that Flaherty diminished the importance of his contributions. The upshot was Flaherty's dismissal of LaDuke in the fall of 1915, when their competitiveness over expeditionary leadership reached a flashpoint.

9 Conjurer's House was at the juncture of the Missinaibi and Moose rivers. Its fame had been fostered by the popular adventure-story writer, Stewart Edward White (1873–1946), whose *Conjuror's House* (1903) made the place a literary landmark. In their journey downstream to Moose, the Leith brothers also passed the site, describing it as "a great monolith of granite standing in the middle of boiling rapids, and rendered inaccessible by them, and since time immemorial regarded by the Indians as an object of superstitious veneration" (*Summer and Winter on Hudson Bay*, 25).

10 The *Nastapoka* was a 36 ft York boat, on which had been constructed a deck cabin to house four people snugly. The Steamer engine proved to be woefully inadequate, breaking down frequently. The *Nastapoka*, at best a coastal cruiser, was beached, near

wrecked, at Great Whale River a little under two months after leaving Moose. There it remained until Flaherty oufitted it for use as local transport during the fourth Mackenzie expedition.

11 During their stay at Great Whale River the Leith brothers met John Meluktuk, the man Flaherty hired as captain (spelling his name Mulucktoo). Meluktuk was the driver of the post's dog team and was described as follows by the Leith brother: "John is a handy man with a needle and always carries a kit with him ready to mend clothes, boots or harness as necessary. He talks Cree but not English, although he understands much that is said. Many Eskimos can talk the Cree language, but we did not see one Indian who could talk Eskimo. John has a remarkable sense of location and when out hunting with others is the one depended upon to find the way home. If there is a difference of opinion as to direction, John's choice settles the matter and is invariably correct. His knowledge of ice is phenomenal. Neither white man nor Indian would venture on ice John called unsafe" (*Summer and Winter on Hudson Bay*, 151, where there is also a photograph of Meluktuk).

12 A whaling station and a small HBC post, subsidiary to the main HBC post at Great Whale River, were established at Little Whale River in 1851. The whaling station was discontinued in 1870, and the HBC's trading activities were transferred to Great Whale in 1890.

13 The HBC factor at Great Whale River, Lewis G. Maver (1874–?), sometimes spelled Mavor, was of great assistance to Flaherty, and the two men remained correspondents over the next decade. They would have shared a fondness for the violin, an affinity we can surmise from what the Leith brothers reported about Maver: "Before going to the Whale River post we were told that the post manager had one weakness – he played the violin, and was especially fond of one piece, Schubert's Serenade – and if we wished to please our host we should approach the post whistling his favorite melody. While we did not follow this advice, before leaving Whale River post we were convinced that his reputation has not been exaggerated. Mr. Maver is not a musician, and above all not a violinist; but having heard the visiting parson [William Walton] play Schubert's Serenade, had fallen in love with it and was putting in his best efforts trying to master it. Morning, noon and night while we were at the post, whenever the violin was picked up, we heard the opening parts of Schubert's Serenade. The last part he never mastered, although we whistled it many times for his benefit. It is altogether likely that he is still persevering and, we hope, enjoying his music. As for us, Schubert's Serenade does not have the attractions it once had" (*Summer and Winter on Hudson Bay*, 94–5).

14 After this date there are no entries until Flaherty resumed the diary in January 1912. Since the Fort George HBC post journals for this period have not survived, we can only speculate on how Flaherty spent his time.

15 The Leith brothers photographed William Snowboy, an influential Cree hunter and camp leader (see *Summer and Winter on Hudson Bay*, 170). Snowboy's sons assisted both the Leiths and Flaherty as guides and dog drivers.

16 The Leith brothers also camped at Jimmy Salt's: "We snacked at the Indian camp of Salt, his wife cooking us some partridges. This is the dirtiest Indian camp I have yet seen. Salt is away at Fort George having a good time. He has a place in the Labrador edition of "Who's Who" through being mauled severely by a black bear some years ago" (ibid., 176).

17 In miscellaneous field notes to this expedition, Flaherty observed that the Eskimo

were "very fond of checkers" and often became very good players (Butler, MN1912).

18 This inventory of equipment and supplies is interesting not only for its particulars – especially those regarding the camera equipment – but also because it invites comparison with the inventory list that Flaherty prepared for his 1921 bear-hunting expedition (which appears just before the 17 Jan. 1921 entry in his diary). This is the first time Flaherty mentions his stills camera equipment. Although there was no mention of the camera(s) he used on the first expedition, it would not be a stretch of imagination to suggest that one or two were among his outfit. The Eastman plate camera was a workhorse piece of equipment; it required a tripod but was excellent for portrait and scenic studies. By contrast, the Graflex, an early hand-held SLR camera, was in its time a high-speed camera favored by photojournalists. George Eastman had purchased the maker of Graflex, Folmer and Schwing, in 1905, retaining its original brand name, and the firm continued to produce it well into the 1970s.

19 The ice break-up that prevented Flaherty from trying to reach the Belchers by sledge freed him to attempt what he had already considered as an alternative expedition (see entry for 23 February). Flaherty was clearly in a "discovery" mode. Using the work of Albert P. Low as the high-water mark, he attempted what Low had failed to accomplish in early 1900 when Low and Nero Fleming had tried to sledge seven hundred miles across the Ungava Peninsula to Fort Chimo. They got as far as Lake Minto, but finding no caribou and thus being unable to feed their starving dogs, they turned back.

20 Flaherty had mentioned that "Huskie Bill" Fleming had determined to accompany him on the trip to Fort Chimo, but he was unable to do so, as the HBC post journal for 12 March records: "Bill Fleming came to also accompany Robert Flaherty to Chimo. But since they had left already he returned to his camp" (Hudson's Bay Company Archives [HBCA] B372/a/18).

21 The Leith brothers also stayed at Jim Crow's camp: "This Grand Old Man of the West Labrador Coast is a fine looking Eskimo, and in his prime was a very powerful man. The early journals of the Little Whale and Great Whale posts mention him frequently. For a great many years he was a servant of the Hudson's Bay Company and retired when too old to longer hunt or voyage. He was always efficient, reliable, and good-natured. The Hudson's Bay officials and all who know or meet him have great respect for old Jim Crow. How old he is no one knows, not even himself. Harold says positively he is over one hundred years of age, and Rev Walton, the missionary, does not deny it. Now that his active career is over he lives by fishing and the bounty of the Company" (*Summer and Winter on Hudson Bay*, 175–6).

22 For many, the barrenness of the Barren Lands was epitomized by the Ungava Peninsula, which Flaherty was attempting to traverse. As early as Jacques Cartier's first voyage along the Labrador coast in 1534, Europeans had heard the first of many oft-repeated commentaries about this region. In his account, Cartier observed: "If the soil were as good as the harbours, it would be a blessing; but the land should not be called the New Land, being composed of stones and horrible rugged rocks; for along the whole of the north shore I did not see one cart load of earth and yet I landed in many places. Except at Blanc Sablon there is nothing but moss and short, stunted shrub. In fine, I am rather inclined to believe that this is the land God gave to Cain" (*The Voyages of Jacques Cartier*, 9–10).

23 If only from the perspective of a photographer, Flaherty was fascinated by arctic dogs, and he did not omit their snarling presence when filming *Nanook* some years later.

They were archetypal creatures to him and were necessary (since they sustained the life of those who could whip them into submission) but were cunningly dangerous in their appetite for any living or dead object, even before it was hit or put into the ground.

24 Although Flaherty never attained even an adequate fluency as a speaker of Inuktitut, he did retain key words and phrases; his efforts are manifested in the word lists he assembled in his diary for this second expedition and in the sixteen typed pages of words and phrases found in Butler, (MN1910), both of which are dated September 1911.

25 In miscellaneous field notes to the second expedition, Flaherty commented on standards of health: "Eskimo of higher health standards than Indian peoples. Pneumonia responsible for the greater number of deaths. Epidemic disease is an influenza or 'a la grippe.' No measles are discovered. Eskimos and half-breeds who live near or at posts suffer and are more susceptible to disease. The more primitive the most healthy. Fur system responsible to a great extent for present condition of natives. Diet is deplorable – coupled with native cooking had produced havoc among them" (Butler, MN1912). For a reference to an "epidemic" introduced by a visiting ship, see the opening of Flaherty's 1920–21 "Port Harrison Diary" in chapter 8, below.

26 Fort Chimo (renamed Kuujjuag), at the mouth of the Koksoak River in Ungava Bay had had an HBC presence since 1830. Draulette and Romanet established a Revillon post there in 1903.

27 The HBC men who accompanied Flaherty were: Harold Parker (1884–?), who had been with the HBC since 1909 and left the company to enlist in the Royal Navy in 1916; and David Edmonds (1871–1967), who served the HBC in the Ungava area 1910–35.

28 Though he made no mention in the diary of the departure of Wetunik and Omarolluk, he did so in his expeditionary report to Mackenzie: "Omarolluk and Wetunik were outfitted with a canoe and grub and sent back to Great Whale River post as soon as the ice conditions would permit. Though they capsized in a rapid on their first attempt, and were forced to return overland to their starting point, they were reoutfitted by the Hudson's Bay Co. and they finally reached Hudson Bay sometime in September" (Butler, MN1910).

29 Partridge, an influential hunter, was relied upon by incoming ships to pilot them through the dangerous tides of the Koksoak River. Maud Watt, the wife an HBC employee, met Partridge in 1915, photographed him, and recalled: "Partridge was a very tall old Eskimo, with a white beard. There was a big island in Ungava Bay named Akpatok where the white bears live in dens in winter. Partridge was the only Eskimo with sufficient courage to enter these dens for the white bearskins. He said it was not dangerous for the bears were sleepy, but nobody else cared to try" ("Chimo Days," 32). Partridge's son, Anghick ("Jimmy"), accompanied Flaherty on his traverse back to Hudson Bay from Fort Chimo.

30 Literary history has not been as approving of John Fox, Jr (1863–1919) and Winston Churchill (1871–1947) as it has of Twain and Balzac. At the turn of the century, both were hugely popular and widely read, Fox for his Tennessee Mountain adventure novels such as *The Little Shepherd of Kingdom Come* (1903) – reputedly the first American novel to attain sale of a million copies – and Churchill for his carefully researched historical romances such as *Richard Carvel* (1899) and *The Crossing* (1904).

31 In miscellaneous field notes to the second expedition, Flaherty commented on contemporary burial practices: "Method of burial at Fort Chimo consists of storing bod-

ies in boxes in a 'dead' house during winter and in June when the ground can be dug a wholesale burial in long trench – the bodies being piled in their boxes on Eskimo sledges and hauled by dog teams – people following. Gruesome to see dogs nosing about the remains of the people" (Butler, MN1912).

32 In his miscellaneous field notes to the second expedition, Flaherty reported: "Omarolluk has created sensation by saying that world was coming to an end very soon. Poor natives are frightened badly and keeping the missionary here busy replying" (Butler, MN1912).

33 Flaherty was describing an Inukshuk – those "monuments" that had been attracting his attention in caribou-hunting areas. They served not only as caribou lures but were frequently arranged so as to funnel the animals into water crossings or culs-de-sac, where they could more easily be killed by bowmen. When constructed at headlands, these piled-up boulders had the look of humans and often served as landmarks for travelers or as markers for caches.

34 Flaherty's plan was to materialize as he hoped. At the Wolstenholme post on 20 August he boarded the HBC supply ship *Nascopie*, inbound on her virgin voyage. On board, Flaherty met Samuel Sainsbury, who was to join his crew on the third expedition and greatly assisted Flaherty in his Baffin Island filmwork. The *Nascopie* brought Flaherty for the first and last time to the western coast of Hudson Bay, where he visited the HBC posts at Chesterfield Inlet, Fort Churchill and York Factory before disembarking at Charlton Island. From there he went to Moose Factory and then by canoe to the railhead at Cochrane. While at Fort Churchill, Flaherty photographed the dramatic ruins of Fort Prince of Wales, which had been captured and burned by the French in 1782. For an account of the *Nascopie*'s first voyage (written by its second officer) and a notice of Flaherty's boarding, see Mack, "The *Nascopie*," 5–9.

35 Flaherty was to remember this episode well. At this moment he was a photographer, while Nawri, Ambrose, and Nuckey were hunters. Their shots spoiled his. This incident was the basis of Flaherty's later reconstruction (in *My Eskimo Friends*, 133–4) of an alleged "conversation" he held with Nanook about the forthcoming filming of a walrus hunt:

> "Suppose we go," he reports, "do you know that you and your men may have to give up making a kill, if it interferes with my film? Will you remember that it is the picture of you hunting the iviuk that I want, and not their meat."
>
> "Yes, yes the aggie will come first," earnestly he assured me. "Not a man will stir, not a harpoon will be thrown until you give the sign. It is my word." We shook hands and agreed to start the next day."

36 On 8 August, Flaherty arrived at the HBC post at Cape Wolstenholme (renamed Ivujivik), its English place name having been given it in 1610–11 by the ill-fated Henry Hudson to honor one of his sponsors, the merchant-adventurer Sir John Wolstenholme (1562–1639). The HBC post, established in 1909 by John Ford and Ralph Parsons, was a particularly isolated one, and in its first years it struggled to survive. In his report to Mackenzie, Flaherty simply described it as "three flat roofed buildings." He placed a supply order for $126, including such items as a harmonica and three pounds of walrus tusks (HBCA, B368/6/2, folios 19–20). While there, Flaherty heard a story that stayed lodged in his imagination for the remainder of his life. The tale was first told as an entry in the HBC post's journal for 3 August 1912, three days before Flaherty's arrival: "When we returned from our hunt, we were surprised to see a small skin boat here, a family of 10 Esquimaux having come in from Mansfield Is-

land part on ice and part by Komatik to Digges Island and then after staying there nearly two months gathering small pieces of drift wood together managed to make a skin covered boat having been on Mansfield ten years and only living on what they could kill with bow and arrows. All their clothing is made of Bear Skin and their trading bought five white foxes and report a fine place for bear. The man's name is Koomak, a good hunter" (HBCA B368/a/1).

Flaherty mentioned meeting "Comock" in his report to Mackenzie but gave no further details. This is a story that he fashioned and refashioned in his later years. It first appeared, apparently co-authored with Chapman Hilder, in five installments, in the *Elks Magazine*, in 1928–29; then as an inset chapter 18, "The Story of Comock," in Flaherty's narrative of the North, *The Captain's Chair*, published in 1938. This version was condensed as "The Grim, Gallant Story of Comock the Eskimo" for *Reader's Digest*, July 1949, 169–80. A reading of it for the BBC was broadcast in January 1950 and reprinted in *The Cinema 1952*, edited by Roger Manvell and R.K. Nelson Baxter. Finally, the BBC version, illustrated with Eskimo drawings that Flaherty had privately published in 1915, was edited by Edmund Carpenter and published in 1968 as *The Story of Comock the Eskimo as Told to Robert Flaherty*. Flaherty regarded the story of Comock as the quintessential arctic narrative, epitomizing the ingenuity of the Inuit to survive in a relentless environment. The tale's migrations and its variations reveal Flaherty's ability as a narrator to take a casually related story and convert it into a minor arctic epic of human fortitude.

CHAPTER FIVE

1 Robert Flaherty Papers in Butler Library (hereafter Butler), MN1910
2 Ibid.
3 Little is known about Knight (who was elected in 1903), other than that he served as the nominator of Machin's election as a fellow in 1904. Machin probably knew of Flaherty's work through his earlier association with Flaherty's father, since Machin, an Ontario legislator, also had mining interests in the western Ontario areas where Flaherty senior had worked.
4 The accounts of the crossings by Clouston and Hendry are in Davies, *Northern Quebec and Labrador Journals and Correspondence, 1819–35*. Peck (1850–1924), the first Anglican missionary in the region, pioneered a mission at Little Whale River in 1859. Much regarded as an Inuktitut linguist, he published *Eskimo Grammar* and included an account of his 1884 crossing in his autobiographical work, *The Eskimo: Our Brethren of the Arctic*.
5 Flaherty to Mackenzie, undated report [November 1912?], Butler, MN1910
6 Ibid.
7 Ibid.
8 Flaherty to Mackenzie, 26 May 1913, Butler, MN1910
9 Ibid.
10 Flaherty to Mackenzie, 16 November 1914 and 24 February 1915, Butler, MN1910
11 Flaherty to Mackenzie, 26 May 1913, Butler, MN1910
12 Butler, MN1927
13 Flaherty to Mackenzie, 2 February 1915, Butler, MN1910
14 For the third expedition, the longest of the four he led, Flaherty kept the most com-

prehensive diaries yet. Typescript copies were made, under the supervision of Frances Flaherty, of all the diary notebooks except those of the fourth edition.

15 The captain of the *Laddie* was Harold Bartlett of Brigus, Newfoundland. The first mate was Stewart Gushue, who was to join Flaherty on the fourth expedition too. William ("Salty Bill") Robertson was cook-seamen and Eugene LaDuke was again Flaherty's assistant, as he had been on the second expedition. Sam Sainsbury, it will be recalled, had been on the *Nascopie* when Flaherty boarded at Cape Wolstenholme in the fall of 1912. He had been employed at Lake Harbour for two years, and Flaherty must have struck up a friendship with him. Hired as an interpreter and crew member, Sainsbury also kept a diary for the period 24 September 1913 to 14 October 1914 (Butler, MN1912), and it provides us with many particulars about daily life and, most importantly, filmmaking activities (in which Sainsbury actively participated as assistant and cameraman). These diary entries will be selectively noted when they parallel the dates and events in Flaherty's diary.

16 Wilfred Thomason Grenfell (1865–1940), an Oxford MD. To serve the fishing fleets and settlements of Labrador, he promoted the use of hospital ships and established throughout Labrador a chain of hospitals, medical stations, orphanages, and schools. Knighted in 1927 and the recipient of many honorary degrees, he published, among many other works about Labrador, *A Labrador Doctor*.

17 Flaherty photographed Robertson and published the portrait in "Winter on Wetalltok's Island," 542.

18 Flaherty's note to himself tells us at least one title among the "comprehensive range of reference and general literature" he included in his outfit for this expedition. Starting in 1818, Sir John Franklin (1786–1847) was associated with a succession of land and sea expeditions in search of that fabled waterway to Cathay, the Northwest Passage. These expeditions made him the preeminent arctic commander of his time. Parliament in 1818 provided an extra incentive for such ventures by promising an award of £20,000 to the discoverer of the Northwest Passage. Franklin's most ambitious expedition occurred in 1845, when, in the *Terror* and *Erebus* with a company of a hundred and forty, he set out only to disappear without a trace. A host of search expeditions were dispatched, and it was only in the late 1850s that evidence made clear that the ships had been abandoned sometime in 1847 and that all had eventually perished. The fate of the Franklin party was the centerpiece arctic disaster of the century. Although scraps of evidence were the only finds, the surge of expeditionary search activity did result in the charting of the hitherto unknown archipelago of the central Canadian Arctic.

19 The skipper of the *Laddie*, Captain Harold Bartlett, was not Flaherty's favored candidate for the assignment. In his proposal to Mackenzie for this expedition, he had suggested Captain Norman Freakley "of the Hudson's Bay Co. service, who is desirous of undertaking this work, and who is probably the best informed navigator of Hudson Bay and Straits at the present time. He has wintered on both James and Hudson Bay, and is also well experienced in the fur trade, and has had altogether an experience of 15 years in that country" (Butler, MN1910). Freakley's name is included in Flaherty's first expeditionary notes among the people he had been recommended to meet. In the fall of 1912, Bartlett had served as skipper of the *Jeanie*, which sank near Fort Churchill, an event that may have exacerbated Flaherty's growing unease about Bartlett's seamanship.

20 The Hudson's Bay Company had established posts at Cape Wolstenholme in 1909

and at Chesterfield Inlet and Lake Harbour (renamed Kimmirut) in 1911. By 1913 James Cantley (1895–1969) was serving as an HBC apprentice clerk and S. Hayward Parsons (1885–1965) as clerk. The area was still being serviced by the *Pelican*, which in 1901 had been decommissioned as a British man-of-war for service as an HBC supply ship. In 1911 Julian W. Bilby (1871–1932) and Archibald L. Fleming (1883–1953) established the Anglican mission at Lake Harbour with the help of the Rev. Peck. Bilby remained in arctic service only until 1913, but the experience of Baffin Island so left its mark on him that he later published *Among Unknown Eskimo*, which includes thirty photographs taken by Fleming, and *Nanook of the North*, a narrative which has nothing to do with the film but does include fifteen publicity photographs taken by Flaherty. Fleming went on to serve as the first bishop of the arctic and in his autobiography, *Archibald the Arctic*, he recalled that Flaherty was present on 21 December 1913 when the new mission church at Lake Harbour was consecrated: "Robert F. [sic] Flaherty was present at the opening. He was in charge of a mining and photographic expedition wintering more than a hundred miles to the west. He was to become famous as a motion-picture producer of such unusual films as *Nanook of the North*. At the time, however, we thought of him only as a vivid, entertaining guest, an excellent violinist and an incomparable raconteur" (145). In the fall of 1915, Frances Flaherty, homeward bound from having accompanied her husband to James Bay on the first leg of his fourth expedition, met Fleming aboard the *Nascopie*. She noted in her diary their meetings aboard and later visited him and Mrs Fleming in Toronto.

21 The Murray brothers, John and Alexander, of the *Active*, and the Canadian-born George Comer of the *Era* out of New Bedford, Massachusetts, were among the last of the whalers who were once as thick as birds in the Arctic of the mid-nineteenth century. None of them could sustain themselves totally on whaling. The Murray brothers, for example, sought profit in small-scale mining, as in these mica operations, as well as trading and hunting walrus and seal. Fleming knew John Murray well, extolling him in his autobiography as a fair and generous "father" to the Eskimo: "He was the old-time whaling captain at his best"(*Archibald the Arctic*, 164). John Murray later re-entered the Flaherty story when, in filming *Man of Aran* (1934), Flaherty hired him as a consultant to help direct the shark-harpooning scenes.

22 The pilot mentioned here is most likely Navolia, a Lake Harbour resident upon whom skippers such as Captain Mack of the *Nascopie* relied for piloting their ships into harbor. Of Navolia, Mack later wrote: "We had speculated ... as to whether Navolia would take the *Nascopie*, a much bigger ship than the *Pelican*, up the Lake Harbour run and through the Narrows as well as he had guided the Pelican. Navolia never turned a hair nor batted an eyelid, but was calm and cool. When it comes to pilots, Navolia is in the same class as Old Partridge was for the Koksoak River going up to Chimo – a pretty high class. To appreciate this, one must see these places at low tide, especially the Koksoak River" (Mack, "The *Nascopie*," 8). According to R.H. MacAulay, in 1934 Navolia was still piloting ships into Lake Harbour (Trading into Hudson Bay, 43).

23 The journals for all the northern Revillon posts are not to be found, so details about Devine and other Revillon employees are scarce. Although Ford (1880–1950) worked for Revillon between 1900 and 1917, he became an HBC man, retiring in 1938. He died in a helicopter accident, crashing into the very Koksoak River where Flaherty

had met him on the second expedition at Fort Chimo.

24 In a log that Captain Bartlett kept of the *Laddie*'s position, he noted that as early as 23 August they were concerned about the prospect of safely getting through the straits and down into Hudson Bay and the Belcher Islands. "The serious drawback of the delay in St. John's," he added, "is making itself apparent" (Butler, MN1912).

25 The Inuktitut word *Chimo* is an ever-present greeting in the western narratives of the North. Its general purpose was as a salutation, but more particularly it suggested on the speaker's part the sense of "Are you friendly?" with the desired reply being "Yes, we are friendly."

26 Flaherty certainly covers the range of musical taste, from the tenor ecstasies of Enrico Caruso (1873–1921) to Harry Lauder (1870–1950), who by 1913 ranked among the preeminent music hall performers of his age. Lauder's Highland tunes and homely patter were especially appealing to this generation of Orkney émigrés doing service in the North. As so often happened, native people were given the names of sports ("Jack Johnson") and entertainment celebrities, and a "Harry Lauder" was to assist Flaherty in his filmmaking work at Port Harrison in 1920–21.

27 We get a different perspective on Sainsbury's bilingual skills from the Cape Dorset artist and camp leader Peter Pitseolak who, in his autobiography *People from our Side* (88) gives a sharp vignette of Sainsbury as Flaherty's interpreter: "There were two white men. One was the boss and one was the interpreter, Samuellie. The interpreter could not speak Eskimo. He told them that he was able to speak the Eskimo language but he could not. That was why he was along on this trip!"

28 Bartlett's log entry for 17 September 1913 records the agreement Flaherty ultimately struck with the crew: "Mr. Flaherty has offered the Boatswain the wages of the Mate from the time Gushue left to work on shore until I am finished with him in Brigus. This gives him an additional $20 per month for his wages from September 13th to end of the voyage. The engineer is to receive $100 per month from August 14th until the end of the voyage instead of $50 as agreed on articles. The cook and sailors are to receive wages up to November 30th, 1913. These terms have been accepted by the crew and they agree to sail a man short according to the articles and give up the cooking stove in the forecastle. The master's wages will be paid monthly until the end of voyage 1914" (Butler, MN1910). Although this agreement undid Flaherty's wish to "effect a slight saving in salaries," his gain was bountiful in that he rid himself of the human tempests that would have most certainly erupted had he tried to winter a crew of ten in a building of 450 square feet.

29 The diary that Sainsbury kept on this expedition begins at this date. He too dwelt on the final unloading of cargo, and he recorded on 26 September: "When the work was finished and nothing more could be done for the day, we opened a barrel of candy and threw them in the air for the natives. This was great fun to watch the natives, especially the men, who were so excited running after the candy, bumped into their wives right and left throwing them on the ground – some of them received very nasty bruises" (Butler, MN1912).

30 Relying on contemporary identifications and the comments of Peter Pitseolak, the 1979–80 Vancouver Art Gallery exhibit identified Noahasweetow as Noogooshoweektok (Nungusuituq) and included a Flaherty photograph of him (illustration no. 36 in the exhibit's catalog, Danker, ed., *Robert Flaherty*, 10). Pitseolak recalled: "The moving picture boss got Noogooshoweetok, Joe and Attachie as Eskimo guides

and helpers. The real worker was Joe's son Avaleeniatuk. He was just a young man, Avaleeniatuk. Attachie was their dog team driver. Noogooshoweetok was the one they took pictures of – and he also made pictures for them. Noogooshoweetok was the first one to draw; the picture makers made him draw. I have seen Noogooshoweetok's drawings recently in books. He was my close relative. I remember he told me it was tiring to make drawings" (Pitseolak, *People from Our Side*, 88). The Vancouver exhibit also included a Flaherty photograph of Avaleeniatuk, no. 48 (Danker, *Robert Flaherty*, 44). In an unpublished "Early Account of the [1913–14] Film" (Butler, MN1913), Flaherty said of Noahasweetow that he "was easily first in either sledge driving or hunting amongst the motion picture retainers of the post and more than that he was the Eskimo artist par excellence at either drawing or carving on ivory." His only fault, Flaherty added, was that he was too controlled by his wife, Luliakame, who "through her jealous envy of the rival stars of the film work," frequently torpedoed her husband's participation in the filming.

31 Sainsbury amplifies this event, recording: "After reaching the camp I learned that several boats owned by different natives were going to leave for their winter quarters. At this opportune moment the moving picture camera was raised for the first time and several hundred feet of film was taken of the Esquimaux and the way they travel with their families at this particular time" (diary, 1 October 1913, Butler, MN1912).

32 It is likely that this nearly two-month gap occurs because the diary book that Flaherty kept for this period is lost. We get some assistance from Sainsbury, who reports intense trapping, including the capture of live foxes for filming purposes, and hunting activity, ventures that did not include Flaherty. As there was sufficient snowfall for packed snow, igloo construction for filming purposes began in late October and continued through November. Some entries Sainsbury made about filming are as follows:

> 31 October 1913 Several Esquimaux were employed building the broken igloo for moving pictures. This igloo had to be built 22 ft. in diameter in order to get the natives who are acting on the raised floor of the igloo, in the first interior scene. Later several feet of film were developed. It proved to be no good owing to under exposure.
>
> 15 November 1913 We started again to build a large igloo for moving pictures. The igloo took quite a long time to build owing to the softness of the snow. After that was finished another one was started. The second being attached to the large one enabled the Governor, who was operating the camera, to get sufficient space from the background to the outer dome ... Later in the night we started developing films that were taken during the last few days.
>
> 21 November 1913 Started taking motion pictures. When everything was ready, camera was set up at a given distance from the subjects that were to be taken. In order to get a good igloo view with the Esquimaux performing in the background, the camera had to be set up in another place in order to get this picture. While operating the camera some little thing went wrong with the film that could not be fixed in the intense frost but had to be taken into the house, which hindered us from doing any work during the forenoon (Butler, MN1912).

33 Anunglung was Noahasweetow's son, and according to later newspaper reviews and Flaherty's "Early Account of the [1913–14] Film," was the central figure in the Baffin Island film – an early counterpart, as it were, of Nanook.

34 Sainsbury's diary entry (11 December 1913) of the festival dinner is worthy of equal presentation: "Although it was not Christmas Day we decided to have our dinner.

Knowing that we would not be together for several weeks, this was agreed to. At 6 p.m. the work of decorating this camp for the coming event was started. The billiard table in the middle of the room was dressed for the occasion. At 7:30 it stood as follows: there were four kinds of candy, of the richest quality, Huyler's chocolates, and fruits of different kinds, which looked so rich and appetizing one could scarce keep from eating them; there was aspic jellied chicken, aspic jellied pigeon, olives, Boston brown bread, Chinese ginger, English plum pudding with rum sauce, champagne, brandy and grape juice to suit the occasion. The table was decorated with colored candles, while raisins burning in alcohol caused a great sensation among the Esquimaux waiters. The natives wondering at this great display of food asked if they could be permitted to look over the table. This was granted by the Governor, who seemed to be the jolliest man in the camp at this particular time. With Chinese fireworks darting about among the festoons and decorations made it all the more exciting. The natives who danced and shouted while a few quick tunes were played on the gramophone, asked for an explanation of this dinner, which was kindly explained to them by the Interpreter of the expedition. The Governor and Stewart drank freely of the champagne and scotch while LaDuke and myself enjoyed the fun ... That was a time, said the Esquimaux, that will never be forgotten by us, and long to be remembered in the history of Baffinland" (Butler, MN1912).

35 The deceased Murray whom Flaherty refers to here is Alexander, who died on 11 November 1912 aboard the *Active* off the Ottawa Islands. Murray's son, Ikidluak of Lake Harbour, whom Dorothy Harley Eber interviewed, recalled: "The captain died on that last trip. Before we spent the winter, the captain was already gone. He died probably not from illness but from alcohol, and he was bound up by his crew. Probably the crew was afraid of him. Why they tied him up, I didn't know. Maybe he didn't get along with his crew. I don't know for what reason he was bound. He was shouting out for Inuit people by their names, but the crew would not allow them to go to him. I don't remember hearing whether there was a lot of alcohol on the ship, but I know there was some because the captain died of drink. The crew bound him up" (Eber, *When the Whalers Were Up North*, 142).

In *My Eskimo Friends*, 37, Flaherty comments on the lethal presence of alcohol aboard the *Active*, noting that two of the crew also died from alcohol toxicity. Flaherty later met Alexander's brother John on the *Active* as he headed south toward the Belcher Islands.

36 The HBC post's journal for Cape Wolstenholme recorded the disasters that befell Ford and the Shepherds:

30 July 1913 This evening the burial service was read over Mrs Shepherd's body which was put into a coffin and sealed up so that it may be sent south. I cannot bear the idea of burying her here as this post may be abandoned at anytime and the grave left neglected and forlorn.

18 August 1913 It is with deep regret that I have to record the death by drowning of Mr. C.C. Shepherd and Mr. William R. Ford this afternoon through the capsizing of their canoe while out shooting. We have searched diligently for them but without success, only picking up Mr. Ford's cap.

21 August 1913 Continued with the search for missing men but found no trace and compelling us to give up hope of finding them alive. Read the funeral service today. (Hudson's Bay Company Archives [HBCA], B368/a/3)

37 Ralph Parsons (1881–1956) had been instrumental in establishing that second gen-

eration of HBC posts north of Great Whale River, beginning with the post at Wolstenholme in 1909 and at Cape Dorset (renamed Kingnait) in September 1913. Rising to the position of district manager and then fur trade commissioner (1931–40), he was the last to hold that title. J.W. Anderson observed that Parsons, "one of the outstanding personalities in the history of modern HBC fur trade, was the man responsible for the development of this trade with the Eskimos of the eastern and central Arctic" (Anderson, *Fur Trader's Story*, 208). Bishop Fleming knew Parsons well and spoke of him as "a fabulous image of power and fame" (Fleming, *Archibald the Arctic*, 259–60).

38 Flaherty's photograph of Allego (Shining Water) was included in the Vancouver exhibition as no. 33, (Danker, *Robert Flaherty*, 27). Dorothy Eber was told by Baffin Island informants that Allego was Flaherty's darkroom assistant and that she particularly enjoyed listening to his gramophone. The Vancouver catalog noted that Allego "was probably living with Noogooshoweetok [the Noahasweetow of Flaherty's diary] at the time but later moved away with an older man from a northern region. She returned many years later with very beautiful tatoos, shaman's powers and the fire and seaweed as helping spirits. She married Alariak, another shaman, and they became famous South Baffin shamans. Allego and Alariak also posed for the camera of Peter Pitseolak [*People from Our Side*, 28]. Allego eventually left Alariak and went to Churchill where she was trampled to death by intoxicated people around 1957" (Danker, *Robert Flaherty*, 86).

39 Luke Foxe (1586–1635), like his English predecessors Frobisher, Davis, Baffin, and Bylot, sought the Northwest Passage. In 1631 he sailed north through the channel that bears his name and then south into James Bay and back out through Hudson Strait in one season. The voyage was accomplished without loss of crew and was remarkable beyond its time for its disciplined seamanship.

40 Flaherty in his entry for 5 February speaks of this shipwreck again, but with a less dire outcome for its crew. Sainsbury, in his entry of 2 April 1914, provides additional details: "Owing to its heaviness and strong wind we did not reach Polar Star land until 5:30 p.m. This place is really the south end of Gordon Bay, but called Polar Star Land by the Esquimaux. Some 15 years ago a Scotch whaler named *Polar Star* was lost at this place, and it has always been called by the Esquimaux Polar Star Land. This old vessel has been very useful to the Esquimaux in making kayaks, sledges, and hunting utensils. A part of the old wreck can now be seen projecting out of the tidal ice" (Butler, MN1912). The bonanza of the *Star* still thrived in the memories of the contemporary Cape Dorset residents whom Dorothy Harley Eber interviewed in the early 1980s. Their memories and the drawings of the *Star* by Pitseolak Ashoona appear in Eber's *When the Whalers Were Up North*, 69–75. The *Polar Star* also proved useful to the local white traders: the Cape Dorset HBC journal of 6 April 1914 recorded that one of the ship's oil tanks had been salvaged to serve as a storage container for seal oil. It took fourteen men and twenty dogs – humans and beasts in harness alike – to haul the 2,500 lb tank to the post (HBCA B397/a/1).

41 The Vancouver exhibition identified Cunayow (Kanajuq, "Devil Fish") as the sitter for Flaherty in photograph no. 29, (Danker, *Robert Flaherty*, 28). The attribution was made by Peter Pitseolak and others. In *My Eskimo Friends*, 75, and elsewhere Flaherty captioned Cunayow as Allego. This "little lady of the snows" – as the *Toronto Star* featured her among three other Flaherty photographs in its article "Fellow Citi-

zens 1500 Miles Away" (28 March 1915) – became in its wide circulation the touchstone image of the arctic beauty.

42 The HBC post journal at Cape Dorset reported the disappearance of Shee on 10 November 1913. The return of the third party that Flaherty describes was entered in the HBC post's journal on 3 February 1914, a few days before his arrival. The notice of the disappearance of the second party, Senejot and Luketak, was reported in an entry on 15 December 1913, which closed with the lament, "The loss of these hunters means a no small loss to the Company" (HBCA, B397/a/1).

43 John Edmonds (1894–?) was reputed to be a skilled interpreter, having been born in the Davis Inlet area. Although Flaherty perceived this new HBC post as useful to his expeditionary supply needs, the Parsons brothers – not quite through their first season – regarded Flaherty with some suspicion, having heard of his heavy trapping activity, and before his visit to the post they viewed him as a competitor: "Up to the present none of the Dorset customers have been visited by these traders which I understand is managed by R.J. Flaherty and located at Amadjuak Bay" (Cape Dorset HBC journal, 25 December 1913). During his visit, it is interesting to observe how Flaherty tried to allay their concerns by the way he presented his purposes to them for being in the area: "Mr. Flaherty is engaged in Ethnological work, moving pictures and portrait making, mineral prospecting and collecting old Eskimo curios and costumes" (HBCA, B379/a/1), 6 February 1914.

44 The Stewart mentioned here was on the threshold of a legendary career as an HBC man. Stephen J. ("Lofty") Stewart (1893–1967) served from 1913 to 1949 in various posts about Hudson Bay and the Baffin Island area, his name and zestful personality being a household reference among seasoned northern hands.

45 Flaherty does not elaborate on his note other than to record in his entry for 1 March that Ralph Parsons took his revenge upon the "crooked" Tuckpannie by demolishing his two rifles with an ax.

46 Like Flaherty, Sainsbury was riveted by the spectacle of the northern lights: "The rays shoot up more rapidly, then they become shorter – all rise together and approach nearer and nearer to the zenith where a great circle is formed. Then they dart out in all directions, all at once the great circle falls asunder ... All at once as if some great voice calls them they rush to the great circle, down they shoot and up again until the circle becomes like a sea of fire of the richest colors. What are the shades – who can describe them. All four colors dart out at the same time – the whole sky is in flames. Nature displays before us such an exhibition of fireworks as transcends the power of the imagination" (diary, 26 February 1914, Butler, MN1912).

47 In *My Eskimo Friends* (123), Flaherty elaborates on his filmmaking activities during this period: "February came, cold but glowingly clear and calm. Then we began our films. We did not want for cooperation. The women vied with one another to be starred. Igloo building, conjuring dances, sledging, and seal-hunting were run off as the sunlit days of February and March wore on. Of course there was occasional bickering, but only among the women – jealousy, usually, of what they thought was the over-prominence of some rival in the film. One young mother, whom, with her baby, I was in the midst of filming one clear day, suddenly got up, and despite my threats and pleas, walked away. Neither she nor her husband had been up to snuff of late, so I decided to send them away. 'Don't care,' she said, when in the most impressive way we announced her fate, 'seals are the best food anyway.' But old Yew, ever father of

his flock, interposed, and what was finally picked out from the crazy-quilt of his pidgin English was that she was not altogether wrong. Two times in as many days I had given Luliakame's (her rival's) baby candy, but I 'no see him.'"

48 Sainsbury reported the success of his haul with a flourish of self-approval: "During the last month our cooking range gave out and it was impossible to cook with it. Knowing that the Hudson's Bay Company had a spare range we decided to buy it. It had to be brought 160 miles over portages and rough ice, which took all of my time to keep it from breaking. However, I succeeded in making the trip to Dorset and back again with the stove without even breaking a screw" (diary, 4 March 1914, Butler, MN1912). By this point, Ralph Parsons was getting increasingly irritated by Flaherty's habit of enlisting whomever he wishes to serve either his expeditionary or his film goals. Parsons wrote to Flaherty on 26 March 1914 providing a list of thirty-nine Eskimo who, he declared, were under irrevocable five-year contracts as HBC servants. He added, "Should you require any of the above named Eskimos to work for you for a short term, please communicate with this office" (Butler, MN1910).

49 In an undated, untitled narrative which David Flaherty, for cataloging purposes, entitled "Early Account of the [1913–14] Film" (Butler, MN1913), Flaherty detailed the printing process he conducted in the field:

> The technical side of the film work, owing to our peculiar circumstances and location were interesting. The bulk of the film development occurred during the later days of March and all through April when for five or six days on end the combined services of all hands at camp were called into requisition. A ten dog team, a fourteen foot sledge with two water casks lashed thereon and the whole manipulated by three boys of the camp ("Kitchen Hangers-On," as the cook called them collectively and "Tooth Brush," "Button Hole," and "Doughnut" individually), were kept constantly on the go bringing water from a half a mile distance from a hole through the ice that had been kept open all through the winter. The water haulage amounted to over four tons a day, all of which had to be carried by hand through the long tunnel into our own quarters where it was poured into a wash tank of developed film and then carried out and thrown away. At night our camp crowded quarters held the drying film at center, suspended from the ceiling, a thousand feet of it and more, and around which it was necessary to circulate with the greatest care, for fear of dust and fire.
>
> How the natives and visitors of an evening used to gather around the bands of tiny pictures, hardly larger than a postage stamp … and listen patiently whilst we tried to make them understand the intricacies of motion pictures generally. They used to listen in great interest when we tried to explain how many people far to southward would see them again in the very actions they had gone through for the camera, all of which old Atchaweek in his quaint point of view: 'I do hope that many "kaplunak" will like us, but I cannot see why anyone would want to see a common igloo and just an ordinary team of traveling dogs.' That was all that seemed to be the queer part of their attitude. They could never quite understand why we bothered about such ordinary affairs of life.

The above narrative contains minor editorial changes in Frances's hand.

50 On their journey Sainsbury reported a close encounter with marauding wolves: "After leaving the camp we saw several wolves at which several shots were fired, but none secured. At noon whilst crossing the lake some fifty miles from the camp we were attacked by a band of 4 or 5 wolves, these animals being very hungry and vicious made

a dash for my dogs, knowing that if they were allowed to enter the team I would lose quite a number of my dogs. The Esquimaux boy being excited, the safety of the team remained with myself, pulling my rifle from the sledge I aimed and in a few seconds one big fellow was tumbling in the deep snow about 25 yards from the sledge. Two shots were fired at the second one ... If there had been a full band of these animals I fear we would have shared the worst fate. This is my first experience of being attacked by wolves in this country, and the natives say it is an unusual thing, the animals must have been in a starving condition" (diary, 12 April 1914, Butler, MN1912).

51 Sainsbury's entries for May provide us with further particulars on filmmaking activities:

> 24 May 1914 The morning was spent arranging for moving pictures. After breakfast a snow platform was raised so many feet from the ground for the purpose of feeding the dogs. While the picture was taken many dogs broke into the provision tent, which hindered us from taking any other pictures during the afternoon. Later in the evening a special igloo was built for pictures.
>
> 25 May 1914 A series of pictures were taken of the Esquimaux making a fire with pyrites and willowdown, which was specially prepared for the purpose. This picture took quite a lot of film owing to the slowness of the woman operating the lamp – one needs much patience in taking pictures of the Esquimaux, who are the slowest people under the sun. 4 p.m. it began to freeze and snow, making it impossible to work outside.
>
> 28 May 1914 At 12:30 started developing films ... kept us busy until midnight. We have at present in the camp 11 Esquimaux families for moving picture purposes. Later retired quite tired and sick of this work and the Esquimaux. (diary, ibid.)

52 Flaherty's account of this in *My Eskimo Friends* (123–4) is at odds with his diary report that the dogs, but not the sledge, went through the ice:

> On the tenth of June I prepared for our long-planned deer-filming expedition, and on the following day, with camera and retorts of film and food for twenty days, Anunglung and I left for the deer grounds of the interior. Through those long June days we traveled far ... We were picking out a course when Anunglung pointed to what seemed to be so many boulders in a valley far below. The boulders moved. "Tooktoo!" Anunglung whispered. We mounted camera and tripod on the sledge. Dragging his six-fathom whip ready to cow the dogs before they gave tongue, Anunglung went on before the team. We swung in behind the shoulder of an intervening hill. When we rounded it we were almost amongst them. The team lunged. The deer, all but three, galloped to right and left up the slope. Three kept to the valley. On we sped, the camera rocking like the mast of a ship at sea. From the galloping dogs to the deer not two hundred feet beyond, I filmed and filmed and filmed. Yard by yard we began closing in. The dogs, sure of victory, gave tongue. Then something happened. I am not altogether clear as to how it happened. All that I know is that I fell headlong into a deep drift of snow. The sledge was belly-up, and across the traces of the bitterly disappointed team Anunglung was doubled up with laughter.
>
> Within two days we swung back for camp, jubilant over what I was sure was the film of films. But within twelve miles of the journey's end, crossing the rotten ice of a stream, the sledge broke through. Exit film.

53 In the "Early Account of [1913–14] Film," Flaherty detailed the circumstances of this stream-fording scene:

In one of the film scenes, Anunglung with his two wives and family were to ford, with sledge and dogs, a tumbling stream to its far shore. The stream selected was a stiff little river for we were keen of course to get an effective picture. None of them funked it for a moment, though the two wives carried babes on the hoods of their kooletahs. They were to sweep down from the hills, the dogs galloping from the river's edge, while Sainsbury and I with the machine located on a rock in midstream were to film their approach and fording. The signal given, down the hillside they came pell mell, the dogs howling like a band of wolves. At the edge of the bank they halted a moment but with a few threatening reaches of the long cracking whip they plunged into the swirl of water and slowly toward midstream they worked their way, the women at the sledge's side often waist high in the rush of frigid water. So perfect was Anunglung's control of the leader dog that even amidst the roaring of water he responded. They reached midstream, then halted and turned in whining fear of the deep swift water before them, but dreading still more the long lash which presently sang through the air above them, they plunged, the smaller of them caught beyond their head-high depths, swept down the rapids to their trace ends which alone held them and prevented them from being carried down on the tongue of water which writhed its way under the ice edge of the sea shore. The deep channel of the rapid's center caught the women breast high but over it they went like Spartans, their babes' little eyes round with bewilderment and within their own little arm's reach of the river's surface. I omitted to mention that a Winchester, tobacco and beads lay waiting for them on the far bank. (Butler, MN1913)

There are good grounds to believe that Flaherty photographed Sainsbury operating the camera midstream. The photograph in question first appeared in a Bell & Howell advertising brochure (24 March 1915) in which Flaherty provided a testimonial to the motion-picture camera he used on the third expedition. The photo appears with the caption "At the ford, Kokjuak River, Baffins [sic] Island, March 1914" (Butler, MN1910). The photo also appears in Rotha, *Robert Flaherty* (51), which incorrectly, in my view, identifies the camera operator as Flaherty and the photographer as unknown. The Vancouver exhibition catalogue includes the photo (no. 111) and suggests, I believe correctly, that Sainsbury was the camera operator and Flaherty the photographer. A sticking point is Flaherty's dating of the photograph in the testimonial as March 1914. Neither he nor Sainsbury mentioned shooting a stream-fording sequence in March, an unlikely month in which to shoot such a sequence, but he did mention two stream-fording shots in July (on the fourth and seventh). This was much more the season for such a sequence, as Flaherty noted in his entry of 11 July: "River a roaring torrent now and sounds very distinct at camp."

54 In his log, Bartlett reported the many hazards and delays they experienced in trying to reach Amadjuak: "14 August 1914. We left St. John's a month ago today, and have only come 1,000 miles from Cape Mugford to our present position, ice of the heaviest nature has been met, we have tried to get inshore and offshore to get through since July 29th, also Grey [sic] Strait there is no other way to try now but wait until the ice opens again. The ice today is different from any we have met, being in big sheets and flat with an average thickness of about 15 feet. Our present position is the best possible to avoid danger from crushing, being midway between Buttons and Resolution" (Butler, MN1912).

55 In this entry, Flaherty glided past a problem – making purchases on credit without ei-

ther he or Mackenzie making good on the invoices – an omission that stalked him in his future commercial relations with the Hudson's Bay Company. Sainsbury was more explicit about the conflict over credit advances that Flaherty had with Ralph Parsons: "After we dropped anchor [at Cape Dorset] the commander of the expedition went on shore to see the factor in charge of the post. After a short conversation, which was not very friendly, between the two men he returned to the boat again in an unpleasant temper. During the winter there had been some grievances between the district manager and the Governour, which brought the two parties to unfriendly terms, not having enough food to take the vessel to James Bay we tried to purchase some from the Hudson's Bay Co. Post at Cape Dorset, but this could not be done without cash on delivery. Later there was enough money raised among the members of the party to buy provisions enough to keep the expedition moving. At 7 p.m. of the 25th we left Cape Dorset for Cape Wolstenholme" (diary, 24 August 1914, Butler, MN1912).

56 Alexander Mackie Chalmers (1892–1956) from Aberdeen was at the beginning of his HBC career, as a clerk. Apart from three years service in the First World War, he remained an HBC employee until 1952.

57 Bartlett's log of 27 August 1914 shows increasing traces of friction between him and Flaherty over the conduct of the expedition. Fretting over the wisdom of harboring in Erik Cove, Bartlett did so only upon Flaherty's order to drop off Sainsbury "to go out by the *Pelican* with Mr Flaherty's results of the past winter, as Sainsbury is Mr Flaherty's servant and not a member of the crew it is unnecessary and not in my place to make any comment about it" (Butler, MN1912).

58 In one of his last entries, Sainsbury described his homeward voyage: "On the morning of the 21st the *George B. Cluett*, an auxiliary schooner chartered by the Carnegie Institute of Washington arrived at Wolstenholme to take on board a supply of water for her homeward trip. After a short interview with the Captain I managed to secure a passage from Wolstenholme to St Anthony, on the east coast of Newfoundland. During our passage, which lasted 10 days, we nearly perished having nothing but salt water to drink for 10 days. Owing to a mistake of the sailors when filling the tanks putting in salt water rather than fresh. On reaching Battle Harbour, I was four days continually drinking before my thirst was properly quenched" (diary, 29 August 1914, Butler, MN1913).

59 Flaherty was alluding to one of many conjectures that surrounded the sinking of the Scottish whaler *Seduisante* ("The Seducer") with all its crew off Nottingham Island on 24 September 1911. Its captain and owner, Osbert C. Forsyth-Grant, who at Cape Heaven maintained one of the last independent whaling-trading stations, was described as follows by Bishop Fleming: "Grant was an intense man; intense in his love of justice, equally intense in his hate. There was something arrogant in his handsome head, in the sensitive mouth that could curl into a sneer ... I am sure he could be dangerous if thwarted" (*Archibald the Arctic*, 123). On the eve of the *Seduisante*'s sinking, Inuit crew members, whom Grant had sent ashore, returned to urge all to abandon ship and met a drunken and mutinous crew. They later reported hearing gunfire aboard the ship during the night. This speculation-riven disaster and the career of its captain is examined by Robert J. Fraser in *Arctic Adventurer: Grant and the Seduisante* and by Dorothy Harley Eber in *When the Whalers Were Up North*, 135–9.

60 Bartlett's log shows him increasingly on edge with Flaherty's wish to sail south to

Hudson Bay rather than east through Hudson Strait and then on to Newfoundland – the original sailing plan for the expedition. In his log of 30 August 1914, he noted that he had told Flaherty that by 10 September they should head for St John's because provisions would not last beyond 10 October (Butler, MN1912).

61 Flaherty, it is now clear, was determined to carry out the functional purpose of the third expedition: to find and explore the Belcher Islands. His order to sail south rather than east resulted in a second mutinous response from Bartlett and the crew. Although Flaherty's diary is silent on this point, Bartlett's log for 5 September 1914 records the following agreement:

> Ordered to proceed to Moose Factory via the Belcher Islands. The *Laddie* will winter at Moose and the crew sent to St. John's Nfld. via Cochrane by canoe. The following agreement was signed by Robt. J. Flaherty.
>
> (1) I, Robt. J. Flaherty of Port Arthur, Canada, Commander of the expedition on the schooner *Laddie* agree to the following conditions should the said schooner winter at Moose Factory, James Bay or at any place in the vicinity.
>
> To pay to the master and crew the full value of all instruments, clothing, stock, etc. belonging to the said master or crew, if such instruments, clothing, stock, etc. be left at Moose or any other place that the *Laddie* may winter and if the same is not delivered to final port of discharge this season in good condition. (St. John's Newfoundland or Brigus, Nfld. either port to be considered final port of discharge.)
>
> (2) That all transportation expenses, outfit for crew, extra clothing for crew, etc. to be paid by owners of *Laddie*, value of instruments, clothing, stock, etc to be based upon cost of same in Nfld. (Butler, MN1912)

Flaherty was to be spared most of these contracted expenses, for Bartlett's log of 25 September 1914 noted that Flaherty arranged for him and the crew to travel outbound to Newfoundland, with their goods, on the *Nascopie*. Stewart Gushue, the first mate, was to stay with Flaherty and Eugene LaDuke, while William Robertson and Michael O'Leary were to remain in Moose Factory with the *Laddie*. Captain Harold Bartlett was to board the *Nascopie* with the following crew members: James Robinson, Ken French, James Way, John Kelly, and Richard Leary (Butler, MN1912).

62 What with the news that England had declared war, and the arrival of the annual supply ship *Nascopie*, these two weeks at Great Whale River and Moose Factory took on the heady spirit of a revival meeting. There would have been meetings with the Nero Fleming–Harold Udgaarden clan, as well as with Flaherty's companions of the second expedition, Wetunik and Omarolluk. There was also Ernest Renouf (1893–?), first mentioned in the 17 September entry. Renouf was serving as clerk to the HBC factor Lewis Maver, and Robert and Frances Flaherty met him again in the fall of 1915. Aman is perhaps Harold A. Calkins, an assistant to Tees (W. Tees Curran, 1866–1936). Both made several exploratory trips along the eastern coast of Hudson Bay and wrote of their travels in *Glimpses of Northern Canada* and *In Canada's Wonderful Northland*. The Wilson and Mackenzie whom Flaherty met on the way to Moose were Frank D. Wilson (1856–1925), the HBC district manager for James Bay, and N.M.W.J. ("Alphabetical") Mackenzie (1857–1945), HBC district manager for the Lake Superior district and author of *The Men of the Hudson's Bay Company*. The annual arrival of the *Nascopie* was no doubt the reason for their presence in the area when Flaherty arrived.

CHAPTER SIX

1 The anecdote appears in a memorial article written on Flaherty's death (Evans, "Wander No More," 13).
2 Letters and papers related to Frances Hubbard Flaherty's early years are housed at the Butler Library in the Hubbard Family Papers (hereafter HFP).
3 Frances Johnson Hubbard [Flaherty], *Decennial Record of the Class of 1905 in Bryn*, 53–6
4 Ibid.
5 These newspaper cuttings can be found in Butler, MN1910.
6 Ibid.
7 One item not found among the Butler papers is "Rare Pictures of Baffinlanders Secured by Sir William Mackenzie's Geographical and Motion Picture Expedition, 1913–1914" (*Canadian Courier*, 27 March 1915).
8 HFP, Frances Flaherty's diary, 4 November 1915
9 Ibid., 22 November 1915
10 Ibid., 22 February 1916
11 Ibid., 10 March 1915
12 Ibid., 2 March 1915
13 Ibid.
14 Ibid., 1 February 1915
15 Butler, MN1910
16 HFP, box 1
17 HFP, Frances Flaherty's diary, 1 February 1915
18 Audiotape interview with Frances Flaherty Ruttan by Susan Boyd-Bowman for the Vancouver Art gallery, 23 July 1979. During the interview, Flaherty Ruttan observed, "He never did like to make public speeches till much later on in life anyway."
19 HFP, Frances Flaherty's diary, 1 February 1915
20 Butler, MN1910
21 Ibid.
22 The most comprehensive effort so far made to reconstruct the content and context of Flaherty's Baffin and Belcher Islands films appears in the "First Films" section of the Vancouver Art Gallery catalogue (Danker, *Robert Flaherty*, 52–7).
23 HFP, Frances Flaherty's diary, 19 April 1915
24 *Toronto World*, March 1915, Butler, MN1910
25 Unspecified Toronto newspaper cutting, March 1915, MN1910
26 For the quotations from Sainsbury, see his diary in Butler, MN1912.
27 Butler, MN1912, Sainsbury's diary, 27 February 1914. Although we can appreciate Flaherty's zeal to promote the Bell & Howell camera, his closing comment in his testimonial about it – "We at no time had any trouble from static sparking" (Butler, MN1910) – ignores the static problem which Sainsbury reports.
28 HFP, Frances Flaherty's diary, 9 April 1915
29 Eber, "On Koodjuk's Trail," 81
30 HFP, Frances Flaherty's diary, 3 March 1915
31 Bridle, "Sir William MacKenzie," 67–8
32 HFP, Frances Flaherty's diary, 13 April 1915

33 Ibid.
34 Ibid.
35 Robert and Frances Flaherty Study Center at Claremont University (hereafter Claremont), audiotape 231A/side 2
36 HFP, Frances Flaherty's diary, 3 October 1915
37 The typescript, prepared by Frances, is at Butler, MN1913. The diary is a compilation of entries into which are woven numerous letters. In addition to Robert, other correspondents are her mother, Frances Lambard Hubbard (1852–1927), and her elder sister, Charlotte Hubbard Goodell (1876–1960). Frances and Charlotte were lifetime correspondents, and the "Dear Tottie" and "Patsy" letters also formed the core of diary narratives that Frances kept later in life.

In December 1914, when the diary begins, Frances and Robert were living at 36 Roxborough Drive, a house they were renting in Toronto.
38 There had been some discussion of Mackenzie visiting the Belcher Islands, a visit that Flaherty was encouraging in order to gain support for the proposed expedition of 1915–16. Although Mackenzie was the sponsor of the expedition, he commissioned Flaherty's father to assess the iron ore potential of the Belchers, as he again did in August 1916.

In this entry, Frances erroneously refers to Canadian National Railways as "the Canadian National Railroad," and she speaks of "Hudson's" Bay instead of Hudson Bay. Such errata often occur in her diary.
39 These drawings, twenty-one in number, were published privately in 1915 by Flaherty under the title *Drawings by Enooesweetok of the Sikosilingmint Tribe of the Eskimo, Fox Land, Baffin Island*. Although Frances was keen to have Robert convert his exploratory work into literary currency, he did not write the introduction she so urged but instead included a headnote: "These Drawings were Made at Amadjuak Bay, Fox Land, the Winter Quarters of Sir William Mackenzie's Expedition to Baffin Land and Hudson's Bay, 1913–1914." A limited facsimile edition of the drawings, edited by Edmund Carpenter, was published in 2001.
40 Alan Sullivan (1868–1947), a Canadian author of some forty novels, was noted for picturesque wilderness novels such as *Under the Northern Lights* (1926). He shared Flaherty's affinity for the North since, educated as an engineer, he had been an employee of the Canadian National Railways.
41 Sir John Franklin's career has already been outlined in chapter 5, note 18. In the convoluted chronicle of Sullivan's wish to transform Flaherty's diaries into a Franklinlike narrative, it was Frances who eventually wished Sullivan to vanish.
42 Charles T. Currelly (1876–1957), the first curator (1907–13) and founding director (1914–46) of the Royal Ontario Museum of Archaeology provided the first public venue for Flaherty's Baffin Island film. The ethnographic material – the "curios" mentioned throughout the diaries – collected on behalf of Mackenzie by Flaherty were donated to the museum. In his autobiography, *I Brought the Ages Home*, Currelly alludes to Flaherty's later fame as a filmmaker and acknowledges that he gave "a magnificent lot of material from his expeditions" 296. Frances's diary entry of 1 February 1915 gives us a decidedly different report on Mackenzie's view of the donation: "All you brought down was a lot of damned curios and we had to give those away."
43 As befits Toronto's Arts and Letters Club, it displayed paintings by noteworthy Canadian artists: John W. Beatty (1869–1941), known for his landscapes, one of which – a snowscape – Frances later received as a Christmas present from Robert; also Alexan-

der Y. Jackson (1882–1974) and James E.H. MacDonald (1874–1932), both of whom became founding members of the "Group of Seven." The Flahertys' association with the Arts and Letters Club gave them entree to Toronto's elite, including the gentleman whom Frances shortly mentions, Augustus Bridle (1869–1952), an early admirer of Flaherty's photographic work.

44 Alvin L. Coburn (1882–1966) was a master portraitist of artists and writers. In addition to those mentioned by Frances, he did photographs of Matisse, Augustus John, Gertrude Stein, W.B. Yeats, Alfred Stieglitz, Mark Twain, and Henry James, among others, which can be seen in his autobiography, *Alvin Langdon Coburn: Photographer.*

45 Frances is referring to George Bryce's *The Remarkable History of the Hudson's Bay Company.*

46 Sir William Howard Hearst (1864–1941) served as premier of Ontario 1914–19. In general, Flaherty and Mackenzie had little success in getting government support for their expeditions. The "Mr E" is the Mr Englehardt (Jacob Lewis, 1847–1921) whom Frances mentions on 11 March 1915. As president of the Temiskaming and Northern Ontario Railway, he, like Mackenzie, was eager to explore the use of Hudson Bay, and a rail spur to it, as a transport gateway to the European market.

47 Frances provides a rollcall of the leading polar explorers of her day. Robert F. Scott (1868–1912) lost the race to reach the South Pole to Roald Amundsen (1872–1928). The Norwegian reached the pole in December 1911, a month ahead of Scott who, with his entire party, perished before they could return to base camp. The Australian, Sir Douglas Mawson (1882–1958), led major scientific expeditions to the Antarctic, his most celebrated one being that of 1911–14 when, as the lone survivor of a small surveying party, he suffered the privations of a near fatal trek to safety. The Manitoba-born Vilhjalmur Stefansson (1879–1962) lost his ship, *Karluk*, and lived for two years in the Arctic among Inuit groups, an experience that led him to argue for greater adaptation by explorers of Native knowledge and techniques. A prolific lecturer and writer, he became a vigorous promoter of northern development with such booster works as *The Friendly Arctic* and *The Northward Course of Empire.* Frances knew of his work, for she cites a passage from his *My Life with the Eskimo* in her diary on 7 January 1915. Finally, there is Sir Ernest H. Shackleton (1874–1922), who gave early assistance to both Scott and Mawson and who came within 100 miles of the South Pole on his 1907–9 expedition. Shackleton, too, endured shipwreck and privation, but in a heroic open-boat rescue effort he brought aid to his stranded crew during his 1914–17 expedition, the one that Frances refers to as just having departed that fall.

48 The Bartletts were a distinguished family of Newfoundland seamen. Harold Bartlett of the *Laddie* was a distant cousin of Robert A. Bartlett, who served as skipper of arctic expeditionary vessels commanded by Robert Peary and Vilhjalmur Stefansson. See Horwood, *Bartlett: The Great Canadian Explorer.*

49 Letter to her sister Charlotte. The book quoted from is Stefansson's *My Life with the Eskimo*, 241.

50 Frances's sister Charlotte was probably on holiday in Florida, a long way off, whereas Buffalo was an easy journey by rail from Toronto.

Given Frances's impending plans to travel north, the Cabot reference must be to William Brooks Cabot (1858–1949) author of *In Northern Labrador.* There he describes his 1903 journey with Leonidas Hubbard (1872–1903) who, pursuing an exploratory route independent of Cabot's, perished from starvation in October 1903. To dismiss rumors that Leonidas was unprepared for the journey, and to realize his wish to map the Naskaupi and George rivers, his widow, Mina Benson Hubbard (later Ellis), set out in June 1905 from the Labrador coast with a party of three in two canoes to trace the flow of these rivers 600 miles north to Ungava Bay. She reached the bay in August. In her book *A Woman's Way through Unknown Labrador*, she recounted, as a woman, the challenges of the journey and vindicated the plan and reputation of her husband. It is difficult to imagine Frances not knowing of her work, since its account of an indomitable woman fiercely loyal to her husband's exploratory vision would have moved her greatly.

51 William Henry Moore (1872–1960) was indeed clever. At the time he was secretary to Canadian National Railways, and later was a writer on Canadian national causes. A Liberal, he served a s a member of parliament, 1930–45.

52 It was Frank Hurley (1885–1962), the Australian photographer and filmmaker, who shot the footage for the Mawson film. The Flahertys had most likely seen it on 22 January when Mawson had screened his film, accompanied with a lecture, at Toronto's Massey Hall. A press notice in the *Star* on 23 January 1915 spoke of it as the "Explorer's Vivid Story" and said that "one of the most interesting features of the movie display was the animal and bird life shown." Hurley also served as Shackleton's photographer and described his Antarctic work in *Shackleton's Argonauts*.

53 The richness of the "curios" donated to the museum can be estimated from a letter from the Royal Ontario Museum to Flaherty dated 20 September 1917 (Butler, MN1910). It inventories about five hundred items that comprise "The Flaherty Collection." The items represent a wide variety of clothing, tools, utensils, games, and toys, including a full-sized sledge and a kayak. A sample of the many superb ivory carvings donated can be seen in Carpenter's *Eskimo Realities*.

54 The clipping's headline would indeed have been fuel for Frances's ire: "Bartlett Saw a New Land: First White Man There. Tells of East Coast of Hudson Bay" (*New York Times*, 19 February 1918, 8). No mention, of course, is made of Flaherty.

55 The Albright exhibition brought together a group of painters, most of whom were known to Frances, including John Singer Sargent (1856–1925), Charles Webster Hawthorne (1872–1930), and Beatrice How (1867–1932). The artist new to her was the Canadian, Homer Ransford Watson (1855–1936), a painter known for his landscapes of pioneer rural life.

56 Lukes is Lewis Lukes, assistant to Mackenzie. His name weaves in and out of Frances's diary, including two telegrams from him that she notes on 26 July 1915.

57 The Flahertys took these letters to the meetings they had with Walter Leighton Clark (1859–1935) on 8 March and William Mason Grosvenor (1873–1944) on 9 March. Clark had been retained by J.P. Morgan to serve as arms purchaser for the British and French, while Grosvenor was a chemist who advanced film technology and manufacturing through his work on slow-motion and high-speed film photography. Another writer of these letters of reference was Dr Charles Stockton (1854–1931), a professor of medicine at the University of Buffalo, who had been Frances's personal physician since her undergraduate days. She probably had met him through her sister Charlotte, a Buffalo resident, and throughout her life she revered his memory.

58 W.G. Griffith's *Birth of a Nation* premiered in New York on 4 March 1915. The brief review in the *New York Times* noted that it was "the advent of the two dollar movie" and that it was an "impressive illustration of the scope of the motion picture camera."

59 "Cousin R" is Dr Royal Whitman (1858–1946), a noted orthopedic surgeon. It was at his home in New York City (1212 Fifth Avenue) that the Flahertys were married.

60 There is no record that the *New York Herald* interview came to anything. The Flahertys apparently did meet Charles Ransom Miller (1849–1922), chief editor of the *New York Times*, 1883–1922, and Miller thought well enough of the material to include it as a feature, with photos and map, in the Sunday Magazine section of 14 March 1915: "Lost Land Found in Hudson Bay."

61 Armit is another nickname for Frances's elder sister "Tottie," whose full birth name was Charlotte Armitage Hubbard. Ordinarily a good judge of character, Frances missed the mark badly on Armit's friend, the no "back-bone" Stephen Galatti (1888–1964). A volunteer in the American Ambulance Corps and a recipient of the Croix de Guerre, Galatti later served as director of the corps (now the American Field Service) during the Second World War.

62 Here again, Arts and Letters Club contacts proved useful in that another member, Arthur Heming (1870–1940) – a well-known Canadian author, artist, and illustrator who contributed to *Scribner's Magazine* – wrote on Flaherty's behalf to Joseph Hawley Chapin (1869–1939), who was Scribner's art editor for forty-six years. Maxwell Perkins, who had joined Scribner's in 1910 and later came to dominate the firm's literary matters, mentoring such authors as Scott Fitzgerald, Ernest Hemingway, and Thomas Wolfe, also encouraged Flaherty as a writer. Scribner's published the American edition of Flaherty's *The Captain's Chair*, and in the early 1940s Perkins advanced Flaherty $2,000 to write his autobiography, "The Odyssey of a Filmmaker." But Flaherty never delivered on the contract. He is reported to have said, "Let them shoot me." Frances later used the proposed title for her version of their film life together.

63 The Flahertys' determination to open doors through contacts continued with Frances calling upon another Bryn Mawr classmate, Isabel Ashwell (1885–1960), for an introduction to the founder of the New York Society for Ethical Culture, Dr Felix Adler (1849–1933). Adler's thought and work on ethical values, education, and the cultivation of the child would have greatly interested Frances. Boas's *The Central Eskimo* was a seminal text in Eskimo studies.

64 George H. Sherwood (1876–1937) joined the Natural History Museum in 1901, rising to director 1927–1934. Clark D. Wissler (1870–1947), whose name Frances incorrectly transcribes as Whistler, was a protégé of Boas and headed the museum's anthropology department. Henry Fairfield Osborn (1857–1935), a distinguished paleontologist, held the chair in zoology at Columbia University and served as president of the museum, 1908–33.

65 Frances's impression of Marguerite Bertsch would have been noteworthy, since Bertsch is among that group of forgotten women who worked in the silent film industry, though not as an actress. Associated with Vitagraph as editor and scriptwriter between 1914–19, she was given directorial credit in the *International Film Index 1895–1990* (vol 2) for four Vitagraph films. She later published *How to Write for Moving Pictures*.

66 It was Captain George Comer (1858–1937), not Cromer, to whom Boas referred. The skipper of the last of the American New Bedford whalers, Comer was a man of wide ethnographic, photographic, and exploration interests. In 1903–4, his ship the *Era* wintered alongside Albert P. Low's *Neptune* and led Low and his company on a Southampton Island survey. It was Low's judgment that except for the Reverend Ernest Peck, Captain Comer was "probably the greatest authority upon the manners and customs of the Eskimos" (*Cruise of the Neptune, 1903–04*, 163). Boas knew Comer well, since the captain had collected notes and artifacts on his behalf. James William

Ellsworth (1849–1925) was an important sponsor of these efforts; an American banker and philanthropist, he was interested in arctic exploration. For a discussion of Comer, see Thomas, "George Comer, A.P. Low, Geraldine and J.D. Moodie," 5–29.

67 It is possible that Frances's typescript confuses which of the Lunds is the painter, since it is likely that it was Mrs Lund – (Belle Jenks Lund (1879–?) – not her husband, whose exhibit Frances was going to see.

68 Frances learned that Sullivan's arctic article was to appear in the *Century* under the title "In Baffin Land: A True Story." Sullivan's story had nothing to do with Flaherty's diaries and, true to Frances's judgment, he wrote a trivial tale of love and treachery. However, he did include eight of Flaherty's photographs, all of which were credited to "R.J. Flaherty, F.R.G.S."

69 On Flaherty's behalf, Currelly proved to be an artful publicist, showcasing the Baffin Island film in a major debut before Toronto's elite. The guest list included Lieutenant Governor John S. Hendrie of Ontario; Byron Walker, the Canadian Bank of Commerce president; and the University of Toronto president, Sir Robert Falconer. Although Robert and Frances thought the presentation went badly, Currelly considered it a great sensation, writing to them on 14 April 1915: "I cannot too strongly congratulate you on the moving pictures you exhibited in Convocation Hall. I think every member of the University who has seen them has said the same. The Museum members who were able to be in the huge audience that night said that they were delighted and that those who were sitting near them seemed to be enthusiastic. I have never known anything received with such great enthusiasm and this is by all classes too, not merely the members of the University but the poorer classes also. Please let me offer you the most sincere congratulations" (Butler, MN1910). No doubt Flaherty was much amused by this capacity to please the groundlings.

70 Lee Keedick (1880–1959) served as agent for many notable personalities, but his first high-profile clients were polar explorers such as Mawson, Shackleton, Amundsen, and Stefansson. Keedick spent a considerable amount of time suing or being sued by his polar clients over contract disputes.

71 Edward S. Curtis's (1868–1952) twenty-volume *The North American Indian* (1907–30) remains unrivaled in its effort to photograph the Native peoples of North America. To support this massive project, Curtis was in New York trying to find a distributor for a motion picture, his *In the Land of the Head Hunters*, which had first been screened in New York in late 1914. He had completed the film among the Kwakiutl people of Vancouver Island, an area familiar to the Flahertys. Given the remarkable convergence of interest in photography and film between Curtis and Flaherty, Frances vacillated in her view of Curtis as model and as rival. While Robert remained her model of excellence, she was not immune to the polished theatricality of Curtis's work, and she responded, perhaps in spite of herself, to the solidity and generosity of Curtis's advice by saying, "I am inclined to think he is right – absolutely."

72 Of all those present, John Collier (1884–1968) was to have substantive influence on the fate of Native American peoples. A founder of the National Board of Review of Motion Pictures, Collier promoted self-regulation of the industry. He later became a student of American Indian culture and served as commissioner of Indian affairs, 1933–45, when he sought to bring to the agency more enlightened pro-Indian policies.

73 The Flahertys put themselves into the midst of the 1915 season of progressive theater. Harley Granville-Barker (1877–1946), best known for his *Prefaces to Shakespeare* (1927–47), had championed the production early in the century of such playwrights

as Gerhart Hauptmann, Henrik Ibsen, and Arthur Schnitzler. In 1915 he was producing in New York, in repertoire, George Bernard Shaw's *Lion* and Anatole France's *Dumb Wife*. Arnold Daly's (1875–1927), association with *You Never Can Tell* reflected his theatrical advocacy of Shaw, for which in 1905 he was arrested – and just as quickly released – on moral charges after producing and acting in Shaw's *Mrs. Warren's Profession*. The Little Theater (renamed the Helen Hayes in 1983), where the Flahertys saw Cyril Harcourt's *Silk Stockings*, was built in 1912 and first bore the name of its builder, Winthrop Ames (1871–1937), a leader in bringing to America the European concept of the "intimate" theater; it originally seated 299.

74 Wyllys Terry (1864–1949), was a major insurance broker and amateur sportsman. Even at his death he still held the record for the longest collegiate run in football history – 115 yards for Yale against Wesleyan in 1894.

75 Frances's intuition about McCord proved solid. On 12 March 1916 a *New York Times* item reported that a Percy A. McCord, secretary of the Scenograph Feature Film Co., had been arrested for theft of "the original film of the Amazon River from the source to the mouth, taken early in 1914 by the expedition which Captain J.C. Beasley was the head."

76 As Frances relates so vividly, the meeting with Alfred Stieglitz (1864–1946) was a "peak experience." Stieglitz's gallery 291 had become a mecca for modernism in photography, and *Camera Work* (1903–17) was its articulate text. Frances's familiarity with British pioneers in photography is suggested by her allusion to David Octavius Hill (1802–70) who, in collaboration with Robert Adamson (1821–48), did important and influential work in photography and portraiture in the 1840s.

77 The "class of '05" reunion that Frances attended at Bryn Mawr brings us into the circle of friends that had been so influential in shaping her early womanhood. The absent Jaynesie, "the fly in the ointment," was Alice Dickson Jaynes (1883–1951) with whom Frances maintained a lifelong friendship, as she also did with Margaret Thurston, who accompanied Frances to James Bay in the summer and fall of 1915. Gertie is Gertrude Hartman (1876–1955), an educator, editor, and writer. Bess was Elizabeth P. Henry who, as Elsey Henry Redfield, wrote short stories for the popular magazines.

78 Frances is referring to Ontario's Humber River. Miss Weil is the American Florence Wyle (1881–1968), who studied sculpture in New York, 1909–12, and lived with Frances Norma Loring (1887–1968), also a sculptor. Frances mentions both in the 21 July entry. The two women became life companions living and working together, first in New York and later in Toronto, where they maintained a mutual household and studio from 1913 until their deaths. They were founding members of the Sculptors' Society of Canada. Frances clearly enjoyed Florence's company and actively discussed the possibility of Florence joining her and Margaret Thurston on the journey they were intending to make to James Bay (letter to Margaret dated 13 July 1915, Claremont, audiotape 321A/side 1). Frances had visited their Toronto studio and was attracted to the sculptors' bohemian life. For reasons unknown, Florence did not accompany Frances and Margaret on their journey north. Margaret joined the Flahertys in Toronto on 22 July, preparatory to their departure.

79 Jocko, as Flaherty named the creature, frolics in and out of the diaries. Upon his return to the Belcher base camp from a trip to the mainland, Flaherty learned of Jocko's death (see his journal of 9 March 1916).

80 The party that was to travel north to Moose Factory on James Bay included Flaherty's

father and brother David as well as Frances and Margaret. This was the first of many associations that David Flaherty (1900–69) had with the Flahertys' work. Apart from *Nanook*, David was associated with nearly every film project the Flahertys ever conducted. A self-effacing individual of retiring manner, he was invariably eclipsed by his more demonstrative brother and most likely will remain unacknowledged for the many quiet contributions he made to the Flaherty enterprise. After Robert's death, David worked to sustain his brother's reputation by working with Frances to develop the Flaherty Foundation. David was also the prime mover in the early 1960s in assembling and cataloging the Flaherty papers housed at Columbia University. For David's comments on his brother and on the collection, see his "Poet of the Cinema," 3–12.

81 The problems that Flaherty had experienced at Cape Dorset near the end of his 1913–14 expedition (the HBC bills incurred but not paid either by him or by Mackenzie and Mann) had not been resolved; thus the hold the HBC placed on the extension of credit. A letter of 28 January 1915 from the fur trade commissioner, N.H. Bacon, to the HBC's London office reflects the company's exasperation with Flaherty's high-handed spending and its embarrassment at having to dun Mackenzie, a member of the HBC's board of directors:

> In view of my suggestion made last year to Sir Wm. Mackenzie that a letter of credit should be taken out for any supplies being required by Flaherty, having been ignored, I have written to Sir William to the effect that these transactions in the Bay must be put on a business basis. It is ludicrous for a party of men to arrive at one of the Company's Posts, give orders for the repair to boats involving some Three to Four Thousand Dollars, take a quantity of supplies and for the question of payment to be ignored every time it is brought up.
>
> I propose to absolutely refuse to ship these goods without pre-payment of freight. The Company at present appear to be financing this prospecting in the Bay under present conditions, and I have pointed out to Sir William that unless some arrangement is arrived at I may have to stop supplies, which are of necessity very valuable to the Company. (HBCA A12/FTmisc/260)

Later HBC correspondence by the commissioner (14 April 1916) indicates that Mackenzie's balance of $4,133 had still not been paid and that to solve the supply problem, Mackenzie turned to the HBC's competitor, Revillon Frères, for a letter of credit (HBCA PAM, RG2/2/91).

82 The trio who motored out to meet the Flahertys were Samuel Sainsbury and Eugene Laduke – veteran members of Flaherty's previous expeditions – and William Robinson, a new member.

83 After Flaherty's departure on the *Laddie*, Frances, Margaret Thurston, David, and Flaherty senior waited on Charlton Island for the *Nascopie*, which appeared on 24 September and took them to St John's, Newfoundland.

84 The story of salvaging the *Fort Churchill* contained sufficient adventure and marvel to burnish its retelling for years after. Slipping its mooring in the fall of 1913, the crewless *Churchill* disappeared. It was thought by all to have been lost until a party of Inuit hunters found the schooner in the spring of 1915, grounded ashore on the Belcher Islands. When they brought news of their find to Great Whale River, the HBC clerk Ernest Renouf sledged out to the Belchers and confirmed the find. Later that summer, Frank D. Wilson (HBC inspector whom Frances had met on the train to New

York City in May) set out in the *Inenew* to retrieve the *Churchill*, picking up at Charlton two of Flaherty's old companions, Omarolluk and Wetalltok, to serve as pilot and interpreter, respectively. The Flahertys were edgy about Renouf's trip to the Belchers. They feared that he would make claims, both geographical and mineralogical, about the islands that would overshadow Flaherty's accomplishments. Their fears were not entirely groundless, since in an article that Renouf later wrote, he declared: "Incidentally mine had been the privilege of being the first white man to visit the islands and see the natives in their homes, if one except the landing on the outer edge of the islands the year previous by Messrs. R.J. Flaherty and E.E. Leduc to repair their schooner 'Laddie' which had struck a shoal off the islands as they made their way south from Baffin's Land" ("Salvage," 20). William Cameron years later interviewed Wilson about the salvaging of the *Churchill* and wrote an article about it ("Runaway Ship," 5–9). The Cameron article is of additional interest in that it includes a number of Wetalltok's drawings of the salvage operation.

85 Frances indeed had reason to triumph, since John Jobin, as a representative of the Canadian Hydrographic Survey, embodied the skepticism Flaherty had encountered in his dealings with government officials about the location and size of the Belcher Islands. Additional confirmation about the Belchers also came from the respected George Redfern (1879–1933), skipper of the *Inenew*, an HBC captain of many years' service, whose log entries about the Belchers provided further proof.

86 Frances is quoting the first stanza of "Open the Bay" by the Canadian poet and dramatist Charles Mair (1838–1927). The poem, a celebration of Canada's emerging northern frontier, was published in Mair's *Tecumseh, A Drama, and Canadian Poems*, 169–70.

87 Mr Fleming is the Reverend Archibald Lang Fleming, whom Flaherty met at Lake Harbour at the beginning of his third expedition. Mr Mackenzie is the HBC district manager whom Flaherty met near the end of the third expedition.

88 Arthur Flaherty, Robert's other brother. At the time of his brother David's death in 1969, Arthur Flaherty was living in Traverse City, Michigan.

89 Given Frances's devotion to her music, the opportunity to hear the great piano recitalist Ignace Paderewski (1860–1941) would surely have been another "peak" for her.

90 "Harry" is Harry A. Ruttan, the husband of Robert Flaherty's only sister, Frances. In 1969 they were still living in Port Arthur (Thunder Bay), Ontario.

91 The Jobe article Frances read in the July 1915 issue of the *Bryn Mawr Quarterly* was an abbreviated reprint of one published in the *Bulletin of the American Geographical Society*, "Mt. Kitchi: A New Peak in the Canadian Rockies," 481–97. Yet another version appeared as "The Expedition to 'Mt. Kitchi': A New Peak in the Canadian Rockies," in *Canadian Alpine Journal*, 188–200. A prolific promoter of her accomplishments, Jobe also persuaded *Harper's Magazine* ("My Quest in the Canadian Rockies: Locating a New Ice Pack," 813–25) to print a less scientific rendition of her mountain explorations. Mary Lee Jobe (1886–1966), like Flaherty, was a Fellow of the Royal Geographical Society. She first met Frances when she was a graduate student at Bryn Mawr (1903–5). Other bonds had formed between them as can be seen from Jobe's *Harper's* comment: "Obviously, here was a chance for personal achievement – not merely achievement for public approbation, but achievement for our own pure delight. Here was a chance to see what on the government maps was only a blank white spot. Who knew, save a solitary Indian or two, what was hidden in the recesses

of those dense forests and forbidding ranges" ("My Quest in the Canadian Rockies," 813). Such views would have resonated with the Flahertys in their journey to confirm the reality of the Belcher Islands.

But the paths of Jobe and the Flahertys also intersected in other unanticipated ways in that in 1924 she married Carl Akeley (1864–1926). Combining taxidermy and the theatrical diorama, Akeley enhanced the presentation of museum animals by placing them in artful reconstructions of their natural habitats, a conception and design he brilliantly executed in the African Hall of the American Museum of Natural History. To aid his understanding of the motion of animals in their habitats, Akeley also designed and patented, in 1916, a motion-picture camera that was light, versatile, functional in extreme field conditions, and operable by one person. The rugged effectiveness of the camera was confirmed by its being the camera of choice for the first established photography division of the U.S. Signal Corps.

When Flaherty left for Port Harrison to film *Nanook*, he took two Akeley cameras. Many years later he recalled, "The Akeley then was the best camera to operate in extreme cold, since it required graphite, instead of oil and grease, for lubrication. These cameras fascinated me because they were the first cameras ever made to have a gyro-movement in the tripod–head whereby one could tilt and pan the camera without the slightest distracting jar or jerk or vibration" ("Robert Flaherty Talking," 13).

Owing to Akeley's efforts to use photography to construct "natural history," Flaherty, always receptive to new cinematic technologies, benefited immensely in his own efforts to photograph, fluidly and with continuity, the natural motions of people within their native habitat. For Akeley's influence on the presentation of natural history and his camera on outdoor photography, see Bodry-Sanders, *Carl Akeley: Africa's Collector, Africa's Savior*.

92 Edwin Prescott Grosvenor (1875–1930) was the twin brother of Gilbert Hovey Grosvenor (1875–1966), who through the articles and photographs of the *National Geographic* reshaped western perception of other peoples. Edwin served as special counsel to the U.S. attorney and successfully led federal anti-trust suits against the tobacco, glass, and film industries. It was through Grosvenor's legal efforts that in 1915 the Motion Picture Patents Company lost its grip on the industry and the way was opened for the new competitive "chaos" which the Flahertys encountered in their efforts to find a sponsor for the Baffin Island film.

93 As was expected of a fellow of the Royal Geographical Society, Flaherty periodically submitted reports on his explorations. They were duly printed in "The Monthly Record" section of the society's *Geographical Journal* under such titles as "Reported Discovery of Large Islands in Hudson Bay" and "Mr. Flaherty's Explorations in Hudson Bay," the latter being the report that Frances refers to here.

94 It is not surprising that Frances failed to get satisfaction from Louis Francis Brown (1865–1925), a theatrical manager; he would have regarded the Flaherty's Baffin film as a competitor to his own enterprise. Brown was manager and partner of Burton Holmes (1878–1958), the man who is credited with the naming and methodology of the "travelogue," a visual presentation on travel accompanied by a lecture-talk. In his way, Holmes internationalized the understanding of thousands worldwide. Over his 65-year career he collected anecdotes as a magnet attracts shavings. *Variety* spoke of him as the longest one-man run in show business. See Brownlow's essay on him in *The War, the West, the Wilderness*, 418–20.

95 Frances had mentioned the Mawson film (photographed by Frank Hurley) on 17 January 1915. It was on her mind again, since she had learned that the film, managed by Lee Keedick, had opened for an extended run in New York City at the Lyric Theater with an accompanying lecture by Dr W.A. Honsberger. The moving pictures of Robert Scott's British Antarctic Expedition (1910–12) were taken by the Australian Herbert G. Ponting (1870–1935), whose film began to circulate in 1913 under such titles as *With Captain Scott, R.N., to the South Pole* and *The Great White Silence*. Paul James Rainey (1877–1923), inheritor of a coal fortune, was a celebrated sportsman, explorer, and big-game hunter, who traveled to and took moving pictures of the Arctic in 1910 with Harry Payne Whitney (1872–1930), also a son of the Gilded Age and a renowned sportsman. It was from Rainey's exploits as a big-game hunter in Africa that his reputation as a moving-picture photographer arose. Rainey's film *African Hunt* (1912) was probably the one that Frances had in mind, since Rainey, for philanthropic causes, frequently screened and lectured on his African experiences. For McCord and his Scenograph Feature Film Company, see note 75 above.

96 The reference is to Pietro Antonio Locatelli (1695–1764), a violinist and a writer of piano sonatas.

97 Frances had in mind the Italian Guarneri family, makers of violins between 1650 and 1750, one of which was the violin that Flaherty, flush with cash, had purchased, to Frances's dismay. In pursuing her goal of advocating Flaherty's work, Frances, turned to those in her Bryn Mawr network, such as Avis Putnam (1884–1943), to gain access to others. For advice on the repair of the fiddle, she turned to Putnam's husband, Edouard Dethier (1886–1962), a violinist and teacher at the Juilliard School of Music. To Avis's father, the publisher Irving Putnam (1852–1931), she turned for advice on publishing Robert's work. In the winter of 1916, Frances sent him Robert's diaries, observing: "A thread of romance binds these diaries together, which is the story of the Lost Islands in Hudson's Bay, the rediscovery of which in conception and accomplishment is the beginning and ending of these chronicles" (Butler, MN1913). Despite Putnam's apparent enthusiasm over the material, nothing came of the exchange.

CHAPTER SEVEN

1 Robert Flaherty Papers in the Butler Library (hereafter Butler), MN1927,48/104

2 See chapter 4, above, diary entry of 6 March 1912.

3 Ibid., 16 August 1911

4 Flaherty, *My Eskimo Friends*, 133–4.

5 As noted earlier, the motion-picture camera that Flaherty used was a Bell & Howell. In Rochester, he received two weeks' instruction on it, most likely the only formal technical schooling that Flaherty ever had in camera operation. The testimonial that Flaherty wrote for Bell & Howell (see chapter 5, above) included three photographs: Sam Sainsbury operating the camera midstream in the Kokjuak River; Eugene LaDuke and Stewart Gushue positioning the camera along Hudson Strait; and Eugene LaDuke shooting the interior of an igloo.

6 Butler, MN1910

7 Butler, MN1927

8 For the final report of 2 February 1915, see Butler, MN1910.

9 There is no record that Frances prepared a typescript for the fourth expedition, as she had for the first three. The text is therefore a transcription of Flaherty's original handwritten diaries, kept in four notebooks.

10 In contrast to the "lone wolf" mode of travel of the earlier expeditions, there is an atmosphere of *jour de fête*, with Flaherty prideful at bringing his family to the portals of the Arctic. In the company are family members central to his being in 1915, including his mentor and guide, Robert H., whose role Flaherty had described in the "Islands" narrative: "My father, who had recently taken charge of Sir William's mining interests, decided to come along with me as far as Charlton Island. His purpose was to get an idea of transportation facilities and general conditions on the Bay; and if the forthcoming exploration through the winter disclosed deposits of iron ore of economic importance, he would come to the newly-discovered islands himself the following year with his own expedition, and make a final report to Sir William" (Butler, MN1927).

Also present, as described in Frances's journal (see chapter 6), were Frances, her Bryn Mawr classmate Margaret Thurston, and David, Robert's youngest brother. After Flaherty's departure, they waited on Charlton Island for the arrival of the *Nascopie* (24 September), which took them to St John's by 18 October 1915.

11 Wilson is the district inspector, Frank D. Wilson, whom Flaherty had met briefly near the end of the third expedition; George Snapes was an HBC man at Moose Factory.

12 The departure of LaDuke was the flashpoint of what had doubtless been a continuing conflict over the expeditionary leadership. In a letter (24 February 1916) to his father, Flaherty reported:

> LaDuke deserted the expedition on the 17th of October on account of my refusal to allow him to live in the house with an Eskimo concubine whom he secured from one of the Charlton Eskimo by promise of marriage.
>
> This affair put me up against the wall pretty hard, and I was forced under the stress of the circumstances to give him the big cruising launch with which to make his get away to the mainland. The details of this affair the men [Gushue and Sainsbury] will explain to you. I cannot do it well here. The whole secret of LaDuke's failure I believe lies in his absurd belief that he was practically offered my position while in Toronto by Mr Lukes [Mackenzie's assistant] or one of his representatives. (Personally I don't believe this is so.) Also the fact that he was given the preliminary Letter of Credit on his trip down to Moose to put the *Laddie* in commission. These things swelled him with the belief that he was in co-charge or something. All in all I have had a very harrowing time of it but which has been largely offset by the results of our work, otherwise non compus mentis. (Butler, MN1910)

Given the tight world of the Arctic brotherhood, the ripple of this conflict could reach all the way to Toronto. Frank Wilson, the HBC inspector, wrote to Flaherty on 28 March 1916: "I am sure the Toronto people will not listen to him [LaDuke] until they hear from you" (Butler, MN1910, 15).

Sainsbury, writing on 14 February 1916 to William Robertson, a shipmate from the third expedition, had a more in-your-face view of the affair: "I must tell you about LaDuke. He certainly has made a lot of bad remarks concerning the expedition and us personally. We were all no-to-good from his point of view. He tells Mavor [HBC factor Lewis G. Maver] that when he got to Toronto he was going to give us the sack and that we were no use on the trip. He also said that Bob and him could have got to the Belchers without us and explored all the islands. Now what do you think of that? I cannot tell you all that he told Mavor. It would fill a large book. The only thing I can say, Bill, is God help him. If we get a chance we'll punch the shit out of him and give his carcass to the crows, the nasty bastard" (Butler, MN1910).

Flaherty's strong sense of violation about LaDuke's behavior was as much about his discomfort over the public airing of sexual matters as it was about the community dangers of jealousy and conflict if "concubinage" were to be practiced. What Flaherty did not wish to confront was the linkage of leadership with sexual power and the challenge provoked by LaDuke's behavior. Flaherty could be deferential in the matter of an outsider's behavior, as in the case of Captain Murray's keeping of an Eskimo concubine (see chapter 5, above, 15 December 1913), but in regard to his own captaincy of the expedition, sexuality was a taboo subject. If addressed at all, it was only in the most oblique terms, as in the instance of Sainsbury having sexual relations with Simonie's elder wife (ibid., 12 December 1913).

Apart from one more mention of LaDuke (on 17 July 1916), the diary is silent on the subject. Overall, the intensity of Flaherty's anger can be gauged from the many occasions among the Butler Library papers where in drafts of reports or other narratives of the expeditions, the word "assistant" is crossed out after LaDuke's name, or where editorial slash lines have been drawn across passages that noted LaDuke's contribution to the expeditionary work. It is as if Flaherty wanted to erase him from the record.

13 There are more than enough references throughout Flaherty's diaries to confirm his use of both live and dead animals to simulate hunting episodes. During the shooting of the Belchers film, Flaherty used a live fox in a fox-trap scene, as he later also did in *Nanook*. Similarly, a dead seal served as the quarry in the sequence on seal hunting through a breathing hole both in *Nanook* and in the Belchers film. Live quarry – ducks, geese, walrus – hunted in their own habitat proved more illusive. For example, Flaherty reported during the third expedition that the duck were "much too scary for pictures" (12 July 1914), and during the fourth expedition that a snapped harpoon line had ruined his walrus-hunting shoot (11 July 1916).

14 The baseball episode, like many other Flaherty tales, was to have a serendipitous migration through the layers of his multiple narrative outlets. Regardless of whether or not a baseball game occurred at the Christmas festivities, the post-diary narrative of *My Eskimo Friends* recalls the event vividly, suggesting its ongoing vivacity in the Flaherty oral repertoire – an assumption validated by the reappearance of the tale, now via the raconteur pathway, in a newspaper account of 1922:

> The most interesting account of a baseball game we have listened to recently was given by Robert J. Flaherty, the explorer, who made the remarkable picture "Nanook of the North." He said that his ship was frozen in a harbor of Belcher Island ... The ice was smooth, with just a little covering of snow, and it seemed a shame not to use it for something. So they decided upon a baseball game.
>
> One of the sailors was such a fan that he had taken a big league ball North with him. That ball constituted the entire baseball paraphernalia in that part of the world. They had to improvise a bat. The diamond was laid out so that the side of the boat formed the backdrop. The deck was the grand stand and the rigging the bleachers. They both were crowded ... Among the spectators were many Eskimo belles. They cheered with an enthusiasm that scared all the polar bears for forty miles.
>
> Each nine consisted of two Americans and seven Eskimos. In addition there were countless volunteer marathon runners. If a ball got beyond the outfielders these

runners formed relay teams and chased it. Refreshments were served while they were gone, because the ball traveled like a duck going south over that ice, and Mr Flaherty says that some of those Eskimos certainly could sock the horsehide.

The baseball uniforms were of a pattern seldom seen in St. Louis in July or August. They were made of sealskins, with mitts and a hood. Altogether it was some game, and in a sense historic, since it introduced baseball to that part of the frozen North. (Trumbull, "The Listening Post")

This retelling provides us with an interesting skein of renderings and embellishments, both Flaherty's and Trumbull's, which ultimately make such tales fugitive pieces for which there is no temporal or narrative master text.

15 Although the diaries do not suggest that Flaherty bathed often, he did on occasion do so, for he included a bathtub in his outfit. On his departure he gave it to the HBC post, and we hear of it again from James Houston, the Canadian artist and writer who, recalling a visit to Great Whale in 1950, observed as he took a piss: "I stood there wetting the snow, staring in surprise at a battered tin bathtub whose outside was painted green, the inside a peeling, white enamel. It was tipped crazily, half-buried in the snow, and was pierced through with three finger-sized bullet holes. There were even marks where someone had thrown a harpoon through the tub. I had heard earlier about that famous bathtub, recently taken from the Company's fur shed, for it was considered another of Flaherty's many extraordinary eccentricities. Imagine that man having the temerity to bring a bathtub and a piano this far north with him, loading them into the Revillons' little herring smack called *Laddie*. Seeing that stabbed tub made me think of the large painting hanging in the Louvre in Paris of Marat murdered by Charlotte Corday in his bath during the French Revolution" (*Confessions of an Igloo Dweller*, 41).

16 Sainsbury arrived in Cochrane on 16 March, and from the Cedric Hotel he sent Robert H. and Frances Flaherty a night message: "Have just arrived with important packet from the islands – samples, plans, etc. All well up north. Please send expense funds for Stewart and myself to cover expenses here" (Butler, MN1910, 15).

17 Thevenet, along with Thierry Mallet, had established many of the first Revillon posts in the bay. At the time Flaherty met him, he was serving as inspector of Revillon's posts in the eastern district.

18 By the 1860s, carbon printing had advanced to the point where it was the print process of choice for detailed, high-resolution photographs of museum sculptures and paintings, an application that greatly influenced the study and methodology of art history scholarship from books. This process, which Flaherty could conduct in the field, is described in Crawford, *Keepers of Light*, 69–74.

19 36 Roxborough Drive was the house the Flahertys rented in Toronto after their marriage.

20 Flaherty had photographed the interior of the Anglican mission church at Great Whale River before and had included in the 1911 album a print of Nero Fleming standing in it (see the illustration on p. 72, above). The catalog of the 1979–80 Vancouver exhibition incorrectly attributes to Flaherty a photograph (no. 69) of twenty or so Inuit men, women, and children seated on church pews. William C. James later identified this as a cropped version of a Great Whale River congregation photograph taken by Albert A. Chesterfield (1877–1959), a-turn-of-the-century HBC trader who worked at Fort George and Great Whale. See James, "Inuit in Church," 59–62, and "Inuit in Church – Once More," 129–30. Flaherty's 1911 album includes the full

print (but damaged on the right side) of this Chesterfield church interior, as well as a Chesterfield print of hay boats being loaded. Another photograph of the Great Whale congregation, which Flaherty did take on the first expedition, was published in the *Canadian Courier* (28 October 1911, 6) with the title: "Home Mission Work in Canada's Northland" and the following caption: "The Esquimaux are the most northerly citizens of the Dominion and this picture is evidence that the missionary finds them willing to learn. This photograph was taken in a little church on the Ungava shore of Hudson's Bay. Copyrighted by R.J. Flaherty."

21 It is at about this point in the fourth expedition that Flaherty abruptly ended his "Islands" narrative.

22 In addition to his father, other members of the party included W.H. Howard and E.S. Moore. Howard, a Canadian government surveyor, was to validate Flaherty's claims about the Belchers, and this eventually led to a revision of the Admiralty charts. In the mid-1930s the Canadian government officially named the largest of the Belchers "Flaherty Island." Moore, a professor of geology at Pennsylvania State University, had been acquainted with the Flahertys from the northwestern Ontario days, when as a mine inspector, he had mentioned Flaherty senior in his reports. He published his Belcher Islands findings in the *Journal of Geology*, 412–38, and the *Monthly Bulletin of the Canadian Mining Institute*, 196–206. Robert H. Flaherty's report to Mackenzie and Mann is not among the Butler Library papers.

23 In *My Eskimo Friends*, Flaherty elaborated on the gifts he distributed when he departed: "Since the Nastapoka could carry only our food, instruments, and personal gear, I divided the hut and its furnishings among Wetalltok, Tookalook, Mukpollo, and their families. There was everything – dishes, an old mirror, old magazines, powder, caps, and cartridges, knives, axes, old clothing, cloth, and old shoes. As a special payment the gramophone and records went to Calla, our cook; a rifle to Mukpollo; the canoe to Tookalook, and to Wetalltok our poor old pianola, much scarred and stained and out of tune from rough transport and misuse. But to Wetalltok it was the most wonderful thing in all the world – big box with the many insides" (74).

Flaherty and Frances claimed that they later received a letter from Lewis G. Maver of Great Whale River which said: "Perhaps you will remember having given your pianola to Wetalltok just before you left the Belcher Islands last fall. Well, Wetalltok was stuck with that pianola on his hands; he couldn't take it into his igloo, and he couldn't leave in your cabin for he had, of course, no fuel. So he conceived the idea of sledging that pianola over to me – it seemed that you told him I would be keen to buy it – but how could he transport a full-sized pianola over eighty-five miles of sea ice, and some of it rafted mighty high at that, was more than I could see, but he did it – brought it right into Great Whale Post, only to find that I wasn't there, for I had been transferred in the fall, south to Fort George (186 miles away). So he kept on down the coast having obtained supplies from the factor on the strength of the sale of the pianola to me, and after the Lord knows how many days, he came sledging in one day at nightfall, right into my post yard, with a 'Chimo' and a 'Here, Angarooka, is the box with the many insides.' The thing worked, you'll be surprised to hear, though some of its notes were what Wetalltok called 'sick sounds'" (*My Eskimo Friends*, 75).

The original of the letter that Maver wrote to Flaherty on 16 April 1917 survives, and it is considerably different: "Wetalltok brought the pianola in the other day in fairly good condition. Some of the notes are out of tune (most of the bass ones) and the pianola part skips over some notes when passing over the perforated brass part in front" (Butler, MN1910). Comparison of the two letters shows how Robert and Frances "wrote up" the northern experiences to cater to their audience's wish for more detail and drama. The durability of the survivor power of this pianola is impressive; during James Houston's visit to Great Whale in 1950, he was told by the HBC trader in residence: "That's Flaherty's wee piano in the factor's parlor. Can ye play us a tune?" (*Confessions of an Igloo Dweller*, 40).

In attempting to cross by water to Great Whale River in the canoe that Flaherty had given him, Tookalook drowned. A final requiem in *My Eskimo Friends* (74–5) is also given to Rainbow (the Thomas of the diary) who, Flaherty tells us, "had gone mad, the result of starvation. For many days he had been at large with the Winchester and cartridges I had given him, spreading terror among the islanders. To save themselves they had to kill him."

24 There exists no story among the papers which takes as its subject the stranding of Omarolluk on an ice floe in Hudson Bay. The stranding on the ice floe motif prevails in many tales of the North and is present in Flaherty's treatment of the Comock story.

CHAPTER EIGHT

1 Ramsaye, "Flaherty, Great Adventurer," 125. Although John Grierson – founder of the British documentary movement and the National Film Board of Canada – declared that Flaherty was scarred by the fire, members of the Flaherty family attest that he bore no burn scars on his hands or face as a result of the accident.

2 Flaherty, "How I Filmed 'Nanook of the North,'" 553.

3 Flaherty, "Robert Flaherty Talking," 12.

4 Letter to Margaret Thurston from Frances Flaherty, Norwalk, Conn., 27 August 119, housed in the Robert and Frances Flaherty Study Center at Claremont University (hereafter Claremont), audiotape 231A/side1

5 Robert Flaherty Papers in Butler Library (hereafter Butler), MN1911

6 Ibid.

7 Ibid.

8 Flaherty, "The Belcher Islands of Hudson Bay: Their Discovery and Exploration," 433–58, and "Two Traverses across Ungava Peninsula, Labrador," 116–32.

9 Flaherty, "The Belcher Islands of Hudson Bay," 456

10 Ibid.

11 Butler, MN1913

12 Butler, MN1911

13 Butler, MN1913

14 Mallet's diary, 49–50. A typed manuscript of sixty-seven pages, the diary is in the Revillon of Paris collection. A microfilm copy is housed at the Library and Archives Canada in Ottawa.

15 Mallet's diary, ibid., 53

16 Ibid., 52

17 Ibid., 51

18 Ibid., 54

19 Most of the Port Harrison entries are not found in the leather-bound field notebooks that Flaherty had customarily used. Since the purpose of this expedition was to make

a film, not to gather scientific information, Flaherty used a different methodology, relying more on impressionistic entries rather than sequential diary narratives. He reverted to his traditional diary mode only on the two expeditions to Walrus Island (22 September – 19 October 1920), and for a portion of the Cape Smith bear hunt (22 February – 9 March 1921). All other narrative passages, including film notes, were made on unnumbered, three-ring sheets, which more often than not were undated.

As organized by David Flaherty in the Butler collection, the microfilmed sheets reside in no narrative sequence whatsoever. For example, the pages that narrate the initial portion of the bear hunt (17 January to 22 February 1921) had to be transcribed sheet by sheet and then reassembled as if they were the scattered sheets of an unpaginated and unbound book. Using contextual clues such as references to season, relationship to previous or forthcoming events, and, on occasion, dates, other sheets were provided placement in the sequence. Apart from the self-contained entries of 22 September – 19 October 1920 and 22 February – 9 March 1921, where the film notes appear in the order that Flaherty wrote them, readers should regard the sequence of all film notes as the best-laid hunches of the editor.

20 Flaherty had followed a now familiar route, taking the railroad to Cochrane and then traveling by canoe down the Groundhog River to Moose Factory. From there he took the *Annie Geele* along the eastern coast of Hudson Bay to the Hopewell Sound area and the Revillon Frères post of Port Harrison at the mouth of the Innuksuak River, where he arrived on 15 August.

21 Flaherty makes no further mention of the epidemic or its nature. Given the date, 1920, it was probably influenza. Some commentators have projected Flaherty as the contaminator, corrupting the primitive by his Western intrusion. But that had been done long before Flaherty ever arrived in the North. Several generations of whalers, missionaries, and traders had already left their biological signature on the people of the North.

22 "Showing the film" most likely refers to the walrus hunt scene that Flaherty had recently shot, rather than to the Baffin-Belcher film, for which the walrus hunt had failed when the harpoon line broke. This screening of the Harrison walrus hunt was later embellished by Frances in Flaherty's *My Eskimo Friends*:

> Three days later the post bell clangs out the welcome news that the kablunak is about to show his iviuk aggie. Men, old men, women, old women, boys, girls, and small children file in to the factor's house. Soon there is not an inch of space to spare. The trader turns down the lamps. The projector light shoots over the shocks of heads upon the blanket which is the screen.
>
> Then the picture. A figure appears. There is silence. They do not understand. "See, it is Nanook!" the trader cries. The Nanook in the flesh laughs in his embarrassment. "Ah! ah! ah!" they all exclaim. Then silence. The figure moves. The silence deepens. They cannot understand. They turn their heads. They stare at the projector. They stare at its beam of magic light. They stare at Nanook, the most surprised of all, and again their heads turn toward the screen. They follow the figure which now snakes toward the background. There is something in the background. The something moves. It lifts its head.
>
> "Iviuk! iviuk!" shakes the room. The figure stands up, harpoon poised in hand.
>
> "Be sure of your harpoon! be sure of your harpoon!" the audience cries.
>
> The figure strikes down; the walrus roll off into the sea. More figures rush in; they grab the harpoon line. For dear life they hold on.

"Hold him! hold him!" shout the men. "Hold him! hold him!" squeal the women. "Hold him!" pipe the children.

The walrus's mate dives in, and by locking tusks attempts rescue. "Hold him!" gasps the crowd.

Nanook and his crew, although their arms seem to be breaking, hold on. But slowly and surely the threshing walrus drags the figures nearer sea.

"Hold him! hold him!" they despair. They are breathing hard. "Dig in! dig in!" they rasp, as Nanook's feet slip another inch through the sand.

Deep silence. Suddenly the line sags, the crew, like a flash, draw in the slack, and inch by inch the walrus is pulled in to shore. Bedlam rocks the house.

The fame of the film spread far up and down the coast. Every strange Eskimo that came into the post Nanook brought before me and begged that he be shown the iviuk aggie.

It had become Flaherty's practice to show prospective participants previous or current examples of film. It was a technique he continued with his next film, *Moana*, he screened *Nanook* for the Samoans. The polar severities of that film meant nothing to Samoans, and the showing had the effect of the proverbial snowball in hell. By contrast, when he screened *The Golem* (1920), the sudden animation of the clay monster in the film stirred its Polynesian viewers deeply, and Golem became the name of choice for a generation of Samoans born in the 1920s.

23 "Snowing up" refers to the practice of encasing a building with blocks of snow to insulate it.

24 The arrival of the *Nascopie* signaled the establishment of a competing post by the HBC at Port Harrison. According to financial reports for 1924, Harrison remained Revillon's most lucrative post on Hudson Bay, grossing over $28,000 in profits.

25 Maggie is Alice Nevalinga the woman who played Nyla, Nanook's wife in the film. This identification of Nyla is also suggested by the Vancouver exhibition catalog (89). As so often occurred, Flaherty and others ascribed Anglo names to Native persons (e.g. "Harry Lauder"). That Maggie was the Anglo nickname of the woman who played Nyla is confirmed by a photograph of her taken by Bob Stewart, the trader in *Nanook*, and published in the *Beaver* (September 1938, 23) with the caption: "Maggie of Port Harrison, the Heroine of Robert Flaherty's film 'Nanook of the North.'" Attata ("father") was the honorific name of the man who played the part of Nanook ("The Bear") in the film, a name that denotes less paternity than his standing as a leader in the community. Relying on Inuit oral history and knowledge, the Vancouver exhibition catalog (93), proposed that the man who played the lead was Allakariallak, an attribution that can be confirmed by a series of photographs published in the *Beaver*, June 1921, 32, by Ralph Parsons, who was the HBC district manager at the time. The series, entitled "A Galaxy of Baffin's Land Types," includes a photograph of a man who bears a decided likeness to the film's Nanook, and is identified as that "Allakarallok."

When Flaherty's diaries use the names Nanook and Attata, Flaherty is referring to one and the same man – Allakariallak. This equivalence is further confirmed by the fact that when Robert and Frances later revised portions of the Harrison diaries, they inserted "Nanook" where "Attata" had appeared originally.

26 Flaherty, "How I Came into Motion Pictures," unpublished and undated narrative, Butler MN1927

27 In what appears to be a fragment of a letter to Frances, Flaherty listed the locations

where she and the children might be staying: New Canaan, where they had resided since 1918; Florida, where her sister Charlotte Goodell lived; North Michigan, the Hubbards' residence; and with the Gutmans in Florida. The Gutmans, Bernhard and Bertha, were close friends of the Flahertys and lived in the Silvermine area of Connecticut as well as Florida. Berhard (1869–1936), an American Impressionist painter, did a portrait of Frances playing the piano.

28 Although there were infrequent cases of the berserk threatening the community, Eskimo justice, when it occurred, could be decisive. In his autobiography, Bishop Fleming wrote of an instance where an Eskimo, having killed his family and others who crossed his path, was surrounded by eight men who simultaneously fired at his silhouette in an igloo, killing him: "Who killed David? Not one man but all the men. In each man's rifle there was one empty cartridge" (*Archibald the Arctic*, 202).

29 In later writings Flaherty tells us more about the preparations for the bear hunt and the supplies the party took:

> The walrus hunting having proved successful, Nanook aspired to bigger game – a bear hunt, no less, at Cape Sir Thomas Smith, some two hundred miles northward. "Here," said Nanook, "is where the she-bear dens in the winter, and it seems to me that we might get the big, big aggie there."
>
> He went on to describe how in early December the she-bear dens in huge drift banks of snow. There is nothing to mark the den save a tiny vent, or airhole, which is melted open by the animal's body heat. His companions would remain at either side of me, rifles in hand, whilst he with his snow knife would open up the den, block by block. The dogs in the meantime would all be unleashed and like wolves circle the opening. Mrs Bear's door opened, Nanook, with nothing but his harpoon, would be poised and waiting. The dogs baiting the quarry – some of them with her lightning paws the bear would send hurtling through the air; himself dancing here and there – he pantomimed the scene on my cabin floor, using my fiddle bow for harpoon – waiting to dart in for a close-up throw; this, he felt sure, would be a big, big picture (aggie peerualluk). I agreed with him.
>
> "With good going ten days will see us there." Ten days for hunting on the Cape, then ten days for coming home again. But throw in another ten days for bad weather, and let's see (counting on his fingers) – that makes four times my fingers – more than enough to see us through."
>
> "All right," said I, "we'll go." And Nanook, his eyes shining, went off to spread the news.
>
> For two weeks we prepared. First of all Nanook and "Harry Lauder" sledged out over the sea ice for walrus meat we had cached under boulders on the Walrus Island. Every night we cooked our big iron pot full of pork and beans and poured them into a large sack, which hung from a hook out of doors, to freeze them. Nanook relashed with tough sealskin thongs and smoothed the runners of his staunchest sledge, whilst his and the wives of his crew on my cabin floor sewed and sewed boots, kooletahs, and dogskin mitts, and fashioned a new sealskin dog whip six fathoms long. Most important of all were the bows and arrows and bear spears, all to be headed, not with the kablunak's iron, but with stones, as in days of long ago. (*My Eskimo Friends*, 142–3)

30 Flaherty had in mind a sun-dog illustration, plate 9, in the first volume of Fridtjof Nansen's *Farthest North*, 96.

31 Another of the "conversations" that Flaherty later reported he had with Nanook and

others appears in *My Eskimo Friends* (154–6), where he described how Nanook told him the story of Comock, a story that became the premier Arctic narrative in Flaherty's imagination. As Flaherty finally fashioned the narrative in published form, it took on the elemental force of the first human family:

Through the evening Nanook talked of ice; of how he and his two hunting companions were nearly caught on the ice pack which drove out to sea. "Where it happened is not a half-day's sledging from this igloo. We were out on the rough ice after bear. We had made a kill and were on our way in to land, when we came upon a lane of open water which stood between us and the ice foot of the Cape. Far off in the distance the lane narrowed. We dropped our kill and made off as fast as we could travel, but nowhere was the lane narrow enough to leap. Just in time we spied an ice pan. It was about the length of a sledge. With the ice pan for boat, our harpoons for paddles, we paddled across."

Then each of the crew told of some misadventure he had had at some time or other on the ice. "Harry Lauder," with his father and mother, the mother carrying a babe in arms, were adrift all through one moon off the Gulf Hazard coast. When the west winds packed the ice field in to the mainland where they landed was Cape Dufferin, two hundred and fifty miles north of Gulf Hazard. The winter was almost done before they saw home again.

"I remember Comock of Kovik, just north of here," said Nanook. "Comock and three men, wives and children were out on the ice. The ice broke while they slept. Two of the men, a woman, and three children drifted off one way and Comock and the rest off the other. The others were never seen or heard of again. But Comock and his crowd, after days and days adrift, touched land. It was the big island off from Kovik (Mansfield Island, seventy miles off the coast). On this island did Comock and his people live. They were very poor. They clothed themselves with skins of the bear. Their sinew (thread) they cut from the intestines of the salmon. They got very hungry for their old friends and homeland, so one day they put out upon the ice as it was parting from the shoreline, hoping that the west winds would blow long enough to carry them over to the mainland. But for a moon they drifted here and there and everywhere, and when they landed it was on an island off Cape Wolstenholme.

"They were very poor," Nanook repeated. "They lived on sea pigeons which they killed with stones. With what sealskins they had and what driftwood, walrus bones and a deer horn they found along the shore, they made an omiak [umiak]. But the omiak was not large enough to hold them all, who now numbered thirteen men, women, babes, and children. So they blew up seal bladders and tied them on the sides of their omiak. Comock's head wife held a long stick in her hands so that the she might keep the children still. Where they reached the mainland was on the straight up-and-down coast of Cape Wolstenholme. On the first narrow ledge that they could see they landed, for a strong wind was rising. The landing was barely big enough to hold their omiaks and themselves, but here for two days they had to stay. The seas drenched them. When the water was calm again they launched their omiak, paddled around the big nose of the Cape, and landed in the snug cove on the other side. Old friends greeted them when they walked out on shore. They must have been glad," said Nanook in conclusion.

"How long was it," I asked, "from the time they were swept out to sea before they reached their homeland again?"

"Ten summers and ten winters were the number of the notches that Comock cut in the handle of his harpoon," Nanook replied.

The Comock story was widely known in the North. Peter Pitseolak, the Baffin Island photographer and painter, recalled in his autobiography that he had heard the story from Comock's son on Nottingham Island in 1927 or 1928 (*People from Our Side*, 98). Pitseolak also recalled, incorrectly, that Comock told the story to Flaherty in 1914. Though Flaherty could have been told a version of the story by Nanook, he heard it first from Comock himself in August 1912 on the second Mackenzie expedition. In his report to Mackenzie, Flaherty observed:

At Cape Wolstenholme I fell in with a family of Eskimos, who had been marooned on Mansfield Island, the north extreme of this island range, for a period of ten years. They crossed to the island on drifting ice floes, but owing to the hazardous undertaking, they were for years afraid to recross, in the meantime existing on this island with bow and arrow. Comock, the head man of these people, gave me interesting information concerning the Right Whale of the Mansfield Island country.

Mansfield Island, with the exception of Comock and his group of people, has been and is uninhabited by natives, and is of course unknown to white men. This information is reliable and was checked subsequently by the same information from other members of this group of Eskimos." (Butler, MN1910)

32 Flaherty gives us the vivid circumstances of the white whale hunt in an article he wrote for the *World's Work*:

Nanook was restless, the wanderlust again was upon him. He knew, he said one day when we were making the whale boat ready for sea, where there were many white whales that played in a little bottle-necked harbor some three days kayaking up the coast. We might, he continued, hopefully, get the "big aggie" (picture) there.

Ice fields still lay along the coast, the blue-green ribbons of water lanes amongst them ever changing with the working of the winds and tide. Came a driving nor'easter herding the floes to sea and before the day was ended all that remained of those vast fields was a thin line far out in the west.

Wild fowl in multitudes we encountered on the way. Under the leaning brows of great cliffs that rose three hundred feet in air were strata of sea gulls and clouds of sea pigeons and big eiders. A weird medley were their wild cries and screams, the re-echoing of our guns, and the deep booming of the sea.

Where we landed for sea pigeon eggs the sea pigeons swarmed like flies hardly an arm's length above us. Waiting until they approached circling toward him, Nanook with a piece of wood would hurl it breast on, bringing down three or four birds with a single throw.

With a gale from the west the ice fields again came in and, rafting high along the bare rock masses of the coast, kept us prisoners. We went inland during the detention, goose hunting among the tundra's tiny discs of ponds. The geese, having shed their wing feathers, were unable to fly. By running them down the men secured them, a task, however, that with the spongy nature of the moss-carpeted ground, was sporting enough.

For two days we worked through every winding lane that opened with the tides, or hauled the boat up on to the floes as the lanes closed in again, until a providential offshore wind finally freed us and we bowled in to a bare rock strip of point which proved to be Nanook's "Culelulewak noona" (the white whale land).

We dared not camp too near the bottle-necked entrance to the whale ground for even from a mile away the banging of an oar against a gunwale might frighten the whales and drive them out to sea. We camped under the lee of a cliff a mile and a half distant, and upon the crest one or another of the men took turns as lookouts for whale. It was two weeks to a day when a school of some twenty all told, came swinging in from the sea. Nanook leading the fleet of kayakers slowly paddled toward the harbor's mouth. "Harry Lauder" carrying the Akeley camera, and myself with the hand camera and film retorts walked overland to the harbor head. We were hardly more than half way over when the lookout signaled that the whales were in. The kayakers at their fastest speed raced for the entrance, and side by side with paddles beating gunwales and all the shouts and yells their lungs could stand came slowly in. The deafening din threw the quarry into a panic. The whales' ear drums, Nanook had explained, are so sensitive that sound not only frightens them but hurts them. Their snow white bodies flashed in the sun as they came up to blow or to rush around the small loop of the harbor's end only to meet the barrier of land. Time after time they tried to break through the kayakers' cordon only to be driven back again or harpooned if they came too near. For an hour the fight kept on until five, all told, were harpooned.

With their kayaks hitched in line, Nanook and his companions spent the remainder of the day towing in the kill and hauling them out on shore. Two days were consumed in cutting up the kill and apportioning it, and then with the whale boat full of meat which Nanook was taking as presents to his people at the post, we left for the south, all the film I carried exposed on Nanook's last "big aggie." ("Life among the Eskimos," 636–8)

33 Flaherty, *My Eskimo Friends*, 638–40

CHAPTER NINE

1 Robert Flaherty Papers in the Butler Library (hereafter Butler), Flaherty diary entry of 4 February 1921
2 Hudson's Bay Company Archives (HBCA), B467/a/2
3 The interview appeared in Sherwood's *The Best Moving Pictures of 1922–23*, which was partially reprinted in Jacobs's *The Documentary Tradition*, 18–19.
4 "Restoring Robert Flaherty's *Nanook of the North*," *Film Library Quarterly*, 10–11. In his discussion, Dobi relies heavily on Shepard's restoration of *Nanook*, which was released in 1976 under the auspices of International Film Seminars, the successor of the Robert Flaherty Foundation which Frances had formed after Flaherty's death in 1951 to advance understanding of his career. See Shepard "The Restoration of *Nanook*," and "Authenticating Films."
5 Butler, MN1913
6 Butler, MN1913
7 Grierson's review appeared anonymously (as "Moviegoer") in the *New York Sun*, 8 February 1926. It is reprinted in Jacobs's *Documentary Tradition*, 25–6.
8 A full study of this movement can be found in Sussex's *Rise and Fall of the British Documentary*.
9 The quotation is from an expanded discussion of *Nanook* entitled "Screened Snow and Esquimaux" (Butler, MN1913), which was later abbreviated as a film review for the *New Republic*, 9 August 1922.

10 Bruce Bliven, *New York Globe*, 9 August 1922
11 Butler, MN1913
12 Mackenzie had traveled to New York in June 1922 to see *Nanook*, and he spoke of his stake in the film in a Toronto *Telegram* interview, 15 June 1922.
13 Butler, MN1913, *Morning Telegraph*, 23 March 1922
14 Butler, MN1913
15 HBCA, B467/a/3

Bibliography

ARCHIVES

British Broadcasting Corporation Written Archives, Reading, Berkshire
British Library, London, England
  Canadian Copyright Collection
Bryn Mawr College Alumnae Archives, Bryn Mawr College, Pennsylvania
Butler Library, Columbia University, New York City
  Robert Flaherty Papers
  Hubbard Family Papers
Harry Ransom Humanities Research Center, University of Texas, Austin, Texas
Library and Archives Canada, Ottawa
  Revillon Collection
  Robert Flaherty Photography Collection, on loan from Claremont University
Mashantucket Pequot Museum and Research Center, Mashantucket, Connecticut
Museum of Modern Art Film Archives, New York City
New York Public Library, Research Division, New York City
Provincial Archives of Manitoba, Winnipeg, Manitoba
  Hudson's Bay Company Archives
Queen's University Archives, Kingston, Ontario
Robert and Frances Flaherty Study Center, School of Theology, Claremont University, Claremont, California

Royal Geographical Society Archives, London, England
Thunder Bay Historical Museum, Thunder Bay, Ontario
Vancouver Art Gallery Archives, Vancouver, British Columbia

SECONDARY SOURCES

Adams, Samuel Hopkins. *The Clarion*. Boston: Houghton Mifflin, 1914
Anderson, J.W. *Fur Trader's Story*. Toronto: Ryerson Press, 1961
Arthur, Eric, Howard Chapman, and Hart Massey. *Moose Factory, 1673–1947*. Toronto: University of Toronto Press, 1949
Bachman, Gideon. "Talking of Robert Flaherty." Film 20 (March–April 1959): 23–7
Barnouw, Erik. "Robert Flaherty (Barnouw's File)." *Film Culture* 53 (Spring 1972): 161–85
– "Robert Flaherty: Explorer." In *Documentary: A History of the Non Fiction Film*, 33–51. New York: Oxford University Press, 1974
Barry, Iris. *Let's Go to the Movies*. New York: Payson & Clarke, 1926
Barsam, Richard. *The Vision of Robert Flaherty*. Bloomington: Indiana University Press, 1988
Bell, Robert. "Report of an Exploration on the Northern Side of Hudson Bay." In *Geological Survey of Canada*. Ottawa: Queens's Printer, 1901
Berton, Pierre. *The Arctic Grail*. New York: Penguin, 1988
Bertsch, Marguerite. *How to Write for Moving Pictures*. New York: Doran, 1917
Bilby, Julian W. *Among Unknown Eskimo*. London: Seeley Service, 1923
– *Nanook of the North: The Story of an Eskimo Family*. New York: Dodd, Mead, 1926
Billings, David K. "Mackenzie's Pictures." *The Moving Picture World*, 17 April 1915, 426
Boas, Franz. *The Central Eskimo*. Lincoln: University of Nebraska Press, [1888] 1964
Bodry-Sanders, Penelope. *Carl Akeley: Africa's Collector, Africa's Savior*. New York: Paragon House, 1991
Boon, T.C. *The Anglican Church from the Bay to the Rockies*. Toronto: Ryerson Press, 1962
Bow, James A. "Mines of Northwestern Ontario." In *Report of the Bureau of Mines*, 7: 365–84. Toronto: Legislative Assembly of Ontario, 1898
– "Mines of Northwestern Ontario." In *Report of the Bureau of Mines*, 9: 35–88. Toronto: Legislative Assembly of Ontario, 1900
– "Mines of Northwest Ontario: Part 1." In *Report of the Bureau of Mines*, 10: 69–90. Toronto: Legislative Assembly of Ontario, 1901
Bridle, Augustus. "Fur Folk of Labrador." *Canadian Courier*, 13 May 1911: 16–17, 20
– "Sir William Mackenzie." In his *Sons of Canada: Short Studies of Characteristic Canadians*. Toronto: J.M. Dent, 1916
Brownlow, Kevin. *The War, the West and the Wilderness*. New York: Knopf, 1979
Bryce, George. *The Remarkable History of the Hudson's Bay Company*. New York: Scribner's, 1900
Cabot, William Brooks. *In Northern Labrador*. Boston: Badger, 1912
Calder-Marshall, Arthur. *The Innocent Eye: The Life of Robert J. Flaherty*. New York: Harcourt Brace, 1963

Cameron, W.B. "Runaway Ship." *Beaver*, June 1948, 5–9
Canavor, Natalie. "Robert Flaherty's Eskimos." *Popular Photography*, October 1980, 88–9, 148–9
Canudo, Ricciotto. "Another View of *Nanook*." In *L'Usine aux images. Paris*, 1927. Reprinted in *The Documentary Tradition*, ed. Lewis Jacobs, 20–4. New York: Norton, 1979
Carpenter, Edmund, *Eskimo Realities*. New York: Holt, Rinehart and Winston, 1973
– ed. *The Story of Comock as Told to Robert Flaherty*. New York: Simon and Schuster, 1968
– *Drawings by Enooesweetok* [1915]. New York: Rock Foundation, 2001.
– *Comock*. New York: Rock Foundation, 2003
Carter, W.E.H. "The Mines of Ontario." In *Report of the Bureau of Mine*, 11: 231–98. Toronto: Legislative Assembly of Ontario, 1902
Cartier, Jacques. *The Voyages of Jacques Cartier*. Toronto: University of Toronto Press, 1993
Christopher, Robert J. "Through Canada's Northland: The Arctic Photography of Robert J. Flaherty." In *Imaging the Arctic*, ed., Jonathan King and Henrietta Lidchi. Seattle: University of Washington Press, 1998
Coburn, Alvin. *Alvin Langdon Coburn: Photographer*. New York: Dover, 1978
Coleman, A.P. "Iron Ranges East of Lake Nipigon." In *Report of the Bureau of Mines*, 16 (pt. 1): 105–35. Toronto: Legislative Assembly of Ontario, 1907
Coleman, A.P. and E.S. Moore. "Iron Ranges East of Lake Nipigon." Report of the Bureau of Mines, 17: 136–69. Toronto: Legislative Assembly of Ontario, 1908
Collins, W.H. "A Geological Reconnaissance of the Region Traversed by the National Transcontinental Railway between Lake Nipigon and Clay Lake, Ontario." In *Canada Department of Mines: Geological Survey*, 1–62. Ottawa: Government Printing Bureau, 1909
Cooke, Alan. "A Woman's Way." *Beaver*, June 1960, 40–5
– "Robert Flaherty: Filmmaker and Explorer." Unpublished study, 1963
Corliss, Richard. "Robert Flaherty: The Man in the Iron Myth." *Film Comment* 9 (November–December 1973): 38–42. Reprinted in *Nonfiction Film Theory and Criticism*, ed. Richard M. Barsam. New York: Dutton, 1976
Cotter, J.L., and Clifford Wilson. "Moose Factory: Yesterday and Today." *Beaver*, June 1946, 22–9
Crawford, William. *Keepers of Light*. Dobbs Ferry, NY: Morgan & Morgan, 1979
Curran, W. Tees, and H.A. Calkins. *Glimpses of Northern Canada*. Montreal: Cambridge Corporation, 1907
– *In Canada's Wonderful Northland*. New York: Putnam, 1917
Currelly, Charles T. *I Brought the Ages Home*. Toronto: Ryerson Press, 1957
Custer, George F. "The (Re)Framing of Robert Flaherty." *Quarterly Review of Studies* 7 (Winter 1982): 87–94
Danker, Jo-Anne B., ed. *Robert Flaherty, Photographer/Filmmaker: The Inuit 1910–1922*. Vancouver: Vancouver Art Gallery, 1980
Davies, K.G., ed. *Northern Quebec and Labrador Journals and Correspondence 1819–35*. Hudson's Bay Record Society, 1963
Davis, Hasselt. *World without a Roof*. New York: Dell, Sloan & Pearce, 1957
De Kalb, Courtenay. "The Condition of Ontario Mines." In *Report of the Bureau of Mines*, 8: 29–48. Ottawa: Legislative Assembly of Ontario, 1899

Dobi, Steve. "Restoring Robert Flaherty's *Nanook of the North*." *Film Library Quarterly* 10. nos. 1–2 (1977): 9–18
Dratfield, Leo. "Robert Flaherty's Daughter Remembers: An Interview with Frances Flaherty Rohr." *Sightlines*, Fall–Winter 1984/85, 10–14
Durant, Mary. "The Man Himself." *The Bicentennial of John James Audobon*, ed. Alton A. Lindsey. Bloomington: Indiana University Press, 1985
Eaton, Walter P, "Class-Consciousness and the Movies." *Atlantic Monthly*, January 1915, 48–56
Eber, Dorothy Harley, "On Koodjuk's Trail." *Natural History* 88 (January 1979): 79–85
– *When the Whalers Were Up North*. Montreal: McGill-Queen's University Press, 1989
Ells, Sydney C. "Exploration Trip, Cochrane to James Bay, June 9th to Sept. 12th, 1911." In *Tenth Annual Report of the Temiskaming and Northern Ontario Railway Commission for 1911*. Toronto: Legislative Assembly of Ontario, 1912
Evans, Ernestine. "Wander No More." *Film News* 11 (September 1951): 13, 22
Evans, Walker. "Out of Anger and Passion: A Review of *The World of Robert Flaherty*." *New York Times Review of Books*, 3 May 1953
Flaherty, David. "A Few Reminiscences." *Film Culture* 2 (1959): 14–6
– "Poet of the Cinema," *Columbia Library Columns* 15 (February 1966): 3–12
Flaherty, Frances. "The Call of the Wind." In *Tipyn o' Bob*, 8–9. Bryn Mawr: Bryn Mawr College, 1905
– *Decennial Record of the Class of 1905 in Bryn Mawr*. Brooklyn: Hunter Collins Press, 1915
– "The Camera's Eye." *National Board of Review Magazine*, April 1927, 4–5. Reprinted in *Spellbound in Darkness*, ed. George C. Pratt, 344–7. New York: New York Graphic Society, 1973
– "Bob Flaherty Was an Explorer." *Saturday Review*, 13 September 1952, 50–2
– "Flaherty's Quest for Life." *Films and Filming*, January 1959, 8
– *Odyssey of a Film-Maker*. Urbana: Beta Phi Mu, 1960
Flaherty, Robert. "Reported Discovery of Large Islands in Hudson Bay." *Geographical Journal* 45 (May 1915): 440
– "Mr Flaherty's Explorations in Hudson Bay." *Geographical Journal* 56 (September 1915): 241–2
– "The Belcher Islands of Hudson Bay: Their Discovery and Exploration." *Geographical Review* (June 1918): 433–58
– "Two Traverses across Ungava Peninsula, Labrador." *Geographical Review* 6 (August 1918): 116–32
– "How I Filmed *Nanook of the North*." *World's Work*, September 1922, 553–60. Reprinted in *Film Makers on Film Making*, ed. Harry M. Geduld. Bloomington: Indiana University Press, 1970
– "Indomitable Children of the North." *Travel*, August 1922, 16–20
– "Life among the Eskimos." *World's Work*, October 1922, 632–40
– "Wetalltok's Islands, I." *World's Work*, January 1923, 324–36
– "Wetalltok's Islands, II." *World's Work*, February 1923, 422–33
– "Winter on Wetalltok's Island." *World's Work*, March 1923, 538–53
– (with Frances Flaherty). *My Eskimo Friends*. New York: Doubleday, 1924
– "How I Went to the Far North to Find Iron." *Sunday Referee*, 22 July 1934

– "North, North with the Dogs through Barren Snow-Swept Wastes." *Sunday Referee*, 29 July 1934
– "Facing Death in a Land of Cold and Hunger." *Sunday Referee*, 5 August 1934
– "If We Had Lost the Canoe, How Should We Have Come Out Alive?" *Sunday Referee*, 12 August 1934
– "By Ship to the North." *Sunday Referee*, 19 August 1934
– "Nearly Wrecked." *Sunday Referee*, 26 August 1934
– "How I Made the First Motion Pictures with Nanook of the North." *Sunday Referee*, 2 September 1934
– "Filming Real People." *Movie Makers*, December 1934, 516, 545. Reprinted in *Documentary Tradition*, ed. Lewis Jacobs, 97–9. New York: Norton, 1979
– "Filming in the Frozen North." In *Living Dangerously*, ed. Cecil Madden. London: George Allen, 1936
– "North Sea." *Sight and Sound*, Summer 1938, 62–3
– "A Whaler Goes Down." *World Film News*, August 1938, 152–3
– *The Captain's Chair: A Story of the North*. New York: Scribner's, 1938
– *White Master*. London: Routledge, 1939
– "The Islands That Were Not There." Unpublished manuscript. Butler Library, Columbia University. N.d.
– "Robert Flaherty Tells the Story of Sorine." *Who*, August 1941, 38, 47, 58
– "The Grim, Gallant Story of Comock the Eskimo." *Reader's Digest*, July 1949, 169–80
– "Robert Flaherty Talking." In *The Cinema 1950*, ed. Roger Manvell. London: Penguin, 1950
– "Film: Language of the Eye." *Screen Director*, January 1951, 1–9. Reprinted in *Theater Arts*, May 1951, 30–6
– "The Story of Comock the Eskimo." In *The Cinema 1952*, ed. Roger Manvell and R.K. Nelson Baxter, 100–25. London: Penguin, 1952
– "Explorations." *Film Book 1*, ed. Robert Hughes. New York: Grove Press, 1959
– *Nanook of the North*, ed. Robert Kraus. New York: Windmill Books, 1971
– *The Drawings of Enooesweetok of Sikosilingminut Tribe of the Eskimo, Fox Land, Baffin Island*. Toronto: Privately printed, 1915

Flaherty, Robert, and John Chapman Hilder. "The Captain's Chair." *Elk's Magazine*, November and December 1928, January, February, March 1929

Fleming, Archibald L. *Archibald the Arctic*. London: Hodder & Stoughton, 1957

Fleming, Rae B. *The Railway King of Canada*. Vancouver: University of British Columbia Press, 1991

Fraser, Robert J. *Arctic Adventurer: Grant and the Seduisante*. Lincoln, Ont.: W.F. Rannie, 1972

Froelick, Louis D. "Flaherty: New 'Movie' Prophet." *Asia* 23, June 1923: 396–400

Gibson, Thomas W. "Statistical Review." In *Report of the Bureau of Mines*, 13 (pt. 1): 1–45. Toronto: Legislative Assembly of Ontario, 1904

Grace, Sherrill. "Exploration as Construction and Nanook of the North." *Essays on Canadian Writing* 59 (Fall 1996): 123–46

Grenfell, Wilfred T. *A Labrador Doctor*. Boston: Houghton Mifflin, 1917

Grierson, John. "Flaherty's Poetic Moana." *New York Sun*, 8 February 1926. Reprinted in *Documentary Tradition*, ed. Lewis Jacobs, 25–6. New York: Norton, 1979

– “Flaherty – Naturalism – and the Problem of the English Cinema.” *Artwork*, Autumn 1931, 213–15
– “Flaherty.” *Cinema Quarterly*, Autumn 1932, 12–17
Griffith, Richard. *The World of Robert Flaherty*. New York: Dell, Sloan & Pearce, 1953
Harris, Lynda. “Revillon Frères Trading Company Limited: Fur Traders to the North, 1901–36.” Ottawa: Ministry of Culture and Recreation, 1976
Hille, F. “Report on the Examination of Some Iron Ore Deposits in the Districts of Thunder Bay and Rainy River, Province of Ontario.” *Canada Department of Mines*. Ottawa, 1908
Holm, Bill, and George Quimby. *Edward Curtis in the Land of the War Canoes*. Seattle: University of Washington Press, 1980
Hopkins, P.E. “Kowkash Gold Area.” In *Report of the Bureau of Mines*, 25 (pt. 1): 264–74. Toronto: Legislative Assembly of Ontario, 1916
Horwood, Harold. *Bartlett: The Great Canadian Explorer*. New York: Doubleday, 1977
Houston, James. *Confessions of an Igloo Dweller*. New York: Houghton Mifflin, 1995
Hoyle, Gwyneth. “Capt. Thierry Mallet: Adventurer, Businessman, Writer.” In *The Fur Trade Revisited*, ed. Jennifer Brown et al., 427–46. East Lansing: Michigan State University Press, 1994
Hubbard, Lucius. *Hubbard’s Guide to Moosehead Lake*. 3rd edn. Boston: A. Williams, 1882
– *Woods and Lakes of Maine*. Boston: J.R. Osgood, 1884
– *History of University of Michigan*. Ann Arbor: University of Michigan Press, 1923
Hubbard, Mina Benson. *A Woman’s Way through Unknown Labrador*. New York: McClure, 1908
Hurley, Frank. *Shackleton’s Argonauts*. Sydney: Angus & Robertson, 1948
Jacobs, Lewis. *The Documentary Tradition*. 2nd edn. New York: Norton, 1979
James, William C. “‘Inuit in Church’: Clearing a Photographic Misatribution.” *Archivaria* 12 (Summer 1981): 59–62
– “Inuit in Church-Once More.” *Archivaria* 13 (Winter 1981–82): 129–30
– ed. *A Fur Trader’s Photographs: A.A. Chesterfield in the District of Ungava, 1901–04*. Montreal & Kingston: McGill-Queen’s University Press, 1985
Jobe, Mary L. “The Expedition to ‘Mt. Kitchi’: A New Peak in the Canadian Rockies.” *Canadian Alpine Journal* 6 (1914–15): 188–200
– “My Quest in the Canadian Rockies: Locating a New Ice-Peak.” *Harper’s Magazine*, May 1915, 813–25
– “Mt. Kitchi: A New Peak in the Canadian Rockies.” *Bulletin of the American Geographical Society*, 47, no. 7 (1915): 481–97
Knight, James B., Commissioner of Mineral Statistics for Michigan. *Annual Report 1892–93*. Lansing, 1895
Lasky, Jessie. *I Blow My Own Horn*. New York: Doubleday, 1957
Leechman, Douglas. “The Father of Place Names.” *Beaver*, September 1954, 24–8
Leith, Charles K. “An Alkonkian Basin in Hudson Bay: A Comparison with the Lake Superior Region.” Economic Geology 5 (April 1910): 227–46
Leith, Charles K., and Arthur T. Leith. *A Summer and Winter on Hudson Bay*. Madison: University of Wisconsin Press, 1912

LeVasseur, N. "La baie d'Hudson: deux îles redécouvertes." *Bulletin de la Société géographie de Québec* 9, no. 3 (1915): 140–9

Lewis, Arthur. *The Life and Work of E.J. Peck among the Eskimos*. New York: A.C. Armstrong & Son, 1904

Low, Albert P. "Report on an Exploration of Part of the South Shore of Hudson Strait and of Ungava Bay." In *Geological Survey of Canada Annual Report*. Ottawa: Queen's Printer, 1899

Low, Albert P., and Robert Bell. "Reports on Explorations of the Coasts of Hudson Strait and Ungava Bay." In *Geological Survey of Canada Annual Report*, vol. 11, pts. L and M. Ottawa: King's Printer, 1901

– "Report of an Exploration of the East Coast of Hudson Bay from Cape Wolstenholme to the South End of James Bay." In *Geological Survey of Canada Annual Report*, vol. 13, pt. D. Ottawa: King's Printer, 1902

– "Report on the Geology and Physical Characteristics of the Nastapoka Islands." In *Geological Survey of Canada Annual Report*, vol 13, pt. DD, 1–31. Ottawa: King's Printer, 1903

– *The Cruise of the Neptune, 1903–04*. Ottawa: Government Printing Office, 1906

MacAulay, R.H. *Trading into Hudson Bay*. Winnipeg: Hudson's Bay Company, 1934.

Mack, Edmund. "The *Nascopie*." *Beaver*, September 1938, 5–9

Mackenzie, N.M.W.J. *The Men of Hudson's Bay Company*. Fort William, Ont.: Times-Journal Press, 1921

Maclellan, David. "Classic Photos of Indians and Eskimos." *Canadian Geographic*, August/September 1980, 58–65

Macmillan, J.G. "Investigations at James Bay during 1912." In *Temiskaming and Northern Ontario Railway Commission Report no. 3*. Toronto: Legislative Assembly of Ontario, 1913

McRae, James A. *Call Me Tomorrow*. Toronto: Ryerson Press, 1960

Maher, W.R. "Reconnaissance for Extension." In *Temiskaming and Northern Ontario Railway Commission Report no. 3*. Toronto: Legislative Assembly of Ontario, 1913

Mair, Charles. *Tecumseh, A Drama, and Canadian Poems*. Toronto: William Briggs, 1901

Mallet, Thierry, "Filming a White Bear on Land." In his *Plain Tales of the North*. New York: Putnam, 1926

– *Glimpses of the Barren Lands*. New York: Revillon Frères, 1930

Manvell, Roger. "Robert Flaherty." In *Cinema 1952*, 126–9. London: Penguin, 1952

– "Robert Flaherty, Geographer." *Geographic Magazine* 29 (February 1957): 491–500

Marcus, Alan Rudolph. *Relocating Eden*. Hanover: University Press of America, 1995

Miller, Willet G. "Iron Ranges of Northern Ontario." In *Report of the Bureau of Mines*, 12: 304–17. Toronto: Legislative Assembly of Ontario, 1903

Moore, E.S. "The Iron Ranges East of Lake Nipigon, Part II." In *Report of the Bureau of Mines*, 17: 163–72. Toronto: Legislative Assembly of Ontario, 1908

– "Geology of Onaman Iron Range Area." In *Report of the Bureau of Mines*, 18 (pt. 1): 196–53. Toronto: Legislative Assembly of Ontario, 1909

– "Lake Savant Iron Range Area." In *Report of the Bureau of Mines*, 19 (pt. 1): 173–92. Toronto: Legislative Assembly of Ontario, 1910

– "Iron Ore Deposits on Belcher Islands." In *Journal of Geology* 26 (July–August 1918): 412–38

– "Iron Deposits on Belcher Islands," *Monthly Bulletin of the Canadian Mining Institute* 82 (February 1919): 196–206

Murie, Olaus J. *Journeys to the Far North*. Palo Alto: Wilderness Society, 1973

Murphy, William T. *Robert Flaherty: A Guide to References and Resources*. Boston: G.K. Hall, 1978

Nansen, Fridtjof. *Farthest North*. 2 vols. New York: Harper, 1897

O'Neill, Patrick B. *Checklist of Canadian Copyright Deposits in the British Museum 1895–1923*. Vol 5. Halifax: Dalhousie University Press, 1989

– "Canadian Photographs in the British Library." *Archivaria* 38 (Fall 1994): 240–1

Parsons, John, and Burton K. James. *The King of Baffin Land*. St John's, Nfld: Creative Publishers, 1996

Patterson, Frances T. "*Nanook of the North*." *New Republic*, 9 August 1922, 306–7. Reprinted in *Spellbound in Darkness*, ed. George C. Pratt. 342–4. New York: New York Graphic Society, 1973

Peck, Edmund J. *Eskimo Grammar*. Ottawa: Surveyor General's Office, 1919

– *The Eskimo: Our Brethren of the Arctic*. Missionary Society of the Anglican Church in Canada, 1922

Petersen, O.M. *Land of the Moosoneek*. Toronto: Bryant Press, 1974

Pierce, Patricia. *Canada: The Missing Years. The Lost Images of Our Heritage 1895–1924*. Don Mills, Ont.: Stoddart, 1985

Pitseolak, Peter. *People from Our Side*, ed. Dorothy Harley Eber. Edmonton: Hurtig, 1975

Pratt, George C. *Spellbound in Darkness: A History of the Silent Film*. New York: New York Graphic Society, 1973

Ramsaye, Terry. "Flaherty, Great Adventurer." *Photoplay*, May 1928, 58, 123–26. Reprinted in *Spellbound in Darkness*, ed. George C. Pratt. 342–54. New York: New York Graphic Society, 1973

Ray, Arthur. *The Canadian Fur Trade in the Industrial Age*. Toronto: University of Toronto Press, 1990

Renouf, Ernest. "Salvage." *Beaver*, November 1921, 16–21

Rotha, Paul. *Robert J. Flaherty: A Biography*, ed. Jay Ruby. Philadelphia: University of Pennsylvania Press, 1983

Ruby, Jay. "A Reexamination of the Early Career of Robert Flaherty." *Quarterly Review of Film Studies* 5 (Fall 1980): 431–58

– "'The Aggie Will Come First': The Demystification of Robert Flaherty." In *Robert Flaherty Photographer/Filmmaker: The Inuit 1910–1922*, ed. Jo-Anne Danker, 66–73, Vancouver: Vancouver Art Gallery, 1980

Rutledge, J.L. "Flaherty of Belcher Island." *Maclean's*, 1 February 1920, 25–6, 53

Ruttan, Frances. "Audio Interview by Susan Boyd-Bowman." Vancouver: Vancouver Art Gallery, 1979

Seegmiller, H.A. "Ungava Stewart." *Journal of the Canadian Church Historical Society* 10 (June 1968): 164–8

Shepard, David. "The Restoration of *Nanook*." *Blackhawk Bulletin*, February 1975, 50

– "Authenticating Films." *Quarterly Journal of The Library of Congress*, Summer/Fall 1980, 342–54

Sherwood, Robert. "Driven." In *Best Moving Pictures of 1922–1923*, 54–8. Boston: Small & Maynard, 1923.
Silver, L.P. "The Animikie Iron Range." In *Report of the Bureau of Mines*, 15 (pt. 1): 156–72. Toronto: Legislative Assembly of Ontario, 1906
Slaght, A. *Report of the Bureau of Mines*, 6:247–63. Toronto: Legislative Assembly of Ontario, 1897
Smith, W.N. "Loon Lake Iron-Bearing District." In *Report of the Bureau of Mines*, 14 (pt. 1): 254–60. Toronto: Legislative Assembly of Ontario, 1905
Stefansson, Vilhjalmur. *My Life with the Eskimo* [1913]. New York: Collier Books, 1962
– *The Friendly Arctic*. New York: Macmillan, 1921
– *The Northward Course of Empire*. New York: Macmillan, 1922
Stewart, Robert. "Eskimo Women and Hunters from Hudson Bay." *Beaver*, September 1938, 22–5
Sullivan, Alan. "In Baffin Land: A True Story." *Century*, September 1915, 703–9
Sussex, Elizabeth. *The Rise and Fall of the British Documentary*. Berkeley: University of California Press, 1975
Taylor, Robert Lewis. "Profile of Robert Flaherty." *New Yorker*, 11 June 1949, 30–41; 18 June 1949, 28–40; and 25 June 1949, 28–43. Reprinted in *The Running Pianist*. New York: Doubleday, 1950
Thomas, Lowell. *Kabluk of the Eskimo*. Boston: Little Brown, 1932
Thomas, Alan. "George Comer, A.P. Low, Geraldine and J.D. Moodie: Fullerton Photographs, 1903–1905." *Northward Journal* 40 (1987): 5–29
Thornton, Gene. "Flaherty's View of Eskimo Life." *New York Times*, 4 May 1980, 29–30
Townsend, Charles W. *A Labrador Spring*. Boston: Dana Estes, 1910
Tremblay, Alfred. *Cruise of the Minnie Maud*. Quebec: Arctic Exchange, 1921
Trumbull, Walter. "The Listening Post." *New York Herald*, 22 July 1922
Twomey, Arthur C. *Needle to the North*, ed. William C. James. Boston: Houghton Mifflin, 1942
Watt, Maud. "Nascopie Honeymoon." *Beaver*, March 1938, 18–26
– "Chimo Days," *Beaver*, September 1939, 30–35
Wild, Roland. *Arctic Command: The Story of Smellie of the Nascopie*. Toronto: Ryerson Press, 1955
Williams, Glyndwr. "James Clouston's Journey across the Labrador Peninsula in 1820." *Beaver*, Summer 1966, 4–15
Wilson, Clifford P. "Nascopie: The Story of a Ship." *Beaver*, September 1947, 3–11
Winston, Brian. "The White Man's Burden: The Example of Robert Flaherty." *Sight and Sound* 54 (Winter 1984/85): 58–60
– "Before Flaherty, Before Grierson: The Documentary Film in 1914." *Sight and Sound* 57 (Autumn 1988): 277–9
Wolf, William. "*Nanook of the North*, 1922: Reality on Film." In *Landmark Films: The Cinema and Our Century*, 24–31. New York: Paddington Press, 1979
Young, G.A. "Iron Bearing Rocks of Belcher Islands, Hudson Bay." In *Canada Department of Mines: Geological Survey*. Summary report 1921, part E. Ottawa: King's Printer, 1922

Index

Page numbers in italics refer to illustrations

Active, 139, 159
Adler, Dr Felix, 238, 419n64
Akeley, Carl, 424n91
Allakariallak (Nanook), *369*, *377*, 380, 432n25; death of, 387–8
Allego, 163, *164*, 408n38
Aman, 199, 414n62
Amundsen, Roald, 417n47
Anunglung, 153, 406n33
Atta. *See* Allakariallak

Bartlett, Capt. Harold, 229, 235, 403n19
Belcher Islands, 78, 285–7, 390n15; press reports on their rediscovery, 203–4
Bell, Robert, 65, 393n15
Bilby, Rev. Julian W., 139, 403n20
Boas, Franz, 238, 419n63; Frances's meeting with, 239–40
Bridle, Augustus, 70, 397n4; review of Baffin film, 216

Calkins, Harold A., 414n62
Cape Dorset, 173, 409n43; settlement history of, 166
Cape Wolstenholme, 120, 124, 265; settlement history of, 401n36
Chalmers, Alexander Mackie, 191, 413n56
Charlton Island, 50
Chesterfield, Albert A., 428n20
Christmas celebration, 155, 292, 406n34
Comer, Capt. George, 240, 404n21, 419n66
Comock story, 401n36; as told by

Nanook, 434n31
Crow, Jim, 92, 399n21
Cunayou (Kanajuq), 168, *169*, 408n41
curio collecting, 60, 127, 156–7, 168, 178, 185, 371, 416n42, 418n53; Royal Ontario Museum of Archaeology recipient of, 210
Curran, W. Tees, 199, 414n62
Currelly, Charles T., 223, 240–1, 416n42
Curtis, Edward: comparison of his photographs and Flaherty's, 242–3; development of the documentary, 384; meeting with, 217–18

Draulette, Y., 63; profile of, 396n31

Edmonds, David, 104, 400n27
Edmonds, John, 173, 409n43
Era, 404n21
expeditions: budget for Port Harrison trip, 326; cargo manifest for 3rd Mackenzie, 132; cost of 1st and 2nd Mackenzie, 130–1; cost of 3rd Mackenzie, 282; supply inventory for Foxe Channel journey, 174–5

filmmaking. *See* motion-picture making
film screenings, 215–16; at Convocation Hall, 240–1; at Toronto Arts and Letters Club, 241
Flaherty, Arthur (brother), 4, 172, 423n90
Flaherty, Barbara Lee, later Van Ingen (daughter), 319
Flaherty, David (brother), 4, 260, 273, 422n80; camping on Charlton Island, 264
Flaherty, Frances Farnham, later Rohr (daughter), 319
Flaherty, Frances Hubbard (spouse), *44*, *47*, *48*; Bryn Mawr biography, 41–2; first meeting with Robert, 42–3; marriage to Robert, 201–3; post-*Nanook* literary endeavors, 385
Flaherty, Frances, later Ruttan (sister), 4, 390n3; interviewed, 24–5
Flaherty, Joseph (son of Alice Nevalinga), 387
Flaherty, Monica Lambard, later Frasseto (daughter), 327
Flaherty, Robert Henry (father), *9*; ancestry, 4; arrival on Belcher Islands, 317; camping on Charlton Island, 264; career of, 4; first iron ore explorations, 16; labor strife, 10–11
Flaherty, Robert Joseph, *9*, *46*, *49*, *74*, *75*, *76*, *77*, *321*, *345*, *370*; apprenticeship to father, 6–7; birth, 4; compares Indians and Inuit, 65; early education, 23–5; early reading, 12, 390n16; encounters with Indians, 11, 14–16, 30, 33–4, 36–7, 65; first meeting with Frances, 42–3; later education, 25–7; love of violin and camera, 25; post-*Nanook* literary publications, 385; relations with Inuit women, 387, 291n12
Flaherty, Susan Klöckner (mother), *10*; ancestry, 4
Fleming, Archibald L. (future bishop), 139, 404n20; Frances's meeting with, 268, 271, 423n87
Fleming, Mary. *See* Udgaarden, Mary
Fleming, Nero, 58, *61*, 72, 394n24; forthcoming ordination, 95; Flaherty's opinion of, 98
Fleming, William ("Husky Bill"), 52, *54*, 299, 394n24, 399n20
Ford, Sam, 141, 404n23
Fort Chimo, 91, 103, *105*, 265; settlement history of, 400n26
Fort Churchill, 266, 422n84
Fort George, 299; settlement history of, 394n21
Franklin, Sir John, 136, 403n18
French Company. *See* Revillon Frères
fur trade, 22, 58, 139, 148, 170, 395n26; collapse of, 25; scarcity of furs, 367

Gillies, Donald, 51, 393n17
Goodell, Charlotte Hubbard. *See* Hubbard, Charlotte Armitage

Grant, Capt. Forsyth, 191, 413n59
Great Whale River, 58, 85, 288; settlement history of, 394n23
Grenfell, Dr Wilfred Thomason, 134, 403n16
Grierson, John, 384, 436n7
Griffith, Neville Owen, 51, 393n17
Gushue, Stewart, *205*, *206*, 403n15

Holmes, Burton, 278–9, 425n94
Houston, James, 428n15, 430n23
Hubbard, Charlotte Armitage, later Goodell (FHF's sister), 40, 274, *321*, 416n37
Hubbard, Frances Johnson. *See* Flaherty, Frances Hubbard (FHF)
Hubbard, Frances Lambard (FHF's mother), 40, 416n37
Hubbard, Julia, later Platt (FHF's sister), *321*
Hubbard, Lucius (FHF's father), 40, 41, 273, 392n1
Hudson's Bay Company: disputes over unpaid bills, 260, 422n81; expansion of northern posts, 403n20; Moose Factory, *68*
Huskies, *See* Inuit
Husky Bill. *See* Fleming, William

Inuit: beauty of the Inuit women, 56; first sighting of, 51, 393n18; Flaherty much impressed with, 55–6
Inuit drawings: Christmas celebrations, by Wetalltok, 292; 1915 publication of, 222; salvaging of *Fort Churchill*, by Wetalltok, 423n84
Inukshuk, 112, 186; description of, 401n33
iron ore, 39, 73, 130, 172, 221, 392n13, 395n27, 416n38; on Belcher Islands, 286–7, 305; search for Minnesota lode, 6
"Islands That Were Not There,"429n21
"Iviuk, Son of Nanook," 386

Jobe, Mary L., 267; marriage to Carl Akeley, 423n91
Jobson, Christopher J.R., 62; profile of, 396n28
Jocko, 262, 300, 421n79

Knobel, Capt. H.E., 7, 17, 390n19

Laddie, 132–3, 148–9, *295*; dismantling of, 300; plans to use as firewood, 294
LaDuke, Eugene, 80, *206*, 397n8; falling out with Flaherty, 290, 426n12; Frances's first meeting with, 224
Lauder, Harry, 146, 405n26
Little Whale River, 84; settlement history of, 398n12
Louttit, Alec, 53, 394n22
Loutitt, Teddy, 53, 394n22
Low, Albert Peter, 50, 390n15

McAlpine, George Emmett, 63; profile of, 396n32
Mackenzie, N.M.W.J., 200, 414n62; Frances's meeting with, 268, 423n87
Mackenzie, Sir William, 49, *52*, 233–4, 250, 392n13; and bankruptcy of Canadian Northern Railway, 216; Frances's profile of, 224; royalty share in *Nanook*, 386, 437n12
McNab, Alexander C., 50, 51, 63, 393n17
Mallet, Capt. Thierry, 322, 327–8
Mann, Sir Donald, 329n13
Maver (Mavor), Lewis G., 87, 88, *200*, 288, 298; profile of, 398n13
Mawson, Douglas, 228, 232, 417n47
Miller, William, 51, 393n20
Moose Factory, 50; settlement history of, 393n16
Moosonee. *See* Moose Factory
motion-picture making, 131, 150–1, 183–4, 185, 187–8, 192, 196–7, 302–3, 306, 406n31, 409n47, 411nn51 and 53; developing the film, 146, 184, 189, 231, 298, 301–3, 311, 314, 336–7, 410n49;

of dismantling *Laddie*, 300, 302; of hunting on Walrus Island, 331; list of film subjects, 315–16; reconstructing Baffin film, 211–14; screening of Baffin-Belcher Islands film, 322; New York screening of Baffin film, 217; use of animals in filming, 291, 427n13; use of film subjects in *Nanook*, 380–1
Mulucktoo (John Meluktuk), 82, 398n11
Murray, Capt. Alexander of *Active*, 159; death of, 407n35
Murray, Capt. John of *Active*, 139, 404n21

Nanook of the North ("Nanook of the Barren Lands"), 3; contract for, 382; critical response to, 383; first release of, 382; Flaherty's financial rewards from, 385–6
Nascopie, 126, 401n34; arrival at Port Harrison, 333; Frances's voyage on, 265
Nastapoka, 80, 288–9, 397n10; near wrecked on reef, 311; repaired for service, 307
Nastapoka Falls, 61, 67, 85–6, 94–5
Navolia, 140, 404n22
Nevalinga, Alice ("Maggie," cast as Nyla), *369*, *374*, *375*, 387, 432n25
Noahasweetow (Noogooshoweektok), *152*, 405n30

Omarolluk, 66, *71*, 310

Parker, Harold, 104, 106, 400n27
Parsons, Ralph, 159, 407n37
Partridge, 105; profile of, 400n29
Peck, Rev. James Edward, 128; profile of, 402n4
Perkins, Maxwell, 207, 238, 419n62
photography: cameras used, 79, 91, 132, 175, 283, 285; developing photographs, 58, 81, 84–7, 133, 134, 229, 302–3; equipment, 283, 285, 336; first public exhibition of photographs, 215; Graflex camera damaged, 330; picture taking on first expedition, 50–1, 55, 60–2; on second expedition, 65, 66–70, 80, 84–7, 92–4, 123; on third expedition, 176, 187, 197; on fourth expedition, 297, 303; use of Akeley camera, 285, 336, 424n91
Polar Star, 171; wreckage of, 167, 408n40

Renouf, Ernest, 197, 414n62; salvaging of *Fort Churchill*, 266, 423n84
Revillon Frères, 29, 30, 37, 391n9
Robertson, William ("Salty Bill"), 136, *137*, 403n17
Royal Geographical Society, 128; Flaherty's election to, 402n3
Rupert House, 63; settlement history of, 396n30
Ruttan, Harry (brother-in-law), 276, 423n90

Sainsbury, Samuel, 138, 147, *189*, *310*, 403n15, 405n27; letter about Flaherty-LaDuke conflict, 426n12; participates in filming, 212–14
Salt, Jimmy, 88, 398n16
Salty Bill. *See* Robertson, William
Scott, Robert F., 228, 417n47
Shackleton, Sir Ernest, 228, 417n47
Simonie, 157–8; recollection of Flaherty's photography studio, 215
Snapes, George, 282, 426n11
Snowboy, William, 88, 299, 398n15
Sorine, 51, *69*
Stefansson, Vilhjalmur, 228, 230, 417nn47 and 50
Stewart, Robert, 327, *369*; writes of Allakariallak's illness, 387
Stewart, Stephen ("Lofty"), 174, 409n44
Stieglitz, Alfred, 247, 421n76
Stockton, Dr Charles, 236, 418n57
Strutton Islands, 288; Revillon's supply depot, 62, 396n29
Sullivan, Alan, 234–5, 416n40; first meeting with, 222–4

"Through Canada's Northland": copyright registration of album of 102 photographs, 65, 396n3
Thurston, Margaret, 44, 48, 287, 390n8, 392n3; camping on Charlton Island, 264
Tookalook, 261–3
Toronto Arts and Letters Club, 210; Flaherty's first visit to, 225
Turner, Mary Louise, 51, 393n19

Udgaarden, Harold, 58, *59*, 298, 394n24
Udgaarden, Mary, *59*

Walton, Rev. William G., 88, 394n21
Wetalltok, 76, 263; drawing by, 292; gift of pianola from Flaherty, 430n23; Flaherty's fictional transformation of, 323–4; his map of Belcher Islands, 77–8, *79*
Wilson, Frank D., *198*, 199, 288, 414n62, 426nn11 and 12; Frances's meeting with, 251